Calvin's Company of Pastors

OXFORD STUDIES IN HISTORICAL THEOLOGY

Calvin's Company of Pastors

Pastoral Care and the Emerging
Reformed Church, 1536–1609

SCOTT M. MANETSCH

OXFORD
UNIVERSITY PRESS

Oxford University Press is a department of the University of Oxford.
It furthers the University's objective of excellence in research, scholarship,
and education by publishing worldwide.

Oxford   New York
Auckland   Cape Town   Dar es Salaam   Hong Kong   Karachi
Kuala Lumpur   Madrid   Melbourne   Mexico City   Nairobi
New Delhi   Shanghai   Taipei   Toronto

With offices in
Argentina   Austria   Brazil   Chile   Czech Republic   France   Greece
Guatemala   Hungary   Italy   Japan   Poland   Portugal   Singapore
South Korea   Switzerland   Thailand   Turkey   Ukraine   Vietnam

Oxford is a registered trademark of Oxford University Press in the UK
and certain other countries.

Published in the United States of America by
Oxford University Press
198 Madison Avenue, New York, NY 10016

Library of Congress Cataloging-in-Publication Data
Manetsch, Scott M.
Calvin's company of pastors : pastoral care and the emerging Reformed Church, 1536–1609
/ Scott M. Manetsch.
p. cm.
Includes bibliographical references (p.) and index.
ISBN 978-0-19-993857-5 (hardcover); 978-0-19-022447-9 (paperback)
1. Geneva (Switzerland)—Church history—16th century.   2. Reformed Church—
Switzerland—Geneva—History—16th century.   3. Pastoral theology—Reformed Church.
4. Religious refugees—Switzerland—Geneva—History—16th century.   5. Calvin, Jean,
1509—1564.   I. Title.
BX9415.M36 2013
284'.249451609031—dc23
2012018345

To my wife, Catherine,
and daughters Hannah and Melissa

CONTENTS

ACKNOWLEDGMENTS

The idea for this book was first conceived nearly ten years ago during a summer in residence at the H. Henry Meeter Center for Calvin Studies (Grand Rapids, Michigan) as I read through the published sermons of Theodore Beza and became intrigued by the prominent pastoral themes that they contained. The vital spirituality and practical ministry concerns that I encountered in the sermons did not match popular caricatures which portrayed Beza's theology as stagnant, speculative, or scholastic. That initial discovery served as the impetus for a more expansive study of the pastoral theology and practical ministry activities of John Calvin, Beza, and the other members of the Company of Pastors who served Geneva's church during the sixteenth and early seventeenth centuries. The gestation of this book over the past decade has required four summer research trips to Geneva, consumed two sabbaticals, and invited rich and valuable conversations with scholarly colleagues on both sides of the Atlantic Ocean. Along the way, my daughters Hannah and Melissa, who were preschoolers when I began this book project, have grown into beautiful teenagers. The passage of time is unrelenting, but God has been good to us.

It is with sincere gratitude that I would like to thank several institutions and the many friends and colleagues that have contributed to this writing project over the years. Research trips to Geneva were made possible by generous financial support provided by the Christian Scholars Foundation and the Lilly Foundation-ATS Faculty Research Grant. The Institut d'histoire de la Réformation at the University of Geneva also awarded me a research stipend and served as my scholarly "home away from home," providing me with research space and access to its outstanding collection of early modern books. I am greatly indebted to the director and professors of the Institute, Maria-Cristina Pitassi, Irena Backus, and Philip Benedict, as well as the remarkable group of scholars who work there, including Alain Dufour, Nicolas Fornerod, Hervé Genton, Béatrice Nicollier-de Weck, Max

Engamarre, and Christian Grosse. Many thanks to all of these colleagues for sharing their scholarship and rich life-experiences with me—often over a cup of coffee in Geneva's old town. In a similar fashion, I am very grateful for the expert advice and competent assistance provided by the librarians at Geneva's State Archive, where I spent many hundreds of hours reading the difficult handwriting of the secretaries of the Consistory. The summers that our family spent in Switzerland over the past decade were especially memorable due to the kind hospitality of a number of precious friends. As a family, we have been immeasurably enriched by our friendships with Reinhard Bodenmann, and Mme. Anne-Marie and M. Jean-Louis Valaud, who opened their hearts and homes to us, sharing with us rich feasts of Swiss and French cuisine, history, and culture. So too, we are so very grateful for dear friends at the Evangelical Baptist Church of Geneva, including Anna Chung, Al and Susan Goff, and especially Derek and Beryl Adamsbaum, who were a constant source of Christian fellowship, spiritual encouragement, and good counsel. And to the Pollard family, thank you for sharing your beautiful apartment with our family; your generosity has meant so much to us.

Closer to home, I would like to thank the administration and Board of Regents of Trinity Evangelical Divinity School, the academic institution where I presently serve on faculty, for supplying research funds each year and granting me periodic sabbaticals to complete this writing project. Thanks are also in order to the H. Henry Meeter Center for Calvin Studies, directed so capably by Karin Maag and her assistant Paul Fields, for welcoming me as a resident scholar in the summer of 2002 and making available valuable resources related to Calvin and Calvinism. Throughout the research and writing of this book, I have been greatly helped by the support of a number of faculty colleagues and graduate students here at Trinity. In this regard, I am so very grateful to my wonderful colleagues in the Church History department, John Woodbridge and Douglas Sweeney, as well as other colleagues and friends, D. A. Carson, Eckhard Schnabel, and Stephen Greggo, who helped me conceptualize aspects of the project, read drafts of the manuscript, and contributed a lot of encouragement and common sense. Similarly, I would like to thank present and past members of the Deerfield Dialogue Group, including professors Richard Averbeck, Dana Harris, Te-Li Lau, Thomas McCall, Robert Priest, Elizabeth Sung, Kevin Vanhoozer, Robert Yarbrough, and Lawson Younger, who have patiently read and commented on chapters of this book, to my great benefit. I am also grateful to my fine student assistants Jeffrey Fisher, Timothy Padgett, Adam Bottiglia, and Ethan McCarthy for their help in editing the manuscript, tracking down bibliographical references, and creating the index. Finally, I wish to thank the people who have helped navigate this book to publication: the anonymous reviewers whose insightful recommendations strengthened my manuscript considerably; Cynthia Read and Sasha Grossman at Oxford University Press for their expert editorial advice and meticulous labors; and E. William Monter for granting permission to reproduce maps from his book *Calvin's Geneva* in the first chapter of my monograph. Thanks so much to each of you.

Most of all, however, I would like to express my gratitude and abiding love to my wife, Catherine, and my daughters Hannah and Melissa. This book would never have been written had it not been for their patience, encouragement, good humor, and sense of adventure as we encountered together the fascinating, foreign, vibrant and wonderful city of Geneva— both old and new. This book is dedicated to them, with thankfulness for the adventures we have shared together.

ABBREVIATIONS

AHR	*American Historical Review*
ARG	*Archiv für Reformationsgeschichte*
BHR	*Bibliothèque d'humanisme et renaissance*
BSHPF	*Bulletin de la société de l'histoire du Protestantisme français*
CB	*Correspondance de Théodore de Bèze.* Vols. 1–35. Edited by Hippolyte Aubert, Henri Meylan, Alain Dufour, et al. Geneva: Librairie Droz, 1960–2011.
CDM	Paul Chaix, Alain Dufour, and Gustave Moeckli, *Les livres imprimés à Genève de 1550 à 1600.* Geneva: Librairie Droz, 1966.
CNTC	*Calvin's New Testament Commentaries.* 12 vols. Edited by D. W. Torrance and T. F. Torrance. Grand Rapids, Mich.: Eerdmans, 1959–1972.
CO	John Calvin. *Ioannis Calvini opera omnia quae supersunt.* Edited by G. Baum, E. Cunitz, and E. Reuss. 59 vols. Brunsvigae: C. A. Schwetschke, 1863–1900.
COTC	*Calvin's Old Testament Commentaries.* 3 vols. Edited by D. W. Torrance and T. F. Torrance. Grand Rapids, Mich.: Eerdmans, 1959–1972.
CTJ	*Calvin Theological Journal*
CTSOT & *CTSNT*	Calvin Translation Society edition of Calvin's *Old Testament and New Testament Commentaries.* 46 vols. Reprint. Grand Rapids, Mich.: Baker Books, 1989.
CTS	Calvin Translation Society edition of *Selected Works of John Calvin. Tracts and Letters.* 7 vols. Edited by H. Beveridge. Reprint. Grand Rapids, Mich.: Baker, 1983.
EO (1541)	*Ecclesiastical Ordinances* (1541). In Henri Heyer. *L'Église de Genève, Esquisse historique de son organization,* 261–275. Geneva: A. Jullien, 1909.

FP	*La France protestante ou vies des protestants français.* 9 vols. Edited by Eugène Haag and Emile Haag. Geneva: Slatkine Reprints, 1966.
FP 2nd ed.	*La France protestante ou vies des protestants français.* 2nd ed. 6 vols. Edited by Eugène Haag and Emile Haag. Paris: Sandoz and Fischbacher, 1877–1888.
Institutes	John Calvin. *Institutes of the Christian Religion.* 2 vols. Edited by J. T. McNeill and F. L Battles. Philadelphia: Westminster Press, 1960.
LR	*Le Livre du Recteur de l'Académie de Genève.* 6 vols. Edited by Sven and Suzanne Stelling-Michaud. Geneva: Librairie Droz, 1959–1980.
LW	*Luther's Works.* Vols. 1–30. Edited by Jaroslav Pelikan. St. Louis: Concordia, 1955–1986. Vols. 31–55. Edited by Helmut Lehmann. Philadelphia: Fortress, 1955–1986.
OER	*Oxford Encyclopedia of the Reformation.* 4 vols. Edited by Hans Hillerbrand. New York: Oxford University Press, 1996.
PC	Unpublished folders of the *Proces Criminel.* Archiv d'État de Genève.
RCP	*Registres de la Compagnie des Pasteurs de Genève.* 13 vols. Edited by Jean-François Bergier, Robert Kingdon, et al. Geneva: Librairie Droz, 1962–2001.
RC	Unpublished volumes of the *Registres du Conseil de Genève.* Archiv d'État de Genève.
R. Consist.	*Registres du Consistoire de Genève au Temps de Calvin.* 5 vols. Edited by Thomas Lambert and Isabella Watt. Geneva: Librairie Droz, 1996–2010.
R. Consist.	Unpublished volumes of the *Registres du Consistoire,* 1551–1609. Archiv d'État de Genève.
SC	*Supplementa Calviniana Sermon inédits.* Vols. 2, 3, 5, 6, 7, 8 10.3, 11.1, 11.2. Edited by Erwin Mülhaupt et al. Neukirchen: Neukirchener, 1936–.
SCJ	*Sixteenth Century Journal*
WA	*D. Martin Luthers Werke. Kritische Gesamtausgabe.* 62 vols. Weimar: Böhlaus, 1883–.
WTJ	*Westminster Theological Journal*

Calvin's Company of Pastors

Introduction

THE SCENE COULD SCARCELY have been more poignant. On April 28, 1564, the Geneva reformer John Calvin summoned the city's ministers to his residence on the rue des Chanoines to give them final instructions as he lay dying of tuberculosis. The pastors who crowded into Calvin's sitting room that day were, like Calvin himself, religious exiles, men who had left families and fortunes behind in France and had come to Geneva for the sake of the evangelical faith.[1] Among the company were several of Calvin's closest friends and long-time colleagues: the gifted Hebraist Michel Cop; the ferocious preacher Raymond Chauvet; the brilliant, but precocious, Nicolas Colladon; the noble-born poet and theologian Theodore Beza—all companions-in-arms with Calvin in the struggle to establish reformed Protestantism in Geneva and France.[2] Calvin spoke to his colleagues for around a quarter hour.[3] He reminisced about the early years of Geneva's Reformation and the intense hostility that he had faced. He defended his teaching ministry and his role as an interpreter of Scripture. He expressed public support for his chosen successor, Theodore Beza. He apologized for his short temper during his long illness. Finally, he exhorted his pastoral colleagues to be on guard against all religious innovation in the future. "I beg you also to change nothing and to avoid innovation," Calvin stated, "not because I am ambitious to preserve my own work...but because all changes are dangerous, and sometimes even harmful." At the end of his speech, Calvin shook the hands of each of his pastoral colleagues, who left his bedside with heavy hearts and (according to Beza) not a few tears. A month later John Calvin, the reformer of Geneva, was dead.

John Calvin was undoubtedly the leading theologian and chief architect of Geneva's Protestant church in the sixteenth century. But the long-term success of his religious program depended in large part on the company of reformed ministers who worked alongside Calvin with daily responsibilities for preaching the Word, performing the sacraments, enforcing discipline, and providing pastoral care in Geneva's three city churches and a dozen countryside parishes. During the mid 1540s, Calvin organized this group of ministers into a formal church institution known as the Company of Pastors which met every Friday morning to examine candidates for ministry and discuss the theological and practical business of the church, both locally and internationally. In time, the membership of the Company of Pastors—or the Venerable Company, as it was sometimes called—included eight to ten ministers from the city's churches, four professors from the Genevan Academy, and another ten or eleven pastors who served the small parish churches in the surrounding villages under Geneva's jurisdiction. From 1536 to 1609, more than 130 men belonged to the Company at one time or another. Several of these ministers who worked alongside Calvin and his successors Theodore Beza and Simon Goulart were highly regarded churchmen and theologians in their own right, with reputations that extended far beyond the shores of Lac Léman. Historians have studied the more prominent of these ministers, including Guillaume Farel, Pierre Viret, Lambert Daneau, Antoine de Chandieu, Jean de Serres, and Jean Diodati.[4] But most of Geneva's pastors during these seven decades, both those who occupied city pulpits and those who served countryside parishes, have received little scholarly attention and are all but forgotten—men such as Michel Cop, Raymond Chauvet, Jean Trembley, Charles Perrot, Antoine de La Faye, Gabriel Cusin, Jean Gervais, and Jean Jaquemot. Fortunately, precious details of their lives and ministries have been preserved in a variety of sixteenth- and early seventeenth-century sources, notably the register of the Company of Pastors, the register of the Genevan Consistory, and the register of the Small Council of Geneva. These archival deposits provide a fragmentary, but rich, mosaic of the color and texture of religious life in early modern Geneva, offering intriguing insights into some of the particular difficulties, dilemmas, and demands that Geneva's pastors encountered as they proclaimed the Word of God and shepherded their Christian flock.

The central purpose of this book is to examine the pastoral theology and practical ministry activities of this cadre of men who served as pastors in Geneva's churches during nearly three-quarters of a century from 1536 to 1609. It explores not only how Calvin, Beza, Goulart, and their colleagues defined the office and functions of the reformed pastorate, but also the manner in which this conceptual ideal was translated into everyday practice in their ministries of preaching, pastoral care, church discipline, visitation, catechesis, and the administration of the sacraments. At the same time, this study will attempt to shed light on the "culture" of Geneva's pastoral company, that is, the regnant assumptions, attitudes, and rules that defined the ministers' identity and self-awareness as a clerical community, an identity that affected how they related to the laypeople in their congregations and to Geneva's civil magistrates.[5] Along the way a variety of important questions will also be explored: How receptive were Geneva's townspeople and country folk to their ministers' preaching and pastoral supervision? To what extent did Calvin's successors in Geneva remain faithful to the reformer's theology and religious program during the final decades of the sixteenth century? In what ways did the practice of pastoral ministry change in Geneva after Calvin? In sum, this book explores the degree to which Geneva's ministers after Calvin obeyed his admonition to "change nothing."

The structure and practical shape of religious life in Protestant Geneva was set in place during the first two decades following Geneva's political revolution in 1536. The city's reformed church was codified by legal statute in the *Ecclesiastical Ordinances* (1541), forged through the protracted struggle between political and religious leaders, and shaped by the formidable theological vision and moral authority of the person of John Calvin. When measured by these early, volatile decades, the leadership of Beza and his pastoral colleagues after 1564 appears on the whole conservative. Styling themselves as defenders rather than innovators of Geneva's religious establishment, Geneva's ministers in the late sixteenth century took seriously their responsibility to uphold the *Ecclesiastical Ordinances*, teach Calvin's *Catechism*, and conserve Calvin's biblical vision of a religious community faithful to God in doctrine and discipline. Consequently, during the period 1536 to 1609, the basic elements of Calvin's conception of the pastoral office, with its commitment to Christian proclamation, collegial ministry, and church discipline, remained unchanged. The minister Antoine de La Faye echoed Calvin's sentiments, and spoke for most of his colleagues, when he advised Geneva's city council in 1605 that "everyone has recognized that change and novelty is extremely dangerous, especially in ecclesiastical matters."[6] Nevertheless, this book will demonstrate that religious life in Geneva and the texture of pastoral ministry *did* change during the generation after Calvin due to a variety of political, religious, social, and polemical factors. In some cases, Geneva's magistrates forced religious change upon the Company of Pastors through negotiation, or even intimidation, in an effort to extend their jurisdiction over church policy in the city. On other occasions, reforms were initiated by the ministers themselves, as they attempted to work out the implications of Calvin's ecclesial program and theology in the face of new religious contexts and challenges. Even if Calvin's legacy loomed large over Geneva's church throughout the period, the theory and practice of pastoral ministry changed in subtle ways during the half century after Calvin's death in 1564.

My analysis of Geneva's pastors has been significantly shaped by the methods and findings of other historians who have investigated the evangelical clergy during the era of the Reformation. As late as 1983, Robert Kingdon could still express bewilderment at the dearth of scholarly literature available on the clergy in the sixteenth century, even though it was the social class most affected by the Reformation.[7] In the decades since, an impressive harvest of specialized studies has been produced that has added considerably to our understanding of these social elites. Research on the Protestant clergy and the pastoral office in early modern Europe has followed a number of different trajectories, including (1) local and regional studies of Protestant clergy and clerical institutions; (2) comparative studies of the theological structure and practical function of Catholic and Protestant ministers; (3) long-term statistical studies of the social profile of European clergy, employing the method of "social biography"; and (4) specialized studies of clerical activities, including preaching, moral discipline, and the celebration of the sacraments. Here I will briefly discuss the first three trajectories. The literature on preaching, moral discipline, and the sacraments will be introduced in later chapters.

Bernard Vogler's magisterial study of religious life in the Rhineland during the second half of the sixteenth century (published in 1976) has done much to spark renewed interest in clergy and clerical institutions.[8] Drawing upon visitation reports, sermons, and disciplinary records, Vogler tracked the economic, social, intellectual, and religious behavior of nearly 2,200 reformed and Lutheran ministers between 1555 and 1619. Following his lead, social historians examined pastoral ministry and religious life in other regions of Western Europe such as Ernestine Saxony, Strasbourg, Zurich, Geneva, Württemberg, and Basel.[9] These local and regional studies broadened our understanding of the clergy's background and training, economic conditions, family life, pastoral duties, and relationship with parishioners. Many of these studies address the provocative thesis, proposed by Gerald Strauss thirty years ago, that the Reformation failed in its objective to root out Catholic and popular beliefs from among the laypeople, despite the best efforts of Protestant clergy to indoctrinate them through sermons, schools, and catechisms.[10] Although scholars of early modern Europe now frame the debate rather differently, the question of how parishioners in the city or countryside understood and responded to Protestant teaching remains a fertile subject for investigation. For example, Bruce Gordon's study of Zurich's rural parishes between 1532 and 1580 illustrates the many difficulties faced by the city's ministers as they taught reformed doctrine and attempted to eradicate traditional folk practices and Catholic rituals among villagers who continued to value popular religious practices, proscribed festivals, and drunken revelries. At least during Heinrich Bullinger's lifetime, popular spirituality proved to be "unassailable" to the pastors' instruction and correction.[11] Amy Nelson Burnett's recent book on clerical education and pastoral ministry in Basel draws a more positive assessment. She argues that by the early seventeenth century one can identify "a fundamental transformation of belief and conduct" among Basel's city and rural parishioners, thanks to nearly a century of Protestant instruction and pastoral care, along with the magistrates' commitment to enforce moral discipline.[12] These examples remind us that Protestant ministers occupied a crucial, yet awkward position in sixteenth-century society. They were called to straddle the divide between God and sinful humanity, between city and countryside, between a written educated culture and a (largely) oral culture.

So too, their sacred vocation made them duty bound to transmit the evangelical message of theologians such as Luther, Calvin, or Zwingli to ordinary burghers and rustic peasants, translating these gospel truths into a vernacular that spoke to everyday life and experience.

A second trajectory of research has explored the way in which Protestant reformers dismantled the traditional conception of the Catholic priesthood and erected in its place a radically new construction of pastoral office and ministry that transformed religious life in the parishes.[13] Protestantism shattered the ritualistic universe of medieval Catholicism and desacralized the clerical office: the power and privileges of the Catholic clergy were truncated; saints' days were replaced by the Lord's Day; the Latin Mass was replaced by vernacular sermons; the celibate priest was replaced by the married pastor.[14] As R. Emmet McLaughlin has shown, evangelical doctrines such as justification by faith alone, the supreme authority of Scripture, and the priesthood of all believers elicited new understandings of Christian ministry.[15] Martin Luther's message that sinners were righteous before God through faith in Christ alone (*sola fide*) not only undermined the Catholic penitential system, but also cut at the root of the medieval priest's sacral role as a dispenser of salvific grace through the sacraments of the church. The Protestant reformers elevated instead the biblical office of the Christian minister or pastor, whose primary responsibility was to preach the Word of God and supervise the behavior of the spiritual community. "[W]hoever does not preach the Word," Luther insisted, "is no priest at all" because "the sacrament of ordination can be nothing else than a certain rite by which the church chooses its preachers."[16] That is not to say that late medieval Catholics ignored the ministry of preaching, nor that Protestant life and worship was empty of religious ritual. Historians now recognize a significant revival of preaching in the century before the Reformation, most evident in the work of mendicant friars and the creation of municipal preacherships.[17] At the same time, despite Protestant criticisms of Catholic "ceremonies" and "superstitions," and despite explosive acts of iconoclasm against Catholic images, the evangelical reformers preserved in modified form traditional rites surrounding the Eucharist, baptism, and reconciliation.[18] Nevertheless, the general pattern still holds true: for Catholics, the primary role of the clergy remained sacramental and liturgical; for the Protestant reformers, it was to preach the Word of God.

In a similar fashion, the Protestant doctrine of *sola scriptura*—the conviction that Holy Scripture was the unique, final authority for the Christian community—had important consequences for pastoral ministry. The scripture principle gave gravitas to the office of preacher. It also made the educational formation of Protestant clergy an urgent priority, especially in those academic disciplines most necessary for biblical exposition such as classic rhetoric, theology, and biblical exegesis. By transferring the locus of authority from the Catholic magisterium to the written Word of God, the reformers enhanced the personal authority of the minister, who was now entrusted with special responsibility to interpret and proclaim the sacred text. Over time, the Protestant clergy emerged as a well-educated group of religious specialists, separated by social position and training from most of the laypeople whom they served.[19] The ministers' authority and the creation of a clerical estate could—and no doubt sometimes did—run counter to the Reformation commitment to the priesthood of all believers, but countervailing factors were at work as well. As Steven Ozment has shown, clerical marriage on the whole assured that Protestant pastors were better integrated into the familial, social, and economic networks of their local communities.[20] Furthermore, evangelicals rejected the Catholic view that ordination conferred on clergy the "indelible character" of objective holiness and sacred power. "I cannot understand at all why one who has once been made a priest cannot again become a layman," Luther opined, "for the sole difference between him and a layman is his ministry."[21] If the magisterial reformers were less sanguine about the spiritual discernment of the common folk following the Peasants' War of 1525, they nonetheless continued to encourage laypeople to proclaim gospel truth to one another and believed divine pardon could be achieved without clerical mediation.[22] In all these ways, then, the office of Protestant pastor brought significant structural changes to the landscape of religious life in early modern Europe.

A third trajectory of research is seen among scholars who have attempted to create a comparative social profile of Protestant and Catholic clergy in the century after the Reformation. Luise Schorn-Schütte and a team of researchers affiliated with the Johannes Wolfgang Goethe University are employing the methodological tool of social biography (*Sozialbiographie*) to draw a composite picture of Lutheran, reformed, and Catholic clergymen in early modern Europe, identifying common patterns in their social and geographical backgrounds, their training and educational levels, their professional duties, and their perceptions of themselves and others.[23] Although cross-confessional social research on early modern clergy is still in its infancy, Schorn-Schütte argues that preliminary findings already challenge long-held misconceptions. By the beginning of the seventeenth century, the educational levels and social backgrounds of Protestant pastors were not significantly different from that of Catholic priests. More often than not, pastors and priests had some university education, though not always theological training. The heightened social prestige assigned to the clerical office made it particularly attractive to the sons of prosperous burghers, wealthy peasants, and territorial officials.[24] According to historians Wolfgang Reinhard and Heinz Schilling, it was this professional competence, social prominence, and moral leadership of early modern clergy that positioned them to play a strategic role in the historical process of "confessionalization," that is, the process of political centralization and social disciplining that proved decisive for the emergence of the modern state in early seventeenth-century Europe. For Schilling, this collaboration between political rulers and compliant churchmen—the former enforcing confessional orthodoxy, overseeing clergy, and compelling religious conformity in their territories; the latter creating ecclesiastical bureaucracies and institutions to manage church life, educate the young, and supervise moral discipline—was a key factor in the creation of "rationalized" states, characterized by bureaucratic efficiency, disciplined subjects, and obedient clergymen and lesser magistrates.[25] While Schorn-Schütte concurs that pastors and priests during this time period frequently served the interests of centralized political authority, her research indicates that the clergy's self-perception as moral guardians of their Christian flocks often led them to adopt a critical stance toward secular authority. Early modern clergymen were much more than mere "agents of the state."[26]

In recent years the theology and practice of pastoral ministry in Calvin's Geneva has also attracted scholarly attention. The person of John Calvin has traditionally dominated Geneva's religious history in the same way that the Reformation Wall, with its larger-than-life granite figure of John Calvin, towers over park Bastion in modern-day Geneva. Calvin has long been a boon for biographers and theologians, some canonizing him as saint, others vilifying him as incarnate demon, but all intrigued by the "bookish, secretive Reformer of Geneva" (to quote Bernard Cottret's memorable phrase).[27] The historical portrait of Calvin that has too often emerged is of a dispassionate "theologian," or a rarified "mind," disengaged from the practical responsibilities and concerns of everyday parish life.[28] Moreover, the commanding presence of Calvin has often relegated to the shadows the contributions of pastoral colleagues who worked alongside him as well as those so-called epigones who served the Genevan church after his death. In the past forty years, scholars have taken a very different tack. Following the lead of Robert Kingdon, social historians have explored in detail the religious institutions that Calvin established in Geneva, particularly the Venerable Company of Pastors, the Consistory, and the Genevan Academy.[29] As a result, we now know a great deal more about how Calvin and his colleagues preached[30] and conducted public worship,[31] enforced moral discipline over their parishioners,[32] and interacted with Geneva's magistrates.[33] So too, valuable studies now exist that describe the form and function of the church office of elder and deacon,[34] as well as the manner in which the Academy prepared men for Christian ministry.[35] This new accent on Calvin's practical concern for church ministry has also prompted scholars to consider the reformer's self-understanding as a pastor and his commitment to *pietas* and spiritual nurture.[36] Elsie Anne McKee's anthology of Calvin's writings on pastoral piety (published in the Classics of Western Spirituality series) provides eloquent testimony to Calvin's own vibrant spirituality, and his commitment as professor, preacher, and pastor to guide his parishioners toward a deeper awareness of God and love for one another.[37]

Customarily, Calvin's death in the year 1564 has served as the *terminus ad quem* for scholarship on religious life in early modern Geneva.[38] As a consequence, historians have never systematically studied the manner in which Calvin's vision for preaching and pastoral care was implemented and modified by Geneva's ministers during the final decades of the sixteenth century. Eugène Choisy's study of political and religious life in Geneva during the ministry of Theodore Beza remains the best survey of pastoral activity during this period, even though it is more than a century old.[39] Choisy's purpose was not so much to illuminate the clerical office or theology of Geneva's pastors, as to chart the protracted struggle between the ministers and magistrates for prerogative over ecclesiastical affairs in the city. Choisy shows that by the early seventeenth century, the "balance of power" established by Calvin had clearly swung to the side of the magistrates, thanks in large part to Theodore Beza's less combative style of leadership. In the century since Choisy's work, a handful of other relevant studies have appeared treating Theodore Beza's sermons and pastoral theology, as well as the Consistory's role in church discipline after Calvin.[40] The most important contribution is Christian Grosse's study of the ritual of the Lord's Supper in sixteenth- and early seventeenth-century Geneva.[41] He not only places Eucharistic practice within its historical, theological, and liturgical contexts, but also examines the strategic role that ecclesiastical discipline and moral supervision played in daily religious life in early modern Geneva. Grosse's expansive study invites further research on pastoral ministry that explores how "high theology" was translated into daily religious practice in late Reformation Geneva.

This present book provides a systematic study of Geneva's ministers, their pastoral theology, and practical ministry activities during nearly three-quarters of a century from 1536 to 1609. The chronological scope of this book requires some explanation. The year 1536 is an appropriate starting point in that it marked the decisive year of Geneva's religious Reformation and the commencement of Calvin's ministry in the city. The choice of the year 1609 is less clear, though not altogether arbitrary. By the first decade of the seventeenth century, four prominent city pastors, whose combined service to the Genevan church totaled more than 160 years, had passed from the scene. In their place, Simon Goulart and a new generation of pastoral leaders was emerging that would guide the church deep into the new century. As we shall see, this transfer of leadership brought important changes to the Genevan church, particularly in the years immediately after Theodore Beza's death in 1605. Examining the pastoral office in Geneva over the course of seven decades—a period spanning Calvin's pastoral career, the duration of Beza's ministry, and the four years following Beza's death—allows us to trace out in detail Calvin's pastoral legacy and the efforts of his successors on the Venerable Company who were committed to preserving it.

This study is made possible by the rich collection of historical resources found in Geneva's State Archive that relate to religious life during the early modern period. In addition to the published registers of the Company of Pastors, I make extensive use of manuscript sources such as the thirty-eight volumes of Consistory minutes from this period,[42] pertinent city council minutes, ministers' correspondence, criminal proceedings, parish reports, and baptismal records. This archival material will be supplemented with a variety of published materials coming from the pens of Calvin, Beza, Goulart, and their colleagues, including sermons, biblical commentaries, prayer books, catechisms, spiritual discourses, and theological writings. This study of pastoral ministry in reformed Geneva is divided into two general sections. The first part, chapters 1 through 5, explores the history and nature of the pastoral office and details the personnel who belonged to the pastoral company from 1536 to 1609. In the first chapter, I describe the events leading to Geneva's political and religious revolution of 1536 and show how principles codified in the *Ecclesiastical Ordinances* (1541) as well as John Calvin's strategic leadership shaped the structure of the ministerial office over the decades that followed. Chapter 2 introduces the ministers who worked alongside or succeeded Calvin between 1536 and 1609 and highlights the career paths and leadership patterns of the most prominent of these ministers. The three chapters that follow describe the recruitment and election of Geneva's ministers (chapter 3), the pastors' family relationships and their financial conditions (chapter 4), and the general rhythm of pastoral work in both the city and countryside churches (chapter 5). The second part of the book examines more closely the specific duties that Geneva's ministers performed as a part of their pastoral vocations, whether preaching (chapter 6); supervising moral behavior (chapter 7); writing books (chapter 8); or providing pastoral care to their parishioners through sacraments, catechesis, visitation, and spiritual consolation (chapter 9). In each case, I consider the dynamic interplay between theory and practice, showing how social and political factors, as well as theology and biblical exegesis, shaped the way Geneva's pastoral company conceived of and performed these ministry tasks.

The reader will encounter three important themes wending their way through the chapters of this book. First, the ministers of Geneva (and indeed, of early modern Europe in general) cannot be understood rightly unless one appreciates the religious nature of their sense of vocation. More than purveyors of spiritual "commodities" or "agents of the state," the pastors in this book emerge as men committed to the reformation of the church and devoted to the spiritual instruction and care of God's people. If their vocation was invariably expressed within a complex matrix of social, political, and economic relationships, this in no way diminished the essential religious nature of their self-identity as preachers and pastors. Second, it is inaccurate to portray Calvin and his pastoral colleagues as ivory-tower theologians, disengaged from the everyday concerns of their parishioners. On the contrary, as evident in their ministries of preaching and pastoral care, the pastors of Geneva devoted much of their time and energy to addressing practical matters of Christian discipleship, enjoining townspeople and peasants alike to conduct lives characterized by faith, hope, love, and repentance. Carter Lindberg's general assessment of Reformation theologians certainly holds true for the ministers of Geneva during the sixteenth and early seventeenth centuries: "Theology for them was not an abstract academic enterprise, but rather was always related to ministry through Word, Sacrament, and service. Theology for them was indeed always 'practical.'"[43] Third, it will be demonstrated that while Beza, Goulart, and their pastoral colleagues jealously guarded the legacy of John Calvin, they made subtle changes to the expression of pastoral ministry in Geneva in response to the practical challenges they faced. Recognizing this, however, does not mean that Geneva's ministers after Calvin should be judged as bold innovators who betrayed Calvin's theological and ecclesiastical program—their innovations were far too modest for such an assessment. It will be suggested that a more fruitful historical approach is to treat Calvin and his so-called epigones on their own terms, evaluating their theology and religious behavior according to the standards that they set for themselves. When Geneva's ministers are viewed from this perspective, they take on an altogether different character as men of enormous complexity who, even as they frequently displayed courageous commitment and unbending moral conviction, were subject to the same moral frailties, pettiness, and pride that they so scrupulously attempted to correct in their parishioners. It is my primary concern, then, not to employ a hermeneutic of suspicion when judging Geneva's ministers, but to exercise both charity and critical subtlety in evaluating the pastoral behavior of Calvin and his colleagues in light of their unique historical and religious contexts. Peter Brown's penetrating observation regarding the historian's role in elucidating the complexities of human experience should serve as our model in this regard: "To explore such people with sympathy, with trained insight, and with a large measure of common cunning, is to learn again to appreciate...[that] 'Man is a vast deep.'"[44]

| Geneva and Her Reformation

FOR OVER THREE CENTURIES before John Calvin arrived in Geneva, the cathedral of St. Pierre stood like a stone sentinel maintaining vigil over the city. Built on the spine of a hill that ran the length of the Upper City, the bishop's church was in command of a broad horizon: the teeming markets and boutiques below in the Lower City; the blue waters of Lac Léman with small fishing boats and larger *barques* plowing its surface; the surrounding countryside, rich with vineyards, pastures, and grain fields; and further in the distance, the jagged snow-crowned peaks of the Prealps. If Geneva's cathedral seemed a silent, impassive witness to the passing of seasons and years, her six bells—the "voices" of St. Pierre—were neither silent nor inattentive to change. In the late Middle Ages, the bells of the cathedral marked the boundaries of daily existence and heightened the drama of urban life. Bells were rung to announce the beginning (4 a.m.) and end (9 p.m.) of the day; bells called people to worship and prayer; bells sounded the alarm of plague and fire; bells celebrated the glad tidings of feast days and the arrival of distinguished visitors; bells mourned the dead. The largest and best known of St. Pierre's bells was La Clémence, a five-ton bell commissioned by the bishop of Geneva, Guillaume de Lornay, and placed in the north tower of the cathedral in 1407. The Gothic inscription around the base of La Clémence described well her responsibilities: "I praise the true God, I summon the people, I assemble the clergy, I weep for the dead, I chase away the plague, I adorn feast days. My voice strikes terror in all demons."[1]

The cathedral of St. Pierre and her bells stood at the epicenter of the unfolding political and religious crisis that ultimately gave birth, in 1536, to an independent republic and a Christian church intended to be reformed in doctrine and practice. This "reformation," or, better, this "revolution," fundamentally changed the structure of political and religious life and set Geneva on a new and dangerous course.[2] Once a relatively obscure Catholic city nestled in the European heartland, the small republic of

Geneva was now thrust to the center stage of Europe's religious drama. Within a few short years, she emerged as a haven for Protestant refugees, a publishing center, and an intellectual brain trust—the center of French-speaking Protestantism—praised by admirers as a "mirror and model of true religion and virtue," maligned by enemies as the "synagogue of the Antichrist."[3] The account of John Calvin's arrival in Geneva in the summer of 1536 and of his strategic leadership of the church in the decades that followed has been told many times. Less well-known is how Calvin's theological and pastoral vision was preserved and shaped by Geneva's ministers in the generations after his death. In order to understand and appreciate the challenges faced by Calvin and his successors, I first summarize the revolutionary era that culminated in the birth of a new church as well as explore Calvin's conception of the pastoral office and the ecclesiastical institutions that he established in Geneva. The final section of this chapter describes the texture of religious life and worship in Geneva during Calvin's lifetime.

1. The Bells of St. Pierre

La Clémence and the bells of St. Pierre's cathedral were not only witnesses but also accomplices to political revolution and religious change. At the dawn of the sixteenth century, Geneva remained very much a traditional, Catholic city. She was the episcopal seat of a vast diocese, spanning 4,200 square miles and including around 450 parishes. The prince-bishop was not only the spiritual head of the diocese but also the temporal lord of Geneva and the surrounding districts which he governed—usually in absentia—with the assistance of the episcopal council and the thirty-two canons that made up the cathedral chapter.[4] The city and its immediate environs boasted seven parish churches and five monasteries. All told, about five hundred secular and regular clergy ministered in the city, constituting around 5 percent of Geneva's ten thousand townsfolk.[5] The privilege to sound St. Pierre's bells belonged to Geneva's four syndics (chief magistrates in the city) and especially to the cathedral chapter, which paid a bell ringer five sols per year to perform this duty. Accordingly, throughout each day, bells were heard summoning the faithful to the Mass, marking the monastic office, announcing meetings of the cathedral chapter, and celebrating the anniversaries of notable churchmen and honored saints. From time to time, the towers of the cathedral pealed with song to proclaim special religious occasions, such as when the bishop paid a visit to Geneva in 1525 or when a procession was held in support of a crusade against the Turks five years later.[6]

By 1520, the prince-bishop's temporal authority over Geneva was becoming increasingly attenuated due to the expansionist aims of the powerful dukes of Savoy. During the course of the Middle Ages, the House of Savoy emerged as one of the most powerful kingdoms in Western Europe, a vast duchy that stretched from the Jura Mountains to northern Italy. In the fourteenth century, Savoy gained control over the territories immediately surrounding Geneva and, recognizing the city's strategic importance as a prosperous commercial center standing at the crossroads of Europe, began maneuvering to annex the city.[7] Over the next century, the dukes expanded their influence within Geneva, achieving the prerogative to appoint judges and execute capital justice in the city. In the mid-fifteenth century, the dukes of Savoy managed to secure from the pope the privilege of nominating candidates to the episcopal office; henceforth, all of Geneva's prince-bishops were either members of the House of Savoy or noble patrons of the dukes.[8] Savoyard sovereignty over Geneva appeared a fait accompli in 1515, when the bishop of Geneva, Jean de Savoy, agreed to cede all his temporal authority to Duke Charles III (who was the bishop's nephew)—a grant approved by the pope but later nullified by the college of cardinals.[9] The expansion of Savoyard influence in Geneva was not welcomed by all the citizens, however. A "republican" faction of Geneva's townspeople, under the leadership of Philibert Berthelier, took the decisive step in 1519 of securing a treaty of *Combourgeoisie* (an agreement to provide mutual defense) with the Swiss canton of Fribourg in hopes of preserving the freedom of the commune. Charles III acted swiftly to crush this challenge to his authority: in short order the treaty was annulled and Berthelier was executed. The duke marched into Geneva with a show of military force, declaring, "The Genevans are my subjects."[10] For the moment at least, the pro-Savoy faction (known as the Mamelus) was in control of the city, and the duke's victory appeared complete. The high point of Savoyard rule arrived six years later, on December 10, 1525, when Charles III forced Geneva's citizens at a general council known as the Council of Hallebardes to recognize him as the sovereign protector of the city.

But the spirit of republicanism had not died with Berthelier. Since the early 1520s, a small group of Genevan patriots known as the Eidguenots had been working tirelessly to forge a political alliance with the Swiss that would preserve Geneva's freedom from Savoy. In the aftermath of the Council of Hallebardes, the fugitive Eidguenot leaders succeeded in concluding a second treaty of *Combourgeoisie* with the cantons of Fribourg and Bern. In February of 1526, the Eidguenot leader Besançon Hugues returned from exile with the treaty in hand and rallied his fellow citizens against the Mamelus-dominated Small Council. On February 25, as La Clémence tolled in the tower of St. Pierre, a general assembly of Geneva's townspeople defied the prince-bishop and the Duke of Savoy by ratifying the treaty of alliance with Savoy's enemies.[11] In the same year, the Genevans created a new political body, the Council of 200, which embodied this same communal spirit and reflected the citizens' growing determination to govern themselves. Thus, by 1526, the primary political institutions of the future republic were in place, namely the Small Council (made up of four syndics and twenty senators); the Council of 60 (the Small Council, supplemented by thirty-five representatives from the Council of 200); the Council of 200 (consisting of elected representatives from every neighborhood in the city); and the General Assembly (comprising all the citizens and burghers in the city).[12] With this remarkable turn of events, the Duke of Savoy was no longer welcome in Geneva.

Pealing bells punctuated each successive crisis during the turbulent decade that followed. In 1530, Geneva's churches sounded the alarm when the Duke of Savoy attacked the city in an effort to reestablish control over his prized possession. In desperation, Geneva called for the assistance of her powerful ally and (since 1528) Protestant neighbor Bern. A Bernese contingent of fourteen thousand soldiers with nineteen cannons secured the city in October, though unruly troops vandalized churches in the suburbs and smashed and burned Catholic images. Soldiers even took control temporarily of the cathedral, ringing the bells and installing a reformed chaplain in the pulpit who delivered Protestant sermons in German.[13] Bern's political and military support proved to be a Trojan horse that brought with it unforeseen religious consequences. Beginning in the autumn of 1532, Protestant missionaries from Bern including Guillaume Farel, Antoine Saunier, and Antoine Froment regularly visited the city to preach the gospel and lend support to a small, clandestine community of evangelicals. Around the same time, religious propaganda and illegal French Bibles began to circulate through the city.[14] The activities of the missionaries did not go unnoticed by Geneva's religious authorities. During their first missionary tour, Farel and Saunier were arrested and brought before the bishop's council. Michel Roset's *Chronicle* (1562) reported the interview as follows: "Come now, you wicked devil Farel, what are you doing, going here and there?...Who sent you here to trouble this city?" Farel replied:

I am not a devil. I proclaim Jesus Christ, who was crucified and died for our sins, and resurrected for our justification, so that anyone who believes in him will have eternal life, but those who do not believe will be condemned. For this purpose I was sent by God, our good Father, as an ambassador of Jesus Christ, called to preach to all those who wish to listen to me.[15]

Farel was beaten and expelled from the city, only to return the following year with assurances of Bern's protection.

The evangelical community, now numbering around eighty persons, held its first public worship service during holy week of 1533 in a private garden located two hundred yards outside the city gate. A French hat maker named Guérin Muète who had organized the service and distributed the Lord's Supper was arrested and banished.[16] That same spring religious tensions boiled over into violence. Rumors spread that the evangelicals were making plans to attack and desecrate the city's churches. On May 4, with St. Pierre's tocsin ringing, a Catholic mob of more than one thousand five hundred persons attacked a group of Protestants at the place du Molard.

In the vicious melee that followed, several Protestants were wounded, and a Catholic native from Fribourg named Pierre Werli was killed.[17] In an effort to punish the perpetrators of this murder and halt the advance of the Protestant heresy, Prince-Bishop Pierre de La Baume, after a five-year absence, returned to Geneva in the summer of 1533. The Small Council refused to recognize the bishop's jurisdiction over the crime. He angrily departed the city after only two weeks, never to return.[18]

Events were now turning in favor of the reformers. In December, a Dominican preacher from Chambéry named Guy Furbity in his Advent sermon in St. Pierre launched a verbal attack against the Protestants while defending the doctrine of transubstantiation. In the middle of the sermon, Antoine Froment and Alexandre Canus jumped up and demanded that the preacher justify his teaching from Scripture. In the ensuing uproar, Canus shouted that Furbity was preaching lies and was a false prophet.[19] The following spring, Protestant sympathizers seized the Franciscan monastery of the Rive, making it the permanent outpost for Farel and Pierre Viret and their evangelical supporters. More than four hundred people packed the monastery's auditorium to hear Farel preach and to receive the Lord's Supper on Easter Sunday, 1534. The ringing of "Protestant" bells from the Franciscan monastery served as a very public and provocative reminder that evangelicals were meeting within the walled city.[20] During this period a number of Catholic clergy began to show interest in the reform. At Pentecost, one of the chaplains of the cathedral named Louis Bernard attended a Protestant sermon and then publicly declared his allegiance to the evangelical faith. The Catholic chronicler Jeanne de Jussie noted with disgust that Bernard married a young Lutheran widow two days later.[21] The next year, Thomas Vandel, priest of the parish church of St. Germain, also converted. Throughout these turbulent months, the bells of St. Pierre rang time and time again, raising the alarm and, invariably, intensifying religious passions. In May 1534, the syndics of Geneva put La Clémence under lock and key and prohibited the cathedral canons from ringing it in an effort to calm the tensions.[22]

Geneva's magistrates were caught on the horns of a dilemma. Political independence from Savoy was their primary objective. But such independence required close ties with powerful Bern, a Protestant territory that was not without its own expansionist designs. And Bernese support brought with it reformed missionaries, whose inflammatory preaching regularly ignited iconoclasm and sectarian violence. From time to time, city officials arrested and punished evangelicals who distributed Protestant literature, disturbed the public peace, or desecrated Catholic property, but they had no stomach for a general purge of the Protestant preachers. In fact, by the spring of 1535, the magistrates had more or less conceded to Farel the monastery of the Rive for public worship. This moderate policy indicates that the city magistrates were divided in their religious commitments. Several of Geneva's city councilors were sympathetic to the Protestants' message and had become advocates of Reformation. Most were more cautious, seeking a middle way that placated Bern and restrained religious violence, while at the same time remaining faithful to the traditional church.

By late spring of 1534, this policy of moderation was becoming nearly impossible to sustain. In May of that year, the Catholic canton of Fribourg, the third member of the *Combourgeoisie*, withdrew from the alliance in protest against Geneva's all-too-passive stance toward the Protestant heresy. Two months later, the city repulsed a surprise attack staged by the bishop and the Duke of Savoy. In response, Geneva's magistrates ruled the office of prince-bishop vacant in October 1534.[23] The city roiled in a new crisis the following March when several Protestant leaders, including the reformer Pierre Viret, became ill from spinach that had been laced with poison. A canon from the cathedral was implicated in the crime. This scandal, and the renewed iconoclasm that it provoked, forced the Small Council to convene a public disputation between Protestant and Catholic partisans on May 30, 1535, in the auditorium of the monastery of the Rive.[24] The chief disputants on the Protestant side were Farel, Viret, and a former Franciscan named Jacques Bernard; the Catholic side was represented by the prior of the Dominican monastery of Plainpalais, Jean Chalais, along with a Sorbonne doctor named Pierre Caroli. For more than three weeks, the two parties debated central Protestant propositions, including justification by faith alone, Scripture's authority over the church, Jesus Christ as the sole mediator between God and man, the futility of praying to saints, and the abomination of the papal Mass. In their closing arguments, the evangelicals demanded "the abolition of the great abuse of the Mass, images and all human inventions by which the holy name of God is greatly blasphemed and the poor people are led to perdition."[25] The Catholics had a ready rejoinder, one that must have crystallized the most trenchant fears of the city's magistrates:

> If you tear down the images, the Masses and all the Papal things as preachers and those who favor them want you to do, know that for every enemy you now have there will be a hundred: and in place of your old and great enemy, the Duke of Savoy, you will have the King of France, who is his nephew, as your adversary, as well as the Emperor, who is also his brother-in-law...and they will all be against you as mad wolves chasing prey, to destroy and ruin you.[26]

The disputation ended on June 24 with the magistrates still divided, unwilling to decide in favor of either religious party. For many of the councilors, it seemed that Geneva had too little to gain, and far too much to lose, by embracing the Protestant religion.

The crisis in Geneva between 1532 and 1535 had much in common with the pattern of reformation that occurred in other cities in Switzerland and Germany during this period: the ingredients of evangelical preaching, print propaganda, and public disputations (with civil authorities serving as judges), mixed with popular religious violence, often became a recipe for explosive social and religious change. In Geneva, the continued belligerence of the Catholic Duke of Savoy and the prince-bishop served as an additional factor that pushed the townspeople toward the Protestant faith. Increasingly, political independence and religious reformation were seen as part of the same holy cause. This twofold concern was stamped onto Geneva's newly minted *trois deniers* coin in 1535: one side stated, "Our God fights for us"; the reverse side read, "After darkness, light."[27]

The final stage of Geneva's Reformation was now at hand. On Sunday, August 8, 1535, as La Clémence called townspeople to worship, Guillaume Farel and his Protestant supporters seized control of St. Pierre's cathedral. Farel, standing in the pulpit, delivered a fiery sermon to the congregation. Later in the day, a mob rushed into the cathedral during the vesper service; threatened the priests; and began ransacking the church, smashing religious statues, desecrating the host, and breaking open trunks that held sacred relics.[28] Geneva's magistrates were helpless to stop the destruction. One syndic who watched this violent episode is reported to have said: "If the images really are gods, then they can defend themselves if they want; we do not know what else to do."[29] The next day, August 9, iconoclastic riots spread to other city churches, St. Gervais and Nôtre Dame de Grace, as well as to the Dominican monastery outside the city walls. These riots broke the religious stalemate.[30] On August 10, the Council of 200 voted provisionally to suspend the Mass and ordered that all iconoclasm cease. A week later, the magistrates decreed that sacred objects taken from vandalized churches—crucifixes, reliquaries, plates—be melted down in order to pay Geneva's war debt to Bern.[31]

Religious violence had not yet run its course, however. On August 24, Protestant mobs wielding hammers and axes attacked the convent of the Sisters of Saint Clare in Bourg-de-Four, hacking at statues and devotional benches, and destroying books and breviaries. Jeanne de Jussie and twenty-three of her religious sisters departed for Annecy six days later, protected by an armed escort.[32] Most, but not all, of Geneva's Catholic clergy had left the city by late autumn. In December, the magistrates ordered the Dominican and Franciscan monks who remained in Geneva to attend Protestant sermons or be banished. Thirteen of the twenty Franciscans chose to renounce their religious vows and embraced the Reformation; several even married.[33] On the whole, however, it appears that only a small percentage of regular and secular clergy converted to the Protestant religion and remained in the city in 1535.[34] In the span of two years, Geneva had renounced its bishop, cleansed its churches of "idolatry," and run off hundreds of Catholic religious personnel. The city on the shores of Lac Léman had decisively broken from her Catholic past.

But Geneva's political independence and religious Reformation were not yet secure. During the winter of 1535–1536, the Duke of Savoy laid siege to Geneva in one final attempt to regain control of his prized city. Once again, a Bernese army marched to the rescue, liberating the city on February 2, 1536. Having conquered the Pays de Vaud on the north shore of the lake, the canton of Bern made overtures to assume political sovereignty over Geneva as well. This suggestion the magistrates bluntly declined: they had not overthrown one master to be ruled by another. Later that spring, on May 21, as La Clémence rang forth from the north tower of St. Pierre, the citizens and burghers of Geneva gathered in the General Assembly to adopt the Protestant religion as law. The assembly voted unanimously "to live in this holy Law of the Gospel and the Word of God," as well as to reject "all masses and other ceremonies and papal abuses, images, and idols."[35] The bells that had joyfully welcomed the prince-bishop to the city in 1525 now celebrated Geneva's independence from him.

2. The Reformation of the Parishes

Shortly before his death, John Calvin recalled the desperate condition of Geneva's church when he first visited the city in July of 1536: "When I first arrived in this church there was almost nothing. They were preaching and that's all. They were good at seeking out idols and burning them, but there was no Reformation. Everything was in turmoil."[36] Calvin's memory of this desperate situation was for the most part accurate. The departure of most of the Catholic clergy from the city by the summer of 1536 created a vacuum in leadership and a crisis in pastoral care, especially in the countryside parishes. There was no church constitution or plan to instruct the children. The Mass had been abolished, but no liturgical form had been created to replace it. The relationship between the church and city magistrates had yet to be defined. Guillaume Farel and Geneva's leaders quickly discovered that it was one thing to demolish the existing religious order, quite another to construct a new one in its place.

It is not surprising, then, that Farel discerned the hand of divine providence when John Calvin stopped off in Geneva en route to Strasbourg in July 1536. Neither Calvin's timidity nor his stated intention to pursue a private life of scholarship discouraged the missionary from Bern. Instead, like an Old Testament prophet, Farel threatened God's judgment upon the twenty-seven-year-old Calvin if he did not stay and assist Geneva's church in its hour of great need. The outcome of this dramatic encounter is well-known: a frightened Calvin agreed to stay on in Geneva, first as a "reader" of theology and soon as a city pastor. Over the next twenty-eight years, with the exception of a three-year exile in Strasbourg from 1538 to 1541, Calvin emerged as the chief architect of the Genevan church and the most prominent minister and theologian in the French-speaking Protestant world. One of the most important dimensions of his legacy was to consolidate the Reformation in the city and establish religious institutions that preserved his distinctive theological vision well beyond his lifetime.

Among the most pressing concerns that Farel and Calvin faced in July 1536 was the need to set forth with clarity Geneva's new evangelical faith and create basic structures for religious practice in the city. In the fall of 1536, Farel (probably assisted by Calvin) produced a brief *Confession of Faith* that defined in twenty-one articles Geneva's public theology, beginning with the affirmation that Scripture alone is "the rule of faith and religion."[37] Several months later, in January 1537, the ministers delivered a rudimentary constitution to Geneva's civil magistrates, entitled *Articles Concerning the Organization of the Church*, which proposed a basic outline for religious life in the city that included monthly celebrations of the Lord's Supper, the practice of church discipline and excommunication, congregational singing of the Psalms, catechetical instruction for children, and the creation of marriage courts to judge matrimonial cases.[38] Geneva's magistrates approved most of the provisions in the *Articles*, although they mandated that the Lord's Supper should be celebrated quarterly, not monthly, and they effectively ignored the ministers' call for church-controlled moral discipline in the city. As a complement to the *Articles*, Calvin also drafted in 1537 his first *Catechism* intended for the religious instruction of boys and girls in the city.[39] These documents presented a program for church reform that was in no way original. Calvin's *Catechism*, for example, was closely patterned after his *Institutes of the Christian Religion* (1536), which itself showed significant dependence on the writings of Martin Luther, Philip Melanchthon, and Ulrich Zwingli.[40] Similarly, the theology of the *Confession of Faith* and the practical reforms proposed in the *Articles* reflected key concerns and commitments shared by other reformed churches in the Swiss confederation.

Daily religious life changed in significant ways in the first years following Geneva's Reformation.[41] The city churches—which the French reformers called *temples*—were reduced in number from seven to three, and the outlying parishes consolidated. A company of around fifteen Protestant pastors soon replaced the roughly five hundred priests, curés, cathedral canons, monks, and nuns who had once ministered in and around the city.[42] Reformed ministers officiated at public worship services wearing the attire of scholars—black gowns, white starched collars, and black caps—rather than the colorful vestments of the traditional clergy. Their primary public responsibility was to preach expository sermons in the French vernacular rather than recite the Latin Mass. Geneva's churches no longer observed the Catholic sacraments of confirmation, penance, holy orders, ordination, marriage, and extreme unction. Though the Lord's Supper and baptism were still celebrated, the liturgical form and theological substance of these two sacraments were substantially changed. Public worship in reformed Geneva was simpler and less ornate than in the medieval church. Gone were the processions, the incense, the candles and acolytes, the monastic choirs, and the melodious organs. Instead, the reformers created a liturgy that gave priority to public prayers, the proclamation of the Word of God, and a cappella singing of the Psalter. Even the rhythm of religious time was transformed, as Calvin and Geneva's magistrates stripped nearly all religious holidays from the calendar. With the monasteries closed, and the Divine Office no longer recited, the bells of the city churches now rang only to mark time, announce the daily sermons, and summon Geneva's magistrates to their meetings. In all these ways and more, the texture of daily religious life in Geneva was radically altered in the months following the summer of 1536.

Geneva's revolution also brought with it significant changes to the parish structure of the city's church. Even before the iconoclasts had finished their destructive work, Geneva's magistrates had begun seizing Catholic property and confiscating the churches, chapels, monasteries, and convents in and around the city. Of Geneva's seven parish churches, two were demolished, one converted to a lecture hall (the Auditoire), and three left open for public worship: the temple of St. Pierre in the Upper City, the temple of the Madeleine in the Lower City, and the temple of St. Gervais across the Rhone River (see map 1.1). A fourth temple, St. Germain, located near the town hall (Hôtel de Ville), was initially loaned to the guild of butchers; later in the century, it was used variously as a powder store, a granary, a home for Italian and English refugee congregations, and even as an alternative worship site on those winter days when St. Pierre was too cold.[43] In a similar fashion, the magistrates seized the monastic houses. They razed the Dominican monastery located outside the city walls, converted the convent of the Sisters of Saint Clare into the public hospital, and turned the Franciscan monastery of the Rive into a public school. The city also sold property belonging to the prince-bishop, the cathedral chapter, and private Catholic residents who had fled the city. This financial windfall, which amounted to 10,647 écus for the year 1536 alone, the magistrates applied to Geneva's enormous war debt to Bern, as well as to pay ministers' salaries and staff the newly founded city hospital.[44]

The three permanent temples within the city walls, St. Pierre, the Madeleine, and St. Gervais, were not parish churches in the strictest sense of the term. Before 1541, townsfolk had freedom to move between temples and attend the preaching service of their choice. This practice, Calvin feared, fostered the perception that the ministers were preachers, not pastors.[45] The *Ecclesiastical Ordinances* (1541) addressed this concern by requiring that children hear the weekly catechism sermon and adults take the Lord's Supper in their local parish temples.[46] Although men and women were still permitted to attend sermons of their choice in other parishes, this stipulation assured at least a degree of pastoral oversight. Another factor that blurred parochial boundaries was Calvin's commitment to ministerial rotation within the city's temples. After his return from Strasbourg in 1541, Calvin routinely preached at St. Pierre on Sundays and at the temple of the Madeleine during the work week. This practice of rotation was designed by Calvin to ensure that Geneva's townspeople would be edified

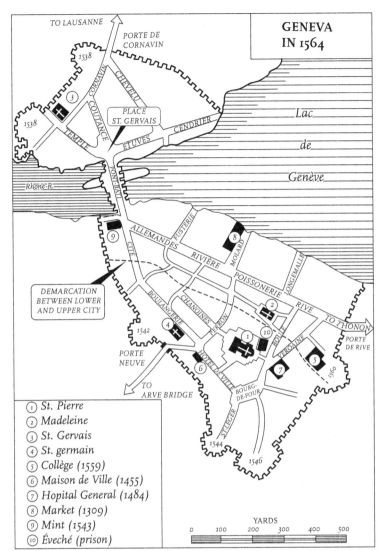

MAP 1.1 Geneva in 1564
Reproduced by permission from E. William Monter. *Calvin's Geneva.* New York:
John Wiley & Sons, 1967.

by a variety of preachers; it also affirmed the collegial nature of pastoral
ministry in the city and discouraged ministers from viewing their preaching posts as personal fiefdoms.[47]

The parish structure was somewhat better defined in Geneva's countryside possessions. As a result of its political revolution, Geneva assumed
sovereignty over a rural population of perhaps two thousand people, living
in around fifty hamlets and small villages in the surrounding countryside
(see map 1.2). In addition to the lands immediately adjacent to the city,

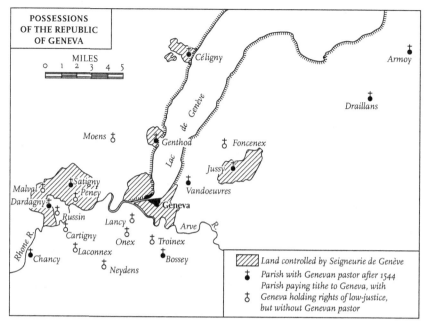

MAP 1.2 Geneva's Countryside Parishes
Reproduced by permission from E. William Monter. *Calvin's Geneva*. New York: John Wiley & Sons, 1967.

Geneva's magistrates governed a patchwork of small rural holdings called *mandements* scattered throughout the surrounding territory within a ten-mile radius of the walled city. In addition, Geneva shared with Bern jurisdiction over several small villages in the bailliages of Ternier and Gaillard that had once belonged to the monastery of St. Victor and the cathedral chapter of St. Pierre. Geneva's magistrates acquired seigneurial rights over most of these rural territories, which included the responsibility to supply pastors for the village churches, as well as the right to collect the traditional tithes and duties from the peasants. Ecclesiastical revenues harvested from the countryside—which totaled more than a third of the republic's income in 1544—were intended to repair and maintain parish buildings, including temples, parsonages, and barns, and to pay the salaries of the new ministers. In point of fact, city officials were often slow in responding to the needs of the rural parishes and often used revenue from the tithe to service Geneva's debts rather than support the temples in the countryside.[48]

One of the first steps in reforming the countryside was to consolidate the parishes and assign competent ministers to the village churches. As William Naphy has shown, this process of organization was slow and difficult, requiring more than a decade to complete.[49] Because of financial constraints, Geneva's magistrates and ministers grouped rural congregations together, assigning a single minister to two or three parish churches who was responsible to preach, catechize the young, and provide pastoral care at the different village temples or chapels on a weekly basis or on alternate weeks. Since sermon attendance was required, rural parishioners sometimes had to travel several miles to attend sermons at a neighboring parish church. By the mid 1540s, several dozen rural congregations had been consolidated into eleven separate parishes, scattered along the north shore of Lac Léman (Céligny, Genthod-Moëns), along the right bank of the Rhone River downstream from Geneva (Satigny-Peney, Russin-Dardagny-Malval), between the Rhone and the Arve rivers to the south of Geneva (Chancy-Cartigny-Valleiry, Bossey, Neydens, Lancy-Onex-Bernex), and between the Arve River and Lac Léman to the west of Geneva (Vandoeuvres-Cologny, Jussy-Foncenex, Draillans-Ursel).[50] Securing well-qualified reformed pastors for these parishes proved to be difficult. The largest and most important parishes such as Jussy and Satigny were staffed with competent reformed ministers almost from the start. In the village of Céligny, the Catholic priest named Jacques Baud converted to the Protestant religion at the time of the Reformation and served his parish for another eight years.[51] The situation was very different in the parish of Russin-Dardagny, however, where the Catholic priest retained his post until 1544, even though he never renounced the traditional religion. Taken as a whole, five of Geneva's eleven countryside parishes did not have a resident Protestant pastor before 1543. It was only in the mid-1540s that Geneva's church finally succeeded in organizing its rural parishes and assigning a resident reformed minister to each.

Farel and Calvin did not have complete freedom in constructing Geneva's church order. From the outset the city's magistrates were careful to guard their prerogatives, wary lest the tyranny of Catholic bishops from which they had been recently liberated be replaced by the domination of Protestant clergymen. The ministers' authority in the city was also weakened by the fact that nearly all were French-born; any attempt on their part to impose right doctrine or right behavior on Geneva's citizens was invariably perceived as a dangerous form of foreign interference. Problems initially arose over enforcing subscription to the city's *Confession of Faith*. In the first months of 1537, the Small Council, after much delay, finally approved the ministers' request that all citizens, burghers, and inhabitants of the city be required to take an oath of allegiance to Geneva's reformed faith as stated in the *Confession*.[52] The councilors made it clear, however, that the magistrates, not the ministers, had the prerogative to punish those who refused to comply.[53] In the months that followed, various efforts to pressure Geneva's population to subscribe to the *Confession* failed. First, a house-to-house canvass came up short. Next, the city's inhabitants were ordered to appear at St. Pierre by neighborhood in hopes of pressuring compliance—a large number of people simply chose to be absent. Finally, in November 1537, the Small Council ordered all recalcitrants to leave the city, yet the senators lacked the political clout (and will) to enforce this unpopular measure. By this time, it was clear that opponents of universal subscription to Geneva's *Confession of Faith* included not only residents who harbored Catholic sympathies, but also prominent patricians who supported the Reformation yet feared that the city's new religious faith was becoming too narrow and too divisive. Exasperated by this widespread resistance, Farel and Calvin appeared before the Small Council in January 1538 demanding the right to refuse communion to those who broke the unity of the church by refusing to take the oath of allegiance. The council rejected their request out of hand.[54]

The city elections of February 1538 attested to how much political capital Calvin's and Farel's supporters who served on the Small Council had lost over the previous months. As a group, the new councilors were less sympathetic to the concerns of Geneva's pastors and more firmly committed to a policy of religious accommodation with Geneva's political ally Bern. This became apparent in the months that followed, as the magistrates began to demand that the ministers adopt a number of liturgical rites practiced in Bern, including the use of baptismal fonts; the use of unleavened bread in communion; and the celebration of religious festivals such as Christmas, New Year's, the Annunciation, and Ascension. Although Calvin was not adverse to the first two proposals in principle, he and most of the other ministers were strongly opposed to what they saw as blatant interference by the magistrates—to say nothing of Bern—in the affairs of the Genevan church.

Things quickly went from bad to worse. In March, the Small Council commanded the city's ministers to desist from making pulpit attacks against the city's leaders. A blind minister named Elie Courauld defied this order several weeks later and was imprisoned after he preached a sermon in which he called Geneva a "kingdom of frogs" and the magistrates "drunkards."[55] In early April, the Small Council announced that the city ministers would be required to distribute unleavened bread, in accordance with the Bernese rite, at the quarterly celebration of the Lord's Supper later in the month. When Farel and Calvin issued a strenuous protest against this decision, they were forbidden to preach. The ministers disregarded this interdiction. On Sunday, April 21, 1538, Calvin and Farel mounted their respective pulpits at St. Pierre and St. Gervais, preached their sermons, and then announced to their outraged parishioners that because of the hostility in the city they would not perform the holy sacrament as scheduled. Having defied the civil authorities, Calvin and Farel faced the magistrates' wrath. In short order the Small Council and the Council of 200 condemned the ministers' actions and ordered them expelled within three days. Calvin did not wait that long; on April 23, he slipped out of reformed Geneva with no intention of returning.

3. Building a New Church Order

Calvin's "exile" in Strasbourg over the next three years proved to be the happiest period of his life. During these years, he served as the pastor of a congregation of French refugees in the city numbering five hundred people, taught biblical exegesis at the *collège* where he lectured on the Gospel of John and Paul's Epistles, and completed a number of writing projects, including the second Latin edition of the *Institutes* (1539) and a biblical commentary on Romans (1540). It was also in Strasbourg that Calvin married Idelette de Bure, the widow of an Anabaptist convert and mother of two young children, who met his criteria for a wife who was "chaste, considerate, modest, economical, patient," and "attentive" to his health.[56] Even as Calvin tasted the fruits of marital bliss, he was also learning important practical lessons about church life and pastoral ministry from Strasbourg's veteran minister, Martin Bucer. It is only a slight exaggeration to say that it was in Strasbourg that Calvin learned to be a pastor.[57] Bucer had recently published a reformed pastoral handbook entitled *Von der waren Seelsorge* (*Concerning the True Care of Souls*, 1536), and though Calvin could not read German, he certainly benefited from Bucer's seasoned judgments regarding the nature of the four offices of Christian ministry, the use of the profession of faith to define the Christian community, the importance of church discipline to promote sanctification, and the political acumen required to negotiate church reforms with city magistrates. With Bucer's encouragement, Calvin implemented in his refugee congregation a mandatory pastoral examination for all members wishing to commune at the Lord's Table. Also, Calvin's congregation employed Bucer's liturgy in daily worship, which included the singing of the metrical Psalms in French. More than anything, however, it was Bucer's friendship and fatherly support that helped Calvin regain his sense of vocation to Christian ministry and proved decisive in shaping his future career as a church reformer.[58]

By the first months of 1540, the political winds were again shifting in Geneva. In the years since the departure of Calvin and Farel, the city church had struggled to establish doctrinal cohesion and to retain qualified pastors in office. When Cardinal Jacob Sadoleto wrote to Geneva's authorities in 1539 in an effort to entice the city back into the Catholic fold, the magistrates were forced to petition Calvin to write the formal response defending Geneva's Reformation.[59] At the same time, political entanglements with Bern were becoming viewed with outright suspicions. In the city elections of February 1540, a political faction named the Guillermines (after Guillaume Farel) gained control of the Small Council and soon initiated efforts to recall Calvin from Strasbourg. In October 1540, an emissary from Geneva arrived at Calvin's doorstep with a formal invitation to return: "On behalf of our Small, Large, and General Councils...we beg you very affectionately to decide to come to us and return to your former place and ministry."[60] Calvin, who had not forgotten the rough way he had been treated two years earlier, was not at all inclined to accept this offer. In response to a letter from Pierre Viret urging him to return to Geneva, Calvin stated, "It would be better to die at once than to suffer repeatedly on that torture rack."[61] Calvin gave a similar response to his friend Farel in Neuchâtel: "Whenever I call to mind the state of wretchedness in which my life was spent" in Geneva, "how can it be otherwise but that my very soul must shudder when any proposal is made for my return?"[62] In the end, Calvin's sense of divine calling and personal duty, as well as the urgent appeals of Geneva's magistrates, caused him to lay aside his anxiety and wounded pride and return to the city on the shores of Lac Léman. He arrived in Geneva on September 13, 1541, and immediately recommenced his preaching ministry, starting at the very place in the biblical text where he had left off three years earlier. The conditions that Calvin had established for his return were twofold: the city's children must be catechized, and church discipline must be exercised in Geneva's churches.[63]

Thanks in large part to the influence of Martin Bucer, the Calvin who returned to Geneva in the autumn of 1541 was more mature and politically astute, and better equipped to lead the struggling church. At thirty-two years of age, Calvin was ready to translate theological conviction into tangible institutional forms. On the same day that he arrived in the city, Calvin appeared before the Small Council to request that a commission be established to draw up a new constitution for the church. Within a week, he had written a rough draft of this church order. The proposed constitution went through several slight revisions at the hands of Geneva's magistrates before being approved by the General Assembly and published as the *Ecclesiastical Ordinances* in November 1541. It would serve as the cornerstone of the Genevan church for the next two centuries. The following year, Calvin published a new liturgy entitled *The Form of Ecclesiastical Prayers and Hymns*, which prescribed a simple and unembellished order of worship centered on preaching, prayers, and the administration of the sacraments.[64] This liturgy also included thirty-five versified French Psalms, five composed by Calvin and the rest written by the famous poet Clément Marot. The tradition of congregational singing of the Psalter which had long impressed Calvin, and was practiced in the refugee church of Strasbourg, now became established practice in the Genevan church.[65] The third major ecclesiastical document that burst from the reformer's pen during these months of prolific activity was the Genevan *Catechism* (1542). Like Bucer's catechisms of the previous decade, Calvin's second catechism adopted a question-answer format (with 373 questions) that addressed, in turn, the Apostles' Creed, the Ten Commandments, the Lord's Prayer, and the sacraments.[66] The importance of this pedagogical tool for Calvinist churches throughout Europe is attested by the number of editions that appeared in short order, including translations into Latin, English, Spanish, German, Italian, and even Greek and Hebrew. The Genevan *Catechism* became the primary means of instructing children in the Christian faith not only in Geneva but also in the reformed churches of France.[67]

If John Calvin was the primary architect of the new religious order in Protestant Geneva, what type of ecclesiastical structure did he wish to construct? Popular legends that depict the city as a theocracy or Calvin as the dictator of Geneva miss the mark. Calvin's objective was not to subjugate the state to the church, but rather to protect the church from being annexed by the state as had occurred in other reformed cities, such as Zurich, Basel, Bern, and even Strasbourg. In a letter to his friend Viret, Calvin voiced grave concerns about this prevailing trend: "See what a sad precedent our brethren would establish if they came to recognize the head of the state as the judge of doctrine.... Certainly, if we permit the yoke to be imposed on us in this way, we betray the holy ministry."[68] Accordingly, the *Ecclesiastical Ordinances* prescribed a Christian commonwealth in which the religious and civil authorities exercised jurisdiction over distinct, yet overlapping, spheres and were expected to cooperate with and assist one another. The church was responsible for interpreting revelation and exercising jurisdiction over spiritual matters; the state had power over temporal affairs and was responsible for protecting the church.[69] Both of these jurisdictions were established by the authority of God's Word and were legitimate only so far as they kept within these scriptural limits.[70] It is important to note that Calvin's principle of distinct, but interdependent, domains was very different than the model of the separation of church and state that appeared in the Constitution of the United States two hundred and fifty years later. In sixteenth-century Geneva, the magistrates prosecuted heretics and serious moral offenders, maintained the city's temples, appointed elders and deacons to their offices, dictated the schedule for public fasts and the Lord's Supper, disbursed tithes and offerings, and paid the salaries of the city's clergy. For their part, Geneva's ministers were employees of the state who could be dismissed at any time (as Calvin's exile to Strasbourg attests), and who were not permitted to sit on any of the citizen councils.[71]

Although Calvin and his pastoral colleagues did not possess formal *civil* authority, they did exercise substantial *moral* authority within Geneva due to their intellectual stature and prominent social position, as well as to the crucial role that the pulpit played in mass communication and indoctrination.[72] During Calvin's lifetime, and in the half century that followed, Geneva's ministers regularly assumed the role of public prophets and moral watchdogs, warning the magistrates from the pulpit and in city council chambers about a variety of dangers, including religious heterodoxy, breaches of justice, and social immorality. The trial and execution of the anti-Trinitarian Michael Servetus offers a good example of the complementary, yet distinct, roles exercised by Geneva's civil and religious leaders during this period. When Servetus arrived in Geneva in August 1553, it was Geneva's city councilors that ordered his arrest, interrogated him, prosecuted his case, and ultimately commanded his execution in late October. Calvin's role in this tragic affair was less official but significant nevertheless: having called for Servetus's initial arrest, he served as theological adviser to the council during the trial, met privately with the defendant in an effort to dissuade him from his heretical opinions, and finally recommended that Servetus be put to death. Calvin's last minute petition for a more humane form of execution, by sword rather than burning, was ignored by the Small Council.[73]

The *Ecclesiastical Ordinances* organized the Genevan church around four offices: the offices of pastor, doctor, elder, and deacon.[74] Calvin believed that this fourfold division of church offices reflected the practice of the apostolic church and was faithful to the pattern prescribed in Paul's Epistles.[75] The pastors or ministers were responsible for preaching the Word of God and administering the sacraments. The ordinances envisioned a city pastoral corps numbering five or six ministers that delivered twenty-six sermons per week between the three parish temples. Although Calvin's initial draft of the church order had stipulated monthly communion services, the final version of the ordinances legislated that the Lord's Supper be celebrated only four times per year, at Christmas, Easter, Pentecost, and the first Sunday in September.[76] In addition to their normal pastoral duties, ministers were required by the *Ecclesiastical Ordinances* to meet every Friday in the Congregation and four times each year for the Ordinary Censure. The Congregation, patterned after Zurich's *Prophetzei,* was intended to be a kind of adult Bible study where ministers and interested laypeople listened to the exposition of Scripture by one of the city's ministers, then discussed matters of exegesis and theology related to the chosen passage.[77] The Ordinary Censure, by contrast, was a private session of the city and countryside ministers that addressed doctrinal differences within the pastoral company or confronted immoral behavior among one of its members. A third institution, the Company of Pastors, was not actually created by the *Ecclesiastical Ordinances,* but emerged during the mid-1540s. This body, which included the clergy and theological faculty, met on Fridays immediately after the Congregation to address concerns related to religious life in Geneva and in reformed churches elsewhere in Europe. Under Calvin's leadership, the Company of Pastors became the external face of the Genevan church: the institution by which Geneva's ministers provided intellectual and religious leadership for the international Calvinist movement.

The church office of doctor or teacher is a unique feature of Geneva's ecclesiastical constitution and a distinctive characteristic of Calvin's ecclesiology. Doctors, like pastors, were charged to interpret the Scriptures and teach sound doctrine. Their mandate extended beyond the local congregation to the larger church, however, and included the responsibility to teach future pastors and protect the church from doctrinal error.[78] The *Ecclesiastical Ordinances* anticipated the creation of a *collège* in which these doctors would prepare Geneva's youth for service to the church and state. This vision took institutional shape with the founding of the Genevan Academy in 1559, consisting of a lower-level Latin school (*schola privata*) and an upper-level "seminary" or "university" (*schola publica*) to train students for Christian ministry, law, and medicine.[79] Even though pastors and doctors occupied distinct offices, Calvin believed that on occasion doctors might also be called by God to exercise the pastoral functions of preaching and administering the sacraments. In his Commentary on Ephesians (1548), Calvin noted:

> Pastors, to my mind, are those to whom is committed the charge of a particular flock. I have no objection to their receiving the name of doctors, if we realize that there is another kind of doctor, who superintends both the education of pastors and the instruction of the whole church. Sometimes he can be a pastor who is also a doctor, but the duties are different.[80]

Calvin believed that this was true of his own vocation: God had called him to be both pastor *and* teacher in the Genevan church.[81] As we shall see, in the half century after Calvin's death, this paradigm of pastor-doctor was reflected in the ministries of a number of Geneva's most notable religious leaders, including Theodore Beza, Lambert Daneau, Bonaventure Bertram, Antoine de La Faye, Jean Diodati, and Theodore Tronchin.

The third order established by the *Ecclesiastical Ordinances* was the office of elder. Twelve lay elders were to be chosen by the magistrates from among the three levels of Geneva's civil government: two from the Small Council, four from the Council of 60, and six from the Council of 200. These elders were responsible "to take care of the life of everyone, to admonish in a friendly manner those whom they see weakening or leading a disorderly life, and, where it may be needful, to make a report to the company which will be deputed to apply brotherly correction."[82] At the same time, the *Ecclesiastical Ordinances* created an institution called the Consistory, a church court consisting of the city pastors and lay elders that was to meet each Thursday at noon for the purpose of overseeing public morality and doctrine, and admonishing and disciplining people guilty of flagrant sin. The Consistory had no power to impose corporal punishment; it had authority to wield only "the spiritual sword of the Word of God." Consistorial discipline was intended to serve as a form of pastoral care, administering spiritual "medicine to bring sinners back to our Lord."[83] What remained unclear in the *Ecclesiastical Ordinances*, however, was whether the power of excommunication belonged to the Consistory or to Geneva's magistrates. As we shall see later in chapter 7, Calvin and the city council battled over the prerogative to exercise this form of public censure until 1555 when Calvin's allies won a majority of the seats on the Small Council and expelled their opponents from the city. From that time on, the Consistory had a free hand to practice excommunication in the church, enabling Geneva's ministers to pursue with vigor their vision of a godly society reformed in doctrine and behavior according to the Christian gospel.[84]

The fourth office established by the *Ecclesiastical Ordinances* was that of deacon. Here, Calvin attempted to provide biblical justification for two offices that already existed in Geneva, the *procureurs* and *hospitalliers* of the city's public hospital.[85] During the revolutionary autumn of 1535, the magistrates had consolidated the charitable work of eight Catholic religious orders and lay confraternities into a single public hospital, housed in the convent formerly belonging to the Sisters of St. Clare in Bourg-de-Four. Geneva's public hospital served as an all-purpose social-welfare institution, offering lodging for people passing through the city; providing medical care for the ill (there was a surgeon-barber on staff); and offering food and shelter to orphans and widows, the crippled and the elderly. The *procureurs* were responsible for soliciting financial support, overseeing bequests, and administering the hospital. The *hospitalliers* lived at the hospital and were charged with the daily care of the sick and indigent, as well as the weekly distribution of bread to poor households. In the church order of 1541, this program of social welfare was incorporated loosely into the structure of the Genevan church: *procureurs* and *hospitalliers* were together given the title "deacons," and the ministers and elders, along with one of the syndics, were appointed as a board of examiners commissioned to visit the hospital four times each year. Although not specifically mentioned in the *Ecclesiastical Ordinances*, the city ministers adopted the practice of choosing a young theological student to serve as chaplain of the hospital to deliver regular sermons and give catechism classes for orphan children. The chaplain and *procureurs* also occasionally distributed Bibles and Psalters to townspeople who could not afford them.[86] Notwithstanding these spiritual functions, the city hospital was a public institution, conceived of and run by the magistrates, not the ministers. Though Calvin incorporated the "diaconal" offices of *procureur* and *hospitallier* into the structure of the city church, Geneva's program of social welfare predated the *Ecclesiastical Ordinances* and owed little to Calvin.

Geneva's political revolution was over by the summer of 1536, but her religious Reformation remained incomplete for several additional decades. As we have seen, it was only after Calvin's return from his Strasbourg exile in 1541 that the constructive work of church building began in earnest. In short order, Calvin had produced a catechism, a liturgy, and a church order that fundamentally reshaped religious life and practice in the city. Equally important were the church institutions that Calvin established—such as the Congregation, the Company of Pastors, the Consistory, the Ordinary Censure, and the Genevan Academy—which both consolidated the Reformation in Geneva and preserved his distinctive theological legacy for the future. Calvin's formulation of the fourfold Christian ministry, with its inclusion of the office of doctor, became a defining characteristic of the Genevan church, although it was not widely duplicated by reformed churches elsewhere in Europe.[87]

Several dimensions of Calvin's ecclesiastical vision are particularly significant for my study. First of all, the careful balance that Calvin envisioned between the authority of the church and the state, assigning to each a distinct sphere of influence and jurisdiction, yet insisting on their mutual cooperation and assistance, represented an important departure from regnant models of his day. He was particularly concerned to avoid the Erastianism practiced in reformed cities in southern Germany and Switzerland where the state dominated the church and usurped the right of excommunication.[88] Calvin's ecclesiastical vision embodied in the *Ecclesiastical Ordinances* sailed against prevailing political winds in Europe that blew in the direction of political centralization and magisterial control of the church. These winds also blew in Geneva. As we shall see in a later chapter, during the half century following Calvin's death, Geneva's ministers struggled against, but ultimately succumbed to, the magistrates' efforts to diminish clerical jurisdiction over the election of city ministers and the right of excommunication.

Another important aspect of Calvin's ecclesiology was its commitment to a plurality of church ministries. For Calvin, church governance was never intended to be the prerogative of one person nor even the responsibility of pastors alone.[89] Rather, as the *Ecclesiastical Ordinances* make clear, authority in the church was to be shared by duly appointed ministers and doctors, as well as lay elders and deacons, each using his own gifts according to the dictates of Scripture for the benefit of the Christian community. The need to work out these general principles in specific circumstances inevitably raised thorny questions and sometimes led to conflict between officeholders in the church. After Calvin had passed from the scene, a series of important controversies forced Geneva's pastoral corps to bring greater clarity to several fundamental issues, including the nature of clerical ordination, the specific roles of pastors and elders in administering the sacraments, and leadership within the Company of Pastors.

The most controversial (and misunderstood) institution that Calvin introduced in Geneva was the Consistory. Calvin's brand of ecclesiastical discipline produced its share of enemies in the sixteenth century, and modern-day critics continue to see in such discipline evidence of Calvin's harsh, even dictatorial, personality. In point of fact, Calvin's broad vision to create a holy community, living under the "yoke" of Christian discipline, was a dream shared—though never realized—by other Protestant churchmen, including Farel in Neuchâtel, Johannes Oecolampadius and Oswald Myconius in Basel, and Bucer in Strasbourg.[90] The ministers who came after Calvin in Geneva were committed to this same program of moral supervision and ecclesiastical discipline. For them, as for Calvin, church discipline was necessary for the spiritual well-being of God's people, an indispensable mark of a Christian community that was reformed in doctrine and practice according to the Scriptures.

4. The Reformation of Worship

Calvin's doctrine of right worship formed the gravitational center of his entire ecclesial vision. The liturgy of the church, the offices of the church, the discipline of the church, the preaching ministry of the church were all intended to bring praise and glory to Jesus Christ, the Lord of the church. Calvin's fervent commitment to right worship pervaded his critique of medieval Christianity and was a central theme to which he returned again and again in his theological writings over the course of his career. Moreover, the conviction that true Christian worship must follow the pattern defined by Scripture led Calvin and Geneva's other pastors to restructure the physical setting and the content of public worship in the city. The final section of this chapter explores Calvin's ambitious program to reform worship in sixteenth-century Geneva.

In late 1554 or early 1555, a French Franciscan named Antoine Cathelan visited reformed Geneva for several days. In addition to roaming the city and talking to locals, he attended a preaching service in one of the city's churches. Shocked by the entire experience, Cathelan returned to France to write a salacious satire entitled *The Parisian Passwind* against Calvin and Geneva's Reformation in which Cathelan provided the most detailed eyewitness account of a reformed worship service in sixteenth-century Geneva.[91] Through the character of Passwind, Cathelan described the interior of the reformed temple he visited: "It is altogether like the interior of a college or school, full of benches, with a pulpit in the middle for the preacher. And in front of the pulpit there are benches for the women and small children. And around them, raised up, the men are seated, without any distinction of personal rank. The stained glass windows are just about all knocked out, and the plaster dust is up to the ankles." Passwind next described the worship service that he witnessed:

> And immediately [the townspeople] entered the church, each person choosing his own place to sit, as in school, and then they waited for the preacher to come to the pulpit. And immediately, when the preacher appeared, all the people knelt down, except the preacher. And he began praying, with uncovered head, and his hands joined. His prayer was entirely in French, created out of his own imagination, which was concluded with the Lord's Prayer, but not the Ave Maria. Then all the people responded quietly "Amen." And two times a week, [they] sing a Psalm before the sermon (but only in the cities). Everyone sings together while seated, men, women, girls, and infants. And if any one recites a prayer on entering the church, he is pointed to and mocked, and held to be a Papist and idolater.[92]

Cathelan clearly found the entire experience disorienting. The cluttered sanctuary that looked more like a school than a church; people sitting on benches without regard for social rank; the vernacular liturgy; extemporaneous prayers; congregational singing of the Psalms—all these features of worship in Geneva scandalized the religious sensibilities of this Franciscan monk.

Similar feelings of shock and horror were no doubt experienced by many of Geneva's townspeople and country folk who witnessed Calvin's program to "cleanse" the temples and reform public worship in the city.[93] The reformers did not hold back in their assault on the physical and sensory elements of traditional worship: all sacred objects such as crucifixes, statues of saints, and holy relics were removed from the temples. Most were systematically destroyed; a few were stored away or sold.[94] The rood screen that had traditionally separated the lay congregation from the chancel and high altar was torn down. Geneva's reformers also removed the altars on which priests had performed the Mass and the tabernacle in which the consecrated host was stored. Over several decades, the walls and pillars of Geneva's temples were whitewashed to cover over Catholic iconography.[95] Stained-glass windows—which served the double function of inspiring religious devotion and keeping the churches dry and warm—were not removed but were left in disrepair. In 1577, the city council ordered that the broken windows of St. Pierre be covered with netting to prevent swallows from flying into the sanctuary and soiling the clothing of members of the congregation.[96] Likewise, the organ of St. Pierre sat unused until 1562, when the pipes of the organ were melted down, and the metal was used to make tin plates for the city hospital and communion vessels for the temples.[97]

Having "stripped the altars" from the Catholic churches, Geneva's authorities reordered sacred space to give priority to the proclamation of the Word of God.[98] In each of the temples, a large wooden pulpit for the preacher was erected against a pillar toward the front of the sanctuary. Around the pulpit were placed benches and chairs, where women, children, and the hard of hearing sat on benches immediately in front, to the right, and to the left of the pulpit, while the men sat behind them.[99] In the temple of St. Pierre, the syndics, senators, judicial officers, and visiting dignitaries were given privileged places in large wooden chairs (formerly the choir stalls) in the chancel and against the wall facing the pulpit. The location of the pulpit in the middle of the congregation had both practical and symbolic importance. Practically speaking, the elevated pulpit facilitated communication, permitting even a large congregation of several thousand people to hear the minister's sermon. It was from this same pulpit—or sometimes from a smaller pulpit stationed below—that a professional cantor led the congregation in the antiphonal singing of the Psalms. The pulpit's location also bespoke the reformers' theological conviction of the essential spiritual equality of ministers and laypeople. No longer did an altar separate the "spiritual" clergy from the rest of the congregation. Further, the proclamation of Scripture in the middle of the congregation was a potent symbol that Christ, the living Word, continued to speak and dwell among his people.[100] Whereas the Catholic Mass was largely a visual event, culminating in the dramatic spectacle of the priestly sacrifice of the body of Christ upon the altar, the reformed worship service was primarily an auditory experience, centered on the proclamation and hearing of the Word of God and the singing of the Psalter.

Geneva's campaign against altars, religious images, stained-glass windows, and organ music has led some scholars to argue that this austerity is indicative of an abstract piety or a deep-seated aversion to the material world within reformed spirituality. A more convincing explanation for reformed Christianity's "war against idolatry" is found in its theological understanding of right worship.[101] For Calvin, Farel, Heinrich Bullinger, and other reformed churchmen of this period, authentic worship lay at the foundation of true Christianity and was a prerequisite for any genuine religious reformation.[102] Calvin treated the subject of right worship in a number of theological works composed shortly after his return from Strasbourg, notably in *On the Necessity of Reforming the Church* (1543) and in his *Treatise on Relics* (1543), as well as in several of his biblical commentaries, especially his commentary on the Gospel of John (1553).[103] Based on Jesus' words in John 4:24—"God is spirit, and his worshipers must worship in spirit and in truth"—Calvin identified two principal qualities of authentic Christian worship: it is *spiritual* and it is dependent upon the divine Word. Worship is "spiritual" in that it originates in the ministry of the Holy Spirit who initiates faith in the Christian man or woman and then stimulates this faith to prayers and praise, purity of conscience, self-denial, and submission to God.[104] For Calvin, the source of worship is the Holy Spirit, the locus of worship is the inward faith of the heart, and the purpose of Christian worship is to bring glory to God alone (*soli Deo gloria*). At its foundation, therefore, right and legitimate worship

> is to acknowledge God as he is, as the only source of virtue, justice, holiness, wisdom, truth, power, goodness, mercy, life and salvation, and so to ascribe and render to him the glory of all that is good, to seek all things in him alone, and to rely upon him in every need. From this arises prayer, praise, and thanksgiving, all of which testify to the glory we attribute to him.[105]

Calvin believed that true worship was also dependent on the Word of God. In Scripture, God not only reveals aspects of his character but also discloses the manner in which he wishes to be worshiped by his human creatures. "The Word of God is the standard by which we discern true worship from that which is false and defective," Calvin wrote. Indeed, "God disapproves of all forms of worship not established in his Word."[106] Here the reformer endorsed what would later be called the "regulative principle," that is, the precept that all religious ceremonies and expressions of piety that are not explicitly permitted in Scripture must be rejected. Furthermore, Calvin believed that the Word of God is the usual instrument by which the Holy Spirit evokes true worship in the human heart. Through the ministry of the written and proclaimed Word, the Spirit solidifies the faith of God's people, calls forth their prayers and praise, purifies their consciences, intensifies their gratitude—in a word, guides them into spiritual worship. Calvin summarized his theology of worship this way: "God is only worshiped properly in the certainty of faith, which is necessarily born of the Word of God; and hence it follows that all who forsake the Word fall into idolatry."[107]

Calvin's understanding of authentic worship comes into sharper focus when it is contrasted with its antithesis, false worship. Religious ceremonies are legitimate expressions of piety only so far as they "lead us straight to Christ."[108] Unfortunately, because of the devastating consequences of original sin, human beings do not by nature seek God nor do they desire to worship him aright in spirit and in truth. Instead, Calvin believed, the human mind is a veritable factory of idolatry that produces a steady stream of "carnal" and external ceremonies intended to manipulate God and win his favor through legalistic righteousness. At face value these religious rituals bear the appearance of devotion, but at their root they are only extravagant forms of idolatry. Rather than elevating the mind and heart to worship God in heaven, external ceremonies and cultic objects attempt to bring God to earth to domesticate him. Religious images such as statues and icons, which Calvin understood to be expressly forbidden in the second commandment of the Decalogue, are particularly toxic in this regard in that they invite worshipers to transfer God's glory to mortal creatures and inanimate objects.[109] For Calvin, therefore, the essential difference between true and false worship was that whereas spiritual worship is prompted by the Holy Spirit, engages the inner life of faith, is subject to the divine Word, and leads to God's glory, false worship springs from the flesh, is concerned with external righteousness, violates God's commands, and is thoroughly idolatrous.[110]

John Calvin and his pastoral colleagues in Geneva believed that the medieval Catholic Church had fundamentally corrupted true Christian worship. Instead of honoring Jesus Christ as the unique mediator between God and sinful humanity, Catholic authorities encouraged layfolk to honor dead saints and martyrs, to pray to them, and even to solicit spiritual power from their clothing and bodily remains. In his *Treatise on Relics*, Calvin noted:

> For they have prostrated themselves and bowed before relics, as before God, lighting torches and candles as a sign of homage to them. They have put their confidence in them and have appealed to them, as if they possessed divine power and grace. If idolatry is the act of transferring the honor of God to others, then can we deny that this is idolatry?[111]

Calvin also criticized the traditional church for its multitude of ceremonies, masses, processions, and festivals, as well as its various cultic accoutrements, including colorful clerical vestments, incense, stained-glass windows, beautiful organs, and trained choirs. Catholic ceremonies like these originate in the human imagination rather than in the Word of God, Calvin believed, and promote a superficial piety characterized by external acts of devotion and obedience to religious rules. Laymen and laywomen might be entertained by "theatrical trifles" of this sort, but these rituals fail to instruct them in any way; indeed, these carnal ceremonies obscure the gospel and distract the devout from the pure exercise of faith, prayer, and praise. Calvin put the matter in the sharpest of terms: "Therefore all who burden the Church with an excessive host of ceremonies despoil her of the presence of Christ, so far as lies in them."[112] But, his opponents might well ask, are not Catholic practices such as incense, candles, lavish vestments, altars, and fasts patterned after Jewish temple worship commanded by God in the Old Testament? Calvin anticipated and answered this question. The Levitical ceremonies of the Jews were intended to serve as prophetic types, pointing to the advent of Christ. But since the coming of Christ, God has given the Church a different set of instructions with regard to true worship. External forms have been replaced by spiritual worship of the heart, and ceremonies and practices once permitted, are now "not only superfluous, but vicious and absurd."[113] For Calvin, therefore, the Catholic Church of his day, with its external pomp and carnal rites, continued to cling to the shadows of the Old Covenant rather than celebrate the light of the gospel in the New Covenant. Through their ceremonies and manifest idolatry, even the most devout among Catholics "choose to wander in a perpetual labyrinth, rather than worship God simply in spirit and in truth."[114]

The foundation on which Calvin and early reformed Christians constructed their aesthetic of worship is now evident. The sine qua non of true Christian worship is the preaching of the Word of God and the congregation's heartfelt response to the divine message. Consequently, the chief adornment of public worship must always be the precious Word of God and the beautiful message of the gospel of Jesus Christ, proclaimed in both sermon and sacraments. Calvin's insistence that the liturgical content and physical space of true worship be "bare and simple" was thus not primarily the result of his personal austerity or an aversion to the material world.[115] Rather, it reflected his conviction that only through pure and simple worship might the beauty of the gospel shine forth resplendent.[116] Calvin's aesthetic of worship was not unique or even original to him, of course. Reformed churchmen in Switzerland and Germany also waged war against Catholic ceremonies and defended pure and simple worship.[117] Likewise, Calvin's aesthetic of worship was shared by his colleagues and successors in the Genevan church. Guillaume Farel succinctly articulated the reformed aesthetic of worship in his *On the True Use of the Cross* (1560):

> The Church should be decorated and adorned with Jesus Christ and the Word of his gospel and his holy sacraments. This great Sun of Righteousness, Jesus Christ, and the light of his gospel, have nothing to do with our burning torches and our candles and candelabras. God has instead ordained that by true preaching and by the holy sacraments practiced in their simplicity this light might be manifested and illumine us with all glory.[118]

Twenty-five years later, in a sermon delivered from the pulpit of St. Pierre, Theodore Beza reiterated this primary conviction. The house of God is not a building

> that we enter to see the beautiful shapes of vaults and pillars, or to admire the splendor of gold and silver and precious stones. Nor is it a place that we visit in order to fill our ears with the singing of choirs and the music of organs. Rather it is a place where the pure Word of God is clearly preached in the presence of each person, with words of exhortation, consolation, warning, and censure necessary for salvation.[119]

A decade later, in 1604, the Genevan minister Antoine de La Faye published a spiritual meditation that summed up Jesus Christ's redemptive work with this stanza:

> You are my wisdom, you are my redemption, full of righteousness and sanctification. All of these truths are summed up in the history of your death and resurrection. And to your holy Word my spirit clings, not to stone or wood. As I praise you with mind, will, and memory.[120]

In their aesthetic of worship, Calvin and his pastoral colleagues in Geneva gave priority to the virtues of simplicity, modesty, and gravity so that the Word of God and the message of salvation in Jesus Christ might sound forth in all its clarity and beauty. This was an aesthetic discerned by the sense of hearing rather than of sight. On this point, Calvin and the ministers of Geneva would have been in full agreement with a statement once made by the German reformer Martin Luther: "the ears alone are the organs of a Christian."[121]

Geneva's Reformation of 1536 brought with it profound and permanent changes to religious life in the city. As we have seen, within a few short years, Geneva's ministers and magistrates had restructured the city's parishes, reduced the number of clergymen in the city, redefined the clerical office, replaced the Mass with daily preaching services, and removed from the city's churches most of their physical ornamentation. At least in the minds of Calvin and his colleagues, these changes reflected a fundamental shift in religious identity: once a Catholic city where "idolatry reigned," Geneva had now become a Protestant republic where "the true Reformation of the gospel" was "purely preached and announced."[122] The city on the shores of Lac Léman was now a strategic gospel-outpost, a religious beacon and refuge, a city "where one preaches the gospel publicly" and where "good people come to hear the gospel."[123] Though Calvin emerged as the central architect of Geneva's reformed church after 1541, the responsibility for constructing and preserving this ecclesial program fell in large part to Calvin's colleagues who worked alongside him, and then succeeded him, in the ministerial office of Geneva. The next chapter will examine in detail the backgrounds and contributions of this Company of Pastors who assisted Calvin during the decades that followed Geneva's dramatic reformation of 1536.

CHAPTER 2 | The Company of Pastors

OVER THE COURSE OF his ministry in Geneva, John Calvin recruited hundreds of men to be pastors of reformed congregations in various corners of Europe, but none of these ministers proved to be of greater importance for reformed Protestantism than Theodore Beza (1519–1605). Calvin first met Beza in the fall of 1548, several weeks after the young Frenchman had converted to the evangelical faith and, with his wife Claudine Denosse, fled Catholic France to find a safe haven in Geneva.[1] Though not yet thirty years of age, Beza's credentials were already impressive. The product of Burgundy's lower nobility, he was refined in his cultural tastes and at ease in the presence of people of power and wealth. His academic training and intellectual gifts were also impeccable: as a young man he had been trained in civil law and the humane letters; at the time of his religious conversion, he was a member of a distinguished sodality of Catholic humanists in Paris; and he was an accomplished poet with a superb command of classical Greek. Calvin possessed a keen eye for talent and immediately recognized Beza's enormous potential as a churchman and scholar. Not only did Calvin encourage him to employ his intellectual and literary gifts on behalf of the evangelical cause, but he helped him secure an academic post teaching Greek at the reformed Academy of Lausanne. Ten years later, Calvin again recruited Beza, this time inviting him to return to Geneva to serve as the rector of the newly founded Genevan Academy and as a city preacher. Over the years, a deep bond of friendship and trust was forged between the two men, due in large part to their shared labors for the gospel, their common concern for France, and Beza's unflinching loyalty to his spiritual mentor. "I would be very cold-hearted," Calvin noted, "if I did not care deeply for Beza, who loves me more than a brother and honors me more than a father."[2] Clearly, Calvin became for Beza what Bucer had once been for Calvin: a spiritual father, a theological mentor, a trusted friend, a guide who helped him discover his pastoral vocation. When Calvin died in May

1564, Beza was the natural choice to succeed the reformer as leader of the Genevan church.

Theodore Beza was the most distinguished of a battalion of reformed ministers who worked alongside or succeeded Calvin in the Genevan church during the sixteenth and early seventeenth centuries. Between 1536 and 1609, Calvin, Beza, and the Company of Pastors recruited over one hundred and thirty men to preach and provide pastoral care in Geneva's city and countryside churches. Several of these ministers were well-known churchmen and highly regarded theologians whose influence extended well beyond the shores of Lac Léman. The majority of the pastors, however, were men of more modest abilities and stature who served their congregations and died in relative obscurity. In this chapter I will describe Calvin's initial efforts to recruit a competent pastoral company for Geneva's churches, and provide quantitative evidence as to the geographic origins, social location, and educational backgrounds of these ministers. These findings will be compared to the profile of Geneva's ministers following Calvin's death in order to highlight general trends and important changes in the composition and backgrounds of the Venerable Company during the seven decades following the revolution of 1536. The men who served Geneva's church as pastors during these years fit into one of three general categories: long-term foreign ministers, short-term foreign ministers, and native ministers. The second section of this chapter will illustrate each of these ministerial "models" through the careers of several of the more prominent pastors. In the final section of this chapter, I will briefly explore the ways in which leadership of the Company of Pastors was constructed and sometimes contested during the generations immediately following Calvin's death.

1. *Geneva's Ministers in Profile*

When Calvin returned to Geneva from Strasbourg in September of 1541, one of the most urgent tasks at hand was to recruit a new group of ministers for the churches of the city and countryside. Unfortunately, Calvin was unable to secure from Lausanne the permanent services of the eloquent preacher Pierre Viret. Instead, the Genevan church was forced to recruit a group of pastors who, although they showed promise, were still far from ideal.[3] Calvin provided a blunt assessment of some of his colleagues' more blatant weaknesses in his correspondence during the following year. "Our other colleagues are more a hindrance than a help to us," Calvin wrote to Oswald Myconius in March 1542. "They are proud and self-conceited, have no zeal, and less learning. But what is worst of all, I cannot trust them, even though I very much wish that I could."[4] The reformer provided specific details in letters to Farel and Viret later that summer: The city minister Philippe de Ecclesia was a poor preacher and unpopular with the people. The minister Pierre Blanchet was engaged in a bitter dispute with his brother-in-law Sebastian Castellio that had become the talk of the town. Blanchet was showing tendencies "which are not very satisfactory," Calvin noted. The other city ministers were making progress in their preaching, though two of them displayed an unhealthy penchant for vainglory. As for the pastor Louis Treppereaux, he "has more levity and less self-control in his conversation and behavior than becomes a minister of the gospel." Calvin also reported that the pastor of Jussy, Nicolas Vandert, had unwisely criticized Geneva's magistrates in a judicial case and would soon be deposed from his post. His likely replacement Henri de La Mare was scarcely better. Surely men like these are "nothing in comparison with Viret," Calvin bemoaned.[5] Overall, this first group of ministers recruited to serve Geneva's churches in the early 1540s did not fare very well. Calvin aside, the average length of service of the ten city ministers hired from 1541 to 1544 was three years; of this group two men died, three were deposed, and three were transferred to countryside parishes. The overall effect of such high turnover was to sow instability and turmoil, weakening the church's ability to provide competent pastoral care.[6]

The appointment of Nicolas Des Gallars to Geneva's pastoral company in 1544 signaled an important new stage in Calvin's recruitment efforts. Des Gallars was from Paris, a man of noble birth, who possessed legal training, rich exposure to the humanities, and polished Latin.[7] Des Gallars served the Genevan church for over a dozen years both as a pastor and as a translator and editor of Calvin's writings. Thereafter his career path led him to pastoral posts in London and Orléans, a role as deputy at the Colloquy of Poissy (1561), and a brief chaplaincy in the court of the Queen of Navarre, Jeanne d'Albret. Other men of Des Gallars's stature and quality soon followed him to Geneva. Between 1545 and 1559, Calvin attracted to Geneva's pastoral company an impressive group of talented and well-educated French ministers who shared his reformed commitments—and who were loyal to him. These pastoral recruits included Michel Cop, noblemen François Bourgoing and François Morel, a former Franciscan monk named Raymond Chauvet, the future theologian Nicolas Colladon, and Theodore Beza. The city ministers recruited by Calvin from 1545 to 1559 enjoyed much longer tenures in office—fourteen years on average—which elevated the quality of preaching and brought greater stability of leadership to the city's churches. It was also in the mid-1540s that the Company of Pastors began to take shape as a formal ecclesiastical institution. By 1546, the Company was meeting for several hours every Friday morning to transact the business of the local churches and maintain formal contact with reformed congregations elsewhere in Europe. In time, the membership of the Company numbered around twenty men, including between seven and ten city ministers, nine to eleven rural pastors, and several professors from Geneva's Academy (usually the professors of theology, Greek, Hebrew, and the arts).[8] During the three-quarters of a century after the revolution of 1536, a total of 135 men belonged to Calvin's Company of Pastors (see the appendix).[9]

The next important period in the development of the Company of Pastors occurred in the years surrounding Calvin's death in 1564. Around a half-dozen prominent city ministers died or departed during these pivotal years, including Jean Macard (d. 1560), Michel Cop (d. 1566), Louis Enoch (d. 1567), and Jean-Raymond Merlin (deposed 1564). They were replaced by a younger cadre of pastors, nearly all expatriate Frenchmen, who were well-trained and deeply committed to the work of pastoral ministry. These new arrivals who joined Beza included Jean Trembley (minister from 1560–96), Jean Pinault (1560–1606), Charles Perrot (1564–1608), Jean Jaquemot (1566–1615), and Simon Gouart (1566–1628). To this elite group were added a decade or so later two other foreigners, the Frenchman Antoine de La Faye (1577–1615) and a Swiss pastor named David Le Boiteux (1577–1612). These eight men—Beza, Trembley, Pinault, Perrot, Jaquemot, Goulart, La Faye, and Le Boiteux—quickly became permanent fixtures in the city pulpits and provided primary leadership for the Company of Pastors into the seventeenth century. Their combined service to the Genevan church was more than three hundred fifty years, with an average tenure of more than four decades. This "long" generation of pastoral leadership brought with it several important consequences for religious life in Geneva. Lengthy pastoral tenures no doubt served to stabilize religious life in the city and appear to have translated into growing professional competence on the part of the ministers. But gray hair often brought with it increased frailty and illness, and probably contributed to a conservative spirit resistant to change. In addition, pastoral longevity in Geneva's city's churches may have made it more difficult for Beza and the Company of Pastors to recruit younger men, particularly those Genevan youths who aspired to the pastoral vocation in service of their mother church.

A fourth stage of pastoral recruitment began in the mid 1590s as the leaders of Geneva's pastoral corps who had made up this "long" generation—Beza, Trembley, Pinault, and Perrot—began to pass from the scene and were replaced by younger men who would lead Geneva's church for the next several decades, pastors such as Gabriel Cusin (minister from 1598–1617), Jean Gros (1601–42), Jean Diodati (1608–45), and Théodore Tronchin (1608–57). This new group of ministers represented the future of Geneva's Company of Pastors. Most were native Genevans, nearly all had formal theological training, and many were the sons of pastors. By way of summary, then, during the seven decades following the revolution of 1536, one can discern four periods, or "generations," of pastoral leadership in Geneva: a period of disruption (1536 to 1544), a period of construction (1545 to around 1559), a period of consolidation (1560 to the mid 1590s), and a period of indigenization and professionalization (after 1594).

To this point, I have described the pastoral personnel who served Geneva's three city temples, St. Pierre, St. Gervais, and the Madeleine. Recruiting pastors for Geneva's rural churches was an altogether different matter. As previously noted, several of Geneva's countryside parishes did not have a reformed minister until the mid-1540s. Even then, the quality of these ministers frequently left something to be desired. In the following decades, the Company of Pastors did succeed in recruiting higher caliber pastoral candidates for Geneva's rural churches, but these ministers rarely stayed long in their posts. Between 1540 and 1609, the duration of clerical assignments in countryside parishes remained static, averaging around five years. The brevity of rural assignments had several causes. Countryside pulpits were often filled with theological students or young graduates of the Academy who had no intention of remaining in Geneva long term. So too the Company of Pastors often treated rural parishes as testing grounds for inexperienced pastors, with the most promising among them soon transferred to the city church. As we will see later, this pattern was far from Calvin's ideal, but it proved to be the reality nonetheless. That is not to say that all rural assignments were of short duration. Abraham de La Maisonneuve, for example, spent the first six years of his career in the parish of Céligny, moved to the church of Genthod-Moëns, where he served for seventeen years, before spending the last seven years of his life as pastor at St. Gervais within the city walls. As a general rule, however, rural parishes could expect their pastors to remain for only five or six years, before they died, were transferred to a city post, or quit the Genevan church altogether.

Having described the pattern of development of the Company of Pastors between 1536 and 1609, I now explore the geographic origins, social locations, and educational backgrounds of the men who staffed Geneva's churches. Of the 135 ministers who labored in Geneva during these years, the geographic origins of 114 of them are known. Table 2.1 identifies the geographic regions from which these ministers came, categorized by the time period in which they were first enrolled in the Company of Pastors. During the years 1536 to 1609, most of Geneva's ministers whose geographic origins are known were recruited from France (72 percent), with a smaller percent of pastors drawn from Geneva (22 percent), the region of Vaud (4 percent), and other Swiss Cantons (3 percent). The French presence within the Company of Pastors was especially strong before 1570, when fifty-nine of the sixty-four (known) ministers were Frenchmen. The percentage of French ministers working in Geneva declined somewhat between 1570 and 1609, but still more than half the ministers appointed during this period were French born. Not surprisingly, recruitment was highest from regions of France located nearest to Geneva (e.g., Dauphiné, Burgundy) or in areas where Huguenot strength was concentrated (e.g., Provence, Languedoc, Guyenne, Poitou). On the other hand, only a handful of ministers came from the Swiss Confederation, although several of them were more prominent members of the Company, such as Jean-Baptiste Rotan from the Grisons, as well as Pierre Viret, Antoine Chauve, and David Le Boiteux from the Pays de Vaud.

TABLE 2.1 Geographic Origins of Geneva's Ministers, 1536–1609

PERIOD APPOINTED	PASTORS FROM GENEVA AND ENVIRONS	PASTORS FROM FRANCE	PASTORS FROM PAYS DE VAUD	PASTORS FROM OTHER SWISS CANTONS	PASTORS FROM UNKNOWN ORIGIN
First Period: 1536–1544	2	20	1	0	8
Second Period: 1545–1559	0	20	0	0	1
Third Period: 1560–1594	12	38	3	3	9
Fourth Period: 1595–1609	11	4	0	0	3
TOTALS	25	82	4	3	21

The relatively small number of Geneva-born men who served the church between 1536 and 1609 is surprising. As table 2.1 indicates, only twenty-five Genevan natives are known to have held pastoral posts in the city and countryside parishes over these seven decades. During the early periods of the Company's existence (1536–1559), the only local men who belonged to Geneva's pastoral corps were two former Catholic clergymen, the priest Jacques Baud and the one-time Franciscan Jacques Bernard.[10] Both of these men came from prominent families in and around Geneva; at the time of the Reformation they converted to the evangelical religion and were assigned to countryside parishes. Other than these two men, no native Genevans were admitted to the Company of Pastors during Calvin's lifetime. This dearth of local leadership began to be corrected during the 1570s. In that decade, five native sons entered Geneva's pastoral corps, all assigned to rural parishes. Twenty years later, in 1594, Abraham Grenet along with Abraham de La Maisonneuve became the first Genevans assigned to the more prestigious parish churches within the city walls. The middle years of the 1590s thus represent an important period of transition in the composition of the Company of Pastors, as graph 2.1 makes clear. After 1594, hiring patterns swung decidedly in the favor of local candidates, and the number of native Genevans serving parishes in the city and countryside began to increase steadily. Of the eight city posts that became available from 1594 to 1609, six were filled by Genevans. By the year 1609, four native pastors held posts within the city walls, and another seven were serving parishes in the countryside.[11]

The recruitment of ministers in sixteenth-century Geneva runs counter to the pattern witnessed in most other reformed territories. Scholars have shown that in reformed cities such as Zurich, Bern, Basel, and Strasbourg,

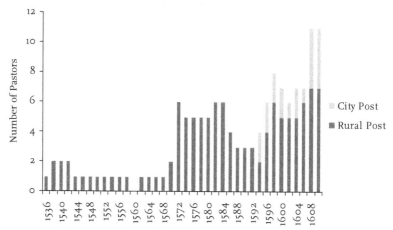

GRAPH 2.1 Parish Assignments of Native Genevan Pastors, 1536–1609

a significant number of Catholic clergy converted to the Protestant faith at the time of the Reformation in the 1520s, forming the nucleus of the new ministerial order.[12] Not so in Geneva, where the vast majority of all Catholic secular and regular clergy abandoned the city at the time of the revolution. So too, the indigenization of Geneva's pastoral corps occurred much more slowly than in most other reformed churches. In Basel, for example, by the 1550s, more than half of newly appointed ministers came from Basel or its rural territory.[13] The same pattern is evident in Zurich, where by the middle of the century the majority of reformed pastors were natives, with many coming from clerical families.[14] In Geneva, by contrast, recruitment of local talent to the pastoral office became common practice only at the very end of the sixteenth century. As a consequence, supervision of religious life in Geneva fell almost exclusively to foreign-born ministers during the first generations after Calvin's death—a fact that many townspeople in Geneva were acutely aware of and resented deeply.[15]

What might explain the Company of Pastors' slow assimilation of native-born ministers into its ranks? Theodore Beza saw the dearth of local leadership as a serious problem and had clear opinions as to its root causes. Writing to the Zurich minister Rudolf Gwalther in 1584, Beza complained about the local situation:

> I congratulate your church, because God has blessed you. For not only do you not have to borrow pastors and professors from elsewhere, but you have a surplus and can assist other cities.... The opposite is the case here in Geneva, where if it had not been for foreigners, either the sheep would have been without shepherds and the schools without teachers, or God would have had to do something extraordinary.[16]

Beza blamed the problem primarily on the spiritual apathy and greed of Geneva's parents who slighted their children's education, neglected the

Word of God, and encouraged sons to pursue more lucrative careers in the trades or commerce rather than in theology and the sacred ministry.[17] Though there may be some truth to Beza's accusation, there were several other factors that were probably equally as important. First, the academic training expected of ministerial candidates was rigorous, time-consuming, and expensive. As these requirements increased over the course of the sixteenth century, some young men in Geneva lacked the intellectual ability or economic resources to pursue theological studies. Second, whereas Protestant churches elsewhere set in place generous stipendiary systems to support ministerial education, the Company of Pastors was not successful in establishing a viable scholarship program for needy students, local or otherwise.[18] In the generation following the foundation of Calvin's Academy, Beza and his colleagues were never able to raise sufficient funds to support more than a handful of students; only two local youths who were the beneficiaries of these scholarships ever became pastors in Geneva's church.[19] A third factor that must have discouraged local young men from pursuing pastoral vocations in Geneva was the preponderance of foreign ministers in the most important pulpits of the church. Even if well-known foreign ministers like Calvin, Beza, and Goulart added luster to Geneva's reputation in the Protestant world, their presence also reduced the availability of desirable city posts and may well have left the impression that clerical careers were for high-placed foreigners, not local young men of less illustrious pedigrees.

To these three factors, which point toward an inadequate supply of qualified native candidates, we must add a fourth factor that addresses the dynamics of power within the Company of Pastors: namely, Beza and his foreign-born colleagues regularly chose to appoint ministerial candidates who were like themselves, foreigners and (usually) Frenchmen. An episode from 1585 is most telling in this regard. In that year, the ministers elected to a city post the Vaudois pastor, David Le Boiteux, who had served the countryside parish of Russin-Dardagny for the previous eight years. The Small Council objected to this choice, however, concerned that Le Boiteux's voice wasn't strong enough for a city pulpit and fearful that Abraham de La Maisonneuve—a native Genevan and son of a syndic who had already served rural churches for fifteen years—would be disheartened and angry for being passed over. Despite the magistrates' reservations, the ministers persisted and Le Boiteux was installed at St. Gervais.[20] Another decade was to pass before La Maisonneuve was finally appointed to a city post. As this case suggests, Beza and many of his French colleagues did not attach a high priority to cultivating native ministers to lead Geneva's church. Their concern was to find the best qualified man for the post— and in their eyes, that usually meant appointing a foreign candidate. This culture of preference finally began to change in the early seventeenth century, however, when Geneva's magistrates started mandating that the Company of Pastors hire local ministers to prominent city posts. In January

TABLE 2.2 Social Origins of Geneva's Ministers, 1536–1609

OCCUPATION OF FATHER	NUMBER OF MINISTERS
Noble	
French	10
Italian	2
Bourgeois	
Artisan	1
Clergyman	9
Judge of French *parlement*	3
Lawyer	3
Merchant	2
Military Officer	1
Notary	3
Physician or Apothecary	2
Professor	2
Syndic of Geneva	4
Peasant	0
TOTAL	42

of 1607, the Company of Pastors nominated Samuel Perrot, a foreign-born minister serving the rural parish of Satigny, to fill a pastoral post in the city. The Small Council rejected this choice and ordered the Company to hold a new election "giving preference to citizens."[21] Spokesmen for the ministers protested strongly against this injunction, arguing that it "seemed entirely without precedent to the Company, since in such elections one had never before considered the distinction between bourgeois and citizens, but only the abilities and capacities that God had given to the candidates."[22] The magistrates would not back down, however, and the ministers were forced to capitulate. In a second election, the Company of Pastors selected a Genevan citizen named Matthieu Scarron, who had received only one vote on the first ballot, to fill the pastoral vacancy in the city.[23] From this point on, the criteria for evaluating ministerial candidates included not only educational training and ability but also geographical background. By the early seventeenth century, the office of minister had become a more attractive and accessible vocational option for a growing number of Genevan young men.

What is known about the social backgrounds of the men who worked alongside Calvin, Beza, and Goulart? The profession or social location of the fathers of around one-third of the 135 ministers who served Geneva's churches between 1536 and 1609 has been identified in table 2.2. This table indicates that Geneva's pastoral company was recruited almost entirely from the urban classes of French-speaking Europe as well as France's nobility. No ministers are known to have come from the world of rural agriculture or from the ranks of day laborers. The prominence of noblemen is especially striking. According to my sample, more than one-quarter (twelve out of forty-two) of Geneva's ministers whose social background is known came from aristocratic families. More often than not, these ministers of high birth were prominent French pastors who migrated to Geneva during seasons of severe persecution and served alongside Calvin and Beza for a short period of time, before returning to their churches in France. The roll call of these noble churchmen includes some of the most important leaders of French Protestantism in the middle decades of the sixteenth century: François Morel, Nicolas Des Gallars, Pierre d'Airebaudouze, Adam Dorival, Lambert Daneau, and Antoine de Chandieu. Two other French refugees with noble pedigrees—Theodore Beza and Jean Trembley—settled in Geneva permanently and had long careers as pastors of the city's church.[24] After Calvin's death the practice of appointing noblemen to Geneva's pastoral offices became less common, with only three ministers of aristocratic backgrounds known to have been recruited between 1564 and 1609.[25] This development reflected (in part) changes in immigration patterns among France's Protestant nobility during the protracted Wars of Religion. So too, longer tenures among Geneva's clergy and (as a result) greater stability of the Company of Pastors meant that there was less need for noble foreigners to fill pastoral posts on a short-term basis.

Scholars have long recognized that Protestantism in sixteenth-century France was primarily an "urban religion," attracting converts predominantly from the ranks of artisans, merchants, and the liberal professions.[26] This same pattern is seen in the social makeup of Geneva's clergy during this period, with a majority drawn from the middling rank of urban society. As table 2.2 indicates, four of the ministers were the sons of Geneva's chief magistrates (syndics). Three other ministers whose backgrounds have been identified came from families of merchants or artisans, including a merchant, a goldsmith, and a tailor.[27] A larger number of Beza's colleagues (thirteen out of forty-two) were the sons of lawyers, judges, notaries, professors, and physicians—members of the "liberal professions" who formed the intellectual elite of urban society. Several ministers from this group came from French families of influence and social prestige: Charles and Denis Perrot, for example, were the sons of a councilor of the *parlement* of Paris. Michel Cop was the son of Guillaume Cop, royal physician to Francis I, and the brother of Nicolas Cop, the famous rector of the University of Paris. Pierre Prevost's father was a professor of the humanities at Lausanne

TABLE 2.3 Educational Backgrounds of Geneva's Pastors, 1536–1609

PERIOD APPOINTED	UNIVERSITY ONLY	GENEVAN ACADEMY ONLY	GENEVAN ACADEMY & UNIVERSITY	PROFESSOR/ TEACHER OR MAÎSTRE[a]	UNKNOWN	TOTAL
First Period: 1536–1544	6	N/A	N/A	9	16	31
Second Period: 1545–1559	5	1	0	9	6	21
Third Period: 1560–1594	11	26	7	6	15	65
Fourth Period: 1595–1609	1	8	6	1	2	18
TOTALS	23	35	13	25	39	135

[a] Denotes a minister known to have served as a professor or regent in a *collège* or academy, or identified as a Maîstre in the sources, for whom other educational information is not available.

and, briefly, the principal of the *collège* of Geneva. To this list of prominent urban professionals should be added the ministers who came from clerical homes. Nine of the ministers in the sample are known to have been the sons of reformed pastors, including Etienne Trembley, whose father served the Genevan church for nearly four decades, as well as Jean Gros and his brother Etienne the Younger who were born in the parish of Jussy where their father was pastor. Although it is too soon to speak of clerical "dynasties," what is clear is that by the beginning of the seventeenth century an increasing percentage of pastoral candidates were coming from pastoral households.[28] The large representation of men from the liberal professions; the absence of candidates drawn from the peasant class; the growing number of ministers coming from clerical homes—in each of these ways pastoral recruitment in Geneva reflected similar patterns evident in other reformed cities and territories during the period. Where Geneva was unique was in the large number of foreign noblemen who served as city ministers, particularly during the first decades of the Genevan Reformation.

Having examined the geographical and social backgrounds of Geneva's ministers, I now turn to their educational training. Table 2.3 breaks down the educational backgrounds of Geneva's ministers between 1536 and 1609 by period in which they were first enrolled in the Company of Pastors. Unfortunately, it is impossible to construct a detailed profile of the educational backgrounds of Geneva's first Protestant ministers between 1536 and 1544 because nothing is known about the formal training of over half the ministers. Though several of Calvin's first colleagues possessed university training, and even doctorates in theology, other ministers appear to have been ill-equipped to serve their churches.[29] Many years later, the pastor Antoine de La Faye quipped that these first ministers belonging to the Venerable Company were not even qualified to watch goats.[30] As Calvin set about building Geneva's pastoral company between 1545 and 1559, the percentage of ministers who possessed university education appears to have increased. Not only Theodore Beza, but Michel Cop, Claude Baduel, Nicolas Colladon, and Jean-Raymond Merlin all received education in the humane letters, and with it the knowledge of Greek or Hebrew, or both.

The founding of Geneva's Academy in 1559 represented an important milestone in Calvin's efforts to elevate the theological competence of ministers both in Geneva and throughout the reformed world. Well over half—forty-seven out of eighty-three—the pastoral candidates admitted to the Company of Pastors between 1560 and 1609 are known to have received theological training at the Academy. Students were drawn to the Academy by its excellent faculty and uncompromising commitment to reformed doctrine. In addition to Calvin, early professors included such illustrious Protestant scholars as Beza and Lambert Daneau (theology), François Berauld and Isaac Casaubon (Greek), Bonaventure Bertram (Hebrew), Claude Baduel and Esaie Colladon (the arts), François Hotman and Jacques Lect (law). During its first five years in existence, the Academy matriculated 339 students, the majority of who came from France in order to prepare for Protestant ministry.[31] By the end of the century, nearly one thousand five hundred students had studied at the *schola publica*, including the sons of princes and magistrates, and many of Europe's leading reformed pastors and theologians. One of the institution's first students was Daneau, who later recalled:

> In 1560, I came to your Academy, full of enthusiasm, not because it was near the French border, for there were others nearby, but because it offered to me the purest source of that heavenly doctrine held by my mentor, the martyred jurist Anne Du Bourg.... I will say freely that so many leading lights, so many talented and famous men in all branches of knowledge were in that city, that it seemed to me to be one of the richest markets for intellectual commerce in the world.[32]

Unlike Europe's universities, Calvin's Academy did not impose matriculation fees and had no authority to confer academic degrees.[33] Students were often in residence for only several months or a year, acquiring basic instruction in reformed theology and scriptural exegesis, before returning to their home countries to undertake gospel labors. While in Geneva, they were formed not only through lectures and academic disputations but also through daily sermons, Sunday worship services, as well as the culture of moral discipline present in the city. Consequently, the substance and quality of theological education provided was viewed favorably in many corners of Protestant Europe. A Genevan magistrate named Jacob Anjorrant who was sent to the Low Countries on a fund-raising mission in 1597, reported back on how the Dutch churches perceived Calvin's Academy:

> The Academy has flourished thanks to the reputation and worth of the out-standing people whose fame was and is known throughout the world be it in theology, law, or in Hebrew, Greek, and Arts. Therefore, those who have had the opportunity to study under such professors are considered to be very learned. However, this would be of very little value if good discipline did not flourish as well. Geneva's reputation in this field is not small, because of the order and discipline that prevails there. As such, the young men who have spent time in Geneva are well thought of, as being well-trained, and because of this, they are placed more quickly in parishes.[34]

In addition to theological training at Calvin's Academy, many of Geneva's ministers during the half-century from 1560 to 1609 could boast a university education as well. I have been able to identify twenty-five of Geneva's pastors (out of eighty-three total) during this period who attended university. Several studied civil law in France before their conversions to the Protestant religion, notably Daneau, Bonaventure Bertram, Simon Goulart, Antoine de Chandieu, and Gaspard de La Faverge. Four ministers appear to have earned doctorates: Daneau in law, Antoine de La Faye in medicine, and Jean-Baptiste Rotan and Jean Diodati in theology. Table 2.3 suggests that during the last decades of the sixteenth century the percentage of Geneva's ministers overall who acquired some university education increased. Many pastoral candidates supplemented their training from the Genevan Academy with theological study at foreign universities. The most popular destinations were the reformed universities of Heidelberg, Basel, and Leiden, whose theological faculties included such renowned scholars as Jerome Zanchi, Jean-Jacques Grynaeus, Amandus Polanus, and Franciscus Junius.[35] Thus, for example, a promising young Genevan named Théodore Tronchin, after having completed his academic work at the Genevan Academy in 1600, made a tour of Basel, Heidelberg, and Leiden in order to study theology and prepare for (what turned out to be) a long career as a pastor and professor in his home church. Six other sons of Geneva are also known to have matriculated in one of these three theological faculties in the final decades of the sample. In fact, after 1580, 40 percent of native Genevans who entered the Company of Pastors had studied abroad, a harbinger of the professionalization of Geneva's clerical office that occurred later in the seventeenth century.

Even if Geneva's ministers as a group were better educated in 1600 than in 1560, their level of formal theological training was probably not exceptional when compared with Protestant ministers elsewhere. Social historians have shown that, at least until the early decades of the seventeenth century, most Protestant ministers in Europe received some theological education, although formal academic qualifications or degrees in theology remained rare, limited to the most important officials of the church. This was true in most regions of Lutheran Germany, as well as in the reformed Palatinate.[36]

Such was also the case in late sixteenth- and early seventeenth-century Geneva, where most of the ministers had received basic theological training from the Academy, but only a few held advanced academic degrees.

The fact that many members of the Company of Pastors shared the same educational background is important for several reasons. At the most basic level, the Academy's intensive program in theology and exegesis helped prepare Geneva's future ministers for their vocation of interpreting and preaching the Word of God. In addition, the students who received their theological training at the Academy were exposed to a single system of doctrine *and* a common religious culture. If the lecture hall introduced them to reformed theology, the pattern of religious life in the city shaped their understanding of public worship, moral discipline, and ministerial comportment. So too, the fact that a sizeable group of Geneva's ministers had learned reformed theology at the feet of Beza in the Academy established the reformer's theological leadership within the Company of Pastors and solidified his moral authority over Geneva's church. This common program of theological education and religious enculturation—as well as Beza's formidable leadership—goes far in explaining the confessional solidarity and cohesiveness displayed by the Company of Pastors during the half century after Calvin's death.

The evidence presented thus far allows us to identify four general trends. First, during the half century after Calvin's death, the membership of the Company of Pastors went from being almost entirely foreign-born to becoming increasingly Genevan-born. By 1609, recruitment of native sons to the pastoral office was more the rule than the exception. Second, during the same period, the social location of Geneva's ministerial corps became more firmly rooted in the middling level of urban society, a development suggested both by the reduction of the number of French noblemen serving the church and by the increasing number of ministerial candidates drawn from clerical homes. Third, as we have seen, the Academy of Geneva was of strategic importance in creating an educated and cohesive clerical company. By the beginning of the seventeenth century, however, more and more pastoral candidates chose to supplement their training from the Academy with advanced theological education at reformed universities elsewhere in Europe. Finally, the length of pastoral careers in Geneva increased steadily during the sixteenth century and the average age of city ministers grew progressively older. Nevertheless, the fact that clerical assignments in the countryside remained of relatively short duration raises questions about the overall quality of pastoral care provided in Geneva's rural parishes.

2. Pastoral Models in Geneva

Throughout the 1540s, Calvin worked tirelessly to construct a pastoral company of men who were committed to the reformed faith, competent in

their pastoral duties, and loyal to him—and no one satisfied these requirements any better than Michel Cop. Calvin and Cop had been boyhood
friends since their student days in Paris.[37] Thereafter, Cop was ordained as
priest and served as a cathedral canon in France for several years before
he went over to the evangelical side and immigrated to Geneva in April
1545, where Calvin quickly recruited him to join the city's pastoral staff.[38]
Writing to a friend in Bern, Calvin described Cop as "a man of exceptional
piety and doctrine," with an intelligence "more profound than his appearance suggests."[39] Over the next twenty-one years, Cop served Geneva's city
parishes through his preaching, pastoral care, and biblical scholarship.
A gifted Hebraist, Cop tutored Calvin in the Hebrew language and published sermons on the books of Proverbs and Ecclesiastes. In the pulpit
Cop was a powerful, sometimes controversial preacher. And always, he was
Calvin's friend and faithful lieutenant. Hence in 1551, when Jerome Bolsec
attacked Calvin's doctrine of predestination in a meeting of Geneva's
Congregation, it was Cop who jumped to Calvin's defense, arguing that
the doctrine of double predestination was "an infallible doctrine, which it
is necessary that all Christians affirm."[40] When Michel Cop died of a fever
in September 1566, his colleague Jean Pinault noted his passing with these
words: "He served happily and fulfilled his ministry in this church without blame since the year [1545]. For God had given him the grace to leave
behind the honors and delights of Egypt—that is France—to settle down
in this city."[41]

The reformed church of Geneva was established and preserved in large
part through the efforts of ministers like Michel Cop, men who had fled
privilege and promising careers in their native France and sought refuge
in Calvin's Geneva, determined to build a new church "reformed" according to the Word of God. Some of these foreigners remained in Geneva
for only a brief period of time; others, like Cop, became long-term, career
members of the Company of Pastors. Only at the end of the sixteenth century did native-born ministers begin to replace foreign clergy as leaders of
the Genevan church. In the present section, I will briefly illustrate each
of these three "pastoral models"—career foreign ministers (i.e., those serving more than ten years), short-term foreign ministers, and native-born
ministers—through the lives of several of the more prominent members
of Geneva's pastoral corps.

Career Foreign Ministers

With the notable exception of Theodore Beza, none of Geneva's ministers
during the second half of the sixteenth century played a more important
role in maintaining the day-to-day practice of reformed Christianity in
Geneva than three career foreign ministers, Jean Trembley, Charles Perrot,
and Simon Goulart. Jean Trembley was one of Beza's closest colleagues
and friends. The two men had several things in common: they were the

same age, both had been born into France's lower nobility, and both had fled to Geneva for the sake of conscience. In addition, Beza was the god-father of Trembley's third son, Théodore, who died in infancy in 1568.[42] Jean Trembley, along with his brothers Etienne and Louis, immigrated to Geneva in 1552. His brothers assimilated rapidly into Geneva's commercial and political life; within a few years, they had become successful merchants and elected to the Council of 200.[43] Jean, on the other hand, found his vocation in the church. In 1560, the Company of Pastors appointed him as minister of the village parish of Satigny-Peney. Four years later, he was transferred to a city post. For the next thirty-five years, Trembley served the congregations of St. Gervais and St. Pierre, preaching several times per week, leading catechism classes, visiting parishioners, and supporting Beza as he directed the business of the church. Trembley's career in Geneva was on the whole unremarkable. He is not known to have published anything. There were only a handful of occasions when his actions stirred public controversy or warranted official comment: when, for example, in the heat of a sermon he compared the city of Geneva to Sodom and Gomorrah, or when, during the great plague of 1568, he consoled victims from the win-dow rather than from bedside.[44] Trembley suffered poor health and physi-cal exhaustion during the final years of his ministry. When he was finally permitted to retire at the ripe old age of seventy-six, he was utterly spent, "broken with age and deprived of all strength and vigor," as Beza report-ed.[45] At his death in 1599, he was survived by a daughter and three sons, two of whom were reformed ministers.

The Genevan pastor Charles Perrot was of a very different temperament than either Beza or Trembley. Perrot was an idealist prone to discour-agement, a man of deep piety who valued Christian charity as much as theological precision. His motto—"groan and remain silent"—reflected the quietism, resignation, and even despair that he felt at the end of his life as he confronted his own sins as well as the failures of the church that he served.[46] Born in 1541 to a councilor of the *parlement* of Paris, Perrot proba-bly briefly belonged to a monastic order before converting to the Protestant religion. In 1564, he immigrated to Geneva and joined his elder brother Denis studying theology under Beza at the Academy. In that same year, the two brothers were admitted to the reformed ministry and appointed to rural parishes. The Company of Pastors soon discharged Denis from his pastoral responsibilities on account of mental illness,[47] and he returned to France where he was a victim of the massacres of St. Bartholomew's Day (August 1572). Charles elected to stay behind and settle down. In 1566, he married Sara Cop, daughter of the minister Michel Cop. The following year he was transferred to the city to work alongside Beza at the temple of St. Pierre, a post that he occupied for the next forty years. Perrot's intel-lectual abilities appear to have been superior to most of his colleagues, given that he was occasionally asked to teach theology on an interim basis at the Academy. In his half dozen writings—none of which were published during his lifetime—he displayed an expansive knowledge of the early church fathers, including Ambrose, Chrysostom, and especially Augustine.

Studies from the past century have highlighted Perrot's compassion for the poor, his concern for personal and social holiness, and his irenic spirit. There is ample evidence for each of these characteristics. His pulpit jeremiads against social injustice and his advocacy for the poor sometimes put him at odds with Geneva's magistrates.[48] Although he was firmly committed to the Protestant doctrine of justification by faith alone (*sola fide*), he was critical of the Genevan church for neglecting repentance and love— the fruit of sanctification.[49] In the last decades of his life, Perrot became increasingly disillusioned with the moral effects of the Reformation. He bemoaned the fact that while the reformers had "searched for right doctrine (*l'orthodoxie*)," they had too often "left right practice (*l'orthovie*) far behind."[50] In one unpublished manuscript, Perrot even accused Protestants of "schism" and asserted that it would have been better if the early reformers had remained in the Catholic Church, groaning quietly about her many faults without disrupting the unity of the Church.[51] Such were the words of a disappointed idealist, not a subversive, however. During his long career in Geneva, Perrot was a loyal and respected member of Geneva's pastoral corps.[52] On those occasions when his colleagues asked him to give account of controversial dimensions of his theology, he did so to their satisfaction. Nonetheless, after Perrot's death in 1608, the magistrates confiscated the pastor's manuscripts from his heirs and submitted them to the city ministers for examination. In the end, statements judged to be erroneous or "Papist" were expurgated, and these manuscripts were returned to Perrot's family under the condition that they were never to be published or allowed to see the light of day.[53]

Apart from Calvin and Beza, probably the best known of the foreign ministers who settled permanently in Geneva was Simon Goulart. Born in Picardy in 1543, Goulart devoted himself to the humane letters and the study of law before his conversion to the reformed faith.[54] He arrived in Geneva in the spring of 1566 and enrolled in the Academy for several months. By the fall of the same year, he was appointed minister of the countryside church of Chancy-Cartigny. Four years later, at age twenty-seven, Goulart married Suzanne Picot, the fifteen-year-old daughter of a prominent Genevan family, with whom he had nine children (six survived infancy). In 1571, Goulart was transferred to the temple of St. Gervais to begin a pastoral tenure in the city that lasted more than fifty years. The young minister was particularly impressed by Beza: "Here in Geneva, Beza is valuable in every way," he wrote in 1576. "On his shoulders my colleagues and I place all of our burdens, with utter confidence."[55] Beza for his part acknowledged this young protégé as "my brother and friend."[56] During his long career in Geneva, Goulart had the reputation of being an eloquent but controversial preacher, unafraid to speak out against what he judged to be the ills of society, whether they be promiscuous styles in clothing, miscarriages of public justice, or the hypocrisy of public officials. Goulart was also one of the most prolific authors of the Genevan Reformation in the second half of the sixteenth century. His literary corpus numbered no less than sixty-five works, including martyrologies, collections of poetry and psalms, spiritual meditations, histories of the kingdom of France, as well as a bevy of editions and translations of classical and contemporary writings (of such authors as Chrysostom, Seneca, Tertullian, Calvin, Beza, Chandieu, Hotman, and William Perkins).[57] As an author Goulart was more of a publicist than a theologian, but his stature in the reformed world was unquestioned. Churches in France and Switzerland regularly tried to woo this "wise and experienced navigator" away from Geneva.[58] The Company of Pastors consistently resisted these efforts, judging Goulart to be "one of the pillars of the Church."[59] Consequently, around the time of Beza's death in 1605, Goulart emerged as the spiritual leader of the Company of Pastors and elder statesman of the Genevan church.

Considering the cases of these three men—Trembley, Perrot, and Goulart—as well as the other foreign-born ministers who immigrated to Geneva and became career members of the Company of Pastors, one is impressed by how rapidly many of their families assimilated into Geneva's political and social life. As we have seen, Jean Trembley's brothers were admitted to the Council of 200 in short order. Trembley's nephews also became important political figures: one was elected to the Council of 200; another served on the Small Council in the early 1600s. In a similar fashion, the sons of ministers Charles Perrot, Jean Jaquemot, and Gaspard de La Faverge were all elected to the Council of 200 at one time or another. Perrot's son Timothée had a particularly illustrious career as a public servant, including a term as the city *auditeur* and as member of the Small Council. The fact that many of these foreign ministers were well-educated or laid claim to French nobility made possible their association with some of Geneva's most advantaged citizens. Several of them married into prominent Genevan families. Thus, for example, the minister Jean Du Perril married the daughter of the syndic Henri Aubert. Simon Goulart's wife Suzanne was the daughter of a member of the Council of 200. One of Nicolas Colladon's sisters became the wife of city councilor (and wealthy French nobleman) Laurent de Normandie; a second sister married the city notary Jean Ragueau. Social ties were forged not only through marriage but also in the weekly meetings of the Consistory, where the ministers supervised church discipline side by side with twelve lay elders, all drawn from Geneva's magistracy. These elders represented some of Geneva's most powerful and wealthy families. The majority of them appear to have been men of solid Calvinist convictions, who supported the city's pastors and were committed to work with them in the cause of moral reformation. Their common religious labor and shared convictions must have frequently strengthened the bonds of friendship and social association. This was true of Theodore Beza, for example, whose closest friends included two syndics

Jean Favre and Jacques Lect, the Italian patrician Pompeo Diodati (who served on Consistory and belonged to the Council of 200), and the Italian marquis Galeazzo Caracciolo (who served on Consistory and belonged to the councils of 200 and 60).[60] Familiarity could also breed contempt, of course, as seems to have happened between Jean Trembley and an elder (and wealthy merchant) named Claude de La Roche, when a nasty marriage dispute between Claude's son and Trembley's niece devolved into heated confrontations in the presence of the Consistory in the mid 1560s (see chapter 7). But even this conflict between Trembley and La Roche highlights this general pattern of social assimilation. Over time, many of these foreign-born ministers and their families came to occupy a respected and influential place in Geneva's urban life during the latter half of the sixteenth century.

Short-Term Foreign Ministers

A second pastoral model, which I designate "short-term foreign ministers," identifies those foreign clergymen whose pastoral service in Geneva was limited to a decade or less. Several different career paths are included under this rubric. A number of these were seasoned pastors from France who sought temporary refuge in Geneva and were briefly employed as city ministers during the harshest periods of religious violence in their homeland. The list of exiled ministers who spent time in Geneva includes some of the leading lights of the French church, including François Morel,[61] Jean-Raymond Merlin,[62] and Pierre d'Airebaudouze.[63] Other foreign ministers came to Geneva to study at the Academy and were recruited to serve one of the rural parishes for several years before returning to their native country. A good example of this career path was Léonard Constant, who matriculated at the Academy in 1571, served as pastor of the parish of Satigny-Peney from 1576 to 1583, and then took voluntary leave to begin a prestigious career providing leadership for the churches of Basel, Bordeaux, and Lyon. Still other short-term foreign ministers relocated in Geneva but died prematurely or were forced to depart when they fell afoul of city authorities. Here we might cite the case of Jean Le Gaigneux from Tours, whose exceptional talents were matched by such an explosive temper and independent spirit that he was finally deposed in 1571 after nine years of controversial ministry. Of the many short-term foreign ministers who worked in Geneva, Lambert Daneau and Antoine de Chandieu were particularly important for the theological contributions they made to French Protestantism.

Lambert Daneau was born around 1530 into a noble family near Orléans.[64] During his twenties, he studied law under the jurist Anne Du Bourg at Orléans and then (apparently) took his doctorate in law at the University of Bourges. In December 1559, on learning that Du Bourg had been executed as a Protestant martyr, Daneau himself embraced the evangelical faith and thereafter set out for Geneva to study theology at Calvin's Academy. Daneau's first sojourn in Geneva lasted less than a year. Soon he was back in France pastoring a reformed congregation in Gien under the most difficult of circumstances. He later recalled: "During the twelve years that I exercised the ministry [in France], I was seven times forced to flee, recalled, condemned, absolved, forced to wander about...but the Lord was my refuge throughout all these calamities."[65] This dangerous assignment was cut short by the bloody massacres of St. Bartholomew's Day in the summer of 1572, which forced Daneau to flee once again to Geneva. Recognizing Daneau's substantial intellectual talents, the Company of Pastors in short order appointed him to the parish of Vandoeuvres and made him a lecturer in theology assisting Beza at the Academy. The following year, Daneau was transferred to the temple of St. Pierre in the city. During his nine-year residence in Geneva, Daneau grew into an internationally recognized theologian, a champion of Calvinist orthodoxy with the expansive vision of establishing and extending the domains of secular knowledge (whether politics, history, moral philosophy, or physics) on the basis of Scripture through the use of the scholastic method of dialectic.[66] He also became a formidable polemicist, battling with his pen both Lutheran and Catholic opponents. During his sojourn in Geneva, Daneau published around thirty works on a breath-taking range of subjects: several moral treatises (on Christian friendship; against sorcery and games of chance); a commentary on the first book of Peter Lombard's *Sentences*; theological writings in defense of the Trinity and against Lutheran "ubiquitarians"; a political treatise justifying armed resistance against royal tyranny; a commentary on 1 Timothy; a work devoted to biblical hermeneutics; several editions of Augustine's writings; and studies on Christian physics and ethics.[67] While in Geneva, Lambert Daneau became close friends with many of the leading French pastors in the city, especially Beza, Perrot, and Goulart, who judged him to be (in the words of Beza) "a person very learned and a virtuous defender of the truth."[68] Despite their best efforts to hold on to this prized colleague, Daneau accepted the call to teach theology at the University of Leiden and took leave of the Company of Pastors in February 1581.

Antoine de Chandieu was also a refugee of the storms of St. Bartholomew.[69] Born in 1534 to an aristocratic family in the province of Dauphiné, Chandieu was influenced by evangelical ideas first as a student in Paris and later during his legal training at Toulouse. After studying briefly with Calvin in the early 1550s, he returned to France and became a co-pastor of the underground church in Paris. Though still in his twenties, Chandieu quickly emerged as one of the chief leaders of French Protestantism. He appears to have played a role in drafting the Gallic Confession (1559) and the French *Ecclesiastical Discipline*; he wrote two apologies defending the reformed churches before the French king; he was elected as moderator of the third National Synod of Orléans (1562).

During the decades that followed, as France writhed in civil war and religious violence, Chandieu and his family were repeatedly forced into exile. After St. Bartholomew's Day, they fled to the safety of Geneva—where Chandieu's name was inscribed on the role of the Company of Pastors—and then relocated down the lake to Lausanne for most of the next decade. Chandieu's prayers and poems from this period capture both his fear and deep Christian faith:

> O God, you who are powerful and awesome, you who are always the same, look thus upon my captivity. Change my weakness into power, my fear into joy and confidence, my servitude into freedom.[70]

During the mid 1580s, Chandieu shuttled between France, Geneva, and Switzerland, serving as a chaplain and an adviser to Henri of Navarre, encouraging the French churches, and raising financial and political support for the Huguenot cause throughout Protestant Europe. Finally, in the fall of 1589, he settled permanently in Geneva and was appointed to preach (without remuneration) Sunday evening sermons in the city's temples.

By the time Chandieu arrived in Geneva he was recognized, along with Daneau and Beza, as one of the foremost theologians of French Protestantism. Beginning in the late 1570s, Chandieu's theological acumen had been displayed brilliantly in a seven-year battle of books with the Jesuit Francisco Torres concerning the true church and legitimate ordination of pastors. Over the next decade, Chandieu published other important writings that addressed Scripture and tradition, purgatory, the Lord's Supper, the forgiveness of sins, and the human nature of Jesus Christ. In the crossfire of theological polemics, Chandieu championed a new "scholastic and theological method" of argumentation whereby syllogism and logical demonstration (drawn largely from Aristotle) were employed to bring clarity to disputed points of doctrine. Though the substance of theology must be drawn from Scripture alone, Chandieu insisted, philosophy might serve as a valuable tool for clarifying what was true and demolishing errors caused by sophistical reasoning and misleading rhetoric.[71] Theodore Beza's admiration and affection for Chandieu were nearly boundless. As a result, when Chandieu caught a fever and died suddenly in March 1591 at age fifty-seven, the old reformer was crushed. "One could create a stream with all the tears that have been shed in Geneva and elsewhere by those who understand the consequences of such a gaping wound," he wrote a correspondent back in France. "As for me personally, I have lost a friend for whom I would sacrifice my life—even many lives—if I could. But because this is the will of God, may his name be praised."[72]

Short-term foreign ministers such as Chandieu, Daneau, Constant, and Le Gaigneux were important to the Genevan church in several ways. Most obviously, they provided the Venerable Company with a pool of talented, experienced candidates to fill the pastoral vacancies that sometimes appeared in the countryside or city temples. The fact that several of these foreign ministers possessed substantial wealth and were thus willing to work for parsimonious wages (or even for free!), made them all the more attractive as candidates. In addition, the theological stature of exiled churchmen like Daneau and Chandieu added luster to the reputation of Geneva's pastoral company and Academy during the 1570s and 1580s, reinforcing the city's identity as a nursery for French pastors and the brain trust of international Calvinism.

More subtle perhaps, but no less important, was the impact that both career and short-term foreign ministers had on Geneva's religious culture during the sixteenth century. As we have seen, many of these foreign ministers and their families had weathered grave dangers and experienced tragedy and loss during periods of religious violence in France. For many, the flames of persecution had galvanized and greatly intensified their religious convictions. Consequently, nearly all the refugee ministers brought to their pastoral work in Geneva a fierce opposition to Catholic doctrine and practice, a deep suspicion of the Valois monarchy, and an uncompromising commitment to reformed Christianity. This attitude was exemplified by Simon Goulart. During a brief visit to France in the summer of 1572, he had been caught in the maelstrom of St. Bartholomew's Day and only narrowly escaped with his life. Back in Geneva, he wrote to a friend: "I have a profound love for my country. Thus, I have decided to stab with my pen those tyrants as long as I live."[73] The perception that Catholicism was a real and present danger to Christian faith was further reinforced in Geneva by the smoldering menace of Catholic Savoy, which burst into open war from 1589–93 as well as in the surprise attack on the night of the Escalade (December 11, 1602). Whereas clergymen in reformed cities such as Basel or Zurich were insulated from direct contact with Catholics by the middle decades of the 1500s, Geneva's geographical location and her refugee population made confessional engagement and hostility an ever-present reality.[74] This religious orientation, with its concern for theological precision and its suspicion of all things "Papist," significantly shaped the content and style of the ministers' sermons, theological instruction, and moral supervision throughout the sixteenth century. The religious experience of these foreign ministers—brimming with courage and commitment, suspicion, and fear—was clearly an important factor shaping the way in which pastoral ministry was conceived of and practiced in Geneva during the half century after Calvin's death.

Genevan-Born Ministers

The third ministry model evident in the Genevan church during this period was that of "native-born minister." As we have seen, the indigenization of Geneva's pastoral corps took place quite slowly, and it was not until the 1590s that local candidates began to be appointed to ministerial posts with some regularity. Who were these twenty-five native sons who served the Genevan church during this period? A significant number of them came from families that were well-connected with the city's political or religious establishment. Abraham and Louis de La Maisonneuve, Jean Chabrey, and Pierre Chevalier were all sons of Geneva's syndics. Similarly, the fathers of Théodore Tronchin, Jean Gervais, and Enoch Mollet had all sat on the Council of 200 at one time or another. Six other men—Paul Baduel, Honoré Blanchard, Etienne Gros the Younger, Jean Gros, Jacob de St. André, and Etienne Trembley—came from pastoral households in the city. The majority of these families that produced local ministers, however, did not come from the illustrious ranks of old Genevans, but had become established in the city more recently, after the revolution of 1536. In a real sense, therefore, many of the native-born ministers were the scions of religious exiles.

The Company of Pastors had only limited success with the first cohort of Genevan-born ministers. Of the eight native sons hired during the 1570s and 1580s, only two ministers were still serving churches in 1590; the rest had either died, been deposed, been transferred to an academic post, or accepted pastoral assignments in France. By contrast, the second cohort of local candidates who entered the Company of Pastors beginning in the mid 1590s—the men who replaced the old guard of Beza, Perrot, Pinault, and Trembley—remained in office for much longer terms. This new generation of native ministers that became the backbone of the Genevan church for the next half century included Jean Gervais (minister 1594–1618), Jean Diodati (1597–1645), Gabriel Cusin (1598–1617), Jean Gros (1601–42), Enoch Mollet (1605–47), and Théodore Tronchin (1606–57). The best known of this group were the two minister-theologians Jean Diodati and Théodore Tronchin.

Diodati was born in Geneva in 1576, the descendant of an aristocratic family that had emigrated from Lucca.[75] While he was still a young boy, Jean's parents made a vow to God that their son would become a Protestant pastor.[76] Consequently, Diodati was sent to the Academy to study theology and scriptural exegesis with Beza and Isaac Casaubon. The young man demonstrated such remarkable ability that after completing his studies, he was appointed professor of Hebrew in 1597 at the age of twenty-one and enrolled in the Company of Pastors.[77] Two years later, he was chosen to be Beza's successor in the chair of theology, a post that he held until 1645. In addition to these academic responsibilities, Diodati was elected to the office of minister in 1608 and given regular preaching duties. During his long ministry in Geneva, Diodati was especially well-known as a theologian and translator of Scripture. In 1618, he and his colleague Théodore Tronchin were sent to the reformed Synod of Dort, where they played a minor role in the formulation of the Canons that espoused reformed orthodoxy against the followers of Arminius.[78] During his sojourn in the Netherlands, Diodati also delivered a sermon before the court of Maurice of Nassau, Prince of Orange, and conducted a preaching tour in the cities of Dordrecht, Rotterdam, Delft, The Hague, and Amsterdam.[79] Until his death in 1649, Diodati maintained an extensive correspondence with many of the most prominent reformed leaders in Europe such as the Prince of Orange, the Huguenot leader Philippe Du Plessis-Mornay, the Patriarch of Constantinople Cyril Lucaris, the French theologian André Rivet, and the chief pastor of Zurich J. J. Breitinger.[80] In retrospect, however, it is clear that Diodati's contribution as a linguist and Bible translator surpassed his work as a theologian. His monumental Italian translation of the Bible, *La Sacra Bibbia* (1641), originally published with annotations, was still the standard Bible of Italian Protestantism at the end of the twentieth century.[81]

Théodore Tronchin was another native-born son who gained prominence in Geneva's church at the dawn of the seventeenth century.[82] Born in 1582, Tronchin studied first at the Genevan Academy before making his way to Basel, Heidelberg, and Leiden for advanced theological training. While in the Low Countries it appears that he attended lectures of the controversial Dutch theologian Jacob Arminius, as well as encountered the more mainstream reformed teaching of Sibrandus Lubbertus and Franciscus Gomarus.[83] Tronchin returned to Geneva in 1606 and was immediately chosen by the ministers to succeed Diodati in the chair of Hebrew at the Academy, despite the magistrates' concern that, at twenty-four, he was too young for the post.[84] For the next fifty years, Tronchin served the Genevan church, as professor of Hebrew (1606–18), professor of theology (1615–56), rector of the Academy (1610–15), and city minister (from 1608). At age thirty-eight, he married Théodora Rocca, the granddaughter of Beza's second wife, Catherine del Piano.[85] Tronchin was certainly not in the top tier of theologians of his age. His contribution at the Synod of Dort was slight, although he did give a public speech in defense of the doctrine of the perseverance of the saints.[86] His published writings—which were few in number—included a collection of theses on the doctrine of original sin (1606), a ponderous apology for the Genevan translation of the Bible against the Jesuit Jean Cotton (1620), and a brief funeral oration in honor of his colleague Simon Goulart (1628).[87] On the whole, the careers of Tronchin and Diodati indicate a declension in the theological clout of the Company of Pastors in the decades immediately after the departure of Daneau and the deaths of Chandieu and Beza. Geneva's theological prestige would soon reemerge, however, through the formidable talents of the minister Bénédict Turretin (1589–1631) and his son François (1623–87) several decades later.

3. The Moderator of the Company

Throughout the sixteenth century, Catholic apologists as well as disgruntled Genevans sometimes complained that Calvin and Beza had elevated themselves to the ranks of "lords" and "popes" of Geneva.[88] Accusations like these illustrate Calvin's and Beza's stature and prominence in Geneva's religious life, even if they overstate the authority the men actually exercised within the church. As an institution, the Company of Pastors was built on the basic principle that all Christian ministers possessed equal authority under the Word to proclaim the gospel and administer the sacraments. Hence, Calvin and his colleagues rejected any notion of preeminence or hierarchy of authority within the pastoral company. All ministers had an equal say in decisions of the Company; no parish assignment whether in the city or countryside was to be viewed as superior to another. At the same time, it was understood that the Venerable Company as a collective possessed authority over its individual members. Geneva's pastors were expected to submit to the judgment of the majority of their colleagues; though the ministers of the Company might vehemently disagree with one another behind closed doors, they must always speak with a single voice when addressing the magistrates or Geneva's public. The day-to-day business of the Company of Pastors was directed by the "moderator," one of the pastors chosen by his peers, who was given responsibility to preside at the Company's weekly meetings and to serve as the Company's chief spokesperson in the church's interaction with Geneva's city magistrates. The moderator was also given precedence at ceremonial functions and was the first to be examined by his colleagues at the quarterly Censure. The mode of selection and the role the moderator played in the Company of Pastors changed in significant ways during the seven decades after Calvin's return from Strasbourg in 1541.

Though, in principle, all of Geneva's ministers possessed equal authority within the church, in point of fact Calvin's star was the brightest light in Geneva's ecclesiastical firmament during his pastoral career. The reformer was the unquestioned leader of Geneva's church, serving as moderator of the Company until shortly before his death in 1564 without election or serious discussion. Equally important, Calvin possessed substantial moral authority within the Company thanks to his formidable theological and biblical knowledge, as well as the strong support of Geneva's magistrates, and he was not averse to leveraging his influence and intellectual brilliance to convince his colleagues, shape church policy, and silence opponents. People who challenged Calvin's theological judgment or spiritual leadership risked incurring the full force of his mental acuity and verbal invective—as Jerome Bolsec found out when he attacked Calvin's doctrine of predestination in a meeting of the Congregation in 1551. But even so, Calvin's authority within the Company was never absolute, and he routinely submitted to the collective will of his colleagues on daily matters of lesser importance.[89]

The controversy that swirled around the minister Jean Ferron in 1549 clarifies the dynamics of power, personality, and influence that existed within the Company during Calvin's lifetime.[90] Jean Ferron had come to Geneva from France in 1544 and was one of Calvin's earliest pastoral colleagues as the minister of the temple of St. Gervais. In the spring of 1549, a servant girl in Ferron's household lodged a complaint that the minister had spoken lewd words to her and touched her body in a dishonorable fashion while his wife was away in Lausanne. Ferron later admitted to groping the young woman but insisted that he had done this "in order to test if she was a good girl."[91] With rumors of the minister's lechery racing through the city, the Company examined Ferron at the quarterly Censure in April and voted to reprimand him and transfer him to a countryside parish. Outraged by this treatment, Ferron delivered a blistering rejoinder to the accusations of Calvin and several of his colleagues. He complained that there was no brotherhood among the Company and then attacked Calvin for being vindictive and for harboring a grudge against him. Calvin's inflated ego hungered for flattery, Ferron asserted, and several of the ministers were only too happy to feed this hunger. At the conclusion of his speech, Ferron stormed out of the Company's chambers. The ministers met in emergency session two days later to deliberate the case further, at which time Calvin requested that the Company judge whether he had exceeded his authority as moderator and minister. The ministers dismissed Calvin and Ferron from the meeting and discussed the case in private before finally exonerating Calvin and upholding the charges against Ferron. The sad episode concluded several months later when the Small Council suspended Jean Ferron from the ministry and he departed Geneva. The controversy surrounding Ferron clarifies several aspects of Calvin's position of leadership within the Company of Pastors. Clearly, many of Calvin's colleagues admired him and deferred to him; others did not. In his role as moderator, and because of his forceful personality, Calvin's disapproval could make a colleague's tenure in Geneva both uncomfortable and brief. But at the same time, Calvin was but one member of a *company* of pastors and he was willing to submit to its authority and judgment. Calvin's Company of Pastors was never Calvin's per se.

Following Calvin's death in May 1564, the mantle of leadership fell on the shoulders of Theodore Beza, an ideal choice given his noble pedigree, his growing theological stature, and his prominence in French Protestantism. In the first meeting of the Company of Pastors after Calvin's death, Beza recalled with affection Calvin's life and friendship and then argued in an impassioned speech that the office of moderator should thereafter be filled by an annual election—this was the pattern of the early church, he believed, and this would best protect the church in the future from ambitious men who might aspire to become perpetual bishops within the church.[92] The ministers approved Beza's recommendation, and then elected him to a one-year term as moderator of the Company. Beza was reelected to the presidency of the Company each of the next sixteen years. Beza's leadership style was significantly different than his predecessor's. Whereas Calvin by temperament had been brilliant, uncompromising, independent, and decisive, Beza was more cultured, sympathetic, collaborative, and politically astute. These personal qualities, along with Beza's aptitude for friendship, proved especially beneficial over the next decades as he guided the Company of Pastors into a more constructive, less combative, relationship with Geneva's magistrates. One consequence was that, by the early 1570s, several of Geneva's ministers had become openly critical of Beza's more conciliatory stance toward the magistrates, fearing it undermined the prophetic ministry of the pulpit and threatened the church's independence from the state. The celebrated controversies surrounding Jean Le Gaigneux and Nicolas Colladon in 1571 laid bare these competing visions and internal debates within the ranks of the Company of Pastors.

Calvin and Geneva's ministers had long asserted the right to reprove the sins of the magistrates in their public sermons. During the spring and summer of 1571, however, the ministers Le Gaigneux and Colladon became ever more vitriolic and independent in their pulpit attacks against the city government, deriding what they saw as its abuse of authority as well as its neglect of public justice and moral discipline.[93] Colladon and Le Gaigneux also expressed frustration with the leadership of Theodore Beza, the moderator of the Company of Pastors, whose policy of accommodation toward the magistrates they feared was diminishing the power and independence of the church. At least for Colladon, it appears that his hostility toward Beza was also borne of professional jealousy at the reformer's ascendance within the Company after Calvin's death.[94] These long-standing tensions exploded into public controversy in May of 1571 when Le Gaigneux and Colladon once again launched scorching jeremiads against the magistrates. An embarrassed Beza complained bitterly to the Small Council that he found the two ministers "so completely intractable and hopeless" that he could no longer work with them.[95] Fearing civil punishment, Le Gaigneux fled the city several days later and took up residence in Lyon, where he continued his attack against Geneva's magistrates and the Company of Pastors for the next six months. In December, the city councilors finally voted to depose the disgruntled minister for insubordination and for abandoning his pastoral post. In the meantime, the minister Colladon's situation became equally perilous. In August 1571, Colladon delivered a particularly inflammatory sermon against the magistrates for permitting the city bank to charge interest at the rate of 10 percent in order to pay off the municipal debt. Theodore Beza was so exasperated by Colladon's harangue that he likened his colleague to a false prophet and threatened resignation if Colladon was not punished. Colladon was subsequently deposed from his office, censured by the Consistory, and sent packing. As with his colleague Le Gaigneux, Colladon left Geneva embittered and eager to announce to anyone who would listen the injustice he had suffered at the hands of Beza and other city leaders. In the long run, the cases of Le Gaigneux and Colladon further strengthened Beza's leadership within the Company of Pastors and clarified the acceptable boundaries within which Geneva's ministers could safely criticize ecclesiastical and civil authorities.

Beza never had designs to become either the "bishop" or "superintendent" of the Genevan church. For five years, from 1573 to 1578, he repeatedly asked to be relieved of the burdensome role of moderator of the Company—requests that his colleagues blithely disregarded as they continued to elect him to the office year after year.[96] Finally, in February 1579, at the time of the annual election, Beza convinced his colleagues to approve a plan where the office of moderator would change hands every year or every three years. Beza then presented this proposal to the Small Council, emphasizing that the present situation, where one man was effectively serving as the permanent president of the pastoral company, was both unwise and dangerous, for "this was the way that the authority of bishops and popes was first introduced [into the church], joined with the fact that there is no support for it in the Word of God."[97] After discussing the matter, the senators rejected the ministers' proposal because they found Beza's leadership style and irenic spirit too valuable to be lost to another candidate. The next year, in February and March of 1580, the pastors once again requested that the magistrates revise the mode of election of the moderator of the Venerable Company. Beza and Trembley delivered several long speeches before the magistrates, explaining the biblical arguments for the equality of the ministerial office, providing a historical survey of the advent and growth of episcopal primacy in the church, and urging the councilors to adopt a plan where the presidency would be rotated within the Company. This time, Beza and the ministers were successful. The Small Council decreed that, henceforth, "as long as it remained in the magistrates' good pleasure," the presidency of the Company of Pastors should rotate among all of the city pastors on a *weekly* basis.[98] One of Beza's most notable political achievements was, paradoxically, to secure a method of shared leadership in Geneva's church that effectively limited his own power.

The custom of the weekly presidency was in place for the next twenty-five years. Week to week, the moderator was the public voice of the Venerable Company; he attended sessions of the Small Council (sitting on a bench at the back of the room); he took the lead in the weekly Consistory meetings; he answered the correspondence of the Company and directed its daily business. Nevertheless, throughout this period, Beza remained the de facto leader of the pastoral corps due in large part to the weight of his reputation and theological judgment, as well as his political connections with Geneva's chief magistrates, especially his friend, the syndic and professor of law, Jacques Lect.[99] The close relationship between Beza and Lect was especially significant in fostering the climate of cooperation and trust between Geneva's temporal and ecclesiastical authorities that prevailed during the final decades of the sixteenth century. Unfortunately, this congruence of political priorities and goodwill dissolved in the early 1600s as the octogenarian Beza declined in health and passed from the scene. In August 1604, the Small Council communicated to the Company its desire that the weekly moderatorship be discontinued, replaced with a longer term of leadership to allow more effective communication between the two bodies. The Company discussed the matter, and then voted to retain the weekly presidency, "given that change, especially at this time, would be neither honorable nor profitable to the Company."[100] Several weeks after Beza's death in October 1605, the syndic Jacques Lect on behalf of the Small Council once again broached the subject of the presidency of Geneva's church, but this time the magistrates had no intention of backing down: they demanded that the ministers elect an annual moderator who, as Calvin and Beza had once done, might provide consistent leadership for the church and represent her before the Council and the larger Protestant world. Over the next seven weeks, a decisive struggle for power between the ministers and magistrates took place, with the Small Council asserting its authority not only to preserve and support the church but to restructure it as well. As one syndic put the matter indelicately: "the emperor is above the church" (*imperator est supra ecclesiam*).[101] The Company of Pastors strenuously resisted what it perceived as an unprecedented encroachment on the church's prerogatives that undermined principles fundamental to Geneva's Reformation. The ministers feared that two cherished principles, in particular, were threatened by the magistrates' actions, namely, that "ecclesiastical matters should be governed by the church," and that the sacred ministry should allow "no degree or preeminence or domination" between pastors.[102] By the end of December 1605, after a series of bitter confrontations in which the interpretation of Scripture, the practice of the early church, and the legacies of Calvin and Beza were fiercely debated, Lect and the magistrates finally achieved their objective as they strong-armed the ministers to adopt an annual, elected presidency of the Company (called the *proestasie*). This victory, which effectively broke the Company's primary jurisdiction over spiritual affairs within Geneva's church, marked the beginning of a new era in which the magistrates would assert ever more authority over religious life in the city.[103]

These turbulent years also witnessed the emergence of Simon Goulart as the chief pastor of Geneva's church. As we have already seen, Goulart was a talented preacher and one of the most prolific authors within the ranks of the Company of Pastors at the turn of the century. In the elections of 1607, Goulart's colleagues elected him to a one-year term as *proestos* of the Company. The following year, the ministers strongly objected when the magistrates attempted to force the Company to make Goulart's role as *proestos* permanent; the ministers sent a delegation to the Small Council, led by Goulart himself, that delivered a 28-point memorandum defending the freedom of the ministry and warning of the dangers of a perpetual presidency.[104] Even so, the members of the Venerable Company selected Goulart to the annual *proestasie* in each of the elections of 1609–1612, a fact that testifies to his leadership abilities and his stature within the Company. When the *proestasie* was abolished and the weekly presidency restored in 1613, the ministers agreed to the magistrates' recommendation that Goulart should remain the ceremonial head of the Company, responsible for presiding at public functions, giving the customary exhortations to the General Assembly and the Council of 200 each year, and answering the Company's extensive correspondence with foreign churches.[105] Though Goulart was not a theologian, and though he never taught at the Academy, he became the true successor of Theodore Beza in Geneva, serving as the spiritual head of the Company of Pastors until his death in 1628.

During the half century following Calvin's death, the profile of Geneva's ministers changed in several important ways. As Calvin and several of his contemporaries passed from the scene, leadership of the Company of Pastors fell to a new generation of talented foreigners, men like Beza, Trembley, Perrot, and finally Goulart, who supervised religious life in the city for the next five decades. Thanks to the leadership and committed labor of these men, Geneva's church experienced a high degree of institutional stability and confessional uniformity. Pastoral tenures in the city grew longer, the frequency of pastoral vacancies declined, and more ministerial candidates received theological training. But one thing did not change: nearly all of Geneva's ministers were foreign born. It was only at the very end of the century, as the "old guard" grew older and retired from public life, that leadership of the Genevan church was gradually handed over to a new generation of ministers, men whose backgrounds were firmly rooted in the soil of bourgeois Geneva. At the same time, the first decade of the seventeenth century witnessed renewed tensions between Geneva's magistracy and church authorities, as the Small Council attempted to gain greater control over the way leaders were selected and leadership was structured within the Venerable Company. This controversy, as we shall see in later chapters, was part of a broader, more protracted struggle as the city's political leaders worked to clarify and diminish the scope of the church's authority in Geneva following the deaths of Calvin and Beza.

CHAPTER 3 | The Pastoral Vocation

BY LATE SUMMER 1576, Theodore Beza and his colleagues were losing all patience with the minister Pierre Des Préaux. Des Préaux had come to Geneva from Rouen six years earlier to study at the Academy. Elected pastor of the parish of Russin-Dardagny in 1571, he had soon run into problems. When the plague had visited the village in 1574, he had abandoned his post and shamelessly fled for his life. The following year he was again censured by the Company of Pastors, this time for turning a blind eye to his wife's immodest behavior and for habitually inviting himself over for free meals at his parishioners' dinner tables. Rather than receiving the ministers' correction in a spirit of humility, Des Préaux had become obstinate and combative. The Company of Pastors decided to give him one last chance.[1] At the end of August 1576, Des Préaux appeared before the Company to demand a four-month leave of absence to look after family business back in France. Geneva's ministers begrudgingly approved a shorter leave, contingent on Des Préaux finding a minister to fill the pulpit during his absence. A week later the minister from Russin returned to the Venerable Company, seething with resentment, and threatened to quit his ministerial post if his original request was not granted.

The Company of Pastors chose this occasion to lecture the angry young minister about the nature of his pastoral vocation. Beza and his colleagues warned Des Préaux not to abandon the work of God and his pastoral calling out of concern for his personal affairs. They reminded him of Jesus' admonition that once putting the hand to the plow, God's workmen must never look back (Luke 9:62). Indeed, Christian discipleship demanded that persons sacrifice not only their self-interest, but their very lives. Further, they warned the minister from Russin to be on his guard lest he follow in the steps of the biblical character Demas whose unbridled love for the world led him to abandon the Apostle Paul and gospel ministry (2 Tim 4:10). These stern injunctions had little effect on Des Préaux. He insisted that he was no Demas and that his family's affairs back in France could not wait. He continued to threaten to quit his post if he was not granted a four-month leave of absence. In the end, neither side was willing to budge, and the Venerable Company accepted the minister's resignation. Pierre Des Préaux left Russin at the end of September and returned to France, where he soon spread reports of the harsh treatment he had received from his colleagues back in Geneva.[2]

For the ministers of Geneva, the pastoral vocation was a high and holy calling. A minister of the gospel should not accept a pastoral charge lightly nor should he leave his spiritual flock except under the most exceptional circumstances. Time and time again, whether in sermons, academic lectures, or published writings, Calvin, Beza, and their colleagues explained the nature of their calling and defended it against local critics and Catholic apologists who challenged them. Their conception of the pastor's vocation found practical expression in the routine of their daily work, as they preached the Word and performed the sacraments, as they disciplined recalcitrant sinners and gave comfort to the dying, as they elected candidates to the sacred ministry and dismissed colleagues who failed to fulfill their pastoral responsibilities. This chapter will explore the nature of the pastoral vocation in sixteenth- and early seventeenth-century Geneva. First, I describe the manner in which Calvin and his colleagues defined the pastoral office and understood its chief duties. Next, this chapter outlines Geneva's public theology that formed the substance of the gospel message that the ministers proclaimed and which invariably shaped their vocational self-understanding. In sections three and four I will explore the process by which ministerial candidates in Geneva were recruited, elected, and ordained for pastoral posts between 1536 and 1609. The final section of this chapter recounts the protracted struggle between the magistrates and the city ministers over the prerogative of pastoral election. During the final years of this period, the ministers and magistrates regularly crossed swords over these volatile issues; almost always they were settled in favor of the magistracy. In fact, by the early seventeenth century, the ministers' right of election had been significantly attenuated by the Small Council, indicative of a more general ascendance of Genevan political authority over the city church.

1. The Minister's Calling

The idea of "calling" or vocation (*vocatio*) lay very near to the heart of both Lutheran and reformed understandings of the Christian life. Across his theological writings, Martin Luther highlighted a doctrine of Christian vocation (*Beruf*) that included three elements: Christians were responsible to serve God in their worldly occupations; all legitimate human occupations were equal in God's sight; the purpose of human vocations was to serve God and neighbor.[3] In the *Institutes of the Christian Religion* (1559),

John Calvin also defended the concept of "worldly" vocation and distinguished it from two other kinds of divine callings. On the one hand, there is a *general calling* to salvation by which God exhorts all men and women to believe in the gospel of Jesus Christ through the voice of the preacher. Christ's statement in Matthew 22:14—"many are called but few are chosen"—indicates, however, that not all who hear this general proclamation of the gospel are elect to salvation. Accordingly, Calvin believed that God gathers his chosen people into the church through a *special* or *effectual* calling, whereby he illuminates the hearts of the elect and brings them to saving faith in Christ. This effectual calling is accompanied by the gift of the indwelling presence of the Holy Spirit, who serves as a "seal" guaranteeing the Christian's spiritual inheritance.[4] The effectual calling brings with it a new kind of life invested with divine purpose and special responsibilities. Christians now receive a *worldly* calling to serve God and their neighbors through everyday duties and earthly occupations. In a famous passage in the *Institutes*, Calvin described this third type of vocation:

> [T]he Lord bids each one of us in all life's actions to look to his calling. For he knows with what great restlessness human nature flames, with what fickleness it is borne hither and thither, how its ambition longs to embrace various things at once. Therefore, lest through our stupidity and rashness everything be turned topsy-turvy, he has appointed duties for every man in his particular way of life. And that no one may thoughtlessly transgress his limits, he has named these various kinds of living "callings." Therefore each individual has his own post so that he may not heedlessly wander about throughout life.[5]

As with Martin Luther before him, Calvin rejected medieval Catholic teaching that elevated clerical or "spiritual" offices above the mundane occupations of ordinary lay believers.[6] Calvin insisted that Christian men and women were called to live out their discipleship within the particular sphere of work and responsibility that God had appointed to them. Whether one was a cobbler or a cook, a mule-driver or a magistrate, every legitimate human occupation possessed divine significance; each could become an expression of praise and gratitude to God.[7] "From this will arise also a singular consolation," Calvin noted, "that no task will be so sordid and base, provided you obey your calling in it, that it will not shine and be reckoned very precious in God's sight."[8] Attentiveness to one's calling brought benefits to the human community, serving as a tangible expression of neighborly love. In addition, believers would find in their earthly vocations a remedy for anxiety, a bridle for ambition, and a stimulus for hard work.[9] Calvin's doctrine of earthly vocation represented a profound legitimization of human labor and the sanctification of ordinary human life.[10]

This conception of Christian vocation became a distinctive feature of the theological and psychological inheritance of later generations of Calvinists, including those ministers who served the Genevan church after Calvin's death. In his *Brief Remonstrance on Games of Chance* (1573), Lambert Daneau insisted that commitment to one's individual calling, along with spiritual devotion and works of charity, should form the substance of the Christian's life. In place of gaming and gambling, "there is....reading the Word of God, then books by other authors; there is the consolation of the sick, the visitation of prisoners, the relief of suffering, and then the attention that every person can and should have to his particular estate and vocation."[11] In a similar fashion, Theodore Beza highlighted this doctrine of vocation in a sermon preached to the congregation of St. Pierre in the early 1590s. Beza explained that all Christians have received a *general* calling to glorify God and seek the well-being of their neighbors. In addition, many people are entrusted with *special* callings from God, obligating them to exercise special authority over and express special concern for people around them. Hence, husbands are commanded to care for their wives, parents are called to instruct their children, masters are responsible to supervise their servants, civil magistrates are to govern the political community, and Christian ministers must provide leadership within the church. These various callings—both general and special—determine the boundaries and general obligations of men and women as they seek to honor God and serve their neighbors in everyday life. Faithfulness in the Christian life demands that men and women fulfill their God-appointed duties without transgressing the limits of their vocations.[12]

Not surprisingly, Calvin and his colleagues believed that the vocation of the Christian minister was of crucial importance for the spiritual well-being of God's people on earth. For Calvin, the office of minister of the Word was the "chief sinew by which believers are held together in one body." Indeed, "[n]either the light and heat of the sun, nor food and drink, are so necessary to nourish and sustain the present life as the apostolic and pastoral office is necessary to preserve the church on earth."[13] In a similar fashion, Beza asserted that the Christian ministry "surpasses every other dignity in the world."[14] Faithful pastors are "more necessary than the air that we breathe."[15] Geneva's Company of Pastors articulated this same conviction to the minister Jean de Serres, in the summer of 1572. Weary of his demanding pastoral work in the rural parish of Jussy, Serres had decided to quit his post and return secretly to France. Catching wind that Serres was packing up his household, Beza and the Venerable Company confronted the disgruntled minister and demanded that he explain his actions. Serres gave a long list of excuses: his health was poor, his mother-in-law was ill, he had family business back in France. Moreover, he had grown so angry and frustrated with his parishioners that "he would go completely crazy if he stayed there a moment longer." The ministers of Geneva did not accept these excuses. They upbraided and excommunicated Serres for abandoning his sacred vocation, reminding the delinquent pastor that "his ministry should be one hundred times more precious to him than all of these things."[16] The pastoral vocation was an "exceedingly sacred and honorable charge," a most serious responsibility that should neither be taken up nor laid aside without divine permission.

What did Calvin and Geneva's ministers believe to be the precise nature and particular duties of the pastor's vocation? Calvin's conception of the pastoral office was in no way original with him; it was drawn in large part from the writings and practices of other evangelical reformers such as Luther, Melanchthon, Bucer, and Oecolampadius, who for several decades had been challenging long-held customs in the medieval church in light of patterns of leadership they discerned in the New Testament. Already in the first edition of the *Institutes* (1536), in a chapter devoted to the "Five False Sacraments," Calvin rejected the Catholic teaching that episcopal ordination conferred an indelible mark of sanctity upon priests that set them apart from lay Christians and gave them special power to confer grace through the sacraments. While acknowledging that the custom of ordaining men to Christian ministry was an ancient practice, Calvin insisted that it did not meet the scriptural standard of a sacrament per se: the ceremony had never been instituted by Christ nor was it conjoined to a divine promise of grace.[17] True ordination, he asserted, was "to call to the governing of the church a man of proved life and teaching, and to appoint him to that ministry."[18] Ordination and calling to ministry were inseparable. At the same time, Calvin argued that the medieval Catholic priesthood was a monstrous caricature of the pattern observed in the apostolic church. He viewed as nothing less than an "impious sacrilege" the Catholic doctrine that episcopal ordination conferred on priests the power and responsibility to perform the expiatory sacrifice of Christ's body and blood on the altar of the Mass. Christ's death was the final, perfect sacrifice of expiation and reconciliation for sinners, he insisted.[19] For Calvin, Christian ministers were not heirs of the Aaronic priests of the Old Testament who performed sacrifices, but successors of Christ's apostles, entrusted with the responsibility to proclaim the gospel in Word and sacrament. "Therefore those who do not devote themselves to the preaching of the gospel and the administration of the sacraments, wickedly impersonate the apostles."[20]

Throughout his discussion of the false sacraments in the *Institutes* (1536), Calvin not only attacked the medieval Catholic conception of priesthood but also defended and described the evangelical model of pastor. The scriptural office of Christian minister, he asserted, involved nourishing and instructing God's people on the divine Word by means of sermon, sacraments, catechism, spiritual conversation, and corrective discipline. The ministers' authority was ultimately derived from and delimited by the Word of God that they proclaimed. The model of pastoral ministry that emerged in Geneva during the decade that followed embodied this new evangelical understanding of ministerial office: the celibate Catholic priest whose primary role was to hear confessions and perform the miracle of the Mass was replaced by the married Protestant pastor whose chief responsibility was to proclaim the Word of God through sermon and sacraments.

Calvin and his pastoral colleagues in Geneva drew upon the rich vocabulary of Scripture to highlight the importance and describe the functions of the pastoral calling. In their writings they avoided speaking of ministers as "priests" or "clergy."[21] Rather, they identified Christian ministers variously as servants, elders, supervisors, messengers, heralds, ambassadors, shepherds, and men of God. They are "builders of God's house," "ministers of the Word of God," "friends of the bridegroom," "dispensers of the secrets of God," "officers of the king," and "pastors of souls for whom Jesus Christ died."[22] Of all these appellations, the most frequently used were ministers (*ministri; ministres*) and pastors (*pastores; pasteurs*). These designations indicate the primary roles of Christian ministers: they proclaim the Word of God; they intercede on behalf of the congregation before God; they care for the souls of their people; they build up and help govern Christ's church. So too, the pastoral office contributes to God's larger mission in the world. The minister's highest goal is the glory of God and the salvation of his spiritual flock.[23] As servants of the divine King, Protestant ministers have the responsibility to "advance the kingdom of our Lord Jesus Christ."[24]

These characterizations of the pastoral office make clear that Geneva's ministers believed that their authority was always derivative. Christ the King speaks and rules through the officers whom he appoints in his church. Ministers are God's spokespersons, God's ambassadors on earth who proclaim glad tidings of salvation through faith in Jesus Christ. In his commentary on John 3, Calvin highlighted the secondary, supporting role that ministers of the gospel must play as they prepare the bride of Christ, the church, for her rightful husband:

> Similarly, Christ does not call his ministers to the teaching office that they may subdue the Church and dominate it but that he may make use of their faithful labors to unite it to himself. It is a great and splendid thing for men to be put in authority over the Church to represent the person of the Son of God. They are like the friends attached to the bridegroom to celebrate the wedding with him, though they must observe the difference between themselves and what belongs to the bridegroom. It all comes to this, that whatever excellence teachers may have should not stand in the way of Christ alone having the dominion in his Church or ruling it alone by his Word.... Those who win the Church over to themselves rather than to Christ faithlessly violate the marriage which they ought to honor. And the greater the honor that Christ confers on us when he puts his bride In our charge, the more wicked is our faithlessness if we do not study to defend his rights.[25]

Moreover, Calvin and his colleagues believed that legitimate Christian ministers and professors were successors of the prophets and apostles— though without the prophetic charism—set apart to teach and administer the Word of God. Beza made this point in his commentary on Song of Songs 1:7: "Finally, pastors and doctors have succeeded the Apostles, not to establish truth itself, but to build good and solid teachings, exhortations, consolations, [and] warnings upon the foundation of the Apostles."[26] In the context of spiritual renewal in the sixteenth century, Beza believed, Protestant ministers had special responsibility to repair the apostolic foundations of the church that had been nearly destroyed by the two Antichrists: the Roman Church and the religion of Islam.[27] Christ calls faithful ministers to be both demolition experts and wise builders, investing them with authority to battle false doctrine, dismantle superstition, and proclaim the gospel.

One of the most succinct descriptions of the roles and duties of the pastoral office coming from a reformed churchman was found in Beza's popular *Confession of the Christian Faith*, an apology for the Protestant religion that he wrote for his Catholic father in 1559.[28] According to Beza, God gave Christian ministers the keys of the kingdom—namely the authority to proclaim the divine Word and administer the sacraments—by which they warn sinners of God's judgment and announce the good news of deliverance from sin, death, and the devil through faith in Jesus Christ. The pastoral vocation also requires that ministers pray faithfully for and on behalf of their congregation. Whereas theological professors are responsible for explaining the Scriptures and instructing catechumens, pastors "apply the doctrine by preaching to the needs of the church, teaching, rebuking, consoling, and exhorting as is required" and "making public prayers." Pastors are thus spiritual shepherds who "watch over their spiritual flock day and night, feeding them on the Word of life both in public and in private."[29] In practical terms, Christian ministers perform a specific set of duties: they preach, they pray, they administer the Lord's Supper, they baptize children, they officiate at weddings, they perform household visitations, they provide spiritual counsel, and they exercise church discipline.[30]

2. The Minister's Message

It would be misleading to reduce the pastoral vocation to a "job description" of religious activities, however. For Geneva's ministers, their vocation could never be separated from the message of salvation that they proclaimed. Calvin and Beza frequently reminded their congregations of this fact from the pulpit of St. Pierre: Christian ministers are legitimate only to the extent that they preach the true gospel. But what was the substance of this Christian gospel, this "good news," that reformed ministers in Geneva were expected to proclaim? As we have seen in chapter 1, Geneva's official theology was articulated in several city documents that Calvin either authored or played a role in drafting, including the *Confession of Faith* (1536), the Genevan *Catechism* (1541), and the Genevan liturgy (1542). In subsequent decades, Geneva's civic and religious authorities attempted to enforce subscription to these basic confessional standards in a number of ways.[31] Children were required to study Calvin's *Catechism* and affirm its doctrine in front of the public assembly when they were first admitted to the Lord's Supper. Likewise, students at the Academy were expected to sign a formulary promising to "follow and hold to the doctrine of faith which is contained in the *Catechism* of this Church" at the time of their matriculation.[32] As for Geneva's ministers, the *Ecclesiastical Ordinances* required them to "receive and hold the doctrine approved in the Church"— that is, the system of theology found in the *Confession of Faith* as well as the Genevan *Catechism*.[33] In the wake of the Bolsec controversy in 1551–52, Geneva's Small Council went even further by decreeing that the theology found in Calvin's *Institutes of the Christian Religion* was "the holy doctrine of God" from which neither minister nor parishioner should deviate.[34] Consequently, Calvin's reformed understanding of Scripture's message and his theological legacy lived on in Geneva's official theology, providing the doctrinal foundation and establishing a confessional framework for his successors as they crafted their sermons, engaged in written polemical debates, and offered spiritual counsel to their parishioners.

The central message of Christianity, Geneva's ministers believed, was the dramatic story of God's mission to rescue the people he had graciously chosen from among Adam's fallen race. There is one true, almighty God, who created the heavens and the earth and who continues to govern the world and the affairs of humankind by his wise providence. This one God exists as three eternal persons: Father, Son, and Holy Spirit. Although men and women are incapable of comprehending God in his essence, God has taken the initiative to make himself known through the "mirror" of the natural world and especially through his sacred Word, found in the Holy Scripture, which is "nothing less than certain truth come down from heaven."[35] Scripture must therefore serve as the "rule of our faith and religion"; no other doctrines or human traditions should be added to it.[36]

According to the Genevan *Catechism*, the chief purpose of human existence is to know the one true God and worship him alone. God is honored when his creatures trust in him, serve him with their entire lives, call upon him for help and salvation, and acknowledge him as the author of all good things.[37] In point of fact, men and women refuse to honor God as God. Through Adam and Eve's original disobedience in the Garden of Eden, the entire human race rebelled against its creator and became both spiritually corrupt and morally culpable. Consequently, Scripture teaches that all human beings are now born in a sinful condition, blind in their spiritual understanding, corrupt of heart, devoid of all natural righteousness, and subject to God's wrath and judgment.[38] Geneva's official theology depicted human depravity in these stark terms: "before we are reborn and remade by the Spirit of God, we are able to do nothing but sin, just as the bad tree produces only bad fruit (Matt 7:17)." Hence, "we cannot anticipate God by any merits or evoke his beneficence. Rather, whatever works we proffer or attempt fall under his wrath and condemnation."[39]

In view of the desperate predicament of human depravity, the Christian gospel is truly "good news." Out of his immeasurable mercy and love, the heavenly Father sent his Son to earth where, as the God-man Jesus Christ, he took on human flesh, was born of the Virgin Mary, lived a sinless life, proclaimed the truth of God, suffered a shameful death on a Roman cross, and rose bodily from the dead. In his person and ministry, Jesus perfectly fulfills the three Old Testament offices of King, Prophet, and Priest. In his office as King, Jesus proclaims the kingdom of heaven, shares spiritual riches with God's people, and empowers them to overcome the enemies of their souls (namely sin, the flesh, the devil, and the world). The resur- rected and ascended Christ now governs his church from heaven. In his office as Prophet, Jesus announces divine truth and the perfect will of his Father, thereby silencing all other revelations and prophecies. In his office as Priest, Jesus serves as sole mediator between God and humanity, having once and for all offered himself as a sacrifice to purchase forgiveness for sinners.[40] This, then, was the central message of Christianity as found in Geneva's official theology: sinners who believe the gracious promise of sal- vation in Christ and repent of their sins are declared righteous before God and receive complete forgiveness, a new spiritual nature, and the assur- ance of eternal life in heaven. Salvation is by God's grace alone, "without any consideration of our merit or works," the *Confession* emphasized, so that "all glory and praise might be rendered unto God."[41] In the *Catechism*, a child was taught the doctrine of justification *sola gratia, sola fide* with these words:

> It is therefore by [God's] sheer mercy and not in respect of works that he graciously embraces us in Christ and holds us acceptable, by attributing to us his accepted righteousness as if it were our own, and by not imputing our sins to us (Titus 3:5).... Because in embracing the promises of the gospel with a sure and heartfelt confidence, we in a manner obtain possession of this righteousness of which I speak.[42]

Furthermore, persons who embrace Christ by faith are not only reconciled to the heavenly Father but also receive the precious gift of the Holy Spirit who creates in them a new spiritual life that gradually—though never entirely on earth—overcomes the sin nature, producing good works and a heart tuned to right worship. In this process of sanctification, the law of God, which previously condemned the sinner, now serves as a "rule of life" to guide the believer toward obedience and righteousness.[43]

The Christian faith was to be expressed and nurtured in the context of the Christian church. The *Catechism* defines the true church as the "body and society of believers whom God has predestined to eternal life."[44] Although it is scattered about in different places, there is one universal church, and Jesus Christ is its only head. The visible church on earth is distinguished by two marks: the pure and faithful preaching of the Word of God, and the right administration of the sacraments.[45] According to

Geneva's official theology, Jesus Christ instituted only two sacraments during his earthly ministry, baptism and the Lord's Supper. Sacraments are joined to the preaching of the Word of God and confirm it. Sacraments strengthen and nourish faith, they serve as badges and pledges of Christian discipleship, and by them God announces, represents, and seals his grace to his people.[46] Baptism, when received by faith, effects what it symbolizes, namely the forgiveness of sin, the mortification of the old nature, and spiritual regeneration.[47] Both the *Confession* and *Catechism* stipulate that the sacrament of baptism should be administered to the infant children of believing parents, as a sign that they too are heirs of God's covenant of grace.[48] On the contentious issue of Christ's presence in the Lord's Supper, Geneva's confessional documents rejected both the Catholic teaching of transubstantiation and the Lutheran doctrine of real presence. The physical body of Jesus is now in heaven, not on earth. But that does not mean that the communion elements of bread and wine are "mere" symbols or that the Lord's Supper is only a service of remembrance and commemoration. Rather, as the *Consensus Tigurinus* (1549) states, "all who in faith embrace the promises there offered receive Christ spiritually, with his spiritual gifts." It is Christ alone "who in the Supper makes us partakers of himself, who, in short, fulfills what the sacraments figure, and uses their aid in such manner that the whole effect resides in his Spirit."[49] Finally, Geneva's public theology also mandated the practice of barring unrepentant sinners from the Lord's Supper, asserting that Jesus Christ had instituted this practice of excommunication to guard the sacrament from profanation and to encourage the repentance and spiritual restoration of the wicked.[50] In this manner, the church of Jesus Christ on earth was to be reformed according to the Word of God in doctrine and discipline.

For Calvin, Beza, Goulart, and their colleagues, the pastoral vocation could not be separated from the message of salvation that ministers proclaimed. As we have seen, that message was substantially defined by the city's catechism, liturgy, and confessional documents, highlighting such characteristic reformed doctrines as the sovereignty of God, the authority of Scripture, total depravity, the unique mediatorial role of Jesus Christ, justification by grace alone through faith alone, the Lord's Supper as spiritual feeding on Christ, and church discipline. This theological inheritance, which owed so much to Calvin's interpretation of Scripture, was one of the major benchmarks by which prospective ministers were evaluated and served as the confessional standard for preaching, catechetical instruction, and pastoral ministry in Geneva's churches. Of course, what was prescribed as the city's public theology was not always faithfully announced in the pulpit or reflected in print.[51] And too, Geneva's official theology in some cases allowed for more precise definition and logical clarification, which was illustrated later in the sixteenth century in Beza's, Daneau's, and Chandieu's openness to employing Aristotelian categories and syllogistic logic in defense of Calvinist doctrines.[52] But if Geneva's confessional tradition was not entirely static, neither was it open to significant doctrinal innovation and change. When the Company of Pastors received the report that the fourteenth National Synod of Saumur (1596) was debating whether French reformed churches should discontinue the regular public exposition of Calvin's *Catechism*, Geneva's ministers responded with a long, strongly worded letter to the synod. The Company described Calvin's *Catechism* as "a very excellent and able summary of the whole of the Christian religion" and "one of the greatest treasures that the Lord has bestowed on us in our days." The Venerable Company warned against making any changes to the content or public use of the *Catechism*, reminding their French counterparts of the Apostle Paul's admonition to Timothy "not only to hold on to right doctrine, but also to remember from whose hands you have received it" (1 Tim 1:10–11).[53] Evidently, by the last decade of the sixteenth century, Geneva's ministers were no longer *reformers* per se, but *conservers* and *defenders* of what they understood to be the true system of biblical doctrine, taught by Calvin, and enshrined in Geneva's confessional documents. Herein one sees the decidedly conservative character of their understanding of the pastoral vocation. As pastors, they were called to proclaim God's unchanging gospel, guarding it from all revision or modification, and in so doing defend Calvin's formidable legacy within Geneva's church.

3. The Minister's Ordination—in Theory

We have seen that, for Geneva's ministers, the pastoral vocation was closely tied to the message of salvation that they proclaimed. But what constituted a "legitimate" call to Christian ministry? And how might one distinguish a genuine pastoral vocation from a counterfeit one? These were crucial questions, of course, and ones that Catholic apologists raised regularly in their polemical battles with Protestant opponents throughout the early modern period. Calvin encountered the problem in a most personal way following his humiliating banishment from Geneva in 1538 when a close friend named Louis Du Tillet (who would soon abjure the Protestant religion) raised the subject of vocation in several painful letters to him.[54] Calvin's sudden dismissal from Geneva's church was clear indication, Du Tillet believed, that God had never called him to the pastoral office in the first place. "I doubt whether you have a true calling from God, having been called there only by men," he wrote. Du Tillet returned to this theme several months later, "I know very well that our Lord has given you a lot of gifts that are useful for a person working in church ministry, but in my judgment this does not mean that you have been established in this ministry or called to it by God."[55] In his response, Calvin wrote that he had taken up the pastoral office in obedience to a clear Jonah-like call from God, and that this calling continued to be confirmed by trusted friends and by God himself. Even so, it is clear that Calvin was wounded deeply by Du Tillet's insinuation that his vocation was the product of presumption and personal ambition rather than divine will.[56]

The Catholic argument against the legitimacy of the Protestant office of minister was formulated in a more general way several decades later in the speech that Bishop Claude d'Espence delivered against Theodore Beza and the reformed delegation at the Colloquy of Poissy in September 1561. D'Espence pointed out that the ordinary manner in which God called men to ministerial orders was through the imposition of the hands of a Catholic bishop, something that very few Protestant ministers had ever received. Scripture did allow for cases where God raised up prophets and apostles to sacred ministry through a direct and special call, without episcopal ordination, but such extraordinary vocations were always accompanied by miraculous signs. On this basis, d'Espence challenged the reformed office of minister: "Show us, I pray you, which of you have performed miracles, or disclose to us which passages of Scripture have prophesied or adverted to your extraordinary vocation, and then we shall believe you and gladly receive your new doctrine."[57] From a Catholic perspective, Protestant ministers like Calvin and Beza had no biblical grounds for claiming either an ordinary or extraordinary calling to clerical office. Consequently, both their vocation and their teaching were illegitimate.

The question of legitimacy was not merely the subject of Catholic polemics but also a matter of serious concern among Protestants themselves. Reformed churches in France regularly confronted the problem of self-appointed itinerant ministers known as vagrants or vagabonds (*coureurs*) who traveled about, causing dissension and usurping leadership of local churches without official authorization or a legitimate vocation. Some of these vagabond ministers had been deposed from previous charges for moral failure or doctrinal error; others had never been properly ordained to the pastoral office; still others were self-styled prophets who spewed forth all manner of confusion and heresy. The problem was so widespread that the official minutes of the French national synods maintained a "list of vagabonds" (*role des coureurs*) to warn reformed congregations about specific preachers. The minutes of the sixth National Synod of Vertueil (1567), for example, listed eight different vagabond preachers for whom the churches should be on the lookout, including these two men:

> Chartier, who claims he was a councilor of Grenoble....is a man of moderate stature with a beard that is graying. He was deposed from the sacred ministry at Usarche by the brothers of Limousin for a number of offenses, including lies, cheatings, forging of signatures, lewd kissing, and rebellions. He intrudes himself into all our churches that will accept him.
>
> Jean Clopet, also named L'Enfant and Child, is a wretched heretic and champion of the Mass, except that he rejects praying to the Saints and prayers said on behalf of the dead. He holds that the good and wicked have the same right to commune in the Body of Christ. He also approves celibacy, and argues that people should turn to the east when they pray to God. Likewise,

he holds that Calvin committed a great error in writing about predestination, and that people are able to follow perfectly all the Commandments of God. He is a minister of smallish stature, with a yellowish beard, blue eyes, a tawny face, and he speaks with a thick accent. He is a Savoyard, 25 years of age, and born in the country of Bresse.[58]

Despite warnings like these, vagabond preachers continued to trouble the French churches throughout the sixteenth century.[59] Beza himself recognized the danger. From the pulpit of St. Pierre he warned his congregation about "those men who run about (*courent*), that is to say, who have the audacity to teach in the church both in public and secret, without having been elected and chosen by the order established by Jesus Christ [and] by the Apostles in his Church." These vagabonds should be "repudiated and chased away."[60] For Beza and French Protestants in general, the problem of self-appointed preachers lent urgency to the question of what constituted a legitimate calling to pastoral work.

In the early editions of the *Institutes*, Calvin laid out an answer that became the standard response of reformed Protestants in France and Geneva. Already in 1536, Calvin rejected the idea that episcopal ordination conferred an indelible spiritual mark that set persons apart for the vocation of minister.[61] In this early phase, the reformer argued that a legitimate vocation was based on the moral character and sound theological understanding of the candidate, combined with a lawful election by magistrates, senators, or elders, in consultation with competent bishops. After he was established in Geneva, Calvin modified these requirements slightly. In the 1543 edition of the *Institutes*, Calvin appealed to the example of the early Christian church to show that it was the responsibility of the ministers— not the magistrates—to appoint candidates to the ministry, with the consent and approval of the people.[62] In this edition, Calvin also developed for the first time his understanding of a twofold call: ministers were set apart for their sacred office by the Holy Spirit through both an internal and external calling. The inner or secret call was the divinely conceived conviction of heart whereby men aspired to the sacred ministry, not out of ambition or greed but out of sincere fear of God and a desire to build up the church.[63] This inner calling needed to be ratified by a subsequent external or "objective" call, that is, the affirmation of the Christian church through lawful election and ordination. The pattern for identifying a legitimate external calling, first articulated in 1543, was included in all subsequent editions of the *Institutes*. Lawful ordination was based on four elements, Calvin argued: First, ministers elect the candidate based on a careful examination of his life and doctrine; second, the magistrates give their approval to the candidate; third, the congregation gives its common consent to the choice of the pastoral candidate; and fourth, the candidate is ordained to his office by the rite of laying on of hands. Under normal circumstances, therefore, a legitimate calling to ministerial office required both the personal leading of the Holy Spirit and the public affirmation and election of the church. But Calvin also recognized that the religious or political situation might not always permit such an orderly procedure of election in the church. In periods of spiritual declension and gross idolatry, God sometimes raised up "apostles" or "evangelists" with an *extraordinary* vocation in order "to lead the church back from the rebellion of Antichrist." (Is Calvin perhaps thinking of himself in this regard?) This extraordinary vocation, where God issues the call immediately without ratification by the church, would always be the rare exception rather than the rule, however. "I call this office 'extraordinary,'" Calvin averred, "because in duly constituted churches it has no place."[64]

This general procedure for electing and ordaining ministers outlined in the *Institutes* found specific institutional form in Geneva's *Ecclesiastical Ordinances* (1541), though with several variations. For one, the *Ordinances* omitted any reference to Calvin's concept of the internal call to ministry and made no mention of an extraordinary vocation. Likewise, Geneva's magistrates revised Calvin's draft of the *Ordinances,* rejecting the practice of ordination by the laying on of hands, a decision prompted by the senators' concern that this ancient ceremony would too easily be confused with Catholic practice.[65] Notwithstanding these minor deviations, Geneva's religious constitution outlined a four-step process for appointing ministers to their offices that was nearly identical to what Calvin prescribed in the *Institutes*: First, the prerogative to elect clergy was given to Geneva's ministers, who were responsible for examining candidates to be certain that they possessed a solid and accurate understanding of Scripture, were competent to teach God's Word, and were persons of exemplary moral character. Second, the names of those elected were then forwarded to the Small Council, which had authority to approve or reject the nominees. Third, once the magistrates had approved a candidate, he was to be presented to the local congregation for its affirmation and was then installed in his office. Finally, the new minister was required to return to the council to take the oath of office. For Calvin and the reformed ministers who succeeded him in Geneva, a legitimate pastoral vocation required election by the ministers in conjunction with the approval of the political authorities and the affirmation of the religious community.

4. The Minister's Ordination—In Practice

It was upon the foundation of both Calvin's doctrine of vocation and the legal requirements of the *Ecclesiastical Ordinances* that Geneva's ministers constructed the pastoral office and conceived of their own pastoral identities during the generations that followed. Recruitment of ministerial candidates was predicated on the basic principle that the church (guided by the Holy Spirit) should seek the candidate, not the candidate the church.[66] Ministers were expected to be humble and willing servants of Christ's church rather than greedy mercenaries for hire. Accordingly, Calvin, Beza, and their colleagues were especially suspicious of candidates who displayed personal ambition or greed, or who appeared more concerned with self-advancement than providing pastoral care for the people of God.[67] The bond between the pastor and the local church was a sacred one—almost like marriage—that should not be broken except with clear divine guidance. As the minutes of the Company of Pastors noted: "Because such a bond and obligation is a kind of marriage, as the ancients have observed, it is a thing very unseemly and inappropriate that one who is married with one party should think of another or even be involved with another."[68] It was God through the church that called candidates to pastoral service, and it was God alone who might transfer a pastor to a different post.

The Company of Pastors recruited candidates as young as twenty-two years of age and as old as sixty-five, although most were in their late twenties or early thirties.[69] Older candidates were normally refugee ministers from France who brought with them extensive pastoral experience. By contrast, young men fresh out of the Academy were regularly recruited to serve pastoral positions in the surrounding countryside. Several of Geneva's most influential ministers were elected to the Venerable Company when they were still in their early twenties, including Nicolas Des Gallars (age 24), Charles Perrot (age 23), Simon Goulart (age 23), Jean Diodati (age 23), and Théodore Tronchin (age 24).[70] The Company of Pastors insisted that competence and spiritual maturity, not age, were of primary importance in a good minister. Thus, when a twenty-two-year-old minister named Jacques Pierre left Geneva to serve a congregation in Arnay-le-Duc, France, in 1600, he carried a letter from the Company which commended his knowledge, wisdom, and zeal, and exhorted the church to receive him as a "precious gift of God's grace" despite his tender years, following the instruction of the Apostle Paul who "enjoined the churches of his time not to despise Timothy on account of his youth"(1 Tim 4:12).[71] Youthful immaturity and inexperience sometimes caused serious difficulties for a minister, however. Such was the case of Nicolas Le More, who studied at the Genevan Academy in 1559 and was sent by the Venerable Company to serve a reformed church in Guyenne in 1560. Barely a year later, Le More wrote to the Company requesting that he be recalled to Geneva, noting that "people have received me very badly here, in part because of my inability, and partly, they say, because I am too young and that it is impossible that I should be learned. For this reason, God's Word does not carry its accustomed authority."[72]

What academic training was required for a person aspiring to the office of pastor in Geneva? The *Ecclesiastical Ordinances* was silent on this question. What was most important, indeed essential, was that pastoral candidates possess "a good and sound knowledge of the Scripture," have the ability "to communicate [God's Word] to the people for their edification," and be persons of "good morals" whose lives were above reproach.[73] Notwithstanding these stated qualifications, the Venerable Company clearly preferred candidates who also possessed formal training in the liberal arts, biblical exegesis, and theology, as well as some practical experience. From 1559 on, these priorities were reflected in the course of study offered at Calvin's Academy (*schola publica*) where students attended lectures each week that treated Hebrew and Greek exegesis, the arts (including readings from ancient Greek philosophers, poets, and rhetoricians), and theology (comprising exegetical and dogmatic studies of select Old and New Testament books).[74] Students also participated in weekly theological disputations intended to strengthen their grasp of biblical doctrine and sharpen their skills in rhetoric and dialectic. Finally, students who sensed a calling to pastoral ministry were required to prepare and deliver sample sermons in the presence of some of the city ministers on Saturday afternoons; on occasion, students were also invited to present sermons at the weekly meeting of the Congregation. The most promising of these candidates were sometimes given temporary preaching assignments in Geneva's rural parishes. Thus, Geneva's program of ministerial formation not only emphasized the acquisition of theological knowledge but also helped students acquire practical skills in interpreting biblical texts and delivering sermons.

As we have seen, by the final decades of the sixteenth century, most of Geneva's ministers had received basic theological instruction at either Calvin's Academy or a reformed university elsewhere in Europe. Even so, Theodore Beza and his colleagues resisted making formal theological education a prerequisite for the pastoral office—at least in theory. The question of the value of formal academic training for Calvinist pastors was raised in a polemical exchange between Beza and a Scottish Jesuit named John Hay. In a booklet published in 1580, Hay had posed 166 theological questions to the reformed church of his native Scotland. Among other things, the Catholic author challenged the legitimacy of the pastoral vocation in Protestant churches and ridiculed the humble backgrounds of reformed ministers in Scotland: many were young and poorly educated; a good number had been drawn from the ranks of street vendors and tailors, belt makers and bakers.[75] Beza answered these criticisms in his *Response to the Five Principal Questions of Jean Hay* (1586). He insisted that the reformed were committed to eradicating spiritual ignorance and moral degeneracy within the churches. However, too often the people most educated in the theological and humane sciences were not the best versed in Scripture or the most zealous to serve God. Indeed, Beza noted, throughout salvation history God had frequently called simple, ordinary people to positions of spiritual leadership, endowing them with exceptional gifts so that they might confound the strong and humble the proud. Certainly, an ideal pastoral candidate should possess knowledge of the humane letters as well as demonstrate Christian piety and zeal. But if one must choose between formal book learning and godly character, Beza clearly opted for the latter:

an unschooled, but godly artisan is "more worthy of handling the sword of the Word of God than even those who have studied their entire lives."[76]

Simon Goulart echoed Beza's sentiments regarding the value and limitations of a liberal education in the second volume of his *Christian Discourses* (1595). Book learning was of value only when it was attentive to moral reformation and pursued with the proper motivation. "If you love to study the humane letters," Goulart commented, "this is a good thing, as long as Christ is your goal. If you desire to gain knowledge so that, through it, you might understand more clearly Jesus Christ contained in the holy Scriptures, to love and worship him there, to enjoy him, and to make him known to others, you study with zeal." By contrast, liberal education was of little value, Goulart believed, if it was not pursued with a pure and right conscience. For, "it is better to know little and love much, than to know a lot and yet be an enemy of God."[77]

What role did a candidate's inward sense of calling play in the process of recruitment of Geneva's ministers between 1536 and 1609? Karin Maag has recently shown that as the sixteenth century progressed, the doctrine of inner calling espoused by magisterial reformers like Calvin and Zwingli was gradually displaced by criteria of selection that focused on education, examination for professional competence, and formal approval by ecclesiastical and civil authorities. In other words, the "inner call" was preempted by the "external" process of selection and ordination.[78] This trend toward objectifying the process of clerical selection is also apparent in late sixteenth-century Geneva. As we have seen, the notion of an "inner calling" does not appear in the *Ecclesiastical Ordinances* at all. Likewise, the subjective sense of divine calling is almost completely invisible in documents describing the recruitment and selection of Geneva's pastors. That does not mean, however, that candidates for ministry lacked a sense of divine direction and confirmation as they pursued the pastoral office. Antoine de Chandieu marked his election to the pastoral office in Geneva in 1589 by penning this prayer in his journal: "O Lord God, you who have called and consecrated me to the holy ministry of the church, teach me and strengthen my soul and body. Bless this work with which I have been charged, and restore me happily to the churches of France."[79] In a similar fashion, when Léonard Constant was loaned for several months to the church at Trémilly, France, he believed that it was God himself who had assigned him to this post. In a letter that he sent back to the Venerable Company describing the difficulties of his pastoral appointment, Constant made this observation:

> Nevertheless, because it is God's pleasure [that I serve in Trémilly], it is more than reasonable that I acquiesce to it. And further, having this testimony in my conscience that it is God who has called me, I rest completely in his holy providence, trusting (with the assistance of your good and holy prayers) that he will give me in his goodness all the strength....that he knows I will need for his glory and for the good and edification of his Church.[80]

For ministers like Chandieu and Constant, the "inner" call of God could not be separated entirely from the "external" call of the church. Indeed, one of the ways in which the subjective call of God was to be discerned was through the judgment and support of other church leaders. The young minister from Guyenne, Nicolas Le More, articulated this most succinctly in his letter back to the Company: "Gentleman and revered fathers: A year ago, God called me to the ministry of his Holy Word *through you*."[81] Although these examples indicate that at least some candidates for ministry experienced an inner sense of divine leading as part of their call to the pastoral office, it does not appear that the process of selection and ordination itself placed much weight on this subjective criterion. To be sure, candidates needed to indicate a sincere willingness to undertake the responsibilities of the pastoral office, but the Company of Pastors was far more interested in assessing theological competence and personal character than probing the recesses of conscience or evaluating the validity of a subjective call to ministry.

Once a candidate for a pastoral post had been identified, the Company initiated the process of election and ordination. Ministerial candidates who had previously been ordained to church office in the Genevan church, and were simply being transferred from one parish to another, were elected to the new post but did not undergo a formal examination. Candidates who had never before served the Genevan church, however, were required to undergo a series of rigorous examinations as part of the process of election to evaluate their knowledge of Scripture and doctrine, as well as fitness for ministry. The theological examination regularly lasted for two hours and was usually conducted by Calvin, Beza, or one of the other theologians from the Academy, who probed the candidate's doctrinal convictions and knowledge of the biblical text. When more than one candidate was under consideration, the examination sometimes took the form of a theological disputation.[82] Beginning in 1576, candidates were also required to make a public statement that they believed in "the doctrine of the holy prophets and apostles, as it is comprised in the books of the Old and New Testaments" and taught in the Genevan *Catechism*. A second examination explored the candidate's character, assessing his life and morals against the qualifications set forth by the Apostle Paul in 1 Timothy 3 and Titus 1. Finally, candidates were expected to preach one or several trial sermons in the presence of the ministers to demonstrate their exegetical and homiletic skills. Once the candidate's character, knowledge of Scripture, theological competence, and preaching ability had been determined, all the members of the Company (from both the city and countryside) gathered in a closed-door session to discuss his strengths and weaknesses, to petition divine guidance, and to vote. Election was determined by a simple majority of all Geneva's ministers. Following a successful election, the moderator of the Company exhorted the candidate as to the duties of the pastoral office, addressed any remaining concerns about the candidate's life or doctrine, and charged him to maintain the confidentiality of the Company's proceedings. The session was concluded with prayers on behalf of the new colleague.[83]

Some candidates such as the French pastor Pierre Servier passed through this demanding process of examination with little difficulty. Considered as a replacement for the departed Des Préaux in the fall of 1576, Servier was examined on September 10, preached a trial sermon from Isaiah 55 four days later, and was elected to the Company of Pastors on September 17, on the condition that he would accept "purely and simply the vocation to serve whatever post this church might judge to be appropriate." He took the oath of office before the magistrates and was installed in the parish of Russin-Dardagny on October 15.[84] Other candidates, however, did not navigate the examination process as easily as Servier. Candidates were routinely dismissed because they were poor preachers or unable to answer basic theological questions. Men of timid bearing or weak voice could also be disqualified. Occasionally, men were rejected because of concerns about their moral character, as seen in one candidate who was sent away when it was discovered that he had been party to a usurious business deal.[85] Sometimes the Company of Pastors approved a candidate but with stated reservations. Though Léonard Constant was judged very knowledgeable in theology, he was "still not trained or fashioned in preaching" and was thus "not yet ready to step into the pulpit"; the ministers decided to give him a trial period of one month in the parish of Satigny before assigning him permanently to the church.[86] The Company of Pastors was even more circumspect about the candidacy of the schoolmaster Théodore Gautier, appointed as a temporary replacement for the minister of Russin in 1602. As regent at the *collège* since the mid-1590s, Gautier had been unable to control his unruly class and had several times been reprimanded for his violent temper and harsh treatment of students. Wishing to relieve the *collège* of an instructor ill-suited for his post, and, at the same time, to fill a one-year vacancy in the church of Russin, the Company of Pastors examined and elected Gautier to the ministry but with this explicit caveat:

> [H]e must learn the nature and responsibilities of the pastoral calling, in general and particular, and display affection not only as one who pastors the sheep of the State, but as one who pastors souls for whom Jesus Christ died. And he must do this with warm affection. Also, he must work to change his gloomy and withdrawn manner of behavior into an attitude that is open and willing, which will relieve him in his work and will greatly assist him in fulfilling his charge.[87]

Gautier appears to have conducted himself reasonably well and remained the pastor of Russin for the next seventeen years.

Following his election, the successful candidate was sent to the Small Council, which had the responsibility either to approve or reject the decision of the Company of Pastors. In point of fact, Geneva's magistrates assumed an ever more prominent role in election during the period after Calvin's death. Deputies from the council regularly audited the trial sermons of pastoral candidates and, during the final decades of the sixteenth century, even began to attend (and occasionally intervene in) theological examinations held in the chambers of the Company of Pastors.[88] Consequently, by the time a candidate appeared before the council, the senators were usually well apprised of his capabilities and liabilities. In the council chambers, men elected to the pastoral office faced further scrutiny regarding their attitudes toward the civil authorities and Geneva's laws. The magistrates normally ratified the ministers' choices, but such approval was never *pro forma*. In January 1585, for example, the Small Council refused to lend its support to the nomination of Pierre Petit to the pastoral post at Armoy. As it turned out, the council knew something of Petit's troubled past in Geneva: ten years earlier he had been imprisoned and then banished from the city for employing false weights; more recently, he had been involved in a contentious lawsuit with his mother-in-law. Given this information, the ministers withdrew Petit's name from consideration.[89] The Petit case highlighted the fact that the ministers were sometimes not privy to judicial information that might disqualify a pastoral candidate. As a result of this affair, it was decided that, henceforth, the Company of Pastors should inquire privately of the magistrates about a candidate's moral stature and legal standing, *before* proceeding to election.[90]

The penultimate step in the process of ordination was the presentation of the candidate to the local congregation and the ceremony of installing him to the pastoral office. Customarily, the candidate preached the Sunday morning sermon and afterward was presented to the congregation either by the outgoing minister (in the countryside) or by a fellow-minister (in one of the city parishes). This presentation appears to have included a brief charge to the new minister and congregation, as well as public prayers for his future ministry. Revisions to the *Ecclesiastical Ordinances* in 1561 and 1576 formalized the congregation's role in this process of affirmation: on the Sunday before installation, the name of the pastoral candidate was announced from the pulpits of all Geneva's churches, and members of the congregation were invited to report to one of the syndics any concerns that they might have about the candidate's doctrine or life.[91] Despite this provision, there is no evidence before 1609 that members of a local parish ever attempted to block the installation of a ministerial candidate. Indeed, parishioners in both the city and countryside appear to have received their new ministers with a fair degree of equanimity. The *Ecclesiastical Ordinances* of 1576 included one other significant revision: it removed the provision that prohibited ordination by the laying on of hands. Notwithstanding this change, during the next several decades, Beza and his colleagues continued to install ministers without the ceremony of the imposition of hands, hesitant to introduce any "novelty" into the Genevan church, even though Calvin himself had once endorsed this practice. It was only in the first years of the seventeenth century—due in part to pressure from the seventeenth National Synod of Gap (1603) *and* Geneva's magistrates—that the Venerable Company began to install ministers in their offices utilizing the rite of imposition of hands.[92]

After a ministerial candidate was elected by the Company of Pastors, approved by the Small Council, and presented to the congregation, one final step was required for ordination: he must return to the council chambers to take the oath of office. In the presence of the syndics and senators, the new minister read a formal statement in which he pledged to preach faithfully the Scripture for the edification of the church, to uphold the *Ecclesiastical Ordinances*, to protect the honor of the magistracy, and to set a good example as an obedient subject of the civil authority.[93] He was thereafter enrolled in the Company of Pastors and placed on the city payroll.

As already noted, the ministers of Geneva insisted on the equality of the pastoral office. Every minister regardless of age, education, years of experience, or parish responsibility "was called to the same charge" and possessed the same authority.[94] Even if veteran ministers like Calvin, Beza, or Goulart might fill the prestigious pulpit at St. Pierre and wield substantial moral authority as the moderator of the Company of Pastors, their vocation and the power of their office was believed no different than that of the most inexperienced minister in a countryside parish. In everyday practice, however, rural posts were normally much less desirable than service in Geneva's city churches. Countryside parishes were used as the training ground for students or young ministers in need of experience; they sometimes also served as the final destination for ministers of mediocre talent. The *de facto* valuation of city parishes over countryside churches is illustrated in the controversial election of Jean Le Gaigneux in 1562. In that year, when a pastoral vacancy in the city became available, the Company of Pastors chose to bypass all the ministers in the countryside and elect instead the French refugee Le Gaigneux, who had never served a rural parish. Calvin and the majority of the ministers justified this decision by arguing that quality pastoral care necessitated that the rural ministers be kept in place, because "frequent changes in such matters would not at all be profitable to the poor peasants, who are more able to receive and understand doctrine from the mouths of [pastors] with whom they are familiar." Several of the countryside ministers saw the matter entirely differently, however, and voiced their deep disappointment at having been overlooked. Fairness dictated, they believed, that Le Gaigneux should have been required to serve first in the countryside before being transferred to the city. They complained that "they would never have accepted the ministry if they had imagined that they would be left in the countryside." This dispute left Calvin horrified and speechless. Later, in the privacy of his home, Calvin is reported to have lifted his hands in the air and cried out: "Who would have imagined that I would see such a thing before I died?"[95]

As it turned out, the choice of Le Gaigneux was ill-advised, and after nine tumultuous years in the pastoral office he was finally deposed from the pastoral corps. The Le Gaigneux case served as both a painful lesson and an important precedent: henceforth, Geneva's Company of Pastors required all ministerial candidates to serve first in a countryside parish before being elected to a more prestigious post in the city.

5. Struggles over Ordination

The *Ecclesiastical Ordinances* was clear that the ministers, not the city magistrates, had the authority to elect pastors for Geneva's churches. But during the first years of the seventeenth century, as the old guard of Beza, Perrot, and Pinault declined in health and as leadership of the Company of Pastors passed to a new generation of ministers, Jacques Lect and other senior magistrates of Geneva made a concerted effort to secure greater control over the process of pastoral ordination and the right to assign ministers to specific parishes. One of the first skirmishes in this struggle between ministers and magistrates occurred in May 1603, when the Company of Pastors appointed the veteran city pastor Jean Pinault to fill the vacant pulpit of St. Pierre during the short-term absence of Jean Jaquemot.[96] Hearing of this decision, the Small Council intervened and commanded the Company to appoint Simon Goulart instead.[97] The council argued that Goulart was a better preacher than Pinault and that "the church of Saint Pierre is the most important church in this city and the majority of foreign visitors attend there."[98] The Company of Pastors objected to the magistrates' unbridled "appetite" for ecclesiastical power and for privileging one parish over the others, but they hesitated to antagonize the secular authorities. Hence, they instructed Goulart to obey the council's directive and accept the preaching duties at St. Pierre, something he resolutely refused. At the same time, Jean Pinault—who had served the Genevan church for over forty years and who was no doubt angered that his effectiveness as a preacher was being questioned—lashed out at the council's heavy-handed tactics. He accused the magistrates of being proud and presumptuous, and lectured them that "they would have the preacher whom we give to them and no other."[99] Geneva's senators had no patience for such insubordination: Pinault was called into the council's chambers, interrogated, and reprimanded for his ill-advised outburst. Next, syndics from the Small Council met with the city ministers and ordered them to install Goulart in the pulpit of St. Pierre immediately. Goulart was forced to comply, but not before he had registered a strong protest. He complained that the action was illegal, and he bemoaned the fact that "our Company is now losing all its dignity and freedom." Ecclesiastical authority had become subservient to the commands of the city councilors, he believed. As a result, "we will not deliver the Church to those who come after us in the same condition as it was left to us by our predecessors."[100] After thirty-three years of service to the parish of St. Gervais, Goulart was (permanently) transferred to the temple of St. Pierre in mid-June 1603.[101]

The struggle over parish assignment continued in the following months. In July 1603, the magistrates informed the Company of its plan to transfer the flamboyant young preacher Gabriel Cusin, pastor at Jussy, to a city post. In a speech before the council, Simon Goulart begged the magistrates to follow the protocol for pastoral elections mandated by the *Ecclesiastical Ordinances*: "Leave us this right over the ministry!"[102] While assuring the ministers of their goodwill and their intentions to abide by church law, the magistrates, nonetheless, forced the pastors to lay aside their reservations and elect Cusin to a city parish. The ministers' discomfort with the procedure is indicated by the sharp reminder that was given to Cusin on the event of his election: "he had received his calling, not from the magistrates, nor by compulsion, but from God through the Company."[103] The following month, August 1603, the city council asserted its authority even further by taking the unprecedented step of loaning a member of the Genevan pastoral corps to a foreign church without first consulting the Company of Pastors. The ministers Jaquemot and Le Boiteux were sent hastily to the Small Council to protest: "ecclesiastical matters should be treated within the church," they insisted.[104] But such objections went unheeded. Two years later, in March 1605, the council again intervened in a foreign appointment, commanding that Antoine de La Faye be sent for six months to serve the church of Neuchâtel.[105] When La Faye refused to go, the council ordered the Venerable Company to draw lots to determine whether La Faye or Jean Jaquemot should be sent. Not surprisingly, the ministers challenged the magistrates' right to issue such a command; they also questioned using lots in such a circumstance. But more than anything, the members of the Company objected to the sustained attack on their traditional ecclesiastical prerogatives: "we cannot understand or allow such a procedure which seems to us a strange novelty, for while they have every right to command us in political matters, in ecclesiastical matters and in that which pertains to our callings, everything has always been done through the church and with the counsel of the Company."[106] Geneva's magistrates were in no mood for a prolonged debate. They called the city ministers to their council chambers and roundly scolded them. Jaquemot was assigned to go to Neuchâtel. Ominously, in the week that followed, the Council of 200 recommended that in the future the Company of Pastors should not be permitted to meet without a member of the Small Council in attendance.[107] Though never enacted as law, this bold initiative indicates the increasingly aggressive stance that Geneva's political leaders were taking toward the city ministers and their traditional prerogatives.

Up until 1605, the epicenter of controversy between magistrates and ministers was over who had the right to assign duly elected ministers to their specific parishes. The Company of Pastors argued that determining where a candidate would serve was part of the church's prerogative in ordination. The Small Council, on the other hand, attempted to disjoin the privilege of assignment from the right of election, wanting a greater role in the placement of pastors to ensure that the most talented—and sometimes the more compliant—ministers were in the largest city churches of Geneva. As I have shown, the magistrates of Geneva succeeded in gaining a more significant role in assigning ministers to their pastoral posts, despite the repeated complaints of the city ministers. After 1605, Jacques Lect and Geneva's magistrates asserted their authority over the church even further by attempting to wrest control of clerical election and ordination itself. This is seen most dramatically in the drawn-out controversy surrounding the foiled election of the minister Michel Le Faucheur.

Le Faucheur was born into a prominent Genevan family in 1582, the grand nephew of Nicolas Des Gallars.[108] His father (also named Michel) had high expectations for his son and thus sent him to the Genevan Academy in 1599 and then to the University of Heidelberg. Le Faucheur finished his schooling in 1603, but because there were no permanent pastoral posts available in Geneva, the magistrates loaned him to the reformed church in Bourg-Arental for two years, after which he became pastor of the church in Annonay, France. Michel Sr. displayed very much of an entrepreneurial spirit as he supervised, and intervened in, his son's pastoral career. In 1606, for example, he made arrangements to have his son appointed to a prestigious church post in Grenoble in the hopes of procuring a larger salary for him. The Company of Pastors was scandalized by this blatant act of "buying and selling the sacred ministry," and sent the elder Le Faucheur to the Consistory.[109]

By all accounts, the young Le Faucheur was a spectacular preacher as well as a brilliant controversialist, and, as his reputation soared in France, the city councilors of Geneva began to eye with great interest their native son.[110] In July of 1608, the Small Council ordered the Company of Pastors to recall this talented minister and install him in the city post left vacant by the ailing Charles Perrot (who died later in November). The ministers refused and with good reason. As we have seen, it had always been the prerogative of the Company of Pastors to elect ministerial candidates. And besides, the established practice was to elect a minister to a city post only after he had first served a countryside parish. Further, the ministers argued, Le Faucheur had been placed in his current post by an official act of the National Synod of La Rochelle (1607). Consequently, Geneva could no longer lay claim to him. An additional concern—which remained unstated until later—was Le Faucheur's personal ambition and flamboyant preaching style, which several of Geneva's ministers found very troubling. "We in Geneva do not need beautiful speakers (*beaux parleurs*)," they argued, "but men who firmly teach the truth, following in the footsteps of that great servant of God, John Calvin, whose style was straightforward, fruitful, and altogether edifying."[111] For the Company of Pastors, the candidacy of Le

Faucheur raised important matters of principle and perhaps also stirred a touch of professional jealousy. The city magistrates also believed that matters of principle were at stake. They had never withdrawn their claim to Le Faucheur. And they resented Geneva's ministers' refusal to obey their commands. The decease of Beza, and now the failing health of Perrot, made it all the more imperative that the talented young Le Faucheur be brought back to Geneva to adorn the city's church and Academy.

From July to December 1608, the Company of Pastors and Geneva's Small Council were locked in a fierce struggle over Le Faucheur's candidacy. Jacques Lect and the other councilors repeatedly demanded that the ministers write a letter inviting the pastor of Annonay to join the Genevan church. The ministers stubbornly refused. Heated debates invariably cycled back to the issues of who had the right to call a minister, and what jurisdiction Geneva held over native sons who were serving churches in France. The Small Council's position was stated succinctly in a closed door meeting held on July 29.

> We must not speak of [Le Faucheur] as the servant of anyone else because he is from this city, where he was born and for which he has been reserved. Nor should we imagine that either provincial or national synods will try to block this, given that such an action would be a gross injustice to the [Genevan] church, depriving her of her rights.... We should not think of this as an "election" nor as relating to the procedure followed in the appointment of a pastor, since Le Faucheur has already been elected and is presently serving as a minister. We should think instead about the well-being and honor of this church, and the fact that this person would be very useful given his remarkable gifts, and especially his strengths in religious controversies with opponents.[112]

The Small Council also appealed to the example of John Calvin, pointing out that the Council of 200 had invited the reformer to return to Geneva from Strasbourg in 1541—without ever consulting the city ministers. On August 3, the Small Council summoned the pastors to its chambers and took the unusual step of demanding an explanation from each minister in turn. Once again, the ministers refused to comply with the council's command to invite Le Faucheur to join the city's pastoral corps: "We are not able to consent to the summons and calling of [Le Faucheur] seeing that such a calling is not legitimate and is in violation of the *Ordinances* that we have sworn to uphold, in which it is stipulated that ministers are those responsible for election." The ministers argued, furthermore, that the example of Calvin's return from Strasbourg was not relevant to the situation at hand. Calvin had been "unfairly chased" from his pastoral post and then "recalled from exile, rather than reappointed to the ministry." And besides, most of Calvin's colleagues in those days were utterly incompetent and thus the magistrates had been forced to exercise exceptional authority to restore good order to the church.[113] To recall a legitimately elected minister (like Calvin) to his post was altogether different than to appoint a pastor from the outside (like Le Faucheur) who had never before been elected to pastoral office in Geneva. The ministers concluded their defense by insisting that there were several capable ministers in the countryside who should be given preference over the gifted, but controversial, Michel Le Faucheur.

The matter was not concluded so easily. On November 4, four representatives from the council, among them Jacques Lect, confronted the ministers and ordered them to elect Le Faucheur to a city pulpit without delay. Recognizing that the ministers of the countryside would certainly oppose Le Faucheur, the councilors mandated that only city ministers should be allowed to cast votes in an election to fill a city post. Moreover, the magistrates had taken the liberty of inviting Le Faucheur (who was visiting his family in Geneva) to preach in the pulpits of St. Pierre and St. Gervais on the following Sunday, an obvious attempt to rouse public support for this popular preacher and increase the pressure on the Company of Pastors. The Small Council's patience was clearly wearing thin: to defy the magistrates' commands would be perceived as an act of rebellion.[114] Yet, Geneva's ministers held firm. They protested that they had not been consulted when the magistrates invited Le Faucheur to preach in the city. Likewise, they feared that denying countryside ministers the right to vote would create a schism in the body of the Company of Pastors; the *Ecclesiastical Ordinances* affirmed the equality of the ministry, and hence for sixty years ministers from both the city and countryside had participated in all pastoral elections. Additionally, the ministers emphasized that to elect Le Faucheur to the Genevan pastoral corps would be an infringement on the rights of the church of Annonay and a violation of the decision of a French national synod.[115] The senators minimized these concerns and cited Scripture against the ministers: "The Son of God predicted that frequently salt would lose its taste and that sometimes the people most responsible to show forth light to others would be mired in the greatest darkness" (Matt 5:13). Indeed, the Bible promised that "God would destroy the wisdom of the wise and the discernment of the understanding" (1 Cor 1:19, quoting Isaiah 29:14).[116] It was their God-given responsibility, the magistrates insisted, to provide for the well-being of both the state and church, and thus it was imperative that Geneva's churches be supplied with the most capable and illustrious ministers available.

Le Faucheur preached to much acclaim at both St. Pierre and St. Gervais on Sunday, November 13, 1608. The next day, his father produced letters from the elders of the church of Annonay in which they renounced absolute right over their pastor and indicated that they might be willing to accept a replacement for him. Armed with this information, the magistrates demanded, once again, that the Company of Pastors draft a formal letter recalling Le Faucheur from France. One last time, the ministers protested, now explicitly criticizing Le Faucheur's ambitious character and his willingness to sell "his vocation for money."[117] But after voicing these final concerns, the ministers capitulated. On December 1, Jean Jaquemot, the moderator of the Company of Pastors, wrote to the church of Annonay requesting that Le Faucheur be released so that he might serve his home church in Geneva.[118] The letter was delivered to France by one of Geneva's senators, who also carried an official letter of request from the Small Council.

In the end, however, the church of Annonay frustrated Geneva's efforts. The elders of the church changed their minds and refused to grant Le Faucheur leave, noting the fruitfulness of his ministry and predicting that his departure would lead to the ruin of the church.[119] Geneva's appeal to the nineteenth National Synod of Saint Maixant in the summer of 1609 was also rejected.[120] The synod judged that Le Faucheur's call to Annonay had been legitimate and that his ministry was so crucial to the French churches that his departure would lead to "several drawbacks and dangerous consequences."[121] Though the magistrates' designs were thwarted in the case of Le Faucheur, their strong-arm tactics against the Company of Pastors had on the whole been successful. The ministers had been forced to bow to magisterial authority and compromise their traditional prerogative to recruit and elect ministers to pastoral offices in Geneva.

The Le Faucheur case and the pitched battle over clerical election in Geneva in the first decade of the seventeenth century can be interpreted from a number of different vantage points. A narrow interpretation of these struggles brings into focus the different priorities and values that existed between the city's political and spiritual leaders. Magistrates and ministers alike recognized the pastoral office as a sacred vocation from God that was of vital importance for the spiritual well-being of the men and women who lived in their Christian commonwealth. So too, both the magistrates and ministers placed a high priority on ensuring that the men who served Geneva's churches were morally upright, competent, and committed to the city's official theology. But here their priorities diverged. For the Company of Pastors, an overriding concern was to preserve the jurisdiction of the church over religious matters, and thus it guarded jealously the ministers' prerogative to recruit, elect, and ordain ministers to pastoral posts as stipulated in the *Ecclesiastical Ordinances*. The ministers were guided by several basic principles as they chose new colleagues, including the belief that no pastoral vocation was superior to another; a commitment to the equal value of every parish assignment (whether in city or countryside); and the conviction that pastors must be motivated by a sincere desire to serve Christ's church rather than by ambition, greed, and overweening pride. Jacques Lect and Geneva's magistrates, by contrast, were animated by a different set of concerns and priorities. While acknowledging in principle the distinct spiritual jurisdiction of the church, the Small Council adopted a policy of intervention aimed at limiting ecclesiastical authority and restricting the ministers' prerogative in recruitment and ordination. Over several years, through confrontation and sometimes by outright intimidation, Geneva's magistrates gained new powers to assign pastors to specific parishes and dispatch ministers to foreign churches, even as they pressured the Company of Pastors to elect ministerial candidates that were otherwise unacceptable. From the perspective of Geneva's magistrates, it was imperative that the city's largest and most prestigious churches be served by the most gifted and eloquent ministers who might enhance the reputation of the city and prove cooperative in their dealings with civil authorities.

A second interpretive frame focuses attention on the broader religious and political context in which the struggle over recruitment and election took place. Controversies surrounding clerical election, as evidenced in the Le Faucheur affair, were neither accidental nor isolated; rather, they were part of a larger campaign waged by Geneva's political authorities against traditional ecclesiastical rights and privileges in the first years of the seventeenth century. As we saw in chapter 2, Jacques Lect and the Small Council imposed on the city ministers a new method for selecting the moderator of the Company of Pastors immediately following Theodore Beza's death in 1605. During this same period, the magistrates successfully attenuated the Consistory's exclusive right over the excommunication of unrepentant sinners (see chapter 7). These important precedents appear to have been part of the council's overall strategy to subject the church to civil authority and assure that those who succeeded Beza as leaders of the church would be compliant and cooperate with the magistrates' rule. A somewhat more nuanced description of these important developments is offered by Eugène Choisy and Matteo Campagnolo, who argue that the leadership vacuum created by the death of Beza invited a new kind of spiritual-political leader in Geneva, embodied in magistrates such as Jacques Lect, who, having been formed by Calvin's theological vision, attempted in their role as Christian magistrates to supervise and govern the affairs of the church as part of a single spiritual commonwealth.[122] Though Choisy overstates the situation slightly, his central insight remains valid: "The true head of the spiritual government will henceforth be the Seigneurie, the Magistracy of Geneva.... [I]t is one of the senators of the Small Council, Jacques Lect, who demonstrates himself to be the true successor of Theodore Beza."[123] At the dawn of the new century, Calvin's vision for a Christian commonwealth in which the Company of Pastors was given primary responsibility to govern the church, elect ministers, judge biblical doctrine, and (with the elders) impose Christian discipline had been substantially altered. To be sure, ministers retained the privilege to interpret the Scripture in their public sermons and, when necessary, speak out against political abuses and societal wrongdoing. But the independence of the spiritual sphere had in large part been undermined. Simon Goulart recognized these ominous developments when he complained in 1603 that "our Company is now losing all of its dignity and freedom."[124]

A third interpretive lens through which the crisis surrounding clerical election in Geneva may be viewed is that of confessionalization. Modern social historians such as Heinz Schilling and Wolfgang Reinhard have theorized that during the period from roughly 1560 to 1650, a process of confessionalization occurred within Europe's major religious communities (Lutheran, Reformed, Catholic) whereby the establishment of territorial churches, the development of confessional identities, and a growing commitment to social discipline contributed to early modern state formation.[125] This process of confessionalization modernized churches and transformed the clerical office in a number of important ways. Church life became more carefully regulated, supervised, and documented through the codification of confessions, catechisms, and church ordinances; the establishment of ecclesiastical bureaucracies; and the creation of disciplinary courts (such as Calvinist consistories). Likewise, the clerical office was increasingly professionalized with the establishment of formal educational requirements and more detailed guidelines for examination and ordination. In this process of modernization, Schilling and Reinhard note, clergymen emerged as quasi-agents of the state, serving as a crucial link for communication between political leaders and their subjects; supervising public discipline; and providing administrative resources for the state (such as maintaining baptismal, marriage, and death registers). It is not my purpose here to evaluate the overall validity of the confessionalization thesis nor to assess its usefulness in describing the history of a small city republic like Geneva. However, Schilling and Reinhard's description of the "new" clerical office in confessional Europe does provide a helpful frame of reference for understanding important changes occurring in Geneva's religious life in the half century following Calvin's death. As we have seen, during Beza's tenure the process of recruitment, election, and ordination became more carefully defined and regulated. A growing number of ministers received formal theological education. At the same time, as we shall see in chapter 7, Geneva's Consistory played a crucial role in maintaining moral discipline and enforcing public order. Likewise, the Small Council's campaign to gain control over clerical recruitment and election was indicative of a broader strategy to bring the city's pastors in line with the political objectives of the governing authorities. The ministers were gradually transformed into quasi-agents of the state who were not only paid out of the state coffers but were also hired, supervised, and dismissed with significant involvement of the magistrates. In all these ways, the "history" of Geneva's pastoral office during the second half of the sixteenth century runs parallel to developments in other confessional traditions.

But, as we have seen, to depict Geneva's ministers as merely—or primarily—quasi-agents of the state is to ignore the ministers' self-understanding. For Calvin, Beza, Goulart, and their colleagues, Christian ministers were called to their sacred office first and foremost by God, not by human beings; their primary responsibility was to proclaim the Word of God, not to enforce the commands of magistrates; their chief concern was to raise up servants of the heavenly kingdom, not produce citizens of an earthly one.[126] The first clause of the oath of office that Geneva's ministers recited in the presence of the Small Council testified to this fact:

> I promise and pledge that in the ministry to which I am called, I will serve God faithfully, proclaiming his Word in purity for the edification of this Church to which he has appointed me, and that I will not at all abuse his doctrine to serve my own carnal desires or to please any living person. On the contrary, I will make use of it to serve his glory and to benefit his people, to whom I am a debtor.[127]

This distinctly religious conception of their vocation did not prevent the ministers from actively supporting the political authorities and their laws, of course. As members of an earthly commonwealth, Christians of all walks of life—pastors included—were required by God to obey and pray for the magistrates as well as promote the well-being of the republic. However, for Geneva's pastors, their vocation as ministers of the Word fundamentally shaped their self-identity, serving as the lodestar of their life work and labors. They were servants of God before they were servants of the state. As Christian pastors, they were called first and foremost to be guardians of the church and spiritual guides for God's flock. The chapters that follow will explore more fully the ways in which this religious identity shaped the rhythm of the ministers' daily work and fortified them as they undertook their challenging ministries.

CHAPTER 4 | Pastors and Their Households

"VANITY OF VANITIES.... All is vanity. What does man gain by all the toil at which he toils under the sun?"—so intoned the world-weary Preacher of Ecclesiastes (1:2–3). In a similar fashion, Antoine de Chandieu, in a collection of poems entitled *Octonaires on the Vanity of this World*, reflected on the ephemeral nature of human existence driven by ambition and dominated by material concerns:

> Never having and always desiring,
> Such are the consequences for him who loves the world.
> The more he abounds in honor and riches,
> The more he is seen aspiring for more.
> He does not enjoy what belongs to him:
> He wants, he values, he adores what other people have.
> When he has everything, it is then that he has nothing.
> Because having everything, he desires everything still.[1]

Such commentary against the vanities of the world, against the lust for wealth, prestige, and power, runs as a leitmotif through many of the sermons and devotional writings of Christian authors in early modern Europe. In this Chandieu and Geneva's pastors were in no way exceptional: they saw it as their responsibility to call God's people to turn their faces away from the baubles and bangles of this world, to lift their eyes above the fleeting pleasures of human life, so as to focus instead on spiritual life with God with its pilgrimage of faith in the here and now, and its promise of glorious hope for the hereafter. The life of the Spirit required attention to things divine and eternal—a God-centered life of submission and worship—rather than a mindless chasing after the shadows of this present world.

It would be wrong, however, to picture Calvin, Beza, Chandieu, and Geneva's other ministers as cut off from the everyday cares and concerns common to humanity. Quite the contrary, even as they proclaimed the life of the spirit, their lives were spent attending to a host of mundane matters, domestic, economic, and pastoral, that were part of their vocational identities and inextricably bound to Geneva's bustling urban life. Geneva's pastors lived in the crowded neighborhoods of the walled city or in small hamlets in the surrounding countryside. Nearly all of them were married, and many had households that included a quiver full of children, a couple of student boarders, and at least one or two servants who needed to be clothed, fed, and instructed. Sons needed to be apprenticed, or sent to school; daughters required dowries to attract potential suitors. Geneva's ministers were never entirely free of these domestic requirements, even if the weight of them often fell upon their wives or household servants. Economic duties also intruded upon the life of spiritual contemplation. In their distinct black ministerial robes, the pastors were invariably under public scrutiny—the subject of gossip, criticism, and curiosity—as they walked through Geneva's dirty, narrow streets, on their way to visit the shop of the butcher, baker, or watchmaker. On market days, on Wednesdays and Saturdays, some of the ministers were no doubt among the throngs of city folk, peasants, and merchants doing business in the place du Molard, looking for bargains on fruits, vegetables, fish, and meat, and hoping to acquire information about the outside world. Several of the wealthier ministers are known to have purchased and sold property, and to have overseen family fortunes back in their native France. So too, the weekly business of the church encroached upon a life of undistracted spiritual solitude. Sermons needed to be preached, and books written. Geneva's ministers were expected to perform baptisms, catechize the young, unite couples in holy matrimony, conduct household visitations, discipline the wicked, and comfort the sick and dying. To be sure, these pastoral responsibilities required attentiveness to the life of the Spirit, to spiritual meditation and prayer. But these responsibilities also called Chandieu and the other ministers away from a life of contemplation, to an active, public life devoted to instruction, persuasion, moral correction, and conflict mediation.

In the chapters that follow, I will explore the daily rhythm of the ministers' work in Geneva between 1536 and 1609, as well as examine in detail the various pastoral duties that made up their vocation as ministers of the Word of God. But first, this present chapter will focus attention on the pastors' households, looking for clues to the nature of the ministers' marriage and family relationships, and describing the physical and financial compensation the pastors received to enable them to carry out their daily work. As will become apparent, their vocation as ministers of the gospel could never be disentangled from the cares and responsibilities of the world. The demands of family life, sick children, deceased spouses, parsonages in disrepair, critical neighbors, and parsimonious wages—these were some of the real emotional and physical challenges that the ministers faced as they performed their ministries day to day. Even as they called their parishioners to trust in Christ and serve the kingdom of heaven, the pastors of the Venerable Company embraced a spiritual calling that required rigorous toil "under the sun."

1. Domestic Life

Few theological convictions of sixteenth-century Protestant reformers had greater impact on the structure of early modern European society than that regarding the goodness of clerical marriage. The pastor's household as an institution was birthed during the 1520s and 1530s, as evangelical church leaders in Germany and Switzerland began to defy canon law and Catholic tradition by renouncing vows of celibacy and taking wives. In their sermons and published writings, but also in their own marriages, reformers like Ulrich Zwingli, Martin Luther, and (somewhat later) John Calvin challenged the medieval church's teaching that the celibate, contemplative life was superior to the active life of marriage and family.[2] The magisterial reformers argued that the medieval church's requirement of clerical celibacy was a human invention that tyrannized the consciences of priests and distorted the Bible's teaching on the value and proper function of marriage. As Calvin saw it, marriage was a "good and holy ordinance" which God had created and offered to men and women from all walks of life for the purpose of procreating children, restraining fornication, and promoting love between husband and wife.[3] Guillaume Farel concurred, crying out in his *Summary and Brief Declaration* (c. 1529): "O holy estate of marriage, you who are sullied and dishonored [by the priests]. O brutal world, devoid of all sense and understanding, do you not have eyes? Are you so blind that you grope about at noontime as if you were in utter darkness? Do you think that in our day this holy estate should be prohibited, that it is sin to fulfill the commandment of God?"[4] The construction of clerical marriage brought with it a new identity and new responsibilities for the Protestant minister: his spiritual calling as a "shepherd of souls" now extended beyond the parish church to his family and household, where he served as husband, father, son-in-law, and *paterfamilias*. It was expected that the pastor's household, including his wife and children, should serve as an example to the surrounding community, a model of Christian piety and domestic tranquility for neighbors to emulate. Susan Karant-Nunn has rightly observed, "The home of the pastor and his wife became a symbol of active spirituality second only to the church itself."[5] Although the magisterial reformers did not mandate marriage for young ministerial candidates, they did anticipate that the majority of evangelical ministers would marry, raise children, and participate in the life of the local community.

This was certainly the case in sixteenth-century Geneva. Nearly all of the 135 ministers who served Geneva's parish churches from 1536 to 1609 were married men, and most had children. In the early decades, a number of Geneva's first pastors came out of Catholic orders and took wives shortly after converting to the Protestant faith. Thus, for example, Jean Chapuis, the former prior of the Dominican monastery in Geneva, embraced the evangelical religion in 1536, married in 1537 (when he was around forty-six years of age), and was appointed to the parish of Chancy a decade later.[6] On the other hand, many of the veteran ministers who emigrated from France to join Calvin were already married when they arrived on the shores of Lac Léman. As the century wore on, especially after the opening of the Genevan Academy in 1559, it became common for younger ministers to wait until they had finished their theological training and commenced their first pastoral assignment in Geneva before looking for a wife. At least two dozen members of the Venerable Company during these decades are known to have married within one or two years after assuming their first pastoral position. For these young men, ordination not only signaled the beginning of a new vocation but also held out the promise of domestic life, providing financial resources necessary to support a wife and set up a household.

Identifying and courting a prospective spouse required discretion, of course, paying due attention to social mores and standards of moral behavior. The socially inept minister from Genthod-Moëns named Georges Druson learned this lesson the hard way in the summer of 1577. Desperate to find a suitable wife with wealth or political connections or both, Druson made proposals of marriage to no less than twenty different women within several months; a number of these young women were from distinguished Genevan families, and two were the daughters of his pastoral colleagues, Michel Cop and Nicolas Colladon. Making matters worse, in several cases Druson was guilty of reneging on marriage proposals offered and accepted. As reports of the minister's bizarre conduct spread through the city, Geneva's ministers and elders summoned him to the Consistory's chambers where they reprimanded and then excommunicated him for behavior judged "unworthy of an honorable and God-fearing man." The Consistory then sent Druson to the Small Council, recommending that he be deposed from office, not only for the scandal caused by the marriage proposals but also for his avarice, his reclusive personality, and his incompetence as a pastor and preacher.[7]

How old were Geneva's ministers at the time they entered marriage? In thirty-five cases where data is available, the average age of Geneva's ministers at the time of their first marriage was thirty-one years. After 1559, the average age of first marriage appears to have declined somewhat, to around 28.5 years, due to the fact that the pastoral ranks were being filled by younger men who came from Protestant families, studied at the Academy, and had never taken Catholic vows of celibacy. Demographic patterns suggest that pastors' wives were probably seven or eight years younger on average than their husbands at the time of their first marriage.[8] Individual cases often departed from these norms, however. Simon Goulart was twenty-four, and his bride Suzanne Picot fifteen at the time of their wedding in 1570.[9] The one-time Franciscan monk Antoine Chauve finally decided to "tie the knot" when he was fifty-five years of age. Michel Cop was a respectable forty-four years old when John Calvin arranged his marriage to Ayma Waremberg—a woman who had already been widowed three times.[10] Most controversial of all was the marriage of Guillaume Farel, who waited until he was sixty-nine years of age before marrying Marie Thorel, a young woman fifty years his junior. Farel's voyage into connubial bliss left Calvin absolutely flabbergasted and irate, fearing that his friend's scandalous action would inflict irreparable damage on the cause of the Reformation throughout Europe.[11]

Marriages in the sixteenth and seventeenth century were typically brief, averaging only fifteen to twenty years, due to the perils of childbirth, the scourge of war, poor nutrition, and regular visitations of disease.[12] Consequently, widows and especially widowers were a common feature of early modern European society. Many of Geneva's most influential ministers, including Beza, Viret, Goulart, Daneau, Perrot, and Pinault, knew the sorrow of burying a first wife, and the comfort and hope that came with remarriage. When Simon Goulart's wife Suzanne died in 1587, the pastor remained a widower for less than four months, before marrying his second wife Geneviève Boucher, in large part to provide maternal care for his six young children.[13] The haste with which Goulart remarried may have raised eyebrows, but it was not without precedent during this period. John Calvin began searching for a new spouse for his friend Pierre Viret less than a month and a half after Viret's first wife, Elizabeth, died in 1546.[14] In a similar fashion, when Beza's wife Claudine Denosse died in 1588, the reformer waited only four months before taking a new bride, a refugee from Piedmont named Catherine del Piano. The seventy-year-old Beza was forthright about his reasons for marrying Catherine, who was twenty-seven years his junior: he anticipated that her companionship would soften the pain of solitude and ease the difficulties of his old age.[15]

The women who married Geneva's ministers came from families spanning the social spectrum, though few, if any, of them were born of peasant stock. Calvin's wife Idelette de Bure was a poor woman, the widow of an Anabaptist convert to reformed Christianity, and the mother of two young children.[16] Theodore Beza's first wife, Claudine Denosse, was the orphaned daughter of a merchant family from Paris.[17] Other ministers had wives who came from more distinguished backgrounds. The wife of Pierre d'Airebaudouze was the daughter of a royal judge from Nîmes.[18] Etienne Trembley married the daughter of the secretary of the French ambassador to the Swiss League.[19] Jean de Serres's father-in-law was an engineer who designed fortifications.[20] The French ministers Lambert Daneau and

Antoine de Chandieu both married women who shared their noble pedigree. Several of the pastors married into Genevan families that had wealth or belonged to the city's aristocracy. What is particularly striking is how many pastors within the Venerable Company married the daughters or close relatives of other Genevan ministers. Calvin and Guillaume Farel had nieces who married pastoral colleagues. Théodore Tronchin married the granddaughter of Beza's second wife, Catherine del Piano. Antoine Chauve and Abraham de La Maisonneuve each claimed the minister Raymond Chauvet as his father-in-law. In a similar fashion, both Etienne Gros the Younger and Osée André married daughters of David Le Boiteux. In total, no fewer than fourteen of Geneva's ministers between 1536 and 1609 married the daughters of their colleagues, creating bonds of trust, loyalty, and dependence that were "thicker than blood." Marriages between pastoral families established relational networks that contributed to the cohesiveness and common vision of the pastoral corps during the second half of the sixteenth century. This point bears emphasis. The explanation for Geneva's conservative ministerial culture in the late sixteenth century, with its solid commitment to preserving Calvin's religious legacy, is found not only in the common theological training of Geneva's pastors and the stable leadership offered by ministers, such as Beza and Goulart, but also in the networks of familial and social alliances that bound the members of Geneva's ministerial corps into a single Company.

If marriages between pastoral families often fostered goodwill and common purpose, unhappy marriages sometimes created deep rifts between members of the Venerable Company. The troubled marriage of Honoré Blanchard, minister of Vandoeuvre, and Marie, daughter of Jean Pinault, is a good example. In 1583, after only sixteen months of marriage, the relationship between Honoré and Marie began to unravel when it came to light that Blanchard had lied about the extent of his personal wealth, was accruing huge debts, and was sexually impotent to boot. The improvident pastor was first excommunicated and then deposed from the ministry as "a man of bad conscience, a liar, a braggart" and "an insulter." Over the next months, Honoré and Marie endured a series of humiliating interrogations and physical examinations to determine whether or not their marriage had been consummated and whether the husband could fulfill his sexual role in marriage. At the end of this torturous process, Geneva's magistrates finally granted Marie's request for a divorce from her husband on account of conjugal abandonment.[21] Not surprisingly, the sad affair left Jean Pinault and Blanchard deeply alienated from one another. At least in this case, an ill-advised marriage divided rather than united members of Geneva's pastoral company.

Geneva's ministers and their wives maintained busy households. The crying of infants and the happy chattering of children at play were common sounds filling their homes. Most of the pastors' households were blessed with children, and not a few were bursting with them: Abraham de

La Maisonneuve and his wife Rachel had twelve children. Simon Goulart was the father of nine children in all. Etienne de Brulères and his wife had eight children. Antoine de Chandieu and his wife Françoise de Felins welcomed thirteen children into the world, although only eight of them survived into adulthood. In his personal journal, Chandieu recorded the date of birth and baptism for each of his children, and wrote a brief prayer marking the occasion. The proud father penned these words for his fifth son Esaïe, born in September 1576:

> May the Lord, the very kind Father, to whom I and my family owe our life and salvation, preserve and help this child to grow up, and provide him in abundance with every blessing on earth, and especially with those of heaven. May he answer these prayers by which his father consecrates him to the holy and happy propagation of the kingdom of Jesus Christ, my Lord.[22]

Like modern-day parents, Geneva's pastors and their wives sometimes worried about the well-being of their children. Pierre Viret and his second wife, Sébastienne de La Harpe, had special cause for concern about their mischievous daughter, Marie. While at play in 1550, little Marie tugged on the cord of the bell attached to the family's house, and the heavy bell with its iron clapper fell on the toddler's head. "By divine providence," Viret later reported, "God turned aside the blow," and his daughter suffered only a few scratches and bruises but no lasting injuries. Later that same year, Marie was involved in a second accident that had a much less fortunate outcome. While playing with a red-hot bed warmer, the infant received severe burns on her face and body that scarred her for the rest of her life.[23]

In addition to the presence of daughters, sons, and servants, most of Geneva's city ministers also boarded students in their households; an arrangement that not only supplemented the family's income but also assured that boys enrolled at the Academy would stay out of trouble and learn to speak acceptable French. Oftentimes these boarders came from influential Protestant families elsewhere in Europe; they included future counts and mayors as well as the sons of famous churchmen, sent to Geneva so that (as one student's father expressed it) "they might be instructed in piety, virtue, and good letters, and so that they can one day serve both God and their *patria* usefully and with praise."[24] These living arrangements invariably required Geneva's ministers to function *in loco parentis* as they monitored the students' spending habits, offered advice and encouragement, corrected sinful behavior, and provided periodic updates to parents back home.[25] This is how the pastor Claude Baudel described his approach to supervising student borders: "As a good pastor, I constantly inspect the pensioners that are in my home. In my household we maintain a well-regulated discipline; and I am very careful to offer a lot of advice and many lessons so that a student cannot live with me without being forced to behave well."[26] One of Beza's former pensioners, Edward Bacon, the son of the chancellor of England, remembered fondly the months he had spent in the reformer's household, listening to Beza's conversation at the dinner table and observing on a daily basis his mentor's godly manner of life. Bacon compared his experience to the prophet Samuel in the household of Eli—his time in Geneva with Beza, he averred, had prepared him better to serve his country.[27]

Although no document survives describing the day-to-day domestic activities of ministers like Calvin, Cop, Beza, Daneau, or Goulart, it is likely that they undertook a variety of practical duties required of the heads of most Christian households: they oversaw the family's financial accounts and correspondence; they supervised the household servants and student boarders; they attended to their children's education; they meted out corrective discipline; and they instructed their sons and daughters in the catechism.[28] It is likely that many of the countryside ministers experienced a somewhat more rugged existence: in the absence of household servants, their daily duties may well have included feeding livestock, tending a garden, drawing water, or gathering firewood. Many of Geneva's ministers no doubt also conducted daily times of Scripture reading and prayer for their households. Calvin recommended in the *Institutes* that Christians should establish regular times for prayer "when we arise in the morning, before we begin daily work, when we sit down to a meal, when by God's blessing we have eaten, when we are getting ready to retire."[29] Toward that end, Beza wrote a collection of twenty-seven prayers that became a regular part of his household's spiritual exercises.[30] These daily prayers, which included selections for a family in the morning, at the meal table, and in the evening, as well as prayers for use in household devotions, were later published (in English) under the title *Maister Beza's Household Prayers* (1603). In the preface to this work, Beza encouraged readers to establish a regular rhythm of prayer in their households. Christians should pray and meditate "if not incessantly, yet at least daily at certain set hours...as well in the congregation, as in our families, morning and evening, among our household as also in our secret chambers." Daily prayers like these constituted "acceptable sacrifices of sweet savor" to God and made it possible for Christians to experience divine blessing in their daily work.[31]

Not everything about the ministers' domestic life was duty and drudgery. Undoubtedly, for many ministers, the love of family and friendships with colleagues added luster to daily life. During a time of intense stress and difficulty in his ministry in Lausanne, Pierre Viret remarked in a letter to Calvin: "One thing alone refreshes me: the peace of my family, the mutual affection and harmony that I share with colleagues and professors, [and] the progress of the school. If I did not have these things, I would no longer live."[32] Geneva's ministers found physical relaxation and pleasure in a variety of other activities. Nicolas Colladon's biography of Calvin reports that the reformer occasionally relaxed by playing popular games such as tossing a disc or playing keys with friends—but "only very rarely" and "in response to the urging of his friends."[33] A number of Geneva's ministers composed poetry, and several of them maintained extensive correspondences with friends around Europe. Simon Goulart was a musician who found particular inspiration from French composers such as Roland de Lassus, Jean de Castro, and Noé Faignient. For Goulart, music was a "beautiful gift of God" that helped relieve the worries of life and provided healing for the wounds of the soul.[34] Theodore Beza shared Goulart's love for music. He is also known to have found recreation in hunting from time to time.[35] For longer holidays, a number of the ministers sought refreshment in the thermal waters of neighboring Pays de Vaud or Thonon. Closer to home, many of Geneva's pastors probably enjoyed—as Beza did—taking regular walks in the countryside, drinking in the natural splendor of lake and mountains. The delight that Beza found in the expansive Alpine landscape was expressed in a lovely poem, found in the dedicatory epistle of his French Psalter (1553):

> As for me, as small as I am,
> I intend to praise my God, as much as I can.
> Cold mountains bear witness of my holy fervor,
> as do pastures, Lake Geneva, foaming rivers,
> that shout forth God's glorious praise.
> This name, Most High, above misty clouds,
> rumbles from Alpine peaks with echoes loud.[36]

It is likely that many of Geneva's pastors also found pleasure and spiritual renewal in their religious experience with God. The ministers' poems, private letters, and written prayers—all intimate windows into their inner lives—regularly attest to a buoyant hope and confidence, drawn from their meditation on the person of God, their trust in divine providence, and their contemplation of eternal rest. For Antoine de Chandieu, the radiant light of a sunrise could spark thoughts of the joys of eternity;

> O Son of sun, as the light of dawn ushers in the new day,
> and adorns the mountains with its golden rays,
> My mind recalls that eternal day most blessed,
> when this world will be o'er and the night finally past.[37]

In a similar fashion, the birth of baby chicks in Beza's household prompted him to contemplate the fruitfulness of his life and reaffirm his desire to follow Christ:

> A hen that I bought for a very small sum,
> bore fifteen chicks before one month was done.
> But to you, kind Christ, what fruit have I given,
> during the seventy-seven years I have been living?
> ....

Forgive me Lord, and to my humble prayer attend,
that I may be your chick, and you to me a hen![38]

In their formal theology, but also in their private writings, the ministers affirmed the doctrine of God's providence and drew comfort and courage from the fact that the heavenly Father wisely ordered the events of their households and governed the lives of both the righteous and the wicked.[39] In the face of danger and tragedy, poverty and loss, the ministers reminded correspondents of the words of Scripture, *Dominus providebit* (Genesis 22:8)—God will provide for his chosen people.[40] Theodore Beza repeated this comforting message in his sermons:

> This is a doctrine of singular consolation for the children of God, that whatever wicked men and Satan (who directs them) have planned and are prepared to do against us, there will be nothing...that God has not ordained, because not even a single sparrow falls to the earth apart from the command and will of God.[41]

Geneva's ministers also expressed confidence that God's providential care would sustain them through death and usher them into the delights of heaven beyond. Beza concluded his meditation on Psalm 130 with this prayer: "I embrace you, O Jesus Christ, my Savior, for you have reconciled me to the Father and assured me by your Spirit of the comfort of my salvation in you. And as I embrace you, I receive the promises of eternal life and joy."[42] This eschatological hope was also articulated in one of Simon Goulart's final letters: "My wife is now 76 years old...and I am 82. Death summons us to the heavenly banquet and the happy life."[43]

Calvin, Beza, and their colleagues would not have recognized, nor been sympathetic with, hard and fast distinctions between public responsibilities and private devotion, between work and worship. The Christian's life with God was to be lived in and through the regular activities of household and community. In even the most mundane of domestic duties, God's people were expected to contemplate divine things and promote God's glory. Thus, in the opening lines of his *Catechism* (1542), Calvin offered this summary of the Christian life:

> MINISTER: "What is the chief end of human life?"
> CHILD: "To know God....Because he created us for this, and placed us in the world so that he might be glorified in us. And it is certainly proper for us to direct our life to his glory since we have our source in him."[44]

Echoing this attitude toward life, Beza stated that "We are put in the world to serve the glory of God with both body and soul."[45] Moreover, as Christian men and women submitted their daily work and household responsibilities to God, they would find hope and strength, and even joy, for their earthly pilgrimage. These themes are summarized in the advice that Simon Goulart inscribed in a friend's friendship journal (*Album Amicorum*) in 1585:

1. Live with other people as if God were watching. Speak with God as if others were listening.
2. Endure with the greatest patience what you are not able to change, and walk with God (by whose authority all things occur) without complaining. Evil and wretched is the person who follows after the commander of Hell.
3. In times of activity as much as in periods of rest, all dimensions of life ought to be beautiful.
4. Commit your way to God. Hope in him, and he will do it.

Goulart concluded this summary of his life philosophy with the following words: "[Only] eternal things endure."[46]

This high-minded vision of the Christian life was often tested by the challenges of daily living. For one thing, the ministers and their families could never escape the intense gaze and gossip of Geneva's residents. As *personnes de qualité*—men of learning and social importance—Geneva's pastors occupied a prominent place in city life, and their households were constantly in public view.[47] Ministerial families were scrutinized and criticized, the topic of conversation and the object of juicy gossip that raced through the marketplace, city taverns, and rural villages. City residents monitored the ministers' spending habits, judged the behavior of their children, commented on the style of clothing worn by their wives—always on the lookout for ministerial hypocrisy or pretense. Hence, in 1565 a widow named Charlotte Pinou criticized Beza in public for preaching about generosity and charity, while at the same time outfitting his home with superfluous decorations that should have been donated to the poor. Certainly Calvin had never lived so ostentatiously, she insisted! A violent husband named Jacques de Sartenbaud angrily denounced his minister Goulart for meddling in his affairs: "those who try to reform the church would be well advised to first reform their own households," he argued. In a similar fashion, when the minister of Bossey named Jean d'Espoir preached a sermon against taverns and drunkards in 1563, one of his parishioners complained that the sermon was better directed against the pastor's own wife who (it was reported) had recently become so inebriated in the city that she had to be carried back to her rural parsonage. When Marie Pinault, the divorced wife of Honoré Blanchard, wore clothing in public that indicated she was still a virgin, heads turned and tongues wagged...and reports of the scandal reached all the way to Scotland.[48] Slanderous reports about Geneva's ministers were also not uncommon. One rumor announced that, in his final days, Calvin had prayed to the devil. Another reported that city ministers had impregnated several servant girls. Yet another announced that Geneva's pastors were meeting secretly in Beza's home to play cards and gamble.[49]

Pastoral households were subject to the same difficulties faced by other households in sixteenth-century Geneva. Petty theft was a recurrent problem: A linen cloth was pilfered from Calvin's home; a thief took Jean Pinault's personal Bible and sold it for 30 sols; a dishonest servant stole scissors belonging to the wife of Raymond Chauvet; a peasant woman took eggs, butter, and wine from the parsonage of Antoine Chauve in Russin; a thief snatched Beza's prized pocket watch and never returned it.[50] As we shall see in subsequent chapters, Geneva's ministers were frequently criticized and sometimes even threatened for things they announced from the pulpit or for the corrective discipline they applied to moral offenders. Occasionally, members of their families or households were also subject to verbal or physical abuse. In 1589, for example, a servant boy from David Le Boiteux's household was beaten within an inch of his life when he grazed his cows in the field of the local butcher.[51] Likewise, when the wife of the minister Gilles Chausse attempted to intervene in a shouting match between neighbors from the perch of her windowsill in 1568, one of the aggrieved parties turned on her, calling her a "drunkard" and ridiculing her velvet headdress.[52] Only rarely did resentment harbored toward Geneva's ministers result in hostile actions directed against their families. One such example took place in 1567, when Raymond Chauvet and his wife were pelted with stones by a disgruntled parishioner named Christoffle Mercier, who was angry that the minister did not allow him to bring his musket to church. One of the stones—judged large enough to kill its intended target—narrowly missed Madame Chauvet.[53] As these various anecdotes indicate, Geneva's ministers and their households were constantly in the public eye, the subject of conversation and sometimes controversy. Membership in a pastoral household brought with it a kind of social notoriety, but also a measure of uncomfortable scrutiny.

2. Pastors and Family Relationships

Descriptions of the ministers' domestic duties shed only meager light on more important questions about the emotional quality of pastoral marriages and family life in late sixteenth- and early seventeenth-century Geneva. Did the ministers and their wives share emotional intimacy and affection in their marriage relationships? Were the pastors and their wives devoted and loving parents, committed to the emotional well-being and nurture of their children? Historians in the 1970s, following the ground-breaking study of Philippe Ariès, argued that European parents before the nineteenth century were, on the whole, indifferent to their children and avoided emotional attachments to them, in large part because so many children died in infancy. According to this thesis, the very idea of "childhood" as a separate stage of human development only emerged in the seventeenth century, as the dominant model of family life based on open lineage and the strong authoritarian father was replaced by the modern "closed domestic nuclear family."[54] Other scholars drew similar conclusions about the quality of relationships between husbands and wives, asserting that marriages in traditional European society were usually void of affection, characterized by cool formality, emotional isolation, and a lack of love.[55] More recently, social historians who study marriage and family life in early modern Europe have discredited such sweeping generalizations, arguing that even if traditional marriages and families were structured differently than today, they were not bereft of emotional attachment or affection.[56] In the case of ministerial families in Geneva, different kinds of historical sources point toward different conclusions: disciplinary and criminal records report marriages and households that were in trouble; on the other hand, private correspondence, poetry, and (rare) journal entries occasionally describe family relationships characterized by intimacy and love.

The registers of Geneva's Consistory for the years 1542 through 1609 call attention to several clerical households and marriages that were dysfunctional and troubled. Members of Calvin's household experienced deep sadness and shame due to the unhappy marriage of Calvin's brother Antoine and his wife Anne, who lived with him in the parsonage on rue des Chanoines. After nearly a decade of suspicion, mutual recrimination, and public scandal, Anne was convicted of committing adultery (a second time) with her husband's servant and their marriage ended in divorce in 1557.[57] A number of Geneva's pastoral families experienced similar kinds of problems. The minister of Bossey, Pierre de L'Escluse, abandoned his wife and children in 1547 and returned to the papal church. In the disciplinary hearing that followed, Geneva's ministers supported his wife's request for a divorce.[58] In the case of the household of Jean Chapuis, preacher in Chêne-Valeiry, it was the wife who threatened to abandon the family due to the fact that the couple had too little money, too many children, and a parsonage that was falling apart.[59] During the sixteenth century, five ministers in all were disciplined for marital infidelity, all of whom were subsequently removed from office by Geneva's magistrates.[60] Perhaps the most notorious case of marital conflict between a pastor and his spouse belongs to Bonaventure Bertram and his wife Geneviève (who was Beza's niece through his first wife). In 1570, Geneviève was suspended from the Lord's Supper and imprisoned for committing adultery with the surgeon who had nursed her to health after she had contracted the plague. From prison, Geneviève gave birth to a child who soon after died—under suspicious circumstances. When the attending pastor urged her to seek God's help, the distraught woman complained in his hearing that "she did not want to pray to God, because he would not help her." This blasphemous statement—or so it was judged by several members of the Venerable Company—further aggravated her situation. In the midst of the crisis, Geneviève and her embarrassed and angry husband began to have bitter arguments: on one occasion he hit her, and she responded by calling him a "villainous pig." In the end, despite the intervention of Madame Beza and Bonaventure Bertram, Geneviève was convicted of blasphemy and forced to undergo the humiliation of making public reparation, walking through the city with torch in hand, crying to God for mercy.[61]

By contrast, a number of Geneva's ministers appear to have had healthy and happy marriages. A sad encomium at the death of a spouse often offers the best (or only) testimony of such domestic contentment. For Calvin, the loss of his wife Idelette after nine years of marriage left a gaping hole in his life. "I am no more than half a man, since God recently took my wife home to himself," Calvin wrote.[62] When Pierre Viret's first wife Elizabeth died in 1546, the distraught husband poured out his heart in similar terms: "With the death of my beloved wife, the Lord has struck me—indeed, my entire family—with the hardest possible blow. He has stripped me of half of myself, and deprived me of a faithful companion, a woman who was a good mistress of the household, a spouse who adapted marvelously to my character, my work, and my whole ministry."[63] Theodore Beza's marriage to Claudine Denosse also appears to have been characterized by mutual respect and deep affection. Beza and Claudine met and were secretly married in Paris in 1544 or 1545 when he was an aspiring young Catholic humanist, and she a chambermaid working for a noble family. Their clandestine marriage was solemnized in a public ceremony in Geneva in November 1548, several weeks after the couple fled France for the sake of the Protestant religion. In the first years of their marriage, Beza wrote a poem in honor of his dear spouse, comparing her to the virtuous wife of Proverbs 31: "Who among men will discover a woman steadfast and virtuous? To find her is to find a treasure. No pearl is more precious!"[64] Beza and Claudine were never able to have children of their own, but even so their home was full of relatives, student boarders, visitors, and maids and servants. When Claudine became ill and died suddenly in 1588, her husband was devastated. Writing to a close friend, Beza poured out the sadness of his heart:

> She was a woman endowed with all the virtues of a wife, with whom I spent 39 years, 5 months, and 28 days in complete harmony. She never undertook formal studies, but she possessed so many remarkable virtues that I found it easy to endure this lack. Nothing more bitter in this life could have happened to me, and I have never craved the comfort of friends more. Just when I am in need of help—soon to be 70 years old, if the Lord wills it—I have lost an incredibly devoted wife. Yet blessed be the name of the Lord.[65]

Although Beza remarried shortly after his wife's death, the memory of his beloved Claudine remained fresh. In his *Poemata* (1597 ed.), the old reformer penned this tribute to their life together: "My Claudia, faithful companion of my exile, you with whom I lived happily through all the various vicissitudes of life during forty years....You were united to me in the flower of youth. You have been so faithful a companion, in sickness and health. No wife was more loved by her husband, and no woman loved her husband with more devotion." Beza's last will and testament instructed that his body be interred next to "my late, and beloved first wife, Claudine Denosse, who for so many years lived with me and assisted me, and performed every duty of a truly Christian wife."[66]

These poignant examples indicate that at least some of Geneva's ministers had great affection for their wives and acknowledged emotional dependence on them. Godly wives provided companionship for their husbands. They gave birth to their children and nurtured them. They brought good order to their households. Calvin, Beza, and their colleagues did not question cultural and religious stereotypes about the inferiority of women in marriage or the husband's responsibility to "rule" the Christian household. But neither did they promote a model of patriarchal marriage characterized by emotional isolation and physical abuse. Calvin once commented: "The man who does not love his wife is a monster (*portentum*)."[67] Beza addressed these matters directly in one of his sermons, speaking to husbands:

> It is true that you are the heads of your wives by the command of God above....But remember that God did not draw the woman from Adam's heel, but from Adam's side. This shows you that she is truly below and inferior to you, but also that she is beside you, which should make clear that she is not your slave. Thus, have nothing to do with all these arguments full of insults, these blows, these beatings, and other violent acts! I do not call such behavior "mastery," but "tyranny" and unbearable inhumanity in the Church.[68]

The death of children offers another precious glimpse into the emotional makeup of Geneva's pastoral households. In the early modern period, nearly half of all children born in Geneva died before reaching adulthood, the victims of such common childhood diseases as dysentery, scarlet fever, the measles, and, most dangerous of all, smallpox.[69] Antoine de Chandieu and his wife Françoise de Felins were well acquainted with this suffering, having witnessed five of their thirteen children die in childhood. In the fall of 1571, Chandieu's daughter Marie came down with a serious lung infection. In a journal entry dated October 4, the distraught father wrote: "Marie, after having coughed for some time, has come down with pneumonia. Lord God, living God, God of life, eternal God, have pity on this dear little one and her two parents. Preserve us in your infinite power, which your great and fatherly goodness has mercifully given to us." The following day, the bereaved Chandieu reported the sad news:

> Towards noon, which was the hour of her birth, Marie fell asleep in the Lord. She had lived seven years, four months, and fourteen days. Her speech and life left her as she was praying to the Lord Jesus. Oh most high and righteous God, righteous judge of all the earth, I worship your judgments. I recognize that I deserve much more than this so harsh a wound. Have pity on me and my family. Comfort the father and mother who are suffering. Withdraw the scourge of your anger. Do not pass judgment on your servants, Lord, for the sake of the love of Jesus Christ, my Master and Savior![70]

Chandieu's anguished response to Marie's death in 1571 serves as eloquent testimony to the deep emotional attachment that this father had for a much-loved daughter. And, in the case of the minister Chandieu, this affection of parent for child was reciprocal. Several years after Chandieu's death, his son Esaïe, paging through his father's personal journal, came across the prayer that his father had written on the occasion of his baptism in 1576. Now, twenty years later, Esaïe added his own inscription to the margins of the journal:

> Grant, oh very kind God, the vow of my pious father, and, as you have blessed him, please bless also his offspring, in keeping with your holy covenant. Oh, all-powerful Father, you who have led me safe and sound by your immense goodness from my birth to this my twentieth year, please welcome me. I place myself under your tutelage. I am yours because of the Lord Jesus Christ. Inspire in me a life lived in such a way that by it, I might serve you and your Church. My God, allow that I might come to deserve to bear the name of my father.[71]

It would be reaching beyond the evidence to suggest that the warm familial relationships experienced by Antoine de Chandieu and Theodore Beza were typical of most clerical households in Geneva. But it would be equally unwarranted to assume that Gilles Chausse's troubled, unhappy marriage was any more representative of the majority of Geneva's ministers. In all likelihood, the emotional temperament of pastoral households in sixteenth- and early seventeenth-century Geneva varied from family to family, ranging from close and intimate to cold, distant, and abusive, depending on the personalities, social conditioning, and moral character of parents and children. What the examples of the households of Beza and Chandieu do show us, however, is that sweeping generalizations that characterize family relationships and pastoral marriages in early modern Europe as "cold and formal," "emotionally detached," or "loveless" are not at all convincing in the face of documentary evidence. For at least some of Geneva's pastors, marriage and family commitments were perfumed by the wonderful scents of mutual devotion, emotional intimacy, and abiding human love.

3. Material Support

In his Commentary on 1 Timothy, John Calvin provided a spiritual rationale for the financial support of good and faithful pastors. Because Christian preachers are the ordinary instruments by which human beings gain knowledge of God and of his salvation, those who are called to the ministry of gospel proclamation are true messengers of God who deserve special honor in the Christian church. In fact, Calvin insisted, where the Word is prized, faithful ministers will be treated with generosity and receive necessary financial support. Satan, on the other hand, attempts to destroy the Word of God by depriving the church of faithful ministers. And one of his chief strategies for accomplishing this is by frightening would-be preachers with the dread of poverty and hunger.[72] In his comments on Paul's well-known statement in 1 Timothy 5.18—"The worker deserves his wages"—Calvin was uncompromising in his insistence on pastoral support: "How intolerable is the ingratitude of those who refuse support to their pastors, to whom they cannot pay an adequate salary!"[73] But the rule of moderation should be observed, as Calvin explained in his treatment of another biblical text (Galatians 6:6): the Apostle Paul "does not want them to have an immoderate and superfluous abundance, but merely that they should not lack any of the necessary supports of life. Ministers should be satisfied with frugal fare, and the danger of luxury and pomp must be avoided."[74] A generation later, the minister Simon Goulart echoed this sentiment in one of his moral discourses, noting that "the pastor of the church ought to live in great simplicity, whether in his lifestyle, his dress, or his interactions with great and ordinary people."[75] This principle of modest pastoral support was observed in practice in Geneva's church during the second half of the sixteenth century. As employees on the city payroll, Geneva's pastors received lodging and wages that enabled them to maintain their parish ministries—but such support was on the whole modest and, at times, even meager.

All of Geneva's pastors were supplied with parish housing, situated either within the walls of the city or in the surrounding villages. When Calvin returned from Strasbourg in 1541, he was assigned the large parsonage on the rue des Chanoines (modern-day rue de Calvin), which he occupied until his death in 1564. The home was conveniently located less than two hundred paces from the temple of St. Pierre and the Hôtel de Ville, in the heart of Geneva's bustling Upper City. Although the precise floor plan of Calvin's residence is not known, it most likely included a sitting room, at least one kitchen, several bedrooms, a study, a courtyard, and a garden—enough space to accommodate Calvin, Idellette, her two children, student borders, and several servants, as well as Antoine Calvin and his wife Anne.[76] Other than his books, Calvin owned little by way of physical possessions. Thus, Geneva's magistrates took it on themselves to outfit the parsonage with necessary furnishings, including three beds, a wash basin, several tables and benches, three trunks, and a dozen stools.[77] Calvin was sensitive to the accusation that he or any of Geneva's ministers were getting rich on the city's payroll; the modesty of his household served as proof that this was not the case: "Everyone knows how simple things are in my home," he once wrote. "They can see that I spend no money on nice clothes, and it is further well known that my brother is not rich, and that what he does have he did not receive from me."[78]

Calvin's residence must have been among the more desirable parsonages in Geneva; after his death, the home was given to Theodore Beza, Calvin's successor, as moderator of the Venerable Company. In his early years in

Geneva, Beza was significantly wealthier than Calvin. Consequently, Beza and Claudine Denosse outfitted the parsonage more sumptuously than the previous tenant, which invited criticisms from some of Geneva's citizens that they were living too extravagantly. Later in life, Beza hung on the walls of his sitting room a half dozen portraits of Protestant leaders, including Calvin, Peter Martyr Vermigli, Wolfgang Musculus, and two of himself—precious reminders of departed friends and God's faithfulness through the years.[79] Several other pastors and their families also lived on the rue des Chanoines during the sixteenth century, including Beza's next-door neighbors Michel and Ayma Cop, the noble-born François Bourgoing, and a much-poorer pastor named Abel Poupin.[80] When Cop died in 1566, he bequeathed the house to his colleague and son-in-law Charles Perrot, who had married his daughter Sara two months earlier. The magistrates did not permit the Perrots to move into the family's dwelling on the rue des Chanoines for nearly a decade, however, due to the minister's pastoral responsibilities elsewhere in the city.

The location of the households of Beza and Perrot indicate the general pattern: ministers who served the three city temples (St. Pierre, St. Gervais, or the Madeleine) were normally given city-owned homes near their parish assignments. The city council frowned upon pastors living too close to one another or inhabiting private homes too far from the churches that they served. Each minister was expected to provide moral supervision and attend to the pastoral needs of the people living in his surrounding neighborhood.[81] One consequence of this arrangement was that when ministers were transferred to different pastoral positions within the city, they were sometimes required to move their households.[82] If frequent complaints from Geneva's ministers are any indication, many of the city-owned parsonages afforded less than ideal living conditions. Gabriel Cusin complained that his house was "too melancholic" and did not provide adequate fresh air. Antoine de La Faye found his parish residence inconvenient and too noisy (it was located next door to a forge). Charles Perrot disapproved of his city-owned parsonage because it was unhealthy and unsuitable for study.[83] When city officials in 1608 inspected Goulart's parsonage in the quarter of St. Gervais, they found it to be "very old and ruinous" and too expensive to repair; they thus recommended that the property be sold and the minister relocated. Goulart stubbornly refused to leave the residence in which his family had lived for nearly forty years, judging such a disruption to be "very aggravating, and hardly beneficial for the general good of the Church."[84] Because of these sorts of problems, by the end of the sixteenth century, Geneva's magistrates increasingly encouraged a rental system where the city subsidized ministers to engage comfortable private homes located in their parishes.

The difficulty of securing adequate pastoral housing was even more acute in the countryside. Most of the ministers who worked in Geneva's surrounding territory lived in parish dwellings that had once belonged to

Catholic priests and vicars before the Reformation. At least some of these parsonages had attached stables and accompanying gardens, fields, or vineyards.[85] Unfortunately, many of these dwellings were also in serious disrepair. Throughout the sixteenth century, Geneva's ministers beat a well-worn path to the city council to complain about the poor condition of ecclesiastical buildings in the countryside. As early as 1544, the minister Henri de La Mare complained about the horrible state of the parsonage at Jussy; even after a wall of the house had collapsed, the magistrates and Calvin seemed to remain unconcerned.[86] As we have seen, the parsonage occupied by Jean Chapuis and his family in the parish of Chêne-Valeiry was so substandard that his wife almost left him because of it. The pastor of Peissy complained that his eyesight was all but ruined by the dank and dirty condition of the parish house.[87] So too, the pastors of Satigny and Russin repeatedly petitioned the Company of Pastors and city officials for more comfortable accommodations for their families.[88] That is not to say that the magistrates completely ignored the situation. Genevan financial records indicate that from time to time the Small Council approved disbursement of funds for the repair of parish buildings in the countryside and to equip them with adequate furnishings. Thus, for example, from 1563 to 1566, the senators approved 53 florins in all to reimburse Gaspard de La Faverge, the minister of Russin, "for the repairs made on his lodging."[89] During this same period, they dispersed another 77 florins 9 sols for repairs on the parsonage at Genthod-Moëns.[90] Nonetheless, it appears that the deplorable condition of Geneva's parish buildings in the countryside constituted a fiscal black hole that the cash-strapped city government could never adequately address.

Surprisingly, some parishes did not have designated lodging for the ministers at all. Osée André, minister of Cartigny, was forced to live outside the bounds of the parish and travel long distances to visit and comfort sick parishioners during most of his fifteen years of ministry there.[91] Similarly, in 1601, the Company of Pastors announced to the magistrates that Jean Gros, minister of Chancy, "still has no means of lodging in his parish to the great detriment of his ministry." The ministers requested that the magistrates arrange for suitable housing for Gros or at least supply him with a horse so that he might provide pastoral care to the people of his far-flung parish.[92] For the Venerable Company, the problem of non-residency in Geneva's countryside parishes was especially galling given long-standing Protestant polemics against the practice of clerical absenteeism in the medieval church. The ministers were uncompromising in their requirement that rural pastors live in their parishes, even when many of these pastors preferred the comfort and security of life in the city. In 1604, parishioners from the village of Jussy complained to the Company of Pastors that their minister Etienne Gros the Younger was not resident in the parish. Having found the parsonage in Jussy in substandard condition, Gros had chosen to live in the city and commute back and forth the six miles to the village. Geneva's ministers would have none of this arrangement. They demanded that Gros "make his ordinary lodging within the parish, whether it be the parsonage or another room of his choosing." This would make it possible not only for him "to preach there each week," but also "to gain a more personal knowledge of his sheep, that desire his presence there."[93] Competent pastoral care required that ministers live in close proximity to their people.

In addition to the parsonage, Geneva's ministers also received a quarterly salary and were given periodic allowances of wheat and wine. Around the time of Calvin's return to Geneva in 1541, the magistrates established a three-tiered salary structure for Geneva's ministers, distinguishing between the moderator of the Company, the other city ministers, and the countryside pastors. The moderator's salary was normally 25–40 percent higher than his city colleagues, in recognition of his special leadership responsibilities within the church. Similarly, the city pastors were paid 25–40 percent more than pastors working in Geneva's rural parishes. Ostensibly, countryside ministers could expect to supplement their regular incomes by grazing livestock and harvesting agricultural products in their gardens. Table 4.1 indicates the salary levels for Geneva's ministers from 1541 to 1609. During these seven decades, the annual salary of the moderator of the Company of Pastors increased from 500 florins to 900/1000 florins; the annual salary of Geneva's city ministers increased from 300 florins to 800 florins; and, the annual salary of Geneva's countryside ministers grew from 200 florins to 500/540 florins. These figures are meaningful, of course, only with respect to their buying power. In the year 1602, for example, one florin (= 12 sols) could purchase at market around six-and-a-half liters of wheat, seven liters of wine, eight loaves of bread, two to three pounds of butter, three pounds of lamb, a dozen oranges, or one hen.[94] Books were somewhat more expensive: the Bible stolen from the minister Pinault in 1567 was sold for two-and-a-half florins.

Despite increasing wages, the buying power of the pastors' salaries actually decreased during the latter half of sixteenth century due to runaway inflation that affected not only Geneva but all of Western Europe. The prices of most basic commodities such as wheat, milk products, fruits and vegetables, meat and fish, wine, salt, clothing, and domestic goods increased significantly. The augmentation of the price of wheat—often employed by historians to measure inflationary pressure in early modern Europe—is indicative of this general increase in living costs in Geneva over these decades. Selling at 8 florins per coupe in 1575, the price of wheat spiked at 23 florins per coupe in 1587, and then fluctuated between 10 and 21 florins per coupe over the following three decades (see graph 4.1).[95] Based on data like this, Jean-François Bergier calculates that the relative value of average clerical salaries in Geneva fell around 40 percent between the years 1569–76 and another 40 percent during the decade spanning 1584–94.[96] The economic situation was especially desperate during Geneva's war

TABLE 4.1 Annual Salaries (in Florins) of Geneva's Pastors, 1541–1609[1]

Year(s)	Moderator	City Ministers	Country Ministers
1541	500	240/300?	200
1542–1558	500	240	200
1559–1562	500	300	240
1563–1569	600	400	260/300
1570–1574	700	500	400
1575–1576	600	400	300
1577–1592	700	500	400
1593–1601	1000	800	500
1602–1604	1000	800	500/540
1605–1609	900	800	500/540

[1] This table is an abridged version of Table I that appears in Jean-François Bergier, "Salaires des Pasteurs de Genève au XVIe Siècle," in *Mélanges d'histoire du XVIe siècle offerts à Henri Meylan*, ed. Henri Meylan (Geneva: Librairie Droz, 1970), 168. The principle currency used in Geneva during this period was the florin (= 12 sols = 144 deniers). Also used was the livre tournois (= 20 sols tournois = 240 deniers tournois), particularly in transactions between French refugees. For the fluctuating value of the florin and the livre tournois relative to the French écu d'or sol, see Annex VII in Liliane Mottu-Weber, *Économie et refuge à Genève au siècle de la réforme: la draperie et la soierie (1540–1630)* (Geneva: Librairie Droz, 1987).

with the Duke of Savoy from 1589 to 1593, when the city was blockaded and crops and livestock in the surrounding countryside were destroyed by marauding armies.

In an effort to soften the impact of rising prices, the Venerable Company in the 1570s petitioned the Small Council to pay a portion of their annual salary "in nature" rather than "in coin." Accordingly, in 1575, the magistrates reduced clerical salaries by 100 florins and began providing each member of the pastoral company with a supplement of 20 coupes of wheat per year (worth 165 florins in that year).[97] This supplement, which became a regular part of pastoral compensation thereafter, was increased to 28 coupes per year by the end of the century.[98] The wheat given to the ministers was not always of the highest quality—indeed, sometimes it was judged "extremely bad." But as the price of grain soared, these payments "in nature" became an ever-larger proportion of the ministers' annual compensation.[99] Geneva's magistrates also furnished the pastors with occasional gifts of wine to compensate for their modest wages and offset the erosive effects of inflation. As the moderator of the Company of Pastors, Beza received each year a

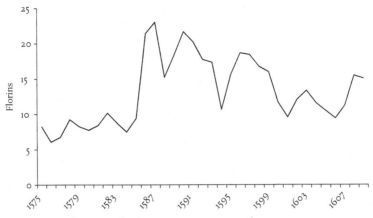

GRAPH 4.1 Price of Coupe of Wheat in Geneva, 1575–1609

payment of one char (649 liters) of wine—he requested that it be *white* wine, befitting his aristocratic taste.[100] In 1577, the magistrates also began to provide occasional allocations of wine (whether red or white) to the other ministers in the city and countryside.[101] Despite these provisions, it seems that Geneva's pastors were not paid particularly well during the generations after Calvin. In the early seventeenth century, the salary of a countryside minister was roughly equivalent to the annual income of a cobbler's assistant.[102] Geneva's city ministers were somewhat better off, but their annual compensation still fell well below the salary of 1,500 florins (plus subsidies of wheat valued at 324 florins) that the illustrious professor of law Denys Godefroy received when he was called to the Academy in 1604.[103]

The overall financial condition of Geneva's pastors between 1536 and 1609 varied widely. Ministers from noble families that boasted significant wealth such as Nicolas Des Gallars, Jean Trembley, or Antoine de Chandieu were probably affected little by soaring prices or the pinch of modest pastoral salaries. Robert Kingdon has shown that several of these ministers engaged in economic activity during their tenures in Geneva, including buying and selling property and lending money at interest.[104] In addition, the account books of the *Bourse française* indicate that no fewer than fourteen ministers made contributions to this welfare fund for poor French immigrants between the years 1550–1559. Listed among the donors one finds the names of John Calvin, Guillaume Farel, Nicolas Des Gallars, Michel Cop, Antoine de Chandieu, François Bourgoing, Nicolas Colladon, and Jean Trembley.[105]

But if some of Geneva's ministers possessed adequate resources to support their households, many others did not. Pastors with large families faced the greatest difficulties. The countryside minister Abraham de La Maisonneuve found it impossible to provide daily bread for his wife and seven (surviving) children on his salary and had to supplement his household's income by "working with his hands." Jean Jaquemot requested transfer to the church of Neuchâtel because his family of six was "unable to live on the wages provided by the magistrates." Etienne de Brulères left his countryside post and returned to pastoral ministry in France because he was unable to support his household of eight children in Geneva.[106] The financial pressure was particularly acute in the early 1570s and during the war with Savoy in the 1590s. In June of 1574, the ministers in the countryside petitioned the Company of Pastors to intervene on their behalf before the Small Council to alleviate their poverty. They argued that even for a pastor without children "it is extremely difficult or even impossible for him to maintain his household well on his wages." On this occasion, the Venerable Company encouraged impoverished ministers to communicate their particular concerns to the magistrates but decided not to lodge an official request lest it appear that Geneva's pastors were ungrateful or greedy for material wealth.[107] Twenty years later, the Company of Pastors did petition the Small Council for more adequate financial support for the ministers, noting that "for the last seven years wages have only covered six months worth of expenses."[108]

Geneva's magistrates provided alms and small gifts of grain to those ministers who were in the greatest need. In the 1540s and 1550s, the minister Abel Poupin received special donations from the city treasury on no fewer than eight occasions to relieve his extreme poverty. In 1556, the secretary noted in the council's minutes: "The councilors have received a report about the misery and poverty of the minister Abel Poupin, who has been sick for a long time and lives in a house that is in total ruin." On this occasion, the senators voted to give Poupin a gift of 25 florins and six coupes of wheat, as well as reimburse him for a robe he had purchased out of his meager resources.[109] Over the decades that followed, Geneva's magistrates gave similar charitable gifts to other ministers: 10 florins to Nicolas Petit in 1564; 25 florins to Charles Malbué in 1566; 14 coupes of wheat to Nicolas Petit in 1567; 25 coupes of wheat to Gilles Chausse in 1573; 6 coupes of wheat to each of Geneva's ministers in the city and countryside in 1574.[110] Beza and the ministers of the Venerable Company recognized that debt and desperate poverty constituted a "great impediment" to effective ministry for several of their colleagues but could do very little to alleviate the situation.[111] In the end, a number of Geneva's pastors died penniless. This was the case with Gilles Chausse. In June of 1574, as Chausse lay dying of the plague, he summoned the Company of Pastors to his bedside. He confessed his faith in Christ and stated his readiness to "depart this miserable life" and "go to God who was calling him." However, he was worried about the well-being of his wife and three children, whom he was leaving "poor and burdened with debts without any means to pay them." After Chausse's death, the magistrates of the city agreed to provide his widow and children with a pension of ten florins and a coupe of wheat each month.[112]

Severe financial hardship is witnessed even in the case of Theodore Beza, the best-paid member of the Company of Pastors during the generation after Calvin's death. Although born into France's lower nobility, he had renounced his rights of inheritance when he fled to Geneva in 1548. Forty years later, Beza found his economic resources depleted and his annual salary inadequate in the face of inflation to support the expenses of his household. In 1591, the register of the Small Council reported that "Monsieur Beza is in some need."[113] The following year, Beza contributed 10 écus to a special collection for the city poor, even though he now had only 200 écus (around 1600 florins) to his name, not counting furniture and books.[114] During the last decade of his life, Beza attempted to stave off creeping poverty by soliciting financial assistance from Geneva's magistrates and foreign friends in Bohemia, Germany, and France—including Henry of Navarre, king of France. The sale of his library to a Czech nobleman in 1599 for 600 gold crowns also helped alleviate his poverty and assured a pension for his widow after his death.[115]

Beza's experience was far from unique. As we have seen, many of the ministers of Geneva battled financial hardships during the last decades of the sixteenth century. Pastoral ministry in Geneva may have been viewed as a high and sacred calling, but it did not pay very well. In a sermon delivered from the pulpit of St. Pierre in the early 1590s, the elderly Beza reminded his congregation of its responsibility to provide necessary financial support for the ministers. Christians "are guilty not only of theft, but sacrilege" when they "refuse to provide support (*nouriture*) to their poor pastors, who fulfill their duty to them." They should "pay their pastors what they deserve." At the same time, Beza warned his pastoral colleagues against becoming religious mercenaries who served the church for the sake of money, for "holy things are not to be sold, but given from the hand of God by means of his servants." So too, pastors must guard against covetousness and greed, lest they become like those priests in the Old Testament whom the prophets condemned for "devouring the people as bread." Instead, faithful Christian ministers must follow Paul's injunction in 1 Timothy 6:8, learning "to be content with food and whatever else is provided them, even if it is much less than what is needed."[116] With these words, then, Beza captured the principle of moderate pastoral support articulated by John Calvin decades earlier: reformed ministers are not mercenaries for hire nor are they mendicants who beg for daily bread. Instead, they are servants of Christ's church, called to share freely the means of grace offered by God to his people. Certainly, Christian workers deserve their wages, but they must never demand them as a right.

As we have discovered, the pastoral vocation in late sixteenth-century Geneva was not at all an ivory-tower affair. Geneva's pastors were called to a lifetime of study, godly conversation, Christian proclamation, meditation, and prayer. But this God-intoxicated manner of life needed to be expressed within, and accommodated to, an everyday world full of leaky roofs, rising prices, critical neighbors, misbehaving children, sick spouses, and modest wages. Goulart's life philosophy—summarized in the maxim "only eternal things endure"—was not a call for otherworldly asceticism but served as a sober reminder that the eternal and the mundane were never very far apart. God's work needed to be accomplished in the Christian household as well as in the Christian church. God's will was to be done on earth as well as in heaven.

CHAPTER 5 | Rhythms of Ministry

EVERY SUNDAY MORNING IN all of Geneva's temples, the minister concluded the 8 a.m. preaching service with a long prayer of intercession. Reciting words taken from Calvin's liturgy, the presiding minister prayed for princes and magistrates, for men and women living in spiritual darkness, for those suffering bodily afflictions and persecutions, for Christians in their daily struggles against sin and temptation. The pastoral prayer also included special petitions for workers in Christ's church:

> We pray to you, true Father and Savior, for all of those whom you have cho-
> sen to be pastors of your faithful people and to whom you have entrusted
> responsibility for souls and the administration of your holy gospel. We pray
> that you might guide them by your Holy Spirit that they might prove to be
> faithful and loyal ministers of your glory, always having this goal: to gather
> together all of the wandering sheep and to bring them to the Lord Jesus
> Christ, the chief pastor and the prince of all bishops, so that, day by day,
> God's flock might benefit and mature in him, with all righteousness and
> godliness. Likewise, we pray that you might deliver all of your churches from
> the jaws of hungry wolves, and from all mercenaries, who seek only their
> own ambition or benefit, and not the praise of your holy name (which is
> primary) and the salvation of your flock.[1]

The words of this prayer summarize the nature and purpose of ministry in Calvinist Geneva: the minister is a servant of Christ and a shepherd of God's people, responsible for proclaiming the gospel and protecting the church from spiritual predators. The purpose of ministry is first and foremost to declare the glory of God, as well as to promote the salvation of the elect. This vision for ministry—impressed on pastors and layper-sons alike through the cadence of the liturgy—took tangible form in the various duties that ministers engaged in week by week, year after year. Geneva's ministers preached sermons and performed the sacraments; they consoled the sick and instructed the wayward and ignorant. In their weekly assemblies, they studied Scripture together, supervised church life, and exercised church discipline. A sizeable number of Geneva's ministers also expressed their sacred vocations by writing books that commented on sacred Scripture, defended reformed doctrine, promoted Christian devotion, and battled the "wolves and mercenaries" that constantly threatened the flock of God. Although the specific "job description" of Geneva's ministers varied slightly depending on personal giftedness and parish assignment, nonetheless, one can identify a definite pastoral rhythm, as well as specific duties that were shared by all members of the Venerable Company who served the Genevan church from 1536 to 1609. This chapter will shed light on these pastoral rhythms by describing the manner in which Geneva's ministers structured liturgical time over the course of the year and performed their regular duties week to week. As will become clear, pastoral ministry in sixteenth-century Geneva was inseparable from the rigorous study and regular proclamation of the Christian Scripture. In the final section of this chapter, I will describe the special responsibilities and difficulties encountered by Geneva's ministers who worked in the countryside parishes. Though Calvin and his colleagues insisted that all Geneva's pastors possessed the same religious calling and the same spiritual authority, in point of fact, countryside ministers faced a unique set of challenges that made their daily lives more lonely, difficult, and dangerous than the ministers in the city.

1. *Liturgical Time*

The Protestant Reformation dramatically restructured liturgical time in sixteenth-century Geneva. The Catholic tradition had organized the liturgical calendar and celebrated the passage of time according to a sequence of church festivals and saint's days. The Catholic liturgical year was divided into two parts.[2] From late November to June, Catholics observed the ritual enactment of the life and ministry of Jesus Christ through the major feast days of Christmas (preceded by four Sundays of Advent), Epiphany (January 6), Easter (preceded by Ash Wednesday and forty days of Lent), Ascension (forty days after Easter), Pentecost (fifty days after Easter), and Corpus Christi (eleven days after Pentecost). The second half of the year, from late June to late November, contained the majority of saint's days, including five of the seven major feasts to the Virgin Mary[3]; days commemorating each of the twelve apostles and the fourteen auxiliary saints; as well as the Feast of All Saints (November 1) and All Soul's Day (November 2). In the region of Savoy and Geneva, festivals dedicated to minor saints such as Saint Claude were especially important. Throughout Catholic Europe, between forty and sixty days a year were set aside as "holy days," marked by abstaining from work, special processions and Masses, and communal celebrations.[4] In addition to religious festivals, the traditional liturgical year also included several dozen fast days—during Lent and on the eve of festivals—for the purpose of self-mortification and to imitate Christ's own forty-day fast and temptation in the wilderness.

Reformed churchmen attempted to dismantle this ritualistic universe, arguing that prescribed days of feasting and fasting promoted a theology of "works-righteousness," and encouraged superstition, drunkenness, and idleness. Ulrich Zwingli recommended that the annual number of religious holidays be reduced to five, namely, Christmas; Annunciation; and three newly created feast days commemorating the martyrs, the evangelists, and the prophets and church fathers.[5] The reformed church of Bern observed only the four festivals of Christmas, the Circumcision of Christ (January 1), Annunciation, and Ascension during which normal work activities were suspended. Most radical of all was the proposal made by Martin Bucer in his Strasbourg liturgy of 1525 that eliminated all religious holidays, with the exception of the weekly observance of the Lord's Day. As we saw in chapter 1, Geneva's magistrates after the revolution of 1536 followed the example of its political ally Bern by mandating that the four festivals of Christmas, the Circumcision of Christ, Annunciation, and Ascension should be observed in Geneva each year. Calvin and Farel voiced their strong opposition to this decision, both because they believed it constituted undue magisterial interference in the church's affairs, and because they feared that observing traditional festivals would cause confusion and reinforce long-standing superstition as to the sacred value of certain days and seasons. After Calvin's return from Strasbourg in 1541, he and his pastoral colleagues renewed their efforts to expunge feast days from Geneva's religious calendar. In 1545, they convinced Geneva's magistrates to suppress the feasts of the Circumcision of Christ, Annunciation, and Ascension. Five years later, after a protracted campaign on the part of the city ministers, the Small Council passed an edict that proscribed all religious holidays in the city, including the feast of Christmas, requiring Geneva's citizens to treat them as ordinary workdays. The Lord's Supper, customarily celebrated on Christmas Day, would henceforth be observed on the Sunday nearest to December 25. Calvin insisted that the Lord's Day, or Sunday, was the Christian's true "holiday," the day when ordinary work was set aside so that believers might worship God and be instructed in his Word.

Geneva's decision to abolish traditional Catholic festivals met with stiff resistance from many city residents, some of whom did not hesitate to voice their criticism in public. In 1554, a woman named Michée bluntly informed her pastor Raymond Chauvet that "the festivals had been observed before [the magistrates' edict] and would continue to be observed thereafter."[6] Several years later, Antoine Cadran was summoned to Consistory for complaining to his neighbors that the church of Geneva was out of step with the territory of reformed Bern by not celebrating Christmas, even though the festival (Cadran asserted) was mandated by Scripture as a commemoration of Noah's flood. The Consistory suspended Cadran from the Lord's

Supper for his impertinence and lies; at the same time, the ministers and elders felt the need to justify their restrictive policy: "in regard to the observance of the day of Christmas, things that are indifferent should not be formalized, and we do not condemn [other reformed cities] that observe such a day, provided that they do so without superstition." In the case of Geneva, however, it was necessary "to remove this festival because it was apparent that the people treated it in a superstitious manner."[7] Despite this explanation, a sizeable number of Genevans remained opposed to the city's policy on feast days and resented the ministers who enforced it. A widow named Clauda Boisier probably spoke for many when, in 1568, she stated that "the day of Noel was a good festival and that Monsieur Calvin and Monsieur Beza had abolished it."[8] Many other men and women ignored the city's edict and secretly observed traditional festivals and fast days, either in the privacy of their homes or by traveling to territories adjacent to Geneva to celebrate them. Though the ministers attempted to put a stop to such activities, they were never entirely successful.

During the second half of the sixteenth century, the Consistory sporadically investigated and reprimanded people suspected of celebrating the feasts of Christmas, Epiphany, Ascension, or of observing the Lenten fast.[9] Besides Christmas, the feast day of Epiphany on January 6—the celebration of the three kings who visited the infant Jesus—was especially popular. In this traditional holiday, celebrants feasted upon a cake with a bean baked inside of it. The fortunate person who found the bean in his piece of cake was proclaimed king and permitted to rule over "his subjects" for the remainder of the day. Oftentimes, the privilege of being "king" brought with it the obligation to provide abundant quantities of wine to make glad the hearts of the celebrants.[10] Traditional festivals like these were particularly difficult to eradicate from peasant life in Geneva's rural territories. Drawing from his experience in the parish of Genthod-Moëns, Charles Perrot reported as follows: "The servants also have a custom of abstaining from work on the days of Christmas, Circumcision, Ascension and Annunciation, under the guise that previously in their country they were required to observe these particular festivals. I have not had much success in keeping them from doing this." Perrot wondered if the ministers' efforts to suppress traditional religious holidays might be ill-advised, particularly given that Geneva's practice was based on "a political, not a spiritual ordinance."[11]

By the turn of the seventeenth century, it appears that other members of the Venerable Company were beginning to share Perrot's doubts about the wisdom of prohibiting all religious festivals. In December of 1604, rumors circulated through Geneva that many of the city's ministers were now in favor of reinstating the feast days of Christmas, Circumcision, Annunciation, and Ascension in keeping with the example of Bern and other reformed cities in Switzerland.[12] Four months later, the Council of 200 requested a formal statement on the subject from the ministers. On this occasion, the Company of Pastors adopted a unified stance, sending Antoine de La Faye to the council chambers to exhort the magistrates to allow no modification in Geneva's religious practice. Appealing to the happy memory of John Calvin, La Faye warned the senators that reestablishing religious festivals would cause scandal and give the impression that Geneva was sliding back toward the papal church. Change was, by its very nature, perilous: "we have always recognized that change and novelty are extremely dangerous, especially in ecclesiastical matters," he insisted.[13] It was crucial that the religious reforms instituted by Calvin be preserved.

Calvin and the ministers of Geneva replaced the traditional church calendar with a new conception of religious time structured around the celebration of the Lord's Supper and the weekly observance of the Lord's Day. The *Ecclesiastical Ordinances* (1541) stipulated that the Lord's Supper should be celebrated in Geneva's churches four times a year, at Christmas time, Easter, Pentecost, and on the first Sunday in September.[14] Over the next century, these four annual communion services provided the basic structure for Geneva's religious life and shaped pastoral ministry in a variety of important ways. The rhythm of church discipline, of censure, repentance, and restoration, was tied closely to the quarterly communion cycle. The Consistory faced an especially heavy load of disciplinary cases in the weeks leading up to the four annual celebrations of the Lord's Supper, and a disproportionately large number of people were suspended from or restored to the sacrament of the Table during this period. To handle this increased workload, the Consistory met twice rather than once during the week prior to communion Sunday. Likewise, Geneva's church constitution required that ministers visit the households in their parishes during the weeks prior to the celebration of the Lord's Supper at Easter to ensure that all men and women who partook of the bread and wine possessed a basic understanding of the Christian message.[15] The quarterly communion cycle also informed the practice of worship and preaching in reformed Geneva. Although the seasons of Advent and Lent were no longer formally recognized, Calvin and his colleagues sometimes set aside the normal *lectio continua* method of biblical exposition to deliver sermons on the nativity of the Lord at Christmas time or a sermon series on the passion and resurrection of Jesus Christ during the weeks prior to the Lord's Supper at Easter.[16] In addition, on communion Sunday, city ordinances required ministers to devote part of their sermons "to explain to the people what the Lord wishes to say and signify by this [sacramental] mystery, and in what manner we should receive it."[17]

Another institution of the Genevan church that was tied to the quarterly communion cycle was the Ordinary Censure. Four times a year, on the Friday before the Lord's Supper, the ministers of the city and countryside, and professors from the Academy met behind closed doors to air their grievances and offer fraternal correction on matters of doctrine and personal moral character.[18] As a visible sign of their unity, the ministers concluded the Ordinary Censure by sharing a meal of soup together.[19] Although the issues addressed during the quarterly censure were normally cloaked in secrecy, the registers of the Company of Pastors provide occasional glimpses into these sessions, testifying to the fact that Geneva's pastors did not always agree on matters of policy and doctrine, and sometimes struggled to get along with one another. It was in the Ordinary Censure of spring 1549 that the minister Jean Ferron was examined and reprimanded by the Company of Pastors for propositioning and groping one of his female servants.[20] Around a decade later, the pastor of Draillans, Nicolas Petit, was censured for (among other things) slandering one of the magistrates, behaving in an arrogant fashion, and refusing to receive the correction of his colleagues—actions that were deemed "unworthy of a minister of the Word of God."[21] In September 1575, the ministers censured Bonaventure Bertram for harboring animosity toward Theodore Beza (his wife's uncle) on account of a financial disagreement between the men. Ten years later, in 1585, the ministers devoted one of the quarterly censures to examining the contents of Beza's book against the French Hebraicist Gilbert Genebrard and discussing whether it should be published. The following year, the Company called on Charles Perrot to explain a controversial document that he had written and to examine more carefully his convictions regarding justification by faith and the sacraments. In 1598, the Venerable Company censured the pastor of Vandoeuvres Jean Du Perril for beating one of his parishioners, who had arrived late to the Sunday service, in full view of his congregation. Again, in 1601, the ministers investigated and then censured city pastor Jean Jaquemot for an inflammatory sermon in which he stated doubts as to whether any of Geneva's magistrates were truly Christian men.[22] The fact that the Ordinary Censure was held shortly before the quarterly celebration of the Lord's Supper was not accidental. These sessions provided a regular venue for Geneva's ministers and professors to redress moral infractions, personal hostilities, and theological differences with colleagues in private, thereby enabling them to approach the Lord's Table with pure consciences and at peace with their brothers. Conflicts and disagreements were inevitable, but the Ordinary Censure was one important way in which Geneva's ministers adjudicated those differences and maintained the unity of the Venerable Company.

Although Calvin and the Venerable Company stripped Geneva's religious calendar of those traditional fast days associated with Lent and observed on the eve of Catholic festivals, it was not their intention to eliminate the practice of fasting altogether. In the *Institutes*, Calvin recommended both private and public fasting as important spiritual disciplines to help Christians subdue the lust of their flesh, foster prayer and meditation, and express their self-abasement and sin before God. Calvin believed that public fasts were especially crucial in times of disaster or trouble: "if either pestilence, or famine, or war begins to rage, or if any disaster seems to threaten any district and people—then also it is the duty of the pastors to urge the church to fasting, in order that by supplication the Lord's wrath may be averted."[23] Accordingly, as the religious fortunes of reformed churches in France deteriorated in the 1560s, and as Geneva's own political security became more tenuous after Calvin's death, the Venerable Company began to call for public fasts with increasing regularity. The first public fast in reformed Geneva was organized in October 1567 in response to the Catholic take-over of the city of Lyon and the massive flow of Protestant refugees that ensued. Theodore Beza and his colleagues organized a second day of com-munity-wide fasting and prayer in September 1572 as reports of the horrific slaughter of reformed Christians on St. Bartholomew's Day filtered back to Geneva. Six years later, amidst rumors that Spanish and Savoyard troops were preparing a surprise attack on Geneva, the Venerable Company once again called for a day of public fasting "so that it might please God to turn his wrath away from our sins and by his grace break the machinations of the enemies who plot so strongly against this Church."[24] This fast, which lasted from early morning until 3 p.m., included sermons in all three of the city's temples, readings from the Old Testament prophets Isaiah and Joel, and congregational singing of the Psalms, notably Psalm 69: "Save me, O God! For the waters have come up to my neck." The ministers added special exhortations for Geneva's townspeople to humble themselves as well as words of comfort "to console them in the grace and truth of our Lord."[25] The practice of holding public fasts during times of extreme danger, or to celebrate occasions of divine deliverance, became a common aspect of Geneva's religious life thereafter.[26] In 1640, the "Genevan Fast" (Le jeûne genevois) was adopted as an annual religious holiday in Geneva—testifying both to the popularity of this spiritual exercise and to how far it now departed from Calvin's original vision.

2. The Pastors' Weekly Schedule

In the same way that the quarterly celebration of the Lord's Supper pro-vided basic structure for Geneva's religious calendar during the year, reg-ular worship services in Geneva's temples set the cadence for corporate religious life from week to week. These worship services also formed a significant part of the workload for Calvin, Beza, Goulart, and their col-leagues. By the 1550s, the team of ministers who served Geneva's three urban temples, St. Pierre, St. Gervais, and the Madeleine, was required by city statute to conduct a total of thirty-three worship services each week, including services every weekday morning, the Day of Prayer on Wednesday morning, and three sermons on Sunday. The chief pastors in the city, men like Calvin, Cop, Des Gallars, Beza, Goulart, Jaquemot, and Perrot, bore the heaviest responsibility for these preaching assignments, delivering as many as eight or nine sermons every fortnight. Ministers who possessed more modest homiletic gifts preached less frequently, but all pastors were expected to deliver at least a couple of sermons each week. It was inconceivable that a minister of the Word would not preach. As for the pastors in the countryside parishes, their preaching schedules usually included one or two sermons on Sunday, as well as a weekday sermon on Wednesday or Thursday.

Sunday was a day of worship and spiritual rest in sixteenth- and early seventeenth-century Geneva. Once a year, the Small Council dispatched a town crier throughout the city to remind the inhabitants that they were required by law to attend the Wednesday morning prayer service as well as the Sunday morning and afternoon services each week.[27] City ordinances stipulated that all boutiques and shops remain closed for the duration of these worship services. Moreover, all Genevan workers, with the exception of those who provided essential daily services such as bakers and city guards, were required to refrain from their daily labors on Sunday so that they might participate in sacred services and experience physical and spiritual refreshment. These regulations achieved social as well as spiritual purposes. Participation at the worship service was a public statement that Geneva's townspeople shared the same Christian faith and were members together of the same Christian republic. Attendance at sermons, celebrating the sacraments, treating Sunday as a sacred day—these were civic duties that confirmed the confessional unity and political cohesiveness of the community. Members of the Consistory argued this very point in the case of a notorious sermon-skipper named Pierre Silmandi, whom they sent to the Small Council for punishment in the spring of 1566. The Consistory requested that the magistrates force Silmandi "to fulfill his duty as a Christian and to recognize that he is a citizen and yet is not fulfilling his duty as a citizen."[28]

Evidently, the chief justification that Calvin and Beza gave for Sunday observance was not civic responsibility, but a particular theological understanding of the fourth commandment of the Decalogue and its application to the Christian church.[29] The reformers believed that the Jewish Sabbath, commanded by God in the Old Testament (Exodus 20:8–11), not only set in place political and ceremonial requirements for the ancient Jewish nation but also prefigured the spiritual rest promised with the advent of the messiah. Consequently, the Jewish Sabbath was abrogated in the ministry of Jesus Christ and was no longer binding on Christians, who experience a perpetual Sabbath, finding renewal and spiritual rest from works righteousness each day of their lives through faith in Jesus Christ. However, the fourth commandment of the Decalogue, with its requirement for stated times of worship, meditation, and rest, was not abrogated with the coming of Christ and remains part of God's immutable moral law for all human beings. Calvin believed that the particular day of the week that Christians set aside for corporate worship was an indifferent matter; however, for the sake of good order, he believed that Christians were wise to accept the traditional practice of observing Sunday as a special day of worship and rest. The central concern of the fourth commandment was not that men and women protect the sanctity of a particular day, but that they observe lives characterized by regular rhythms of public worship, prayer, and private meditation on God's works. As Calvin commented:

> For if the stores and businesses are closed on Sundays so that no one has to work as during the week, we have a much greater opportunity to devote our time to things to which God calls us, such as instruction in his Word, coming together to confess our faith, to call on his name and to participate in the celebration of the sacraments.[30]

Beza echoed Calvin's sentiments in his paraphrase to Psalm 92: "Thus, the principle point is this, that there might be one day set aside, dedicated to the normal meeting of the faithful in which the word of God might be taught, the sacraments administered, along with prayers and praises to God and works of grace."[31]

In point of fact, many of Geneva's citizens disobeyed the city's statutes regulating the Lord's Day. Already in the mid 1550s, Calvin complained in a sermon that many Genevans neglected religious instruction and worship on Sundays:

> If there be one day in the week reserved for religious instruction when they have spent six days in their own business, they are apt to spend the day which is set apart for worship, in play and pastime; some rove about the fields, others go to taverns to quaff; and there are undoubtedly at this time as many at the last mentioned place, as we here assembled in the name of God.[32]

Between 1542 and 1609, the Consistory frequently interviewed and sometimes reprimanded people for working on Sunday, whether for pruning trees, making lace, selling tripe, unloading boats, hunting birds, or moving furniture.[33] The Consistory also disciplined people for engaging in recreational activities on Sunday that were deemed inappropriate for spiritual refreshment, such as hunting, dancing, banqueting, playing tennis or billiards, or bowling skittles.[34] When Sunday labor was born out of service to the community rather than avarice, the ministers normally showed leniency. For example, in 1561 they dismissed with only a gentle admonition two cobblers who spent a Sunday afternoon repairing a leather oxen yoke for a traveler passing through the city.[35] The ministers and elders took stronger measures against people who frequently neglected Sunday worship services out of indifference, greed, or desire for pleasure. Hence, Pernette Dupré was suspended for missing three months of sermons without excuse. Louis Curlet was barred from the Table for averring that sermon attendance was for wealthy people, "not for poor workers like himself." Antoine Decroux was suspended from the Lord's Supper for transporting nuts to the countryside instead of attending the Sunday sermon. Hubert Le Sec and Guillaume Morand were suspended and sentenced by the magistrates to three days in prison on bread and water for gambling with keys (*joue aux clefs*) at Plainpalais during the Sunday morning sermon.[36] As each example illustrates, the Consistory's campaign to protect Sunday observance was particularly focused on enforcing attendance at worship services. Between 1542 and 1609, only a handful of Genevans were actually suspended from the Lord's Supper for *working* on Sunday; many more were excommunicated for regular absence from or misbehavior during Sunday sermons. Faithfulness to the fourth commandment required not simply that Christians abstain from physical labor and recreation, but that they perform their holy service to God by hearing the Word preached, participating in the Lord's Supper, and singing psalms of praise and thanksgiving to God. The ministers made this point abundantly clear to Pierre Quemoz, after he missed the Sunday sermons to transport animal hides to Annemasse in the spring of 1571: Christians should "work during the week and serve God on Sunday," they stated.[37]

In addition to sermons and worship services, Geneva's ministers were expected to engage in a variety of other pastoral activities each week. On Thursdays at noon, they met in the Consistory for several hours to address disciplinary cases. On Friday mornings, the ministers convened in the Auditoire for the weekly Congregation, a meeting of clergy and interested laypeople to discuss questions of biblical exegesis and theology. Immediately following the Congregation, Geneva's ministers retired to their private chambers for the weekly session of the Company of Pastors to discuss the business of Christ's church, both locally and internationally.[38] The ministers' regular schedule was further crowded with weddings and baptisms (performed in conjunction with the daily preaching services), household visitations, spiritual counsel of parishioners, personal study, and sermon preparation. In addition, many of Geneva's city ministers were assigned ancillary duties related to religious education or pastoral care in the city: some served as military chaplains or professors at the Academy, others were appointed to visit the hospital and prison, or to administer the city's *bourse* for poor students and immigrants. And on top of everything else, nearly one in six of Geneva's ministers was a published author.

Balancing the daily activities of public ministry with the requirement for private study must have been a challenge for the ministers of the Venerable Company. Sermons and books were not created *ex nihilo*, but required pastors to spend many hours behind their desks, studying the biblical text (in the original Greek and Hebrew languages), consulting commentaries, reading the latest theological work, praying, and writing. The *Ecclesiastical Ordinances* (1541) mandated that Geneva's pastors be lifelong students of the sacred text; ministers who neglected their studies—and particularly the study of the Scriptures—were subject to consistorial admonition and even formal discipline.[39] It is likely that different ministers adopted different habits of study. Calvin's practice was to retire early in the evening after dinner to prepare his sermon for the following day or to make progress on writing projects. Beza was known to work at his desk late into the night by candlelight. Even so, the strain and unremitting demands of pastoral work no doubt made personal study and sermon preparation difficult—at least at times. In 1539, for example, Calvin wrote Farel from Strasbourg, describing his busy schedule:

> I cannot think of a day this year in which I was so overwhelmed with all kinds of things to do as today. For because the messenger wanted to take also the first part of my work, I had to look over the first twenty pages of the manuscript. On top of that I had to lecture, preach, write four letters, settle several disputes and receive more than ten visitors.[40]

Calvin's weekly schedule only became more hectic in the years that followed. In a similar fashion, four decades later, the Company of Pastors deputed Beza and Jaquemot to the Small Council to complain about the unrealistic demands placed on the ministers. Because of the weight of their duties, combined with a shortage of manpower, the ministers had little time to study and were no longer able to preach with "knowledge and edification."[41]

But even as they acknowledged the importance of personal study, Calvin and Beza warned would-be ministers against becoming bookworms, aloof from the problems and needs of their parishioners. Scholarship was always done in the service of the church. As Calvin commented to a pastoral friend back in France:

> In all your studies you must be careful that you are not looking merely for entertainment, but working toward the purpose of being useful to the church of Christ. Those who desire of scholarship nothing more than an honored occupation with which to drive away the boredom of idleness impress me as being like those who spend their whole life merely looking at beautiful pictures.[42]

Beza acknowledged this same problem in his published sermons in the final decades of the century, and he offered guidance to help reformed pastors find a proper balance between the active life of ministry and the private life of study. The primary goal of pastoral ministry, he insisted, is to care for the spiritual well-being of God's people, that is, to administer the Word of God to the Christian flock for their edification and consolation with an eye toward their salvation. Faithful pastors must have a thorough knowledge of the Scripture and biblical doctrine. After all, how will pastors instruct their people on subjects that they themselves do not understand? But tireless study must never distract the shepherd from his sheep.[43] "It is a very holy and necessary desire for a preacher to be diligent and careful in study so that he has something to feed his sheep," Beza observed. "But if he throws himself so much into it that, while he is studying, Satan devours one of his sheep, then he cannot be called a true pastor. A true pastor not only attends to the reading of Scripture...but also guards his flock."[44] The faithful Christian pastor must be a competent student of the Holy Scriptures *and* attentive to the needs of his congregation; he must never be an ivory-tower theologian cut off from the people whom he is called to serve.

One of the most important ways in which Geneva's ministers matured as interpreters of sacred Scripture was through the weekly Congregation. Modeled after Zwingli's *Prophezei* in Zurich, Geneva's Congregation was established by Calvin and Farel in 1536 to provide a regular setting in which ministers, professors, and interested laypeople could study and discuss the contents of Scripture together.[45] The *Ecclesiastical Ordinances* of 1561 described the function and purpose of this reformed institution as follows:

> It will be expedient for all the ministers, in order to preserve purity and unity of doctrine among them, to meet together one day each week for a conference on Scripture, and no one will be exempt unless he has a legitimate excuse.... As for those who preach in the rural villages dependent on the magistrates, the city ministers should encourage them to come [to the Congregation] whenever they can.... And so as to assure that everyone is diligent in study and no one becomes nonchalant, each [minister] will be given a turn explaining the Scripture passage from week to week. Afterwards, the ministers will retire and each member of the Company will advise the person who explained [the text] what was wrong, so that this censure might serve to correct him.[46]

The Congregation was not intended to be a preaching service. Rather, it was a kind of in-depth public Bible study created for the purpose of training clergy and laypeople in the interpretation and application of Scripture, building theological consensus among members of the Venerable Company, and assuring the competence of Geneva's ministers. In a letter to Wolfgang Musculus, professor at Bern, Calvin argued that institutions like the Congregation were "not only useful but necessary" for a healthy church because they served to monitor the zeal and competence of ministers, taught them how to apply the biblical text to their auditors, and helped maintain the unity of doctrine in the church. It was also valuable for motivating laypeople to study and understand God's Word.[47] Calvin insisted that Scripture needed to be interpreted and discussed in community to avoid the rash conclusions of private imaginations. "The fewer discussions of doctrine we have together, the greater the danger of pernicious opinions," he commented.[48] Indeed, "solitude leads to great abuse."[49]

The weekly meetings of the Congregation were part of the normal rhythm of the pastor's life and work during the course of the sixteenth century. Every Friday morning at 7 a.m. (or 8 a.m. in the winter), the city's ministers, a handful of countryside pastors, the professors of Hebrew, Greek, and the arts from the Academy, and perhaps forty or fifty committed laypeople gathered in the Chapel of the Auditoire next to St. Pierre to study Scripture together. The assembly began with a set prayer:

> We pray to you, our good God and Father, asking that you might forgive all our faults and offenses, and illuminate us by your Holy Spirit to have the true understanding of your holy Word. Give us the grace that we need to handle it purely and faithfully to the glory of your holy name, for the edification of the Church, and for our salvation. We ask these things in the name of the only and blessed Son, our Lord Jesus Christ. Amen.[50]

After this prayer, the designated minister for the week (or sometimes a theological student) read the chosen biblical passage aloud and offered a detailed commentary on the text drawn from his knowledge of Greek and Hebrew. He concluded these exegetical and theological remarks by inviting public response and comment. In 1563, for example, Michel Cop finished his exposition of Joshua 1:6–11 with this statement: "This is what God has given me to say briefly on this passage. The passage is very rich and expansive and contains important teaching. Therefore, I beg the brethren to whom God has given much greater gifts than me to supplement my deficiency, and I ask for assistance as each one is pleased to help me."[51] At this point, the moderator of the Company of Pastors took the floor to lead a detailed discussion that explored the meaning and application of the passage under consideration.[52] Each minister and professor in attendance was required to have studied the passage of the week and was expected to participate in the discussion. The many laypeople present in the conference— their number included students, schoolmasters, physicians and lawyers, printers, and artisans—were also invited to participate in this general discussion. The conference was concluded with a second prayer, after which the Company adjourned to its private chambers where more pointed criticisms and more detailed discussion of the exposition of the Congregation might take place.[53]

In the early years of its existence, the Congregation was sometimes roiled in controversy. In 1549, for example, Calvin and his colleagues became so wearied by the torrent of inept, erroneous, and absurd statements that the minister of Vandoeuvres, Phillippe de Ecclesia, habitually poured forth during the weekly Congregation that they censured him and forbade him from speaking in the meeting thereafter. They appealed to the Apostle Paul's words in 1 Corinthians 14 to justify their decision: "he who does not speak for edification in the church should remain silent."[54] More famous still was the celebrated controversy surrounding the former Carmelite monk Jerome Bolsec who attacked Calvin's doctrine of double predestination at a meeting of the Congregation on October 16, 1551. On that morning, Bolsec took the floor to argue that Calvin's teaching that God, in eternity, had predestined some men and women to salvation and others to damnation "makes God into a tyrant, indeed an idol, as the pagans have made Jupiter."[55] Calvin refuted Bolsec's accusations in front of the assembly with a brilliant hour-long speech in which he detailed the biblical basis for the doctrine of election as well as its presence in the teaching of church fathers like Augustine. Immediately following this heated session, Bolsec was arrested by the magistrates and put in the city prison, where he languished for a month before being banished from the city. Outbursts such as Bolsec's were the exception rather than the rule, however. Over the course of the following decades, the Genevan Congregation seems to have settled into a predictable and noncontroversial pattern, working methodically, and with little controversy, through large portions of the biblical canon, verse-by-verse, chapter-by-chapter.[56]

In the end, the Congregation may have been a victim of its own success. For while the weekly assembly appears to have been quite effective for training ministers in biblical interpretation and maintaining doctrinal uniformity, it promoted a scholarly study of the Scripture that became drawn out and tendentious, beyond the capacity or interest of most laypersons. Intense investigation of the biblical text by theologically trained ministers and professors crowded out dynamic interchange between ministers and laypeople. Consequently, following Beza's death in the first years of the new century, the Small Council began to pressure the Venerable Company to change the structure and function of the Congregation. In particular, the magistrates complained that weekly sessions of the Congregation lasted so long that few city councilors or laypeople could endure them; even the most devout townspeople found it very inconvenient "to remain in one place for two-and-a-half hours without budging, especially during the bitter cold of winter."[57] As a solution, the Small Council proposed that the ministers move the Congregation to the time of the 6 a.m. sermon at St. Pierre to shorten the length of the Congregation and (it was hoped) encourage better attendance by the laity. The pastors rejected this proposal, arguing that such a revised format would effectively transform a lesson in Scripture and theology into a public sermon with no time for general discussion. Once again, as they had done so frequently during these years, the ministers sounded the alarm about the dangers of deviating from Calvin's biblical vision of ministry. "Changes and novelties have always been dangerous in both the State and Church," they insisted. Once "the door is opened to changes, it is not easy to close it."[58] For two years, the Venerable Company and the Small Council locked horns over the structure and schedule of the weekly Congregation. Finally, in 1609, the ministers agreed to a significant compromise: the weekly Congregation was moved to the hour of the Friday morning sermon. Instead of preaching a sermon, the officiating minister now explained the biblical text in the form of an exegetical and theological lesson, keeping his comments to the allotted hour and making only a brief application of the text to the assembly. Laypeople were invited to attend the lesson but were no longer allowed to make public comments or ask questions. Discussions of the minister's competence as an interpreter of Scripture were now reserved for the privacy of the chambers of the Venerable Company.[59] Whatever the magistrates' purposes may have been, the new structure of the Congregation after 1609 effectively ended its pedagogical function as an intense, scholarly conference on the sacred text that involved both ministers and laypersons.[60]

3. Challenges in the Countryside

The weekly schedule of pastors in the countryside was somewhat different than that of city ministers. Given their distance from the walled city, the rural ministers were able only occasionally to attend the weekly meetings of the Congregation, the Consistory, or the Company of Pastors. Their pastoral duties centered on preaching in the several village churches within their parishes two or three times a week, catechizing young people, visiting the sick, and providing pastoral care and moral supervision for the country folk. This work was difficult and sometimes even dangerous. Because nearly all the countryside ministers provided pastoral care for at least two rural congregations, and because most of their parishes were spread out over four, six, or even eight square miles, the ministers were forced to travel long distances on foot or horseback, fording rivers, enduring the heat of summer, and braving the snows of winter. In some cases, pastors were only able to visit outlying village churches every second Sunday to conduct worship services and catechism classes.[61] Ministers with weak physical constitutions or of advanced age found it difficult to perform the duties required by a large rural parish. Thus, for example, the minister Paul Baduel was transferred from the church of Russin-Dardagny in 1557 because a physical disability—he had lost an eye—and his "small stature" made it nearly impossible for him to ford the rivers and travel the roads of his far-flung parish.[62] Time and again, the Venerable Company voiced its concern to Geneva's magistrates about this situation and asked for more manpower in the countryside. In 1576, for example, the ministers reported to the Small Council that "there are some parishes with villages so far from one another that it is impossible for one minister to discharge his duty over them, or for one person to serve so many people spread so far apart."[63] Regrettably, financial considerations almost always caused the Small Council to refuse requests for more pastoral support, although it did sometimes provide rural ministers with special funds to purchase and utuble horses to make travel easier.[64] Not only distance but also impassible roads and flooded rivers made pastoral care in the countryside difficult. The pastoral circuit for the minister of Russin-Dardagny required him to wade across the Allondon River that, during the spring rains, often became swollen and treacherous. In April 1576, the magistrates finally agreed to build a footbridge over the river—but only after the minister, while attempting to ford the river on the shoulders of one of his attendants, fell into the water and contracted a fever. He died several months later.[65] Ministry in

Geneva's rural parishes was difficult and lonely work. No doubt many of the countryside pastors missed the collegiality and intellectual stimulation that the city offered.[66]

In addition to these physical demands, pastors who worked in Geneva's countryside faced real challenges instructing and supervising peasant folk whose outlook and concerns often differed significantly from their own. The ministers' cultural background, educational training, and economic status set them apart from most of their parishioners and probably left many of them ill-equipped for the daily demands of rural agrarian life.[67] Because nearly all of Geneva's ministers were recruited from the world of cities and towns, few possessed the practical knowledge of raising livestock, planting and harvesting crops, or repairing farm implements. Men trained in theology and exegesis at the university or Academy, who participated in a humanistic culture focused on classical texts, scholarly discourse, and refined eloquence, no doubt found it bewildering and difficult to instruct rural congregations of men and women who could neither read nor write, and who cared more about prospects for the fall harvest than the finer points of Christian doctrine. Economic disparities may have also exacerbated this cultural divide. Even if pastors were poorly paid compared with other urban professionals, they were better off economically than the majority of their parishioners engaged in subsistence farming, whose livelihoods were vulnerable to the vagaries of pestilence, weather, and war. In all these ways and more, Geneva's ministers and their households stood apart from their rural neighbors. Bridging the cultural divide depended in large part on ministers being attentive to these differences and patiently adapting over time. "Poor peasants," Calvin reminded his colleagues, "receive more willingly and understand more easily doctrine that comes from the mouth of those with whom they are familiar."[68] But this ideal was often not achieved. As noted in chapter 2, pastoral tenures in Geneva's rural parishes were normally of short duration, averaging only around five-and-a-half years. Countryside ministers regularly vied for city posts or left their churches in search of more attractive assignments in France.

The most detailed contemporaneous description of pastoral work in Geneva's countryside is found in a set of instructions that Charles Perrot left for his successor as Perrot prepared to depart the parish of Genthod-Moëns for a city church in the early 1560s.[69] These instructions indicate a conscientious pastor and a demanding regimen of duties. According to Perrot, the pastor of the parish was responsible to preach on Sundays and on Thursdays (when the crops were not in the fields), conduct separate catechism classes for adults and young children, examine all adult parishioners in preparation for the Lord's Supper, investigate reports of immoral behavior, perform baptisms and weddings, and console the sick at their bedsides. Perrot was forthcoming about the unique set of challenges his successor would face. Despite magisterial prohibitions, the peasants continued to celebrate the traditional feasts of Christmas, Circumcision,

Ascension, and Annunciation. During worship services, only a handful of people were able to recite the Psalms, and oftentimes the minister would find no one prepared to lead congregational singing. Preaching services and catechism classes should be limited to one hour—"because otherwise the people notice it and become annoyed." Perrot advised his successor to keep the message of his sermons simple. "I would counsel the minister not to deal with subjects too complex, such as those found in the letters of St. Paul, because the people will remember almost nothing by the time of the next sermon."[70] In the same way, when teaching the catechism, thorny questions such as those related to the Lord's Supper should be explained with simple words over three or four weeks, because there are "some questions and doctrines in the Catechism that one cannot easily teach the people without confusing them."[71] The minister should work hard to establish friendly relationships with his parishioners, but at the same time he must protect principle and preserve propriety. In the case of baptismal banquets, for example, Perrot had arrived at this workable compromise: "When I am invited [to these banquets], I sometimes attend them out of friendship or some other good reason, but not otherwise."[72] Perrot's instructions make it clear that the overriding concern of the faithful pastor should be that his spiritual flock understands the basic Christian message and embraces by faith the gospel of Jesus Christ. These spiritual priorities must particularly be in view when visiting the bedside of the sick and dying. In these cases, Perrot advised, "I exhort, console, and pray for [sick persons], and then I encourage them also to pray and to embrace the forgiveness of their sins in true repentance and with faith in the death and passion of our Lord Jesus."[73] Charles Perrot concluded his pastoral instructions with a simplified version of the catechism, adapted to the capacities of villagers in Genthod and Moëns. This precious document illustrates well that ministry in the rural parishes demanded cultural adjustments, modest expectations, and a great deal of patience—qualities that not all of Geneva's book-learned pastors possessed.

Even in the best of times, pastoral work in Geneva's countryside parishes was difficult. During the final decades of the sixteenth century, the threats of Savoy and the activities of Catholic missionaries made rural ministry nearly impossible. The Treaty of Lausanne (signed in 1564) restored to the dukes of Savoy the frontier around Geneva that had been held by Bern since the victory of 1536. Consequently, the baillages of Gex, Ternier, and Thonon surrounding Geneva were handed over to Savoy in 1567, although the practice of the Protestant religion in those territories was guaranteed by treaty, and a number of the reformed churches continued to be supervised by Geneva and Bern. With the accession of the bellicose Duke Charles Emmanuel I in 1580, Savoy engaged in a new, aggressive campaign to reintroduce the Catholic religion in these territories as well as to capture the city of Geneva. Countryside pastors in the outlying parishes were caught in the crossfire.[74] During the 1580s, Savoyard officials and soldiers increasingly harassed rural pastors and destroyed church property.[75] In the spring of 1588, for example, Savoyard troops stationed a temporary guard in the temple at Bossey and burned some of the church's benches; the soldiers also housed their prostitutes in the church's parsonage.[76] The onset of the Savoyard War (1589–1593) forced most of the countryside ministers to leave their posts and evacuate to the city, where they watched helplessly as members of their congregations were killed by marauding armies and peasant farms and fields burned. According to one gruesome report, the parish church of Genthod was piled high with the corpses of war dead. Several pastors were directly involved in the conflict. Etienne Trembley, the minister of Bossey was captured and held prisoner by the Savoyards for three months. The pastor of Satigny, Guillaume de Morgues, serving as chaplain of Geneva's troops in the field, was taken hostage at the massacre of Bonne on August 22, 1589, and was executed by the Savoyards two years later. In all, more than three hundred fifty Geneva soldiers who laid down their arms in surrender at Fort Bonne were slaughtered, including two sons of the minister of Vandoeuvres Jean Du Perril. In his daily *Journal* of the Savoyard War, Du Perril noted "it has pleased God, who conducts all things by his holy providence, to humiliate us."[77]

The truce of 1594 between Geneva and Savoy brought little security or stability to the countryside parishes. In fact, during the next decade, rural pastors faced even greater dangers from the twin threats of "bandits and wolves"—Savoyard soldiers and now Catholic missionaries as well. With the conclusion of the war, Jesuit priests and Capuchin monks under the leadership of François de Sales began an all-out effort to evangelize the provinces of Thonon and Ternier, reformed strongholds in Savoy on the southern shore of Lac Léman adjacent to Geneva.[78] Sporadically at first, and then with increasing success, the Catholic mission won converts by pursuing public debates, distributing tracts, and conducting processions and Forty-Hour Vigils.[79] In the summer of 1596, three Capuchin friars reestablished the Mass in Ternier, to the south of Geneva. On Christmas Day of the same year, François de Sales ignored Protestant opposition and celebrated the Mass in the parish church of Thonon, the first such service in sixty years. The Venerable Company bitterly protested what it viewed as violations of the Treaty of Lausanne and appealed to Bern for advice and support. But, at the same time, Geneva's ministers resolutely refused to engage the Catholic missionaries in theological debate, fearing it would lend legitimacy to Savoy's efforts to convert the rural population. In the end, the Catholic campaign to evangelize Thonon and Ternier—backed by political pressure and threats from the Duke of Savoy—was a stunning success. By December of 1598, several thousand people had renounced the Protestant religion and embraced the Catholic faith. Almost overnight, the reformed religion had been swept from the southern shores of Lac Léman. Theodore Beza was horrified by what he described as a great "apostasy." He likened the situation to the Jews' betrayal of Jesus in Jerusalem during holy week: the very same people who had welcomed Jesus with cheers on Palm Sunday now shouted "Crucify him!"[80]

Countryside parishes under the direct administration of the Geneva church also experienced intense Catholic pressure during these years. The pastors in the parishes of Neydens, Bossey, and Chancy-Valleiry, between the Rhone and Arve rivers to the south of Geneva, were repeatedly threatened by soldiers and confronted by officials of Savoy, who commanded that they stop preaching. In the summer of 1598, Savoyard troops kidnapped the ministers of both Chancy and Bossey and held them as hostages for ransom.[81] In August, a representative of the Duke of Savoy accompanied by a Catholic priest arrived in the village of Valleiry (three miles south of Chancy) and ordered the residents to restore the altar and Catholic adornments to the parish church. The villagers reportedly refused, answering that "their bodies and possessions belonged to their prince [the Duke], but their souls belonged to God."[82] A very different outcome occurred in the village of Veyrier, located at the foot of the Salève only five miles south of Geneva, where the villagers expelled their pastor and returned to the Catholic faith of their ancestors. In the face of these dangers, the ministers of the Venerable Company back in the city urged their rural colleagues to stand firm in courage and Christian faith: "it is necessary for us to do our duty in our vocation, depending on the providence of God, which will cover us."[83] The re-Catholicization of neighboring Gaillard in May of 1601 shifted the Catholic threat to the parishes between the Arve River and Lac Léman to the west of Geneva, especially Draillans and Vandoeuvres.[84] In July of that year, a Savoyard captain with about forty soldiers and a priest unexpectedly arrived at the temple of Vandoeuvres, forced open the doors, and celebrated the Mass. The next Sunday morning, two priests accompanied by three Savoyard soldiers returned to the church; this time, however, the parish minister Hugues Roy and members of his congregation stood up to them and refused them entrance. Geneva's magistrates instructed Roy hereafter to have an armed bodyguard ready to protect him whenever he preached in the parish church.[85] Dire circumstances like these not only demanded courage on the part of Geneva's pastors and their flocks but also required a renewed commitment to pastoral care and instruction in order to fortify the minds and hearts of the country folk in Geneva's rural territory. The Venerable Company reminded the countryside ministers of this in March of 1602:

> Our brothers of the rural parishes have been urged to work all the more diligently in their parishes in the visitation of individual families and in the instruction of the young in these places. For the priests who are all around are deliberate in instructing the poor people and youth in error.... [Thus] we must guard our parishes where, each day, an infinite number of papists and their households are being introduced, who will bring horrible confusion and impiety to our flocks if we do not watch over them.[86]

One remarkable example of pastoral diligence in the face of difficulty is seen in the ministry of Jean Gervais, pastor of Bossey from 1594 to 1612. Gervais, who was the godson of John Calvin, was in his early thirties when he set aside his craft as a rope maker and enrolled at the Genevan Academy to study theology. In 1594, he was elected pastor of the parish of Bossey (which included the village of Veyrier) four miles south of Geneva, a reformed outpost in the middle of the Savoyard province of Ternier. During eighteen years of ministry there, Gervais and his family were repeatedly at risk from military aggression and Catholic evangelism. In the summer of 1598, the pastor was snatched out of bed in the middle of the night by Savoyard soldiers and was held as a prisoner for several weeks until a ransom of 400 écus was paid.[87] During the next months, Gervais struggled to counteract the influence of Capuchin missionaries throughout his parish, especially in Veyrier, where the villagers finally rejected the reformed faith and returned to the Catholic religion in November 1598. Catholic authorities threatened Gervais that if he ever returned to the village to preach he would be killed and his body thrown in the road. Despite such intimidation, the minister continued at great risk to visit in secret the handful of Protestants who remained in the village until Geneva's magistrates ordered him to discontinue his pastoral work there several months later.[88] Ironically, even while this crisis was unfolding, the magistrates decided to expand Gervais's pastoral responsibilities by assigning the vacant parish of Neydens to him as well. Hence, beginning in the fall of 1598, Gervais had oversight of the churches of Bossey and Neydens (separated by around four miles), as well as congregations in Sierne, Onex, and Lancy—a charge that made it impossible for him to preach in each parish church more than once every two weeks. The villagers of Neydens complained bitterly about this arrangement, and the Company of Pastors echoed their frustration: "it is an intolerable scandal that this parish, with so many souls, should be so poorly provided for," the ministers insisted. Neydens and the surrounding villages were "neglected and exposed to the wolves who are attempting to devour everything."[89] The Small Council remained unresponsive, however, and Gervais was forced to continue his pastoral work without needed support.

Over the next decade, Jean Gervais endured many more difficulties: he and his family were repeatedly threatened, household possessions were stolen, and a convert to Catholicism lodged a lawsuit against him. And, all the while, Capuchin missionaries and Catholic priests traveled about the parish, challenging the minister to public disputations and calling on the country folk to renounce the reformed faith and return to the traditional church. The situation was so dangerous that Gervais did not dare leave his family alone overnight.[90] In 1600, the exhausted pastor asked to be relieved of his post and transferred to another parish, a request that the Venerable Company denied. When open war broke out following the

Duke of Savoy's surprise attack on Geneva on the night of the Escalade (December 12, 1602), Gervais and his family were forced to find refuge within the walled city. After the signing of the Treaty of St. Julien (July 1603), which ended hostilities between Geneva and Savoy, the minister returned to his countryside parish and to the same pastoral problems as before. Savoyard soldiers and Catholic missionaries continued to disturb Bossey-Neydens. The demands of preaching and pastoral care in the far-flung parish remained unrealistic and unremitting. Jean Jaquemot, who visited the parish in 1605 on a fact-finding mission, reported back to the Venerable Company that Gervais's charge was "too weighty for a single pastor."[91] One episode from the spring of 1606 illustrates the tense confessional climate that existed in Bossey-Neydens throughout this period. In May of that year, two high-ranking officers from the territory of Ternier came to Bossey to intimidate the pastor and pressure the villagers to abjure the Protestant religion. When Gervais refused to hand over the keys of the parish church to them, one of the officers (according to the minister's report) began to kick the temple door, shouting blasphemies and threats. Later, he visited Gervais's parsonage and repeated this insulting display, promising to return in the future with a Capuchin missionary.[92]

Throughout these years Gervais was in regular communication with his colleagues in the city, reporting his concerns and asking for pastoral advice: How should he treat parishioners who ignored the summons of the Consistory? What responsibility did he have to console and instruct former parishioners who had converted to the Catholic religion? Was it appropriate for a pastor to help the sick and poor draft their last will and testament?[93] Might he occasionally engage Capuchin missionaries in public debate? The Venerable Company's response to this final question was uncompromising: Gervais must always be "prepared to give a reason for his faith" and respond to his adversaries with "holy prudence and discretion" (1 Peter 3:15), but he must never enter into a formal dispute with the Catholic missionaries.[94] To the very end, Jean Gervais battled overwork and endured an unremitting campaign of Catholic harassment in his pastoral role in Bossey. Finally, in 1612, the Company of Pastors transferred him to the city post of St. Gervais, in part to honor "an old servant who had worked so courageously for such a long time."[95]

The dramatic example of Jean Gervais illustrates how different ministry in the countryside could be from pastoral work in the city. Neither assignment was free from difficulties, of course, but the requirements placed on rural pastors were especially challenging. Countryside pastors were paid poorly and their homes were often in disrepair. The size of rural parishes required many of the pastors to live peripatetic existences, braving bad roads, inclement weather, bandits, and soldiers in their effort to provide care for their spiritual flock. Theirs was an isolated, physically demanding, and dangerous vocation, far removed from the more comfortable, more secure, more collegial existence of Geneva's city ministers. Small wonder, then, that many of Geneva's rural ministers aspired to be transferred to the city. Likewise, one is not surprised that turnover among countryside pastors was much higher than that of their city colleagues. Though some pastors, like the courageous Jean Gervais, served their rural parishes faithfully and well for many years, others found ministry in the countryside too lonely, too backward, and just too difficult.

CHAPTER 6 | The Ministry of the Word

IN EARLY JULY 1595, the veteran minister Simon Goulart submitted his resignation and announced that he would never again preach at the temple of St. Gervais. Goulart's announcement caught his pastoral colleagues completely off guard, though his actions were not precipitous. For weeks his anger had been smoldering over what he saw as a clear miscarriage of justice on the part of Geneva's magistrates in a civil case between two wealthy French immigrants, the elderly Madame de Juranville and her step-daughter Madame de Martinville.[1] Goulart had finally come to the conclusion that, in good conscience, he must either condemn the magistrates' injustice from the pulpit or retire from his pastoral office. To avoid public scandal, the minister chose the latter course. Over the next month, the perplexed and increasingly exasperated ministers attempted to bring their colleague to his senses, granting him a temporary reprieve from his daily sermons while at the same time demanding that he submit to the collective will of the Company and resume his pastoral duties. A minister's conscience "must be instructed by the Word of God and by the discipline of the Church," they insisted.[2] To abstain from preaching was "completely contrary to the nature of the holy ministry."[3] Goulart remained intransigent, however. Under the present circumstances, he believed, the pulpit for him was "worse than the gate of hell."[4] Without the knowledge or permission of Geneva's authorities, Goulart established contact with the church in Lausanne hoping to secure a transfer.

Finally after weeks of arm-twisting, cajoling, and threats, Simon Goulart returned to his pulpit on Sunday morning, August 14, and delivered a sermon that was nothing less than spectacular. In it he decried the fact that the city magistrates had condemned an innocent woman and allowed the guilty party to parade through Geneva's streets with her head held high. More dangerously, Goulart used his sermon to condemn as a prostitute (*putain*) Gabrielle d'Estrée, the mistress of Henry IV, assuring his congregation that God would soon visit his wrath upon the French king and his kingdom.[5]

Such a tirade could not be left unpunished. The day after the sermon, the Small Council had Goulart arrested and imprisoned in the Hôtel de Ville, where he remained for the next seven days. On August 22, Goulart was finally released, but only after he admitted his failure, begged the forgiveness of the magistrates, and promised to remain in Geneva and submit his conscience henceforth to the judgment of his colleagues.[6] The fact that Goulart's pastoral career survived this scandalous episode is a testimony to the strength of his personal ties in the church and city, as well as his sizeable reputation as a preacher, author, and leader of French Protestantism. He remained a central pillar of the Genevan church until his death in 1628.

Goulart's crisis of 1595 illustrates the importance of preaching in reformed Geneva as well as some of its inherent problems. For Calvin and the ministers who came after him, Christian preaching was the primary instrument that God employed to bring sinners to faith in Christ and guide them toward spiritual maturity. It was unthinkable, then, that a reformed minister—especially one of Simon Goulart's stature—would refuse to preach. Moreover, the controversy surrounding Goulart's explosive sermon in 1595 points to the important social function that the pulpit played in Geneva and sixteenth-century Europe. Christian preaching was by far the most important means of mass communication in the early modern era.[7] Protestant and Catholic preachers occupied an influential position in urban life, serving as social commentators, moral watchdogs, and purveyors of public information who shaped popular opinion and either undergirded or undermined established authority in church and society. Small wonder, then, that political authorities such as Geneva's Small Council would attempt to bridle the tongue of a disgruntled preacher like Goulart.

This chapter will explore the important place that the sermon occupied in Geneva's religious life from 1536 to 1609. To do this, I will not only consider Calvin's theology and style of preaching, the frequency of sermons and their position within the Genevan liturgy, but also consider some of the different ways in which Geneva's townspeople "heard" the sermon and reacted to the city preachers. By extending my analysis beyond Calvin's lifetime, I will also demonstrate some of the special challenges faced by Beza and his colleagues as they attempted to preserve Calvin's homiletic legacy. What will become clear is that the pulpit stood at the epicenter of controversy and change in reformed Geneva. In the minds of Geneva's ministers, the proclamation of the Scripture was God's dynamic instrument for bringing about personal spiritual regeneration, the reformation of the church, and the transformation of society according to the righteousness of Christ.

1. Preaching in Calvin's Geneva

"No sermon, no Reformation." This statement, made by historian Susan Karant-Nunn to emphasize the crucial importance of preaching in the

German Reformation, is equally true when applied to Geneva.[8] Preaching was at the heart of religious change in Calvin's city during the sixteenth century. As we have seen, explosive sermons in the early 1530s delivered by evangelical missionaries like Guillaume Farel, Pierre Viret, and Antoine Froment were decisive in challenging popular religious belief and dismantling the traditional church. After the revolution of 1536, preaching served as the primary instrument by which Calvin and the ministers of Geneva constructed a new church order and promoted a new religious ethos among the city's residents. In both of these ways, in demolition and construction, Protestant preaching was of central importance to Geneva's Reformation.

With that said, however, it would be inaccurate to conclude that Christian preaching was unknown in Catholic Europe or Geneva before the Reformation. In fact, scholars have shown that a virtual "homiletic revolution" occurred in Western Europe in the thirteenth century, spurred by the emergence of universities, the recovery of ancient rhetoric, and (especially) the growth of mendicant orders such as the Franciscans and Dominicans.[9] By the late Middle Ages, the typical city dweller in Western Europe may have had the opportunity to hear as many as eight hundred sermons over the course of a lifetime.[10] At the papal court, Renaissance preachers regularly delivered carefully crafted orations that praised God's character and deeds, and articulated the moral ideals of the Christian life.[11] Well-trained humanist preachers were also a common feature of municipal life (at least in the larger cities), hired by magistrates to adorn city pulpits and edify the Christian population. More important still were the mendicant preachers who crisscrossed the European landscape by the thousands delivering vernacular sermons on Sundays, Catholic feast days, and during Advent and Lent that taught basic doctrine, called for repentance in light of final judgment, and extolled the Christian virtues illustrated in the lives of the saints and martyrs.[12] Ironically, even as sermons were becoming an ever more popular aspect of religious life in the fifteenth century, they were, for the most part, absent from the day-to-day ministry of the Catholic parish. Parish priests and curates were not expected (and few were qualified) to preach. Over the centuries, the custom of preaching a brief homily during the *prône* of the Catholic Mass had disappeared almost entirely. As a general rule, preaching on the eve of the Reformation was occasional and performed by mendicants and other specialists—not by parish clergy.[13]

This overall pattern was true of Geneva during the century before Calvin's arrival. In his careful study of the visitation reports of the Diocese of Geneva from 1378 to 1450, Louis Binz found not a single instance of a priest or curate preaching in his parish.[14] Instead, Geneva's townspeople had the opportunity to attend sermons by mendicant preachers on alternative Sundays at the Franciscan and Dominican monasteries in the city. These sermons were supplemented at Advent and Lent by longer sermon series preached by locals or by more famous mendicant preachers from Italy, Spain, or France. People came from far and wide, for example, to hear the Advent sermons of the famous Spanish Dominican preacher Vincent Ferrier in 1403. A generation later the Italian Benedictine preacher Baptiste of Mantua preached to overflow crowds in the city.[15] By the middle decades of the fifteenth century, special preacherships like these were funded by public monies.[16] The importance of the Catholic sermon is perhaps best seen during the religious crisis leading up to the Protestant victory in 1536. During these volatile months, a doctor of the Sorbonne and famous Dominican preacher named Guy Furbity came to Geneva to try to out-preach the evangelicals. In one of his sermons, he warned that the seamless robe of Christ was in danger of being torn into pieces by four executioners, the Arians, the Sabellians, the Germans (i.e., Luther), and the Vaudois (i.e., Farel and the Bernese missionaries). Furbity's homiletic was so volatile—and so politically dangerous—that Geneva's magistrates threw him in prison for his effort.[17]

What was noteworthy, then, was not that Protestant leaders like Luther, Zwingli, or Calvin championed Christian preaching per se, but that they viewed the proclamation of the Word of God as the minister's primary duty and restructured parish life in view of this priority. "For God there is nothing higher than preaching the gospel," Calvin once noted, "because it is the means to lead people to salvation."[18] Church documents in reformed Geneva made this point repeatedly and forcefully. Christian ministers were appointed in the church of Christ "to preach the holy gospel," to "preach the Word of God," and to "announce the gospel."[19] Geneva was identified as the place "where one preaches publicly the gospel."[20] Accordingly, one of the first actions taken by Calvin and Farel after the revolution of 1536 was to establish a regular order of preaching services in Geneva's three urban churches and in the surrounding villages.[21] This schedule was further refined five years later when Calvin returned from Strasbourg. The *Ecclesiastical Ordinances* (1541) envisioned that a pastoral staff of five men and three assistants (*coadjuteurs*) would preach at least twenty sermons in the city each week.[22] According to this original plan, worship services were to be celebrated every Sunday at St. Pierre, St. Gervais, and the Madeleine at 8 a.m. and again at 3 p.m., with a catechetical sermon at noon. The ministers of St. Pierre and St. Gervais were required to offer a fourth service for household servants on Sunday mornings at the break of day (as early as 4 a.m.). The *Ordinances* also stipulated that three morning preaching services (*cultes ordinaires*) should be held during the work week at three different locations in the city, with the services beginning at successive hours to encourage better attendance.[23]

This ambitious program of preaching was more of an ideal than a reality at first. But over the course of the 1540s, the schedule of preaching services in Geneva became firmly established in practice as the number of weekly sermons grew. In 1549, the magistrates ordered the Company of Pastors to provide sermons every day of the week within the walled city.[24] Parishioners were soon able to attend *cultes ordinaires* at St. Pierre,

St. Gervais, and the Madeleine from Monday through Saturday at 6 a.m. (7 a.m. in the winter). Wednesday was designated as a special "Day of Prayer" with the preaching service expanded to include the full liturgy and congregational singing, as on Sundays. When the *Ecclesiastical Ordinances* were republished in 1561, a total of thirty-three services had been established in the city's three parish churches: eleven worship services on Sunday, and twenty-two preaching services during the rest of the week (including four "sunrise" services at 4 a.m. or 5 a.m.).[25] By contrast, there were fewer opportunities to attend sermons in Geneva's rural districts. In countryside parishes, the majority of ministers probably presided at only two or three preaching services per week, the Sunday morning service, the catechetical service at Sunday noon (offered every fortnight), and an occasional midweek sermon on Wednesday or Thursday when the demands of the harvest were not too great.[26] Because many pastors served rural parishes that had multiple congregations, it was typical for them to preach at the same temple every other week.

It was the expectation of both ministers and magistrates that every resident of Geneva would attend at the very least the worship services on Sunday morning and afternoon, and the prayer service on Wednesday (which was moved to Thursday in 1581 so as not to conflict with market day).[27] In addition, at least one representative from each household was required to attend the *culte ordinaire* daily. Those individuals or households that consistently neglected the proclamation of God's Word risked a possible warning from the local warden or a formal rebuke from the Consistory.[28] Likewise, as we saw in chapter 5, shopkeepers, craftsmen, and tavern owners were required to close their businesses and shops on Sundays and during the Wednesday morning prayer service.[29] On the whole, it appears that the majority of Genevans complied with city statutes and dutifully attended worship services, at least those on Sunday mornings. But at the same time, as we shall see, a sizeable number of townspeople viewed Protestant services with less than enthusiasm, born of disinterest, Catholic conviction, or open hostility against Geneva's pastors.

The extensive sermon schedule in Geneva's churches required a high degree of organization and demanded significant commitment from the ministers. Early on, the Company of Pastors established the custom of creating three pastoral teams to provide leadership over Geneva's three city churches. The most gifted or senior ministers on each team—men like Calvin, Raymond Chauvet, Nicolas Des Gallars, (and later) Theodore Beza, Charles Perrot, and Simon Goulart—shared primary preaching responsibilities within their respective parishes, especially for the Sunday morning sermon and the Wednesday Day of Prayer. They were assisted by one or two colleagues who bore a somewhat lighter preaching load and so were entrusted with greater responsibilities for household visitations, baptisms, and catechizing children. Less experienced or less gifted preachers were usually given responsibility for preaching at the dawn services.[30]

Notwithstanding this general structure, parish assignments were subject to constant variation and change. Geneva's ministers frequently preached in other parish churches as part of their normal assignment. Calvin, for example, regularly preached Sunday mornings at St. Pierre and weekday services at the Madeleine; from time to time he also preached Sunday afternoons at St. Gervais.[31] Moreover, sickness, change in personnel, and the special needs of particular congregations often required adjustments to the preaching schedule. Under exceptional circumstances, city ministers were appointed to fill temporary vacancies in rural churches, or country-side pastors were brought to the city for several weeks.[32] All of this meant that it was not uncommon for faithful churchgoers to hear three, four, or even five different preachers at their parish temple over the course of a single week.[33]

The regular rotation of preachers between parish assignments achieved several important objectives. First, it allowed all of Geneva's ministers to preach on a regular basis, something that Calvin viewed as essential to the Christian ministry. This flexible arrangement also illustrated the Company of Pastors' fundamental commitment to the priority of the Word and the equality of the Christian ministry. The preacher was not the proprietor of a pulpit or the captain of his congregation: it was Christ who presided over his church through the Word. At least in theory, ministers of the Christian gospel were interchangeable.[34] So too, the rotation system probably encouraged collegiality between ministers as they worked with different colleagues in different parish churches during the week and sometimes had the opportunity to hear one another preach. For the people who attended sermons in Calvinist Geneva, the rotation system gave them the chance to listen to a variety of preaching styles and preachers, which, no doubt, invited comparisons between effective and poor preaching. Some city residents even "voted with their feet" by avoiding the sermons of ministers known to be boring or overly harsh. In 1545, for example, the Small Council bemoaned the fact that the minister Pierre Ninaux, though well educated, was a poor preacher and unpopular among the people of his parish. The council secretary wryly noted: "When they see [the minister] going to the church of St. Gervais, the people turn around and go home."[35]

The large number of sermons delivered from Geneva's pulpits week to week placed heavy demands on the members of the Company of Pastors, especially on the city's most popular preachers who bore a disproportionate load of the preaching. For most of his career in Geneva, Calvin preached once or twice on Sundays, and every day of the week on alternate weeks, a schedule that demanded around eighteen to twenty sermons per month, or two hundred fifty sermons per year.[36] In all, Calvin probably delivered well over four thousand sermons in the course of his ministry in Geneva. During the next generation, Geneva's most prominent ministers, such as Theodore Beza, Simon Goulart, and Charles Perrot, appear to have preached with comparable frequency, though many of them found it impossible to maintain this punishing preaching schedule as they grew older and struggled with poor health.[37] In 1587, for example, the elderly Jean Trembley petitioned the Company of Pastors to reduce his regular duties, noting that he had been preaching at St. Pierre for "a long time" and now "felt all broken down."[38] The septuagenarian Theodore Beza made a similar request three years later, noting that, though he had the desire, he no longer possessed the physical strength to preach so many sermons each week. In Beza's case, the Venerable Company granted him reprieve from the weekday sermons but asked that he continue to preach at St. Pierre every Sunday and deliver his normal lectures at the Academy.[39] The demands of the pulpit also took their toll on Calvin. During the final year of his life, as he battled tuberculosis, the reformer was no longer able to maintain his regular preaching rotation. He delivered his final sermon on a Sunday morning in February 1564, and he had to be carried to St. Pierre's on a litter.

Throughout the sixteenth and early seventeenth century, Geneva's ministers observed an established schedule of preaching. Rather than selecting biblical texts based on the lectionary or the church calendar, Calvin and his colleagues followed the example of the reformed churches of Zurich and Strasbourg by preaching continuously through books of the Bible (the *lectio continua* method). Calvin believed that this was the practice of the early church. On weekdays they expounded Old Testament books; on Sunday mornings they preached from the New Testament; on Sunday afternoons they preached either from the New Testament or from the book of Psalms. The ministers sometimes deviated slightly from this pattern before Christmas or during Holy Week to preach weekday sermons from gospel texts related to Jesus' birth, death, and resurrection.[40] The ministers appear to have had relative freedom in choosing the part of the biblical canon to expound, although they were expected to consult the Company of Pastors before beginning a new sermon series.[41] Thanks to the labors of Geneva's printers and the determined efforts of a group of stenographers who recorded Calvin's sermons beginning in 1549, scholars have reconstructed in detail Calvin's preaching schedule during the last fifteen years of his life.[42] Thus we know, for example, that during the years 1555 and 1556 Calvin was preaching a long series of sermons through the book of Deuteronomy on weekday mornings (two hundred sermons in all) and expositing the New Testament books of 2 Timothy, Titus, and 1 Corinthians on Sunday mornings and afternoons. During Holy Week of 1555, he took a brief break from this schedule to preach weekday sermons on the theme of Jesus' passion and resurrection drawn from the Gospel of Matthew.

Unfortunately, the homiletic schedules of Geneva's other ministers cannot be described with the same precision. Only two preaching series during Calvin's lifetime have been identified with certainty: those delivered by Michel Cop (Proverbs and Ecclesiastes) and Pierre Viret (Isaiah).[43] Slightly more can be said about Theodore Beza's preaching ministry after Calvin's death. In 1574, Beza was preaching through the book of Hebrews and the Epistle of James. In 1578, his weekday sermons were devoted to the book of Isaiah. Five years later, he was preaching through the Song of Songs. In the spring of 1590 he commenced a series on the death of Jesus Christ (thirty-six sermons), followed immediately by a series on Jesus' resurrection (twenty sermons).[44]

2. *The Worship Service*

Throughout the period 1542 to 1609, the Sunday worship service followed closely the liturgical order established in Calvin's *Forms of Prayers* (1542).[45] The congregation was summoned to the city's churches by the ringing of bells, which commenced around a half-hour before the morning and afternoon worship services. Couples wishing to be married were required to appear before their pastor at the beginning of the service for a brief wedding ceremony.[46] The worship service began with a cantor leading the congregation in singing a Psalm *a capella* from the Genevan Psalter.[47] These Psalms, Calvin believed, were crucial in that they stirred the hearts of those assembled to look to God and glorify his name with holy ardor.[48] Many years after his first visit to Geneva in 1548, Beza still remembered the emotional impact of hearing for the first time the vernacular Psalms sung in worship at the temple of St. Pierre.[49] After the Psalm was sung, the minister stood up in the pulpit and spoke the words of invocation ("Our help is in the name of God"), followed by a brief exhortation to repent and a general prayer of confession. The assembly then sang a second Psalm. Next, the minister recited a prayer of illumination, requesting that God be honored and the church edified through the preaching of the Word. The form of this prayer was left to the discretion of the minister, though it was customary for him to conclude with the recitation of the Lord's Prayer.[50] After the prayer of illumination, the minister read aloud the Scripture text in French and then moved into his sermon. In Calvin's Geneva, the Sunday sermon regularly lasted forty-five minutes or longer. At the conclusion of his sermon, Calvin often included a brief extemporaneous prayer of application that acknowledged God's majesty and human frailty, and expressed the congregation's willingness to submit to the divine Word. For example, Calvin ended his Sunday sermon of April 14, 1560 with this prayer:

> We bow ourselves before the majesty of our good God, acknowledging our faults, and praying that he might help us to feel them more and more so that we might be brought to a true repentance and might seek nothing except to serve and honor him in his Son, our Lord Jesus Christ. And we pray that it might also please him to be patient with our weaknesses and pardon the many sins that still reside in us, until he has completely purged them from us. And may he continue to grant us this grace until he finally receives us to himself and guides us completely into his presence.[51]

Following the sermon and the brief prayer of application, the minister transitioned without pause into a long intercessory prayer in which he prayed for the well-being of earthly rulers and Christian pastors, the advance of the gospel, the consolation of the persecuted church, and the protection and spiritual renewal of God's people. The prayer concluded with a paraphrase of the Lord's Prayer, after which the people affirmed the Apostles' Creed and sang a final Psalm. On Sundays when infant children were baptized, the minister would perform the sacrament after the sermon and intercessory prayer in front of parents, godparents, and the watching congregation.[52] The Sunday service was concluded with the minister dismissing the assembly with the Aaronic blessing ("May the Lord bless you and keep you"). As the congregation filed out of the sanctuary, they were invited to place their alms in collection boxes at the doors of the church.[53]

What was the length of worship services in Calvin's Geneva? For Sunday morning and afternoon services, as well as the Day of Prayer, the different elements of Calvin's liturgy—Psalm singing, liturgical prayers, Scripture reading, sermon, marriages, baptisms—undoubtedly required a service of well over an hour. Weekday services (*cultes ordinaries*) were somewhat shorter, since the Psalms were not sung, and ministers omitted the prayer of confession and modified the intercessory prayer. Geneva's authorities required the *cultes ordinaires* to be concluded within an hour to permit craftsmen and laborers to begin their workday, and city councilors to attend scheduled council meetings. In point of fact, the ministers often preached and prayed much longer than this. Thus, in 1572, the magistrates complained repeatedly about the length of weekday services, particularly those conducted by the pastors at St. Gervais. The Company of Pastors responded by exhorting their colleagues "to study brevity and conclude the sermon and prayers within the hour if it is at all possible."[54] Longwinded preachers continued to be a serious enough problem that in 1580 the city council installed forty-five minute hourglasses in all the city's churches to assure that the sermon remained an acceptable length and that services ended promptly on the hour.[55] Even so, Geneva's magistrates were still complaining about long sermons in the city's churches three decades later.[56]

Calvin's liturgy established authoritative guidelines for worship in Geneva, and the majority of reformed churches in France followed these guidelines as well. Even minor innovations from it were almost always frowned upon. When Charles Perrot invited his congregation to kneel during the congregational prayer in 1584, the city council expressed alarm, both because kneeling was contrary to custom, and because there was too little space between the benches to make the practice convenient.[57] On another occasion, the ministers briefly experimented with having theological students read aloud the Scripture text before the sermon, only to conclude that "it would be better simply to leave things as they had been before."[58] When the city councilors suggested in 1573 that baptisms be moved from the end of the service to the beginning in order to respond to the needs of parents with restless infants, the ministers strongly objected. They reasoned that since the rite of marriage already preceded the sermon, celebrating both weddings and baptisms before the preaching would take up thirty minutes and thus "only half-an-hour would be left for the sermon."[59] One of the clearest examples of the ministers' commitment to preserve Calvin's liturgy without modification is seen in the way the Venerable Company responded to reports in 1609 that reformed congregations in France were considering changes to Geneva's liturgy by shortening the long intercessory prayer and revising the formulae of baptism and the Lord's Supper. In a strongly worded letter to the French churches, Simon Goulart on behalf of the Company registered the ministers' strong objections to such a plan. All changes to Calvin's liturgy were "suspect and dangerous," he emphasized, and would do nothing but undermine the unity and edification of the reformed churches in France and Geneva.[60]

The Genevan ideal of a simple, well-ordered service in which the faithful attentively listened to, understood, and responded to the Word of God was not always achieved in practice. A variety of discomforts and distractions made attendance at sermons a challenging experience for even the most devout at times. The city's churches could be stifling hot in the summer and bitterly cold in the winter. On several occasions the frigid winter weather prompted the ministers to move services from the cavernous temple of St. Pierre to the smaller (and warmer) church of St. Germain a block from the Hôtel de Ville.[61] There were also plenty of human distractions. Between 1541 and 1609, a long litany of nuisances great and small elicited the complaints of ministers as well as parishioners. Members of the congregation frequently arrived late to Sunday worship, missing the congregational singing and the introductory prayers. Others left early, causing a commotion during the concluding baptismal service.[62] At weekday sermons in the church of St. Gervais, parishioners sometimes found it difficult to hear the preacher because of the noise caused by blacksmith shops nearby.[63] In Geneva's churches, babies often wailed, dogs barked, and schoolboys chatted happily through the morning sermon. Worshipers were also distracted sometimes when people succumbed to violent coughing fits, when drunkards vomited in full view of the assembly, or when weary souls fell asleep and snored along with the sermon.[64] Some people caused controversy and invited complaints when they brought more than their Psalter hymnals with them to church. In 1560, for example, Françoise Frochet made a spectacle of herself when she came to the sermon at St. Pierre's carrying apples, pears, and chestnuts, which she noisily shared with those sitting next to her.[65] Pierre Toulieu also got into trouble when he sat through a worship service in a countryside church with his musket propped on his shoulder and his hunting dog sleeping at his feet.[66] It is clear, moreover, that many townspeople welcomed the preaching service as an opportunity to socialize with friends or flirt with members of the opposite sex rather than to listen to the sermon. The case of Benjamin

Maret and Antoine Grifferat is altogether typical. Maret and Grifferat were brought before the Consistory in 1563 for having talked and laughed throughout the Sunday morning sermon at the temple of St. Pierre. After extensive questioning, Maret admitted to flirting with a young woman in a red bonnet while Grifferat confessed to chatting with a friend for part of the service "but not during the entire sermon."[67] Due to such noise and distractions, some people found it difficult to concentrate on the preacher's sermon. Some townspeople who suffered from poor hearing gave up attending services entirely.[68]

The presence of benches in the city's churches was a definite advance over medieval practice in which most laypeople stood or sat on the ground during Mass, but even this convenience sparked controversy.[69] Where people sat in the congregation spoke to their social status and authority, and at least some members of the congregation jealously guarded their places.[70] In 1564, for example, the Consistory reprimanded André Morel for creating a public disturbance during the Sunday morning service when he refused to give his son's seat to the baron of Mont Brissier, and showered the baron with insults when his son was forcibly removed from the bench. Four decades later, an inebriated churchgoer named Issac Chartier caused a "great scandal" at a Sunday afternoon service at the Madeleine when he forcibly removed a woman from her place on a bench designated for men. Women watching this outrageous behavior cried out so loudly that the minister David Le Boiteux had to stop the sermon and ordered the angry women to leave the service.[71] Several years later at the temple of St. Gervais, a widow named Claudine Salomon became so enraged at another woman who had claimed her choice seat that she attacked the woman with a wooden stool, striking her so hard that the victim was "in danger of losing her leg."[72] Not all seating controversies were violent; some seemed almost comical. In December 1567, the Consistory summoned to its chambers a widow named Catherine Orgaine for regularly choosing a seat close to the pulpit, in full view of the Count Palatinate (who was visiting Geneva), and shamelessly flirting with him during the sermon. Catherine informed the skeptical ministers that God had revealed to her that she would one day become the Count's wife. When Catherine could not be dissuaded from her glorious dream or her disruptive behavior at sermons, the pastors finally prohibited her from attendance at St. Pierre and required that she worship elsewhere, on pain of being sent to the city magistrates for more serious punishment.[73]

In addition to sporadic distractions and disturbances like these, more extraordinary events sometimes disrupted preaching services in Geneva. In 1572, a mentally disturbed congregant began yelling during a Sunday morning service at St. Pierre and threw rocks at city councilors seated in the privileged stalls along the wall. The ensuing uproar almost caused a citywide riot.[74] A similar uproar occurred six years later when the Genevan pastors refused to dismiss their congregations and insisted on completing their sermons despite reports of a fire blazing on the island in the Rhone River in the heart of the city. Later, the ministers received a stern reprimand from the city magistrates for their conscientiousness: henceforth, preaching must be suspended when public safety was at stake.[75] Probably the most unusual disruption of a reformed worship service in Geneva during this period occurred in 1607, when a woman believed to be possessed by a demon began barking like a dog during a communion service. The secretary of the Consistory noted (in a classic case of understatement) that such behavior caused "several people to be offended."[76] Anecdotes like these should not lead one to draw the conclusion that misbehavior and controversy was the general rule at worship services in Geneva during the period. The fact that disciplinary records report relatively few disruptions, and that ministers and magistrates alike so energetically combated them, indicates that they were probably outside the norm. Nonetheless, archival evidence of this sort reminds us that attending sermons in sixteenth- and early seventeenth-century Geneva was far from the staid, dispassionate experience often depicted in portrayals of Calvinist services in art and print. Ideals of simplicity, discipline, and good order sometimes fell victim to the complexities and vagaries of human mischief, weakness, and sin.

3. The Art of Preaching

In his biography of Calvin, published several months after the reformer's death, Beza contrasted the deceased reformer's preaching style to that of his famous colleagues Guillaume Farel and Pierre Viret. Farel excelled in a sublimity of mind that caused people to tremble when they heard him thundering from the pulpit. Viret was noted for his eloquence that entranced audiences who hung on his words. As for Calvin, he "never spoke without filling the mind of the hearer with the weightiest of insights." "I have often thought," Beza commented, "that a preacher who was a composite of these three men would have been absolutely perfect."[77] Vehemence, eloquence, doctrinal substance: these were virtues highly valued by preachers in Calvinist Geneva. If one were to add to this list three additional qualities—clarity, simplicity, and concern for Christian edification—one would have arrived very close to the homiletic style that Calvin espoused and practiced during his career in Geneva. Although John Calvin never wrote a treatise on preaching, his sermons and published writings offer extensive advice for preachers, describing (and modeling) in detail the purposes and preferred style of Christian preaching.

Calvin's homiletic theory and practice was substantially shaped by his engagement with the rhetorical culture of Renaissance humanism, his exposure to the homilies of John Chrysostom, and most important, his extensive reflection on the content and style of the biblical writings themselves. During the second half of the fifteenth and the early decades of the sixteenth century, Christian humanists such as Rudolf Agricola, Desiderius Erasmus, Philip Melanchthon, and Jean Sturm had attempted to adapt the classic rhetorical forms of Roman orators such as Cicero and Quintilian to serve the religious instruction of the Christian faithful. Their vision was to mine the wisdom of humane letters (*studia humanitatis*) in general, and the classical orators in particular, to create a program of intellectual, literary, and moral formation that would educate men and women to be wise as well as good. Calvin was a committed partisan of this pedagogical and moral program, first as a law student at Orléans and Bourges, and later, in the early 1530s, as a member of a circle of humanist intellectuals in Paris. Historian Olivier Millet has shown that Calvin's conception of Christian preaching was especially influenced by the rhetorical theories of the German humanist Melanchthon, whose ideas and writings he most likely encountered during his years in Paris.[78] In Melanchthon's preaching manual entitled *On the Duties of the Preacher* (1529) and his textbook on rhetoric entitled *Elements of Rhetoric* (1532), the German humanist had moved beyond the three traditional classifications of rhetoric focused on praise and blame (*genus demonstrativum*), persuasion (*genus deliberativum*), and courtroom pleading (*genus judiciale*) to champion a new genre of rhetoric (*genus didascalicum*) that was particularly well-suited for Christian preachers who wished to elucidate the central doctrines of Scripture. This new approach to Christian oratory, which effectively wedded rhetoric and dialectic, required the preacher to begin with a doctrinal theme or topic drawn from the biblical text; define and distinguish its key terms; identify its different causes (efficient, formal, material, and final); and then apply the doctrine's meaning to the congregation.[79] Melanchthon's theory of preaching based on the common places of Scripture became especially popular among Lutheran expositors for the instruction and moral transformation of the Christian community. Calvin gained several important insights from this new approach.[80] Most important, Melanchthon's work contributed to Calvin's appreciation for the central didactic purpose of preaching, where the truths of Scripture were laid before the audience through such stylistic elements as precise definitions, amplification, dialogue, demonstration, and illustration. So too, Melanchthon's definition of rhetoric as the form of teaching truth in an ornate fashion and the importance he ascribed to clarity of speech were important for Calvin. Even if the Geneva reformer did not employ the formal structure proposed by the *genus didascalicum*, nor adopt a topical approach to preaching, his debt to the German humanist was substantial.

Calvin's commitment to the *studia humanitatis*, with its goal of moral and cultural renewal through the recovery of ancient wisdom, also encouraged him to look to the writings of the early church fathers for insight into the nature of preaching. In this regard the homilies of the fourth-century bishop John Chrysostom were especially important for Calvin.[81] During the late 1530s, Calvin was reading Chrysostom carefully and preparing to publish a French translation of his homilies. Though the reformer never completed this project, he did write a Latin preface in which he praised Chrysostom as an expositor and interpreter of Scripture.[82] One of the primary responsibilities of the preacher, Calvin observed, was to model for the common people the proper way to read the sacred text. And in this Chrysostom excelled. The golden-mouthed bishop was famous for a clear, verse-by-verse exposition of the text of Scripture. "It was his supreme concern," Calvin noted, "never to turn aside even to the slightest degree from the genuine, simple sense of Scripture and to allow himself no liberties by twisting the plain meaning of the words."[83] Chrysostom was unique for his age, however, and Calvin found little good to say about other interpreters in the early church: Origen and Jerome obscured the straightforward meaning of Scripture with their endless allegories; Hilary's commentaries lacked clarity and showed little concern for the mind of the biblical authors; Ambrose came nearer to the true sense of Scripture but was excessively brief; even Augustine, the great doctor of the church, was often undependable as an expositor of Scripture because of his penchant for overly subtle interpretations.[84] For Calvin, then, Chrysostom's homilies provided a precedent and model for the renewal of Christian oratory in the sixteenth century. What characterized Chrysostom's preaching should be shared by all expositors of the Word: to proclaim the simple and natural sense of Scripture in a clear manner to instruct and edify the people of God.

Most important for the development of Calvin's homiletic theory and practice was his engagement with the biblical text itself. As with other reformed expositors, Calvin's preaching bears close resemblance to the method of interpretation he employed as a commentator on Scripture.[85] At the heart of Calvin's hermeneutic and theory of preaching stands a particular understanding of the nature and authority of the sacred text. Calvin and the Genevan ministers who came after him shared the conviction that because the Jewish and Christian Scriptures were the inspired Word of God they should command unique authority within the Christian church (*sola scriptura*). Though Calvin never formalized a doctrine of biblical inspiration, statements scattered throughout his exegetical and theological writings demonstrate his conviction that Scripture was the verbally inspired Word of God, infallible revelation recorded through the agency of the biblical authors.[86] While the reformer acknowledged the significant role that the human authors had played in the transmission of the sacred writings, he insisted, nevertheless, that the prophets, apostles, and evangelists had served as "sure and genuine scribes of the Holy Spirit," the "mouths" by which God communicated "heavenly doctrine," and "divine oracles" to his people.[87] As a result of their divine origin, Calvin believed, the canonical writings were without error and altogether trustworthy. He variously described Scripture as "the unerring standard," "the pure Word of God," "the infallible rule of his holy Truth," "the certain Word of God coming from heaven," "the infallible Word of God," and "free from every stain and defect."[88] To be sure, Calvin recognized that biblical language is always accommodated language as God condescends and "stutters" to the limited capacity of human understanding, like a nurse speaking to a child.[89] But Calvin did not conclude thereby that the biblical authors themselves were guilty of contradiction or error. Such a conclusion, he insisted, would impugn the Holy Spirit and overturn true religion. Moreover, because the words and message of Scripture are God's infallible revelation to humankind, Calvin believed that they should constitute the highest authority within the Christian church. The Word of God "is like the Lydian stone" by which the church "tests all doctrines," Calvin noted. Indeed, "all controversies should be decided by thy Word."[90] Finally, as a corollary to this belief in the divine nature and authority of Scripture, Calvin and Geneva's ministers also affirmed the unity, sufficiency, and clarity of the sacred text: the books of the Old and New Testaments constitute a coherent unity by virtue of their divine authorship and the single covenant of grace; the Scripture contains all doctrines necessary for salvation and for sustaining Christian faith. Moreover, the central teachings of the Word of God are not obscure but accessible to all Christians as they attend to holy writ with the assistance of the Holy Spirit.[91]

Based on their doctrine of Scripture, Calvin and his reformed colleagues drew a number of conclusions that had significant bearing on how they understood the nature of preaching and the specific methods that preachers should adopt in their sermons. First, Calvin believed that the divine message of Scripture was timeless truth and altogether relevant for the men and women in his congregation. For this reason it was critically important "that faithful people be allowed to hear their God speaking and to learn from his teaching."[92] This not only justified vernacular translations of the Scriptures but also added urgency to the recovery and use of the biblical languages of Hebrew and Greek in the study of the Scriptures. Second, the primary manner by which Christians hear their God speaking is through the preaching ministry of the church. Calvin insisted repeatedly that vernacular preaching was vital for the well-being of God's people. Preaching, along with the proper administration of the sacraments, was a distinguishing mark of a true Christian church.[93] Third, the preacher's authority is always derivative. He is like an ambassador or herald who is responsible to hand over the teachings of one who is in authority over him. In his sermons, therefore, the preacher must invent nothing new, but faithfully explain the message of salvation announced by the biblical authors through the inspiration of the Holy Spirit. When the minister does this, it is as if God himself were speaking to the congregation. Calvin notes: "When a man has climbed up into the pulpit, is it so that he may be seen from afar, and that he may be preeminent? Not at all. It is that God may speak to us by the mouth of a man. And he does us that favor of presenting himself here and wishes a mortal man to be his messenger."[94] Fourth, Calvin, Beza, and the ministers of Geneva insisted that the proclamation of

God's Word was *powerful*—indeed, life changing—as the Spirit of God used it in the life of the elect. The Spirit, who at one time inspired the biblical authors, continues to use the reading and proclamation of the Scriptures to illumine the hearts and minds of the audience so as to impart the life-giving knowledge of Jesus Christ to his people. The Word of God, noted Calvin, "will not find acceptance in men's hearts before it is sealed by the inward testimony of the Spirit."[95] For Calvin, Word and Spirit were insepa-rable. Finally, as a consequence of all this, Calvin believed that the Word of God must stand at the center of church life and serve as the focus and unction of the minister's vocation. In a memorable passage from the *Institutes*, Calvin wrote:

> Here, then, is the sovereign power with which the pastors of the church, by whatever name they be called, ought to be endowed. That is that they may dare boldly to do all things by God's Word; may compel all worldly power, glory, wisdom, and exaltation to yield to and obey his majesty; supported by his power, may command all from the highest even to the last; may build up Christ's household and cast down Satan's; may feed the sheep and drive away the wolves; may instruct and exhort the teachable; may accuse, rebuke, and subdue the rebellious and stubborn; may bind and loose; finally, if need be, may launch thunderbolts and lightnings; but do all things in God's Word.[96]

Calvin's intensive engagement with Scripture was also important in shaping his homiletic method. For Calvin, and for his reformed colleagues in Geneva, Christian preaching is expository preaching; that is, it endeav-ors to explain the biblical text in its literary and historical context and applies the message to the needs and problems of the audience. Put sim-ply, the goal of preaching is to explain the intention of the biblical author for the building up of the congregation. To do this, preachers follow the example of Scripture by employing a plain, straightforward style. Calvin recommends that Christian preachers work through their passage verse by verse, "peeling" the text as they explain historical background, define key words, discuss important theological concepts, and occasionally para-phrase the passage to lay bare its meaning. Convinced of the fundamental clarity of scriptural revelation, Calvin warns preachers against speculation and subtle arguments that conceal rather than reveal the truth of God's Word. Expositors must especially shun allegorical interpretations unless the Scripture text absolutely demands it. "Let us know," Calvin states, "that the true meaning of Scripture is the natural and simple one, and let us embrace and hold it resolutely."[97] When treating difficult passages, the expositor must look to the unity of God's revelation, allowing Scripture to interpret Scripture by consulting verses from across the biblical canon to help elucidate the literal meaning of the text. Moreover, the principle of the unity of Scripture requires the preacher to do more than dissect the various clauses and verses of his text, but to demonstrate how these indi-vidual parts relate to the theological meaning of his passage, and indeed, to the larger storyline of the Scripture as a whole.[98] And what is the central focus, or *scopus*, of Scripture? For Calvin, it is the living person of Jesus Christ himself. "[T]he Scriptures should be read with the aim of finding Christ in them. Whoever turns aside from this object...will never reach the knowledge of the truth."[99] Even once the passage is summarized and its doctrine explained, however, Calvin does not believe the task of the preacher is complete. For, just as the biblical authors—especially the Old Testament prophets—employed a holy vehemence that drove God's truth deep into the hearts of their listeners, so the Christian preacher must proclaim *and apply* the Word to God's people for their spiritual profit. "If doctrine is not supported with exhortations, it is sterile and will not pierce our hearts," Calvin observes.[100] In another sermon, he comments: "There are two things required [of preachers], first that we provide a good and pure explanation to the faithful of that which is required for their salvation, and then that we add as much vehemence as appropriate, so that the doctrine touches and enlivens hearts." Teaching and exhortation "must be conjoined, and they must never be separated."[101] In this way, the Holy Spirit achieves his sacred purposes through the ministry of the preacher, declaring God's glory, announcing the gospel of salvation in Christ, and reforming the church.

In his commentaries and sermons, Calvin frequently addressed the role of rhetoric or human eloquence in preaching.[102] While he does not dismiss the value of persuasive oratory altogether, he is adamant that in the church eloquence must always serve the Christian gospel. One of Calvin's fullest descriptions of the nature of "biblical" or "spiritual" eloquence is found in his commentary on 1 Corinthians 1:17—a passage where the Apostle Paul warns against "words of human wisdom." Calvin argues that Paul was not condemning classical rhetoric per se. Rhetoric as a human art is among the "splendid gifts of God" and "useful and suitable for the general affairs of human society."[103] Too often, however, practitioners of the rhetorical arts have been known for their ambition and arrogance, intoxicated by the splendor of words and high-sounding talk. Too often the brilliance of human eloquence has been used to obfuscate God's truth and has despised the crude simplicity of the message of the Cross. Hence, Calvin argues, God chooses to use a different kind of eloquence—a spiritual eloquence— which is powerful to bring men and women to salvation. The Apostle Paul modeled this; although he was not a born orator, he was a "minister of the Spirit" who used "unpolished and ordinary speech" to "bring down the wisdom of the world."[104] In a similar fashion, the Jewish prophets and Christian apostles declared the message of God: sometimes with words that flashed of human eloquence, but always with a message that bespoke the simple majesty, wisdom, and power of the Spirit of God. This spiritual eloquence, Calvin concludes, "is not bombastic and ostentatious, and does not make a lot of noise that amounts to nothing. Rather, it is genuine and efficacious, and has more sincerity than refinement."[105] The Christian preacher, then, should follow the example of the biblical prophets and apostles who proclaimed the Word of God with simple eloquence, wisdom, and power that came from the Spirit of God.

4. Calvin in the Pulpit

What was it like to hear Calvin preach from the pulpit of St. Pierre? It appears that Calvin stood before his congregation without sermon notes, with only the Hebrew or Greek text of Scripture before him.[106] Customarily, the first sermon in a series involved an introduction that summarized the history, general themes, and arguments of the biblical book.[107] Then, in the weeks that followed, Calvin preached successively through the biblical text, usually focusing on one to six verses at a time. A brief analysis of Calvin's sermon on Acts 2:39–40 (the conclusion of the Apostle Peter's sermon at Pentecost) delivered on Sunday, January 19, 1550, demonstrates the chief characteristics of the reformer's pulpit ministry and indicates that he followed closely the homiletic principles he defended elsewhere.[108] One is impressed, first of all, by the plain, straightforward structure of the sermon. After a brief introduction in which he recapitulates his message from the previous week, Calvin proceeds to examine the meaning of his text clause by clause, verse by verse, punctuating major transitions with inelegant phrases such as "We come now to St. Peter's speech," or "Voilà, this is what needs to be noted first of all." Other than following the flow of the passage before him, Calvin's sermon displays no discernible homiletic outline and ignores the elements of a public speech prescribed by the classic rhetoricians.[109] The sermon concludes abruptly as Calvin announces that he has run out of time and "will save the rest for another occasion." Calvin makes a few final comments and then concludes the sermon with prayer.

Throughout the course of his sermon on Acts 2:39–40, Calvin employs a direct and familiar style. He addresses his congregation with the French pronoun *nous* (we), indicating that the preacher identifies with his congregation as together they submit to the authority of God's Word. Calvin employs a variety of rhetorical techniques to hold the attention of his audience. He uses popular idioms and phrases. He supports his conclusions by making reference to other biblical passages outside his text. He is careful to avoid technical theological language and makes no reference to the Greek text behind his French translation. He sometimes paraphrases his biblical text or restates important doctrines or lessons. Calvin the preacher almost never speaks of his personal affairs. Throughout the sermon, Calvin chooses vivid images to grab the attention of his listeners: mendicant preachers are "ministers of Satan"; blasphemers have as much reverence as "dogs"; those who justify the deeds of the wicked are no better than executioners who strangle them. Sometimes Calvin paints dramatic scenes with his words to capture the imagination of his audience and convey urgency to them:

> If I should see a man getting too close to a pit, so that he is only a couple of paces from falling into it and dying, will I say nothing more to him than "Watch where you are walking"? Not at all! Rather I must shout as loudly as possible: "Oh! Do not go any further! Stop right there, otherwise you will break your neck!"[110]

Another effective rhetorical device that Calvin uses is the construction of imaginary dialogues with his opponents. For example, responding to criticisms that his language against Roman Catholics is too harsh, Calvin invents a group of professors who demand, "What need is there to cry this way against the pope and his followers, calling him the Antichrist? Should not a minister simply preach the gospel, without using words like that?" Calvin responds to this criticism by pointing his opponents to verse 40 of his text: "Voilà these terrible professors! They ought to be grieved instead of presuming to teach Saint Peter the correct preaching style or telling him what he should say!"[111]

It is important to recognize that Calvin employs stylistic elements like these in the service of his primary goal, which is to explain the doctrine of the text and apply it to his congregation. And Calvin's exposition of Acts 2:39–40 is extremely rich in the theological lessons it communicates. In a sermon that lasts less than an hour, Calvin assures his congregation of the certainty of God's promises (v. 39a) and explains the relationship between sacrament and the Word (vv. 38, 39), the legitimacy of infant baptism as a sign of God's covenant of grace (v. 39a), and the importance of renouncing the evil of this "corrupt generation" (v. 40b). Throughout, Calvin is concerned to show that the truths set forth in the book of Acts are timeless and thus relevant for the men and women in his audience: "Now all of this that Peter spoke regarding the perverse generation of his own day, we need to understand applies to our own day as well," Calvin insists.[112] Nearly every major theological insight is thus accompanied with an exhortation or a specific point of application. Sometimes Calvin offers words intended to comfort and fortify the weak of faith: "Let us recognize, therefore, that God displays his heart towards us when he opens his mouth to speak, and we must not dispute with him saying, 'Is it so, or not?'"[113] On other occasions, Calvin gives spiritual advice that is universally applicable to his audience: "Let us receive the Word of God with reverence so that it might serve as our bread and medicine."[114] Frequently, Calvin's exhortations are intended to scold sinners and call them to repentance—and it is here that Calvin's vehemence is particularly evident. Pointing to the example of the Apostle Peter, he notes: "When we see that some people have given themselves over to fornication, superfluous habits, usury, pillaging, and other similar wicked deeds, we must cry out with a loud voice: 'Hey! Do not go any further! You are near to the abyss of Hell. If you fall into there you will never be rescued, indeed you will suffer punishment forever!'"[115] Interestingly, Calvin finds it is necessary in this context to justify the fervency of his oratory: if some people are put off by his vehemence, Calvin observes, they must remember that Peter and Jesus used equally strong language to warn sinners of their danger.[116] In a striking fashion, therefore, Calvin's sermon on Acts 2:39–40 illustrates the chief characteristics that he recommends elsewhere for a Christian sermon: it lays bare the plain meaning of the text; it adopts a style that is familiar, vivid, and clear; it imparts rich doctrinal substance; and it employs holy vehemence in applying God's truth to the needs and problems of the audience. Calvin's sermon on this passage from Acts corroborates the testimony once made by Calvin's friend Conrad Badius that the reformer's preaching is "pure, plain, and appropriate for the text that he is examining" and "well-suited for the capacity of his sheep."[117]

5. Preaching After Calvin

Calvin's simple, doctrinal style of expository preaching became the model for homiletics in Geneva and among French Protestants during the generation after his death.[118] But how was one to inculcate this distinctive form of preaching in ministers who did not have the rhetorical gifts of Calvin, or who had never heard the reformer preach? One solution was to publish editions of Calvin's sermons as pedagogical tools for young preachers. So too, as previously noted, the Venerable Company coached student preachers in the weekly meetings of the Congregation and sometimes gave ministerial candidates preaching assignments in the countryside parishes to develop their homiletic skills. Moreover, some of Geneva's ministers took it upon themselves to coach and encourage young preachers through conversation and correspondence. An example of this is seen in the long, affectionate letter that Theodore Beza wrote in 1601 to a former student named Louis Courant, who had recently departed Geneva to begin pastoral ministry in France. Drawing upon forty years of ministry experience, Beza, in his letter, captures succinctly many of the homiletic priorities and pastoral concerns emphasized by Geneva's pastoral company:

> Louis, I did not want to miss this opportunity to tell you of the great pleasure that I received from hearing about the grace God has given you in the undertaking of your vocation. This should compel you a hundred times over to be on your guard and in constant care, both as to the doctrine that you have the responsibility to proclaim in its purity and entirety, as well as to the way you present it to your flock, whether they be individuals or families. Beware of polluting the holiness of true doctrine, either by indulging in vain and curious speculations and subtleties directly contrary to its simple purity, or by using a flowery eloquence that is entirely at odds with the serious and sound…simplicity of the prophets and apostles, a style that is truly divine and heavenly.

Another fault that is equally dangerous comes from a blatant neglect of the conscientious and careful reading of and continual meditation on the Old and New Testaments. It is by this means alone that one can avoid proclaiming some novelty that goes beyond the strong and sure foundation of the Holy Scriptures, which we have been strictly forbidden to do.

For reasons even clearer, one must find blameworthy [the minister] who...does not understand how passion can be used either to hasten or restrain wicked deeds. This defect is all the more dangerous when covered and clothed in the appearance of zeal, which is more aptly named presumption and dangerous indiscretion. To avoid such errors, I would especially recommend above all other books in Holy Scripture the two epistles of the apostle Paul to Timothy, from which we learn the rules that should be followed and how to keep them. Moreover, in addition to the history of the deeds of the apostles and prophets...we have the perfect example in our sovereign pastor and completely perfect teacher, the Son of God himself. The Gospel accounts of his life provide a sure and complete formula for every circumstance.

Beza concluded his letter to Courant by reminding him of what he had learned while a student in Geneva and assuring him of his affection and continued support. "I trust that you will receive all this advice from one whom you know loves you and who considers you to be among the plants that God has graciously allowed him to grow in his holy harvest. May God alone receive the glory, and may it please him to give you abundant growth."[119]

In addition to personal counsel like this, Beza and his colleague Lambert Daneau attempted to standardize in writing the primary elements of Calvin's exegetical and homiletic method and create a template for duplicating it. In the years following Calvin's death, Beza and Daneau became the primary champions of the reformer's homiletic legacy. Both men had been trained extensively in the *studia humanitatis* and were vitally interested in recent developments in rhetoric instruction in the Protestant world. Both men also recognized the strategic importance of establishing formal methods of interpreting and expositing the Scriptures that were faithful to Calvin's example, which might serve as pedagogical tools for future reformed preachers. By the 1560s, there were a number of different homiletic models and resources available for Protestant expositors, but none was more important for Geneva's ministers than the writings of the Marburg theologian Andreas Hyperius (1511–1564).[120] In his two most important works, a preacher's manual entitled *On the Formation of Sacred Sermons* (1553) and a handbook on the training of theological students entitled *On the Proper Formation for Theology* (1556), Hyperius drew a clear distinction between the form of biblical interpretation practiced in the schools, and the way in which the Scriptures should be interpreted and taught in the pulpit to the common people.[121] In popular homiletics, Hyperius recommended a method of preaching that captured a number of the priorities found in Calvin's own sermons. The preacher should briefly explain the natural or literal sense of the passage before moving on to a fuller discussion of key theological themes within the text. During the course of the sermon, it was the preacher's responsibility to confirm and apply central doctrines to his hearers by employing four rhetorical genres: the refutation of error (*genus redargutivum*), correction of vice (*genus correctorium*), instruction in moral virtue (*genus institutivum*), and words of consolation (*genus consolatorium*).[122] Like Calvin, Hyperius believed that the preacher's chief duty was to instruct and edify the people of God through the exposition of Scripture. Christian preaching was intended "to bring all the faithful to the knowledge of their sins, to faith, to the pure invocation of God, to the amendment of their lives and, if possible, to make them new men."[123] Hyperius's homiletic theories were well-known to Beza, Daneau, and their colleagues. French editions of *On the Formation of Sacred Sermons* were published in Geneva in 1563 and again in 1564.[124] Beza praised Hyperius's contribution to theology and Protestant oratory in a brief biographical sketch and poem that he included in his *Images* (1580).[125] Beza also wrote a position paper entitled "A Summary of the Method of Preaching," in which he offered general advice for preachers gleaned in part from the insights of Hyperius's work.[126] In a similar fashion, the theories of Hyperius figure prominently in a book that Daneau wrote on biblical hermeneutics, entitled *The Method of Treating Scripture* (1579).

In his perceptive study of Daneau's theological program, Olivier Fatio demonstrates both the degree to which Daneau attempted to regularize Calvin's exegetical and homiletic priorities and how extensively he drew on the writings of Andreas Hyperius to do this.[127] In the *Method*, Daneau proposed a three-step process for Scripture interpretation which coincides with the steps required for sermon preparation and delivery. (1) In the rhetorical step, the interpreter situates the biblical passage within the broader context of Scripture and then identifies the key rhetorical elements in the text (e.g., summary, solemn declaration, transition, development) to divide it into its cohesive parts. (2) In the dialectical step, the interpreter analyzes the scope of the biblical passage by studying the logical arguments employed by the sacred author, paying particular attention to such things as genus, specie, form, definition, cause, effect, and consequence. (3) In the theological step, the interpreter focuses on what the biblical passage actually means in its context. To do this, the interpreter employs a six-step method, beginning with a presentation of the essential doctrine of the passage (the *summa doctrinae*), followed by the division of the essential doctrine into its constituent parts, the explanation and definition of each part, the comparison of these parts to other biblical passages, and the resolution of apparent contradictions. Daneau recommends that "lively exhortations" be made to reinforce each doctrinal point treated. So too, he encourages interpreters to use the entire canon of Scripture as well as theological common places (*loci communes*) and biblical commentaries to help elucidate the meaning of the passage. Once the theological meaning of the text has been laid bare, the interpreter is encouraged to add four additional elements: the refutation of the errors of papists and heretics, the refutation of profane authors, the exhortation of members of the congregation to live godly lives in Christ, and the application of general moral principles to the church as a whole. As should be apparent, Daneau's *Method* is an effort to standardize several of the most important elements in Calvin's homiletic method. It mandates that a pericope be examined within the larger scope of Scripture; it requires the careful exposition of individual parts (sentences and verses) of the text without losing sight of larger patterns of argumentation and central theological themes; it expects that theological lessons will be accompanied by "lively exhortations." As with Calvin, Daneau's work seeks to promote a method of preaching that is clear and straightforward, rich in theological substance, and devoted to the edification, correction, and consolation of God's people.

Another way in which Calvin's homiletic legacy was preserved in Geneva during the late sixteenth century was through the pulpit ministry of Theodore Beza. In the final decades of his pastoral career, Beza published three sermon collections comprising eighty-seven sermons in all: *Sermons on the Song of Songs* (1586), *Sermons on the Passion of Jesus Christ* (1592), and *Sermons on the Resurrection of Jesus Christ* (1593).[128] Beza's published sermons were intended to serve as a final testament to his ministry, explaining and defending the truths of reformed Christianity, which he had spent his life proclaiming. Taken together, the sermons also function as a kind of primer for Christian ministers as they describe in detail the biblical foundations of church vocation, the duties of the pastoral office, and the nature of reformed preaching.[129] Throughout his published sermons, Beza models Calvin's simple style and instructs a new generation of ministers in the art of preaching.

Echoes of Calvin are heard frequently in Beza's published sermons as he explains to his congregation the purpose and nature of Christian preaching. For Beza, as for Calvin, the pure preaching of the Word of God is one of the marks of the true church. The church is found "where Jesus Christ is preached and no other."[130] Preaching is the ordinary instrument the Holy Spirit uses to bring sinners to repentance and faith in Christ. Citing the Apostle Paul in Romans 10, Beza notes that "faith comes by hearing, and hearing comes by the preaching of the Word of God."[131] This does not mean that the syllables and sentences of the minister hold magical power to save the listener. The locus of power resides with the Spirit of God, who uses the Christian preacher as an instrument to bring God's rich blessings and spiritual regeneration to sinners. Beza comments: "In the simple preaching of the gospel the preacher is not the one who gives to believers the salvation signified by this Word preached. That pertains to God alone."[132] Christian preaching is not only necessary for salvation but also a primary means by which Jesus Christ fortifies the elect during their earthly pilgrimage. As the people of God attend to the public exposition of Scripture, God imparts his graces to them, thereby feeding their souls, convicting them of sin, and strengthening their faith. Further, Beza echoes Calvin's conviction that, as with the sacraments, Christian preaching is an instrument that the Holy Spirit uses to unite the believer to Christ. In "the ordinary administration of the Word," Beza notes, "Jesus Christ also presents his entire self to us, to be received as by the hand of our faith."[133] Indeed, believers encounter Christ through "his holy Word purely proclaimed," which, when received by faith, enables us to "mount even to the high places where he is seated at the right hand of God."[134]

For Beza, as for Calvin before him, good preaching consists in the concise exposition of the biblical text that includes instruction and edification. The preacher instructs the congregation by a careful explanation of the text of Scripture—every word in it should be weighed and considered—with an eye toward bringing clarity to the central doctrines of the Christian faith.[135] The didactic function of preaching is thus of crucial importance. But biblical exposition is more than a recitation of grammatical or theological observations drawn from a verse-by-verse study of the sacred text. Beza shares Calvin's conviction that the good preacher must teach and *apply* the Word of God to the audience.

> First, let us learn here that to preach the gospel is not simply to explain a text and deal with several questions of doctrine, as some people would like to insist who try to shut up their pastors when they exceed these limits. But rather, it is necessary to apply the medicine to the patients, for otherwise preaching would be without fruit.[136]

The faithful preacher is like a spiritual doctor, who not only instructs the people of God, but also applies the "medicine" of God's Word in such a way that they receive edification through words of consolation and correction. This is what sets the pulpit apart from the university lectern, Beza insists. The preacher *applies* Christian doctrine to his congregation for their spiritual edification with the goal of making them mature in Christ.

Theodore Beza insists that a particular homiletic *style* best served these aims of Christian preaching. Trained as a humanist, Beza, like Calvin, recognized the value of studying classical rhetoric and praised the art of speaking persuasively in human affairs. Indeed, in the early centuries of Christianity, God had blessed the church with Greek and Latin theologians who were eloquent in speech and writing. Accordingly, Beza warned preachers against remaining satisfied with a barbaric style (*le barbare jargon*) that ignored conventions of proper speech and despised valid insights gleaned from the liberal arts. With that said, however, Beza emphasized that the Christian preacher must not depend on human eloquence or employ "artificial rhetoric" in the pulpit.[137] The preacher's model should not be the lawyer, pleading a case at the bar, nor a professional orator making a harangue or delivering a pleasant discourse. The pulpit is not the place to show off one's learning, display one's rhetorical skills, or indulge in idle speculation about divine mysteries. Rather, the minister of the Word must emulate the prophets and apostles—and especially Jesus himself—who employed simple and straightforward language, a "holy rhetoric" or "fire" which the Holy Spirit used to illumine, purify, and set ablaze the hearts of those who listened. Beza here differs not at all from Calvin in describing the kind of rhetoric a Christian preacher should adopt:

> One must learn this holy rhetoric, not from the principles of the orators...but from examples in the writings of the Prophets and Apostles, where one will find neither a contrived manner of writing, nor a flowery arrangement of words, but a weight, a gravity, and a vehemence which is apparent to anyone with sound judgment.[138]

The "foolishness" of Christian preaching is that its power comes not from human eloquence or learning but from the Holy Spirit "who has a rhetoric all his own." In its simplicity, clarity, vehemence, and doctrinal *gravitas*, Christian preaching reflects the majesty of God's Word and testifies to the fact that the church is established and built through the power of God alone.[139]

Beza's extant sermons provide rich insight as to how he actually practiced the preacher's craft. Though these sermons were prepared for publication, and several of them appear substantially redacted, overall their form and style still bear striking resemblance to Calvin's homiletic.[140] Beza's sermons are simple in their form and organization. In beginning a preaching series, he usually devotes several sermons to larger preliminary questions related to the historical background or theology of the book under consideration. Once this prolegomena is complete, Beza then employs the *lectio continua* method of exposition, preaching successively through a biblical book several verses at a time.[141] Beza's sermons contain no formal introductions: he normally begins a sermon with only a sentence or two recapitulating the previous week or summarizing the text under consideration. Next, Beza systematically "peels" the passage as he rehearses the narrative, explains the context, and considers parallel passages that shed light on the meaning of the text. Only occasionally does Beza signal the "heads" of his homiletical outline in advance. More often, the preacher highlights his major points in the course of the exposition, employing unadorned transitions ("it follows in our text"; "to return to our text"). Beza regularly digresses from careful analysis of the scriptural passage to draw applications, answer objections, and develop broader theological or ethical lessons for the edification of his congregation. On occasion, he is sensitive that he has departed too far from holy writ: "Some might say that I have gone far from my text, but this is not true."[142] The conclusions of Beza's sermons are as concise and unadorned as his introductions. Usually, he briefly summarizes the passage of the day and offers a final prayer or word of exhortation: "may God give us the grace to understand fully and meditate on this very precious teaching for his honor and glory, and for our salvation."[143]

Although Beza's sermons are plain and straightforward in their organization, they nonetheless reveal a preacher who is skilled both as pedagogue and rhetorician. As with Calvin before him, Beza is committed to the instruction and edification of his audience. The reformer employs a variety of didactic strategies to promote the understanding of his audience: he reiterates themes and lessons; he adopts language that is accessible to his hearers; on the rare occasions that he employs Latin or Greek in his sermons, he is quick to provide translation ("as we say in common language"). Beza does not burden his exposition with syllogisms or appeals to theological authorities, ancient or contemporary; his sermons are garnished instead with hundreds of biblical quotations and allusions.[144] That is not to say that Beza ignores matters of high theology in his homiletic ministry. Like Calvin, he regularly addresses weighty and controversial doctrines such as predestination, justification by faith alone, and the nature of Christ's presence in the Lord's Supper. He does depart from his mentor in this, however: whereas Calvin was somewhat reticent to preach on the doctrine of the Trinity or employ Nicaean language to describe the persons of the Godhead in his sermons, Beza suffers no such compunction.[145] Nevertheless, these dogmatic discussions do not devolve to the abstract or theoretical; they are framed for the purpose of not only instructing but also edifying the Christian community.

One is impressed by the familiar and practical quality of many of Beza's sermons—and here again the parallel with Calvin's homiletic is striking. Beza addresses his congregation as "my brothers" and "people of Geneva" and speaks often in the first person plural. The reformer frequently repeats well-known proverbs and maxims, such as "Good pope, wicked man," or "the wisest men often act the most foolishly."[146] If illustrations are rare, Beza is adept at well-chosen (or at least, arresting) images to capture the attention of his hearers: transubstantiation is worse than cannibalism practiced by natives in America; the Roman Church is like a thief who enters a house, pillages it, and then takes up residence in it after having chased the owners away.[147] From time to time he alludes to the contemporary situation (e.g., an earthquake, a recent legal case, massacres in France), but he almost never refers to his own personal experience from the pulpit.[148] Beza employs a variety of rhetorical strategies to move his audience to repentance and obedience. As with Calvin, he makes regular use of repetition, parallelism, the interrogative, and irony. For example, in the early 1590s, Beza bemoans the moral decline in Geneva that has accompanied war with Savoy.

> Especially now with the moral license spawned by this war, how often the name of God is defiled! How many shocking curses! How many horrible

blasphemies are committed! But who cares about them? Who tries to correct them? Who reports them, or is willing to testify against the offenders?...How then shall we be excused, we who pride ourselves as the reformed Church of God?...Should we not instead cry with bitter tears to avert the wrath of God?...Alas, yes![149]

Like Calvin, Beza uses drama to illustrate important lessons or to evoke the judgment of God. He holds imaginary conversations with his opponents, whether gluttons or skeptics, Nicodemites or Catholics. Similarly, he occasionally speaks through the mouth of a third person—friend or foe—to dramatize biblical truth: "Jesus cries at our gates, 'I am hungry. I am thirsty. I am naked. Will no one give me anything to eat?'"[150] If Beza does not hesitate to address matters of high theology, he nonetheless remains sensitive to the more immediate concerns of his congregation. His sermons contain much that could be described as pastoral theology, addressing such practical questions as how Christians should approach suffering and death, the qualities of good parenting, or the steps involved in making a wise decision.

At the same time, however, Beza employs "holy" vehemence to rebuke sinners and call them to repentance. Beza's sermons are full of strong words against a laundry list of sinners, whether adulterers, blasphemers, greedy merchants, negligent judges, or dishonest tradesmen. He scolds members of his congregation for their spiritual lethargy and stubbornness. He criticizes parents for failing to send their children to catechism and city councilors for showing clemency toward convicted criminals. Beza launches his most scorching homiletic volleys against ostentatious wealth and immodest dress. In one sermon he explodes: "Shame, shame, shame on such stinking and repulsive habits! They have nothing to do with true Christianity!"[151] Beza's prophetic zeal—which was shared by Calvin and most of the other ministers of the period—may well seem overly harsh and vitriolic to the ears of many moderns; indeed, as we shall see, Geneva's townspeople were sometimes angered and offended by such strong pulpit rhetoric. Nevertheless, these sermons portray Beza as a preacher convinced of the importance of his message and passionately committed to the spiritual well-being of his flock. Like Calvin, Beza's preaching is direct and passionate, intended to excite interest, provide instruction, and instill conviction and change in his audience.[152]

The simple style of preaching practiced by Calvin, regularized by Daneau, and defended and modeled by Beza served as the standard homiletic approach in Geneva's pulpits during the sixteenth century. Regardless of whether a preacher was young or old, it was expected that he would follow Calvin's example by preaching expositional sermons in a plain and familiar style, uniting doctrinal instruction and spiritual exhortation. Eloquence was always the servant of the gospel message. Two controversies shortly after the turn of the century indicate the degree to which Calvin's style had become normative in the reformed churches of Geneva and France, and the extent to which that norm was being challenged by younger preachers with more innovative homiletic styles. We have already described in chapter 3 the controversy surrounding the ministry of Michel La Faucheur, whose flamboyant preaching style raised the eyebrows and suspicions of Geneva's Company of Pastors in 1608. On that occasion, the Company exhorted Geneva's preachers to continue to follow in the footsteps of John Calvin, "that great servant of God," who joined the "solid teaching of the truth" with a style that was as "simple as it was fruitful" for the purpose of edification.[53]

Five years before this, another controversy had erupted within the ranks of the Venerable Company which, if anything, had posed an even greater threat to Calvin's homiletic legacy inside and outside of Geneva. The episode began in August 1603 when Gabriel Cusin, the twenty-nine-year-old minister of the parish of Jussy, was examined by the Venerable Company for a pastoral post in the city. Geneva's ministers became sharply divided over his candidacy: while everyone agreed that his doctrine was orthodox, some members raised concerns about his preaching style. His diction and rhetorical style were "new," "overly elegant," and filled with dangerous allegories—a style the Company judged was better suited to entertain his congregation than to instill in them "good and solid judgment." Cusin was ultimately elected to the city post by majority vote, but only after being warned against using allegories in his homiletic delivery and reminded of his responsibility to maintain "an honorable and prudent gravity" in his sermons.[54] The matter was far from resolved, however. Three months later, the Company received letters from reformed churches in Languedoc, complaining that French students at the Genevan Academy were being corrupted in their preaching styles by the controversial example of Gabriel Cusin. Once again, the ministers confronted their colleague and demanded that he employ greater simplicity in both his comportment and pulpit oratory. The Company highlighted several grievances. In his exposition of Scripture, Cusin "should not recite an infinite number of passages which serves more for ostentation than edification." So too, he must strictly avoid using allegories, which are Satan's instruments "to undermine the authority and certitude of the Scripture and profane them." Moreover, Cusin must stop showing off by reciting his prayers extemporaneously and must eliminate all novelties from his sermons that only nourish curiosity among his parishioners.[55] Despite the Venerable Company's continued support of Cusin, several of the ministers had become resentful of their popular colleague, fearing that his sermons were prejudicial to the well-being of the church.[56]

During the next several years, the "new style" of preaching practiced by Cusin and other reformed preachers in France continued to grow in popularity, especially among young students of theology. The situation became so serious that, in February 1605, the Venerable Company summoned to the Auditoire all ministerial students from the Academy to warn them about preaching methods that employed a "new style and new language" borrowed from pagan authors and Catholic preachers. Such "painted" eloquence undermined "the solid simplicity of the Scriptures" and "transformed their preaching of the Word of God into a vain babble." It was feared that in the long run this style would erode the piety, morals, and sound doctrine of the churches. The ministers urged the young scholars instead to read the sermons and emulate the preaching style of those "greatest and most notable servants of God"– among them Calvin and Beza—and devote themselves henceforth to the work of the Lord in all modesty and simplicity.[157] This attempt to block the progress of innovative preaching styles does not appear to have been very successful. The following year, more letters arrived from France complaining that the sermons of some Geneva-trained preachers were "spoiling the Scripture by allegorical expositions that were more subtle than solid." Geneva's ministers organized a second assembly to warn the students.[158] Several months later, in January 1607, the Venerable Company sent a letter to the eighteenth National Synod of La Rochelle defending the simple style of preaching practiced by the reformed churches. The traditional method, with "its solidity and simplicity" as well as its "doctrine and piety," was best suited for the edification of God's people and remains the "chief and natural beauty" of the churches. In their letter, Geneva's ministers made no reference to Gabriel Cusin nor admitted any responsibility for the proliferation of new preaching styles among younger reformed ministers. Instead, Geneva's pastors sounded the alarm about the innovative methods of some preachers. The reformed must eschew all vain eloquence that tickles the ears through its flamboyant style. They must avoid imitating the oratorical methods of Jesuit preachers who seek more to win admiration than edify the people. So too, reformed preachers must show restraint in appealing to the writings of nonbiblical authors such as Seneca, Plato, Aristotle, or the Greek or Latin fathers.[159] This spirited defense of Calvin's simple style was received with approval by the National Synod of La Rochelle which met in the spring of 1607. At the same time, recognizing Geneva's complicity in the crisis, the synod sent a letter to the Company of Pastors admonishing it to provide better supervision over theology students at the Academy and to ensure that all ministers avoided allegories in their sermons.[160] The Company of Pastors took this opportunity once again to remind Cusin and the other city ministers of the virtues of the traditional style of homiletic: their sermons should "treat and explain doctrine in a manner that was simple, clear, and suitable for edification, abstaining from allegories and all other devices not suitable for the sacredness of the Word."[161] Neither Calvin nor Beza could have summarized their style of preaching any more succinctly. Even so, the controversy over preaching styles in the reformed churches was far from settled, as the following decades would show.

6. Preachers and Their Audience

How did Geneva's townspeople and rural folk view their preachers and interact with the sermons they heard during the period from 1536 to 1609? Answering these questions with any sort of precision is difficult. Though the sporadic complaints and criticisms of disaffected Genevans who appeared before the Consistory offer an intriguing glimpse into religious life during the period, such disciplinary cases do not provide a balanced appraisal of public attitudes in general. In a similar fashion, the praise that friends and admirers sometimes lavished on Geneva's more famous preachers cannot serve as a reliable measure of popular sentiment as a whole. Overall, it seems safest to state what is obvious: a handful of Geneva's ministers were exceptionally gifted and popular as preachers; a handful of the ministers had meager homiletic ability and were disliked by their congregations; and the majority of the ministers were competent, though unexceptional, expositors of the Word of God. As we have already noted, Calvin, Farel, and Viret were considered to be excellent preachers in their day and occupied an honored place among French Protestant orators.[162] Following in Calvin's footsteps, Theodore Beza was also a highly regarded preacher. In the heady days after the Colloquy of Poissy (1561), Beza preached to crowds in Paris numbering six thousand people and more.[163] Once installed in Geneva, Beza's sermons attracted large crowds of Geneva's faithful as well as a steady stream of curious outsiders. Former students recalled with pleasure Beza's substantial gifts of communication and the erudition evinced in his teaching and preaching.[164] Here one found (as Antoine de La Faye reported) "an exceptional eloquence, a spirit so pleasant and friendly that he won the hearts of all those who saw him."[165]

Other Genevan preachers such as Simon Goulart, Charles Perrot, and Antoine de Chandieu appear to have been talented preachers as well. When the famous Hellenist scholar Isaac Casaubon heard Goulart preach for the first time in 1599, he recorded in his journal: "I just heard Goulart explain the biblical story of the purification of the Virgin. O what a pious and erudite man! What a blessed people to have such a distinguished man as a preacher!"[166] That Chandieu also had substantial skills as a preacher is suggested from this glowing eulogy delivered by his friend, the Geneva syndic Jacques Lect:

> His manner of speaking was gentle and simple, without external affectation or feigned brilliance, but at the same time not lacking in skill or eloquence. In this way he joined the understanding and richness of the material examined with the beauty of language.... His elocution was full of modesty, his gestures measured, conventional, and naturally soft. All harshness and violence of expression was unknown to him. And such moderation full of wisdom and kindness made a greater impression on people than the anger of so many others. At the same, he was not beyond speaking frankly or with severity in his sermons when it appeared useful to him. And so, people always listened to him with admiration.[167]

By the turn of the century a new group of talented preachers was emerging to replace Beza and Chandieu, and to join Goulart on the Venerable Company. Though none of them achieved the international stature of their predecessors, these ministers, such as Jean Jaquemot, Antoine de La Faye, Gabriel Cusin, Pierre Prévost, and Jean Diodati, did impress listeners with their homiletic abilities. When the English ambassador paid a visit to Geneva in 1628, for example, he made a special point of attending—and praising—the sermons of Prévost and Diodati.[168]

Not all of Geneva's pastors were talented or popular as preachers, however. Soft-spoken men such as Abel Poupin, Claude Baduel, and Lambert Daneau lacked the strength of voice necessary to preach in the large sanctuary of St. Pierre and thus were assigned to smaller parish churches in the city or countryside.[169] Other preachers like Pierre Ninaux and Jacques Bernard were avoided because of their reputation for being boring or difficult to understand.[170] A city dweller named Pierre Mourex complained in 1560, for example, that he could learn as much from his minister's sermons when he was sleeping as when he was awake.[171] More frequently, Geneva's pastors were disliked, not because they were incompetent, but because of their combative personalities, their harsh sermons, and their sharp reprimands. Though nearly all of Geneva's ministers drew criticism from time to time for sermons that were too severe or too pointed, several men were particularly notorious for stirring popular outrage by their vitriolic and abusive preaching. Angry words and incessant scolding too easily masqueraded as the reformed virtue of "holy vehemence." A widow named Aguette Bouliet perceptively described this tendency in an interview before the Consistory in 1581: "The ministers become angry when they show zeal in the pulpit," she complained.[172] Whether this style of preaching was born of holy zeal or bad temper, it invariably created emotional distance and resentment between the preacher and members of his congregation. Hence, an immigrant from Normandy (and supporter of Jerome Bolsec) complained that "the preachers do nothing but insult people."[173] A similar criticism was voiced by a chamber girl speaking of her minister François Bourgoing: whenever he speaks "it seems that he wants to bite people."[174] Geneva's Small Council sometimes felt it necessary to summon the ministers to demand that they moderate their tone, reminding them that sermons should edify, not scandalize, the people of God.[175]

Of all the ministers, Raymond Chauvet was probably the most hated. A ferocious preacher, Chauvet seems to have delighted in excoriating the sins and sinners that he encountered both in the church and marketplace. In 1546, for example, Chauvet pronounced from his pulpit a curse on members of his congregation who were leaving the sermon early: "May evil, plague, war, and famine fall upon you!" he cried.[176] Over the next two decades, dozens of defendants appeared before the Consistory complaining about the abusive verbal attacks of Chauvet, people whom he had variously maligned as wicked foxes, wicked idolaters, good-for-nothings, gossips, papists, prostitutes, whores, and fornicators.[177] Geneva's townspeople returned their minister's venom, giving him the nickname *Torticol*—literally, "pain in the neck."[178] Tybaulde Serralinez said that Chauvet had the soul of a cat or dog.[179] Petit Pierre claimed that he would rather listen to his dog bark than to Chauvet preach.[180] A servant named Monet even admitted that he once contemplated grabbing Chauvet by the neck and stabbing him with a knife.[181] On a number of different occasions Geneva's magistrates and ministers were forced to reprimand their colleague, admonishing him "not to be so angry and to use greater moderation" in his sermons and conversation.[182] But overall, the Company of Pastor's tolerance for such inflammatory preaching was quite high; Chauvet's voice rang out from Geneva's pulpits for twenty-five years until his death in 1570.

Not surprisingly, Geneva's townspeople regularly discussed and harbored strong opinions about the preachers' appearances, words, and behavior. Blanche Firmin was charmed by the adoring glances and sparkling eyes of the (married) Bonaventure Bertram, minister of Chancy.[183] A girdle-maker named Loys Piaget praised the "beautiful words" of the sermon he heard and found the minister's message "very agreeable."[184] Louise de La Cheval also admired the "beautiful sermons" of the minister of Bossey-Neyden, Jean Du Perril: "How happy his mother must be to see him so learned!" she remarked. But her friend Gabrielle Faillon had a different view, opining that Du Perril was a "fool and a beast and that no one liked him."[185] A similar conversation occurred between Bernard Mognet and the (unnamed) sister-in-law of Claude Vellu. When the woman encouraged Mognet to visit Geneva to hear Calvin's preaching, the man retorted that there were two devils in hell, and one of them was Calvin.[186] The fact that nearly all of Geneva's ministers were French born did not escape the notice of Geneva's citizens. Some natives deeply resented—and even made racist slurs or xenophobic comments against—these influential foreigners in their midst, especially during Calvin's lifetime.[187] The ministers were accused of being "bishops" and "cardinals," with Calvin and Beza as their "pope."[188] In 1553, the Consistory confronted a drunkard who, when under the influence of strong drink, regularly cried out "Calvin is the god of Geneva!"[189]

Another topic of conversation was to compare Geneva's pastors with the Catholic preachers in France or Savoy. No doubt many Genevans viewed the sermons of Calvin, Beza, Goulart, and their colleagues as an improvement over the fare offered by Catholic preachers. But not everyone did. Mathieu Brutal when he was visiting from Paris in 1569 commented to friends that the Cardinal of Lorraine preached the Scripture every bit as effectively as Theodore Beza.[190] In a similar fashion, a barber named Mathieu Doussin opined that the mendicant preachers in neighboring Chambéry were more biblical in their sermons than Geneva's ministers.[191] François Le Quiert was probably not alone when he reserved judgment on the question, noting that "there is preaching here in Geneva *and* in the papacy and I do not know which of them to believe."[192]

The deluge of vernacular sermons that poured forth from Geneva's pulpits not only made laypeople consumers of the Word but also empowered them to become critics of their ministers' exegesis and theology. Especially in the early years of the Reformation, Geneva's townsfolk frequently criticized the ministers for preaching doctrines that they did not think were found in Scripture or of which they did not approve. Certainly some of these critics were Catholic believers still loyal to the old church, but others were advocates of the Reformation who remained skeptical about their ministers' teachings. In 1548, for example, Balthasar Sept caused a great scandal during the Sunday service when he burst out laughing and mocked the interpretation given by his minister Abel Poupin about the Great Trumpet on Judgment Day.[193] Several years later, François-Claude Blecheret complained that the minister Nicolas Colladon was "extravagant with his text and did not follow it" but "jumped all over the place."[194] Another parishioner, angered by Calvin's doctrine of predestination, stated in 1556 that "the gospel one preaches here is not the gospel of Jesus Christ."[195] A soon-to-be banished Anabaptist named Martin Guillaume agreed: "the Word of God preached by the ministers was only foolishness."[196] Aimé Plonjon made the novel suggestion that Geneva's ministers should avoid interpreting the Scripture altogether and "preach only the text of the Gospel."[197] On occasion parishioners became confused about—or misrepresented—the message of the sermon. In 1546, for example, Jacques Gruét spread the rumor that Calvin in a sermon had accused all people who danced of being debauched. Calvin corrected him: he had said that dancing often *leads to* moral debauchery.[198] Twenty years later, Jean Paris was accused of spreading the more damaging report that Beza had claimed in a sermon that the Virgin Mary was damned and in hell. Witnesses established that Beza had never said such a thing—but that Paris had.[199]

Another way to gauge popular attitudes toward reformed preaching in Geneva is by looking at attendance at sermons. The fact that only a small number of people were disciplined by the Consistory year to year for frequent absence from sermons probably indicates that most city dwellers attended the mandatory preaching services on Sunday and the Day of Prayer.[200] On the other hand, sermons on weekday mornings were not nearly as well attended. During the final decades of the sixteenth century, Beza and his colleagues beat a well-worn path to the city council, complaining about sparse attendance at the *cultes ordinaries* and bemoaning the spiritual malaise indicated by such neglect.[201] During Advent of 1566, a sizeable group of inhabitants from the parish of St. Gervais were summoned to Consistory and scolded for not attending preaching services. If they did not seek out God at sermons, how could they expect God to seek them out during the rest of the week? they were asked.[202] In 1583, the ministers arranged that a public crier go through the city to remind inhabitants (and the city councilors) of their responsibility to attend weekday sermons.[203] Five years later the Venerable Company expressed its deep concern to the magistrates that there is "a great contempt for the Word of God, zeal has grown cold, and our reprimands both from the pulpit and in Consistory accomplish nothing."[204] Beza lodged a similar complaint in a sermon from this period: it used to be that reformed Christians would go one hundred leagues to feed upon the "celestial bread" of God's Word, but now they despise the divine Word and grumble if they have to walk a short distance to hear it preached. "The heavenly manna that we found so sweet in the beginning has now lost its flavor for us," Beza lamented.[205]

Homiletic hand-wringing like this accomplished little, for in 1592 the Venerable Company was once again forced to send a delegation to the Small Council to report that the city marketplaces were full of men, women, and children during the hour of the weekday sermons. The ministers requested that city officials do something to redress such a "great contempt for the Word of God."[206] Attendance in the parish of St. Gervais was particularly poor, probably due to the minister's reputation for long-winded sermons and the controversy that swirled around Goulart at the time of the Juranville-Martinville affair.[207] During holy week of 1596, barely a dozen people attended weekday sermons at St. Gervais.[208] And so the problems continued, with the ministers complaining in 1600 and again in 1605 about the dismal attendance at their sermons during the week. As they had done several times previously, the city magistrates directed local wardens to remind city residents of their religious duty, while at the same time advising the ministers to shorten the length of their sermons and to be more moderate in their admonitions from the pulpit.[209]

One can only conjecture why attendance at weekday services was often so poor. No doubt some people boycotted these sermons because they did not like the preacher or found the sermons too long, too dull, or too harsh. But probably more often the daily requirements of city life made the *cultes ordinaires* inconvenient and burdensome. For many Genevans, attending preaching services was a regular—and even valued—part of their religious experience, but two or three sermons a week was judged adequate to meet their spiritual needs.

7. Preaching to Power

One group of people that listened with special attentiveness to the ministers' sermons were the civil authorities of Geneva. For the magistrates, passionate sermons that attacked the authority or persons of the city councilors were not merely embarrassing, they could be judged seditious. Between 1536 and 1609, the Company of Pastors repeatedly crossed swords with the Small Council as the ministers struggled to preserve their right to proclaim God's Word without interference from the civil authorities.[210] In the ministers' view, it was imperative that they be allowed to fulfill their prophetic role of preaching truth to power. As Beza saw it, the ministers were called by God to condemn public unrighteousness, otherwise the people would treat them as if they were watchdogs that did not bark.[211] During the second half of the sixteenth century, the ministers "barked" frequently in their sermons, reprimanding the magistrates for interfering in church affairs, for miscarriages of justice, for harsh treatment of the poor, and for neglecting to enforce city ordinances against usury, blasphemy, adultery, and ostentatious displays of wealth. Along the way, this struggle between the church and magistracy produced a number of clerical casualties; the ministers Jean-Raymond Merlin, Jean Le Gaigneux, Nicolas Colladon, and Urbain Chauveton were all dismissed from their posts when their pulpit attacks became too strident or when they refused finally to submit to the magistrates' censure or the collective will of the Venerable Company.

A tenuous compromise of sorts was achieved by the early 1570s, in large part through Theodore Beza's deft and moderate leadership. The magistrates agreed not to interfere in or "gloss" the ministers' sermons. The pastors, for their part, promised to confer as a Company before attacking public vice from their pulpits. So too, the ministers promised not to criticize city councilors by name in their sermons and indicated a willingness to consult the magistracy in private before criticizing it in public. Even so, this compromise was fragile and contested. As Beza disappeared from public life in the 1590s, the magistrates employed increasingly draconian measures against the Company of Pastors in an effort to bridle dissent. As we have seen, Simon Goulart in 1595 was imprisoned for his pulpit attacks against the magistracy. In 1603, Pierre Prévost received a severe reprimand from the Small Council for asking in a sermon why criticism of the magistracy was not permitted in a republic like Geneva. Surprised by their harsh response, the city ministers politely reminded the magistrates that it was the pastors' God-given duty "to admonish the magistracy from the pulpit, for it is the pulpit of truth."[212] Three years later Jean Jaquemot was imprisoned for two weeks for criticizing, with words judged "too biting," the hypocrisy of several (unnamed) city councilors who had danced and become drunk on a Sunday afternoon after attending the morning worship service.[213] Jaquemot defended himself, in part, by appealing to homiletic principles previously stated by Calvin and Beza:

> The Holy Spirit guides his servants in such a manner that when they address people who are docile and teachable, and not filled with malice, they treat them with gentleness. But when they confront people who are impious and profane, who despise the grace of God, then they must speak more harshly to awaken them from their stupidity. For it is like physicians who prescribe mild medicines when the illness is not so dangerous, but must resort to stronger medicine when there is a tumor present.[214]

The level of suspicion between ministers and magistrates heightened further in 1608 when in their Sunday morning sermons the preachers of all three city churches criticized the Council of 200 for extending clemency toward a convicted adulterer and war hero named Ami Pichard. The Small Council summoned and interrogated the three offending preachers—Goulart, Prévost, and David Le Boiteux—and then upbraided each of them for their scandalous sermons: the ministers had embarrassed the magistrates and undermined their authority; they should have lodged their protest in private rather than from their pulpits. The ministers held their ground, insisting that the magistrates' failure to enforce city ordinances was a public injustice that deserved a public rebuke. Moreover, the ministers demanded that the freedom of the pulpit be preserved (here they appealed to the example of Beza) lest the magistrates "close the mouth of the Spirit of God."[215] In the end, the Venerable Company restated the traditional principle while at the same time warning their colleagues who preached in the city to temper their language. In the future, ministers should "continue to reprimand, exhort, and publicly admonish" the magistrates, but with "the wisdom and moderation required and appropriate for the edification of the Church."[216] Though a temporary truce had been achieved, ministers like Simon Goulart, Jean Jaquemot, and Pierre Prévost were very much aware that the traditional freedom granted to Geneva's preachers was slowly being undermined.

Occasional anecdotes and controversies like these offer only an impressionistic view of popular attitudes toward preaching in sixteenth- and early seventeenth-century Geneva. Though disapproval and dissent are not hard to find in the written records of Geneva's city council and the Consistory, the fact remains that throughout the period the magistrates continued to mandate church attendance, most townspeople continued to attend preaching services, and the ministers continued to deliver hundreds of sermons each year. If some residents criticized the city's pastors and did everything possible to avoid the sermons, many others welcomed daily preaching services as a time to socialize with their friends, learn about the outside world, and receive religious instruction and spiritual edification. It is likely that as the decades passed, the majority of Genevans came to understand and even agree with most of what was proclaimed from the city's pulpits. After all, the ministers in their sermons were declaring the city's "official theology" that had been established by popular vote and city statute, and which was taught every week in Catechism class. What must have appeared to many people as strange and confusing in the 1540s, over time became the established, "traditional" doctrine of the Genevan church. In that sense, by the dawn of a new century the ministers' sermons were an essential tool for preserving the religious status quo and defending the orthodox doctrine handed down by Calvin.

Geneva's preachers occupied a prominent position in the city's public life in the sixteenth and early seventeenth centuries. From their pulpits, Calvin, Beza, Goulart, and their colleagues functioned as exegetes, pedagogues, theologians, social commentators, family counselors, and moral watchdogs. More fundamentally, the ministers believed that in their role as preachers they were God's chosen spokesmen, charged with proclaiming the Christian gospel which was God's powerful instrument for bringing about spiritual regeneration and effecting the reformation of the church. This conviction undoubtedly contributed to the ministers' confidence in the importance of their pastoral office and added special urgency to their daily preaching ministries. But at the same time, Calvin and his colleagues recognized that many men and women remained apathetic and resistant, and were even hostile to the message that they proclaimed. Church discipline was therefore essential to ensure that Geneva's townspeople lived in a manner consistent with the Word of God and that the city remained a gospel outpost, reformed in both doctrine and practice.

CHAPTER 7 | The Ministry of Moral Oversight

VISITORS TO CALVINIST GENEVA, both friends and foes alike, frequently commented on the disciplined moral behavior they encountered among the city's residents. The English exile William Whittingham who visited Geneva in the early 1550s praised the republic as the "mirror and model of true religion and true piety." In a similar fashion, fellow exile John Knox admired the saintly comportment of Geneva's citizens: "In other places, I confess, Christ is truly preached, but manners and religion so sincerely reformed, I have not yet seen in any other place."[1] Three decades later, an inquisitive Jesuit priest named Luca Pinelli made a brief stopover to observe religious life in Geneva and to interview Theodore Beza whom he likened to the "pope among the Calvinists." Pinelli recorded his surprise that during his three-day visit he "never heard any blasphemy, swearing or indecent language" in the city, a fact that he ascribed to the devil's cunning who wished to "deceive simpleminded people" with the "appearance of a reformed life."[2] An even stronger impression was left on the Württemberg minister Valentin Andreae, who visited Geneva in 1610. "When I was in Geneva I observed something great that I shall remember and desire as long as I live," he later wrote:

> There is in that city…as a special ornament, a moral discipline which makes weekly investigations into the conduct, and even the smallest transgressions of the citizens…. All cursing and swearing, gambling, luxury, strife, hatred, fraud, etc. are forbidden, while greater sins are hardly ever heard of. What a glorious ornament of the Christian religion is such a purity of morals![3]

The fact that Valentin Andreae was the grandson of Beza's arch nemesis, the Lutheran theologian Jacob Andreae, makes his praise of Geneva's moral practice all the more striking. Whether attributed to God's activity or Satan's deception, Geneva's reputation as a citadel of moral discipline and public probity was widely recognized during and after Calvin's lifetime.

In this chapter, I will explore the manner in which Calvin and the pastors of Geneva attempted to promote personal sanctification and public righteousness through the work of the Consistory. A careful study of all the extant records of the Consistory from 1542 to 1609 provides a unique window into the structure and purposes of reformed discipline, as well as the shifting priorities of Geneva's ministers as they interviewed sinners week to week and applied the spiritual "medicine" of church discipline in an effort to promote repentance, reconciliation, and spiritual growth. Although Calvin's brand of moral discipline was often intrusive and almost always controversial, it served as a crucial dimension of pastoral care in reformed Geneva well into the seventeenth century.

1. The Consolidation of Calvin's Consistory

All of the major Christian confessions during the early modern period—Roman Catholic, Lutheran, the Church of England, Anabaptist, Reformed—were committed to defending orthodox doctrine and enforcing standards of public morality among their adherents. Nevertheless, reformed churches following Geneva's example gave special prominence to moral discipline and created institutions to oversee societal righteousness and encourage personal sanctification. Over the last four decades, historians of early modern Europe have carefully studied Calvinist moral discipline and the tribunals that reformed churches established to enforce it. These moral tribunals, known variously as consistories, kirk sessions, presbyteries, or Kirchenrat, have been of particular interest to social historians, who have found in disciplinary records a rich deposit for understanding popular belief and daily life in the age of the Reformation. Dozens of specialized studies now exist that explore the form and function of reformed discipline in various regions of Europe, from Transylvania to Scotland, from Emden to Nîmes.[4] Accordingly, perceptions of these disciplinary institutions have changed significantly. Whereas consistories were once often portrayed as repressive agents of social control created primarily to punish misbehavior and promote a kind of puritan moral austerity, recent scholarship has highlighted the fashion in which disciplinary institutions helped to establish the structure of Calvinist marriage, preserved the sacral unity of the Eucharistic community, and protected the prevailing moral norms in reformed churches and territories. Scholars have also recently demonstrated the manner in which Calvinist social discipline contributed to the process of confessionalization and state-formation in early modern Europe.[5] At the same time, specialists have gained a new awareness of the penitential and pastoral objectives of reformed discipline. Even as they attempted to regulate public morality, consistories concerned themselves with educating the ignorant, defending the weak, and mediating interpersonal conflicts. My study of Geneva's Consistory from 1542 to 1609 especially demonstrates this *pastoral* dimension of moral supervision and church discipline in Geneva during Calvin's lifetime and over several generations that followed.[6]

As we have seen, Calvin's return to Geneva in September 1541 was a personal triumph that served as a vindication of his ministry and provided the reformer with a unique opportunity to translate into reality a theological conception of the church that had gradually crystallized during his stay in Strasbourg, informed through his study of Scripture and the influence of Martin Bucer and Johannes Oecolampadius.[7] One important feature of this conception was Calvin's conviction that the church must have the authority not only to proclaim freely the Word of God but also to provide spiritual correction to members who rejected right teaching or refused to turn from wicked behavior. The exercise of church discipline by ministers and elders was essential for the well-being of the Christian community, he believed. It was like a "father's rod" that preserved the unity and purity of the church and guided God's people to obedience and spiritual health. Calvin articulated this belief in a well-known passage that appeared for the first time in the 1543 edition of the *Institutes*: "as the saving doctrine of Christ is the soul of the church, so does discipline serve as its sinews, through which the members of the body hold together, each in its own place." Consequently, "all who desire to remove discipline or to hinder its restoration—whether they do this deliberately or out of ignorance—are surely contributing to the ultimate dissolution of the church."[8] For Calvin, a true reformation of the church required that God's people be reformed both in doctrine *and* in personal behavior.

The *Ecclesiastical Ordinances*, drafted in November 1541, represented the first step toward the realization of Calvin's ecclesial vision. As noted earlier, the *Ordinances* for the first time created the Consistory, a church tribunal consisting of the city's pastors and twelve lay elders who were charged to meet every Thursday at noon "to see that there is no disorder in the church and to look for solutions when it is necessary."[9] The Consistory was required to follow the guidelines for church discipline outlined in Matthew 18:15–17. In cases of private vice, the pastors and elders were first to admonish the sinner in private. If the offender ignored these warnings, he or she should be summoned to Consistory for examination and formal rebuke. Those sinners who remained obstinate, who refused to repent or reform their behavior, were to be suspended from the Lord's Supper for a brief period of time so that they might "humble themselves before God and better recognize their error."[10] In cases of public misbehavior, the *Ordinances* stated that the ministers and elders might forgo private admonitions and summon the offender directly to Consistory for examination and censure. Defendants suspected of criminal conduct were to be delivered to Geneva's magistrates for additional civil punishments. In all of its deliberations, the Consistory was expected to treat offenders with moderation and gentleness, recognizing that these "corrections are nothing but medicine to bring sinners back to our Lord."[11] In the view of the *Ordinances*, church discipline was intended to heal, not harm, the wayward Christian; its purpose was primarily remedial, not punitive.

The *Ecclesiastical Ordinances* made it clear that the church's prerogative over moral discipline was limited to the use of "the spiritual sword of the Word of God"—the Consistory's power must in no way encroach upon the magistrates' authority to execute public justice in the city.[12] What remained unclear, however, was whether or not the magistrates could supersede the will of the Consistory in moral cases that held implications for civic life. And too, the language of the *Ordinances* was vague—perhaps intentionally so—as to whether ultimate jurisdiction in cases of suspension and excommunication belonged to the church or civil magistrates.[13] These points of ambiguity triggered a protracted struggle from 1542 to 1555 pitting Geneva's pastors, who were committed to Calvin's vision of a disciplined Christian community, against a sizeable number of Geneva's senators and townsfolk, who were suspicious that the foreign-born ministers wished to impose a new regime of "papal" tyranny on the city. This tug-of-war between ecclesiastical and civil authority was in no way peculiar to Geneva, of course, as many Protestant territories in the first half of the sixteenth century struggled to define the role of the territorial church within the broader interests of the political community. What was unique about Geneva, however, was Calvin's surprising "victory" in 1555 that allowed the city church to gain complete control over ecclesiastical discipline and the right of excommunication, thereby departing from the state-controlled church model practiced by reformed cities such as Strasbourg, Basel, Bern, and Zurich.[14]

Only the general outline of this conflict needs to be recounted here.[15] In March of 1543, the Council of 60 was charged to study the question, "Does the Consistory have the authority to prohibit people from the Lord's Supper?" Not surprisingly, the council ruled in the negative, concluding that the church's power to wield the "spiritual sword of the Word of God" involved the admonition of sinners and nothing more.[16] Not deterred by this decision, the Consistory continued to assert and exercise its right to suspend from the Lord's Supper obstinate sinners who refused to repent of wrongdoing. During the 1540s, Calvin's Consistory suspended a relatively small number of Genevans from the sacrament of the Table—on average one or two dozen per year. The Small Council for the most part turned a blind eye to these ecclesiastical censures, not wishing to revive the politics of confrontation with the city ministers that had led to Calvin's forced departure in 1538. Nevertheless, the ministers' campaign to purify the city of immorality and Catholic "superstition" soon stirred widespread public resentment, especially as the ministers pushed for the closure of the city taverns, suspended several of Geneva's leading citizens for a variety of sins, and (most controversial of all) defied the wishes of parents by assigning biblical names rather than the names of popular Catholic saints to infants at baptism.[17] Several of Geneva's most powerful citizens, men like François Favre and his son-in-law, the future syndic Ami Perrin, ran afoul of the

Consistory and became outspoken critics of Calvin, protesting bitterly that the city's ministers were usurping the traditional rights of the magistrates. By the early 1550s, as the number of annual suspensions began to climb steadily, complaints against Calvin's discipline became common currency throughout the city, even within the chambers of the Consistory itself. When Boniface Conte was interrogated by the Consistory in 1551 for suspected fornication he told Calvin to his face that the reformer was not his prince and that he would not answer Calvin's questions.[18] Later that same year, François Chabod was reprimanded by the ministers and elders for stating publicly that "people should not be suspended from the Lord's Supper unless the magistrates commanded it."[19] Calvin's sharp dispute with Jerome Bolsec and his supporters over the doctrine of predestination in 1551 only intensified this climate of resentment and distrust.

The crisis finally came to a head during the years 1553 to 1555. At the center of controversy were Philibert Berthelier, the son of the famous Genevan patriot-martyr, and the syndic Ami Perrin and his political faction known as the Children of Geneva (*Enfants de Genève*), or the Perrinists. In December 1552, Berthelier was excommunicated and jailed for three days for ridiculing the minister Raymond Chauvet in public—calling out "There's that dandy, there's that dandy!"—and then, afterward, angrily denouncing the ministers and elders for the draconian measures they had taken against opponents of Calvin's doctrine of predestination.[20] Over the next months, Berthelier remained unrepentant and refused to seek pardon from the church. Instead, in early September 1553, he challenged the prerogative of the Consistory by petitioning the Small Council to revoke his suspension, a request that the Syndic Ami Perrin and his allies who controlled the council were more than happy to grant. Calvin and the ministers reacted swiftly and decisively: they announced from their pulpits that they would not give the sacrament to Berthelier at the upcoming celebration of the Lord's Supper, and then they threatened to resign en masse if the magistrates did not reverse their decision.[21] An impasse had clearly been reached. The Small Council was forced to backtrack, asking Berthelier to abstain for the moment from the Supper, while it negotiated with the ministers and solicited political advice from the reformed cantons of Switzerland. The council also sent the question to the Council of 200, which ruled in November of 1553 that "the Consistory has the power to suspend no one [from the Lord's Supper] without the command of the Small Council."[22] Calvin and his colleagues still refused to back down, however.

The matter was finally resolved, not by negotiation, but by the annual elections of January 1555 in which, thanks to the votes of hundreds of newly enfranchised French immigrants, the supporters of Calvin won control of all four syndic posts and gained a slim majority on the Small Council. Calvin's allies quickly solidified their victory at the ballot box by purging Perrin loyalists from the Council of 200 and quickly selling the right of *bourgeois* (and with it the privilege to vote) to more than fifty French immigrants, most of whom were strong supporters of Calvin.[23] For Perrin and his friends, this was the last straw. On the night of May 16, 1555, the Perrinists took to the streets in a drunken protest that quickly degenerated into a riot, in the midst of which Ami Perrin (illegally) seized the syndic's black baton symbolizing the magistrates' authority and waved it over the crowd. Though no one was injured in the melee, the new government judged it to be nothing less than an act of open rebellion and moved decisively to crush Perrin and his faction. By the end of the summer of 1555, more than forty-five Perrinists found guilty of crimes, ranging from disorderly conduct to sedition, had been sentenced to punishments of fines, public reparations, banishment, and even death by hanging. Ami Perrin, Philibert Berthelier, François Chabod, and a dozen other "conspirators" narrowly avoided the hangman's noose by fleeing Geneva. With a stroke, the most vocal opponents of Calvin's vision of church-sponsored discipline were eliminated.

In retrospect, the events of the summer of 1555 were decisive in realigning political power in Geneva and solidifying Calvin's control over church affairs in the city. As William Naphy has shown, the new ruling elite that emerged after 1555 was a coalition of anti-Perrinists, political newcomers, and wealthy French immigrants that threw its full support behind Calvin's moral and religious program, thereby establishing Geneva's identity as a Calvinist bastion for more than a century.[24] In the decades that followed, the office of elder on Consistory became an important stepping stone for political advancement within the magistracy. One important result of Calvin's victory of 1555 was that the Consistory now had complete freedom as it applied church discipline and restored sinners to the church. This prerogative was further strengthened by several important concessions that Calvin was able to secure from the Small Council in the years that followed. In 1556, the magistrates allowed for the first time that formal oaths be administered to witnesses who testified in disciplinary cases; henceforth lying to Consistory constituted the civil crime of perjury.[25] The following year, the council issued an edict that required people who had been suspended from the Lord's Supper to be reconciled to the church within six months, on pain of banishment from the city. The Edict of 1560 extended the ministers' role even further in that it gave them new advisory powers in the annual elections of elders to Consistory, allowed men of bourgeois status (and not just full citizens) to be appointed to the office of elder, required that major excommunications be announced publicly from the church's pulpits, and mandated public reparations for sinners guilty of notorious scandals.[26] These latter two edicts which strengthened the Consistory's power to enforce discipline were incorporated into the revised edition of the *Ecclesiastical Ordinances* (1561). Finally, during the 1560s, Calvin and his colleagues were successful in convincing Geneva's magistrates to adopt tough new civil penalties against adultery as well as to enact sumptuary codes to suppress excessive luxury in clothing and banqueting.[27]

With the turbulent political standoff of the 1540s and early 1550s behind them, Calvin and Geneva's ministers now had free rein to implement their vision of a Christian commonwealth that was reformed both in doctrine and practice.

2. Moral Discipline in Theory and Practice

Geneva's unique brand of church-sponsored discipline emerged from biblical and theological reflection, as well as everyday practice. Calvin's fullest explanation and defense of church discipline appeared in the 1559 edition of the *Institutes* (Book IV, chapter 12). Over the next half century, Geneva's ministers like Beza, Chandieu, and Daneau frequently restated and defended Calvin's formulation in their sermons, private correspondence, and published writings. More often than not, the opponents of consistorial discipline whom they engaged were not Lutherans or Catholics, but other reformed churchmen, such as Jean Morély, Thomas Erastus, and Adrian Saravia, who believed that the power to excommunicate belonged rightfully to the entire Christian congregation, or to the magistrates, or to bishops rather than exclusively to ministers and elders. In the midst of these contentious debates, Beza and his colleagues made explicit what had remained implicit in Calvin's theology, namely, that church discipline rightly practiced was an essential mark (*nota*) of a true church, inseparable from the pure preaching of the Word and the proper administration of the sacraments.[28]

What scriptural warrant did Geneva's ministers provide for their understanding of corrective discipline? Calvin and Beza found biblical justification for the practice of church discipline throughout the Christian Scriptures, but especially in Paul's Letters (e.g., 1 Cor 5; 2 Cor 2:5–11; 2 Thes 3:15; 1 Tim 1:20) as well as in Jesus' mandate to his disciples in the Gospel of Matthew (16:19 and 18:18–19). The reformers believed that when Jesus entrusted the spiritual "keys" of God's kingdom to his disciples, he was granting to the Christian church as a whole the authority to bind and loose sinners through the proclamation of the gospel and corrective discipline. Specifically, the "power of the keys" was exercised by ministers and elders as they declared God's judgment against obstinate sinners through admonition and excommunication ("to bind") and applied God's forgiveness toward those who repented through words of absolution and consolation ("to loose").[29] Calvin insisted that the power of the keys did not give the church the authority to pronounce damnation or salvation—that decision belonged to God alone. Instead, the church's discipline was always provisional, intended to rescue the wayward in a spirit of mildness and gentleness.[30] In this way, Calvin averred, reformed excommunication was to be distinguished from the Catholic pronouncement of anathema, for whereas the latter "condemns and consigns a man to eternal destruction," the former warns the sinner of future condemnation and "calls him back to salvation."[31]

Calvin, Beza, and their colleagues believed that ministers exercised the power of the keys in three primary ways. First, the spiritual authority to "bind and loose" was exercised in a general way when ministers preached the gospel in their sermons, announcing God's righteous judgment upon the wicked and God's promise of salvation to those who turned to Christ in repentance and faith. Second, the power of the keys was employed more particularly when pastors and lay elders conducted annual household visitations to examine the character and doctrine of church members, or when they admonished sinners in private conferences. Finally, ministers and elders employed the power of the keys through the ministry of the Consistory as they confronted people who were guilty of moral failure and excommunicated from the Lord's Table those who refused to repent of their error. At each stage of discipline, church leaders needed spiritual discernment to apply the appropriate measures of rigor and gentleness to bring about the repentance and restoration of the sinner. Wise pastors, Beza once observed, need "not only to discern the illness, but also the situation and disposition of the patient, looking for the best medicine to prescribe, preaching the Law to the hardened, and the gospel of grace to those despairing. In brief, let us always condemn the sin, but try to save the sinner."[32] This was Calvin's view as well. The power of the keys needed to be exercised with wisdom and gentleness, in the hopes of rescuing the sinner. Otherwise discipline might degenerate into "spiritual butchery."[33]

Geneva's ministers believed ecclesiastical discipline had three primary purposes or goals. First, moral correction helped preserve the purity of Christ's church and protected the Lord's Supper from being profaned. Second, church discipline was intended to protect Christians from the bad influence of wicked people. Third, moral discipline was intended to shame rebellious sinners, thereby hastening their repentance and making possible restoration to the Christian community.[34] With these goals in view, Calvin warned the reader of the *Institutes* against trying to create a perfect Christian society through discipline that was too rigorous—that was the mistake of both the ancient Donatists and modern-day Anabaptists, he believed. "[T]o consider the church already completely and in every respect holy and spot-less when all its members are spotted and somewhat impure—how absurd and foolish this is! It is true, therefore, that the church has been sanctified by Christ, but only the beginning of its sanctification is visible here [on earth]."[35] Because of this inherent tension between God's power to trans-form sinners and the persistence of sinful human nature, Calvin believed that Christian pastors needed to have realistic expectations about what could be achieved through moral oversight and correction. On this point, Calvin expressed his agreement with the early church father Cyprian: "Let a man mercifully correct what he can; let him patiently bear what he can-not correct, and groan and sorrow over it with love."[36]

Calvinist discipline in Geneva depended upon an elaborate system of surveillance and pastoral supervision within the city and countryside parishes. The *Ecclesiastical Ordinances* (1541) required that twelve lay elders be assigned to each of the city's neighborhoods so that they might "keep an eye on everything."[37] In a similar fashion, Geneva's ministers lived in different neighborhoods of the city so that they might know the members of their local congregation and be in a better position to exercise pastoral care and corrective discipline. In addition to pastors and elders, city officers known as *dizeniers*—minor magistrates whose primary duties were military and administrative—were given broad powers of supervision over each of the city's twenty-five civil districts to warn sinners and if necessary, send offenders to Consistory. In 1550, the ministers gained permission for the first time to conduct annual visitations of the city's households to examine foreign visitors and domestic servants as to their knowledge of the Christian faith and their preparation for the Lord's Supper. By the time that the *Ecclesiastical Ordinances* were revised in 1561, the scope of annual visitations had been broadened even further: city pastors, accompanied by an elder and *dizenier*, were now required to visit all of the households in their quarter each year before Easter "to examine each person briefly regarding his faith" so that no one would come to the Lord's Table "without an understanding of the grounds of his salvation."[38] These household visitations became a crucial aspect of pastoral care and supervision in Geneva over the next half century. Through these regular interviews Geneva's ministers were able to monitor the religious knowledge of their parishioners, address misbehavior and interpersonal conflict behind closed doors, and identify moral cases that were serious enough to justify further action by the Consistory. A good number of Geneva's residents appear to have chafed at this intense program of moral oversight. Jean Dacront probably expressed the opinion of many when he complained to a friend in 1556 that "the Devil and the Consistory never sleeps."[39]

The network of moral oversight functioned differently in the dozen rural parishes under Geneva's sovereignty. To assist the countryside pastor and the local governor or *châtelain*, the Consistory appointed each year a rural elder (called a *garde*) who was expected to watch for "vice and scandals" in the parish and to deliver offenders to the Consistory in the city.[40] As for rural visitations, the *Ecclesiastical Ordinances* (1561) mandated that a commission of two city councilors and two city ministers be delegated each year to evaluate the quality of ministry in the countryside parishes. The commissioners were required to assess the minister's character, the minister's sermons (were the sermons faithful to the gospel *and* edifying for the people?), and the minister's diligence in visiting the sick and admonishing sinners. The commissioners were also charged to exhort parishioners to attend worship services and to apply them to their benefit.[41]

The large number of disciplinary cases that came before the Geneva Consistory beginning in the 1540s indicates the overall effectiveness of this system of pastoral supervision and oversight. Every Thursday at noon, dozens of people were summoned to the Consistory's chambers for interrogation or to provide testimony. Most defendants came voluntarily; those who did not were brought forcibly by the lieutenant of the Consistory (called the *sautier*) or by the rural *garde*. The hearing began with a member of the Consistory, usually the head elder or the moderator of the Company of Pastors,[42] asking the accused why he or she had been summoned. Sometimes that question alone produced the desired confession, but normally defendants would feign ignorance or insist on their innocence. There then followed a series of pointed questions intended to rattle even the most obstinate sinner. For example, when a student named Louis Braquet was called before the Consistory in 1580 for suspected Catholic sympathies, the interrogation went like this:

> Louis Braquet was asked if he went to the Lord's Supper. He said no. He was asked why not. He said that he was not adequately prepared. He was asked why he was not prepared. He answered that he still had difficulties regarding [the reformed doctrine of] the bodily presence of our Lord Jesus Christ in the Supper. He was asked if he shared his doubts with anyone else. He said no, but admitted also to have doubts about [the church's interpretation of] the passage in the Apostles Creed where it said that our Lord descended into Hell. It seemed to him that this statement proved that there was a purgatory.[43]

In cases where more than one party was involved, defendants were given the opportunity to tell their sides of the story and respond to their accusers. Sometimes the complexity of the case—or all too often the dissimulation of defendants—forced the Consistory to defer discussion to a later session when witnesses might be called to corroborate testimony. In the case of Louis Braquet, the ministers subpoenaed his brother Jean as a witness, who testified under oath that Louis had in fact discussed his Catholic views publicly in a debate with fellow students.[44]

Sessions of the Consistory sometimes became tense and combative. When the ministers confronted Guillaume Torteau for excessive drinking at a tavern, for example, he became so enraged that he threw his hat on the ground in front of the Consistory and demanded a hearing before the magistrates.[45] In a similar fashion, an elderly bachelor named Jaques Du Puis slammed the door of the Consistory's chambers and stalked off angrily after the ministers warned him about the dangers of allowing his chamber girl to sleep in the kitchen next to his bedroom.[46] People of more sensitive temperament sometimes burst into tears when confronted by the intense questioning and stern admonitions of the ministers. Pernette Aberjoux, for example, "wept and cried" in the presence of the Consistory after she was forced to admit abandoning a child that she had born out of wedlock.[47] Similarly, when Jeanne Coulairin was confronted for stealing bread and clothing from the city hospital, she threw herself on the ground and "cried for God's forgiveness."[48] The impression left by the Consistory registers is that the ministers and elders were usually adept at exposing falsehood and determining guilt. Consequently, most hearings achieved an admission of wrongdoing and pleas for forgiveness. Only rarely did the Consistory give up and leave the accused to the "judgment of God" or refer the case to the magistrates with the hopes that they could "more fully determine the truth."[49]

Once guilt was determined, the ministers and elders applied one of several types of corrective discipline to the offender, depending on the gravity of sin and the degree of contrition expressed. In ascending order of severity, these spiritual penalties included: (1) verbal reproof and admonition by Consistory, (2) public confession and reparation before the church, (3) minor excommunication (also known as suspension), and (4) major excommunication.[50] In cases of private sins or minor moral infractions, the ministers and elders delivered a stern lecture to the chastened sinner, variously described in the Consistory registers as holy reproofs (*les sainctes admonitions*), warnings (*les advertisements*), encouragements (*les exhortations*), or strong admonitions (*les bonnes remonstrances*). Occasionally, offenders were required to confess their failure on bended knee or, in cases of unresolved quarrels, to submit to a service of reconciliation with their enemies. More serious "public" sins, that is, offenses that were notorious and caused public scandal, often required public confession in front of the congregation on a Sunday morning. Only rarely do the secretaries of Consistory provide details as to the substance of these rebukes, but evidence suggests that these admonitions often included general pastoral advice and exhortations from the Scripture. To a notorious adulteress, Calvin delivered "beautiful admonitions from the holy Scripture."[51] A city notary charged with usury was exhorted "from the Word of the Lord" to fulfill "his duty of love toward his neighbor and help him in good conscience."[52] The Consistory encouraged an angry wife to "win the heart of her husband and live in peace with him" as well as to seek the honor and glory of God.[53] Louis Braquet was ordered to meet with Theodore Beza and other city ministers so that they might dissuade him from his Catholic views and answer his objections to reformed doctrine.[54] Pastoral reprimands like these were not always well-received, of course. When the ministers scolded a gambler named Guillaume Barbelet for his laziness and neglect of his seven children, Barbelet shouted "arrogantly and uncivilly" that he, not the ministers, was responsible for feeding his children, and that he still had five sols to buy food for them.[55]

In their admonitions and pastoral advice, the ministers were not usually imposing a "foreign law" on the townsfolk of Geneva. Rather, their discipline reinforced standards of behavior and belief that were accepted as normative by most members of the community: Genevans must attend sermons and eschew papal "idolatry"; abusive husbands must stop beating their wives; delinquent fathers must abstain from drunkenness, find work, and instruct their families in the fear of the Lord; women must obey their husbands and attend to the needs of their households; children must go to school or choose a trade and obey their parents. Behind such pastoral advice and admonitions, of course, loomed the threat of more serious action. Sinners who refused to admit their wrongdoing, or who remained resistant to change, faced the unpleasant prospect of suspension from the Lord's Table, major excommunication, or even civil punishment.

The *Ecclesiastical Ordinances* recognized two kinds of excommunication, minor excommunication (usually called suspension) and major excommunication.[56] The penalty of minor excommunication or suspension was the least severe and far and away the most common form of interdiction: around 96–97 percent of all known excommunications in Geneva between 1542 and 1609 were of this sort. Described in the sources variously as a ban (*une interdiction*), a suspension (*une suspension*), or a prohibition (*une défense*), minor excommunication barred the sinner from the sacrament of the Lord's Table but not from social contact with other church members or from public worship services. The ministers and elders expected that suspensions would be of short duration, for one or two of Geneva's quarterly communion services, after which sinners were to be reconciled to the church. The roll call of miscreants who received this form of censure makes for colorful and often tragic reading. It includes adulterers and Anabaptists, blasphemers and wife beaters, drunkards and gluttons, business cheats and petty thieves. People were suspended for neglecting their children, visiting fortune-tellers, praying the rosary, missing sermons, urinating in church, fighting with their neighbors, and singing profane songs. From a modern vantage point, some of these disciplinary cases appear both trivial and heavy-handed: the wife of Denis Courtoys was suspended for cursing during childbirth; Phillibert Binot was censured for wearing a golden necklace on her wedding day; Jean Vignier was excommunicated for throwing his crossbow to the ground in anger following an archery contest.[57] Moreover, on some occasions, the Consistory's discipline seems to be nothing short of cruel and pastorally disastrous, as when the Consistory suspended a young husband and schoolteacher named Job Verat in 1565 for dissimulating about his sexual impotence. In this instance, Verat's parents complained bitterly that "if Monsieur Calvin had still been alive, [the Consistory] would not have behaved in this fashion."[58]

The penalty of major excommunication (*l'excommunication*) was a more severe judgment but was employed much less frequently. Between 1542 and 1609, only around 3–4 percent of all interdictions were of this more extreme variety. "Very rarely must one resort to excommunication," Beza once commented in a letter to Heinrich Bullinger.[59] The Consistory reserved this type of discipline for hardened sinners who stubbornly refused to repent, or who were guilty of egregious public sins such as habitual usury, flagrant sexual misconduct or religious heresy. Thus, for example, a spur maker named Pierre Arman was excommunicated in 1569 for having sold coal at inflated prices to his poor neighbors.[60] In a similar fashion, Maurice de La Fontaine received "harsh and severe censures" and then was excommunicated from the church for the crimes of rape and sexual assault.[61] In cases like these, the *Ecclesiastical Ordinances* stipulated that ministers announce at the end of their Sunday morning sermons the expulsion of the sinner from the spiritual community, which included, at least in theory, social ostracism until repentance occurred.[62] Hence, when Antoine Pellinque stoutly refused to affirm the orthodox doctrine of the Trinity (claiming that a divine spirit had instructed him otherwise), the Consistory finally decided to "proclaim and publish his excommunication in the Church."[63] What was the precise nature of the social ostracism practiced against sinners like these? Though the Consistory registers themselves provide few answers, the Venerable Company did address this question in response to a query from the reformed churches of Normandy in 1564. Writing on behalf of his colleagues, Beza advised the churches to avoid "frequent association" with people who had been excommunicated from the church. He emphasized, however, that this general policy of exclusion did not apply to the relationship shared by husbands and wives or to the civic obligations of magistrates and subjects. Moreover, Beza insisted that excommunicated persons should be welcomed—indeed encouraged—to attend public preaching services, because it was by hearing God's Word that even the most hardened of sinners might be brought to repentance. And was not repentance "the principle goal of excommunication" in the first place?[64]

The ministers and elders of Geneva appear to have been relatively even-handed in meting out discipline, blind for the most part to the status and social prominence of defendants. They suspended not only artisans, merchants, and peasants, but also influential urban professionals, powerful city magistrates, and wealthy aristocrats. In 1568, for example, the Consistory suspended the former syndic Jean Chautemps—one of Calvin's strongest allies—for committing the sin of adultery twelve years earlier.[65] The Consistory also disciplined family members of Geneva's pastors. Over the years, the Consistory scolded and suspended ministers' sons and daughters for various types of inappropriate behavior, including writing lewd letters, ridiculing the schoolmaster, fighting with knives, entering clandestine marriages, and fornicating before marriage.[66] A handful of ministers' wives were also subject to consistorial investigation and discipline, including the spouses of Jean Chapuis, Bonaventure Bertram, and Honoré Blanchard.[67] In addition, Geneva's ministers sometimes watched their extended relatives, sisters and brothers, nieces and nephews, daughters-in-laws and sons-in-laws, endure the humiliation of being called to Consistory.[68]

Geneva's ministers themselves were also subject to consistorial scrutiny and judgment. Between 1542 and 1609 the Consistory summoned and examined no fewer than eighteen members of the Venerable Company for moral failure (see table 7.1). In all, nine ministers from the Venerable Company are known to have been suspended from the Lord's

TABLE 7.1 Consistorial Discipline Against Geneva's Ministers, 1542–1609

NAME	YEAR	OFFENSE	TYPE OF DISCIPLINE	DEPOSED BY MAGISTRATES
Simon Moreau	1545	Accused Fornication	Not Stated	Yes
Aymé Méigret	1546	Fornication	Not Stated	Yes
Jean Fabri	1556	Adultery	Not Stated	Yes
François Bourgoing	1561	Party to Clandestine Marriage	Reprimand	No
Jean-Raymond Merlin	1564	Rebellion vs. Magistrates and Ministers	Reprimand	Yes
Louis Henri	1570	Usury	Major Excommunication	Yes
Bonaventure Bertram	1570	Quarrel with Wife; Lying	Reprimand	No
Nicolas Colladon	1571	Rebellion vs. Magistrates and Ministers	Reprimand	Yes
Urbain Chauveton	1571	Rebellion vs. Magistrates and Ministers	Suspension	Yes
Jean Le Gaigneux	1572	Rebellion vs. Authority; Abandoning Post	Suspension	Yes
Jean de Serres	1572	Abandoning Post; Avarice	Suspension	Yes
George Druson	1577	Scandal; Avarice	Suspension	Yes
Honoré Blanchard	1583	Abandoning Post; Lying; Scandal	Suspension	Yes
Louis de La Maisonneuve	1583	Fornication	Suspension Likely	Yes
Jean Guérin the Younger	1587	Fornication	Major Excommunication	Yes
Simon Goulart	1595	Rebellion vs. Magistrates and Ministers	Reprimand	No
Jacques Royer	1605	Rebellion vs. Magistrates and Ministers	Major Excommunication	Yes
Enoch Mollet	1609	Fighting	Reprimand	No

Supper for the following sins: rebellion against the magistrates (three cases), fornication (two cases), dereliction of duty (two cases), scandal (one case), and usury (one case). Examining such cases of discipline *against* Geneva's ministers provides a number of interesting insights. First, every minister who was suspended from the Lord's Table during this period was also deposed from office by the Small Council—usually with the full support of the pastoral company. Church discipline and magisterial justice worked in tandem. Second, a significant number of Geneva's ministers were deposed from their posts by the Small Council *without* being suspended, or disciplined, or even examined by the Consistory. In all, 16 percent of the ministers (22 out of 135) who served Geneva's churches from 1536 to 1609 were removed from office for misbehavior.[69] This percentage is slightly higher than the rate of dismissal witnessed in other reformed churches during the same period.[70] Third, though ministers suspended from the Lord's Supper were usually restored to the sacrament following repentance and reconciliation, this process of reintegration did not include restoration to their pastoral offices. In fact, none of the ministers deposed from office during the years 1536 to 1609 were permitted to resume pastoral work in Geneva, although several went on to ecclesiastical careers elsewhere in reformed Europe.[71] What becomes clear, then, is that church discipline employed against Geneva's pastors displayed features and achieved outcomes that were unique from most other moral cases. Disciplinary action against ministers served not only to foster repentance and protect the Christian community from bad examples, but also clarified power relations within the Company of Pastors, established boundaries of authority between church and state, defined norms of acceptable clerical behavior, and protected the dignity of the pastoral office.[72]

The decision by the Consistory to impose the penalty of suspension or major excommunication on a sinner brought with it significant religious and social consequences. Most important, the offender was temporarily barred from the Lord's Supper—no small penalty for reformed Christians who believed that the sacrament of the Table was a means of grace offered by Christ for the spiritual nourishment of believers. The decision to suspend a man or woman from the sacrament served as a serious rebuke of the sinner's life and warned of divine condemnation if repentance was not forthcoming. Suspension also entailed social penalties. In a state of suspension, men and women were not usually permitted to contract a marriage, baptize a child, or serve as a sponsor at baptism. These sanctions not only jeopardized the spiritual well-being of the offender and his or her household but might also disrupt the social and financial networks binding families and kinship groups together.[73] The Consistory registers contain many instances in which suspended persons finally submitted to consistorial discipline to obtain permission to marry or serve as a godparent at baptism.[74]

For most Genevans, the prospect of appearing before the Consistory, to say nothing of being publicly disciplined, was both humiliating and frightening. Elisabeth and Marguerite Mége stated that they would rather have their heads cut off than appear before the Consistory.[75] An immigrant named Jean Lefèvre complained that he would experience "great dishonor back in France for having been called to Consistory" in Geneva.[76] The stigma attached to suspension and excommunication damaged reputations and strained relationships; it caused neighbors to talk and enemies to taunt. Benoit Constantin attacked a neighbor for calling him a "jealous and wicked excommunicate."[77] More sinister was the case of Jean Clemencin who threatened to kill his wife if she ever again reported his abusive behavior to Consistory. After demanding that Clemencin stop beating his wife, the ministers and elders suspended him from the Lord's Supper and sent him to the magistrates for punishment.[78] This last example illustrates the legal consequences that sometimes accompanied Genevan church discipline. As an ecclesiastical court the Consistory had no authority to impose corporal punishment. However, in cases where misbehavior was not only sinful but criminal, the Consistory functioned as a de facto advisory board to civil justice both by gathering evidence about the crime and by recommending appropriate punishments, whether fines, imprisonment, beatings, or banishment. These three dimensions of church discipline—spiritual sanction, social shame, and the threat of civil punishment—made suspension and excommunication particularly effective pastoral tools for regulating public behavior and restoring sinners to the church. Whether these sanctions also promoted a change of heart and stimulated personal sanctification is far more difficult to determine.

Once sinners acknowledged their guilt and displayed remorse, they were expected to undergo one of several rituals to demonstrate the sincerity of their repentance before being readmitted to the sacrament. A sinner must "demonstrate the fruit of his repentance," the ministers insisted.[79] For less serious offenses such as dancing, drunkenness, or gambling, the offender usually returned to the Consistory chambers and begged the ministers' and elders' forgiveness, often on bent knee. In the case of a notorious gambler named Pierre Vandel, he was ordered to demonstrate the genuineness of his repentance by burning in public his playing cards "for the common edification."[80] In cases of public arguments and family quarrels, the ministers and elders required that estranged parties participate in a ceremony of reconciliation in which, in the presence of the Consistory, they apologized to one another, acknowledged the other to be a "person of the good," and shook hands or embraced. For sins deemed to be public and especially egregious—including fornication, usury, and Catholic behavior—the Consistory required repentant sinners to confess their sins in front of the entire congregation at the beginning of the Sunday morning worship service. Thus, a widow named Anthoine de Monet, found guilty of participating in an exorcism and attending Catholic Mass, was required by Consistory to attend her countryside church and "beg God's forgiveness before the people as an example."[81] This public ritual achieved a number of different objectives. Not only did it validate the sinner's repentance and serve as a deterrent for others, it also constituted a clear public statement of the sinner's reincorporation into the visible church and union with the faithful company of Christians.[82] But the ritual was also humiliating, and not a few offenders chose to leave Geneva rather than submit to such intense public shame. Still others looked for ways to circumvent the Consistory's discipline. In 1568, for example, Martin Barrette petitioned the Small Council to pardon him of the sin of usury without making public reparation in St. Pierre. When the Consistory learned of Barrette's deceit, they turned his suspension into a major excommunication for his rebellious attempt "to overthrow the order established in this church."[83] The ministers and elders were firm on this point: spiritual discipline and reconciling sinners to the church was the responsibility of the Consistory, not the magistrates. And Scripture required that public confession be made for serious public sins. Personal embarrassment was beside the point. Defendants and ministers alike were duty bound to submit to the yoke of discipline "that God ordains in his Church."[84]

3. Church Discipline in City and Countryside

Scholars have paid insufficient attention to the nature of church discipline in Geneva after Calvin. The handful of studies that treat the subject have usually succumbed to broad and unflattering generalizations. Based on his study of consistorial records from 1559 to 1569, historian E. William Monter concluded thirty years ago that, after Calvin, the Consistory "became obsessed with practically all forms of deviance" and was "not interested so much in religious orthodoxy as in social control— down to minute points of behavior."[85] This judgment has been repeated more recently by Alister McGrath, who argues that after Calvin's death "the Consistory appears to have lost its sense of direction, and degenerated into little more than a crude instrument of social control, verging on the hysterical."[86] Conclusions like these—weighted with modern assumptions and value judgments—do not do justice to the broader patterns of disciplinary activity in Geneva during the half century after Calvin's victory over the Perrinists in 1555. So too, facile generalizations of "social control" fail to penetrate to the foundational pastoral concerns and commitments at the heart of the disciplinary work undertaken by Calvin, Beza, Goulart, and their colleagues. This section will quantify and classify all documented suspensions in the Geneva church from 1542 to 1609, looking for patterns that shed light on the changing priorities and strategies that the Consistory employed to enforce godly behavior and right belief in the city and countryside.[87]

Number of Suspensions

Geneva's ministers employed the penalty of suspension or excommunication with breathtaking frequency during the years 1542 to 1609. (Hereafter, the words "suspension" and "excommunication" will be employed as synonyms unless otherwise indicated.) In all, we have documented 9,256 excommunications during this time period, and this does not include eighteen years for which consistorial registers no longer exist.[88] Graph 7.1 depicts the annual number of suspensions in Geneva's urban and countryside parishes from 1542 to 1609 based on extant Consistory registers. The graph's bell-shaped curve is unmistakable: beginning with only several dozen annual excommunications or suspensions during the first decade of the Consistory's existence, the number of annual suspensions began to climb steadily after 1555, reaching around 300 suspensions in 1559, and spiking at 681 suspensions in 1568. Following this peak, the number of annual excommunications fell sharply in the early 1570s before leveling off during the next four decades, when suspensions ranged between 100 and 150 per year.

Another way of depicting this pattern is by calculating the average number of censures per weekly session of Consistory (see graph 7.2). Before Calvin's victory over the Perrinists in 1555, the average number of suspensions by the Consistory from the Lord's Supper was less than one per session. Over the next decade, the number of weekly excommunications climbed steadily until the year 1568, when the Consistory suspended nearly twelve persons on average per session. Four years later, that number was reduced by over one half. During the final quarter of the sixteenth century and the first decade of the seventeenth century, the average number of suspensions hovered around two per week—a figure that is actually lower than the frequency of suspensions during the final decade of Calvin's life. Later in this chapter I will propose several reasons for this highly variable pattern of discipline from 1542 to 1609. Nonetheless, the overall number of suspensions in Calvinist Geneva during this period is staggering, far

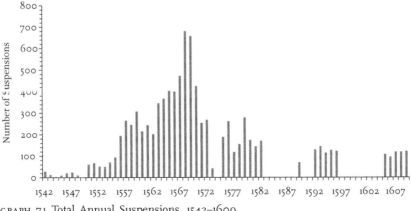

GRAPH 7.1 Total Annual Suspensions, 1542–1609

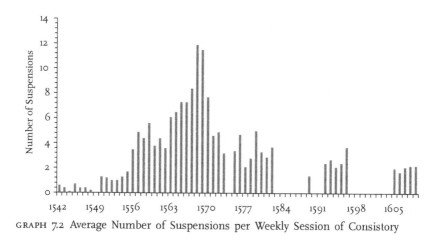

GRAPH 7.2 Average Number of Suspensions per Weekly Session of Consistory

exceeding the rate of excommunications found in reformed churches in Scotland or in southern France during the period.[89]

Types of Suspension Offenses

What types of misbehavior caused people to be suspended from the Lord's Supper? Table 7.2 provides a quantitative summary of the chief reasons for suspensions broken down by gender. The ten most common reasons for suspensions from the Lord's Supper in Calvinist Geneva were quarrels and household disputes (25.4%), fornication and adultery (12.7%), various scandals (7.3%), blasphemy (5.6%), lying and slander (5.0%), Catholic behavior (4.9%), illicit dancing and singing (4.8%), rebellion against authority (4.7%), drunkenness (4.0%), and ignorance (4.0%). Other sins, such as gambling, folk religion, begging and idleness, endangerment, and heresy, were less common.[90] A number of insights can be gleaned from this summary. First, the Consistory censured defendants far more frequently for faulty behavior (such as quarrels, blasphemy, or drunkenness) than for wrong doctrine (such as heresy, ignorance, or Catholic belief). At least in practice, Geneva's Consistory functioned more as a morals court than as a theological tribunal. Second, during the decades of our study, men were nearly twice as likely to be suspended from the sacrament as women (64%–36%), a difference that remained more or less constant throughout the sixteenth century.[91] This gender disparity between male and female suspensions did not go entirely unnoticed by Geneva's townspeople. When a velvet-maker named Jean Mercier was confronted by the pastors and elders in 1609 for beating his wife with a stool, he complained that "the Consistory is the paradise of women" and that the city magistrates "pursue men and protect women."[92] (No doubt, the hundreds of female defendants who appeared before the ministers and elders each year viewed the matter very differently!) Some offenses tended to be gender specific: women were more likely than men

TABLE 7.2 Suspension Offenses, 1542–1609

OFFENSE	NO. MALE/FEMALE	TOTAL	% OF TOTAL
Quarrels/*Mauvais Ménage*	1572/777	2349	25.4
Fornication/Adultery	636/538	1174	12.7
Scandals	447/233	680	7.3
Blasphemy	393/125	518	5.6
Lying/Slander	265/194	459	5.0
Catholic Behavior	298/152	450	4.9
Illicit Dances/Songs	171/274	445	4.8
Rebellion	308/123	431	4.7
Drunkenness	277/97	374	4.0
Ignorance	209/159	368	4.0
Confessional Infidelity	186/169	355	3.8
Petty Theft	159/161	320	3.5
Gaming/Gambling	253/2	255	2.8
Violation of Lord's Supper	163/82	245	2.6
Business Fraud Usury	164/29	193	2.1
Folk Religion	63/99	162	1.8
Sermon Violations	108/34	142	1.5
Clandestine Marriage	61/50	111	1.2
Begging/Idleness	80/24	104	1.1
Endangerment	33/28	61	.7
Anabaptism/Heresy	25/1	26	.3
Unknown	18/16	34	.4
TOTALS	5889/3367	9,256	100%

to be disciplined for illicit dancing and singing, petty theft, and the practice of folk religion. Men, by contrast, account for nearly all of the suspensions for offenses such as gambling, business fraud, and heresy.

As indicated, slightly more than one-quarter of all recorded suspensions in Geneva between 1542 and 1609 were for public quarrels and domestic disputes (called *mauvais ménage*—literally, bad household). Many Genevan households were troubled and violent: reports of vicious arguments, abused wives, neglected children, and mistreated servants fill the pages of the register of the Consistory. Arguments often spilled out of the house into the streets and fields. Genevans attacked their spouses and neighbors with fists and feet, with scissors and swords, with batons and baguettes, with bowls of pottage and wooden plates. One angry butcher even used the head of a dead goat as a weapon against his unfortunate wife.[93] As shall be seen shortly, attempting to reconcile estranged spouses and embittered neighbors was one important way in which the Consistory exercised pastoral care in Geneva.

Nathaniel Hawthorne's *The Scarlet Letter* has sometimes given credence to the stereotype of harsh Calvinist clergymen preoccupied with punishing the sexual sins of vulnerable female victims. During the lifetimes of Calvin and Beza, however, only around 13 percent of all suspensions in Geneva were for sexual sins such as fornication, adultery, and solicitation.[94] In these cases men were censured at a slightly higher rate than women, indicating that the Consistory was committed to maintaining a uniform standard of sexual behavior for both genders. Sexual behavior judged particularly abhorrent or criminal, such as incest, sodomy, abortion, and prostitution, make only rare appearances in the Consistory's caseload.[95] We see only a half dozen accusations of incest (or attempted incest) in the Consistory registers from 1542 to 1609. Claude Dusuit, for example, was excommunicated and sent to the magistrates for committing incest with his grown daughter named Nicolarde in 1566; Claude justified his behavior by appealing to his poor health and insisting that "his daughter treated him better than his (second) wife."[96] Cases involving sodomy, by contrast, did not usually go through the normal channels of ecclesiastical discipline: people suspected of homosexual activity were not excommunicated, but were tried, condemned, and executed by Geneva's civil authorities. Even so, on at least one occasion, the ministers and elders supplied key evidence to the city's magistrates that led to the conviction and capital punishment of a homosexual offender.[97] The Consistory also took action against pimps (*maquereaux*) and prostitutes, as well as the clients who sought their services. In 1566, for example, eleven men were suspended from the Lord's Supper for committing adultery with a prostitute named Loise Maistre. The magistrates interrogated Loise and condemned her to death by drowning on March 28, 1566.[98]

Most cases of sexual misbehavior that the Consistory examined year to year fell under the category of "simple fornication," involving unmarried men and women who engaged in sexual activity or engaged couples who cohabitated before they acquired the necessary approval of parents and received the formal blessing of the church. Geneva's Marriage Ordinance (1546) outlawed this traditional practice of "anticipating" marriage, and the ministers and elders worked strenuously, though without a lot of success, to eradicate it.[99] The account of Siegfried, a student from Nuremberg, is a typical case. In 1578 the Consistory suspended him for having sexual intercourse with a servant girl; in this instance, Theodore Beza delivered the remonstrance in Latin because the boy did not understand French.[100] While the Consistory insisted that legitimate promises of marriage (fiançailles) be honored, it showed little interest in forcing marriage on men and women who had shared physical intimacy, even when children were born from the illicit union. The large number of cases of fornication that involved members of the servant class is especially striking: around one-quarter of all censures for sexual sin involved members of the servant class, and a sizeable percentage of this subset involved a master or male family member having sexual relations with a female servant or wet nurse. The vulnerability of female domestic workers is illustrated in the sad account of the maid Françoise and her master Pierre Chapuis. Pierre imposed his will on Françoise with promises of marriage and assurances that drinking honey would prevent an unwanted pregnancy. In the presence of the Consistory, Pierre denied having said anything about marriage; both were suspended from the Lord's Table and sent away with a sharp rebuke.[101]

Cases of adultery were viewed as far more serious than "simple" fornication. Adulterers violated God's law; defiled the marriage bed; and broke the covenantal bonds that united spouses, families, and community. From the perspective of Geneva's ministers, the sin of adultery "polluted the sanctity of marriage" and was "extremely pernicious to human society," second only to murder in its moral gravity.[102] In the first decades of Geneva's Reformation, the normal penalty for adultery was excommunication, followed by the civil punishments of whipping and banishment.[103] In the early 1560s, however, Geneva's city magistrates began to apply the death penalty in cases of adultery that were judged especially egregious. A few years later, in 1566, capital punishment for adultery was enacted as law.[104] Though Geneva's ministers supported this policy in principle, their general practice was to recommend that leniency be shown adulterers in all but the most exceptional of circumstances. This was also the approach indicated by Theodore Beza in treatises that he wrote on the subjects of polygamy and divorce in 1568.[105] As a result, after Calvin's death, most adulterers were suspended from the church for a term and forced to make a humiliating confession before the church—but they were not executed. In 1595, for example, the Consistory excommunicated Jean Mercier and recommended that he be whipped and banished from the city when it was discovered that he had infected his wife and children with syphilis, having contracted the disease from a prostitute during a trip outside of Geneva.[106]

Catholic behavior was another common reason that Genevans were suspended between 1542–1609, comprising just under 5 percent of all excommunications. I have used the term "Catholic behavior" to denote instances where people *voluntarily* aligned themselves with some dimension of Roman Catholic faith or practice, such as attending Mass or a Catholic festival, marrying a Catholic spouse, reciting the Ave Maria, fasting from meat on Fridays, fighting in Catholic armies, manufacturing Catholic religious objects, or permitting a priest to baptize or bury members of their families. Many of these cases reveal deep attachment to the traditional religion, as when the wife of Pierre Corajod welcomed a priest into her home and received a rosary from him, or when Collet Dumurgier insisted before the ministers that the Virgin Mary "is an advocate for sinners."[107] Clearly, Catholic belief was never completely eradicated from reformed Geneva, especially from the outlying villages in close proximity to Catholic Savoy. Even so, a sizeable number of men and women suspended for "Catholic behavior" were probably not Catholic at all, but partisans of the reformed religion whose familial commitments and commercial interests required ongoing contact with the Catholic world, or whose moral sensitivities allowed for a greater degree of religious accommodation than the Venerable Company permitted.

Suspensions for "confessional infidelity" were different from discipline for Catholic behavior in that this category refers to cases of accommodation to Catholic faith or practice that resulted from coercion or danger rather than voluntary choice.[108] When Catholics regained control of Lyon in 1567, hundreds of Protestant refugees fled to Geneva, many of whom had temporarily abjured the reformed religion or participated in Catholic rites out of fear of persecution.[109] In 1568 alone, the Geneva Consistory suspended 149 French refugees for this sin; the following year another 98 people were censured. Their anguished stories are poignantly recorded in the Consistory minutes: Catholic soldiers forced Marie Bachelet at knifepoint to attend Mass and take "the idol of paste"; Élie Denie wore a crucifix around her neck to avoid being killed as she fled to Geneva; Hannibal Merle was forced to abjure the "evangelical religion" under threat of imprisonment or death.[110] Suspensions for confessional infidelity became much less common after 1569, in part because the flood of refugees temporarily abated, and partly because the Consistory devised different methods for handling these cases of religious accommodation. Hereafter, refugees who confessed this sin were not excommunicated from the sacrament as long as they agreed to make public reparation during a Sunday worship service prior to the quarterly Communion service.[111]

The final group considered here are those who were suspended for "scandals." This is the least coherent of our subject areas, yet it includes some of the cases of greatest interest to historians of society and culture. Under this rubric I included suspensions for sins that caused public outrage or offended moral sensibilities but did not fit neatly into other categories. Most of these cases were, in fact, labeled "scandalous" in the Consistory registers. Minor sexual offenses such as kissing and flirting, dirty jokes, pornography, cross-dressing, exhibitionism, use of love potions, and suspicious frequentation figure prominently in this category. Undoubtedly a few of these sexual scandals were more the result of indiscretion than of evil intention. For example, a widow named Jeanne Bellin and her teenage son Pierre were suspended from the Lord's Supper for sleeping in the same bed, even after their pastor had demanded an end to this unseemly practice. Jeanne insisted that poverty, not promiscuity, dictated these sleeping arrangements.[112]

The Consistory also waged war against boisterous behavior associated with traditional practices such as carnival and the charivari. In March 1572, for example, the ministers and elders tried without success to extract confessions from a group of five young hooligans who had run around town in masks and paint, making noise and mocking the Psalms.[113] The Consistory was more successful later that year when it disciplined fourteen young men for creating a scandal by marching through the village of Lancy on the day of the Lord's Supper, drinking alcohol and playing flutes and tambourines.[114] The charivari—a noisy ritual in which youths serenaded and mocked a newlywed couple—was another type of scandalous behavior that the Consistory attempted to curtail.[115] Hence, the Consistory suspended three men in 1580 for embarrassing a couple on their wedding night: having fastened a bell to the marriage bed, the pranksters pulled on the attached rope to announce the consummation of the happy union. The ministers and elders scolded the men for having committed these "follies" instead of praying to God for the bride and groom.[116]

As these accounts illustrate, the Consistory's campaign against "scandalous" behavior extended beyond the enforcement of biblical morality to the maintenance of cultural standards of decency, honor, and propriety. This is made clear in the case of a retired French minister named Sebastien Jullien, who was suspended for the scandal (*le scandale*) caused when he misused alms received from public charity and wasted time attending tennis matches in the city—actions deemed out of keeping with his social rank and profession as a minister of the gospel.[117] Genevans were disciplined for a variety of other kinds of strange and unseemly behavior such as urinating in public, swimming in the nude, throwing a leg of lamb into a dung heap, nursing a dog with breast milk, and wrapping the tail of a calf in a poor woman's handkerchief.[118] Perhaps the peasant Jean Saddo wins the award for the most bizarre example of scandalous behavior. In 1576, Jean became so frustrated by his cow's unruliness that he extracted one of the animal's eyeballs, which he then placed in the hands of his minister. The young man was suspended from the Lord's Supper for "his cruelty and extreme barbarity" to animals.[119]

Countryside Suspensions

Because the registers of the Consistory distinguish between urban and rural suspensions, it is possible to isolate the primary reasons for excommunications in Geneva's villages and rural hamlets (see table 7.3). Overall, I have identified 1,946 suspensions in Geneva's rural parishes, comprising 21 percent of the total number of excommunications between the years 1542

TABLE 7.3 Rural versus City Suspensions, 1542–1609

RURAL SUSPENSIONS			CITY SUSPENSIONS		
Offense	Number	% Total	Offense	Number	% Total
Fornication/Adultery	416	21.4	Quarrels/*Mauvais Ménage*	2030	27.8
Quarrels/*Mauvais Ménage*	319	16.4	Fornication/Adultery	758	10.4
Illicit Dances/Songs	263	13.5	Scandal	590	8.1
Catholic Behavior	135	6.9	Blasphemy	384	5.3
Blasphemy	134	6.9	Lying/Slander	384	5.3
Scandal	90	4.6	Rebellion	352	4.9
Folk Religion	81	4.2	Confessional Infidelity	341	4.7
Rebellion	79	4.1	Ignorance	325	4.4
Theft	78	4.0	Drunkenness	315	4.3
Lying/Slander	75	3.9	Catholic Behavior	315	4.3
Drunkenness	59	3.0	Theft	242	3.3
Violation of Lord's Supper	57	2.9	Gaming/Gambling	215	2.9
Ignorance	43	2.2	Violation of Lord's Supper	188	2.6
Gaming/Gambling	40	2.1	Illicit Dances/Songs	182	2.5
Clandestine Marriage	18	1.0	Business Fraud/ Usury	178	2.4
Business Fraud/ Usury	15	.8	Sermon Violation	131	1.8
Confessional Infidelity	14	.7	Begging/Idleness	97	1.3
Sermon Violation	11	6	Clandestine Marriage	931.3	1.3
Endangerment	8	.4	Folk Religion	81	1.1
Begging/Idleness	7	.4	Endangerment	53	.7
Anabaptism/Heresy	2	.1	Anabaptism/Heresy	24	.3
Unknown	2	.1	Unknown	32	.4
	1,946	100%		7,310	100%

and 1609. Three types of misbehavior in the countryside were disciplined at a much higher frequency than in the city: fornication and adultery, illicit dancing and singing, and folk religion. Cases of fornication and adultery constitute more than one-fifth of rural suspensions—twice the rate found in the city. This disparity is probably due, in large part, to the challenges of regulating sexual behavior in the less populated countryside, as well as continued resistance on the part of rural villagers to the minister's campaign to institutionalize marriage by prohibiting sexual intercourse until after the publication of the banns and the blessing of the church.[120]

Another category of misbehavior that was especially prevalent in the countryside was illicit dancing and singing. More than 13 percent of all rural suspensions were for dancing or lewd singing (compared to only 2.5 percent in the city). Peasants and village dwellers were censured for singing obscene songs—sometimes with instrumental accompaniment—at times of harvest and carnival, at weddings, as well as on traditional Catholic feast days.[121] When a group of six women was called before the Consistory for singing "wicked" songs along the banks of the Arve River on a Sunday afternoon in May 1577, the ministers exhorted them instead to sing "psalms and praises to God" and sent them away with a firm scolding.[122] Dissolute singing and illicit dancing frequently went together. A favorite pastime of many young people in the countryside was to gather in a field or house to dance, drink, and sing to the music of the violette, the fife, and the drum. From the ministers' perspective, dancing was a vain amusement that fueled fleshly passions and often led to (or was an expression of) drunkenness and sexual promiscuity. One of their colleagues even wrote a treatise against dancing.[123] Before Calvin's death, suspensions for dancing were relatively rare; in fact, the secretary of the Consistory noted in the register for 1560 that "it is not our custom to prohibit people from the Lord's Supper for dances."[124] Over the next decades, however, the number of people suspended for illicit dancing and singing soared. During the spring of 1579 alone, the Consistory suspended more than fifty young men and women for cavorting in the countryside, singing, dancing to music, and drinking. Several decades later, a "sting operation" led to the excommunication of fourteen people who had danced during a wedding banquet in the village of Lancy.[125]

The frequency of suspensions for folk religion was also higher in rural areas than in the city, although overall the numbers are quite modest (4.2 percent of rural and 1.1 percent of city excommunications). Some of these offenses may have been expressions of popular Catholic belief, such as touching for scrofula or the use of healing water.[126] Other practices are more clearly non-Christian or "pre-Christian," such as employing traditional folk medicine, visiting a sorcerer, or consulting a fortune-teller. The witch-craze that gripped much of Western Europe in the second half of the sixteenth century was also present in Geneva. Between 1568 and 1582, forty-three people were tried for witchcraft by Geneva's magistrates, and twelve were executed.[127] Although the Consistory in my sample never disciplined a defendant for witchcraft (witches were burned, not excommunicated), it did play an advisory role to civil justice, interrogated witnesses, and passed evidence and suspects on to city officials.[128] So too, the ministers and elders intervened on behalf of people who were wrongly accused of witchcraft and also disciplined people who participated in occult activity. In December 1567, a short time after an accused sorcerer named Jean Guignard was burned at the stake, the ministers convened an emergency session of Consistory to interrogate seventeen villagers from Bourdigny who were accused of having consulted him. In this session, five people were excommunicated who had sought out Guignard to heal their children and farm animals, and to find lost possessions.[129] Forty years later, the fear of witches and black magic once again swept through Geneva and her countryside. In 1607, the Consistory reported to the Small Council that seventeen demoniacs were walking around the city, making a lot of noise and disturbing worship services. The ministers and elders promised the magistrates that "we will try to do our duty in this matter by visitations and prayers."[130] During this period the Consistory intervened in a significant number of cases related to occult activities; defendants were examined and disciplined for attempting to exorcise demons from children, playing tarot cards, falsely accusing neighbors of witchcraft, having their fortunes read by gypsies, and throwing snowballs at demoniacs.[131]

Not all cases of folk religion involved occult practice or traditional folk cures, however, as the memorable case of Antoine Bonard illustrates. In July of 1568, Bonard was arrested by the magistrates and sent to the Consistory for worshiping the sun in the city marketplace. Because the sun represented the majesty of God, he reasoned, it was appropriate to bend one's knee and worship the sun. The Consistory was of a different opinion and suspended Bonard from the sacrament, threatening banishment if he persisted in his errors. Three months later, Bonard was in trouble again, this time for taking the Lord's Supper in defiance of his suspension. He insisted that since God had forgiven his idolatrous act, he now had divine permission to partake of the holy sacrament, regardless of the Consistory's judgment. Condemning his "arrogance" and "foolishness," the ministers and elders censured Bonard for a second time and sent him to the city council, requesting that he be "purged from the city."[132] On the whole, cases of folk religion and "superstition" like these are relatively rare in the Consistory registers. They serve as a reminder that Geneva's ministers were never completely successful in rooting out traditional folk beliefs and practices in the city and (especially) in the countryside. But with that said, the Consistory registers offer little support for scholarship that argues that Christianity in the sixteenth century was primarily the possession of a small clerical and educated elite that imposed "orthodox" doctrine on an illiterate peasantry that remained essentially committed to traditional folk religion, witchcraft, and magic.[133] Instead, most Genevans who lived outside the city's walls were responsive to their ministers' moral oversight and appear to have been in essential agreement with the Christian message preached from Geneva's pulpits.

4. Moral Discipline After Calvin

Patterns of discipline in reformed Geneva come into clearer focus when we examine different stages in the development of the Consistory during the sixteenth and early seventeenth century. Three distinct stages of consistorial activity can be identified during the first generations of Geneva's reformed church: a period of consolidation from 1542–1555, a period of rapid expansion from 1556–1569, and a period of stabilization from 1570–1609 (see table 7.4). During the period of consolidation (1542–1555), Calvin and his colleagues were still putting in place the institutional structure of church discipline in Geneva. Household visitations in the city and pastoral oversight in the countryside parishes remained undeveloped for much of the period. Moreover, as we have seen, Calvin and the Venerable Company faced strong resistance from Geneva's magistrates over the ministers' prerogative to excommunicate sinners. These factors go far in explaining the relatively modest nature of consistorial activity before 1555. During these years, around sixteen people on average were summoned to the Consistory's chambers each week, either as defendants or witnesses. Of the 509 people

TABLE 7.4 Primary Reasons for Suspension by Period

CONSOLIDATION 1542–1555	EXPANSION 1556–1569	STABILIZATION 1570–1609
Fornication/Adultery (23%)	Quarrels/*Mauvais Mesnage* (22%)	Quarrels/*Mauvais Mesnage* (31%)
Quarrels/*Mauvais Mesnage* (13%)	Fornication/Adultery (11%)	Fornication/Adultery (13%)
Catholic Behavior (12%)	Blasphemy (7%)	Scandal (9%)
Rebellion (10%)	Scandal (6%)	Drunkenness (7%)
Blasphemy (9%)	Ignorance (6%)	Illicit Dances/Songs (7%)
Scandal (9%)	Confessional Infidelity (6%)	Gaming & Gambling (5%)
Ignorance (8%)	Lying/Slander (6%)	Lying/Slander (4%)
Lying/Slander (3%)	Rebellion (5%)	Blasphemy (4%)
Anabaptism/Heresy (2%)	Catholic Behavior (5%)	Catholic Behavior (4%)
Recorded Suspensions: 509	Recorded Suspensions: 4997	Recorded Suspensions: 3750

known to have been excommunicated during this period, only one in seven came from the countryside parishes surrounding Geneva. Moreover, between 1542 and 1555 the Consistory focused its energies on a select group of moral infractions that most of Geneva's citizens would have recognized as reprehensible: blasphemy, family quarrels, scandals, and especially fornication and adultery. The disproportionate number of people suspended for fornication and adultery (23 percent of all excommunications) led some Genevans mistakenly to assume that the Consistory's primary function was to punish sexual deviance. Thus, when the Consistory investigated a suspected Anabaptist named Jeanne Pignier in 1543, she expressed surprise that the ministers had summoned her, for "she had heard that the Consistory was for men and women guilty of fornication, and she had not committed fornication."[134] During this period, moral infractions that townspeople viewed as less serious, or even socially acceptable, such as gambling, heavy drinking, illicit dancing and singing, or begging and idleness, were rarely if ever punished with ecclesiastical suspension.

Following their decisive victory over the Perrinists in 1555, Calvin and the ministers of Geneva gained a free hand to investigate and impose church discipline on the city's residents with little interference from the civil authorities. Consequently, the Consistory's caseload expanded dramatically from 1556 to 1569, and along with it the number of annual suspensions. During these fourteen years, around thirty-four people on average were summoned to the Consistory's chambers each week (either as defendants or witnesses), and nearly 5,000 excommunications were recorded. To put these numbers in sharper perspective: if we assume a combined urban and rural population of 20,000 in 1569, then in that year alone around 3 percent of all Genevans were suspended from the Lord's Supper and nearly one of every twelve people living in the city and countryside was summoned to the Consistory's chambers as a defendant or witness.[135] Evidence indicates that the system of moral surveillance in the countryside was also becoming more effective: around 23 percent of all recorded suspensions came from Geneva's rural parishes outside the city walls. During this period of rapid expansion, the Consistory widened its disciplinary net to excommunicate persons guilty of forms of misbehavior that had previously been ignored or had merited only consistorial admonition. In the decade of the 1560s, sins such as business fraud and usury, confessional infidelity, illicit dancing and singing, drunkenness, folk religion, absence from sermons, and neglect of the Lord's Supper became important targets of consistorial discipline.[136] At the same time, the ministers and elders continued to apply discipline regularly in an effort to resolve household quarrels and pacify disputes between neighbors.

A number of factors are most likely responsible for this significant increase in consistorial activity. Although Geneva's population did increase significantly between 1556 and 1569, the rate of growth only partially explains the sharp rise in excommunications year to year.[137] Another factor that inflated the numbers of excommunications in 1568 and 1569 was the high incidence of confessional infidelity in the aftermath of the re-Catholicization of Lyon. Most crucial, however, was the Consistory's success in wresting ecclesiastical discipline from the control of Geneva's magistrates. With its new-found independence, the ministers and elders launched an aggressive campaign to impose broad moral reforms on Geneva's townspeople and country folk intended to shape every aspect of life, including religious belief, sexual behavior, family relationships, recreation, and business activities. After Calvin's death in 1564, Beza and his colleagues attempted to solidify and expand this moral program. One wonders, in fact, if the high rate of disciplinary activity during the late 1560s was fueled in part by the Consistory's enthusiasm to fulfill Calvin's vision of a godly society once he was gone from the scene.

The upward trajectory of disciplinary activity in Geneva's church was abruptly reversed after 1569. Between 1570 and 1609, a total of 3,750 people are known to have been suspended from the Lord's Supper. Sixteen people on average were summoned to Consistory each week as witnesses or defendants, down from the average of thirty-four people per week from the previous period, and the number of excommunications stabilized at between 100 and 150 suspensions per year. One wonders if the decline in consistorial activity after 1569 indicates that Beza and his colleagues were beginning to recognize that the frenetic rate of censure in the late 1560s had not been successful in transforming moral behavior in the city. Or perhaps the ministers' initial enthusiasm to fulfill Calvin's vision of a godly society had become tempered by the practical difficulties of enforcing discipline *and* restoring a growing number of people to the Lord's Supper. One thing is clear, however: during this period of stabilization important changes were taking place in the caseload of the Consistory. Whereas in the 1540s and 1550s a substantial part of the Consistory's disciplinary activity was aimed at correcting fornication, Catholic belief, ignorance, and blasphemy, by the end of the century the focus had shifted to pacifying violent households, reconciling estranged spouses, and promoting harmony in the community. Indeed, from 1570 to 1609, nearly one-third of all suspensions in Geneva were for domestic disputes and public quarrels. The minister Jean Pinault and one of the elders articulated this primary concern of consistorial discipline in 1605: "the goal of the Consistory is to appease discords so that all might live in peace and harmony," they stated.[38] Moreover, between 1570 and 1609, an ever-greater part of the Consistory's discipline was aimed at discouraging such popular activities as illicit dancing and singing, gambling, banqueting, and heavy drinking. From a broader perspective, the ministers' commitment to peacemaking and their campaign against worldly amusements reflected a general pattern witnessed elsewhere in reformed Europe, as Calvinist communities attempted to promote social holiness and establish their moral identity in distinction from their Catholic neighbors.[39] By the dawn of the new century, corrective discipline in the hands of Beza and his colleagues had become a tool for fashioning a peaceful, well-ordered community in which men and women understood the central message of (reformed) Christianity and conducted their daily affairs with moral seriousness.

One crucial development that occurred during the period 1570–1609 was that the magistrates began to intervene in the Consistory's activities and successfully ended the church's monopoly over the power of excommunication. Already in 1576, Geneva's magistrates were becoming impatient with the scope and severity of the ministers' discipline. In January of that year, the Small Council summoned Theodore Beza to its chambers to complain about the fact that the Consistory "frequently suspended from the Lord's Supper people who had no previous record of wrongdoing and whose sins were of a minor nature—indeed sins for which they had already repented." The council warned that such severity would do nothing but "put consciences in trouble, offend a lot of people who, once suspended, would only fall into worse sins, and create hatred for the Consistory."[140] It is noteworthy that in this reprimand Geneva's magistrates were affirming principles that had been of central importance to Calvin's original vision of church discipline as stated in both his *Institutes* and in the *Ecclesiastical Ordinances*: corrective discipline should be gentle and moderate, and it should be applied only in cases when sinners refused to repent. Responding to this official rebuke, a compliant Beza and his colleagues acknowledged that "heretofore there has been too great a rigor" in their discipline and promised to follow the magistrates' instructions in the future.[141] The diminution of Consistory activity during the final quarter of the century was no doubt in part due to public pressure like this.

Three decades later, the magistrates interfered more directly in the Consistory's business. In December 1602, the ministers and elders issued a subpoena to a prominent senator named François Franc to explain the circumstances surrounding an act of fornication committed by a servant girl from his household. Franc flatly refused to come to Consistory. He argued that this affair involved his servant, not him; moreover, he claimed, the magistrates had already addressed the situation. For the next four months, Franc ignored the Consistory's repeated demands that he appear for questioning. Finally, in April of 1603, the ministers and elders suspended him from the Lord's Supper and then threatened him with major excommunication. At this juncture, Geneva's Small Council intervened in support of Franc, warning the Consistory that if it did not stop pursuing him the matter would be referred to the Council of 200. The councilors made it clear that they, not the ministers, had the prerogative of routing disciplinary cases to either civil or ecclesiastical tribunals. The Consistory had little choice but to back down and accept a compromise, though the ministers were very much aware of the dangerous precedent that had been set. In recording the unhappy conclusion of this affair, the minister Jean Pinault wrote, "O woe! This is the ruin of the Consistory!"[142]

Pinault's prediction was not far off the mark. Three years later, Geneva's magistrates decisively broke the Consistory's exclusive control over excommunication in a controversy that surrounded two city councilors, Jean Rilliet and Jean Sarasin. The Consistory summoned Rilliet and Sarasin to its chambers in February 1606 when it was reported they had attended a private gathering of townspeople that had celebrated the feast of the kings at Epiphany where the participants had "elected" a king and queen and drunk to their health.[143] The two senators insisted that they had not taken part in the festivities and thus refused to appear before the ministers and elders. Yet again the Small Council intervened, advising the ministers that they should ignore this misdemeanor or, at the very least, address the sinful behavior in a private session rather than in Consistory. At the same time, the Council informed the *sautier* that he was not to deliver Rilliet or Sarasin to the Consistory. On March 6, 1606, the ministers and elders deliberated at length the best way to respond to this situation. They recognized the dangers of antagonizing the magistrates. But on the other hand, they agreed that because "the discipline of the Consistory is the central axis (*le seul pivot*) of the Church," it was essential that the Consistory reprove the sinful behavior of even Geneva's most powerful citizens so as to "preserve the good order and discipline" of the church and "not revisit the days of Berthelier in the past."[144] Fortified by principle, the Consistory disregarded the magistrates' pressure to back down. When Sarasin and Rilliet continued to refuse to appear in Consistory, the ministers and elders imposed the penalty of major excommunication upon them, stating that "because they have disobeyed their mother church" their mother "does not recognize them as children of the church."[145] Around the same time, the minister Jean Jaquemot delivered several passionate sermons from the pulpit of St. Pierre in which he criticized the magistrates, condemned Sarasin and Rilliet for their foolishness and pride, and promised that the Consistory would remain firm even though the council was trying "to overturn the two columns of the church" (i.e., the Company of Pastors and the Consistory).[146] Despite these bold statements, the magistrates had the last word. On March 22, Jaquemot was arrested and imprisoned in the Hôtel de Ville. Four days later, the Small Council issued a decree that rendered the Consistory's excommunications of Rilliet and Sarasin null and void. The Council justified this decision by appealing to provisions in the *Ecclesiastical Ordinances* that required private sins to be treated in private, which the magistrates interpreted to mean outside of the Consistory's chambers.[147] The Consistory appealed this decision to the Council of 200, which several weeks later ruled in favor of the Small Council's action. The Consistory was ordered to depute two ministers and two elders to deliver private remonstrances to Sarasin and Rilliet. At the same time, the Council of 200 advised the Consistory in the future to "follow more carefully the *Ecclesiastical Ordinances*" in their disciplinary activity.[148] Though the Consistory still possessed the right to excommunicate moral offenders, this power had been significantly eroded by the events of 1606. The monopoly over church discipline that Calvin had struggled to achieve before 1555, and that the Consistory had carefully guarded over the next half century, was successfully broken by Geneva's magistrates barely six months after Beza's body had been laid in the grave.

5. Church Discipline as Pastoral Care

At first glance, the chambers of Geneva's Consistory would seem an unlikely place to discover expressions of Christian concern and pastoral care. In their weekly meetings, the ministers and elders functioned more as judges than therapists as they confronted sinners in the hopes of achieving repentance and spiritual restoration. As we have seen, sometimes the Consistory's discipline appears heavy-handed, harsh, or punitive—at least to modern Western sensibilities. The reader may well chuckle at the story of Claude Griffat, who was suspended from the Lord's Supper for naming his dog "Calvin."[149] But it is hard not to be appalled in other cases, as when in 1562 a young woman named Claudine Fichet was excommunicated for having attempted suicide by throwing herself into the Rhone River following her mother's death.[150] Church discipline in Calvinist Geneva could be very strong spiritual medicine indeed. Moreover, the large number of suspensions that we have documented in the Geneva church between 1542 and 1609—more than 9,200 in all—raises questions about the pastoral wisdom and spiritual benefits of this model of church discipline.

But numbers and random anecdotes do not tell the whole story. The Consistory minutes also portray Geneva's ministers as conscientious pastors, concerned about protecting their spiritual flock in a variety of important ways. This commitment to pastoral care runs as a common thread through the Consistory's work during Calvin's lifetime and in the decades that followed. One is impressed, first of all, by the enormous effort expended by the ministers and elders to elicit confession and bring about repentance and spiritual restoration. Hour after hour, week by week, Consistory members inquired into the most intimate, the most painful, the most destructive dimensions of their congregants' lives. The ministers and elders met with people face-to-face; they addressed them by name; they listened at length to their grievances. It was not uncommon for the Consistory to meet with a defendant two, three, or four times before applying the "medicine" of church discipline that fit the individual circumstance. The modern reader may well shudder at the severity with which some defendants were treated, but Geneva's pastors and elders cannot be accused of being apathetic to the spiritual needs of their flock nor of being naively disengaged from the pervasive injustice, misery, and sin that surrounded them.

In their role as spiritual shepherds, the ministers of Geneva were not only committed to enforcing right behavior but were also concerned with applying corrective discipline that would help change the inward attitude of the heart. The Consistory regularly urged defendants to "reflect on their consciences," to seek a "clean heart," to "feel and understand [their] fault," or to confess "from the mouth and heart."[151] Discipline was intended to "touch" the hearts of sinners so that they might turn away from their sins and "bear the fruit of repentance."[152] Thus, Rolette Copponex was sent away still under the ban of suspension because she continued to harbor hatred for a neighbor who had wronged her; she was exhorted to return once she had "a better disposition of the heart."[153] When the Consistory rebuked a man and woman guilty of fornication in 1548, one of the ministers explained the soul's journey from sin to spiritual health in these terms: sinners must "repent, recognize their faults and henceforth walk in newness of life, demonstrating signs of repentance, with the heart touched by the Holy Spirit so as to weep and receive the grace of God."[154] Certainly, Geneva's ministers recognized that repentance and spiritual renewal were the work of God, who alone could change the attitude of the heart. Nevertheless, the ministers believed that church discipline was an important ministry that God used to turn sinners back to spiritual health and Christian righteousness.

Another way in which the ministers and elders carried out their pastoral responsibilities was by using corrective discipline to protect the weakest, poorest, and most vulnerable members of Genevan society. The Consistory regularly intervened in cases of child abuse, confronting and often disciplining parents who savagely beat their children or neglected to provide them necessary food, clothing, and shelter.[155] The ministers and elders also disciplined fathers who refused to support bastard children, mothers who refused to nurse sickly newborns, and parents who attempted to marry their prepubescent daughters to older men.[156] When, in 1551, an abandoned infant was discovered in a basket in a field outside the village of Jussy, Calvin and the Consistory summoned witnesses in an effort to locate the parents of the child.[157] Calvin's Consistory employed its disciplinary authority to enforce basic norms of compassion and mercy in the city. It admonished Genevans who refused to care for elderly parents and grandparents.[158] It intervened to force intransigent fathers to allow sons and daughters to marry.[159] It petitioned the Small Council to provide gainful employment for young women, lest they be lured into prostitution.[160] It defended the cause of helpless orphans, poor laborers, mistreated prisoners, despised refugees, and social misfits.[161] In 1589, for example, the Consistory learned that a widow named Jeanne de Claren was guilty of horrific treatment of her ten-year-old niece; she regularly burned her head with live coals, kicked her in the stomach, beat her to the point of blood, and forced her to beg through town. The ministers suspended the woman, advised the magistrates of the situation, and then placed the girl in the city hospital, at the expense of her aunt.[162]

The Consistory also worked to root out social and economic injustice. The ministers and elders confronted landlords for cheating or threatening poor tenants.[163] They warned citizens about incompetent surgeons, and scolded physicians and gravediggers who demanded excessive fees from the sick and bereaved.[164] They disciplined merchants who created monopolies or violated city ordinances by inflating the price of basic commodities such as wood, coal, meat, and bread.[165] They chastised masters for withholding servants' wages or for cruel treatment of their apprentices.[166] On several occasions, the Consistory also censured wealthy citizens who used their financial advantage to oppress those in debt to them. In 1580, for example, the Consistory summoned Colle Anthonio to its chambers for the "cruel inhumanity" that he employed toward one of his debtors, "to whom he had shown no pity and consideration." The ministers rebuked Anthonio with strong words, urging him in the future to act "more gently and kindly" toward this "poor person who for the small debt of 20 florins is crying in prison."[167] The Consistory sometimes extended more tangible forms of assistance to Geneva's poorest inhabitants. When the ministers and elders learned that Jean Marchand had abandoned his wife Catherine and their two small children, leaving them in abject poverty, the Consistory petitioned the deacons to provide Catherine with the money needed to return to her family back in France.[168] In a similar fashion, when the ministers learned that Gaberel Levet was wasting his family's resources at the tavern with the result that his children were in danger of starving to death, they asked the magistrates to appoint a curator to protect the family's resources and provide for the children.[169]

The Consistory's campaign to protect the weak and vulnerable was especially important during visitations of the plague, when death, fear, and suspicions threatened to unravel family loyalties and undermine social harmony. During the plague years of 1568–1572, the ministers and elders intervened in nearly a dozen cases in which plague victims were assaulted or abandoned by terrified family members and neighbors. The account of the Bourgeois family in the village of Malval serves as one shocking example. In September 1571, a daughter of the family contracted the plague while in the final days of pregnancy. Fearing infection, the young woman's mother, brother, and sister abandoned her. Even when the pains of labor overcame the sick woman, neither family members nor neighbors responded to her desperate cries for help. In the end, she delivered her baby alone, all the while screaming for water and assistance. Both mother and infant died within hours. The woman's family, listening to the entire ordeal outside the family's house, had already dug a grave for the woman. The Consistory's response to this horrifying account was more than perfunctory: in addition to suspending family members for their inhumanity, the ministers sent a delegation to the city magistrates, demanding that "sick villagers should be cared for, either by people from the city or from their own villages" so that "no one would suffer a similar thing ever again."[170]

The Genevan Consistory in the sixteenth and early seventeenth century also provided a mechanism to reconcile estranged spouses and pacify arguments between family members and neighbors. In this way, as Robert Kingdon observed, the Consistory functioned as a kind of compulsory counseling service.[71] The ministers and elders mediated hundreds of disputes each year, some that endangered life or marriage, others that disrupted the peace of household and community. In the Consistory's chambers feuding parties aired their grievances, argued with one another, and sometimes reconciled. In cases where financial resources were in dispute, the ministers often helped appoint arbiters to resolve the disagreement.[72] On other occasions, they solicited the intervention of family members, godparents, and civil authorities to hasten reconciliation.[73] The Consistory sometimes offered consolation or encouragement to victims of abuse and misfortune. Hence, Mangin Colin was summoned before the Consistory in 1580 and questioned about his wife, who had stolen money and fled the city. The ministers then encouraged him "to continue to live soberly and to pray that God might give him the patience to endure such affliction."[74] Customarily, the Consistory employed moral persuasion and even threats in an effort to stem destructive behavior, end violence, and foster reconciliation. Thomas Thomasset was told that if he ever again beat his wife, he would be sent to the magistrates.[75] Marguerite Charton received such a stern rebuke for accusing her husband of being a traitor and a "Judas" that she burst into tears and admitted her fault.[76] Many times moral persuasion and threats were not enough, however. In 1561, a wife beater named Jean Pradaire was summoned to Consistory for vicious batteries against his wife. A half dozen witnesses described a gruesome pattern of abuse. In previous attacks, Pradaire had showered insults upon the poor woman, pinched her thighs with hot tongs, hit her in the stomach and face, and tried to strangle her. Now he had struck her in the head with a board and knocked her unconscious. The victim—who was judged "an honorable and virtuous woman"—was still in bed recovering from a cracked skull and other injuries. Hearing this report, the ministers and elders excommunicated Pradaire and commanded him never "to touch or mistreat his wife again." He was then sent to the city magistrates with recommendations that he receive additional corporal punishments.[77]

Because the registers of the Consistory are by their nature more attentive to misbehavior than to personal moral reformation, it is difficult to determine the long-term outcome of the ministers' and elders' efforts to heal troubled relationships. Successes are occasionally noted, however. In June 1578, Gabriel Pottu and Jaques Bottilier were called before the Consistory and suspended from the Supper for fighting in public. In response to the ministers' admonition "to live together as good brothers and fellow-citizens," the two men agreed to be reconciled and shook hands as a sign of friendship. When the two men were readmitted to the sacrament two months later, the register noted that they were now "good friends and reconciled together."[78] The Consistory's intervention in the bitter quarrel between Barthélemy Varin and Jeanne Esply in 1580 demonstrates that the threat of suspension from the Lord's Table could serve as a powerful impetus for reconciliation. Barthélemie had accused Jeanne and her husband of theft; Jeanne responded by saying that Barthélemie was ugly and was a liar (literally, she had a "snake's tongue"). After listening to the charges and countercharges, the ministers reminded both women that, in good conscience, they ought not to participate in the upcoming communion service due to their mutual hostility. The threat of suspension had its effect: Jeanne acknowledged Barthélemie to be a "good woman" and asked her forgiveness. As a sign of reconciliation and friendship, both women shook hands and promised to treat one another better in the future.[79]

In many other cases, however, the Consistory's efforts to pacify conflict and heal broken relationships between spouses or neighbors appear to have failed. Despite the ministers' and elders' best pastoral advice and strong moral pressure, some violent marriages and damaged relationships proved beyond repair. The troubled marriage of Claude de Roche and his wife Pernette is a poignant example of this. Claude and Pernette came from two of Geneva's most prominent families: Claude was the son of a city magistrate (and the nephew of an elder), Pernette was the niece of the minister Jean Trembley. Claude and Pernette had been married for only two years when they first appeared before Consistory in June of 1565 to launch recriminations against one another. Pernette complained that her husband was almost always drunk and regularly accused her of being a whore, a traitor, and a sorceress who poisoned wells (un empoisonnesse); Claude insisted that he was only defending himself against the abusive tongue of his wife, who frequently called him a drunkard and a villain and spoke ill of his family. After listening to the young couple argue, the Consistory tried to reconcile them and then suspended them from the Lord's Supper. Several weeks later, a pastor and elder visited their household to check up on the couple and encourage Claude to find gainful employment.[180] By the end of September, however, the situation had deteriorated further and more disturbing details began to come to light. Witnesses reported in Consistory that Claude regularly came home late at 8 p.m. and ate in his room by himself. In a fit of rage, he had recently thrown his supper and all the plates out the front door. He continued to call his wife a whore and threatened to hit her with his baton. On several occasions, he had driven Pernette out of the house and forced her to sleep in the servants' quarters. Just a few days earlier, Claude had struck his wife with his fists when she refused to hand over her personal trunk to him. Not surprisingly, Pernette was now hesitant to sleep with Claude for fear of her life. In fact, she had recently told her mother-in-law that "she would rather have Claude dead…than to live like this." Given this dangerous situation, the ministers and elders took an unusual step: in addition to renewing the couple's suspension and sending them to the magistrates, the Consistory ordered that Claude return to live with his parents for several months "until he learns what it is to live in a household and becomes employed in a profession."[181]

Unfortunately, the temporary separation of Claude and Pernette did not work to heal their unhappy marriage. In February 1566, the Consistory deputed the two uncles, the minister Jean Trembley and the elder François de Roche, to meet with Claude and Pernette to see if they might be ready to live under the same roof again. Apparently some form of reconciliation was achieved, because the following month Claude and Pernette were once again living in the same house—and once again fighting. Over the next two years, their marriage bumped from crisis to crisis. Claude began to drink again. Pernette refused to sleep with him. Pernette accused Claude (wrongly, it seems) of committing adultery with a servant girl. The couple engaged in name calling that resulted in several vicious fights. When Pernette scolded Claude for not going to Sunday sermons, he punched her. In May of 1568, Pernette's father intervened and brought his daughter home for protection.[182] All the while, concerned family members and Geneva's Consistory repeatedly intervened, counseling, cajoling, and threatening the unhappy couple to live in peace. The last (recorded) time that Claude and Pernette appeared together before Consistory was in August 1568, when they requested to be readmitted to the Lord's Supper. The ministers granted their request while at the same time admonishing them to "live and dwell together in peace and complete harmony."[183] It is unlikely that Claude and Pernette ever experienced the peace and harmony that their families and the Consistory had worked so exhaustively to achieve in their marriage. What is certain, however, is that their marriage ended prematurely. Sometime before January 1576, the tormented Claude de Roche died, leaving behind the bereaved—or perhaps relieved—"Pernette, widow of Claude de Roche."[184]

As the account of Claude and Pernette de Roche graphically illustrates, Geneva's ministers and elders were church leaders intimately involved in the lives of their parishioners, attentive to the complexities and difficulties of broken relationships, bad decisions, wrong belief, and sinful behavior. For Calvin and his colleagues, church discipline in its various forms served as "spiritual medicine" prescribed by God to bring healing to the human heart, making possible repentance, reconciliation, and spiritual growth. Though corrective discipline did not always achieve personal moral reformation, it remained a vital part of a healthy church, the "yoke" that Christ ordained to preserve the unity and purity of the church and guide his people to obedience and spiritual maturity. As we have seen, church discipline was employed by the Consistory to protect the weakest members of Geneva's society, enforcing basic norms of fairness and humanity. Consistory members served as helpers for the poor, advocates for the weak, mediators for the estranged, and defenders of the exploited and abused. Geneva's ministers were not idealists seeking to establish a perfect spiritual commonwealth. Rather, they were open-eyed realists committed to interjecting biblical standards of belief and behavior into the messiness of human life to make possible Christian forgiveness and salvation. Both during Calvin's lifetime, and in the generations that followed, moral discipline was a crucial aspect of pastoral care in reformed Geneva.

Church discipline was not the only form that pastoral care took in Calvinist Geneva in the sixteenth and early seventeenth century. Chapter 9 will describe some of the other ministries in which Geneva's ministers engaged to provide spiritual instruction, guidance, and comfort for the people in their congregations. But first, I will briefly survey the substantial literary corpus of Geneva's pastors and demonstrate how writing books was, for many of them, an important dimension of their pastoral vocation.

CHAPTER 8 | Pastors and Their Books

THE DAILY LIVES OF Geneva's ministers were filled with books. Whether serving a parish in the city or countryside, the ministers were members of a literate humanist culture that was shaped by and engaged with the ideas and opinions found on the printed page. For John Calvin, Theodore Beza, Simon Goulart, and their pastoral colleagues, books were friends, conversation partners, sources of wisdom, and models for cultured eloquence. While still an aspiring Catholic humanist in Paris in the 1540s, Theodore Beza once paid tribute to his classical library with this memorable epigram:

> Warmest greetings, my little books, my dear books,
> my delights, my salvation.
> Greetings, my Cicero, my Catullus, greetings!
> Greetings, my Vergil, and you two Plinys;
> my Cato, my Columella, my Varro, my Titus-Livy!
> Greetings to you also, my Plautus and Terence,
> and you Ovid, Quintilian, Propertius, greetings!
> And greetings to you, eloquent Greeks, whom I should have put first,
> Sophocles and Isocrates!
> And greetings to you, whom popular favor gave a name.
> And you, great Homer, greetings!
> Greetings, Aristotle, Plato, and Timaeus!
> And greetings to the rest of you, who aren't permitted
> to be included in the measures of my Phalaecean verses.
> Finally, I greet all of you, my dear books,
> a second and a third time. Greetings![1]

Beza's religious conversion to Protestantism in 1548 restructured his allegiances and altered his vocational plans; but newfound convictions never diminished his appreciation for books, classical as well as Christian.

Geneva's ministers during and after Calvin's lifetime shared Beza's commitment to this learned culture of letters and books. They studied books at academy and university; they consulted them as they prepared sermons; they discussed them in their correspondence; they bought, loaned, and borrowed them; they censored them; and a good number of the pastors wrote them. Books served as more than conversation pieces and sources for spiritual edification, however. They were also instruments of persuasion and potent weapons for the confessional battles that shattered Europe in the early modern period.[2] In their work as authors, Calvin and the ministers of the Venerable Company defended a vision of spiritual reformation and sought to construct a church reformed in doctrine and practice, that undermined time-honored traditions, overturned the old order, and called forth new identities, loyalties, and doctrinal commitments. This chapter, then, will describe the strategic role that print literature played in Geneva's religious life from 1536 to 1609. In particular, my study of the several hundred books written by Geneva's pastors indicates an intellectual culture that was vibrant, creative, and eclectic, committed to Calvin's religious vision while at the same time in conversation with the broader Christian tradition. Though they remained committed to Geneva's official theology, the ministers who came after Calvin did not merely parrot him but attempted to apply the reformer's theological vision to the ethical concerns, confessional challenges, and spiritual needs of a new generation of reformed Christians.

1. Libraries and Censorship

Most, if not all, of Geneva's pastors owned at least a modest collection of exegetical and theological books that served as a kind of "tool kit" for their daily ministries. Calvin's personal library has been estimated at three hundred to three hundred fifty volumes; after his death, his heirs sold the majority of the books to Geneva's magistrates for inclusion in the library of the Academy.[3] Theodore Beza's library also must have been substantial in that it commanded a sales price of 600 gold crowns shortly before his death—unfortunately most of its contents are not known.[4] Somewhat more can be said about Simon Goulart's library, which probably numbered more than four hundred volumes. In the final decades of his life, Goulart dispersed half his library, including all his theological books, to his three sons, and then sold-off piecemeal another two hundred "good Greek, Latin, and French books" to pay creditors.[5] Among the volumes for sale were philosophical writings (such as Aristotle, Plotinus, Plutarch, and Seneca), historical works (including Thucydides, Herodotus, Appianus, and Diodorus), and various local histories (of Geneva, France, Italy, Germany, England, Scotland, Spain, and Persia).[6] Lambert Daneau, who was also a bibliophile, twice lost all of his books when fleeing the religious wars in

France. During his sojourn in Geneva, Daneau borrowed extensively from the libraries of Beza and Goulart for the necessary materials to complete his various writing projects.[7]

The only complete inventory of a minister's library from Geneva that remains from this period belongs to Jean de Brunes, who served the countryside parishes of Chancy and Russin from 1598 to 1601, and then moved to the church of Lyon where he ministered until his untimely death in 1603. A survey of this booklist brings a number of surprises.[8] First, the size of Brunes's library is impressive, containing 549 titles (662 volumes in all). The library included twelve complete copies of the Bible, in Hebrew and Greek, as well as Latin, French, and German translations. So too, one finds a variety of exegetical tools, including Greek and Hebrew dictionaries and grammars, concordances, harmonies of the gospels, commentaries (on every book of the Bible), and studies of the morals and laws of ancient peoples. Fully half the books in Brunes's library were theological in nature. In addition to the writings of the early church fathers (in the original Greek and Latin), the library contained texts by Chrysostom, Augustine, and Thomas Aquinas. Likewise, books written by nearly all the major Protestant reformers are found there: Calvin, Luther, Zwingli, Beza, Bucer, Oecolampadius, Rudolf Gwalther, along with the works of several Catholic controversialists such as Robert Bellarmine and Alphonso de Castro. Perhaps the most surprising discovery from this inventory is the broad literary taste of minister Brunes. Nearly half the books in his library fell outside the domain of theology or exegesis, covering topics such as jurisprudence, pedagogy, ancient and modern geography, cosmography, astronomy, natural history, medicine, horology, ornithology, even a history of the discovery of America. Works by poets, both ancient and modern, as well as by figures from the French Renaissance, are also found on the booklist: Homer, Virgil, Terence, Pierre de Ronsard, Guillaume Du Bartas, Philippe Desportes, Michel de Montaigne, and Jean Bodin. Of course, to own a book is not to read a book. And, if book inventories of reformed ministers elsewhere in Europe are any indication, it is likely that Brunes's library was unusually large.[9] Nevertheless, the fact that a somewhat obscure countryside pastors owned such a large and diverse collection of books is indicative of the priority that Geneva's ministers gave to humane letters, the culture of ideas, and public discourse.

In addition to buying and reading books, the pastors of the Venerable Company were regularly asked to evaluate the theological content of manuscripts being prepared for publication. City ordinances placed Geneva's printing industry entirely under the supervision and control of the magistrates. To the Small Council was given the authority to regulate the number of printers in the city, to approve or censure the publication of new works, and to oversee the price and quality of each volume produced.[10] From an early date, however, the magistrates adopted the practice of seeking advice from John Calvin and other ministers before granting permission to print theological writings. This privilege to review and recommend religious writings for publication was officially granted to the ministers in the last years of Calvin's life, and Geneva's pastors played an active role supervising the printing industry during the century that followed.[11] Usually the ministers approved a book's publication with barely a comment, but on certain occasions they voiced concern. In 1577, for example, Beza and his colleagues criticized before the magistrates a book published by Henri Estienne in which the pope was called "the great vicar of God."[12] A decade later the pastors asked the magistrates to block the printing of an almanac by Gervais de La Court that included fanciful predictions and a list of saint's days.[13] In a similar fashion, the ministers requested the censure of Ovid's *On Love* and *Metamorphoses* as well as the profane poetry of other classical poets such as Catullus and Horace.[14] When a Genevan printer published an unexpurgated version of Michel de Montaigne's *Essays* in 1602—ignoring corrections that had been made by the minister Charles Perrot seven years earlier—the pastors complained bitterly about this "profane and cynical book" that they feared would "encourage men in atheism" and "sow the seed of scandal" in Geneva and beyond. The magistrates responded by ordering that all remaining copies of the book be confiscated.[15] City officials did not always acquiesce to the Company's concerns, however. In 1588, the magistrates approved the publication of Gaston Dulco's book entitled *On the Production of Precious Stones and Metals,* which defended Paracelsus and the art of alchemy despite the ministers' strong objections that "this art of changing metals is false."[16]

As they kept a watchful eye on Geneva's print shops, the ministers and elders in Consistory also monitored and attempted to regulate the kinds of books that circulated through the city and were read by their parishioners. City statute forbade the sale and distribution of books that espoused Catholic "superstition" or contained materials judged to be "shameful" or "lascivious."[17] Geneva's ministers and elders were primary agents in the enforcement of these laws, always on the lookout for Catholic literature smuggled into the city from nearby Savoy or the print shops of Lyon. In 1560, the pastors voiced alarm that a local merchant was selling a children's book titled *The Fountain of Life* that was full of "idolatry and pollution"; in addition to being decorated with crucifixes, the volume encouraged children to celebrate Catholic festivals and to confess their sins to a priest. The ministers petitioned the magistrates to punish the book dealer and confiscate and burn all copies of the book as a public example so that such false teaching might "not take root but be altogether extirpated."[18] Several years later, the Consistory disciplined three men for circulating a book by Sebastian Castellio titled *Advice to Desolate France* in which Geneva's clergymen were blamed for religious violence back in France.[19] In addition to books that attacked Geneva's ministers or undermined the church's official theology, the Consistory regularly censured literature that they judged dangerous for public morals, including books of the occult, pornography, and ribald humor. After receiving a report that a book "of enchantments and charms" had been found in the boutique of Mathieu Canard, the ministers and elders interrogated Canard and ordered him to burn the book immediately, which the man did.[20] A notorious gambler named Aimé de Chappeaurouge was excommunicated in 1579 for using ill-gotten wealth to fill his library with a collection of "bad books." The rector of the Academy visited Chappeaurouge's house to examine the contents of his library and confiscate those books deemed profane or dangerous.[21] In a similar fashion, the Consistory scolded the merchant Domaine Favre in 1559 for lending copies of the multivolume saga *Amadis of France* to young men in the city. Favre was advised that he should "own other types of books like the holy Bible, the Old and New Testament, and other books about the gospel with which to be instructed." The ministers then forwarded copies of *Amadis* to the magistrates for burning, noting that books of this sort "only serve to corrupt and deprave young people, and moreover are only lies and dreams."[22]

Keeping "bad books" out of the hands of young students at the Genevan Academy posed special challenges for the ministers, as the case of Lucas Cop illustrates.[23] The son of the (deceased) pastor Michel Cop, Lucas was called before Consistory in 1570 charged with neglecting his studies, missing sermons, lying to the ministers, and reading "several profane books," including the works of Rabelais and Catullus. Further investigation revealed that Cop and a dozen other students had also sampled the love poetry of Ronsard, Ovid, Jean-Antoine de Baïf, and Balthasar Castiglione; in fact, Cop had stolen several of these volumes from a local book merchant.[24] The Consistory suspended Cop and three of his friends from the Lord's Supper and sent the young man to the Small Council, which opened a criminal investigation that ultimately convicted him to a public flogging in the presence of the students of the Academy.[25] Efforts like these to regulate the kinds of printed material available to townspeople were never entirely successful. Yet the campaign to purge the city of books judged dangerous continued throughout the early modern era, reflecting the ministers' commitment to defend right doctrine, promote good morals, and exercise pastoral oversight of their flock in reformed Geneva.

2. Pastors as Authors

The pastors not only collected and censured books; they also wrote them. Calvin's literary corpus is well known, with around one hundred discrete volumes published from the time he arrived in Geneva in 1536 until his death twenty-eight years later. During the 1550s, Calvin's literary output ranged from 100,000 to a remarkable 250,000 published words per year.[26] Late nights spent writing at his desk by candlelight or long days spent dictating from bed inevitably took a toll on his health and spirits: "I get so tired from that endless writing that at times I have a loathing for it, and actually hate writing," Calvin complained to Bullinger in 1551.[27] But true religion needed to be defended in print as well as from the pulpit. "I would be a real coward if I saw God's truth being attacked and remained quiet without a sound."[28] Theodore Beza also recognized the strategic value of defending reformed Christianity through print media and he encouraged colleagues such as Chandieu, Daneau, and Goulart to join him in this important endeavor. To a minister friend in Zurich, he wrote in 1575: "I rejoice that my colleagues Daneau and Goulart are friends of yours, and I beg that you also exhort them to write [books]. For you see how few men we have today who are able to write with precision and substance—which is the very thing that we need."[29] From Beza's perspective, the ministry of writing books that defended the truth and edified the people of God was of vital importance for the well-being of the church. Chandieu voiced this same conviction in his poem *Palinode Concerning Pierre Ronsard* (1563). In order to battle the "furious papist," reformed Christians needed "to confound him with well-argued sermons, to restrain him with weapons, to answer him with books, without losing courage in the midst of danger."[30]

From 1536 to 1609, at least 22 of the 135 ministers who served on the Company of Pastors wrote books that were published during the years that they were engaged in parish ministry in Geneva. In all, Geneva's pastors produced around three hundred fifty discrete titles during their tenures in the city—roughly two hundred fifty titles if one discounts the published writings of Calvin.[31] By far the most prolific of Geneva's ministers during the half century after Calvin were Beza (more than seventy-five titles), Goulart (around sixty-five titles), Daneau (around thirty titles), La Faye (more than fifteen titles), and Chandieu (more than five titles). Ministers such as Bonaventure Bertram, Pierre Chevallier, Nicolas Colladon, and Jean Jaquemot who held joint appointments at the Geneva Academy as professors of theology, Hebrew, Greek, or the arts, account for most of the remaining volumes authored by Geneva's ministers. Table 8.1 lists the number of known titles published by Geneva ministers from 1536 to 1609, categorized by subject area.

As table 8.1 indicates, books written by Geneva's ministers covered a broad range of topics and employed a variety of literary genres, including commentaries, sermons, prayers, poetry, songs, biographies, historical narratives, and theological polemics. Themes explored ranged from highly technical questions of Greek exegesis and Hebrew grammar, to more controversial, even spectacular, subjects like witchcraft, martyrdom, and the person of the Antichrist. Several books were best sellers in their day, notably Calvin's *Institutes* (in its various editions), Beza's *Confession of the Christian Faith* (1559), and Beza's and Clement Marot's *Genevan Psalter* (1562). Other works were judged so politically explosive that Geneva's magistrates required them published under pseudonyms or prohibited their publication in Geneva altogether.[32] Although space does not permit a detailed roll call of the battalion of books written by Geneva's ministers from 1536 to

TABLE 8.1 Number of Titles Published by Genevan Ministers During Pastoral Tenure, 1536–1609

SUBJECT AREA	NO. OF TITLES [CALVIN]	% OF TOTAL
Bibles and Exegetical Aids	14	4%
Commentaries on Scripture	34 [26]	10%
Commentaries on Patristic/Classical Texts	6	2%
Correspondence	3 [1]	1%
Devotional Works	20	6%
Ethics	17 [7]	5%
Geography	1	—
History/Biography	29 [1]	8%
Natural Sciences	3	1%
Poetry and Music	9 [1]	3%
Politics	5	1%
Sermon Collections	28 [21]	8%
Theology and Polemics	130 [42]	37%
Translations and Editions	51	15%
Total	350 [99]	100%

1609, I will briefly survey some of the more noteworthy volumes in five general subject areas: theology and polemics, translations and editions, history and biography, Biblical studies and exegetical aids, and practical works of Christian devotion.

Theology and Confessional Polemics

Books of theology and confessional polemics comprise around 37 percent of all volumes written by Geneva's ministers during the seven decades after 1536. Nearly all these titles came from ministers who held joint appointments as professors of theology at the Geneva Academy, men such as Calvin, Beza, Chandieu, Daneau, and La Faye. Without a doubt, the most influential summary of reformed theology in the French-speaking world throughout this period remained Calvin's *Institutes*,[33] but Beza's *Confession of the Christian Faith* (1559), his two-volume *Questions and Answers* (1570, 1576), and Chandieu's *Response to the Profession of Faith* (1585) were also important for popularizing and defending Calvin's theological vision.[34] Theodore Beza published his *Confession* in response to the request of his

Catholic father for a concise statement of the evangelical faith. Choosing the form of an expanded catechism, Beza set out to explain and provide scriptural justification for reformed Christianity in seven chapters ranging from the doctrine of the Trinity to the Last Judgment. In the preface, Beza excoriates the Roman Church for discouraging laypeople from studying the Scripture. By contrast, the reformed teach by word and example that "pastors must feed their flock with the Word of Life, and that the sheep, for their part, need to know and understand what they proclaim, in order to be nourished and consoled by it, and be protected from wolves and false prophets." Beza thus invites his audience to discover the truth of Scripture as they read his book: "I desire that each person who reads [my *Confession*] will compare it carefully with the Scripture, which is the sole and true touchstone for proving true doctrine."[35] Although Beza's *apologia* for the Protestant faith did not achieve the desired conversion of his father, it did enjoy immense success, appearing in thirty-five editions and five languages during his lifetime.[36]

Perhaps the most creative effort to articulate the theology of reformed Christianity and justify its orthodoxy within the broader frame of the Protestant tradition is found in the *Harmony of the Confession of Faith* (1581), a collaborative work by the French minister Jean-François Salvard and Geneva's pastors Beza, Daneau, Chandieu, and Goulart in response to the publication of the Lutheran Book of Concord a year earlier.[37] The *Harmony* contained a catalogue of ten reformed confessions and the Lutheran Augsburg Confession, along with comparative tables intended to show the substantial doctrinal agreement between the different Protestant traditions.[38] The purpose is clear: since the reformed and Lutherans share the same Christian faith, they should lay aside bitter rivalry and form a common evangelical front against their enemies, the Roman Church, the king of Spain, and the Jesuits. More immediately, it was hoped that the *Harmony* would convince Lutheran princes, like Auguste of Saxony, to stop persecuting crypto-Calvinists in their territories and provide military and political support for embattled Huguenots in France. This venture in Protestant ecumenism accomplished little in the end. The *Harmony* quickly fell into almost complete oblivion, "rediscovered" only in the twentieth century by Protestant ecumenists.

Geneva's theologians also spilled rivers of ink in polemical exchanges with critics and confessional enemies of reformed Christianity. Geneva's ministers mounted vigorous attacks against the teachings of anti-Trinitarian writers including François David, Georges Biandrata, Michael Servetus, and Giovanni Valentino Gentile. In his *Refutation of Heretics* (1573), Daneau even proposed a dialectical method to expose the lies of heretics and defeat their sophistical arguments.[39] Calvin, Beza, and their colleagues also waged wars of words against Catholic opponents such as the Dutch theologian Albert Pighius, the French jurist François Bauduin, the Dominican Claude de Sainctes, the bishop and missionary François de Sales, and the English

Jesuit John Hay. In 1547, Calvin wrote a more substantial refutation of the Council of Trent. Invariably, these disputes with Catholics cycled back to such fundamental issues as the source of Christian authority, the definition of the true church, and the nature of the Eucharist. In his commentary on the first book of Peter Lombard's *Sentences* (1580), Lambert Daneau thrust beyond these occasional controversies to strike at the heart of the method practiced by scholastic theologians from the Middle Ages to the present. Because the schoolmen had ignored Scripture and granted Aristotle's metaphysics preeminence within the "temple" of theology, Daneau argued, Catholic theology had become characterized by speculation and endless disputes that rendered Christian truth uncertain and gave false warrant to the Roman pontiffs' vaunted claims to authority.[40] In addition to battling anti-Trinitarians and Catholics, members of the Venerable Company also vied against Protestants closer to home who questioned aspects of Calvin's doctrine or challenged Geneva's theological leadership within the reformed world. During his career, Beza entered the list against reformed opponents such as Claude Aubery, Sebastian Castellio, Thomas Erastus, Antoine de Lescaille, and Adrian Saravia in an effort to defend and define more carefully the theological nuances of predestination, church discipline, justification by faith alone, and Presbyterian church government.

But more than all other opponents, Geneva's pastors waged their fiercest battles with Lutheran scholars over the doctrines of Christ's presence in the Lord's Supper and the ubiquity of Christ's resurrected body. In the mid 1550s, Calvin wrote three treatises defending the *Zurich Consensus* (1549) and the reformed doctrine of the Lord's Supper against attacks of the Lutheran pastor Joachim Westphal. These controversies escalated during the three decades after the Peace of Augsburg (1555) as confessional identities became more rigid and the political fortunes of Lutheran and reformed churches diverged. All together, pastors in the Venerable Company published around thirty-five titles against Lutheran opponents from 1536 to 1609, including works against all the major Lutheran controversialists of the period, Jacob Andreae, Johann Brenz, Wilhelm Holder, Lucas Osiander, Jean Pappus, Nicolas Selnecker, and Joachim Westphal. These theological battles were invariably fought within the creedal boundaries established by the fourth and fifth-century councils of the Christian church.[41] Lutheran theologians condemned Calvin and reformed Christians as "sacramentarians" and spiritual offspring of the ancient heretic Nestorius because they denied Christ's physical presence in the communion elements and rejected the Lutheran claim that the properties of Christ's divine nature were communicated *in abstracto* to his resurrected body.[42] Calvin's theological heirs in Geneva matched insult for insult by condemning the Book of Concord as a Pandora's box and likening Lutheran Christology to the Eutychian heresy which mixed and confused the two natures of Jesus Christ.[43] These protracted controversies culminated in an unhappy stalemate at the Colloquy of Montbéliard in 1586 when Beza and the Lutheran theologian Jacob Andreae failed to reach agreement on any of the disputed articles related to Christ's presence in the Eucharist, the use of art and music in the churches, and predestination. Beza reported the conclusion of the colloquy in his *Acts of the Colloquy of Montbéliard* (1588) in terms tragically reminiscent of the interchange between Luther and Zwingli at the Marburg Colloquy six decades earlier: Beza offered Andreae the "hand of brotherhood" and assured him that the reformed would treat Lutherans with peace and concord. Andreae refused this gesture of Christian fellowship, offering in return only the hand of kindness and humanity. To which Beza responded: "Since you have refused to recognize us as your Christian brothers, we will not accept a handshake that only feigns human kindness."[44]

Translations and Editions

Members of Geneva's Venerable Company also translated and edited a substantial number of books written by other authors, ancient as well as modern. Around 15 percent of the books published by Geneva's ministers from 1536 to 1609 fit this category. Simon Goulart's role as a translator, editor, and publicist is especially noteworthy. Over his long career, he produced a virtual library of French editions of important theological and devotional works written by leading Protestant divines, including Beza, Joachim Camerarius, Chandieu, Jean de L'Espine, Philip Du Plessis Mornay, William Perkins, Peter Martyr Vermigli, Zacharias Ursinus, and Jerome Zanchi. Especially provocative or influential were Goulart's translations of François Hotman's political treatise *The French Gaul* (1574) and Jean Crespin's *History of Martyrs* (1582), works that advocated a spirit of resistance against political tyranny and encouraged embattled Protestants in France to embrace the cross of suffering on behalf of the evangelical faith. Goulart explained his goals as an editor and popularizer in one of his prefaces: He wished "to make the reading [of this book] easier for those who have still not attained an understanding of difficult matters that one encounters here, both in terminology and topics drawn from all domains of knowledge."[45] In addition to contemporary works, Goulart translated into French the writings of important classical and patristic authors for the edification of his audience or for specific polemical purposes. Under this rubric one finds his French translations of Plutarch, Seneca, Basil, Chrysostom, Cyprian, Gregory of Nazianzus, and Tertullian. Goulart's appreciation for music and his penchant for things esoteric are evident in other editions that he published, including a collection of the songs of Roland de Lassus (1576) and translations of volumes on witchcraft and sorcery written originally by Jehann Wier (1579) and Caspar Peucer (1584).[46]

In his work as editor, Goulart was not above modifying and expurgating texts to suit his moral tastes and polemical concerns. As much as he appreciated the music of Roland de Lassus and praised the composer's artistic genius, Goulart found many of his lyrics "foolish, lascivious, and profane"——not at all appropriate for the ears of pious men and women. Accordingly, Goulart announced in the preface to his edition of Lassus that he was taking extensive liberties in revising and removing objectionable material "so that one can sing them with the voice or play them with instruments without soiling the tongue or offending the ears of Christians."[47] Goulart employed this same strategy in his edition of Michel de Montaigne's *Essays* (1595).[48] The Genevan editor suppressed chapters of the *Essays* that championed the Catholic religion and advocated political compromise in France. Gone too were Montaigne's defense of liberty of conscience, his praise of Sebastian Castellio (whom Montaigne had described as a "very excellent personage"), his condemnation of vernacular transla- tions of the Bible, and his suggestion that Lutheranism contributed to the rise of atheism. Goulart also sanitized passages where Montaigne's choice of material or argument violated Calvinist moral sensibilities. He censored, for example, Montaigne's racy anecdote in his chapter "On Virtue," describing a lovesick young gentleman who, when unable to consummate physical union with his mistress, castrated himself and sent the offending member to her as a sign of purification for his moral offense.[49] Given extensive revisions like these, one might wonder why Goulart bothered to publish editions of Montaigne or Lassus in the first place. The most probable explanation is offered by historian Ingerborg Jostock, who argues that Goulart's work as editor reflects a general pat- tern of censorship in confessional Europe during the second half of the sixteenth century. Beginning around 1560, Catholic and Protestant intel- lectuals undertook a project of refashioning vernacular and profane lit- erature according to their ideological perspectives in an effort to guide Christian readers toward literature that would edify and promote moral virtue.[50] Goulart's work as a translator and editor serves precisely this function. By mining the treasures of the ancient fathers and popularizing the work of select contemporary authors, the Genevan pastor made avail- able to the reading public in the French-speaking world a collection of books intended to reinforce Protestant convictions and inculcate Calvinist standards of moral behavior.

History and Biography

Geneva's ministers recognized the strategic importance of producing historical works that preserved and defended the memory of important Protestant leaders and presented reformed interpretations of the momen- tous religious and political events of their century. Accordingly, around 8 percent of all books produced by the ministers from 1536 to 1609 were his- torical in nature. Several of these volumes celebrated the lives of Geneva's two most famous ministers, Calvin and Beza. Pastors Nicolas Colladon and Beza each wrote postmortem biographies of Calvin; La Faye also memo- rialized the life of Beza.[51] Of a different genre was Beza's *Images* (1580), which brought together engraved portraits, brief biographical sketches, and epitaphs *in memoriam* of forty deceased churchmen, martyrs, princes, and princesses who had served the cause of church reform in the age of the Reformation.[52] This constellation of illustrious men and women—among them Savonarola, Erasmus, Luther, Bucer, Calvin, Farel, and Marguerite d'Angoulême—"not only loved and maintained virtue, but also restored to a place of honor the mother of all virtues, namely true religion."[53] Beza believed that it was of critical importance that these heroes of the faith be remembered and emulated, particularly at a time when the light of the Reformation seemed to be fading in many corners of Europe. Beza expressed these sentiments in a letter to a friend in Germany to whom he was sending a copy of the *Images*: "It has always delighted me greatly to remember the era of those great men, which I have come to compare with a golden century. But alas! How quickly it was changed, not into a century of silver or bronze, but into a century of iron!"[54]

In addition to biographies, Geneva's pastors wrote more than a dozen historical works describing the dramatic unfolding of the political and religious crisis in Geneva and France. Ministers Simon Goulart and Antoine de La Faye recounted Geneva's desperate struggle for survival during the Savoyard War (1589–1593) and its victory on the Night of the Escalade (December 12, 1602). Other ministers chronicled the origins and early progress of reformed Christianity in France, the failed attempt to reach religious concord at the Colloquy of Poissy, and the tragic violence that ensued during the French civil wars. The most important of these histories were Jean de Serres's *Commentary on the State of Religion in the Kingdom of France* (1571), Theodore Beza's *Ecclesiastical History* (1580), and Simon Goulart's *Memoires of the State of France under Charles IX* (1576) and *Memoires of the Catholic League* (1587–99).[55] These works wove together eyewitness reports, letters, discourses, and martyr accounts to fashion a moral history of the struggle of God's true church against what were judged to be the forces of false religion and tyranny. For these authors, historical writing had a responsibility to do more than chronicle past events in a precise fashion. The faithful historian is a "minister and trumpet of Divine Providence," averred Serres, who proclaims the purposes of God in human history and applies moral judgments to the activities of kings and commoners.[56] "History not only draws up a list of accusations against wicked men and commits them to eternal memory, but even more it drags them before the tribunal of God whether they like it or not."[57] Writing history was both a polemical and moral undertaking. For some of Geneva's ministers, writing history also satisfied deeply felt personal concerns. Simon Goulart may well have spoken for other colleagues when he commented in the aftermath of the St. Bartholomew's Day massacres: "I am possessed by such a burning love for my fatherland that life will be bitter for me until I describe to my fellow Frenchmen, with historical exactitude, the treachery of the tyrant [King Charles IX]."[58] Writing history was a way of righting wrongs and reminding French Protestants of their identity as a people, suffering beneath the cross of Christ.

Biblical Studies and Exegetical Aids

Far and away the most lasting literary contribution made by Geneva's ministers was in the domain of exegetical aids, biblical commentaries, and translations of the Bible. Around 14 percent of the books written by Geneva's ministers from 1536 to 1609 fall into this category. Calvin's work as a commentator on sacred Scripture is well known. During his lifetime he published commentaries or lectures (*praelectiones*) on nearly one-half of the books in the Old Testament canon as well as commentaries on every book of the New Testament except 2 and 3 John, and Revelation.[59] By comparison, the number of commentaries that other members of the Company of Pastors published between 1536 and 1609 was surprisingly modest— only eight in total—a consequence no doubt of living in Calvin's long shadow. Because Calvin "surpassed by a great deal all the old and modern" commentators, Beza observed, "my advice is the same as the opinion of Cicero...concerning Julius Caesar's commentaries, be it known that he dissuaded through marvel the wisest men from writing after him."[60] Notwithstanding these sentiments, a number of Geneva's pastors did write and publish commentaries on sacred Scripture such as Nicolas Des Gallars's work on Exodus (1560), Daneau's treatment of 1 Timothy (1577), Beza's studies of Ecclesiastes (1588) and Job (1589), and Antoine de La Faye's commentaries on Romans (1608), 1 Timothy (1609), and Ecclesiastes (1609).[61] In addition, Geneva's ministers produced a variety of Bible helps such as Greek and Hebrew grammars, scriptural paraphrases, and even a handbook on scriptural hermeneutics.[62]

It was in the domain of Bible translations that Theodore Beza and his colleagues after Calvin left their most lasting mark. During the second half of the sixteenth century, Geneva was a virtual factory of Bible production. In her inventory of French Bibles printed in the early modern period, Bettye Thomas Chambers identifies more than eighty editions of the complete French Bible produced in Geneva between 1550 and 1600, and roughly the same number of French editions of the New Testament.[63] Geneva printers also produced a steady stream of Old and New Testament editions in other languages, Latin, Greek, Hebrew, Italian, Spanish, and English. Under the leadership first of Calvin, and then of Theodore Beza, the Company of Pastors played a crucial role in this thriving industry. While still a professor of Greek at Lausanne in the 1550s, Beza had applied his humanistic philological training and knowledge of the biblical languages to the task of creating a new Latin translation of the New Testament, based on the best Greek codices available to him. This superior Latin translation appeared for the first time in 1556 under the title *New Testament of Our Lord Jesus Christ* (in-folio).[64] Over the next forty-two years, Beza carefully revised and republished this substantial work four times. With the Greek text supplied in parallel columns, and extensive exegetical and theological notes added to the bottom of each page, Beza's *Annotations* (as it came to be known) served as the gold standard of reformed biblical scholarship in the late sixteenth century.[65] Beza himself viewed it as his *chef d'oeuvre*: "nothing in life is dearer to me," he wrote to a friend.[66]

Of equal or perhaps even greater importance to the history of French Protestantism was Calvin and Beza's contribution to the so-called Genevan Psalter. Almost immediately upon arriving in Geneva in 1536, Calvin recognized the need to translate the Psalms into French meter for use in public worship and commissioned the famous Renaissance poet Clément Marot to undertake the work. When Marot died in 1544, he had completed only forty-nine of the one hundred fifty chapters of the Psalter. Calvin next solicited the assistance of Beza, then a professor of the Academy of Lausanne, who completed the project over the following decade. Published as *The Psalms of David* (1562), the Genevan Psalter consisted of metrical translations of all one hundred fifty Psalms put to music by Louis Bourgeois (and others) in a form that could be clearly heard and easily sung by the Christian congregation. It was a best seller from the start. More than 27,000 copies were printed in the first weeks; an additional sixty editions appeared over the next four years.[67] The power of the metrical Psalms stamped the identity of reformed Christians in a variety of ways. The Genevan Psalter was not only a staple in public worship, but was sung in the marketplace, intoned by martyrs on their way to the scaffold, and even chanted by armies as they marched into battle. In the decades and centuries that followed, the Genevan Psalter served as the distinguishing mark of reformed worship and the *cri de coeur* of embattled French Protestantism.[68]

Two other monuments to Geneva's biblical scholarship deserve mention, the Bible of 1588 and Jean Diodati's Italian translation of the Bible. During the second half of the sixteenth century, the Venerable Company became increasingly convinced of the need for a more accurate French translation of the Bible to supplant Pierre Olivetan's version and to serve as the official Bible for French-speaking Protestants. For sixteen years, the ministers and professors of Geneva—in particular Beza and the Hebraist Bonaventure Bertram—labored over the translation and annotations. It was finally published with much fanfare in 1588 under the title *The Bible, Revised by the Pastors and Professors of the Church of Geneva* and was soon received as the official version of the French churches.[69] The Bible of 1588 proved a spectacular success, measured both by its influence and subsequent history. Published in folio, quarto, and octavo formats, this Bible remained the standard French Bible for over a century and did not undergo significant revision until 1805.[70] Despite its popularity and longevity, however, Catholic opponents—and even several reformed leaders in Geneva and France—expressed strong reservations about the translation's overt confessional bias.[71] One of these later critics was the Genevan minister and theologian Jean Diodati, himself an excellent philologist and exegete, who determined to apply his formidable talents to a new Italian translation of the Bible. He began the project in 1603 and completed it four years later. "I have tried with all my power," he wrote a friend, "to open the door for our Italians to the knowledge of the heavenly truth. May our Lord, who miraculously assisted and strengthened me in this work, grant his blessing that it may bear fruit."[72] He intended his Bible for both edification and confessional battle, an instrument to assist believers in worship and personal devotion, but also to promote the diffusion of evangelical belief in Italy.[73] Diodati later significantly improved this first Italian translation. His *Holy Bible* (2nd edition), published in folio format in 1641, was celebrated throughout Protestant Europe for its philological precision and elegant style, as well as the insightful commentary that accompanied each biblical chapter.[74] In the following centuries, Diodati's *Holy Bible* nearly achieved the status of Luther's German Bible and the English Authorized King James version of the Bible and remained the authoritative Italian Protestant Bible until the second half of the twentieth century.[75]

Practical Theology and Devotional Writings

In the letter preface to the third volume of his *Theological Treatises* (1582), Beza described the critical importance of both dogmatic theology *and* practical religion for the well-being of the church. "How preposterous it is," he writes

> if we desire so much to defend one flank of this sacred city, that is the Church, that we ignore an evident assault by the enemy on another flank. For we must guard against this most beguiling trick of Satan, lest in being so concerned about defending dogma (δογματική) on the one hand...we lose practical religion (πρακτικήν) on the other, which is the end and goal of the Christian religion.[76]

Beza believed that Christian pastors and teachers were responsible not only to defend pure doctrine but also to encourage practical religion and personal piety. Indeed, when ministering among ordinary people, ministers had the responsibility of treating practical religious concerns rather than difficult theological questions.[77] This commitment is readily apparent in the inventory of books published by Geneva's ministers from 1536 to 1609, where nearly 20 percent of titles might be categorized as practical or devotional in nature, including ethical treatises, sermon collections, and devotional literature.

Defining standards of ethical behavior for reformed Christians was a special concern for Geneva's pastors. Calvin, for example, published works treating the use of religious relics (1543), the religious accommodation of so-called Nicodemites (1544), and judicial astrology (1549), as well as a treatise on the Christian life (1550). Pierre Viret's *Diverse Treatises for the Instruction of the Faithful* (1559) offered straight-forward advice and comfort for believers back in France who contemplated disavowing Roman Catholicism and converting to the reformed faith.[78] Somewhat later, Theodore Beza wrote a full-length study against Bernard Ochino that examined the scriptural warrant for polygamy and divorce and a shorter booklet that considered whether or not Christians who trusted in God's sovereignty might still flee a deadly plague. This practical bent is especially evident in the writings of the minister Lambert Daneau, who during the decade that he served on the Venerable Company wrote a textbook on Christian ethics as well as penned a variety of treatises examining practical moral questions such as whether Christians were permitted to play games of chance, dance, wear contemporary styles of clothing and hairstyles, and serve in the military.[79]

Daneau's popular treatise *On Witchcraft* (1573), which was republished ten times, in Latin, English, and German before the end of the century, offers a good illustration of his method of ethical instruction.[80] Taking the form of a dialogue, an interlocutor named Antoine reports to his friend Theophile that a large number of people back in France have been accused of witchcraft, and one suspected witch has even been executed. He inquires of Theophile whether these accusations are a "pure fable and mockery," or whether there are in fact witches in the world who have power to use black magic to harm other people. Drawing upon a rich array of biblical passages, classical sources, and contemporary reports, Theophile proceeds to distinguish eight ways that Satan works through human agents before arriving at the definition of a witch or sorcerer: "We will call [witches] those who by the suggestion, knowledge, and a pact made with the devil, kill, injure, or corrupt human beings or animals."[81] Over the next one hundred pages of the treatise, Theophile answers Antoine's many pressing questions and practical concerns:

ANTOINE: Are there witches in the world?

THEOPHILE: Yes.

ANTOINE: Why is witchcraft more prevalent today than three or four centuries ago?

THEOPHILE: Because God is justly punishing sixteenth-century men and women for rejecting the Word of God and turning a blind eye to the light of the gospel.

ANTOINE: Is it possible for human beings to make a pact with Satan in an effort to become wealthy or gain power over their neighbors?

THEOPHILE: Yes.

ANTOINE: In what manner do witches exercise their power?

THEOPHILE: Witches are agents of Satan who employ hexes, chants, poisons, and drugs, to injure men, women, and children, bewitch animals such as horses, sheep, and cows, and even poison grass, trees, wine, water, and the air—but only with the express permission and sovereign will of God.

ANTOINE: Can Satan then work miracles?

THEOPHILE: No, but through his malevolent power he can manipulate the natural order to accomplish his strange and wicked designs.

ANTOINE: What punishment do witches deserve?

THEOPHILE: Witches are enemies of humankind, apostates of the Christian faith and guilty of high treason against God. They thus deserve death. However magistrates must exercise caution and due diligence when investigating suspected cases of witchcraft lest innocent people be implicated.

ANTOINE: What of good witches? May one seek their assistance for healing or to find lost valuables?

THEOPHILE: There is no such thing as a good witch; therefore, witches should never be consulted for any reason.

The dialogue draws to a close with Antoine asking the most urgent question of all: How then are Christians to protect themselves from these most dangerous emissaries of Satan? Daneau, through the voice of Theophile, has a ready answer: "There is no drug or recipe or medicine that can protect us from witches, except to pray to God night and day, when we rise in the morning or lie down at night...." for God is "the sovereign King who is all-powerful over devils and witches, and who deploys an army of angels to guard his children. So then, since we have placed ourselves in God's safekeeping, who can harm us? For if God is for us, who will be against us?" (Rom 8:30)[82]

Printed sermons also reflect the ministers' commitment to the instruction, edification, and sanctification of reformed believers. During his years in Geneva, Calvin preached around four thousand sermons, and sixteen separate collections of these sermons appeared in print before 1564.[83] Calvin hoped that these printed sermons would not only edify and instruct ordinary believers but also provide a practical model "for many who have been called to the ministry of the gospel during these times of trial."[84] After Calvin's death, his published sermons continued to attract a broad readership in the French-speaking world and beyond. No fewer than thirty editions of Calvin's sermons appeared between 1564 and 1600 in Latin, French, English, Dutch, and German editions.[85] In the preface to the Latin translation of Calvin's sermons on the book of Job (1593), Beza praised his mentor's substantial gifts as an interpreter: in Calvin, one finds "a supreme fidelity in interpretation, a keen judgment to express the truth, a profound erudition, and an attentiveness [to the biblical text] that never sleeps."[86] Beza went on to report that Calvin's sermons remained popular even to his own day. Calvin's sermons were "so greatly appreciated" that in French congregations "which did not have their own shepherd and teacher, these sermons were presented from the pulpit in regular meetings of the congregations." Hence, even "in these very difficult times in France, many people are wonderfully encouraged by them both in the church and in their families."[87]

The popularity of Calvin's published sermons, and the perception that they should serve as models for subsequent reformed homiletics, probably discouraged other ministers in Geneva from publishing their own pulpit expositions. During Calvin's lifetime, the only colleagues whose sermons appeared in print were Michel Cop, who published homilies on Proverbs (1556) and Ecclesiastes (1557), and Jean-Raymond Merlin, who published sermons on the Ten Commandments (1562). The English translator of Cop's sermons on Proverbs (1580 edition) compared the Geneva minister to a bee who first collected and then brought back to the "hive" (i.e., the church) the sweet honey of the Word of God to nourish the people of God. Cop "not onely read [the Proverbs of Solomon] for his own delight, but also sucked out of everie flower of same Garden, most sweete honie: which being faithfully gathered & disposed in the Hive, he left as fruite of his labour to al posterity, for al the godly to be partakers of."[88]

Better known were the sermons of Theodore Beza, published at the end of the century.[89] Numbering eighty-six sermons in all, Beza's published homiletic works mirror the expository style and doctrine of Calvin. They are rich in theological instruction and practical application, concerned to teach, exhort, warn, console, and edify reformed Christians in the face of difficulty and danger. In the preface to the *Sermons on the Song of Songs*, dedicated to his pastoral colleagues in Geneva, Beza described "the enormous consolation" that he had experienced preaching the sublime mysteries contained in this enigmatic portion of the scriptural canon, and expressed his hope that the reader would also receive edification from them. For edification "is the only goal to which our sacred ministries should be directed, as you well know."[90] In a similar fashion, in the dedicatory preface to the *Sermons on the History of the Death of Jesus Christ*, addressed to embattled pastors, elders, and deacons of the reformed churches in France, Beza stated his hope that preaching on the suffering and death of Jesus Christ might provide consolation for Christians in the face of "great confusions" and "so many harsh storms."[91] Beza intended his sermons to serve as a kind of final testament "containing the doctrine that I have proclaimed for forty years," and in which "I desire to persevere until this happy end."[92]

Many of the writings described in this chapter could appropriately be listed under the general category of "devotional literature." Printed sermons, Psalters, catechisms, annotated Bibles, and religious biographies were all intended to encourage spiritual reflection and stir religious fervor among the Christian faithful. But a number of books published by Geneva's ministers were created with the specific purpose to promote meditation, prayer, and joyful submission to the divine will. Books of this sort became especially popular among Geneva's ministers during the final decades of the sixteenth century. As noted earlier, Beza wrote a collection of daily prayers for use in the Christian household. Beza, along with Chandieu and Goulart, also wrote lengthy prose *Meditations* on select chapters of Holy Scripture (Chandieu's meditation on Psalm 32 ran to 248 pages!).[93] The pastor-poet Jean Jaquemot rendered the Old Testament book of Lamentations into Latin verse.[94] Beza produced a similar work on the Song of Songs. One of the most accomplished poets among Geneva's pastoral company was Antoine de Chandieu. His famous poem, the *Octonaires on the Vanity of This World* (1583), presented in a cycle of fifty, eight-line verses a haunting description of the fragile and fleeting nature of human life as well as the vanity of worldly amusements, while at the same time calling men and women to find safe refuge in God alone.[95] The poem concludes with this sober assessment and final prayer:

'Tis both folly and vanity,
to be preoccupied with this world.
All the pleasures of this life
cause only worry and grief.
God, you alone are wise and firm.
Teach me to live content.
Receive me in your bounteous love,
My steadfast and wise one.[96]

Of all Geneva's ministers, it was Simon Goulart who published the largest number of devotional writings during the period. In the final decades of his life, Goulart's mindset appears to have taken a turn toward more sober and contemplative matters, themes that he explored in a variety of moral discourses, spiritual meditations, and handbooks on old age and death. Goulart's *Christian Discourses*, published in two installments in 1591 and 1595, provide an especially good illustration of the depth of the author's reflection upon the complexities of the Christian life.[97] In the preface to the first volume, Goulart states that his central purpose is to give assurance to embattled believers that, no matter how great their suffering, they must not lose courage but submit to God's wisdom because their heavenly Father will sustain them in this life and bring them safely to heaven in the next. In the forty-seven discourses that make up these two volumes, Goulart examines the existential concerns and painful questions that must have concerned many reformed Christians during the generation after Calvin's death: How do good men and women live in a wicked world? Why does God seem to delay in helping his people? Is it permissible to rejoice at the ruin of one's enemies? Can Christians be confident of their eternal election? How should Christians prepare to die? His penetrating gaze scans a broad horizon, including such matters as pride, prosperity and poverty, spiritual warfare, divine providence, the human conscience, and the joys of eternal life. An excerpt from Goulart's treatment of the topic of poverty illustrates well the overall tone and approach of these discourses:

It is in poverty and in contempt for perishable things that the luster of the Church is seen. When religion gave birth to an abundance of earthly goods, the daughter suffocated her mother. When early Christian bishops were made of gold, their crosses were made of wood. But bishops became like wood when their crosses appeared as gold. The more that there was simplicity in the administration of the Word of God and the sacraments, the more that pastors were small and humble in the eyes of the world, and the Church had fewer troubles. Who can dare despise the poverty of a faithful servant of God in the presence of the Prophets, Apostles, Confessors and Martyrs, and Jesus Christ himself—all of whom were poor?[98]

Several of the themes that Goulart treated briefly in the *Christian Discourses* he soon expanded into full length monographs, including the subjects of spiritual warfare (1601), preparation for death (1602), wisdom in old age (1605), the Christian conscience (1607), and Christian assurance (1609). Goulart's concern with practical spirituality as well as his preoccupation with the nearness of death is readily apparent throughout these works. Thus, a woodcut on the title page of *The Wise Old Man* (1605) depicts the elderly Goulart at his writing desk with quill in hand; the Latin inscription reads: Dum Scribo, Morior—"As I write, I am dying."[99]

One cannot help but be impressed by the intellectual vitality and versatility of Calvin's colleagues and successors who published books from 1536 to 1609. Nearly one in six of Geneva's pastors undertook scholarship and writing as a part of their ministries. The most prominent among them, ministers such as Beza, Daneau, Chandieu, and Goulart, were veritable polymaths who applied their training as humanists to a wide breadth of intellectual inquiry. The ministers were biographers and biblical commentators; they were poets, political theorists, philologists, and preachers.[100] Nearly two-thirds of their combined writing lay outside of the domain of formal theological discourse. Nonetheless, most of the literary works penned by members of the Venerable Company had clearly defined *theological* purposes, that is, to persuade doubters and defend true religion, to provide comfort for suffering Christians, and to guide the faithful to mature Christian discipleship. This point deserves special emphasis. Though neither Beza nor his colleagues ever wrote a theological text that rivaled Calvin's *Institutes* in substance or popularity, and though they published only a modest number of biblical commentaries and sermon collections, they went well beyond Calvin in working out the implications of his religious program, applying it to the ethical concerns, the confessional challenges, and the spiritual needs of new generations of reformed Christians in French speaking Europe and beyond. The substantial literary corpus of Geneva's ministers indicates that the *studia humanitatis* were very much in the service of spiritual renewal and religious reformation. Or, to put it somewhat differently, for Beza and many of his colleagues, the writing of books was one important way that they fulfilled their spiritual calling as pastors of Christ's church.

3. Books, Theology, and Calvin's Legacy

Leaders who follow in the footsteps of important religious figures are easy targets for strong criticism: they are condemned for lack of originality if they preserve the status quo, vilified as traitors if they do not.[101] Such has been the unhappy lot of Theodore Beza, Lambert Daneau, Antoine de La Faye, and other reformed churchmen who provided theological leadership in Geneva during the half century after John Calvin's death. When they have not been entirely ignored, they have too often been measured against Calvin's long shadow and found wanting. This final section will explore some of the most important continuities and discontinuities between Calvin's theological program and that of his successors in Geneva. I will begin by describing how scholars of the past half century have presented the relationship between Calvin and the reformed theologians who came after him during the period known as Reformed Orthodoxy.[102] In the second part of this section, I will draw upon my study of the books written by Geneva's ministers to highlight important dimensions of intellectual life in Geneva that remained constant and changed from 1536 to 1609.

Calvin against the Calvinists?

It has become very much of a "cottage industry" for scholars to investigate the transformation of Calvin's theology at the hands of his reformed heirs over the century and a half after his death in 1564. A generation ago, the weight of scholarly opinion followed the interpretation of historians such as Walter Kickel, Basil Hall, and Brian Armstrong who argued that later reformed theologians, beginning with Beza, radically departed from Calvin's exegetical and Christ-centered theology.[103] Kickel's *Reason and Revelation in Theodore Beza* (1967) argued that Beza, by introducing Aristotelian dialectics and a rational system of causality into Calvinist theology, was chiefly responsible for the emergence of Reformed Orthodoxy which placed reason on equal footing with revelation and posited the doctrine of predestination as the central dogma from which the entire scheme of salvation was to be deduced.[104] Clear evidence of this, Kickel believed, could be found in Beza's *Table of Predestination* (1555), which argued for supralapsarian predestination and included a chart that subsumed the entire plan of creation, fall, and redemption under God's eternal purpose of election.[105] Similar conclusions were drawn by Basil Hall in his classic essay "Calvin against the Calvinists." For Hall, Beza was to be blamed for undermining the biblical and exegetical foundations of Calvin's theology by introducing Aristotelian logic into the reformed tradition, an approach that was highly speculative, rationalistic, and dogmatic. The fruit of this speculative approach was particularly evident in Beza's biblical literalism, as well as such idiosyncratic doctrines as supralapsarian predestination, limited atonement, and the immediate imputation of Adam's sin to all humanity.[106] Brian Armstrong developed this line of analysis further by describing the basic structure and content of reformed scholasticism for which Beza was largely responsible. Reformed scholasticism (1) "asserts religious truth on the basis of deductive ratiocination from given assumptions or principles, thus producing a logically coherent and defensible system of belief"; (2) employs reason in religious matters so that "reason assumes at least equal standing with faith in theology"; (3) views the Scripture as a "unified, rationally comprehensible account of Christian truth" and the measuring stick for determining orthodoxy; and (4) demonstrates "a pronounced interest in metaphysical matters, in abstract, speculative thought, particularly with reference to the doctrine of God."[107] Underlying Armstrong's definition was the assumption that the theology of "scholastic" reformed theologians like Beza or Daneau was intrinsically at odds with Calvin's biblical "humanism."[108]

This general paradigm of "Calvin against the Calvinists" defended by Kickel, Hall, and Armstrong continues to find currency among a number of contemporary theologians and historians. In a popular survey of Christian theology, Alister McGrath observes, "It seems to be a general rule of history that periods of enormous creativity are followed by eras of stagnation. The Reformation is no exception."[109] G. J. Spykman concurs: "[T]he promising beginnings embedded in Calvin's thinking were frustrated before the sixteenth century had even run its full course by contrary influences within the Reformational traditions itself on the part of theologians like Theodore Beza."[110] Historian Philip Holtrop in his study of the Jerome Bolsec affair draws the contrast between Beza and Calvin most sharply, asserting that Beza was "primarily a theologian of the 'head,' while Calvin focused primarily on the 'heart.'"[111] Whereas Calvin's theology (at its best) was "more celebrative than cerebral, and more doxological than dialectical," the theological system of Beza and other later reformed scholastics was burdened with Aristotelian philosophical assumptions that rendered it more analytic, dogmatic, and abstract—focused more on God as he is in himself (*Deus in se*) than God as he is for us (*Deus pro nobis*).[112] For scholars like Holtrop, Hall, and Armstrong, John Calvin's Christ-centered, "doxological" theology was fundamentally subverted by Reformed Orthodoxy that followed him, a tradition that they denounced with an arsenal of pejorative adjectives such as "arid," "abstract," "dogmatic," "dead," "dialectical," "rationalistic," "cerebral," "scholastic," "speculative," and "stagnant."

In recent decades, the "Calvin against the Calvinist" thesis has come under increasing scrutiny. A company of scholars, following the lead of Richard Muller, and fortified with important historical insights from Paul Oskar Kristeller and Heiko A. Oberman, have attacked the old consensus from a number of flanks, demanding greater precision in defining key terms such as "scholasticism" or "rationalism," and calling into question overly facile dichotomies made between the Middle Ages and the Reformation, humanism and scholasticism, biblical theology and speculative theology.[113]

The general contours of their arguments need only concern us here, summarized in four points. First, a growing number of scholars challenge the premise that Calvin ought to be seen as the primary well-spring for later reformed theology or the benchmark by which to measure "true" reformed Christianity. The theological structure and substance of Reformed Orthodoxy that emerged in the last decades of the sixteenth century and flourished during the seventeenth century was significantly indebted not only to Calvin, but to other second- and third-generation reformed thinkers, notably Martin Bucer, Heinrich Bullinger, Andreas Hyperius, Wolfgang Musculus, Peter Martyr Vermigli, and Jerome Zanchi.[114] Rather than pitting Calvin against later Calvinists, it is more accurate, they believe, to understand the emergence of Reformed Orthodoxy as development within a single but variegated theological tradition in which a largely uniform set of confessional commitments was formulated and defended in a variety of ways.[115]

Second, it is now recognized that Calvin was more indebted to the medieval theological tradition than first appears. To be sure, Calvin frequently employed the title "scholastics" (*scholastici*) in a derogatory fashion to refer to Catholic theologians who in his opinion obfuscated the central doctrines of the Christian faith through vaunted reason, speculation, and endless disputation.[116] Calvin was at his rhetorical sharpest when he excoriated medieval theology for defending a system of works righteousness that subverted the gospel of grace taught in the Scripture. But, as Muller and others have demonstrated, Calvin did not altogether reject the school theology of the Middle Ages.[117] In his *Institutes*, Calvin several times appeals to the theology of "the sounder Schoolmen" (such as Peter Lombard or John Duns Scotus) to attack "more recent Sophists" such as Gabriel Biel or the doctors of the Sorbonne.[118] Calvin was in conversation with the medieval Catholic tradition, often critical of it, but not beyond learning from it and even appropriating some of its insights. Calvin's theological and exegetical writings bear witness that he was not averse to employing scholastic modes of argumentation from time to time, such as making philosophical distinctions, posing formal questions, and employing dialectical reasoning, when it served his overall purposes. This is seen, for example, in Calvin's appropriation of medieval (and Aristotelian) categories to distinguish between levels of necessity, between the four causes of salvation, between the eternal decree and its execution, and between the sufficiency and efficiency of Christ's atonement.[119] David Steinmetz has put the matter well: "Calvin discovered that some philosophical distinctions, including many of the distinctions drawn by the schoolmen, were too useful to be discarded lightly."[120]

Third, Muller has argued convincingly that reformed scholasticism, as understood in its historical context, was primarily "a matter of theological method rather than of dogmatic content."[121] While Calvin characteristically attacked the school theology of the Middle Ages, his theological heirs in places like Geneva, Heidelberg, and Cambridge frequently employed the term "scholasticism" in a more neutral sense to describe a *method* of theological discourse, developed in the medieval schools and later appropriated and adapted by Protestant academies and universities, which posed formal questions and employed philosophical tools such as dialectics, careful distinctions, and academic disputations to expose error and arrive at correct conclusions about the Christian faith.[122] Reformed scholastics like Beza who applied philosophical tools of analysis to clarify and defend central doctrines of reformed Christianity were not *rationalists* per se: philosophy was to be the handmaiden, not the master, of theological knowledge.[123] Over the course of the century after Calvin's death, this theological approach was further refined in the face of pedagogical and polemical challenges; nevertheless, reformed orthodox theologians consistently affirmed the importance of scriptural exegesis and resisted a metaphysical system that deduced points of theology from a central dogma such as predestination. According to Muller, reformed theologians after Calvin who employed the methods of scholasticism invariably accepted Scripture as the authoritative Word of God and continued to affirm the priority of revelation over reason.

Finally, the common antithesis between "scholasticism" and "humanism" is no longer considered to be defensible. It was the important contribution of Paul Oskar Kristeller to demonstrate major points of continuity between medieval scholasticism and the humanist program of the Italian Renaissance.[124] Historians of Reformed Orthodoxy have applied this insight in various ways. For one, it is now clear that the form of scholasticism advocated by theologians like Beza and Daneau, and institutionalized in the curriculum of reformed academies, was a method forged by humanists such as Philip Melanchthon and Jacques Lefèvre d'Etaples that synthesized traditional scholastic discourse with the Renaissance humanist commitment to classical sources, philology, and rhetoric, organized around a collection of theological topics (*loci communes*).[125] This fusion of scholastic methodology with the program of humanist education was woven into the curriculum of the Genevan Academy from the very beginning.[126] Furthermore, a number of studies have recently demonstrated the significant degree to which Beza and many of his colleagues in Geneva were shaped by the intellectual values of northern humanism, with its commitment to religious reform through the educational program of the *studia humanitatis*, the recovery of the biblical languages, the philological analysis of ancients texts, and the priority of rhetoric and persuasion.[127] Even in old age, reformers like Beza, Daneau, and Goulart remained committed to the values of humanism as reflected in their taste for Greek and Latin authors, their love of the classical languages, and their penchant for poetry, historical writings, and exegetical commentaries.[128]

Thanks to these four advances, scholars have gained a clearer understanding of the nature of reformed scholasticism and a more nuanced view of the development of reformed theology after Calvin. So too, most historians now correctly reject the model of "Calvin against the Calvinists" as both imprecise and misleading. But to recognize important points of continuity between medieval and reformed scholasticism, and between Calvin and later reformed thinkers, in no way diminishes important differences. These points of difference come into clearer focus when one examines more carefully the theological content of the books that Geneva's pastors published before 1609.

Intellectual Life in Calvinist Geneva

There is little doubt that John Calvin's theology and church polity occupied a privileged place in sixteenth- and early seventeenth-century Geneva. To be sure, Beza and his colleagues vigorously defended the normative authority of Scripture in matters of faith and practice—but their interpretation of Scripture was shaped to no small degree by Calvin's theological writings and the institutions he established. The catechism that children memorized; the catechism and *Ecclesiastical Ordinances* that candidates for ordination affirmed; the liturgy that the congregation listened to week by week—all of these had been written by Calvin and articulated the theological and practical content of his religious program. Many of the ministers who worked alongside Calvin regarded him as a kind of spiritual father and were intensely loyal to his ecclesial vision. In the words of Charles Perrot, Calvin was "our good master and our common father."[129] On the other hand, ministers and prominent laymen such as Sebastian Castellio or Jerome Bolsec who voiced strong criticism of Calvin, who challenged his leadership or questioned his theology, were usually sent packing from Geneva in short order. Beza in particular presented himself as Calvin's faithful disciple. "I confess that I am one of those the Lord has instructed in this true and holy doctrine of his gospel by his faithful servant John Calvin," Beza noted. "I will certainly never be ashamed to call myself his disciple and one of many thousands of people that he has won to Christ."[130] Loyalty like this earned Beza the scorn of Catholic apologists, who accused him of "Calvinolatry" or of being "Calvin's creature."[131]

This commitment to Calvin and his theological legacy remained a distinguishing feature of Geneva religious life after the reformer's death in 1564. As we have seen, Beza penned books defending Calvin's memory and theological program. He and several colleagues edited for publication Calvin's correspondence and sermon collections long after the reformer's death. So too, scholars have shown that Beza made extensive use of Calvin's *Institutes* and biblical commentaries in his theological instruction at the Genevan Academy.[132] Perhaps even more importantly, Beza exercised leadership within the Company of Pastors to ensure that Geneva's ministers—including a new generation of men who had never known Calvin—remained faithful to Calvin's theological legacy and articulated it in their sermons and published writings. The ministers' loyalty to Calvin's religious vision was on display when they examined candidates for ordination, when they reprimanded Geneva's citizens for sullying Calvin's memory, or when they blocked the magistrates' attempts to innovate in matters of religious policy.[133] Sometimes this commitment to Calvin's legacy took the form of written *apologiae* against religious opponents. In 1599, for example, the Company of Pastors appointed Charles Perrot to respond in print to Catholic controversialists Thomas Stapleton and Jean Maldonat who had with "vehemence, injury, and malice" attacked Calvin and his doctrine. The Company stated that this project was necessary, "lest it seem that we have contempt for the truth of God proclaimed by his servant [Calvin], to whom we have always maintained our fidelity."[134] This same loyalty to Calvin's theology informed the Company of Pastors' relationship with reformed churches outside of Geneva. This was evident in the Company's letter to the French churches when the fourteenth National Synod of Saumur (1596) considered abandoning the regular exposition of Calvin's *Catechism* in local reformed congregations. Geneva's ministers argued that the *Catechism* was "a very excellent and able summary of the whole of the Christian religion" and "one of the greatest treasures that the Lord has bestowed on us in our days." In the view of Geneva's churchmen, no modification in the content or use of Calvin's *Catechism* was permissible.[135] One final anecdote is particularly revealing of the degree to which Geneva's ministers continued to attribute special authority to the memory and theological vision of Calvin. In 1610, Simon Goulart, who was then serving as moderator of the church, attempted to force the renowned Greek scholar Isaac Casaubon to affirm on oath all the doctrines found in Calvin's *Institutes*. "I know that Monsieur Calvin was a great person," Casaubon noted, "but his disciples have made things worse." For Casaubon, the pastors in Geneva after Calvin had become guilty of "a true pharisaism." Loyalty to Calvin, he believed, had devolved into an unbending orthodoxy characterized by brittle legalism.[136]

Whether the theological conservatism of Beza and Geneva's Company after 1564 deserves to be characterized as "legalistic" or labeled "Calvinolatry" depends very much on the interpreter. What is beyond debate, however, is that even as they honored Calvin's legacy, Beza and his colleagues were not mindless imitators of Calvin. They did not hesitate to question minor points of Calvin's exegesis of Scripture. Likewise, in their theological and exegetical writings they regularly consulted authors from the broader Christian tradition for insight and inspiration. Professors at the Academy, such as Beza, Daneau, and La Faye, advocated for and employed a program of scholastic argumentation in their theological works that finds no direct parallel in Calvin's writings. And finally, in the face of new pedagogical and polemical challenges, Geneva's ministers applied these rigorous methods of analysis to clarify the truths of Scripture and draw out the logical implications of Calvin's thought.

Geneva's pastors and theologians sometimes disagreed with Calvin on minor points of exegesis and Scripture interpretation. For Beza, Calvin was the foremost interpreter of the Bible of his time, but that did not mean he endorsed every exegetical decision of his spiritual mentor. In the preface to the second edition of his *Annotations* (1565), Beza conceded that "sometimes in certain places I disagree [with Calvin], not on matters of doctrine, but in the explication of certain passages."[137] Thus, for example, in his treatment of Acts 2:27 in the early editions of the *Annotations*, Beza translated the Greek phrase οὐκ ἐγκαταλείψεις τὴν ψυχήν μου εἰς ᾅδην as "thou shalt not leave my body (*cadaver*) in the grave (*sepulchrum*)" whereas Calvin had translated it, "thou shalt not leave my soul (*anima*) in Hades (*infernus*)."[138] Jean Diodati's annotations to his Italian Bible reflected a similar independence in interpretive judgment. In his comments on Hosea 6:7, for example, Diodati argued that the Hebrew noun *adam* referred to the biblical character Adam rather than humankind in general—an interpretation that Calvin decades earlier had judged to be "frigid and diluted" as well as "vapid."[139]

Moreover, Beza and his colleagues such as Daneau, Chandieu, and Goulart recognized the value of the Christian tradition and drew extensively from theological and biblical resources well beyond their narrow confessional horizon. This fact was amply illustrated in the diverse contents of their libraries and the books that they translated and edited for publication. It was also reflected in the large repertoire of religious authors, reformed and otherwise, that they consulted for their theological writings. In Beza's three-volume work *Theological Treatises* (1570–82) the most frequently named authorities are Augustine (347 instances), Calvin (213), Cyril (111), Jerome (93), Chrysostom (73), Basil the Great (66), Luther (60), Ambrose and Tertullian (56), Zwingli (52), Theodoret (38), Vermigli (36), Bullinger (35), Cyprian (34), and Melanchthon (28).[140] By way of comparison, in his biblical *Annotations*, Beza cited by name Erasmus more than 2,100 times, followed by Augustine (265 citations), Cicero (197), Tertullian (192), Chrysostom (176), and Jerome (175). Aristotle was cited 44 times, while the name of Calvin—identified as "*that most learned interpreter*"– appeared on 37 occasions.[141] Not all of these references are positive ones, of course; Erasmus and Jerome were regularly used by Beza as foils to defend the "correct" reading of the biblical text. However, the wealth of references to theologians and biblical exegetes outside of the reformed tradition makes clear that Beza was in conversation with Christian authors from a variety of theological traditions, especially the fathers of the early church.

This expansive use of contemporary and ancient sources is easily documented in the published works of other members of the Venerable Company, including theologians Daneau, Chandieu, and La Faye.[142] Simon Goulart's *Common Places of Sacred Statements* (1592) illustrates particularly well this project to root Geneva's moral and theological program in the soil of the broader Christian tradition. The *Common Places* was a kind of encyclopedia of quotations that brought together several thousand notable statements and anecdotes drawn from Christian authors, organized under more than three hundred topics ranging from Abstinence to Idolatry, and Justification to Zeal. Here again, the religious authorities cited are surprisingly eclectic, including not only Protestant leaders (e.g., Luther, Calvin, Beza, Bullinger, Oecolampadius) but also early church fathers (e.g., Cyprian, Cyril, Augustine, Jerome, Chrysostom) and medieval Catholic theologians (e.g., Anselm, Bernard of Clairvaux, Hugh of St. Victor, and Jean Gerson).[143] What these examples demonstrate is that Geneva's ministers in the generation immediately after Calvin's death drew extensively and freely from theological resources well beyond their confessional tradition and their century—just as Calvin had done. Though Beza and his colleagues worked vigorously to defend the theological program of Calvin in Geneva and elsewhere in Europe, their commitment to the ideals of the *studia humanitatis* assured that they would do more than simply echo Calvin and repristinate his theology. The ministers' books written during the generation after Calvin were characterized by a broad catholicity in which theological discourse was founded on Holy Scripture and the larger Christian tradition.

As noted earlier, another important way that Beza and Geneva's theologians departed from Calvin was in their more extensive use of scholastic methodology in some of their theological writings. That they did so self-consciously and programmatically is clear from statements in their correspondence and published writings. In 1568, the Zurich reformer Heinrich Bullinger in a letter to Beza expressed his strongest opposition to the "new" scholastics who employed Aristotle's methods and confused their listeners with questions and endless disputes. "To be frank," he wrote, "I despise this [Aristotelian doctrine] with my whole heart, and I often remind myself of that saying of Tertullian: 'The philosophers are the patriarchs of the heretics.'"[144] In response to stated concerns like these, Beza and his colleagues found it necessary to defend their use of scholastic methods, all the while insisting that divine revelation must always be given priority over reason in Christian theology. For Beza, dialectical argumentation allowed one to rule out false interpretations and construct valid arguments; it did not make propositions of its own.[145] In keeping with this view, the reformer championed the use of logic and disputations in the theological curriculum at the Genevan Academy from the very beginning.[146] In a letter preface that found its way into his *Theological Letters* (1573), Beza criticized "ignorant men" who while correctly arguing that "theology in no way depends on human reason," drew from this the wrong conclusion that "dialectic should be excluded.... This fiction merits no further refutation," Beza insisted, "for who does not see that reason [*ratio*] is one thing and the exercise of reasoning [*ratiocinatio*] another?"[147] A decade later, in his preface to Daneau's *Christian Isagoges*, Beza returned to this matter:

> I neither mix the sacred with the profane, nor bind that divine wisdom to the rules of dialecticians. For far be it from me—far be it from me—that I should consider either the *principia* of theology, or those heads of our religion

that are deduced from the *principia* of theology, to be sought in the books of the philosophers. For from this arises nothing other than that pseudo-knowledge, which Paul lucidly and most correctly repudiates.[148]

Consequently, while praising the philosophical method of Aristotle, Beza did not hesitate to condemn the Greek philosopher as "delirious" for teaching that the world was eternal or for rejecting particular providence.[149] Aristotle and all other philosophers "must be weighed against the norm of the holy Scriptures."[150] Indeed, all religious speculation disjoined from the truth of Scripture was to be eschewed. In a heated interchange with the Lutheran theologian Tileman Heshusius over the Lord's Supper, Beza stated this point succinctly: "We think that it is wicked to investigate the 'how' more fully, since we do not wish to know even a particle beyond the Word."[151]

Both Lambert Daneau and Antoine de La Faye agreed with Beza's conclusion. The *matter* of theology must never be derived from Aristotle or human philosophy. Scripture alone contains the true doctrine of faith. However the *form* of theology allows for a variety of approaches. Dialectic, Daneau noted, "is very useful for Christians because it teaches them to discern the true from the false." Therefore, "[d]ialectic should not be suppressed in the schools and in Christian disputes, nor should pastors be criticized who use it in their writings."[152] Antoine de La Faye made a similar point in the preface to his *Theological Theses* (1586) where he defended the use of scholastic disputations in the training of theological students at the Genevan Academy. La Faye acknowledged the dangers of rational methods of argumentation if they were not practiced modestly, with a desire for the truth and out of reverence for God's majesty.[153] Tertuallian was not entirely wrong in asserting, "Philosophers are the patriarchs of heresies."[154] However, La Faye insisted that the laws of the Genevan Academy established strict guidelines to ensure that theological students engaged in disputations that honored God and served the church: all modes of argumentation that undermined scriptural truth were forbidden, including sophistical assertions, false propositions, undue curiosity, evil contention, and intellectual pride.[155] When conducted properly and piously, academic disputations brought clarity to the Word of God, strengthened the church, and prepared schoolboys to defend God's truth.

The most extensive defense of scholastic methodology from a Genevan minister was written by Antoine de Chandieu in his preface to *Common Place on the Written Word of God.*[156] Chandieu begins by pointing out that the same early church fathers who criticized the sophistical teaching of the heretics also recognized the value of "the true science of disputation" and regularly employed logic against their opponents. For logic rightly used "shatters the illusions and fallacies of the sophists, refutes errors, drives out lies, and places the light of truth before the eyes of the soul for inspection."[157] Chandieu appealed to a biblical similitude to make his point: just as the pagan citizens of Tyre and Sidon assisted in the construction of Solomon's temple (1 Kings 5), so logical arguments can contribute to the building of the church of God.[158] Unfortunately, medieval theologians were guilty of misusing philosophy, mixing sophistical reasoning with theology, thereby propagating falsehood rather than truth. Chandieu described four major errors introduced by the medieval schoolmen: First, they based their major propositions on philosophy rather than Scripture. Second, they introduced uncertainty into Christian theology by encouraging disputations *pro* and *contra* on theological truths beyond controversy. Third, the schoolmen obscured rather than adorned the beauty of truth by their subtle arguments. Fourth, scholastic theologians explored vain and frivolous questions.[159] Particularly grievous was the schoolmen's undermining of Scripture's supreme place in the church: "Since theology is above all the sciences, it is not only foolish but altogether wicked to subject it to philosophical principles. And it is completely intolerable to treat ecclesiastical doctors as equal to the Prophets and Apostles."[160] In the final pages of his preface, Chandieu laid out the proper place of philosophy in theological disputation. He noted that there are two different ways to treat divine questions in speech or writing. The "rhetorical method" allows for a full and pleasing investigation of theological topics in a manner that appeals to the minds and affections of general audiences. This approach is not invalid, Chandieu emphasized, but it does not provide the precision or clarity of the "scholastic method" in resolving difficult theological questions. The scholastic method, by contrast, avoids arguments that "stir the affections of the soul," and instead "strips off the covering of rhetoric [*oratio*]" to "explain things simply and precisely and bring forth bare arguments so that the truth of the matter may be clearly seen."[161] When subservient to theology, the scholastic method penetrates to the "anatomy" of an argument, exposing fallacies and sophistical arguments while defending the Christian gospel. Chandieu thus concluded his preface by urging Protestant intellectuals to undertake divine disputations on behalf of the truth, "not as on a human stage, but in the midst of the whole church before the presence of God and his holy angels, not out of zeal for victory, but for the sake of holding onto the truth."[162]

The distinction that scholars like Beza, Daneau, Chandieu, and La Faye made between the form and matter of theology was of central importance as they defended and promoted the use of scholastic methods both at the Genevan Academy and in their theological writings. They believed that the polemical challenges posed by Catholic, Lutheran, and Socinian opponents justified, even necessitated, more precise methods of argumentation. At the same time, Geneva's theologians affirmed their unbending commitment to the reformed understanding of Scripture, articulated by John Calvin and institutionalized in Geneva's official theology, with its accent on divine sovereignty, human depravity, justification by faith alone, the unique authority of Scripture, and the importance of moral discipline in the church. Even so, a careful study of the theological corpus of Beza and his colleagues makes clear that they did modify and develop aspects of Calvin's theology out of pastoral concern or in an effort to create a more coherent system of thought. These changes were not a betrayal of Calvin's theological program; rather, they represent an effort to interpret Scripture and apply Calvin's thought in light of new questions and new contexts—but always within the parameters of Geneva's official orthodoxy.

Scholars have called attention to a number of areas of discontinuity between Calvin's theology and that of his successors in Geneva. In the domain of epistemology, for example, it is now clear that Beza placed somewhat heavier accent on external (objective) evidence as a basis for religious knowledge than did Calvin.[163] This impulse to objectify religious knowledge was also seen in Daneau's theological corpus. In his *Christian Isagoges*, for example, Daneau discussed the nature of the divine essence and attributes, and posited rational "proofs" for God's existence—topics that Calvin had not addressed formally in his *Institutes*.[164] Other areas where Beza and Daneau modified or departed from Calvin's teaching were in their affirmation of church discipline as a formal "mark" (*nota*) of the true church, and in their provocative justification of political resistance by lesser magistrates in the aftermath of the St. Bartholomew's Day massacres (1572).[165]

Somewhat more needs to be said about Beza's views on predestination, Christian assurance, and the extent of Christ's atonement, three doctrines that have elicited lengthy commentary from scholars of the reformed tradition. As for the doctrine of predestination, Beza shared Calvin's conviction that God in his sovereignty ordained both the salvation of the elect and the damnation of the reprobate but added his own unique "twist" based on his reading of Romans 9:21. Whereas Calvin described God's eternal decree of election and reprobation as occurring logically *after* the decision to create human beings (the infralapsarian position), Beza consistently taught that God's decision to glorify himself through predestination *preceded* the divine plan to create human beings who would fall into sin (the supralapsarian position).[166] In the midst of the heated controversy with Jerome Bolsec over the nature of predestination in 1555, Beza explained his supralapsarian views in a letter to Calvin:

> I think that Paul compares the human race not yet created to a lump in order to show that God, like a potter, not only before he created the human race, but even before he decided to create it, determined to declare his glory in a twofold way, and that he created humankind afterwards for this twofold purpose: to save some people (based on his purpose that no one can fathom) according to his decree by his mercy through Christ, and to damn other people by his just judgment, because of their own corruption and its fruits, that in both his glory might be declared.[167]

Beza's doctrine of supralapsarian predestination, which was original with him, was later embraced by other reformed theologians such as William

Perkins, Franciscus Gomarus, and Johannes Macovius.[168] The doctrine has sometimes been pointed to as conclusive evidence of the speculative turn in Beza's theology. Historical context suggests, however, that Beza may well have been attracted to this interpretation of Romans 9 out of a desire to protect the absolute unconditional nature of predestination and undercut the opinions of opponents like Bolsec who asserted that predestination was based on foreseen faith or foreseen unbelief.[169]

Beza also departed in subtle ways from Calvin on the matter of Christian assurance.[170] In contrast to the teachings of the medieval church, reformed Protestants believed that assurance of salvation was a constituent element of saving faith and should be the normal experience of all Christians. Calvin believed that Christian assurance should be grounded primarily on the promises of God in Christ, with secondary supports provided by the internal testimony of the Holy Spirit and the presence of sanctification in the life of the believer. Christ "is the mirror wherein we must...contemplate our election," Calvin insisted.[171] While not denying this, Beza argued for a graduated process of assurance that reflected, in reverse, the order by which God's decree of election was executed on behalf of his people: beginning with the "lowest stages" of good works and personal sanctification, believers' gaze must ascend to the testimony of the Holy Spirit, who bears witness to genuine faith and spiritual adoption, and ultimately to the highest stage of Christ himself in whom their election is sure.[172] In his *Questions and Answers* Beza explained assurance in these terms:

> QUESTION: But in that most perilous temptation of particular election, where should I flee?
> ANSWER: To the effects whereby the spiritual life is rightly discerned.... [We] are not able to raise ourselves to that highest light unless we climb by those steps whereby God draws His elect to himself according to His eternal decree, as those whom He created for His own glory. Therefore, that I am elect, is first perceived from sanctification begun in me, that is, as I recognize my hatred of sin and my love of righteousness. To this I add the testimony of the Spirit, arousing my conscience.... From this sanctification and comfort of the Spirit we attain faith. And therefore we rise to Christ, to whom whosoever is given, is necessarily elect from all eternity in Him and will never be driven out.[173]

Beza's formalized scheme of assurance was an attempt to balance the objective promises of God in Christ (as the highest grounds of assurance) with the testimony of the Holy Spirit and the subjective experience of the believer (as the initial ground of assurance). On at least one occasion, however, Beza's concern to provide consolation to Christians made anxious by the conundrum of divine election led him to place a particularly heavy accent on sanctification as the source of assurance. Hence, in his *Petit catechism* (1575), Beza noted that "good works are for us the certain evidences of our faith" and bring us "certainty of our eternal election"[174] This bald statement of the so-called *practical syllogism*—that the believer can find proof of saving faith and election in large part from personal holiness—represented a real departure from Calvin's Christological approach to assurance. Over the next century, reformed thinkers including William Perkins, John Downame, William Ames, and John Owen followed the trajectory set by Beza as they encouraged the faithful to practice a kind of spirituality characterized by spiritual meditation on Christ and rigorous self-examination in an effort to identify sin, monitor sanctification and, thereby, arrive at greater certainty of salvation.[175]

Equally as controversial has been Beza's defense of definite atonement and the question of its relation to Calvin's doctrine.[176] Beza, like Calvin, affirmed that Christ's death served as a penal substitution for sinful humanity, that is, that Christ offered himself on the cross as a substitute for sinful men and women, that by suffering God's just punishment he might purchase salvation for them. Both Calvin and Beza also rejected universal redemption, insisting that only the elect would be saved. Might one conclude from this that Christ died only for the elect? Calvin nowhere addressed this question in detail, although on several occasions he did appear to have endorsed the view that Christ's satisfaction on the cross was effective only for the elect.[177] Theodore Beza, on the other hand, was crystal clear on the subject. Throughout his career, he defended the doctrine of definite atonement as a scriptural teaching that preserved the unity of the Triune God's redemptive work and protected divine election from any hint of human synergism.[178] Beza's clearest statements on this subject appeared in his debate with the Lutheran theologian Jacob Andreae during the Colloquy of Montbéliard (1586). In a sharp exchange with Andreae over the extent of God's salvific will, Beza insisted that "the benefit of [Christ's] propitiation necessarily pertains to the elect alone, and because they are elect, they also believe." Indeed, Christ's death in no way benefits the reprobate: "Now is it really true that Christ bore the sins of the whole world, as you interpret it to mean 'each and every person'? Surely your opinion seems intolerable to us, that Christ died on behalf of the damned, and that men are not condemned on account of their sin."[179] From Beza's perspective, Christ died for the sins of the world only in the sense that his sacrifice was of infinite value. The Son of God became man to provide atonement for the sins of the elect whom the Triune God had chosen from eternity. Beza's doctrine of definite atonement was not unique to him nor was it a theological innovation birthed in the Genevan church. Reformed thinkers outside of Geneva such as Peter Martyr Vermigli, Jerome Zanchi, William Perkins, Caspar Olevianus, Zacharias Ursinus, and David Pareus all defended the doctrine, oftentimes in response to Faustus Socinus's unorthodox views on the subject.[180] In the early seventeenth century, Geneva pastors Jean

Diodati and Theodore Tronchin, as representatives of the Genevan church at the Synod of Dort, subscribed to the doctrine of definite atonement as it was formulated in the Canons of Dort (1619).

This study of intellectual life among Geneva's ministers during the generation after Calvin has shown that Beza and his colleagues were neither self-styled innovators nor mindless imitators of Calvin. In the face of new pedagogical and polemical challenges, the ministers in their theological writings sometimes defended and frequently employed scholastic methods of analysis, attempting to arrive at more precise formulations of biblical doctrine and defend core convictions of reformed Christianity. At least before 1609, such theological discourse took place well within the confessional boundaries of Geneva's official religion, which itself was informed by the broader reformed tradition throughout Europe. Moreover, it bears repeating that while Beza and other reformed churchmen advocated the use of scholastic methods of argumentation in their more polemical and doctrinal writings, they were equally committed to the exegetical and philological methods of Renaissance humanism as they studied Scripture and the early church fathers, and articulated their findings in catechisms, biblical commentaries, sermon collections, scripture meditations, prayer books, moral and ethical discourses, and religious poetry. To characterize the reformed theological tradition after Calvin as "scholastic," without nuance, is to overlook the substantial number of exegetical and pastoral writings that were published by Geneva's ministers during the half century after Calvin. Moreover, to caricature this theological tradition as "arid" or "speculative" or "stagnant" is to ignore the rich store of biblical resources and practical devotional materials produced by ministers like Beza, Daneau, Chandieu, and Goulart. These were not simply theologians committed to matters of the "head." Rather, like Calvin himself, they were ministers of the gospel who took seriously their responsibility to instruct and edify the people of God and promote Christian sanctification.

CHAPTER 9 | The Ministry of Pastoral Care

TROUBLES, TROUBLES, NOTHING BUT troubles. So it must have seemed to
Theodore Beza as he walked the two hundred paces from his home on the
rue des Chanoines to the temple of St. Pierre to deliver the eight o'clock
sermon on Sunday morning December 21, 1589. On this particular morning, the seventy-year-old patriarch of the Genevan church was confronted
with a host of difficulties. His physical health had declined significantly
in recent months; he now battled chronic fatigue, partial deafness, painful
arthritis, and occasional bouts of dizziness. In addition, his pastoral duties
had never seemed heavier. There were baptisms to perform. Preparations
needed to be made for the quarterly Lord's Supper, to be celebrated the following week. Boys were once again behaving badly at the weekly catechism
class. A bitter feud between Gideon Adam and his mother-in-law needed to
be pacified. More seriously, the wife of the cobbler Nicolas Fredin had been
raped by soldiers in the village of Gex and was believed pregnant; now
Nicolas was demanding a divorce.[1] On top of these pastoral concerns, Beza
faced the unrelenting pressure of his duties as preacher and professor; he
was still expected to preach several sermons each week and regularly deliver
theological lectures at the Genevan Academy. Under normal circumstances,
Beza's advanced age and growing frailty might well have justified semire-
tirement and a lightening of his pastoral responsibilities. But these were
not normal circumstances. Geneva was at war with her archenemy Charles
Emmanuel I, the Duke of Savoy, and the war was going very badly. And
so, on the morning of December 21, 1589, Theodore Beza climbed into
the pulpit of St. Pierre's and preached to his anxious congregation, most
likely from a passage in the Gospels on the subject of the passion of Jesus
Christ.[2] We do not know the precise content of this sermon, but we do
have evidence of the emotional strain and physical exhaustion that Beza
felt during this difficult time period. In a letter to a friend in Breslau,
dated from mid-December, the weary old minister concluded with these
words: "Remember to pray more and more for your friend Beza as he

looks down the final stretch of his course. Although I am worn out, the Lord has never before given me a heavier load to carry."[3]

Pastoral ministry in sixteenth-century Geneva was demanding work. Calvin and his reformed colleagues shared the belief that God appointed Christian pastors to be spiritual shepherds who cared for God's people by proclaiming the gospel of salvation in such a way that, through the power of the Holy Spirit, sinners might repent and become faithful disciples of Jesus Christ, living lives marked by confident faith, Christian obedience, and fruitful service. The ministry of the Word thus required more than the public exposition of Scripture; it also entailed the declaration and application of God's Word to individual women and men, girls and boys, through the sacraments, corrective discipline, catechetical instruction, household visitations, and spiritual counsel and consolation. As Calvin noted in his liturgy, "the office of a true and faithful minister is not only to teach the people in public, which he is appointed to do as pastor, but also, as much as he is able, to admonish, exhort, warn, and console each person individually."[4] For Calvin, Christian ministers were expected to provide intensive, personal, spiritual support that would nurture their parishioners' Christian understanding and spirituality over the course of a lifetime, from cradle to grave. This vision of Christian ministry, shared by Calvin, Beza, Goulart, and their colleagues in Geneva, was not at all original with them, of course; their understanding of the nature of pastoral care was significantly indebted not only to other Protestant reformers but also to the Christian tradition as a whole. In the chapter that follows, I will explore some of the most important elements of pastoral care in reformed Geneva, noting ways in which the reformed ministers maintained, developed, and sometimes deviated from Calvin's pastoral vision during the course of the sixteenth- and early seventeenth-centuries.

1. The Sacrament of Baptism

From the beginning, evangelical opposition to the teachings of the medieval Catholic Church focused on the doctrine of the sacraments. Already in 1520, in *The Babylonian Captivity of the Church*, Luther leveled a blistering attack on five of the seven traditional Catholic sacraments, arguing instead that only baptism and the Lord's Supper could rightly be called Christian sacraments because they alone had been instituted by Christ in the New Testament as rites that presented through physical symbols the forgiveness of sins and the grace of God. Luther also rejected the traditional Catholic teaching that the sacraments conferred grace through the performance of the rite (*ex opere operato*) as long as no obstacle was erected through mortal sin; rather, he taught that the sacraments were sure signs and promises of God's grace to those who received them by faith.[5] John Calvin and the reformed ministers of Geneva shared the general outline of Luther's sacramental theology—even if some of the particulars became the subject of fierce debates later in the century. In the first edition of Calvin's *Institutes* (1536), the reformer addressed the subject of the sacraments in two lengthy sections. In chapter 4, Calvin offered several definitions of a sacrament and described the nature and benefits conveyed by the two legitimate sacraments of baptism and the Lord's Supper. In the following chapter, Calvin attacked the "Five False Sacraments" practiced in the Catholic Church. Calvin defined a sacrament as "a testimony of God's grace, declared to us by an outward sign." As such, it "confirms and seals the promise" of God's grace and mercy to believers even as it nourishes and strengthens faith. Only in a secondary sense does the sacrament serve as a confession or testimony before others.[6] As with Luther, Calvin rejected the Catholic understanding of sacramental efficacy *ex opere operato*—the sacramental elements do not possess inherent power to impart grace or righteousness, he insisted. Rather, the sacraments "have the same office as the Word of God: to offer and set forth Christ to us, and in him the treasures of heavenly grace." These benefits are always communicated by the Holy Spirit and are received by faith.[7] Although Calvin used slightly different language when defining the Christian sacraments in later editions of the *Institutes*, the basic elements remained unchanged: the sacraments are a means of grace that strengthen the faith of believers and serve to nourish, sustain, and deepen their communion with Jesus Christ.[8]

The rite of baptism in Geneva went through significant changes in form and theological substance at the time of the Reformation. During the Middle Ages, the sacrament of baptism was viewed as a religious rite and public ritual of enormous importance. Drawing especially on the theology of Augustine, the Catholic Church held that baptism washed away the effects of both original sin and actual sin, made the recipient a member of the body of Christ, and initiated the process of justification in the life of the Christian. Because baptism was believed necessary for salvation, the medieval church accepted as legitimate those baptisms administered by laypersons or even infidels in emergency situations, as long as they were performed with water in the name of the Trinity.[9] Given its spiritual importance, canon law required that infants receive baptism within eight days of birth. In addition to its religious significance, the sacrament of baptism also marked a newborn child's entry into the civic community. In the baptismal ceremony the parents of the infant were officially acknowledged; the newborn received a Christian name; and the child began to be incorporated into a social network of godparents and family members.[10]

By the end of the Middle Ages, the Catholic sacrament of baptism included a number of important rituals and liturgical acts. On the day of baptism, godparents brought the infant to the door of the church, where a Catholic priest (sometimes accompanied by an acolyte) met the baptismal party and inquired of the child's Christian name and gender, and what he or she requested of the church.[11] The godparents were expected to answer "faith" or "to be baptized." The priest then recited a series of prayers and performed exorcisms over the child, sometimes using salt to symbolize the child's preservation in the faith. Next, the priest read the Scripture text from Matthew 19:13–14 where Jesus blessed the children, and then he performed the *effeta* (opening) by touching the child's ear and nose with spittal to make her receptive to the Word of God. Following the *effeta*, the godparents carried the candidate across the threshold into the church to the baptismal font, where the priest declared a series of blessings, first on the child with special prayers and then on the baptismal waters. The Catholic liturgy required the godparents to renounce Satan, and, together with the priest, to recite in Latin the Lord's Prayer and the Apostles' Creed. The priest then took the child and dipped her three times in the water invoking the triune God, the Father, the Son, and the Holy Spirit. After the baptism, the infant was dressed in a white robe symbolizing the innocence of Christ and then anointed with oil and presented with a lighted candle. As a general rule, baptisms in the later Middle Ages were conducted in private and the parents of baptized infants did not attend the baptism: mothers were at home recovering from childbirth; fathers were making preparations for the baptismal feast to follow.

Reformed churches in sixteenth-century Europe significantly altered the baptismal rite, and the Genevan church was no exception.[12] Calvin had no patience for what he saw as the gross superstitions with which Catholics had corrupted the pure form of the sacrament practiced in the early church. In his commentary on Acts 10:47–48, Calvin bemoaned the fact that though "the apostles were content with water alone for administering baptism," the papal church had packed all sorts of "nonsensical things" into the sacrament. "They think that the dignity of baptism is enhanced with oil, salt, spittle, wax-tapers, when these are rather filthy abominations which corrupt the pure and genuine institution of Christ."[13] The simplicity that Calvin espoused was clearly seen in Geneva's baptismal liturgy, which he wrote and was published along with the Genevan Psalter of 1542.[14] For Calvin, as for other reformed churchmen, baptism was a sacrament of the Word in which the entire community of believers participated. Hence baptisms were to be celebrated only during a public service of worship in conjunction with the ministry of preaching. In Calvin's Geneva, baptisms were conducted at the conclusion of preaching services throughout the week, although many families seem to have preferred the Sunday services.[15] Moreover, because baptism was believed to be a sign of God's covenantal blessing to believers, Geneva's ministers demanded that the child's parents, or at least the father, be present at the service along with the godparents and pastor.[16]

Geneva's baptismal services observed the following prescribed order.[17] Standing before the congregation and speaking in a loud voice, the officiating minister recited a brief invocation and then inquired of the baptismal party, "Do you present this child to be baptized?" The parents and godparents responded, "Yes."[18] The minister then delivered a five-minute baptismal exhortation that summarized God's plan of redemption through Jesus Christ and the meaning of Christian baptism. According to this liturgical statement, baptism is a sign and testimony of the remission of sins and (secondarily) of spiritual mortification and rebirth through the death and resurrection of Jesus Christ. Participants receive a "double grace and benefit" through baptism: First, that "we have a sure witness that God desires to be our loving Father, not imputing any of our sins and offenses to us," and, second, that "he will assist us by his Holy Spirit so that we might be able to battle against the Devil, sin, and the lusts of our flesh until we have the victory, living in the freedom of his...kingdom of righteousness."[19] The liturgy made clear, however, that these benefits did not derive from the instrumentality of the water itself, but from Jesus Christ. "[A]s he communicates to us his riches and blessings by his Word, so he distributes them to us by his sacraments."[20] After defining the nature and benefits of baptism, the minister's exhortation concluded with an explanation and defense of *infant* baptism by appealing to several biblical passages that showed that infants were sanctified through their Christian parents (1 Cor 7:14) and belonged to the covenant people of faith (Gen 17:7–9; Matt 19:13–15). "God was not only content to adopt us for his children and to receive us into the communion of his Church" but also included "the children of the faithful" among his sons and daughters "on account of this covenant."[21] Once the baptismal exhortation was finished, the officiating pastor read a prayer, led the congregation in the Lord's Prayer, and then addressed the baptismal party before him. At this point in the liturgy, the parents were expected to confess aloud their Christian faith by reciting the Apostles' Creed in French and then promise in the presence of the congregation to instruct the child in Christian doctrine and the teachings of Scripture, and to encourage her to love God and her neighbor. Finally, one of the godparents announced the Christian name of the infant, and the minister baptized the child in the name of the Father, the Son, and the Holy Spirit by means of sprinkling water on the forehead.[22] After the service families customarily hosted a banquet for relatives and friends to celebrate this important event, although Genevan authorities placed strict controls on the amounts of food and drink that could be served.

The baptismal service in sixteenth-century Geneva had a decidedly pedagogical function. According to the rubric, the pastor was required to read the liturgy in "a loud voice" so that "all might be edified" and "learn by heart the fruit and purpose of their baptism."[23] Geneva's townspeople witnessed dozens of baptismal services in the city churches each year and if they were paying attention, they would have soon learned the basic outline of Calvin's theology of baptism.[24] Another pedagogical tool that was crucial for instructing Geneva's inhabitants in a reformed understanding of the sacraments was Calvin's *Catechism*, which was studied by children in their school lessons and explained in catechetical sermons at noon every Sunday.

The *Catechism*'s treatment of the subject of baptism was more extensive than that found in Geneva's liturgy and provided adults and children with a basic summary of reformed teaching on the nature, purpose, and benefits of Christian baptism.

Like the baptismal rite, Calvin's *Catechism* stated that the primary meaning of Christian baptism was the washing away or remission of sins, with a secondary meaning of mortification and spiritual regeneration. The water itself does not wash the soul; rather, it is the blood of Christ that renders God's people pure and undefiled, and this is made visible and sealed for God's people when the "Holy Spirit sprinkles our consciences with that sacred blood." The *Catechism* rejected the Zwinglian teaching that baptism was merely a covenant sign or pledge, for "pardon of sins and newness of life are certainly offered to us *and received by us* in baptism."[25] The *Catechism* also rejected the Catholic view that people were regenerated through the waters of baptism or that the sacrament benefited all recipients indiscriminately. People receive the benefits of baptism only by faith. "Many by their wickedness preclude [baptism's] entry, and so render it empty for themselves. Thus its fruit reaches the faithful only."[26] At this point, the *Catechism* addressed the question of infant baptism, because if faith was necessary to receive the promise offered in baptism, then why should the church baptize infants that do not possess faith?[27] The catechumen was given a ready response: "It is not necessary that faith and repentance always precede baptism.... It will be sufficient if infants, when they have grown up, exhibit the power of their baptism."[28] As with Geneva's baptismal liturgy, the *Catechism* appealed to the concept of the covenant to defend infant baptism. In the old covenant, the infant sons of Abraham and his descendants received circumcision as a visible sign of God's promise of salvation through repentance and faith; so now, in the new covenant, the infant sons and daughters of Christian parents are baptized to testify that they are heirs of that same promise of salvation. The scope of God's grace shown to the children of the faithful was not truncated by the Advent of Christ; rather, it was broadened to include the children of all believers. For this reason, the *Catechism* stated, infant baptism provides "a splendid consolation" to Christian parents that God will extend his grace and mercy to their children.[29] And, for the children themselves, baptism testifies "that they are heirs of the blessing promised to the seed of the faithful, and that, after they are grown up, they may acknowledge the fact of their baptism, and receive and produce its fruit."[30] Though baptism does not guarantee the salvation of the child born of Christian parents, it does constitute a probable sign that the Holy Spirit will one day enable the child to receive, by faith, the benefits of forgiveness and regeneration signified in the sacrament.[31] The *Catechism* made clear, therefore, that baptism benefits Christian believers throughout their lives: it testifies to their justification before God; it reassures them of God's continued love and forgiveness; and, through the enabling work of the Holy Spirit, it empowers them to die to sin and live holy lives devoted to God.

Many of Geneva's townspeople and country folk were slow to embrace the changes in baptismal theology and practice introduced by Calvin and his reformed colleagues. Indeed, some of Geneva's residents were openly hostile to these reforms. Between 1536 and 1609, Geneva's ministers struggled to eradicate a variety of traditional baptismal practices, including emergency baptisms, participation in Catholic baptisms, and naming children after Catholic saints. On rare occasions, Calvin, Beza, and their colleagues also disciplined people who espoused Anabaptist convictions. During the first decades after Geneva's Reformation, the Consistory investigated a handful of baptismal cases in outlying villages where godparents or midwives performed emergency baptisms out of concern for the salvation of a sickly newborn infant.[32] While Lutheran churches in Germany permitted this traditional practice, Geneva's ministers viewed emergency baptisms as pernicious because sacraments should only be performed by ministers in the assembly of the faithful in conjunction with the preaching of the Word, and they were predicated on the false Catholic teaching that baptism was necessary for salvation.[33] It was with these theological concerns in mind that the Consistory sharply rebuked a woman named Claude Mestral in 1548 for allowing a midwife to baptize her sick infant out of the mistaken belief that "if the children of believers do not have the external sign [of baptism] they will perish." The ministers and elders lectured Claude that, because of God's covenant of grace, "the children of the faithful are saved, even as the faithful are assured that God is their God and the God of their children."[34] Though emergency baptisms became extremely rare in reformed Geneva after 1550, nevertheless, the parental instinct to assure the spiritual well-being of sickly children through baptism was very difficult to root out entirely. This is seen in the fact that, in the rural parish of Russin in 1599, parents continued to bring sick newborns to their pastor in the middle of the night to request baptism. The Venerable Company instructed the pastor of Russin and other countryside ministers to remind their congregations that "the doctrine which claims that baptism is necessary for salvation is false" and that all baptisms should be celebrated in the presence of the Christian assembly and in conjunction with Christian preaching.[35]

A more pervasive problem that directly undermined Geneva's public baptismal theology was the fact that some city residents continued to participate in Catholic baptisms. Consistorial activity between 1542 and 1609 indicates that around three dozen men and women were suspended from the Lord's Supper for allowing their children to be baptized by priests in Catholic territories and a somewhat smaller number of people were disciplined for attending or serving as godparents at Catholic baptisms. Cases in which Genevan parents permitted Catholic baptisms for their children are scattered throughout the decades of my study. Many of these Catholic baptisms were undoubtedly motivated by the parents' continued loyalty to the traditional religion, as when a Genevan citizen named Pierre Mercier and his wife attended Mass and had their son baptized while visiting Dijon in 1548, or when three men from the village of Céligny took their newborn children to neighboring Savoy in 1595 to have them baptized by a priest.[36] In one remarkable case, a father named Nicolas Baud from the village of Peissy carried the corpse of his newborn son to "the chapel of Our Lady who performs miracles" in Seysel in hopes that the infant might be resuscitated long enough to receive Catholic baptism before burial.[37] Not all Catholic baptisms indicated Catholic conviction, however. Some reformed parents were forced by circumstance or physical danger to consent to Catholic baptisms when their children were born outside of Geneva. Thus, for example, in 1572 the Consistory suspended from the Lord's Supper a reformed refugee named Gilles de Busegny who had "baptized his child in the Mass" in order "to save his life" during a period of persecution in the Catholic city of Lyon.[38] In a similar fashion, a local goldsmith named Nicolas Flaignec was disciplined by the Consistory in 1581 when he "lightheartedly" took his pregnant wife to Lyon where she gave birth to a son and then presented him to a priest for baptism.[39] A number of Genevan townspeople were also censured for attending or serving as godparents at traditional baptisms in neighboring Savoy or back in France. Though the historical sources do not shed much light on what motivated people to do this, it is likely that social conventions and family loyalties were as important as religious convictions in many of these cases. What is important to emphasize, however, is that even though Geneva's Venerable Company condemned traditional baptisms in the strongest of terms and disciplined people who attended them, the ministers, nevertheless, accepted Catholic baptisms as valid Christian baptisms and consistently rejected Anabaptist claims that rebaptism was necessary. As Calvin stated in the *Institutes*, Christian baptism was "not of man but of God, no matter who administers it." People who were baptized with water in the name of the Trinity received a true Christian baptism, he argued, even if they "were baptized by impious and idolatrous men under the papal government."[40]

As we have seen, Geneva's baptismal rite allowed godparents the privilege of choosing a Christian name for their godchild in the baptismal service. Frequently, godparents named godchildren after themselves. Karen Spierling has observed that this traditional privilege was "a very personal act," for "names were a source of bonding between godparents and godchild and a sign of honor."[41] During the summer of 1546, Calvin and the Company of Pastors launched a campaign to restrict the kinds of names that godparents could give to their godchildren out of concern that many popular baptismal names promoted Catholic belief and superstition. The ministers drafted a list of names they judged to be unacceptable, either because they were blasphemous (e.g., Jesus, Emmanuel, Savior); absurd (e.g., Cross, Sunday, Noel); corrupt (e.g., Tyvan, short for Steven); or superstitious (e.g., names traditionally given to the three Magi: Gaspard, Balthasar, and Melchior).[42] Most controversial of all, the ministers outlawed the common name "Claude" because of its association with the popular Saint Claude whose shrine was located a few miles outside of Geneva. Not surprisingly, the Venerable Company's efforts to change naming patterns in the city bred a lot of ill-will toward the ministers. The controversy began in August of 1546 when the pastor who was officiating at the baptism of the son of Ami Chapuis refused to name the boy "Claude," as requested by the godparent, but instead gave him the name "Abraham" before the congregation at St. Gervais. The angry, embarrassed father refused to accept the baptismal name and even questioned the validity of his son's baptism; he became so contentious that he landed in the city prison.[43] Many members of the congregation who had watched this spectacle were scandalized by this unseemly display of clerical power. The ministers were not willing to back down, however, and several days afterward, they convinced the magistrates to pass a city ordinance which established that, henceforth, only biblical names were to be given to children at baptism. Over the next seven years, the ministers were embroiled in a series of bitter disputes over baptismal names, many of which took place in public view of their congregations. Powerful Genevan citizens like Gaspard Favre and Balthasar Sept were understandably upset that their names were no longer considered "acceptable" titles for the children of family members and friends for whom they were invited to serve as godfathers. Favre complained that "he would no longer bring infants to baptism, because it was illegal for him to give [infant boys] his name."[44] What was a religious principle for the city's pastors was for many townspeople an egregious infringement of a traditional privilege that diminished their personal prestige and threatened to loosen the social ties that bound families and kinship groups together.

Nevertheless, in the long run, the ministers' efforts to reform naming patterns in Geneva proved to be an unqualified success. As E. William Monter has shown, by the decade of the 1560s, 97 percent of the boys and 98 percent of the girls who were baptized in Geneva's churches received baptismal names drawn from the Old or New Testaments (as compared to 57 percent and 51 percent respectively before 1536). Baptismal names that were relatively rare before the reformation—such as Abraham, Daniel, Isaac, David, Sara, or Rachel—became common in Geneva during the second half of the sixteenth century.[45] Ironically, the name "Mary" also increased in popularity as a woman's name in reformed Geneva. At the same time, the names of Catholic saints such as Claude, Martin, Balthasar, and Gaspard disappeared almost entirely from Geneva's baptismal registry. The official protocol regarding baptismal names was added to the revised edition of the *Ecclesiastical Ordinances* in 1561 and remained in force until 1638 when the Company decided to discontinue the prohibition of names because the danger of superstition seemed over.[46] Although Geneva appears to have been the only reformed territory in early modern Europe that instituted naming policies by legal statute, reformed churchmen elsewhere in Switzerland, France, and England shared Calvin's concern to eradicate the names of Catholic saints from the repertoire of acceptable titles for baptized children and in their place, promoted biblical titles that better reflected their identity as the covenant people of God.[47] In this sense, Calvin and his colleagues intended that the very names that identified reformed Christian men and women would point back to the theological meaning of their baptisms, reminding them of their privileged status as members of the covenantal community of believers.

Even as they attempted to eradicate Catholic baptismal practices and beliefs, Geneva's Venerable Company remained vigilant in guarding the city from the influence of Anabaptist teaching. One way that the ministers did this was to keep a watchful eye on new parents, requiring them to present their newborn children for baptism within three or four days of birth. Those who delayed baptizing their children faced a consistorial reprimand or even suspension.[48] More dangerous than delayed baptisms was the threat posed by Anabaptists who passed through Geneva from time to time, often attacking the city's official theology and seeking to win converts.[49] In 1547, a poor dressmaker named Antoine was called before the Consistory for criticizing the magistrates and holding to "the doctrine of the Anabaptists." In this hearing, Antoine challenged Calvin to his face and stated that he had no intention of accepting doctrinal instruction from "monks or priests." He was ultimately banished by the magistrates for his errors.[50] Four years later, amidst reports that two Anabapiststs were in the city "spreading their poison" of perfectionism, Calvin devoted the Friday morning Congregation to refuting their false teachings that "a person is not a Christian if he is not perfect" and "a church is not a church unless it is perfect." Calvin appealed to reason and the testimony of Scripture to argue that even though Christians "are called to perfection" and should strive for it, nevertheless, they will never achieve it until they are liberated from the body at death. In this life "we walk and run" toward perfection, "but we have not yet arrived at the goal."[51] Later, Calvin was called to the city council chambers to confront the two heretics face to face; one of the men was convinced of his errors, the other was not and was banished from the city.

Two decades later, a similar drama unfolded when Theodore Beza was summoned to the Hôtel de Ville in November 1573 to confront an Anabaptist weaver named Bartholomew Carron, who had been arrested for teaching townspeople that the magistrates did not have the right to wield the sword, that Christians should hold all their goods in common, that Geneva's church was not a true church and her ministers only liars, and that Scripture nowhere taught that infants should be baptized. In the face of Beza's rebuttal—and the looming threat of capital punishment—Carron disavowed his teaching and admitted his error.[52] The magistrates ordered Carron whipped and banished from the city, warning him that if he ever returned he would be hung. The case did not end there, however, for Carron relocated to a village in nearby France where he continued to propagate his Anabaptist teachings. In 1581, the Consistory summoned a widow to its chambers that had placed her son under the apprenticeship of "a weaver named Bartholomew Carron who is of the sect of the Anabaptists." The ministers and elders demanded that this arrangement be terminated immediately.[53] In March of the following year, four weavers from Geneva were examined by the Consistory and suspended from the Lord's Supper for visiting Carron and embracing some of his Anabaptist views. Two of the men were restored to communion a month later, but only after they had renounced the "error of the Anabaptists" and reaffirmed the "evangelical doctrine" as it was "preached and purely taught in this city."[54]

Overall, Anabaptism cases like these were relatively rare during the ministries of Calvin, Beza, and Goulart. Between 1542 and 1609, only a half-dozen men are known to have been suspended from the Lord's Supper for espousing Anabaptist views or associating with suspected Anabaptists. Geneva's city magistrates appear to have prosecuted a somewhat larger number of Anabaptist cases without recourse to the Consistory or ecclesiastical discipline—but still the numbers remained modest. It would be wrong to conclude that all Anabaptists who came to Geneva did so with the intention of propagating their baptistic doctrine, for some people with Anabaptist sympathies, no doubt, kept their opinions to themselves and accommodated their convictions as best they could to Geneva's official religion. In one unusual case, an eighteen-year-old Anabaptist named Abraham de La Mare chose to convert to the reformed faith and receive Christian baptism at the hands of Geneva's ministers.[55] Arriving in Geneva in late spring 1577, Abraham de La Mare appeared before the Consistory in August to request instruction in the reformed religion and Christian baptism. The ministers encouraged him to attend sermons, study the catechism, and seek out the city's pastors for private instruction as needed. Four months later, Abraham returned to Consistory to give a reason for his faith, requesting Christian baptism and admission to the church. On Sunday afternoon, December 22, 1577, Abraham de La Mare stood before the congregation in the temple of St. Pierre and disavowed the teachings of the Anabaptists point by point. After he had recited "the chief points of evangelical doctrine" and repeated aloud the Apostles' Creed and the Lord's Prayer, Abraham was baptized by the minister Charles Perrot with sprinkling of water in the name of the Father, the Son, and the Holy Spirit.[56]

2. Catechism and Religious Instruction

The baptism of Abraham de La Mare was not at all typical. Most Genevans received catechetical instruction and made public profession of faith *after*, not before, baptism. The normal pattern observed in Calvin's church was that baptized children received catechism instruction at home, at school, and in the church so that by the time they reached early adolescence, they were prepared to profess their Christian faith and receive admission to the Lord's Table. Geneva's program of religious education and spiritual formation was significantly indebted to the practice of other reformed churches. In 1523 or 1524, Ulrich Zwingli established in Zurich the first formal program of weekly catechism instruction for children, and this model was soon duplicated in other reformed churches throughout Europe. By the early 1530s, catechism instruction was commonplace in reformed territories such as Zurich, Strasbourg, Basel, and Bern, based on catechisms written by prominent reformed leaders such as Leo Jud, Martin Bucer, Wolfgang Capito, Mathias Zell, and Johannes Oecolampadius.[57] These catechisms treated the Ten Commandments, the Apostles' Creed, and the Lord's Prayer with the goal of presenting a basic summary of the Christian message of salvation in such a way that children might embrace it as their own and profess their faith publicly before the church. Catechetical instruction was thus seen as an essential part of the sacrament of baptism, for as children came to understand the gospel and professed faith in Christ they were exhibiting the fruit of the baptism they had received as infants.[58]

Already in the first edition of the *Institutes* (1536), Calvin had recommended a plan of religious education for evangelical churches that included catechetical instruction and a public profession of faith. Once installed in Geneva, Calvin and Guillaume Farel took the first steps toward implementing this vision when they presented to the magistrates a document entitled *Articles Concerning the Organization of the Church* (1537), which proposed that all the children in the city be required to learn "a brief and simple summary of the Christian faith," submit to periodic examinations from the ministers, and finally "make confession of their faith to the Church."[59] Parents were given a primary role in this program of religious instruction. As it turned out, the "brief and simple summary" to which the *Articles* alluded was none other than Calvin's first catechism which appeared several months later under the title *Instruction and Confession of Faith* (1537). In this catechism, Calvin provided a concise summary of the main teachings of his *Institutes*, organized according to thirty-three doctrinal topics that treated the knowledge of God, the Ten Commandments, election and predestination, the Apostles' Creed, the nature of prayer, the Lord's Prayer, and church discipline.[60] These initial steps toward establishing regular catechetical instruction and examination were cut short when Calvin and Farel were banished from Geneva in the spring of 1538.

Mandatory catechetical instruction was one of the chief conditions that Calvin made for his return to Geneva from Strasbourg three years later. For Calvin, recovering the ancient practice of catechesis was critical to preserve reformed Christianity in the future: "The church of God will never preserve itself without a catechism," he noted, "for it is like the seed to keep the good grain from dying out, causing it to multiply from age to age."[61] In the *Ecclesiastical Ordinances* (1541), all children in the city and countryside were required to attend catechetical sermons every Sunday at noon and make "a profession of [their] Christianity in the presence of the Church" before participating in the Lord's Supper.[62] The document gave primary responsibility for catechizing young people to the city's ministers; parents had a secondary role of assuring that their children attended catechism classes and abstained from taking the Lord's Supper until they had made a public profession of their faith. To support this pedagogical program, Calvin wrote a second catechism entitled *The Catechism of the Church of Geneva* (1541) which, as we have seen, remained one of the most important doctrinal standards of Geneva's church for the next two centuries. Calvin's revised *Catechism* was much longer than his previous catechism, written in the form of a dialogue covering 373 questions-and-answers.[63] Beginning with the foundational question "What is the chief goal of human life?" (Answer: "It is to know God"), the *Catechism* goes on to consider the doctrine of the Trinity, the nature and offices of Christ, the atonement, the ministry of the Holy Spirit, the nature of the church, the Law, right worship, prayer, and the sacraments.[64] Interestingly, Calvin's *Catechism* omits any detailed treatment of election or predestination. So too, Calvin modified the structure of this second catechism, discussing the Ten Commandments *after* the Apostles' Creed, to make clear that God's law not only prepared people for the gospel but also served as a guiding principle for Christians as they lived lives of gratitude and obedience to Christ.[65] At the end of the *Catechism*, the reformer appended a brief prayer book containing five model prayers that were to be recited at the beginning and end of the day, at school, and before and after meals. Clearly, Calvin was concerned not only to equip children with the knowledge of the major points of reformed doctrine but also to offer basic instruction in the moral and devotional aspects of Christianity.[66]

How, then, was Calvin's *Catechism* actually used in sixteenth-century Geneva? First, it is important to note that children were not expected to memorize all 373 questions-and-answers of the *Catechism* as a prerequisite for admission to the Lord's Supper. The *Ecclesiastical Ordinances* stipulated only that children must be "sufficiently instructed" in the *Catechism* so that they might "solemnly recite a *summary* of that which is contained in it."[67] In practice, it appears that Calvin's *Catechism* functioned primarily as a doctrinal manual—a kind of theological curriculum—to assist parents, school teachers, and ministers as they instructed children in Geneva's common faith.[68] Over time Calvin's *Catechism* also came to function as a confession of faith that was affirmed by ministers when they were examined for ordination, by young people when they made public profession of faith, and by students when they enrolled at Calvin's Academy.[69]

Recognizing that Calvin's *Catechism* was better suited as a theological manual and doctrinal standard than as a catechetical formula that could easily be memorized, Geneva's pastors approved the use of abridged versions of the *Catechism* and several of them wrote their own smaller catechisms to instruct Geneva's young people.[70] An example of this was Charles Perrot's brief handwritten catechism that he used in his countryside parish of Genthod-Moëns in the early 1560s. Similarly, Beza's *Little Catechism*, first published in 1575, was regularly appended to Calvin's *Catechism* as a concise statement of Geneva's official theology that could be memorized by children.[71] One of the most popular abridgements of Calvin's *Catechism* was *The French ABC's* published by the Genevan printer Jean Crespin in 1551, which went through four editions by 1630.[72] The contents of Crespin's forty-page booklet reveal that it was intended as a basic pedagogical tool for use in Geneva's households and primary schools.[73] The pamphlet included, in order, a table of the ABCs in French, the Lord's Prayer, the Apostles' Creed, the Ten Commandments, the five prayers from Calvin's *Catechism*, a three-page summary of reformed doctrine, forty-four biblical texts drawn from the Old and New Testaments, several short prayers for students, a brief catechism entitled "The manner of examining children who wish to receive the Lord's Supper," and a mathematical table listing numbers from 1 to 100. For our purposes, the concise catechism entitled "The manner of examining children" that was included in the *The French ABC's* is especially revealing, both because it was probably written by Calvin himself, and because it illustrates the modest level of Christian understanding that was expected of children before they were admitted to the Lord's Table. Among the twenty-two questions that made up this brief catechism, several are noteworthy:

> MINISTER: In whom do you believe?
> CHILD: In God the Father, and in Jesus Christ his Son, and in the Holy Spirit.
> MINISTER: Are the Father, Son, and Holy Spirit more than one God?
> CHILD: No.
>
> MINISTER: By what means are you saved and delivered from the curse of God?
> CHILD: By the death and passion of our Lord Jesus Christ.
> MINISTER: How is that?
> CHILD: Because by his death he has brought us life and has reconciled us to God his Father.
>
> MINISTER: What does baptism signify?
> CHILD: It has two parts. Because our Lord represents there for us the remission of our sins and then our regeneration and spiritual renewal.
> MINISTER: And the Lord's Supper, what does it signify?
> CHILD: It signifies for us that by the communion of the body and blood of our Lord Jesus Christ our souls are nourished in the hope of eternal life.

MINISTER: Is it your understanding that the body of Christ is enclosed in the bread, and the blood of Christ is enclosed in the wine?
CHILD: Not at all.

MINISTER: What is the way for us to reach heaven, where Jesus Christ is?
CHILD: It is by faith.

With this one booklet, then, Geneva's children were taught their ABCs, learned to count to 100, received basic instructions in prayer, and were given an easy-to-remember summary of reformed doctrine taught in Geneva's church.

Although the *Ecclesiastical Ordinances* said little about the responsibilities of parents to catechize their children, other Genevan sources make clear that fathers and mothers were expected to play a central role in instructing their children in the Christian faith.[74] In 1549, the magistrates sent a crier through the city announcing that "all fathers of families should be diligent in instructing both their children and their male and female servants, and require them to attend sermons and catechism classes."[75] So too, Geneva's ministers in their sermons exhorted parents to take seriously the religious education of the members of their households. In a sermon on Deuteronomy delivered in the mid-1550s, Calvin noted that "those whom God has honored with the gift of children...are all the more responsible to make every effort that their children are duly instructed. Now if they desire to instruct them well, they must always begin with faith. For even if children display all the virtues of the world, this will amount to nothing unless they fear and honor God."[76] Four decades later Beza repeated this theme in a sermon delivered from the pulpit of St. Pierre. Spiritual conversation and instruction should be a regular aspect of family life, Beza observed,

> with wives asking questions of their husbands at home, fathers instructing their household servants according to the example of Abraham, children being examined by their fathers, and mothers also teaching their children. It is for this reason that the family is honored with the general title of "church."[77]

In accordance with this pedagogical vision, Geneva's Consistory sometimes intervened to hold parents accountable for the religious instruction of their children. In 1542, for example, the ministers and elders ordered a cobbler named Pierre Clerc to "teach well his children the evangelical doctrine."[78] Four decades later, the Consistory confronted the widow Françoise Forestier for the ignorance and laziness of her daughters Jeanne and Pernette. The ministers charged the mother to give her daughters "instruction in the Word of God and require them to work and pray," for "God never abandons those who fear him."[79] Disciplinary cases like these underline the fact that Geneva's ministers expected that families and households would serve as "little churches" where children learned how to pray and acquired a basic knowledge of the reformed faith through conversation and catechism.

Undoubtedly many Genevan parents took seriously their responsibility to provide Christian instruction for the children and servants in their households. A good illustration of this is seen in the fascinating account of a ten-year-old apprentice from Basel named André Ryff, who came to Geneva in 1560 and worked for several years in the household of a grocer named Jean Du Molard. Writing many years later, André remembered Du Molard as a strict disciplinarian and demanding master who had, nevertheless, imparted to his family and servants a fervent piety.[80] Every morning and evening the members of the household knelt next to the stove where Madame Du Molard led them in prayer, giving thanks to God "for his graces and benefits, and passionately praying that he might shower on us his Spirit, his protection, his blessing, and his mercy." Over time, Jean Du Molard taught André how to pray and entrusted to him the responsibility of leading the family's daily prayer services; "in this way," the young man observed, "I believe that I acquired a sincere fervor for religion." In addition to teaching him to pray, Du Molard regularly instructed his young apprentice on the catechism and sent him along with the other servants to the 5 a.m. preaching service each weekday morning. These religious exercises paid off, for when André was examined by the city's ministers, they judged his knowledge of the Christian faith adequate for admission to the Lord's Table. As he looked back on his sojourn in Geneva, André Ryff expressed gratitude to God for the "edification" he had received from learning Geneva's *Catechism*, even as he prayed that the Lord "would see fit by his grace to sustain me in this faith as I have professed it." The spiritual disciplines and piety gained in the household of Jean Du Molard left a lasting impact on André Ryff.

In addition to religious training at home, Geneva's children also received catechetical instruction at school and in the church. Girls and boys who attended one of Geneva's *petites écoles*—small private schools that offered basic instruction in reading, writing, and mathematics—were catechized by means of doctrinal summaries, such as the *The French ABC's*, as well as by the required catechetical sermons on Sundays.[81] Students who enrolled in the Latin school (*schola privata*) that made up the lower level of Geneva's Academy encountered a more intense exposure to Calvin's *Catechism*. In the introductory class, boys of ages five or six were taught the Apostles' Creed, the Lord's Prayer, and the Ten Commandments, and began to study a summary of the catechism in French and Latin.[82] Students were required to attend sermons with their classes on Wednesday mornings and Sundays at noon; on Saturdays, they took turns reciting the section of the catechism that would be treated in the catechetical sermon the following day. In later years, as the boys advanced in their knowledge of the reformed faith, they were expected to move from abridged versions of the catechism to Calvin's full *Catechism* in Latin and Greek editions. By the time that students completed their studies at the *schola privata* at age eleven or twelve, they would have worked through Calvin's *Catechism* six or seven times and most would have mastered its doctrinal contents. It is important to note, however, that admission to the Lord's Table was not tied directly to a child's level of schooling or age. The *Ecclesistical Ordinances* made clear that boys and girls were welcomed to the Lord's Supper only after they had reached the age of discretion (around ten years of age) and were able satisfactorily to articulate the basic doctrines of the reformed religion and confess it as their own. Toward that end, four times a year on the Sunday before Geneva's quarterly communion service, young people who were prepared to confess their Christian faith stood in front of the worshiping congregation and, in response to the ministers' questions, recited the shortened form of the *Catechism* that served as their formal profession of faith. A week later, they were invited for the first time to feed upon the body and blood of Jesus Christ offered in the sacred meal of the Lord's Table.

Religious instruction was provided for adults as well. Calvin and his colleagues wanted to make certain that all the men and women who lived and worked in Geneva, both longtime residents and recent immigrants, were able to demonstrate a basic understanding of and commitment to the reformed faith before they participated in the Lord's Supper. This was not only an educational goal, it was their pastoral vision: Geneva's inhabitants must "know how to declare the reason for their salvation and make a confession of faith, as all good Christians should be able to do."[83] In reality, during the first decades of Geneva's Reformation, the Consistory encountered hundreds of men and women who were unable to articulate the outline of Geneva's public theology and who continued to affirm elements of Catholic doctrine that they had learned as children. People who had grown up in the Catholic Church memorizing in Latin the Creed, the Our Father and the Ave Maria often found it difficult as adults to give an account of their Christian faith in the French vernacular. Hence, in 1542 a mason named Claude Morel was able to recite by heart the Ave Maria and the Apostles' Creed in Latin, but could only repeat the first two words of the Lord's Prayer in French.[84] Many Genevans found it especially difficult to learn the Ten Commandments. Marguerite Danelle, the wife of a pin maker, announced to the Consistory in 1561 that there were three commandments in the Law of God: baptism, the Lord's Supper, and...she could not remember the third.[85] The following year, when the minister Louis Enoch exhorted Aimé Navette at the visitation to memorize the Ten Commandments, Aimé replied, "I knew nothing of it last year; I know nothing of it now; and as for the year to come, the Devil with it!"[86] The Consistory was particularly concerned that people understand that salvation was received by God's grace through faith in Christ rather than the result of human good works. Thus, in 1580 when a day laborer named Jehan Revilliod was unable to give an account of his faith and asserted, instead, that people were saved by good works, the secretary of the Consistory noted in his register that the defendant had "responded very badly because we should have faith and confidence of our salvation based on the death of our Lord Jesus Christ."[87] From time to time, the Consistory encountered men and women who displayed utter confusion not only about Geneva's reformed creed but about the Christian religion as a whole. Thyven Bastard of the parish of Bourdigny was stumped by the minister's question "Who suffered and died on the cross?"[88] A widow named Guillermette Tissot was judged to be "very stupid and ignorant of the way of her salvation" for declaring to the Consistory that the Virgin Mary was the *father* of Jesus. Further questioning revealed that she was unclear as to whether the Virgin was a man or a woman.[89] Similar confusion reigned in the case of a wagon driver named Mermet Foudral, who announced to the ministers that there were three gods in heaven who were all one, that the divine Father named "Pilate" had died for sinners, and that only the devil was in hell.[90] Some defendants who were suspended by the Consistory for the fault of "ignorance," without question harbored doubts or hostility toward orthodox Christianity itself. When the Consistory interrogated a sailor named Pierre Boulard in 1561 as to the definition of a Christian, he said he did not know but insisted that he was one. Asked if the Turks were also Christians, he responded "yes," since they were God's creatures just as he was. Hearing these responses, the Consistory suspended Boulard from the Lord's Supper "for his stupidity and ignorance, and because he speaks out of deliberate malice" toward Christianity.[91]

Geneva's ministers attempted to redress widespread ignorance like this through an intensive program of Christian instruction and spiritual supervision. Sermons served as the cornerstone of this pedagogical enterprise. In addition to regular preaching services, the ministers required adults in need of remedial religious education to attend catechism sermons at noon on Sundays. Hence, when Claude Pascard betrayed utter confusion about the Christian faith in 1560, the Consistory suspended him from the Lord's Table and ordered him to attend catechism classes every week for a year, sitting with the children to be better instructed and to report his progress to his pastor on a regular basis.[92] Though many men and women refused to attend these sermons out of the perception that "the catechism hour is for children," the Venerable Company never backed down from its stated requirement that the catechism sermon should serve both children and ignorant adults.[93]

Religious instruction took place in less formal ways as well. Men and women who could read were sometimes required to purchase and read the Bible or study the *Catechism* on their own. Husbands who possessed knowledge of Geneva's religious creed were responsible for instructing their wives.[94] In some cases, the Consistory ordered ignorant adults to hire a private tutor to help them learn the summary of the *Catechism*.[95] On other occasions, Geneva's ministers themselves took responsibility for tutoring and providing spiritual instruction for ignorant parishioners to expedite their restoration to the church. Thus, for example, the minister Nicolas Colladon agreed to meet the widow Guillermette Tissot every Sunday after the catechism class to help her learn the Lord's Prayer, the Apostles' Creed, and the reason for her faith.[96] Similarly, the pastor Jean Pinault was commissioned "to meet daily" with a citizen named Pierre Genod "until he was properly instructed."[97] These examples make clear that, for Geneva's ministers, helping men and women grow in Christian understanding was one of the ways that they exercised pastoral care within their parishes. On the other hand, men and women who stubbornly refused to apply themselves to acquiring basic understanding of the reformed Christian faith were not welcome for long in Calvinist Geneva. A day laborer named Antoine Amied was reminded of this fact in 1561, when the Consistory threatened to recommend his banishment from Geneva if he continued to ignore its commands to attend sermons, go to the weekly catechism, and seek out instruction "on the way of his salvation" from his pastor.[98] Religious instruction in reformed Geneva was not optional. In the minds of Calvin and his colleagues, the future of Geneva's reformation depended on a godly community of adults and children who shared a common commitment to biblical Christianity. It was their responsibility as spiritual shepherds to instruct God's flock in Christian truth—and to expel from the sheepfold those who refused to embrace that truth as their own.

It is extremely difficult to determine the long-term effectiveness of Geneva's program of religious instruction. On the one hand, archival documents reveal that many children and adults routinely skipped Sunday catechetical sermons and that unruly behavior at these services was commonplace. Occasionally, the ministers and elders complained to Geneva's magistrates about the "great contempt" that townspeople had for the Sunday catechism lesson and about the shocking ignorance that prevailed throughout the city.[99] On the other hand, if the number of ignorance cases in the Consistory's caseload serves as a reliable indicator, one might well conclude that the ministers' campaign to cultivate understanding of the reformed faith among Geneva's inhabitants did achieve a measure of success. Up until 1564, the number of people disciplined for religious "ignorance" was relatively high, accounting for more than 10 percent of all known suspensions. In the generation after Calvin's death, ignorance cases became far less frequent so that, between 1565 and 1609, suspensions for ignorance accounted for less than 1 percent (0.6 percent) of all known suspensions.[100] During the final two decades included in my study, I identified only seventeen people excommunicated for the fault of "ignorance"—and many of these individuals were recent immigrants to the city. Despite this indication of success, however, Geneva's ministers recognized the superficiality and tenuous nature of their educational enterprise. Memorizing a brief summary of the *Catechism* or reciting the Creed and the Lord's Prayer in French did not guarantee that a person had an adequate understanding of Christian doctrine. Beza and his colleagues admitted this fact in 1576, when they expressed their alarm that many people whom they examined were not well instructed and that "our catechisms...do not seem to be accomplishing what they should."[101] Even so, the extensive nature of Calvin's educational program, enforced by visitations, examinations, and consistorial discipline, guaranteed that men, women, and children alike would receive at least a basic introduction to reformed Christianity. Though some Genevans chafed at this, many others probably welcomed the opportunity to grow in Christian understanding.

The positive, pastoral dimension of Geneva's educational program is illustrated particularly well by the Consistory's interaction with a former monk named Master Thomas Sylvester. Having once served as a physician in the court of the King of Hungary, Sylvester arrived in Geneva in July of 1559 desiring "to hear the preaching of the gospel" and "become instructed and live according to the true reformation of the gospel." An initial interview before the Consistory determined that Sylvester was "very ignorant and did not know the principles of Christianity"; consequently, the ministers charged Sylvester to study the *Catechism* in Latin and Italian and to report back in six weeks for a fuller examination of his Christian faith.[102] When Sylvester returned to Consistory at the end of August without having mastered the summary of the *Catechism*, the ministers gave him another three months to be instructed and advised him to consult the city pastors to "discuss with them matters of doctrine."[103] Finally, after five months of formal and informal catechetical instruction, Master Thomas successfully declared "the reason for his faith and the manner of his salvation" before the Consistory in December 1559. As a result, the ministers received him as a "Christian" and granted him admission to the Lord's Table.[104]

3. The Sacrament of the Lord's Supper

For children participating in the Lord's Supper for the first time, the sacramental meal of bread and wine represented an important milestone in a spiritual journey that commenced at baptism. As we have seen, in the sacrament of baptism, children were adopted into the household of Christ, the church, and promised the forgiveness of sins through repentance and faith. In the years that followed, as children were nurtured by their parents, attended sermons and studied the catechism, they received basic instruction in Christian doctrine and practice so that they might know what to believe, know how to live, and know how to pray. When they made profession of faith in early adolescence, children gave public testimony that God's grace, signified in their baptism, had born the fruit of repentance and faith in their lives. Finally, as they participated in the sacrament of the Lord's Table for the first time, they were fully integrated into the community of believers, recognized as members of Christ's church and recipients of the life-giving benefits offered through communion with Christ's body. According to Calvin's theology, the heavenly Father, who graciously adopted the children of believers into his household through baptism, was the same benevolent Father who now provided them with spiritual nourishment in the Eucharistic meal.[105]

In comparison to the traditional Catholic Mass, the celebration of the Lord's Supper in reformed Geneva was simple, almost austere. At the communion table, Calvin and his colleagues offered their congregations bread, wine, and the Word of God in the vernacular language—without the sensory "feast" of processions, incense, candles, bells, and rich clerical vestments experienced in the Mass.[106] The Catholic polemicist Antoine Cathelan described the unadorned character of the reformed communion service that he witnessed when he visited Geneva in the mid 1550s:

> Three or four times a year, according to the will of the magistrates and princes, two tables are set up in the church, and each is covered with a tablecloth, and a lot of hosts are set out on the left, and three or four cups or glasses on the right, with lots of pots full of either white or red wine under the table. And after the sermon the preacher descends from the pulpit and goes to the left end of the table, where the hosts are, and standing with his head uncovered he places a piece [of bread] in each person's hand, saying "Remember that Jesus Christ died for you." Each person eats his piece while walking to the other end of the table, where he takes the wine from one of the elders, or other persons so-charged, without saying anything, while the sergeants with heads uncovered pour the wine and provide additional hosts if they run out. Throughout all of this, somebody else reads from the pulpit in the vernacular, with head uncovered, the Gospel of Saint John, from the beginning of the thirteenth chapter, until everyone has taken their pieces, both men and women, each one at their different tables, along with the boys and girls of around eight to ten years of age.[107]

Cathelan's description of Geneva's communion service is corroborated in large part by other contemporaneous sources. Notwithstanding Calvin's preference for more frequent communion services, the Lord's Supper was celebrated in reformed Geneva four times a year, at Christmas, Easter, Pentecost, and the first Sunday in September.[108] A week before the celebration, the ministers in their Sunday sermons were expected to call their parishioners to spiritual examination and preparation, as well as to warn uninstructed foreigners and children who had not yet made profession of faith to abstain from taking the sacred meal.[109] On the Sunday morning of the Lord's Supper, two communion tables covered with white tablecloths were set up in the front of the sanctuary in Geneva's churches. After the sermon, the minister descended from the pulpit and stood beside one of the communion tables, where he read a brief liturgy that included the words of institution from 1 Corinthians 11:23–29, a statement of formal excommunication that barred notorious sinners from the Table, and a summary of the meaning of the Supper. The congregation then processed single file to the tables, men to one table and women to the other, where they received wafers of unleavened bread from the ministers and drank wine from a chalice offered by the elders (or sometimes by a deacon or schoolmaster). As people awaited their turn to partake of the Lord's Supper, the congregation sang a Psalm or listened to a reading from the Scripture. The service was concluded with prayers of thanksgiving.

Despite the plain format of the sacrament, Geneva's communion celebration was a public ritual rich in religious and social symbolism—a point that Christian Grosse has recently demonstrated in his important study of Eucharistic practice in reformed Geneva. The simplicity of the service served as an antitype to the Catholic Mass: the minister faced the assembly rather than turned his back on the congregation; he recited the communion liturgy in French rather than Latin; the faithful partook of both bread *and* the cup; the focus of the sacrament was on the word of salvation, proclaimed through the signs of bread and wine, rather than on Christ's body located in the consecrated elements. The quarterly celebration of the sacrament ritualized the process of restoration and sanctification, even as it defined the boundaries of the spiritual community and announced the unity of the fellowship of believers. Moreover, the Lord's Supper was a ritual of social and political importance that dramatized the configuration of authority in Geneva. The fact that the ministers used *unleavened* bread rather than common table bread in the sacrament served as a poignant reminder of the magistrates' authority within the church, since they had mandated this practice in 1538 against the strong objections of Calvin and Farel.[110] The fact that elders (all drawn from the magistracy) were given the privilege of administering the chalice to the faithful in the Lord's Supper displayed and enhanced their public status and depicted the cooperative relationship that should exist between religious and civil authorities. Finally, the fact that, from 1574 on, Geneva's magistrates were given priority to commune first at the Table, before the rest of the congregation, was a clear public statement of their privileged place within the Christian community.

Even so, the spiritual and pastoral significance of the Lord's Supper was of primary concern to Calvin, Beza, and their colleagues. Calvin's doctrine of the Lord's Supper has been variously described as "real spiritual presence" or "symbolic instrumentalism": through the sacramental signs of bread and wine, the benefits of Christ are not merely signified but given to the faithful so that they partake of the very substance of Christ's body.[111] Christ's body is not located in the consecrated elements. Rather, in Calvin's view, Christ is physically present in heaven, and it is there that believers feed on the substance of his life-giving flesh and are united with him through the ministry of the Holy Spirit. The gift that the Lord Supper bestows is thus the person of Jesus Christ himself—and this intimate communion occurs by faith, through the Word, and by the power of the Holy Spirit. Calvin explained the relationship of sacrament, the Word, and the Holy Spirit in an important passage from Book Four of his *Institutes*: "For first, the Lord teaches and instructs us by his Word. Secondly, he confirms it by the sacraments. Finally, he illumines our minds by the light of his

Holy Spirit and opens our hearts for the Word and sacrament to enter in, which would otherwise only strike our ears and appear before our eyes, but not at all affect us within."[112]

Calvin articulated his distinctive doctrine of the Eucharist in Geneva's *Catechism* and in successive editions of the *Institutes*. It was also announced from Geneva's pulpits four times a year when the ministers read the liturgy in preparation for the celebration of the Lord's Supper. In the liturgy, Geneva's ministers explained to their congregations that the Lord's Supper was like a "spiritual table" that provided "heavenly bread" for hungry souls and "spiritual medicine" for poor, sick sinners. In the Supper, believers were made "participants" of Christ's body and blood, joined to Christ "to the end that we might possess him entirely in such a manner that he lives in us and we in him." For Christ himself is "the heavenly bread" who "feeds and nourishes us to eternal life."[113] The liturgy made clear that Christ's physical body was not enclosed within the bread and wine; the physical elements were "signs and witnesses" of God's salvation "promised in the Word of God." Hence, instead of focusing on the sacramental elements themselves, the faithful were instructed to raise their hearts on high to feed upon Christ's body in heaven: "Let us not amuse ourselves with these earthly and corruptible elements, which we see with our eyes and touch with our hands.... For our souls will be prepared to be nourished and revived on [Christ's] substance when they are lifted above all earthy things to reach all the way to heaven, and enter the kingdom of God where he dwells."[114] Calvin's liturgy made clear, then, that participating in the Lord's Supper was an essential part of the Christian life, because by it believers received spiritual nourishment and healing, and were united more and more with Christ. For their part, Geneva's ministers believed that as they proclaimed Christ's salvation through the symbols of the sacrament, and as they distributed the holy food to their parishioners, they were providing crucial pastoral support and care to the people of God.

Calvin's doctrine of the Lord's Supper remained the official position of the Genevan church for more than two centuries. After Calvin's death, Theodore Beza emerged as the most important champion of Geneva's doctrine of "symbolic instrumentalism." In a variety of theological writings as well as in interconfessional colloquies held at Poissy (1561) and Montbéliard (1586), Beza defended Geneva's sacramental position against the Catholic doctrine of transubstantiation and against Lutheran teaching that Christ's ascended body was ubiquitous and thus physically present in the sacramental elements. In his popular *Confession of the Christian Faith* (1559), for example, Beza emphasized that, in the Lord's Supper,

> the reality signified (that is, Jesus Christ and all his benefits) is always truly presented...by God, who is faithful to his promise, in such a way that the sign and the reality signified are always conjoined.... But [this conjunction] is achieved by the power of the Holy Spirit alone. Through him, Jesus Christ

(who, as a man, is in heaven and physically absent from us, as Scripture testifies) is presented to us just as truly as the sacramental elements are presented to us. Thus, our faith contemplates Jesus Christ in the sacrament, and by this means climbs up to heaven to embrace him more and more, and joins us with him.[115]

In addition to defending Calvin's distinctive doctrine of the Lord's Supper, Beza and his colleagues also remained protective of the particular rites and customs that became a part of Geneva's communion celebration. The communion bread was to be unleavened, not common table bread. The bread was to be broken by the officiating minister in the sight of the congregation (the so-called *fractio panis*). In the city churches, the wine was to be administered by a lay elder or deacon, not the presiding minister. All forms of private communion, even for the sick and dying, were prohibited. Geneva's ministers recognized that a number of these customary practices were nowhere dictated by Scripture and thus belonged to the category of indifferent doctrines (*adiaphora*). Even so, the Venerable Company during the decades after Calvin consistently rejected various proposals to modify sacramental practice in Geneva's churches—even in the interest of confessional unity with other reformed churches. The conservative stance of Geneva's ministers on the question of whether leavened or unleavened bread should be used in the sacramental meal was especially ironic: whereas Calvin and Farel had run afoul of Geneva's magistrates in 1538 for refusing to adopt the Bernese rite of serving unleavened bread in the sacrament, seven decades later the Venerable Company was unwilling to *abandon* the use of unleavened bread in the Lord's Supper despite overtures coming from the reformed churches of Bern and France.[116] In both cases, the ministers were more concerned with protecting their prerogative to define local church practice than with the actual practice itself.

Geneva's celebration of the Lord's Supper, which was intended to express the unity of the community of faith, sometimes exposed tensions, theological differences, and misunderstandings among church members. Between 1542 and 1609, nearly two hundred fifty people are known to have been suspended by the Consistory for "profaning" or "polluting" the sacrament of the Table. This category of misbehavior included a number of different kinds of "sins," but it most commonly involved Genevans who habitually missed communion services, partook of the communion elements in violation of a prior sentence of excommunication, or indulged in illicit activities such as banqueting or gambling on the "sacred day" when the Lord's Supper was observed. As the Consistory reminded a fisherman named Jean Favre in 1560, feasting at "the holy banquet" of the Lord was far more important than guarding his fishing boats.[117] Especially in the early decades of Geneva's Reformation, "profanation" of the Lord's Supper often signaled Catholic behavior that was no longer permitted in the reformed city. Thus, for example, the Consistory addressed a handful of cases where parishioners, instead of consuming the communion bread at the Lord's Table, attempted to take it home under the belief that it possessed sacred power to heal a sick family member. In one notable instance, in 1560, Calvin even interrupted a communion service to seize a piece of communion bread from a man who had pocketed it rather than eaten it.[118] Thirty years later, the Consistory disciplined a rural elder named Pierre Jaquemin who tried to steal the leftover bread following the communion service in the parish of Céligny—although it is not clear whether this was a case of Catholic behavior or simple theft.[119] Over the years, Geneva's ministers established an informal protocol to regulate some of the special circumstances and difficulties surrounding Geneva's quarterly celebration of the Supper. Ministers were instructed to deny the sacrament to men and women who wore ostentatious or provocative clothing.[120] Likewise, people who were insane or seriously mentally impaired were not allowed to take the sacred elements.[121] On the other hand, deaf and mute congregants who displayed a Christian lifestyle were welcome at the Table.[122] So too, people believed to be demon-possessed (les demoniaques) were permitted to commune—as long as they were "peaceable" and "in their right mind."[123] Remarkably, both Calvin and Beza allowed, at least in principle, water to be substituted for sacramental wine in exceptional cases when the fruit of the vine was scarce or would cause serious health problems for the celebrant. Even so, there is no evidence that water was ever served at a communion service in Geneva over the course of the sixteenth century.[124]

By far the most contentious debate concerning Eucharistic practice during the generation after Calvin was over the question of whether elders should be permitted to administer the communion cup. In keeping with the stated requirements of the *Ecclesiastical Ordinances*, the standard practice in Geneva's churches during the sixteenth century was that ministers distributed the communion bread in the Lord's Supper and that church elders or deacons administered the cup.[125] Due to the dubious moral quality of some of the elders (gardes) in Geneva's small rural parishes, the Venerable Company in 1600 granted countryside pastors permission to administer both the bread *and* the cup in the Lord's Supper when circumstances required it.[126] Four years later, however, the Company rescinded this provision, mandating once again that the cup must be administered by the elders rather than the ministers. Jacques Royer, pastor of the parish of Céligny, was particularly upset by this volte-face and demanded an explanation, which the Company provided in April of 1604, pointing (among other things) to the fact that the custom of elder participation in the Lord's Supper was a long-standing practice in Geneva's church, had been endorsed by Calvin, had not previously been viewed as controversial, and was justified in view of the semi-ministerial function of the eldership attested to in Scripture. At the same time, the Company warned of the scandal that would ensue among reformed churches elsewhere if such "changes and novelty" were introduced into Geneva's church.[127] Royer was not convinced by these arguments, insisting that the role of elder was strictly a *lay* office and noting that Calvin's *Catechism* itself stipulated that only ministers of the Word should administer the sacraments in the church.[128] Appealing both to his conscience and to Calvin's *Catechism*, Royer thereafter refused to allow the elders of his parish to assist in the celebration of the Lord's Supper. What began as a civilized disagreement on a minor point of doctrine soon escalated into a bitter feud between the Company of Pastors and Royer, who lashed out in public against his colleagues and refused to submit to their collective judgment. From Royer's perspective, the Company of Pastors was overly harsh and was abusing its authority under the pretense of remaining faithful to Calvin's legacy. For Simon Goulart, Jean Jaquemot, and the other ministers, Royer was a "rebel against the order of the church" who possessed a "restless and contentious" spirit. This judgment seemed confirmed when Royer began to muster support from foreign reformed churches against both the Company of Pastors and Geneva's magistrates.[129] Jacques Royer was finally excommunicated by the Consistory for the sin of "rebellion" in the summer of 1605, and thereafter deposed from his office and expelled from the territory by Geneva's magistrates.[130] The controversy was far from settled, however. In the years that followed, Royer continued to attack his former colleagues back in Geneva, even as his views regarding a strictly "lay" office of elder won a wide hearing in the French reformed churches. Finally, in 1609, the nineteenth National Synod of Saint-Maixent struck a compromise on the issue that indicated Royer's views had won a favorable hearing among many reformed delegates in France: though elders were allowed to administer the cup in the Lord's Supper, they were not permitted to speak "so that it would be clear that the administration of the Sacrament belongs to the authority of the minister alone."[131] In retrospect, the controversy that swirled around the person of Jacques Royer in 1604–1605 highlights a number of characteristics of religious life in Geneva that we have noted before. Even minor innovations in religious practice were viewed with suspicion. Ministers who voiced public dissent or challenged the collective will of the Company of Pastors did not remain in office very long. And too, the memory of Calvin was formative in shaping religious policy in Geneva after 1564, although his legacy was oftentimes debated and applied in various ways.

4. Pastoral Visitation

Throughout this study it has been evident that Calvin and Geneva's Company of Pastors were committed to a model of pastoral work that involved intensive, personal interaction with Geneva's townspeople and country folk. The proclamation of God's Word in public assemblies was crucial, but not sufficient in itself. The ministers believed that they needed to know and show personal care for the men and women in their parishes, helping them apply the truths of God's Word to their particular life circumstances and challenges to promote personal godliness and spiritual reformation. "It is not enough that a pastor in the pulpit should teach all the people together," Calvin once noted, "if he does not add particular instruction as necessity requires or occasion offers."[132] Consequently, the Venerable Company expected that all of Geneva's ministers would pray for their parishioners, instruct them in the catechism, nourish them on the sacrament, offer them spiritual counsel and consolation, correct their sinful behavior through discipline, and visit them in their homes. Calvin and his colleagues often used the analogy of the shepherd—and appealed to the example of Jesus as the Good Shepherd—to emphasize this important pastoral dimension of the minister's spiritual vocation. In a sermon treating Jesus' famous charge to Peter, "Feed my sheep" in John 21:15, Theodore Beza highlighted these pastoral responsibilities:

> It is not only necessary that [a pastor] have a general knowledge of his flock, but he must also know and call each of his sheep by name, both in public and in their homes, both night and day. Pastors must run after lost sheep, bandaging up the one with a broken leg, strengthening the one that is sick.... In sum, the pastor must consider his sheep more dear to him than his own life, following the example of the Good Shepherd.[133]

One of the primary ways in which Geneva's ministers tried to meet the personal needs of their parishioners was through household visitations. During his years in Strasbourg, Calvin instituted regular personal interviews with the members of his French refugee congregation to assure that they were prepared to take the Lord's Supper. In a letter to Farel in 1540, Calvin argued that this kind of personal oversight served as a necessary replacement for the Catholic sacrament of Penance, giving reformed pastors the opportunity to instruct the ignorant, reprove the unrepentant, and console those who were experiencing spiritual struggles.[134] After returning to Geneva, Calvin and his colleagues won permission from the Small Council in 1550 to visit the households of their parishes four times annually to examine the behavior and doctrine of servants and foreigners.[135] During the years that followed, the Venerable Company expanded this program of visitation to include interviews of all the adults and children in the city while at the same time reducing the frequency of visits to once a year. This system of annual household visitation was enacted as church law in the revised *Ecclesiastical Ordinances* of 1561, which stipulated that every year before Easter, Geneva's pastors, accompanied by an elder and a *dizenier*, were to visit all of the households in their parishes in order "to examine all persons regarding their Christian faith, so that no one will come to the Lord's Supper without a knowledge of the basis of their salvation."[136] These interviews not only protected the sacrament from being profaned, but also provided Calvin and his colleagues a venue in which to engage their parishioners in holy conversation: instructing them in Christian truth, correcting their sinful behavior, and consoling them as circumstances required.[137] The close connection between visitations, moral correction, and the sacrament of the Table indicates that Calvin's program of annual household visitations was intended to fulfill the pastoral need once served by the Catholic sacrament of penance. As Herman Selderhuis has recently observed: for Calvin, "the confessional was not thrown out, but was relocated to the living room."[138]

The annual visitation in reformed Geneva included several key elements. After calling together the members of the household (or several households), the ministers began by examining the parents, children, and servants to determine whether they were able to explain their Christian faith and had a knowledge of the *Catechism*. The pedagogical function of the visitation was thus of great importance. The ministers and elders then inquired whether the members of the family were attending sermons and participating in the sacraments, and investigated possible interpersonal conflicts or behavioral problems within the household. The young apprentice from Basel, André Ryff, who worked in Geneva from 1560–1563, remembered the annual visitation in this fashion: "The ministers gather together the residents of six to eight households, both young and old, to interrogate and examine them, requiring them to give an account of their faith and the *Catechism* before they take the Lord's Supper."[139] The registers of the Consistory indicate that household visitations were a highly effective instrument in identifying troubled households and spotting immoral behavior. In fact, many times the interrogation at visitation served as a prelude for consistorial discipline, as when Calvin discovered in 1554 that a sailor named Jacques Verna was repeatedly soliciting his step-daughter for sex, or when the visitors to the household of Pierre Requens in 1596 learned that the father had so neglected his four-year-old son that the lad had starved to death.[140] Because of the intrusive nature of these interviews, a sizeable number of Geneva's residents resisted opening their front doors and exposing their private lives to their elders and ministers. During the sixteenth and early seventeenth century, it was relatively common for townspeople to hide in their houses or abandon the city when the minister and elder came to visit. The ill-tempered minister Raymond Chauvet was especially hated—and avoided—at visitation time. So too, disciplinary records indicate that the ministers sometimes encountered criticism or open hostility during the visit. An armor polisher named Pierre Vanier mocked the minister and elder who visited him and quoted Scripture against them. A butcher named Jacques de Joux told the *dizenier* that he'd rather go to Consistory than be visited by his minister Jean Pinault, because Pinault only spoke to him about his financial debts. When Jean Trembley visited the household of Jean "the Braggart" Renault in 1569, the minister found the man seething with anger because Trembley in a recent sermon had described his congregation at St. Gervais as a pack of "devils." Had it not been for the grace of God (the Consistory record reports), Renault would have incited his entire household against the visitors.[141]

In addition to the annual visitations at Easter, Geneva's ministers conducted less formal visits in their parishes throughout the year. As noted in chapter 7, Calvin, Beza, Goulart, and their colleagues sometimes visited defendants after they had been disciplined by Consistory in order to monitor their spiritual progress or to assist them achieve reconciliation in personal relationships. Geneva's pastors also visited parishioners who were suffering bereavement and extreme poverty. When the Company of Pastors learned in the summer of 1589 that Geneva's garrison at Bonne had fallen to Savoyard armies, and that three hundred fifty Genevan soldiers had been slaughtered, the ministers all agreed "to try to visit the bereaved families to console them as much as we are able."[142] Two decades later, when seventeen reputed demoniacs arrived in the city, making a racket and causing scandal, the Venerable Company resolved that "all of us will try to do our duty in this matter by visits and prayers."[143] Geneva's ministers also kept a look out for families that were experiencing extreme poverty so as to offer spiritual support and coordinate special assistance through the city hospital. Thus, for example, in 1601 the Venerable Company deputed the elderly pastor Jean Pinault to "visit and assist" a desperately poor family that was struggling to care for a son who was both paralyzed and mentally handicapped.[144] On another occasion, the city ministers along with the *dizeniers* undertook a general canvass of their neighborhoods to identity Geneva's poorest households, in hopes of allocating meager public charity more effectively.[145]

The *Ecclesiastical Ordinances* also required Geneva's ministers to take turns visiting the city prison, the Evesché, every Saturday afternoon to admonish and console the prisoners.[146] During this visit, the appointed minister addressed the spiritual needs of individual prisoners, and sometimes preached a brief sermon for the instruction and edification of all. Over the decades, Geneva's ministers occasionally expressed concern, even horror, at conditions they witnessed in the city prison and took concrete steps to correct the situation. In 1565, the Consistory complained to the magistrates that prisoners were being mistreated at the Evesché. Thirty years later, the city jailer Paul Voisin was reprimanded by the Consistory for striking one of the prisoners—a battery that Simon Goulart himself witnessed during the weekly visit.[147] In 1604, Charles Perrot reported to the Venerable Company the desperate condition of a prisoner named Pierre Gayet who had descended into suicidal depression after being chained to his bed in his dark cell for several months. The Company sent Perrot to the Small Council to request that mercy be extended to Gayet, and then instructed ministers who visited the prison in the future to "give [Gayet] some company, especially at night, and to visit him as often as possible in order to instruct and comfort him."[148]

Another way that Geneva's ministers cared for prisoners was by accompanying criminals to the scaffold to hear their final confessions and to call them to repentance and faith in the last moments of their lives. A striking example of this is seen in the case of the murderer Antoine de Goelles who, in November 1582, was executed for having assassinated one of Geneva's archenemies, a Savoyard nobleman named Gaspard de Grailly, and afterward pillaging his chateau and burning it to the ground. Theodore Beza accompanied Goelles to the field of Plainpalais, where the scaffold had been erected, and then asked him a series of questions intended to elicit his heartfelt confession of the murder, as well as make it clear that Geneva's magistrates had played no role in the crime. Once Goelles had made a full confession, his eyes were covered with a handkerchief, and Beza recited a final prayer: "Lord God, I pray that as the physical eyes of Antoine are now covered, you might open the eyes of his faith so that he might see your son Jesus Christ." Goelles prayerfully responded, "Oh God, I pray that it might be so," and "Oh God, give me your grace." Moments later, Goelles's body swung lifelessly from the scaffold.[149]

The visitation of the sick was among the most important duties expected of Geneva's pastors week to week. The *Ecclesiastical Ordinances* required all inhabitants of the city and countryside to call for a minister when they, or a loved one, had been bedridden for three days or longer so that they might benefit from the minister's spiritual consolation and instruction in the Word of God.[150] Though not all Genevans obeyed this law, most did.[151] Calvin's liturgy of 1542 included general guidelines to assist pastors as they conducted these visitations. According to these guidelines, it was the minister's duty

> to visit the sick, and console them according to the Word of God, showing
> them that everything they are suffering and enduring comes from the hand
> of God and his good providence, and that he sends nothing to his faithful
> people except for their good and salvation.[152]

In the liturgy, Calvin offered special advice for pastors as they consoled ill parishioners facing imminent death. When sick persons were terrified of death, Calvin advised, the pastor should remind them that death was not able to destroy Christians, since they have Jesus Christ as their guide and protector, who will lead them to life eternal. When terminally ill patients found their consciences troubled by their sins, the pastor should remind them of God's mercy and the salvation promised to those who embrace Jesus Christ by faith. Even in the shadow of death, poor sinners could rest in God's goodness and find safe refuge in his Son.[153]

Pastoral care for the sick was never more urgent, nor more dangerous, than when plague visited Geneva. During the sixteenth century, Geneva's hospital for plague victims was located several hundred yards outside the walled city in the field of Plainpalais, next to the place of execution and the cemetery. During seasons when the scourge of disease threatened the city, members of the Company of Pastors were appointed to visit the hospital to offer spiritual consolation to the seriously ill and dying. Some of the ministers undertook this dangerous assignment with compassion and courage; for others, the fear of contracting the contagion reduced them to cowards. The responsibility of providing pastoral care to people infected by the plague invariably placed in sharp relief the gravity of the minister's calling and the personal costs that came with it.

When the plague arrived in Geneva in the fall of 1542, one of the ministers named Pierre Blanchet—whom the magistrates praised as a man with a "big heart"—volunteered to relocate outside the city and visit the plague hospital so that he might "console the poor infected people."[154] Calvin reported Blanchet's election in a letter to Viret, at the same time expressing his personal fears of the potential dangers:

> The pestilence also begins to rage here with greater violence, and few who are at all affected by it escape its ravages. One of our colleagues was to be set apart for attendance upon the sick. Because Pierre [Blanchet] offered himself, all readily acquiesced. If anything happens to him, I fear that I must take the risk upon myself, for as you observe, because we are debtors to one another, we must not be wanting to those who, more than any others, stand in need of our ministry.

Calvin advised Viret that pastors should not jeopardize the well-being of the larger church for the sake of caring for individual persons. But even so, duty must always trump fear: "So long as we are in this ministry, I do not see that any pretext will avail us, if, through fear of infection, we are found wanting in the discharge of our duty when there is most need of our assistance."[155]

The following spring when the plague returned to Geneva, the magistrates took aggressive steps to contain the epidemic: dogs and cats, which were thought to be carriers of the disease, were exterminated; the law courts were closed until after the harvest; the sick were confined at home or sent to the plague hospital. On May 11, 1543, the brave Pierre Blanchet was once again appointed to provide pastoral care for the sick and, three days later, he returned to the plague hospital. By the end of the month he had contracted the disease and died.[156] Blanchet's death precipitated a crisis within the ranks of the Company of Pastors, as Calvin and his colleagues struggled for nearly a week to find a replacement for him. No one from the Venerable Company was willing to undertake the assignment. At the same time, the magistrates mandated that, because of Calvin's international stature and importance for the Genevan church, his name should be removed from the roster of potential candidates—an exemption that must certainly have bred tension, if not outright resentment, among his colleagues. The Venerable Company finally resorted to drawing lots to select pastors for the plague hospital. But the men whose names were chosen refused to accept the charge, declaring in the presence of the magistrates that even though this duty "belongs to their office," nonetheless, "God has still not given them the grace of strength and constancy needed to go to the said hospital."[157] Finally, a young minister named Mathieu de Geneston broke the impasse by stepping forward and volunteering to offer spiritual consolation to the sick at the plague hospital. A short time afterward Geneston began making periodic visits to plague victims in the hospital at Plainpalais; like Blanchet, he soon contracted the disease and died.[158]

The plague of 1542–44 was hardly the Company of Pastors' finest hour. The crisis raised serious concerns about the ministers' level of commitment to their spiritual flock *in extremis*, and, no doubt, gave Geneva's townspeople one more reason to resent the city's foreign-born pastoral company. The plague years also laid bare important questions of pastoral protocol, strategy, and theology that the ministers debated over the next three decades. Given Calvin's principle of the equality of the pastoral office, was it justifiable to exempt Geneva's most prominent ministers from caring for people afflicted with contagious diseases? Should the responsibility of providing spiritual care for plague victims fall on one or two men alone, or should all of Geneva's ministers be involved in this crucial pastoral work, despite the risks? Given the ministers' commitment to the doctrine of God's sovereignty over human illness and death, was it appropriate for them to take steps to protect themselves from infection? Where was the line between necessary precaution and pastoral neglect, between bold faith and rash presumption?

These issues became urgent once more in August of 1564, several months after Calvin's death, when the plague returned to Geneva. The Company of Pastors debated at length the right course to take. Several ministers insisted that each pastor should be responsible for visiting his own parishioners that were quarantined at the plague hospital; in so doing, they would demonstrate that "God is powerful to protect" the person who "devotes himself to helping the victims of such a sickness in accordance with his vocation."[159] The majority, however, saw this as too risky and defended the traditional practice of choosing one colleague by lot for the dangerous assignment. The next question proved equally contentious: should Theodore Beza, as Calvin's successor, be exempt from the lottery? Several members of the Venerable Company argued against such an exemption given that all of Geneva's ministers shared the same charge and the same divine calling. Moreover, they pointed to the examples of prominent reformed ministers such as Oecolampadius in Basel, Bucer in Strasbourg, and Bullinger in Zurich who were known to have fulfilled their pastoral calling by visiting people infected with deadly disease. Even Calvin himself had visited plague victims when he served the French congregation in Strasbourg.[160] Despite this line of argument, Beza's name was removed from consideration, and, after a prayer, the Venerable Company proceeded to the election, choosing the minister Jean Le Gaigneux. Even so, the matter was still not entirely settled. Several days later, wishing to protect "so excellent a man" as

Le Gaigneux, Geneva's senators recommended that the Venerable Company choose in his place two lay superintendents who might provide for the spiritual needs of sick people both inside and outside the city. After still more discussion, the Company of Pastors rejected this proposal, partly out of fear of public perception and partly out of the conviction that God had appointed ministers to fulfill this pastoral office, no matter how dangerous. Several days later Le Gaigneux moved his residence outside the city and began his ministry to the plague victims at the hospital. As a precaution, however, he did not actually enter the hospital but consoled the sick from outside their windows.[161]

The epidemic returned to Geneva with a vengeance four years later. Between 1568 and 1571, as many as three thousand townspeople died of the plague. In the midst of the panic, the civil authorities detained, interrogated, and tortured more than one hundred people under suspicion of being witches or plague-spreaders (les engraisseurs); those who confessed were executed by burning at Champel outside the city.[162] During the course of this protracted crisis, the ministers enacted important changes in their protocol for caring for the sick and dying. Before 1570, the Company of Pastors continued to employ the lottery system (with Beza's name being exempt), electing one minister to console the sick at the plague hospital and a second minister to visit people quarantined in their homes. By 1570, however, Beza as the moderator of the Company found this pastoral approach unacceptable. In an impassioned speech before the Small Council in March, Beza insisted that he should be included in the lottery. As a minister of the gospel, he argued, it was his responsibility before God "to fulfill all the duties that his office required, which included chiefly the consolation of poor sick people." The responsibility for overseeing pastoral care for the sick belonged to the church, not the magistrates. Moreover, Beza pointed out, giving preferential treatment to one pastor over his colleagues was both wrong and dangerous, because it would "give an opening to the devil to stir up schism among those who were all called to one and the same office."[163] In the face of Beza's persuasive appeal, the Small Council relented and permitted his name to be added to the roster in the next lottery (though it was not chosen). More important, the reformer's commitment to Calvin's twin principles of the equality of the pastoral office and the duty of each minister to care for the seriously ill translated into a new procedure for ministering to plague victims. When the epidemic returned in the summer of 1571, the lottery system was dispensed with entirely; instead, each minister was assigned to care for the plague victims within his own parish, and Beza and his colleagues took turns each week visiting the plague hospital.[164] This procedure became the standard practice thereafter. During the plague of 1578, for example, the Company of Pastors rejected with strong words the magistrates' efforts to reinstate the lottery system or to appoint foreign ministers to visit the plague hospital so as to protect the city ministers from the contagion. For the ministers, the pastoral vocation required that each of them "faithfully and courageously" care for "their afflicted sheep" during times of plague. In a similar fashion, the Venerable Company judged the magistrates' suggestion to employ foreign pastors to care for Geneva's plague victims as "against our duty and unworthy of all consideration."[165]

Clearly, seasons of plague not only tested the courage of Geneva's ministers, but also forced them to reconsider the nature and responsibilities of their pastoral calling. It is somewhat ironic that, by the early 1570s, Beza and his colleagues had established a protocol for caring for plague victims that, even though it deviated from Calvin's practice, was more consistent with Calvin's philosophy of pastoral care. Three commitments were primary: the church, not the magistrates, should oversee pastoral care; no minister was to hold superior rank over his colleagues; and all men called to the pastoral office had the responsibility to care for their parishioners who were sick and dying. Important practical questions remained, however, about the limits of the pastor's responsibilities in the face of deadly contagion. Did the minister defy God's providence when he employed safeguards to protect himself from the plague? Did a pastor's obligations to his wife and family supersede his responsibility to his spiritual flock? Was it ever justifiable for a pastor to abandon a sick parishioner in the interest of self-preservation? Beza addressed these questions directly in a small treatise entitled *Questions Regarding the Plague* (1579).[166]

Beza's *Questions Regarding the Plague* was written in part to address local concerns and in part to refute a treatise written by a reformed pastor in Aarberg named Christophe Lüthard, which had argued that plagues are deadly, not because they are contagious, but because they are an expression of God's punishment against sinners. From this, Lüthard had concluded that it was inadmissible for Christians to take precautions or flee from the plague.[167] While Beza agreed with Lüthard's premise that plagues were sent by the providence of God to punish sinners, he rejected his conclusions. To say that diseases were sent by God in no way precluded the possibility that God also accomplished his providential designs to heal or kill through various secondary causes, whether they be medicines or infectious diseases.[168] Scripture made clear that the poison of vipers was deadly and diseases such as leprosy contagious. Experience also demonstrated that "many diseases are contracted by handling and touching," and that medicines were sometimes helpful to counteract the effects of illness.[169] Hence, Beza noted, "even as God has ordained that some people will not die from the plague, so also he has appointed remedies which, as much as it is in their power, people may use to avoid the danger of the plague."[170]

Beza next turned his attention to the practical question of whether and under what circumstances Christians should flee from a deadly plague. Beza's general advice was this: it was perfectly acceptable, indeed wise, for Christians to flee the plague as long as they fulfilled their duty of piety toward God and charity toward their neighbors.[171] Both reason and experience demonstrated that flight was one of the most effective strategies for avoiding infectious disease. Nevertheless, men and women who contemplated flight were warned that they must never place their own safety above that of their spouses, families, neighbors, and fellow citizens. When the choice was not clear, Beza suggested that those Christians were less culpable who remained behind when they might have fled, than those who fled when they should have remained behind.[172] This, then, was Beza's advice for the majority of Christian men and women. However, those whom God had placed in public offices such as magistrates and Christian ministers had greater responsibility for the common good during times of extreme danger and plague. Beza stated the requirements of pastors in uncompromising terms: "It would be something very shameful, indeed wicked, to even imagine a faithful pastor who abandons one of his poor sheep in the hour when he especially needs heavenly consolation."[173] Whereas the sheep might flee danger, under most circumstances the shepherd must not. Beza concluded *Questions Regarding the Plague* with a poignant personal example drawn from the years when he served as a Greek professor in Lausanne:

> About twenty-eight years ago, when I was sick with the plague in Lausanne, my other colleagues, including that exceptional man of blessed memory, Pierre Viret, were prepared to visit me. And John Calvin himself also sent by courier letters in which he offered every type of kindness to me. But I did not permit any of them to visit me, lest I should be judged to have been thinking only of myself. For the disadvantage to the Christian commonwealth would have been very great had those illustrious men died.[174]

Beza's parting comment indicates both his long-standing affection for Calvin and Viret, as well as his own pastoral instincts: had the shoe been on the other foot, with Viret and Calvin stricken with the plague, Beza would have thrown all caution to the wind and visited his two friends at their sick beds.[175] This was not only the responsibility of a friend, it was the duty of a pastor.

5. Spiritual Counsel and Consolation

To live in sixteenth-century Geneva was to live a precarious existence. The world of Calvin, Beza, and Goulart was a world of wars and rumblings of war; it was a world populated by witches and demoniacs; a world where people were afflicted by disease, famine, and sudden disaster. It was a world of foul streets, meager crop yields, poor hygiene, and crushing poverty. In this world death was never far away. "Innumerable are the evils that beset human life," Calvin once noted. "Wherever you turn, all things around you not only are hardly to be trusted but almost openly menace, and seem to threaten immediate death."[176] As we have seen, Geneva's ministers accepted it as their responsibility to proclaim God's hope and salvation to people living and dying in this dangerous world, assuring them that God was both good and wise in his government over human affairs. Traces of this ministry of spiritual consolation appear from time to time in the written records of the Consistory and the Company of Pastors during this period: the ministers comfort parents mourning the loss of beloved children; they speak words of encouragement to husbands and wives experiencing personal tragedy or misfortune; they offer consolation at bedside to men and women who are ill or dying.[77] But as a general rule, these reports offer few details about what the ministers actually said or did to comfort people who were suffering. Greater insight as to the substance of the ministers' consolation is available when we examine their prayers, their letters, and their moral discourses on topics related to persecution, aging, illness, and death.

Throughout this study, we have observed the important place that prayer served in church life in Geneva between 1536 and 1609.[78] Children learned to pray through the *Catechism*. The daily preaching service began and ended with prayers. On Wednesdays and Sundays, Genevans observed a longer service of prayer that included Psalm singing, recitation of the Lord's Prayer by the congregation, and a lengthy pastoral prayer. In times of danger and crisis, the Venerable Company organized public services devoted to community prayer and fasting. More routinely, Calvin encouraged Christians to pray in their households, when rising from bed, before going to work, before and after meals, and when retiring at the end of the day.[79] "Words fail to explain how necessary prayer is," Calvin insisted. "Surely with good reason the Heavenly Father affirms that the only stronghold of safety is in calling upon his name." Through prayer, Christians are reminded of God's providential care for them, experience God's power to heal and help them, and receive assurance of God's grace to forgive their sins and bring them into eternal life. In sum, Calvin believed, "it is by prayer that we call [God] to reveal himself as wholly present to us."[80]

The prayers that Geneva's pastors offered on behalf of those who were suffering—the persecuted, the elderly, the sick, and the dying—provide important clues as to the nature of the consolation they provided their parishioners facing life's most difficult moments. Calvin's liturgy for the Wednesday and Sunday worship services included a long intercessory prayer in which the congregation raised up corporate petitions for friends and family members who were suffering.

> O God of all consolation, we pray for all those who are visited and chastised by the cross and tribulations, for people whom you have afflicted with the plague, or war or famine, for people suffering from poverty, prison, sickness, banishment, or other calamities of body or spirit. We pray that you might help them to recognize your fatherly care in these circumstances as you chastise them for their amendment. We pray that, as a result, they might turn their entire heart toward you, and being so converted, might receive full consolation and be delivered from all evil.[81]

The congregation next prayed for Christians facing persecution elsewhere in Europe, that they might be comforted in their afflictions and strengthened by the Holy Spirit to stand firm to the end. In the last part of the intercessory prayer, the ministers turned their attention to all Christians in general as they struggled against the weakness of their flesh and the enemies of their souls, the world, the devil, and sin: "Please strengthen us by your Holy Spirit and arm us with your graces, so that we might be able to resist continually all temptations and persevere in this spiritual battle, until we obtain the full victory, finally triumphing in your kingdom with our Captain and Protector, our Lord Jesus Christ. Amen."[182] This prayer of intercession on behalf of suffering Christians illustrates important themes in reformed attitudes toward human suffering. Though sickness and afflictions are the result of human sin and rebellion, God in his fatherly care uses them as instruments of his grace in the lives of his children. Christians thus pray, not for deliverance from all bodily afflictions on this earth, but that the Holy Spirit might strengthen the wavering faith of God's people, produce a spiritual harvest of repentance and holiness in their lives, and empower them to persevere amidst the fierce spiritual battles of this life to achieve the victor's crown with God in heaven.

These same themes are evident in the personal prayers of Geneva's ministers. Calvin's extemporaneous prayers, with which he concluded many of his daily sermons, frequently acknowledged that human suffering is part of God's sovereign purpose for his children and reflects his fatherly love for them.[183] Similarly, the three prayers that Simon Goulart included in his treatise *The Wise Old Man* (1605) reminded his readers that God sustains his beloved children through the weakness, diseases, and temptations that come with old age, and even uses these afflictions to set their affections on heaven.[184] This pastoral focus on human suffering, God's providence, and Christian consolation is particularly on display in Theodore Beza's *Household Prayers* (1603).[185] Beza intended this booklet of twenty-eight prayers to be a kind of primer for the Christian life, offering guidance and encouragement to believers as they prepared to read Scripture, conversed around the dinner table, celebrated the Lord's Supper, endured suffering, and faced the shadow of death. Beza's prayer entitled "On the Visitation of the Sick" is especially revealing in that we find a concise summary of the reformer's theology of suffering, as well as evidence of his pastoral approach to comforting sick persons at bedside. Beza begins this prayer by asserting that human diseases are God's "rod" and "medicine" given to remind men and women of their sins, to tame their fleshly desires, and to focus their attention on the future day of judgment when the wicked will be punished and the elect will enjoy everlasting joy in God's presence. The pastor therefore prays that this form of divine correction will accomplish its necessary effect, namely, that the sick person will repent of his sins and submit to God's will with confident faith:

Since it has pleased you, O just and merciful Father, to visit this poor sick person with your rod, afflicting him for his offenses, as he himself has confessed, we beseech you that…he may with quiet obedience bear your visitation, submitting himself willingly with all his heart to your holy will. [May he trust that you] strike him, not as a severe judge, but as a most merciful Father, whereby he may learn to rest his whole trust and assurance in your love, you who are the Author of his life.[186]

Beza goes on to pray that the medicine of affliction will not only serve to awaken the spiritual awareness of the sick patient, but also enable him to apprehend and desire (with the eyes of faith) the joys of heaven in God's presence. Because sick persons are especially prone to doubt and unbelief, Beza also petitions the Lord to strengthen the faith of the suffering believer so that "even to his last gasp, never fearing the temptations of Satan, of death, or of hell," he might be assured that "Christ has overcome them" and "broken their bonds."[187] To this point, Beza has not yet prayed for the physical healing of his sick parishioner. He now does this in a single sentence, entreating God that "if it be your pleasure to restore him to health, with the increase of your grace, may he yet serve among us to your glory." But, recognizing that it may not be God's design to grant physical healing, Beza adds the petition, "receive him into your heavenly Jerusalem…[and] grant him the life of his soul among your angels, until, by the resurrection of all flesh on the great day of the Lord, he may live as a whole man in the contemplation of your glory."[188] At the end of the prayer, Beza turns his attention to the friends and family members of the sick Christian, praying that the illness of their loved one may serve as a "mirror" in which they see the shortness and uncertainty of human life, motivating them to live more carefully for God's honor and service. In concluding the prayer for the sick person, the pastor invites the gathered household to join him in reciting the Lord's Prayer. Beza's prayer "On the Visitation of the Sick" thus reiterates central themes found in Calvin's liturgical prayer of intercession. God is sovereign over human illness and suffering. The Christian pastor offers prayers and words of consolation to help afflicted persons recognize and experience God's larger purposes in their suffering, including repentance, strengthened faith, a more intense desire for heaven, and a greater love for God. The highest goal of pastoral consolation is not physical comfort or healing; rather, it is deeper communion with Jesus Christ.

Geneva's pastors also provided spiritual consolation to God's people through the letters that they wrote. During their careers in Geneva, Calvin and Beza maintained epistolary contact with multiple dozens of correspondents throughout Western Europe, testifying to the fact that their religious influence, indeed their "parish," extended well beyond the shores of Lac Léman.[189] Many of the reformers' letters are brimming with theological insight and pastoral concern, offering modern readers a precious view into the manner in which they carried out the ministry of consolation. A particularly good example of this is seen in the correspondence between Theodore Beza and the Polish humanist Johannes Crato, personal physician to the Habsburg emperors Maximilian II and Rudoloph II.[190] Crato initiated contact with Beza in the mid-1570s to request his theological judgment on the *Confession* of the Bohemian Brethren—which Beza did in expansive detail.[191] Over the next decade, until Crato's death in 1585, the men wrote several letters to one another each year, reporting news from their respective outposts, discussing mutual friends, and sharing good books. By the early 1580s, as his health began to deteriorate, Crato became increasingly terrified of death. In a letter from November 1582, Crato poured out his deepest concerns and questions to his friend Beza. He reported that his physical illness had caused him to lose spiritual courage. Was his fear of death a sign that he lacked sufficient faith, as Calvin had once indicated? Was it a sign of God's judgment against him? Should not all sinners, Christians included, tremble before a holy God? Crato informed Beza that he was spending his days reading and meditating on the Scripture, leaning on Christ Jesus, the bread of life. He concluded his letter by asking for Beza's help and advice: "If I have written anything that in your judgment is wrong, please redirect me to the right path."[192]

Beza addressed his friend's "soul sickness" in a long, moving letter written in January 1583. It is a natural and good thing to think about death, he noted, for otherwise we would deceive ourselves and live like brute beasts. Indeed, the Word of God teaches us that we should be mindful of death, though not frightened by it, and even desire it because it is our entryway into the habitation of eternal happiness.[193] Beza explained that there are three primary reasons people fear death: either they consider life so precious that they do not wish to lose it, or they dread the painful separation of soul from body that comes with death, or they tremble at the dark uncertainty beyond the grave. Over the next several paragraphs, Beza mustered a variety of Old and New Testament passages to demonstrate that these human reasons for being terrified of death are ultimately unfounded. This present life is but a breath, full of evil and vanity. God uses the pain and suffering that Christians experience, even death itself, to bring glory to his name and achieve eternal blessing for his people. Quoting the Apostle Paul, Beza notes: "'Now if we suffer with Christ, we will also reign with Christ.' In the meantime, I admit that righteous people suffer, but through suffering, they will win the victory and obtain the eternal weight of glory that cannot be compared to the suffering of this present age."[194] And what of the grave? The fact that Jesus Christ defeated the grave and rose from the dead provides certain proof of the Christian's future resurrection and life with God in heaven. "Christ has triumphed over the first death so that we are made participants in his victory."[195] In the final paragraphs of Beza's letter to Crato, he addresses some of the specific concerns raised by his friend. How do we know that we are numbered among God's children who will experience divine mercy rather than judgment? Beza asserts that the

Christian's faith, along with the testimony of the Holy Spirit and the fruits of holiness that he produces in the life of the Christian, all bear witness to the believer's spiritual adoption. Moreover, Crato needs to know that even his ongoing struggle with sin is a sign that he is among God's children. "We should not be terrified at all by the contradiction between our fleshly desires that reject the Spirit's good, and the new man who rests in the law of God—as if this were to render our election and salvation uncertain. On the contrary, this is a most certain proof that the Spirit of adoption has been given to us."[196] Finally, Beza addressed the matter of fear itself. The fear of death has been a terrible, but unavoidable, quality of the human condition since the Garden of Eden, and Crato should not torment his conscience because he is afraid. Instead, the fearsomeness of death should motivate him to hate sin all the more and endeavor to shine forth God's light in the darkness of this world. Beza concluded with a prayer for his friend: "May God, our most merciful Savior strengthen us more and more by his Spirit so that, after weathering so many fierce storms and having sailed into that harbor of true tranquility, we might celebrate eternal triumph with him who has secured our victory."[197]

It appears that Johannes Crato found some encouragement from Beza's counsel. By return mail, Crato thanked Beza for his comforting letter and stated that "as long as I have life and eyesight, I will consult it often."[198] Though Crato remained bedridden, his sense of Christian assurance had in large part been revived. Over the next two years, the correspondence between the two men frequently cycled back to topics of death, Christian assurance, and the role that suffering plays in the Christian life. Beza continued to monitor Crato's condition, expressing pleasure that his friend's spiritual depression had abated somewhat, while at the same time sharing insights to console and encourage him. In one letter, from November 1583, Beza observed that "It is the Lord's custom to raise all the way to the heavens those people he has first brought down to hell.... Therefore, come on! Let us continue to fight strongly until we receive from him the prize for our struggle!"[199] On another occasion, Beza wrote, "Although I wish that your physical health were better, nevertheless I congratulate you that in this suffering you are discovering that statement of our most excellent Apostle to be altogether true: 'For those who love God, all things work together for good.'"[200] After struggling with chronic illness for several years, Johannes Crato finally passed from this world in 1585—but not before Beza had pronounced one last benediction on his friend: "Farewell, esteemed man! May the Lord, who hears your continual groans and has wrestled with you during this long and painful disease, sustain you by means of his invincible strength, until that time when, by his Spirit, we trust in his mercy with complete confidence."[201]

The priority that Geneva's ministers attached to pastoral consolation, as witnessed in their prayers and letters, is also evident in many of the books they wrote addressing practical spirituality and Christian devotion. Of all these works, Simon Goulart's two-volume *Christian Discourses* (1591, 1595) stands out, both in the important existential questions it addresses and in the rich insight and comfort it offers Christians facing life's most difficult circumstances.[202] In the conversational style of these discourses, the reader is able to imagine Simon Goulart, as pastor and spiritual guide, sharing words of instruction and consolation with members of his congregation during a household visit or beside their sickbeds. Suffering is inevitable, necessary, and profitable for the children of God, Goulart asserts. "No matter how great and powerful the afflictions might be, the faithful should not lose courage," for "the more the storm rages, the more the Christian's hope of gaining the Lord's help grows in their hearts."[203] In a discourse devoted to "Spiritual Wounds and Their Remedies," Goulart gives ten principles to be followed by Christian pastors, or "consolers" (*consolateurs*), as they apply the medicine of Scripture to the needs of suffering men and women. These principles are:

1. The pastor should know and have true compassion for the person suffering.
2. The pastor should encourage the ailing Christian to adore the judgment of God and be mindful of his mercy.
3. The pastor should conduct a careful examination of the conscience of the suffering person, probing its condition, deportments, and passions, so as to apply the proper kind spiritual consolation.
4. The pastor should have at hand a variety of examples of faithful Christians who faced similar afflictions and yet trusted in the grace of God.
5. The pastor should remind the afflicted Christian that other believers have remained faithful as they faced similar, or even worse, trials.
6. The pastor should listen to and affirm what the suffering person says, while gently expanding upon or correcting opinions that are confused or inaccurate.
7. The pastor should encourage the ailing person to draw God's light from the darkness of his suffering. For example, if the patient complains of weak faith, the pastor should point out that even this desire for more faith provides assurance that God will fortify and increase it.
8. The pastor who instructs the suffering believer should employ sharp warnings, combined with consolation and words of praise—yet avoid all flattery and dissimulation.
9. The pastor who consoles suffering people should know Scripture well and be skilled in fervent prayer. Pastoral counsel should return regularly to these central truths: suffering is part of the human condition; God is faithful to his children; God promises to help believers endure temptation.
10. The pastor must employ the words of Scripture judiciously so that the afflicted person can feed on them and be strengthened by them.[204]

Throughout the *Christian Discourses*, Goulart models many of these principles of spiritual consolation as he considers the pressing questions and concerns that trouble Christians throughout their earthly pilgrimages. What is the purpose of our lives? Why are some people wealthy and others poor? How should we handle sudden changes in our life circumstances? Is it permissible to delight in the destruction of the wicked? Why do the wicked frequently prosper and the righteous suffer? A sizeable number of Goulart's discourses address questions that are especially urgent to men and women facing the shadows of death: How do I know whether or not I am of the elect? Is it wrong to want to live longer? Is suicide an option for Christians? How should I prepare to die? What happens to my soul after death? What is heaven like?

Goulart in his *Christian Discourses* is particularly concerned to prepare Christians for physical death and assure them of God's love and protection during their final hours. In this sense, many of the discourses function as a kind of manual describing the art of dying well (*ars moriendi*). In his discourse "On Death," for example, Goulart lists seven spiritual exercises that Christians should practice as they reach the final hours of their lives: First, keep in mind the promises of the kingdom of God. Second, battle continuously the temptations of Satan by means of the Word of God. Third, pray that God will not allow you to be tempted beyond your strength. Fourth, contemplate with the eyes of your faith Jesus Christ, humiliated and exalted for your salvation. Fifth, forgive those who have sinned against you. Sixth, confess your faith and Christian hope. And finally, seventh, commend your soul to God.[205] As Christians approach death, Goulart recognizes, they are frequently tempted to doubt God's promised salvation and despair of their future hope. In this spiritual drama, Satan is especially active. Goulart's discourse "Remedies Against Satan's Temptations in our Final Hour" enumerates the stinging accusations and doubts that Satan launches against God's children as they struggle on their deathbeds. The voice of Satan accuses: "You are a miserable sinner, worthy of damnation." "Your sins are too great to be forgiven." "How do you know that the promise of the gospel pertains to you?" "Are you certain that your repentance and faith are genuine?" "How do you know that you are among God's elect?" In response to each of these attacks, Goulart provides the faithful Christian a ready answer, drawn from the pages of Scripture. For example, when Satan questions the believer's election, the Christian responds:

All true believers are sheep of Jesus Christ, elected in him to eternal life. Psalm 23 says that "The Lord is my shepherd." And Psalm 100 says "Know that the Lord is God. It is he who has made us, and we are his; we are his people and the sheep of his pasture." So too, Jesus Christ says in John 10, "My sheep hear my voice." I have heard this voice and heeded it. Thus, I am one of the sheep of this Great Shepherd, who has given his life to bring me into his sheepfold, having rescued me from your jaws, O roaring Lion.[206]

Clearly, Goulart believed that God's Word was to serve as the pastor's most important resource in caring for Christians on their deathbeds. Scripture is like a "pharmacy" for wounded souls, he asserted. It offers a "secure harbor for agitated consciences."[207]

For Simon Goulart, the basis for Christian hope was ultimately found in the faithfulness of God himself, who had promised to lead his children through the dark valley of death into his glorious presence in heaven. It was right and good, then, that Christians meditate on their glorious destiny, not only on their deathbeds, but throughout the entirety of their earthly pilgrimage. This was their goal; this was their resplendent reward. Accordingly, Goulart concluded the first volume of his *Christian Discourses* with a lengthy description of the final resurrection and eternal life in God's presence. The pastor's description of heaven is breathtaking:

> The eternal and blessed life with God in heaven, accompanied by rest and unspeakable glory, is the goal of the faith of Christians. This is the harbor of their hope, the refuge of all their desires, the crown of their consolation that they will certainly enjoy, having escaped from the travails of this miserable and fleeting earthly life, indeed, from death itself.
>
> They will receive in heaven...glorified bodies, healed of all evils, no longer afflicted by sin, ignorance, errors, illness, sadness, worry, fear, anguish, or enemies. They will be delivered from all pain and suffering. They will enjoy fully and completely the Lord their God, the fountain and inexhaustible treasure of all good things, who will pour out on them all his goodness, his infinite joy, with which he will satisfy all their thoughts and desires. They will see him and contemplate him face to face, without any clouds to obscure him. They will learn of God's wisdom with regard to the creation and redemption of his elect by means of Jesus Christ, and the reasons for his all-powerful and wondrous works. The eternal Father will disclose his burning and unspeakable love for them, which he demonstrated by sending his Son into the world to draw them from death into eternal life. His children will be moved by his gracious work, filled with wonder, contentment, and ineffable delight, and will love their heavenly Father with a burning love, submitting themselves fully to his wisdom with eager joy. And they will submit to him as their only sovereign and greatest good. And they will rejoice with continuous joy in his presence, magnifying his glory, singing of his goodness along with the holy Angels and the entire Church triumphant. There they will see Jesus Christ, the blessed virgin Mother, the Patriarchs, the Prophets, the Apostles, and all the faithful who have preceded them, including their family members and friends who died in repentance and faith. This entire company together, with one heart and voice, will recall the goodness and infinite blessings God has shown them, celebrating with songs of thanksgiving the praises of the Father, the Son, and the Holy Spirit....
>
> Thus, eternal life is the end and fulfillment of all good things, for which God has purchased us through his Son. This is the goal on which our gaze

should be fixed throughout our earthly pilgrimage. This is the treasure that we should unceasingly desire. This is the hour and the blessing to which all the plans and efforts of our lives should be inclined.... This is our true country, our permanent city, in which our citizenship has been acquired by the merit of the death of Jesus Christ. This is the home that we long for, amidst the banishments, the weariness, the dangerous fears of this valley of misery and the shadow of death. This is the safe refuge and the beautiful harbor toward which we sail amidst so many waves and storms that constantly trouble the world. This is the blessed land where we will dwell by means of death.[208]

For Simon Goulart, perfect fellowship with God in heaven is the ultimate goal of the Christian's life and faith. Pastors provide spiritual consolation to suffering saints by helping them turn the eyes of their faith away from the troubles and afflictions of this life, to focus instead on their safe harbor, their true country, the blessed land that God has prepared for them in heaven.

Geneva's ministers stood between two worlds. They lived their lives and conducted their ministries in the hard-scrabble, trouble-filled, ever-changing world of sixteenth- and early seventeenth-century Geneva. At the same time, they proclaimed the Christian message of hope and salvation, anticipating a permanent city—the blessed land—where all of God's people, men, women, and children alike, would live in peace and unspeakable joy in communion with the Triune God forever. Calvin, Beza, Goulart, and the other pastors of Geneva saw it as their vocation as Christian ministers to bring these two worlds closer together. As seen in this chapter, the Venerable Company promoted this God-centered life through an intensive program of pastoral care and religious instruction that spanned the whole of the Christian life, from the cradle to the grave. As they proclaimed the Word in sermon and sacrament, as they taught and comforted God's people through catechism, visitation, and spiritual conversation, Geneva's ministers believed that they were not only religious workers, constructing a city church, they were spiritual shepherds caring for the Master's flock, serving God's larger purposes for this world and the next.

TOURISTS WHO VISIT MODERN-day Geneva are sometimes surprised to discover that no grave or headstone exists to commemorate the life of the reformed minister John Calvin. In accordance with Calvin's last wishes, his body was buried in a public cemetery outside the walls of Geneva, "without any pomp or show" and with no stone to mark the spot. Today, the precise location of Calvin's final resting place is not known. Even so, Calvin's spiritual legacy has demonstrated tenacious resilience over the centuries. As the French historian Lucien Febvre once observed, "Calvin did not build himself a tomb of dead stones; he constructed it from living stones."[1] The truest monument to Calvin's life was a reformed church, built on the Christian gospel, organized according to the fourfold office, committed to preaching the Word of God and to right worship.

Among the "living stones" that Calvin left behind was the company of reformed ministers who labored in Geneva's city and countryside parishes. As we have seen, the long-term success of Calvin's religious program depended to a significant degree on these lesser known ministers who succeeded him, men who were entrusted with daily responsibilities for preaching, performing the sacraments, enforcing discipline, and providing pastoral care in Geneva's churches. More than one hundred thirty men belonged to the Venerable Company between 1536 and 1609, constituting a colorful cast of characters that included a bookish theologian named Lambert Daneau, a courageous countryside minister named Jean Gervais, a tenderhearted father named Antoine de Chandieu, a wizened patriarch named Theodore Beza, a ferocious preacher named Raymond Chauvet, and a heavenly minded spiritual adviser named Simon Goulart.

Several factors were important in unifying this disparate collection of ministers into a single, largely cohesive Company. The overwhelming majority of Geneva's ministers during the sixteenth century were French refugees whose religious convictions had been galvanized and intensified by Catholic persecution back in their homeland. This alone goes far in explaining the pastors' intense loyalty to the Frenchman John Calvin and the brand of reformed Christianity that he sought to establish in Geneva. After the founding of Calvin's Academy in 1559, the majority of these foreign-born ministers received at least part of their theological training in Geneva where, in addition to studying reformed doctrine at the feet of Calvin and Beza, they were shaped by a common religious culture that included daily preaching services, academic disputations, and rigorous moral discipline. Candidates for pastoral office in Geneva were subject to a uniform process of examination that required them to subscribe to the city's official theology, articulated in the *Confession of Faith*, the *Ecclesiastical Ordinances*, Calvin's *Catechism* and liturgy, and (somewhat later) Calvin's *Institutes*. The unity of the Venerable Company was further strengthened by institutions such as the Congregation and the Ordinary Censure, which served to regularize the ministers' interpretation of Scripture, foster fraternal correction, and encourage the mediation of conflicts. Finally, by the beginning of the seventeenth century, it had become common practice for young ministers to marry the sisters, daughters, and nieces of their pastoral colleagues, forging familial networks and social alliances that intensified their commitment to one another. All of these factors, then, were crucial in shaping the ministers' theology and practice, and creating a relatively cohesive pastoral culture in Geneva during Calvin's lifetime and in the following decades.

Calvin's commanding personality and formidable intellect were also important in giving shape to pastoral life in Geneva and establishing confessional solidarity within the Venerable Company. As we have seen, Calvin was an ardent opponent of ecclesiastical preeminence and throughout his career championed the principle of the equality of Christian ministers. Even so, the reformer possessed special moral authority as the chief architect of Geneva's church and the moderator of the Company of Pastors. Calvin's theological writings and liturgy defined the substance and boundaries of orthodoxy in the Genevan church. So too, Calvin exercised strategic leadership in recruiting would-be pastors and dismissing colleagues whom he judged to be incompetent, theologically unsound, or disloyal to his leadership. During the 1540s and 1550s, Calvin's international stature and theological vision served as a kind of gravitational field that drew to Geneva some of French Protestantism's most gifted preachers and theologians, including men like Nicolas Des Gallars, Michel Cop, Lambert Daneau, and Theodore Beza. At the same time, Calvin's combative personality broached no rivals in Geneva; outspoken critics who attacked his leadership or theology—men such as Jean Ferron, Sebastian Castellio, or Jerome Bolsec—were not welcomed in the reformed city for very long. Consequently, by the final years of his life, Calvin had succeeded in creating a pastoral company in Geneva that was intensely committed both to the reformed faith and to his theological leadership. More than simply the architect and recognized leader of the church, Calvin had become both a theological guide and a spiritual father to many of Geneva's ministers.

Theodore Beza and his pastoral colleagues took very much to heart Calvin's final exhortation to "change nothing." Following the reformer's death in 1564, Beza assumed the role of Calvin's loyal disciple, exercising his sizeable theological gifts and deft political leadership to defend Geneva's church order and preserve Calvin's theological vision. As noted throughout this study, under Beza's leadership the Company of Pastors jealously guarded its prerogative over religious life in Geneva and resisted efforts to modify church doctrine and practice. No change was permitted to Geneva's public theology as expressed in the *Confession of Faith* and Calvin's *Catechism*. So too, though revisions to Geneva's liturgy and practice of worship were sometimes proposed, they were rarely adopted. Thus, for example, the Venerable Company disallowed the practice of kneeling at worship services; it rebuffed efforts to reintroduce religious holidays such as Christmas to the church calendar; it fought against flamboyant preaching styles that deviated from Calvin's unadorned homiletic; it resisted the magistrates' efforts to adopt the use of leavened bread in the Lord's Supper. Such resistance to change was born of a deep-seated conservatism among Beza and his colleagues. From their perspective, religious change was dangerous, not only because it threatened to undermine the biblical foundations of Geneva's reformed church, but also because it too easily sowed confusion among God's people and fostered disunity within the larger world of reformed churches. Antoine de La Faye stated this conservative principle as a basic maxim: "everyone has recognized that change and novelty are extremely dangerous, especially in ecclesiastical matters."[2]

If Beza and his colleagues were not bold innovators, neither were they mindless imitators of Calvin. This study has identified significant ways that religious life and pastoral practice *did* change in Geneva between 1536 and 1609, oftentimes in response to shifting political and religious circumstances. A number of these reforms reflected the Venerable Company's commitment to work out in practice implications of Calvin's theological program. Thus, for example, when the ministers called for periodic community-wide fast days in response to religious and political disasters in France during the 1560s and 1570s, they were introducing a new custom to religious life in Geneva that was, nonetheless, faithful to Calvin's theology of fasting articulated in the *Institutes*. So too, the Venerable Company's commitment to Calvin's doctrine of the equality of ministers led Beza and his colleagues in the early 1570s to abandon the lottery system and begin requiring *all* city and countryside ministers to visit plague victims in their parishes. This same commitment to the equality of the pastoral office was demonstrated in 1580 when Geneva's ministers abandoned the practice of the perpetual moderatorship and adopted, instead, a weekly presidency that rotated between members of the Venerable Company. In each of these instances, Geneva's ministers were more consistent than Calvin himself in working out the practical entailments of the reformer's pastoral theology. To a certain degree, the Consistory's changing approach to moral discipline after Calvin's death also indicates an effort to put into practice the theological values espoused by the reformer. As seen in chapter 7, after Calvin's victory over the Perrinists in 1555, the Consistory launched an aggressive campaign to impose broad moral reforms on Geneva's townspeople and country folk. Reaching a pinnacle in 1568, the annual number of excommunications declined significantly thereafter, so that, during the next four decades, annual suspension totals were actually below those registered during the last years of Calvin's lifetime. Though the decline of consistorial activity after 1568 was due in large part to magisterial pressure, it appears that Beza and Geneva's ministers had come to recognize that their frenetic disciplinary activity was excessive and failed to achieve the biblical purposes for discipline as outlined by Calvin. Church discipline was intended to be spiritual medicine that healed rather than harmed the patient.

Scholars of the reformed tradition have sometimes pitted Calvin against later Calvinists, arguing that Protestant "scholastic" theologians such as Beza, Daneau, Chandieu, and La Faye were guilty of adopting a rationalistic scheme of theology that fundamentally betrayed the doxological and Christological focus of Calvin's theological work. My study of the books published by Geneva's ministers from 1536 to 1609 challenges this thesis. During these decades, around 20 percent of the ministers' books may be classified as practical or devotional in nature, a significant number appearing after Calvin's death. Through their poetry, ethical treatises, Scripture meditations, published sermons, prayer collections, and moral discourses, Geneva's pastors such as Beza, Daneau, Chandieu, and Goulart applied the priorities of reformed theology to the ethical concerns and spiritual needs of new generations of reformed Christians in Europe, offering their readers biblical wisdom, practical instruction, and spiritual consolation. This rich, but largely forgotten, devotional tradition defies the conclusion of those who characterize Geneva's theology after Calvin as "abstract," "speculative," or "rationalistic." It is true that as Beza and his colleagues engaged Catholic and Lutheran opponents in their polemical writings, they frequently employed philosophical methods of analysis and argumentation that were (largely) foreign to Calvin's theology. The scholastic method, the ministers believed, was particularly well-suited to expose logical fallacies, penetrate to the essence of an argument, and lay bare the truth of Scripture. Yet even as they championed scholastic methods of theological argumentation, Beza, Daneau, Chandieu, and La Faye shared Calvin's commitment to the priority of revelation over human reason and consistently affirmed the importance of scriptural exegesis for arriving at Christian truth. Likewise, though in some of their dogmatic work Beza and Daneau modified or developed certain aspects of Calvin's theology (on such topics as Christian assurance, supralapsarian predestination, and the extent of the atonement), these changes were not a betrayal of Calvin's theological program per se, but reflected their commitment to interpret Scripture and apply Calvin's thought in light of new questions and new contexts. And, invariably, these subtle theological shifts occurred within the boundaries of Geneva's official orthodoxy.

The political authorities were the agents most responsible for change in Geneva's churches between 1536 and 1609. Around the turn of the century, Geneva's magistrates commenced an aggressive campaign to expand their jurisdiction over religious life in Calvin's city. Some of these changes were relatively benign, as when the Small Council pressed the Venerable Company to reintroduce the rite of the imposition of hands on pastoral candidates during ordination (a practice that Calvin himself had once endorsed a half century earlier). Other reforms mandated by Geneva's political authorities proved to be far more ominous for the church, prompting Goulart's complaint in 1603 that "our Company is now losing all its dignity and freedom."[3] Led by the powerful syndic Jacques Lect, the city's magistrates programmatically attacked the church's traditional prerogative over appointing preachers to vacant parishes, lending city pastors to foreign churches, electing ministers to the pastoral office, and structuring the role of moderator in the Company of Pastors. The most striking example of the magistrates' campaign to roll back the church's authority was witnessed when the Small Council in 1606 reversed the excommunications of two influential senators, effectively breaking the Consistory's monopoly over church discipline—a prerogative that Calvin had worked so hard to achieve fifty years earlier. It is probably not a coincidence that these important changes in the balance of power between church and state occurred at the same time that Beza was retiring from public life. For nearly four decades, Beza, as Calvin's successor, had forged an effective working relationship with Geneva's governing elites, fostered in large part by Beza's more irenic personality, moderate leadership style, and refined cultural taste that allowed him to relate easily with people of power and wealth. Once Beza's steadying hand was no longer at the helm of the church, this spirit of cooperation and mutual trust with Geneva's city councilors quickly dissipated, signaling a new period of conflict and confrontation between Geneva's religious and political leaders.

My study of pastoral ministry in sixteenth- and early seventeenth-century Geneva has revealed a world that is both familiar and strangely foreign. Modern Western observers will probably recognize the basic outline of Calvin's religious thought and many of the institutions that he constructed in Geneva between 1536 and 1564. At the same time, Geneva's church documents describe a variety of religious customs and practices that appear less familiar, even bizarre and dangerous. Most people today will find incomprehensible—indeed, reprehensible—the practices of witch-burning and heretic-hunting that were accepted almost without question in sixteenth-century Europe. Many will also be troubled by the gender inequalities and rigid class distinctions that existed in the structure of church, society, and households in Calvin's Geneva. But other aspects of religious life in Geneva may well invite curiosity and questions, rather than moral judgment. What are we to make of fathers bringing deceased babies to Catholic shrines for resuscitation and baptism? How are we to understand reports of noisy demoniacs roaming Geneva's streets, brides being excommunicated for wearing gold jewelry, or citizens fighting viciously for choice seats at the Sunday morning sermon? And why on earth did Jean Saddo extract the eyeball from his cow and give it to his minister? The foreignness of Geneva's religious history should alert readers to the dangers of too blithely drawing modern lessons from past realities and practices. Differences of language, culture, and religious worldview create a sizeable gulf between "back then" and "now." The past is always a foreign country.[4]

But even so, the task of the historian is not simply that of an antiquarian who dusts off ancient artifacts that are roped off from the general public with a sign reading "do not touch." The study of religious history invites, even compels, us to investigate the past with an eye toward the present, to explore the foreignness of history with the expectation that "cultural immersion" of this sort will not only expand our knowledge of peoples and events but also enrich our experience by providing needed perspective, timely wisdom, apt warnings, and precious glimpses into the failings, the beauty, and the sheer complexity of the human condition. James O'Donnell has it right when he comments in his recent biography of St. Augustine that "it will be impossible for us not to think of our *now* when we read about his *then*, and that's as it should be."[5] So what insights might we glean for *today* from pastoral life as it was practiced back *then* in Calvin's Geneva? I present these final observations from my vantage point as an academic historian who is a Christian within the Protestant tradition, an ordained minister in a historic reformed denomination, and a faculty member at an evangelical divinity school where it is my vocation and privilege to train men and women preparing for church ministry.

First, this study of the Company of Pastors has shown that the vocation of Christian ministry is a difficult one. As we have seen, Geneva's pastors faced heavy workloads and encountered many hardships in their pastoral careers, including financial deprivation, incessant public criticism, congregational apathy, and sometimes even physical danger. Far more than "agents of the state," Calvin and his colleagues served as biblical interpreters, spiritual counselors, social prophets, and moral watchdogs that regularly challenged popular beliefs and social conventions, and sometimes thundered against Geneva's political authorities. The ministers occupied a crucial, yet awkward, position in early modern society as they sought to translate gospel truths into a vernacular that provided hope, meaning, and forgiveness to men and women who sometimes struggled to believe— and frequently struggled to behave themselves. Too often, the ministers' moral indignation and spiritual blind spots only increased the difficulties they encountered in applying Scripture to the needs of their parishioners. Pastoral effectiveness in Geneva required courage, a clear sense of vocation, thick skin, a generous dose of humility, and solid Christian faith. Pastoral virtues like these are still required of Christian workers today even if their congregational contexts are centuries removed from Calvin's.

Second, my study of Calvin and the Company of Pastors has highlighted the importance of accountability and collegiality in pastoral work. Woven into the DNA of Geneva's reformed church were Calvin's convictions that ministers of the gospel stood beneath the authority of Christ, that no Christian minister should hold preeminence in the church, and that ministers must be accountable to the collective judgment of their colleagues. As we have seen, the Company of Pastors—to which each minister belonged as an equal partner—supervised the pastoral work and monitored the personal conduct of all of Geneva's pastors. Likewise, in the weekly meetings of the Congregation, ministers studied Scripture together, evaluated one another's sermons, and forged a common theological outlook. Christian understanding, Calvin believed, was achieved in community. The Ordinary Censure also promoted collegiality in providing a regular venue for Geneva's ministers to air doctrinal disagreements and address interpersonal conflicts behind closed doors. Finally, when members of the Company committed serious moral failure, they were subject to the judgment and correction of their peers on the Consistory. Though this collegial model of ministry did not foster bold innovation, nor allow for strong dissent, it did create a pastoral culture in Geneva where ministers depended on one another, learned from one another, were subject to one another, and forgave one another. Contemporary Protestantism, with its infatuation for robust individualism, celebrity preachers, and ministry empires, has much to learn from the example of Geneva's church.

Third, this study has shown the leading role that the Scriptures played in Calvin's Reformation, suggesting the central importance of God's Word for Christian renewal in our own day. In one of his first Protestant writings, Calvin summarized his central religious purpose with this concise statement: "I demand only this, that faithful people be allowed to hear their God speaking and to learn from his teaching."[6] Calvin devoted most of his career to making this religious vision a reality. As we have seen, between 1536 and 1609 the language and message of the Bible was nearly omnipresent in Geneva's religious life as it was proclaimed in sermons, recited in catechism, sung in the Psalter, studied in the Congregation, discussed in the marketplace, and read devotionally in households. At the same time, Geneva's pastors produced a virtual tsunami of Bible translations, Psalters, commentaries, exegetical aids, and devotional writings that equipped preachers for their pulpit ministries and provided instruction and spiritual comfort for their parishioners. Calvin and his reformed colleagues believed that where God's Word was faithfully proclaimed and gladly received, there the Holy Spirit was at work in power to effect moral transformation in the lives of men and women. Spiritual reformation and scriptural proclamation went hand in hand. It seems plausible that Geneva's distinctive religious culture in the sixteenth century—described by one English visitor as a "model of true religion and true piety"—was in large part the result of this extensive engagement with the text of Scripture.[7] So too, one suspects that the path to spiritual renewal for moribund churches and tired saints in the twentieth-first century involves, at least in part, recovering the central place of Scripture in the church's ministry.

Finally, this book has demonstrated the high priority that Calvin, Beza, Goulart, and their colleagues placed on the ministry of pastoral care. For the reformers, the ministry of the Word involved more than the public exposition of Scripture; it also entailed the application of the divine message to people in every stage of life, from cradle to grave. Christian ministry needed to be Word-centered *and* people-centered. Geneva's pastors fulfilled their calling when they baptized infants, taught children their catechism, welcomed young adults to the Lord's Table, conducted household visitations, comforted the sick, and consoled people preparing to die. At the same time, in weekly Consistory meetings, the ministers and elders confronted men and women suspected of moral failure or wrong belief, applying the "medicine" of church discipline in the hopes of achieving repentance, healed relationships, Christian understanding, and spiritual growth. Though dimensions of Calvin's program of pastoral supervision and discipline strike our modern sensibilities as heavy-handed and unduly intrusive, the ministers' sustained commitment to the spiritual well-being of adults and children in their parishes seems on the whole quite admirable. Indeed, in our modern world where men and women so often struggle with spiritual dislocation, fractured relationships, and deep-seated loneliness, Calvin's vision for pastoral oversight that includes gospel proclamation *and* intense relational ministry appears especially relevant and important.

In retrospect, this portrait of the Venerable Company has highlighted the virtues, the vices, and the sheer complexity of the men who served alongside Calvin between 1536 and 1609. In the face of plague, they were capable of great courage and utter cowardice. In their discipline, they could be supportive and compassionate or harsh and unforgiving. In their relationships with one another, the ministers often displayed a spirit of cooperation and mutual respect, but they were not immune from petty quarrels, backbiting, recriminations, and vainglory. In their sermons, Geneva's pastors fed their sheep on the bread of the gospel, and yet regularly fulminated against the ills and excesses of their congregations. In their more reflective moments, ministers like Calvin, Beza, and Goulart sometimes acknowledged their limitations and failures in ministry, and expressed their need for divine help to overcome them. They recognized that, ultimately, the success of Geneva's Reformation and the preservation of the church into the future depended, not on them, but on God's sustaining grace. In a sermon delivered at the very end of his pastoral career, the elderly Theodore Beza beautifully articulated this attitude of dependence and trust. "We are able to say, by the grace of God, that we have preached, and continue to preach, the pure truth contained in God's holy Word," he wrote. "But alas, at what price? Where is our zeal, our care, and our diligence as pastors? O Lord, support us therefore by your infinite goodness. Preserve in us a good and right conscience. Fill us with zeal for your glory. Increase in us the knowledge, the wisdom, the love, and the endurance required for such a calling. In sum, be pleased to bless our modest efforts."[8]

APPENDIX

Geneva's Ministers from 1536–1609

Italicized date (e.g., *1560*) denotes year first enrolled in the Company of
Pastors. Asterisk (*) denotes employed in city parish.

*1. Airebaudouze, Pierre d'(d. c. 1571): From Nîmes. Pastor in Jussy (*1555*–60),
  Geneva (1560–61). See *FP*, vol. 1, 19, 26.

2. André, Osée (b. 1567): From **Geneva**. Studied at Genevan Academy. Pastor
  in Chancy/Cartigny (*1595*–98), Cartigny (1598–1609). See *FP* 2nd ed., vol. 1,
  col. 237–38; *LR*, vol. 2, 40–41.

3. Arnaud, Jean (c. 1546–72): From Nîmes. Studied at Genevan Academy.
  Pastor in Chancy (*1571*–72). See *FP* 2nd ed., vol. 1, col. 364; *LR*, vol. 2, 66.

*4. Baduel, Claude (1491–1561): From Nîmes. Studied at Nîmes, Paris,
  and Wittenberg. Pastor in Geneva (*1556*), Russin/Dardagny (1556–57),
  Vandoeuvres (1557–61). See *FP*, vol. 1, 212–13.

5. Baduel, Paul (1545–1626): From **Geneva**. Studied at Genevan Academy.
  Pastor in Chancy (*1572*–84). See *FP*, vol. 1, 213–14; *LR*, vol. 2, 105.

6. Baldin, Jean (d. 1559): From St.-Romain-du-Gard. Designated "Master" in
  Consistory Minutes. Pastor in Jussy (*1546*–48), Moëns/Genthod (1548–59).

7. Baud, Jacques (date unknown): From **Geneva**. Pastor in Céligny (*1536*–43).
  Deposed.

*8. Bernard, Jacques (d. 1559): From **Geneva**. Designated "Master" in Consistory
  Minutes. Pastor in Geneva (*1538*–42), Satigny (1542–59).

9. Berthod (or Berthault), Antoine (dates unknown): Origin unknown. Pastor
  in Bernex (c. *1596*).

*10. Bertram, Bonaventure (1531–94): From Thouars in Poitou. Studied at
  Toulouse, Paris, and Cahors. Pastor in Chancy (*1562*–66), Geneva (1566–
  87). Professor of Hebrew (1567–86). See *FP*, vol. 2, 229–31.

*11. Beza, Theodore (1519–1605): From Vézelay in Burgundy. Studied at Orléans
  and Bourges. Pastor in Geneva (*1559*–1605). Professor of theology (1559–
  1599). See *FP*, vol. 2, 259–84.

12. Bioley, Pierre (dates unknown): From **Geneva**. Studied at Genevan Academy. Pastor in Céligny (*1590–91*).

13. Blanchard, Honoré (dates unknown): From **Geneva**. Studied at Heidelberg. Pastor in Vandeouvres (*1581–83*). Deposed. See *FP* 2nd ed., vol. 2, col. 604.

*14. Blanchet, Pierre (d. 1543): Origin unknown. Pastor in Geneva (*1542–43*). See *FP* 2nd ed., vol. 2, cols. 605–606.

Blesy, Antoine de. See Robert, Antoine.

Boulier, Jean. See La Roche, Jean.

*15. Bourgoing, François, sire of Daignon (c. 1515–65). From Nevers. Pastor in Bossey/Neydens (*1545*), Geneva (*1545–52*), Jussy (*1552–63*). See *FP*, vol. 2, 483.

16. Brulères (dit. De La Fontaine), Etienne de (dates unknown): From Giens-sur-Loire. Pastor in Russin/Dardagny (*1588–90, 1594*). See *FP* 2nd ed., vol. 3, col. 288.

17. Brunes, Jean de (1577–1603): From **Geneva**. Studied at Genevan Academy and Heidelberg. Pastor in Chancy (*1598–1600*), Russin (*1600–1601*). See *LR*, vol. 2, 355.

18. Bussier, Annet (d. 1543). Origin unknown. Pastor in Vandoeuvres (*1540–41*), Satigny (*1541–42*).

*19. Calvin, Jean (1509–64). From Noyon in Picardy. Studied at Bourges and Orléans. Pastor in Geneva (*1536–38, 1541–64*). See *FP*, vol. 3, 109–162.

20. Carmel (or Carmet), Gaspard (d. 1560). From St. Marcellin in Dauphiné. Studied at Basel. Pastor in Moëns/Genthod (*1560*). See *FP* 2nd ed., vol. 3, col. 769.

21. Chabrey, Jean (1584–1615): From **Geneva**. Studied at Genevan Academy. Suffragant in Chêne (*1607–1609*), pastor in Satigny (*1609–13*), Geneva (*1613–15*). See *LR*, vol. 2, 447–48.

*22. Champereau, Edme (or Aimé) (date unknown): Origin unknown. Pastor in Geneva (*1540–45*), Draillans (*1545*). Deposed.

*23. Chandieu, Antoine de (c. 1534–91): From Chabot in Mâconnais. Studied at Paris, Toulouse, and Geneva. Pastor in Geneva (*1572, 1589–91*). See *FP*, vol. 3, 327–32.

24. Chapuis, Jean (1491–1560): From near Lyon. Pastor in Valeiry/Chêne (*1546–57*).

*25. Chausse, Gilles (d. 1574): From Chanteloup in Normandy. Pastor in Vandoeuvres (*1562–66*), Geneva (*1567–74*). See *FP* 2nd ed., vol. 4, cols. 255–56.

*26. Chauve, Antoine (1509–89): From St. Saphorin, Vaud. Studied at Genevan Academy. Pastor in Russin/Dardagny (*1566–71*), Geneva (*1571–89*). See *FP*, 2nd ed., vol. 4, cols. 256–57; *LR*, vol. 2, 482.

*27. Chauvet, Raymond (d. 1570): From St. Celli in Gévaudan. Designated as "Master" in Consistory Minutes. Pastor in Geneva (*1545–70*). See *FP*, 2nd ed., vol. 4, cols. 260–63.

28. Chauveton, Urbain (d. 1616): From La Châtre in Berry. Studied at Genevan Academy. Pastor in Vandoeuvres (*1566–71*). Deposed. See *FP*, 2nd ed., vol. 4, cols. 263–65; *LR*, vol. 2, 485.

29. Chevalier, Pierre (1544–94): From **Geneva**. Studied at Basel, Heidelberg, and Wittenberg. Pastor in Céligny (1584–87). Professor of Hebrew (1587–94). See *FP*, 2nd ed., vol. 4, cols. 310–11.

*30. Colladon, Nicolas (d. 1586): From Berry. Studied at Lausanne and Heidelberg. Pastor in Vandoeuvres (1553–57), Geneva (1557–71). Professor of Theology (1566–71). Deposed. See *FP*, vol. 4, 3–5.

31. Constant, Léonard (d. 1610): From Limoges. Studied at Genevan Academy and Basel. Pastor in Satigny (1576–83). See *FP*, 2nd ed., vol. 4, cols. 589–90; *LR*, vol. 2, 553.

*32. Cop, Michel (1501–66): Near Paris. Pastor in Geneva (1545–66). See *FP*, 2nd ed., vol. 4, col. 615.

*33. Courauld, Elie (d. 1538): Origin unknown. Pastor in Geneva (1536–38). Deposed. See *FP*, 2nd ed., vol. 4, 786–88.

*34. Cugniez, Louis (d. 1552): From Ange. Designated as "Master" in Consistory Minutes. Pastor in Geneva (1544), Russin/Dardagny (1544–52).

*35. Cusin, Gabriel (1574–1617): From **Geneva**. Studied at Genevan Academy and Heidelberg. Pastor in Jussy (1598–1603), Geneva (1603–17). See *FP*, 2nd ed., vol. 4, cols. 982–83; *LR*, vol. 2, 609.

*36. Daneau, Lambert (1530–95): From Beaugency-sur-Loire. Studied at Orléans and Genevan Academy. Pastor in Vandoeuvres (1572–74), Geneva (1574–81). Professor of Theology (1572, 1576–81). See *FP*, vol. 4, 192–98.

*37. Desbordes, Jacques (unknown): From Bordeaux. Studied at Genevan Academy. Pastor in Geneva (1564–66). See *FP* 2nd ed., vol. 5, col. 265.

*38. Des Gallars, Nicolas (1520–81): From near Paris. Pastor in Geneva (1544–53), Jussy (1553–55), Geneva (1558–60). See *FP*, vol. 4, 244–46.

39. Des Préaux (dit De La Tour), Pierre (dates unknown): From Rouen. Studied at Genevan Academy. Pastor at Russin (1571–76). See *FP*, 2nd ed., vol. 5, col. 365; *LR*, vol. 3, 100.

*40. Diodati, Jean (1576–1649): From **Geneva**. Studied at Genevan Academy. Professor of Hebrew (1597–1606). Pastor in Geneva (1608–45?). Professor of theology (1599–1645). See *LR*, vol. 3, 116–17.

41. Dorival, Adam (d. c. 1612): From Aubigny-sur-Nère. Studied at Genevan Academy. Pastor in Chancy (1588–90). See *FP*, vol. 4, 303–304; *LR*, vol. 3, 128.

42. Druson, Georges (dates unknown): From Forez, near Brussels. Studied at Genevan Academy. Pastor in Russin/Dardagny (1571–72?), Moëns/Genthod (1573–77). Deposed. See *FP*, 2nd ed., vol. 5, col. 506; LR, vol. 3, 138.
Duc, Pierre. See Le Duc, Pierre.

43. Du Perril, Jean (1533–98): From **Geneva**. Designated as "Master" in Consistory Minutes. Pastor in Neydens (1561–83), Vandoeuvres (1583–98).

*44. Du Pont, Claude (d. 1559): From Blois. Studied at Genevan Academy. Pastor in Geneva (1557–59). See *FP*, 2nd ed., vol. 5, col. 887; *LR*, vol. 3, 191.

45. Du Pont, François (dates unknown): From Agen. Pastor in Moëns/Genthod (1538–43). See *FP*, 2nd ed., vol. 5, col. 888.

*46. Ecclesia (or Osias), Philippe de (dates unknown): Origin unknown. Designated as "Master" in Consistory Minutes. Pastor in Geneva (1542–44), Vandoeuvres (1544–53). Deposed.

*47. Enoch, Louis (d. 1570): From Issoudun in Berry. Designated as "Master." Pastor in Geneva (1554–67). See *FP*, vol. 4, 538–39.

*48. Fabri, Christophe (dit Libertat) (1509–88): From Vienne in Dauphiné. Studied at Montpellier. Pastor in Geneva (1536). See *FP*, vol. 7, 87.

*49. Fabri, Jean (dates unknown): From Larche in Basses-Alps. Designated as "Master" in Consistory Minutes. Pastor in Geneva (1549–56). Deposed. See *FP*, 2nd ed., vol. 6, col. 360.

*50. Farel, Guillaume (1489–1565): From Gap in Dauphiné. Designated as "Master." Pastor in Geneva (1534–38). See *FP*, vol. 5, 59–72.

*51. Ferron, Jean (dates unknown): From Poitiers. Pastor in Geneva (1544–49). Deposed. See *FP*, 2nd ed., vol. 6, col. 509.

52. Fillon, Pierre (d. 1622 or 1623): From Avallon in Burgundy. Pastor in Armoy (1578–91), Céligny (1592–96). See *FP*, 2nd ed., vol. 6, col. 538.

53. Galtier, Jean (d. 1598): From Aigle in Vaud. Pastor in Lancy (1584).

54. Gautier, Théodore (1562–1636): From Orléans. Studied at Basel. Pastor in Russin (1601–18).

*55. Geneston, Matthieu de (d. 1545): From Geneston, near Nîmes. Pastor in Geneva (1542–45).

56. Gervais, Jean (1560–1618): From **Geneva**. Studied at Genevan Academy. Pastor in Bossey (1594–98), Bossey/Neydens (1598–1612), Geneva (1612–18). See *FP*, vol. 5, 256; *LR*, vol. 3, 453.

57. Godet (or Goudet), Jean (1582–1648): From **Geneva**. Studied at Leiden and Genevan Academy. Pastor in Moëns/Genthod (1607–15), Satigny (1615–47). See *LR*, vol. 3, 487.

*58. Goulart, Simon (1543–1628): From Senlis in Picardy. Studied at Genevan Academy. Pastor in Chancy (1566–71), Geneva (1571–1628). See *FP*, vol. 5, 329–36; *LR*, vol. 3, 509.

*59. Grandjean, Matthieu (d. 1561): From Charité in Macon. Designated as "Master" in Consistory Minutes. Pastor in Geneva (1557–61), with responsibilities at Russin/Dardagny (1557–61).

*60. Grenet, Abraham (1557–1620): From **Geneva** (citizen). Regent at *Collège*. Pastor in Geneva (1594–1604).

61. Gros, Etienne (d. 1584): From **Geneva**. Regent at *Collège*. Pastor in Vandoeuvres (1571–72), Jussy (1572–84).

62. Gros the Younger, Etienne (1581–1659): From **Geneva** (Jussy). Studied at Genevan Academy. Pastor in Jussy (1603–15), Geneva (1615–26). See *LR*, vol. 3, 541.

63. Gros, Jean (1577–1642): From **Geneva** (Jussy). Studied at Genevan Academy. Pastor in Chancy & Valeiry (1601–1605), Céligny (1605–18), Geneva (1618–42?). See *LR*, vol. 3, 541.

64. Guérin the Younger, Jean (d. after 1614): Origin unknown. Studied at Basel. Pastor in Chancy (1585–87). Deposed.

65. Héliod, Pierre (d. 1640): From Belleville in Bourgogne. Studied at Genevan Academy. Pastor in Céligny (1600–1601). *LR*, vol. 4, 34.

66. Hellin (or Herly), Jean (dates unknown): From Picardy. Pastor in Céligny (1563–64).

67. Henry, Louis (dates unknown): From Picardy. Pastor in Céligny (*1564–71*). Deposed. See *FP*, vol. 5, 502.

*68. Jaquemot, Jean (c. 1543–1615): From Bar-le-Duc. Studied at Genevan Academy. Pastor in Peney/Satigny (*1567–74*), Geneva (*1576–1613*), Peney (*1613–15*). See *FP*, vol. 6, 39–40; *LR*, vol. 4, 141.

69. Joubert, Jean-Joseph (dates unknown): From Rochechouart in Haute-Vienne. Studied at Genevan Academy. Pastor at Céligny (*1587–89*). See *LR*, vol. 4, 167.

*70. La Faverge, Gaspard de (d. 1571): From Saint-Joire. Studied at Cahors. Pastor in Russin/Dardagny (*1562–66*), Geneva (*1566–71*). See *FP*, vol. 6, 186.

*71. La Faye, Antoine de (1540–1615): From Chateaudun. Professor of philosophy (*1577–80*), pastor in Chancy (*1579–80*), Geneva (*1580–1615*). Professor of Theology (*1581–1610*). See *FP*, vol. 6, 186–88.

La Fontaine, Etienne de. See Brulères, Etienne.

*72. La Maisonneuve, Abraham de (1542–1601): From **Geneva**. Studied at Genevan Academy. Pastor in Céligny (*1571–77*), Moëns/Genthod (*1577–94*), Geneva (*1594–1601*). See *LR*, vol. 3, 42.

73. La Maisonneuve, Louis de (d. 1610): From **Geneva**. Studied at Genevan Academy. Pastor in Bossey (*1570–83*). Deposed. See *LR*, vol. 3, 42.

*74. La Mare, Henri de (dates unknown): From Rohan. Pastor in Geneva (*1536–37*), Geneva and Jussy (*1537–42*), Jussy (*1543–46*). Deposed. See *FP*, vol. 6, 237–38.

75. La Roche (dit Boulier), Jean (dates unknown): Origin unknown. Pastor in Vandoeuvres (*1560–62*). See *FP* 2nd ed., vol. 2, col. 1014.

*76. Le Boiteux, David (c. 1552–1612): From Lausanne. Studied at Genevan Academy. Pastor in Russin/Dardagny (*1577–85*), Geneva (*1585–1612*).

77. Le Court, André (dates unknown): From Issoire in Puy-de-Dôme. Pastor in Céligny (*1554–57*), Chancy/Cartigny (*1557–62*).

*78. Le Double, Abdénago (1545–1571): From Chaumont. Studied at Genevan Academy. Pastor in Moëns/Genthod (*1567–71*), in Geneva (*1571*). See *FP*, 2nd ed., vol. 5, col. 379; *LR*, vol. 4, 297.

79. Le Duc, Pierre (dates unknown): From St. Didier in Ain. Designated as "Master" in Consistory Minutes. Pastor in Russin/Dardagny (*1561–62*), Vandoeuvres (*1562*).

*80. Le Gaigneux, Jean (d. 1580): From Tours. Studied at Genevan Academy. Pastor in Geneva (*1562–71*). Deposed. See *FP*, vol. 6, 513–514. See *LR*, vol. 4, 304.

*81. Lescluse, Pierre de (dates unknown): From Paris. Pastor in Neydens/Bossey (*1544*), Geneva (*1544–45*). Deposed.

*82. Macard, Jean (c. 1520–60): From Provence. Designated as "Master" in Consistory Minutes. Pastor in Russin/Dardagny (*1553–56*), Geneva (*1556–60*). See *FP*, vol. 7, 160–61.

83. Malesier, Matthieu (d. 1557): Origin unknown. Designated as "Master" in Consistory Minutes. Pastor in Bossey (*1545–57*).

84. Manissier, Jean (dates unknown): From Béthune in Artois. Regent at *Collège*. Pastor in Moëns/Genthod (*1595–96*), Céligny (*1596–1600*).

*85. Marcourt, Antoine (d. c.1560): From Lyon. One-time Doctor in Sorbonne. Pastor in Geneva (*1538–40*).

86. Marion, Martin (dates unknown): Origin unknown. Pastor at Lancy (*1568–78?*).

87. Marquis, Claude (1527–62): Origin unknown. Pastor in Chancy (*1562*).

*88. Martin, Arnoul (dates unknown): From Hauteville in Champagne. Studied at Genevan Academy and Herborn. Pastor in Satigny (*1591–92*) and Geneva (*1592–93*). See *FP*, vol. 7, 295; *LR*, vol. 4, 446.

89. Martin, Barthélemy (dates unknown): From Volonne. Studied at Genevan Academy. Pastor in Lancy (*1587*). See *LR*, vol. 4, 446.

*90. Maubué, Charles (c. 1539–66): From Berry. Regent at *Collège*. Pastor in Moëns/Genthod (*1560–64*), Geneva (*1564–66*).

*91. Méigret, Aymé (dates unknown): From Auxerre. Pastor in Geneva (*1542–44*), Moëns/Genthod (*1544–46*). Deposed.

*92. Merlin, Jean-Raymond (d. 1578): From Romans in Dauphiné. One-time Professor at Lausanne. Pastor in Peney/Satigny (*1559*), Geneva (*1559–64*). Deposed. See *FP*, vol. 7, 385–87.

93. Mollet, Enoch (1578–1647): From **Geneva**. Studied at Genevan Academy and Heidelberg. Pastor in Chancy (*1605–1610*), Cartigny and Onex (*1610–17*), Geneva (*1617–47*). See *LR*, vol. 4, 565.

94. Montliard, Jean (d. 1563): From Beauce. Pastor in Draillons (*1554–57*), Céligny (*1557–63*). See *FP*, vol. 7, 490–91.

*95. Morand, Jean (dates unknown): From Picardy. One-time Doctor in Sorbonne. Pastor in Geneva (*1538–40*).

96. Moreau, Simon (dates unknown): From Tourraine. Pastor in Bossey/Neydens (*1544–45*). Deposed.

*97. Morel, François (dates unknown): From Collonges. Pastor in Geneva (*1557, 1560–62*). See *FP*, vol. 7, 500.

98. Morgues, Guillaume de (d. 1589): From Saint-Léonard in Nivernais. Pastor of Peney/Satigny (*1583–89*).

*99. Ninaux (or Ninault), Pierre (dates unknown): From Touraine. Pastor in Geneva (*1544–45*), Draillans (*1545–54*).

100. Offre, Arnaud (dates unknown): Origin unknown. Pastor in Lancy (*1583–84*).

101. Offre, Martin (dates unknown): Origin unknown. Pastor in Lancy (*1578–83?*).

102. Paquelet, François (d. 1598): Origin unknown. Studied at Genevan Academy. Pastor in Neydens (*1583–98*).

103. Péréry, Jean (dates unknown): From Montauban. Pastor in Neydens (*1545–61*).

104. Perreaud, Eléazar (dates unknown): From Burgundy. Studied at Heidelberg. Pastor in Russin/Dardagny (*1585–88*). Professor of Philosophy (*1587–93*).

*105. Perrot, Charles (1541–1608): From Paris. Studied at Genevan Academy. Pastor in Moëns/Genthod (*1564–66*), Geneva (*1566–1608*). Professor of Theology (*1572, 1586, 1598*). See *FP*, vol. 8, 195–96; *LR*, vol. 5, 132–33.

106. Perrot, Denis (1539–72): From Paris. Studied at Genevan Academy. Pastor in Satigny (*1564–66*). See *FP*, vol. 8, 195–96; *LR*, vol. 5, 133.

*107. Perrot, Samuel (1559–1618): From Langeais. Studied at Genevan Academy. Pastor in Satigny (1595–1609), Geneva (1609–18). See *LR*, vol. 5, 138.

*108. Petit, Nicolas (d. 1578): From near Paris. Designated as "Master" in Consistory Minutes. Pastor in Geneva (1544), Chancy (1544–57), Draillans (1557–78).

*109. Pinault, Jean (d. 1606): From Poitiers. Studied at Genevan Academy. Pastor in Jussy (1560–66), Geneva (1566–1606). See *FP*, vol. 8, 242–43; *LR*, vol. 5, 191.

110. Pleurs (or D'Espoir), Jean de (d. 1570): From Troyes. Pastor in Bossey (1557–70). See *FP*, vol. 8, 261.

*111. Poupin, Abel (d. 1556): From Seiches in Agénois. Designated as "Master" in Consistory Minutes. Pastor in Jussy (1543), Geneva (1543–47, 1548–56). See *FP*, vol. 8, 310.

*112. Prévost, Pierre (1569–1639): From Issoudun in Berry. Studied at Genevan Academy. Pastor in Russin/Dardagny (1597–98), Russin (1600–1601), Geneva (1601–39). See *FP*, vol. 8, 320–21; *LR*, vol. 5, 240.

113. Privé, François (d. 1584): From Provence. Studied at Genevan Academy. Pastor in Céligny (1577–84). See *FP*, vol. 8, 334; *LR*, vol. 5, 247.

114. Ravier, Antoine (dates unknown): From Gévaudan. Pastor in Satigny (1538–41).

115. Regalis, Jean (d. 1545): Origin unknown. Pastor in Draillans (1544–45).

*116. Rhetis, Jean (dates unknown): Origin unknown. Preacher in Geneva (1536?).

117. Robert (dit de Blesy), Antoine (dates unknown): Studied at Basel. From region of Orléans. Pastor in Vandoeuvres (1574–76).

118. Robert, Lazare (dates unknown): From Rouen. Studied at Genevan Academy and Leiden. Pastor in Draillans (1586–95). See *LR*, vol. 5, 358.

*119. Rotan, Jean-Baptiste (d. 1598): From Grisons in Switzerland. Studied at Heidelberg. Pastor in Vandoeuvres (1576–79), Geneva (1579–89). Professor of Theology (1587–89). See *FP*, vol. 9, 8–9.

120. Roy, Hugues (d. 1618): Origin unknown. Regent at *Collège*. Pastor in Jussy (1584–98), Vandoeuvres (1598–1618).

121. Royer, Jacques (date unknown): Origin unknown. Pastor in Céligny (1601–1605). Deposed.

122. Saint-André, Jacob de (dates unknown): From **Geneva**. Pastor in Moëns/Genthod (1571–73). See *FP*, vol. 9, 76.

*123. Saint-André, Jean de (d. 1557): From Besançon. Designated "Master" in Consistory Minutes. Pastor in Moëns/Genthod (1546–48), Jussy (1548–52), Geneva (1552–57). See *FP*, vol. 9, 76.

*124. Saunier, Antoine (dates unknown): From Dauphiné. Rector of schools. Pastor in Geneva (1534–38)

125. Sauvage, Jean (dates unknown): From Casteljaloux in Guyenne. Studied at Genevan Academy. Pastor in Vandoeuvres (1579–81). See *FP*, vol. 9, 193; *LR*, vol. 5, 484.

*126. Scarron, Matthieu (1560–1613): From **Geneva**. Studied at Genevan Academy and Heidelberg. Pastor in Moëns/Genthod (1596–1607), Geneva (1607–13). See *LR*, vol. 5, 490.

127. Serres, Jean de (c. 1540–98): From Villeneuve-de-Berg. Studied at Lausanne and Genevan Academy. Pastor in Jussy (1566–72). See *FP*, vol. 9, 263–68. Deposed. See *LR* V.561.

128. Servier, Pierre (d. 1577): From Lyon. Studied at Genevan Academy and Heidelberg. Pastor in Russin (1576–77). See *LR*, vol. 5, 562.

129. Trembley, Etienne (1556–97): From **Geneva**. Studied at Heidelberg. Pastor in Bossey (1583–94).

*130. Trembley, Jean (1519–99): From Lyon. Rector at *Collège*. Pastor in Peney/Satigny (1560–64), Geneva (1564–96). See *FP*, vol. 9, 413–14.

*131. Treppereaux, Louis (d. 1580): From St. Vincent near Toulouse. Pastor in Geneva (1542–44), Céligny (1544–53).

*132. Tronchin, Théodore (1582–1657): From **Geneva**. Studied at Basel, Genevan Academy, Heidelberg, and Leiden. Professor of Hebrew (1606–1618). Pastor in Geneva (1608–57). Professor of Theology (1615–56). See *FP*, vol. 9, 422–23; *LR*, vol. 6, 75.

133. Vandert, Nicolas (dates unknown): Origin unknown. Pastor in Jussy (1541–42). Deposed.

134. Viret, Maurice (d. 1586): From Chablais. Pastor in Armoy (1562–78), Draillans (1578–86).

*135. Viret, Pierre (1511–1571): From Orbe. Studied at Paris. Pastor in Geneva (1534, 1541–42, 1559–60). See *FP*, vol. 9, 513–21.

Introduction

1. The term "evangelical," drawn from the Greek word *euangelium* (good news), was the self-designation of early proponents of the Reformation in the sixteenth century, before such terms as Lutheran, Calvinist, or Zwinglian came into vogue. The present work employs the word in this sense. See Hillerbrand, "Evangelical (Evangelisch)," in *Encyclopedia of Protestantism*, 2:701–702.

2. See *Theodori Bezae Vita Calvini*, in *CO* 21, cols. 166–68.

3. "Discours d'adieu aux ministres," in *CO* 9, cols. 891–94. Unless otherwise noted, all translations are my own.

4. The most important studies of these more prominent ministers are, for Guillaume Farel, Borel-Girard, Aubert, Piaget et al., *Guillaume Farel, 1489–1565*; Barthel, Scheurer, and Stauffer, *Actes du Colloque Guillaume Farel*. For Pierre Viret, Barnaud, *Pierre Viret, sa vie et son oeuvre*. For Lambert Daneau, Félice, *Lambert Daneau, pasteur et professeur en théologie*; Fatio, *Méthode et théologie*. For Antoine de Chandieu, Bernus, *Le ministre Antoine de Chandieu*; Barker, *Protestantism, Poetry and Protest*. For Simon Goulart, Jones, *Simon Goulart, 1543–1628*. For Jean de Serres, Dardier, *Jean de Serres, sa vie et ses écrits*. For Jean Diodati, Budé, *Vie de Jean Diodati, theologien genevois*; McComish, *Epigones*. The life of Theodore Beza has been recounted by a number of biographers, notably Baird, *Theodore Beza, the Counsellor of the French Reformation, 1519–1605*; Geisendorf, *Théodore de Bèze*; Manetsch, *Theodore Beza and the Quest for Peace in France, 1572–1598*; Dufour, *Théodore de Bèze, Poète et théologien*.

5. I draw my definition of "culture" from Peter Burke's classic work, *Popular Culture in Early Modern Europe*, xxii–xxiii.

6. *RCP* 9:81.

7. Kingdon, "Calvin and the Government of Geneva," 51.

8. Vogler, *Le clergé protestant rhénan au siècle de la réforme, 1555–1619*. See also his "Recrutement et carrière des pasteurs strasbourgeois au XVIe siècle"; and "Formation et recrutement du clergé protestant dans les Pays Rhénans de Strasbourg à Coblence au XVIe siècle."

9. Important contributions include Karant-Nunn, *Luther's Pastors*; Abray, *People's Reformation*; Biel, *Doorkeepers at the House of Righteousness*; Gordon, *Clerical Discipline and the Rural Reformation*; Naphy, *Calvin and the Consolidation of the Genevan Reformation*; Tolley, *Pastors & Parishioners in Württemberg*; Burnett, *Teaching the Reformation*.

10. Strauss, *Luther's House of Learning*. See also Strauss, "Success and Failure in the German Reformation."

11. Gordon, *Clerical Discipline and the Rural Reformation*, 221–222. Gordon notes that this outcome was not that surprising to Heinrich Bullinger, however, who was too pragmatic to expect that the Reformation would result in the complete transformation of society.

12. Burnett, *Teaching the Reformation*, 255.

13. On this topic, see for example Eire, *War Against the Idols*; Green, "'Reformed Pastors' and *Bons Curés*"; Pettegree, *Reformation of the Parishes*; Karant-Nunn, *Reformation of Ritual*; Evans, *A History of Pastoral Care*; Witte Jr., *Law and Protestantism*; Dixon and Schorn-Schütte, *Protestant Clergy of Early Modern Europe*.

14. See, for example, Scribner, *Popular Culture and Popular Movements in Reformation Germany*; Duffy, *Stripping of the Altars*.

15. McLaughlin, "The Making of the Protestant Pastor."

16. Luther, *The Babylonian Captivity of the Church*, in LW 36:113.

17. See, for example, Martin, *Le métier du prédicateur à la fin du Moyen Age, 1350–1520*; Taylor, *Soldiers of Christ*; Swanson, "Before the Protestant Clergy," 47–48.

18. For a helpful survey of interpretations of the role that ritual played in the Reformation, see Grosse, "'En Esprit et en Vérité?'" See also Muir, *Ritual in Early Modern Europe*; and Karant-Nunn, *Reformation of Ritual*.

19. McLaughlin, "The Making of the Protestant Pastor," 75; Pettegree, "The Clergy and the Reformation," 13–16.

20. Ozment, *Reformation in the Cities*, 34, 98.

21. Luther, *The Babylonian Captivity of the Church*, LW 36:117. That Ulrich Zwingli held a similar view, see Gordon, *Clerical Discipline and the Rural Reformation*, 59.

22. For Luther's view of the priesthood of all believers, see Gerrish, "Priesthood and Ministry in the Theology of Luther." Reformed theologians like Heinrich Bullinger also defended this doctrine. See *Second Helvetic Confession* (1566), art. 25, 10, in Beeke and Ferguson, *Reformed Confessions*, 204.

23. Luise Schorn-Schütte provides an excellent review of this expansive literature in "Priest, Preacher, Pastor." See also Schorn-Schütte, "The Christian Clergy in the Early Modern Holy Roman Empire"; Dixon and Schorn-Schütte, *Protestant Clergy of Early Modern Europe*, 1–38; and Burnett, "A Tale of Three Churches."

24. Schorn-Schütte, "Priest, Preacher, Pastor," 9–19.

25. See Schilling, "Confessional Europe"; Reinhard, "Pressures towards Confessionalization?" Several historians have questioned whether this "hard" model of confessionalization adequately explains political and religious developments outside of Germany. See particularly Benedict, "Confessionalization in France?"

26. Schorn-Schütte notes: "The image of the clergyman as an agent of the state, which has long been employed to characterize both Protestant and Catholic structures, urgently requires revision, especially for the era under discussion here.

Even if it is true that Protestant and reformed Catholic states prescribed a role for the clergy that was useful to the temporal authorities, this did not preclude the clergy of either confession from viewing the authorities critically." Quoted in "Clergy in the Early Modern Holy Roman Empire," 727. See also Schorn-Schütte, "Priest, Preacher, Pastor," 29–36.

27. Cottret, *Calvin: A Biography*, xiv.

28. E. William Monter expressed this sentiment when he observed that "Calvin was not so much a personality as a mind who "lived for his work: teaching, preaching, and writing." See his *Calvin's Geneva*, 98.

29. The registers of Geneva's Company of Pastors have now been published for the years 1546–1618 in *RCP*. Over the past thirty years, Kingdon and his students have completed a transcription of the minutes of the Consistory of Geneva between 1542 and 1564. These minutes are in the course of being published by Thomas Lambert and Isabella Watt, eds., in *R Consist*. An English translation of the first of these volumes has been published by Robert Kingdon, Thomas Lambert, and Isabella Watt, eds., *Registers of the Consistory (1542–1544)*.

30. Peter, "Rhétorique et prédication selon Calvin"; Stauffer, "Un Calvin méconnu"; Parker, *Calvin's Preaching*; Millet, *Calvin et la dynamique de la Parole*; Lambert, "Preaching, Praying and Policing the Reform in Sixteenth-Century Geneva."

31. Kingdon, "The Genevan Revolution in Public Worship"; McKee, "Calvin and His Colleagues as Pastors."

32. Kingdon, "The Control of Morals in Calvin's Geneva" ; Watt, "Women and the Consistory in Calvin's Geneva," 429–30; Kingdon, "The Geneva Consistory in the time of Calvin"; Grosse, *Les rituels de la cène*.

33. Naphy, *Calvin and the Consolidation of the Genevan Reformation*.

34. McKee, *Elders and the Plural Ministry*; Kingdon, "The Deacons of the Reformed Church in Calvin's Geneva"; Kingdon, "Social Welfare in Calvin's Geneva"; McKee, *John Calvin on the Diaconate and Liturgical Almsgiving*; Olson, *Calvin and Social Welfare*.

35. The classic study of Calvin's Academy is Borgeaud, *Histoire de l'Université de Genève: L'Académie de Calvin 1559–1798*. More recently, see Lewis, "The Geneva Academy"; Maag, *Seminary or University?*

36. Zachman, *John Calvin as Teacher, Pastor, and Theologian*; Lee, "Calvin's Understanding of *Pietas*." See also Battles, *Piety of John Calvin*.

37. See Brian Gerrish's preface to McKee, *John Calvin: Writings on Pastoral Piety*, xiii–xviii.

38. A notable exception to this pattern is Heyer's *L'Église de Genève*. Less helpful is the old and unreliable survey by Gaberel, *Histoire de l'Église de Genève depuis le commencement de la Réformation jusqu'à nos jours*.

39. Choisy, *L'État Chrétien Calviniste à Genève au temps de Théodore de Bèze*.

40. For Beza's preaching, see Delval, "La doctrine du salut dans l'oeuvre homilétique de Bèze"; Delval, "La prédication d'un réformateur au XVIe siècle." Beza's pastoral theology is treated in Raitt, "Beza, Guide for the Faithful Life"; Wright, *Our Sovereign Refuge*; Manetsch, "'The Most Despised Vocation Today.'"" The role of the Consistory during the generation after Calvin's death is studied by Monter, "The Consistory of Geneva, 1559–1569"; Manetsch, "Pastoral Care East of Eden."

41. Grosse, *Les rituels de la cène.*

42. Consistory minutes for the years 1542–1551 are published in the *R. Consist.* For the years 1551 to 1564, I consulted the transcriptions of the Consistory registers completed by the students of Robert M. Kingdon (available in electronic form at the H. Henry Meeter Center for Calvin Studies, Grand Rapids, Michigan). For the years 1564 to 1609, I read the original manuscripts of the Consistory, available in the State Archive of Geneva. The extant volumes are listed in the bibliography under *Registres du Consistoire* in the manuscripts section. Unpublished volumes of the Consistory minutes will be cited (without italics) as R. Consist.

43. Lindberg, *Reformation Theologians,* 380.

44. Brown, *Religion and Society in the Age of Saint Augustine,* 21. Similarly, Grant Wacker has applied this statement to Pentecostal leaders in early twentieth-century America, in *Heaven Below,* 17.

Chapter 1

1. Deonna, "Cathédrale Saint-Pierre de Genève, cloches, horloges, orgues." For the important role that bells played in the years leading to Geneva's Reformation, see Grosse, *Les rituels de la cène,* 59–72.

2. See Kingdon, "Was the Protestant Reformation a Revolution?" Kingdon employs the definition of "revolution" proposed by the political scientist Sigmund Neumann: "a sweeping, fundamental change in political organization, social structure, economic property control, and the predominant myth of a social order, thus indicating a major break in the continuity of development" (quoted in ibid., 55).

3. Dufour, "Le mythe de Genève au temps de Calvin," 503, 513.

4. Kingdon, "Was the Protestant Reformation a Revolution?" 61; Binz, *Vie religieuse et réforme ecclésiastique.*

5. Naef, *Les origines de la réforme à Genève,* 2:22–25. William Naphy indicates that the number of religious personnel in the city may have been even higher. See Naphy, "The Renovation of the Ministry in Calvin's Geneva," 113–15.

6. Deonna, "Cathédrale Saint-Pierre, clothes, horloges, orgues," 135–51.

7. See Binz, *A Brief History of Geneva,* 18–20; Monter, *Calvin's Geneva,* 29–63.

8. Binz, *A Brief History of Geneva,* 19.

9. Lambert, "Preaching, Praying and Policing the Reform," 52.

10. Binz, *A Brief History of Geneva,* 22.

11. These events are described by the sixteenth-century chronicler Michel Roset in *Les chroniques de Genève,* 110–14. See also Monter, *Calvin's Geneva,* 39–43.

12. For a detailed description of Geneva's councils and civil officers, see Naphy, *Calvin and the Consolidation of the Genevan Reformation,* 38–40; and Lambert, "Preaching, Praying and Policing the Reform," 39–46.

13. Jussie, *Le levain du Calvinisme,* 20; Naef, *Les origines de la réforme à Genève,* 2:256–58. See also Eire, *War Against the Idols,* 126–28.

14. Grosse, *Les rituels de la cène,* 47–51.

15. Roset, *Les chroniques de Genève,* 165. Jussie, *Le levain du Calvinisme,* 48–50.

16. Roset, *Les chroniques de Genève,* 169. This event is discussed in Grosse, *Les rituels de la cène,* 51–52; and Naef, *Les origines de la réforme à Genève,* 2:412–18.

17. Jussie, *Le levain du Calvinisme,* 64–66.

18. Monter, *Calvin's Geneva*, 50–51.

19. Froment, *Actes et gestes*, described in Grosse, *Les rituels de la cène*, 55. See also Naef, *Les origines de la réforme à Genève*, 2:469–75.

20. Jussie, *Le levain du Calvinisme*, 86. These events are also described by Monter, *Calvin's Geneva*, 49–56; Eire, *War Against the Idols*, 122–65.

21. Jeanne de Jussie, as reported in Coram-Mekkey, Chazalon, and Bron, *Crises et révolutions à Genève*, 60–61. Also see Jeanne de Jussie, in Kingdon, *Transition and Revolution*, 90.

22. Deonna, "Cathédrale Saint-Pierre, cloches, horloges, orgues," 135.

23. Monter, *Calvin's Geneva*, 53.

24. For a helpful discussion of this disputation, see Eire, *War Against the Idols*, 140–44; and Catherine Santschi, "Être religieux à Genève à l'époque de la réforme," 10–13.

25. Quoted in Eire, *War Against the Idols*, 143.

26. Froment, *Actes et gestes*, quoted in Eire, *War Against the Idols*, 144.

27. Coram-Mekkey, et al., *Crises et révolutions*, 98–99. This detail is also mentioned in Roset, *Les chroniques de Genève*, 211.

28. Roset, *Les chroniques de Genève*, 200. See also Savion, *Annales*, in Geisendorf, *Les annalistes genevois*, 441.

29. Froment, *Actes et gestes*, 144–45, quoted in Eire, *War Against the Idols*, 146.

30. Carlos Eire correctly notes: "Through iconoclasm the Protestants had circumvented the power of the magistracy," *War Against the Idols*, 147.

31. Ibid., 148.

32. Jussie, *Le levain du Calvinisme*, 152–209.

33. Monter, *Calvin's Geneva*, 54.

34. Gabriella Cahier-Buccelli demonstrates that, as late as 1539, there still remained in Geneva around fifty former Catholic priests and monks, most of whom had abjured the Catholic religion by that time. See "Dans l'ombre de la réforme," 371.

35. Quoted in Coram-Mekkey et al., *Crises et révolutions*, 71–72.

36. "Discours d'adieu aux ministres," *CO* 9, cols. 891–94. See Monter, *Calvin's Geneva*, 95–97.

37. Authorship of Geneva's *Confession of Faith* is disputed by scholars, though most believe that its composition owes more to Guillaume Farel than to John Calvin. The *Confession* is found in Heyer, *L'Église de Genève*, 253–60. An English translation of the *Confession* is found in Calvin, *Calvin: Theological Treatises*. A more detailed discussion of the theological substance of the *Confession* is provided in chapter 3.

38. The *Articles Concerning the Organization of the Church* is in *CO* 10.1, cols. 5–14; an English translation is included in Calvin, *Calvin: Theological Treatises*, 48–55. Scholars continue to disagree whether the *Articles* came from the pen of Calvin or of Farel. On this, see Gordon, *Calvin*, 71–72.

39. See *Instruction et confession de foy dont on use en l'église de Genève*, *CO* 22, cols. 25–74. In 1538, Calvin published a Latin translation of this catechism under the title *Catechismus, sive christianae religionis institutio*, *CO* 5, cols. 313–62. I. John Hesselink has provided a fine English translation and commentary of this translation, in *Calvin's First Catechism: A Commentary*.

40. See Ganoczy, *Young Calvin*, 137–58.

41. See Lambert, "Preaching, Praying and Policing the Reform," 156–58.

42. See Kingdon, "Calvin and the Government of Geneva," 53–54.

43. Kingdon, "The Genevan Revolution in Public Worship," 269. For the various uses of the temple of St. Gervais, see *RCP* 5:135, 143, 161, and 8:178.

44. Coram-Mekkey, et al., *Crises et révolutions*, 112–13. See also Monter, *Studies in Genevan Government*, 12–13.

45. Calvin to Bullinger, February 21, 1538, *CO* 10.2, col. 154. See Burnett's helpful discussion, "A Tale of Three Churches," 111–12.

46. *EO* (1541), 265–66.

47. McKee, "Calvin and his Colleagues as Pastors," 19–23.

48. Monter transcribes Geneva's 1544 budget, receipts, and expenses in *Studies in Genevan Government*, 17–18.

49. Naphy, *Calvin and the Consolidation of the Genevan Reformation*, 53–83.

50. For the complex arrangement and rearrangement of parish assignments see Santschi, "Être religieux," 22; and Heyer, *L'Église de Genève*, 205–31. The parish assignments described here did not remain static. During the course of the sixteenth century, two parishes were disbanded (Lancy and Draillans), one parish was subdivided (Cartigny was separated from Chancy), and two parishes merged (Bossey-Neydens). Thus, by the year 1600, there were a total of nine rural parishes under the jurisdiction of the Genevan church. For photographs of many of these rural temples, along with a brief history of these parishes, see Geisendorf, *Temples de la Campagne Genevoise*.

51. Santschi, "Être religieux," 21.

52. Sixteenth-century Geneva recognized three levels of civic involvement. Citizens (*citoyens*) were those men born within the walled-city of Geneva to a citizen or bourgeois; they had the right to vote in all public elections and could serve in any public office. Burghers (*bourgeois*) were foreign-born men who had either purchased or been granted the rights of citizenship; they possessed all the rights and responsibilities of citizens, except that they could not serve on the Small Council. Inhabitants (*habitants*) were foreigners who were granted rights of residence in the city, but no enfranchisement. See Naphy, *Calvin and the Consolidation of the Genevan Reformation*, 47–48

53. See Gordon, *Calvin*, 78–81.

54. Ibid.; Cottret, *Calvin: A Biography*, 126–31; Lambert, "Preaching, Praying and Policing the Reform," 172–79.

55. Cottret, *Calvin: A Biography*, 130.

56. Calvin to Farel, May 19, 1539, *CO* 10.2, col. 348; *CTS* 4:141.

57. See Gordon, *Calvin*, 85–90; Wendel, *Calvin: Origins and Developments of His Religious Thought*, 59–62; Zachman, *Calvin as Teacher, Pastor, and Theologian*, 22–23; Selderhuis, *Calvin: A Pilgrim's Life*, 88–92.

58. In a letter to Bucer in October 1541, Calvin described the Strasbourg reformer as "my very honored father in the Lord." See *CO* 11, col. 299; *CTS* 4:294–95.

59. See Calvin's "Reply to Sadoleto."

60. Quoted in Cottret, *Calvin: A Biography*, 150.

61. Calvin to Viret, May 19, 1540, *CO* 11, col. 36; *CTS* 4:187.

62. Calvin to Farel, October 27, 1540, *CTS* 4:211.

63. See "Discours d'adieu aux ministres," *CO* 9, col. 894.

64. De Greef, *Writings of John Calvin*, 128–29. The text of *La forme des prières et chantz ecclésiastiques* appears in *CO* 6, cols. 161–224.

65. For the history of the Genevan Psalter, see Candaux, *Le Psautier de Genève, 1562–1865;* and especially Pidoux, *Le Psautier Huguenot.*

66. The French-Latin text of this catechism is found in *CO* 6, cols. 1–159. An English translation is found in Calvin, *Calvin: Theological Treatises*, 83–139. For a discussion of this catechism, see De Greef, *Writings of John Calvin*, 131–33; and Janz, "Catechisms," in *OER* 1:278.

67. The influence of Calvin's *Catechism* in France is attested in several places in the minutes of the national synods of the reformed churches of France. At the ninth National Synod of Foi (1579), for example, the churches were enjoined "de remettre en usage le Catechisme, & les Ministres de l'enseigner & exposer succintement, par des Demandes & des Réponses simples et familiéres: s'accommodant à la capacité & rudesse du peuple, sans entrer en de longs discours sur des lieux communs. Et les Eglises où ledit ordre de Catechisme n'est pas observé, seront exhortées de le remettre en pratique, de telle sorte que les Ministres catechiseront eux-mêmes leur Troupeau, une ou deux fois chaque année, en exhortant un chacun de s'y trouver & de l'aprendre soigneusement." Aymon, *Tous les synodes nationaux des églises réformées de France*, 1:127. For other references to the use of the Genevan *Catechism* in France, see ibid., 1:179, 219.

68. Calvin to Viret, August 23, 1542, *CO* 11, col. 431; *CTS* 4:346.

69. Wendel, *Calvin*, 79. See also Cottret, *Calvin: A Biography*, 159–64; and Witte Jr., *Reformation of Rights*, 39–80 and especially 70–76.

70. *Institutes* IV.viii.1–9. See Wendel's discussion in *Calvin*, 305–307.

71. Initially, city ministers who received the right of bourgeoisie were permitted to participate in the annual General Assembly of Geneva's citizenry. In 1552, even this privilege was revoked. See Naphy, *Calvin and the Consolidation of the Genevan Reformation*, 137–38.

72. Naphy, *Calvin and the Consolidation of the Genevan Reformation*, 154.

73. See Bruce Gordon's even-handed treatment of Calvin's role in the Servetus trial, in *Calvin*, 217–32.

74. *EO* (1541), 261–75.

75. The *Ecclesiastical Ordinances* begins with this statement: "il y a quatre ordres d'offices que notre Seigneur a institué pour le gouvernement de son Eglise..." *EO* (1541), 261. This statement is taken verbatim from Calvin's original draft of the ordinances. See "Draft Ecclesiastical Ordinances," in Calvin, *Calvin: Theological Treatises*, 58. In his *Institutes of the Christian Religion*, Calvin sometimes defines the roles of pastor and doctor as a single office: "Scripture sets before us three kinds of ministers.... For from the order of presbyters (1) part were chosen pastors and teachers; (2) the remaining part were charged with the censure and correction of morals; (3) the care of the poor and the distribution of alms were committed to the deacons," see *Institutes*, IV.iv.1, pp. 1068–69.

76. In a first draft of the ordinances, Calvin required that the Supper "be always administered in the city once a month, in such a way that every three months it takes place in each parish," see "Draft Ecclesiastical Ordinance," in

Calvin: Theological Treatises, 66. The final form of the *Ecclesiastical Ordinances* reduced its celebration to four times per year to distinguish the Lord's Supper from the Catholic Mass. See *EO* (1541), 270. By contrast, in his *Institutes*, Calvin recommended that the Supper be administered "at least once a week." See *Institutes*, IV.xvii.43, p. 1421.

77. For Zurich's *Prophetzei*, see Gordon, *Clerical Discipline and the Rural Reformation*, 180–81.

78. See Zachman, *John Calvin as Teacher, Pastor, and Theologian*, 60–62.

79. Maag, *Seminary or University?* 10–11.

80. Comm. Eph. 4:11, *CO* 51, col. 198. English version in *CNTC* 11:179. See Zachman's discussion of this passage, *John Calvin as Teacher, Pastor, and Theologian*, 62.

81. In Calvin's "Reply to Sadoleto," he notes: "In that Church I have held the office first of doctor, and then of pastor. In my own right, I maintain that in undertaking these offices I had a legitimate vocation," in Olin, *John Calvin-Jacopo Sadoleto*, 50. For Calvin's view of his vocation, see also Zachman, *John Calvin as Teacher, Pastor, and Theologian*, 62.

82. *EO* (1541), 267.

83. "Et néantmoins que tout cela soit tellement modéré, qu'il n'y ait nulle rigueur dont personne soit grevé, et même que les corrections ne soient sinon médecines pour réduire les pécheurs à notre Seigneur," *EO* (1541), 275.

84. See Naphy, *Calvin and the Consolidation of the Genevan Reformation*, 167–235. The 1561 revision of the *Ecclesiastical Ordinances* is somewhat clearer in giving the right of excommunication to the ministers and elders, even as it reiterates that the civil jurisdiction is reserved for the magistrates alone. See *CO* 10, cols. 116–117.

85. See Robert Kingdon's articles, "Calvin's Ideas about the Diaconate: Social or Theological in Origin?"; and "Social Welfare in Calvin's Geneva." Also important is Olson, *Calvin and Social Welfare*, especially 17–32.

86. Olson, *Calvin and Social Welfare*, 32.

87. Benedict, *Christ's Churches Purely Reformed*, 452–54.

88. "Erastianism," named after the Basel reformer and professor Thomas Erastus (1524–1583), is the view that civil government should hold all sovereignty within a commonwealth and that political authority is superior to ecclesiastical authority. Consequently, the church should possess no coercive power. See Baker, "Erastianism," *OER* 2:59.

89. See McKee, *Elders and the Plural Ministry*.

90. Benedict, *Christ's Churches Purely Reformed*, 86–87. See also Heyer, *L'Église de Genève*, 20; Burnett, *Teaching the Reformation*, 75–76; Burnett, *Yoke of Christ*.

91. Cathelan, *Passevent Parisien*. See Philip Benedict's helpful discussion of this work in *Christ's Churches Purely Reformed*, 491–94. Cathelan was responding to Theodore Beza's equally biting satire *Epistola magistri Benedicti Passavantii*, published in 1553.

92. Cathelan, *Passevent Parisien*, 26–27.

93. See Grosse, *Les rituels de la cène*, 256–69; Lambert, "Preaching, Praying and Policing the Reform," 203–21; Kingdon, "The Genevan Revolution of Public Worship," 269–70.

94. In 1566, for example, the minister of Genthod-Moëns asked the Consistory for advice as to what should be done with the relics that remained in the parish temple at Moëns. He requested permission to sell them to finance needed repairs of the parish temple. R. Consist. 23 (1566), fol. 17.

95. Deonna, "Cathédrale Saint-Pierre de Genève. La peinture."

96. Deonna, "Cathédrale Saint-Pierre de Genève. Les vitraux," 88.

97. Deonna, "Cathédrale Saint-Pierre, cloches, horloges, orgues," 186.

98. See Kingdon, "The Genevan Revolution in Public Worship," 269–70; Grosse, *Les rituels de la cène*, 262–69.

99. The placement of benches and chairs in Geneva's temples was not a complete innovation. Grosse notes that benches briefly appeared in Geneva's churches in the late thirteenth or early fourteenth century, only to be removed in the 1440s by order of episcopal officials. In *Les rituels de la cène*, 268–69.

100. Ibid., 266–68.

101. For an historical description and theological analysis of reformed Christianity's understanding of true worship, see Michalski, *Reformation and the Visual Arts*, 43–74; Wandel, "The Reform of the Images"; Butin, "John Calvin's Humanist Image"; and Eire, *War Against the Idols*. Philip Benedict provides an excellent summary of worship patterns among reformed Christians in the sixteenth and seventeenth centuries in *Christ's Churches Purely Reformed*, 491–509.

102. Calvin writes: "There is nothing to which all men should pay more attention, nothing in which God wishes us to exhibit a more intense eagerness than in endeavoring that the glory of his name may remain undiminished, his kingdom be advanced, and the pure doctrine, which alone can guide us to true worship, flourish in full strength." *De necessitate reformandae Ecclesiae*, CO 6, col. 530; CTS 1:228. This passage is discussed in Eire, *War Against the Idols*, 197–200.

103. *De necessitate reformandae Ecclesiae*, CO 6, cols. 457–534. An English translation of this treatise "The Necessity of Reforming the Church" is found in CTS 1:122–234. For Calvin's *Traité des reliques* (1543), see *Calvin, Three French Treatises*, 47–97. For Calvin's commentary on the Gospel of John, see CNTC vols. 4 and 5.

104. "The worship of God is said to consist in the Spirit because it is only the inward faith of the heart that produces prayer and purity of conscience and denial of ourselves, that we may be given up to obedience of God as holy sacrifices." Comm. John 4:24 in CNTC 4:99.

105. *De necessitate reformandae Ecclesiae*, CO 6, col. 460; CTS 1:127.

106. *De necessitate reformandae Ecclesiae*, CO 6, cols. 464, 461; CTS 1:132, 128.

107. Comm. John 4:23 in CNTC 4:99

108. *Institutes* IV.x.29, pp. 1206–1207.

109. *De necessitate reformandae Ecclesiae*, CO 6, col. 463; CTS 1:131. See also *Traité des reliques*, in Calvin, *Three French Treatises*, 51.

110. In his Commentary on Philippians 3.3, Calvin notes: "By spiritual worship [Paul] means that which is recommended to us in the Gospel and consists of trust in God and calling upon Him, self-renunciation and a pure conscience. We must supply an antithesis, for he censures, on the other hand, legal worship, which alone was urged by the false apostles," CNTC 11:269. See Butin's helpful

discussion of this passage in "Calvin's Humanist Image of Popular Late-Medieval Piety," 423.

111. *Traité des reliques,* in Calvin, *Three French Treatises,* 51.

112. Comm. John 4:23 in *CNTC* 4:100.

113. *De necessitate reformandae Ecclesiae, CO* 6, col. 478; *CTS* 1:152. See also Calvin's comments in John 4:20, *CNTC* 4:97.

114. *De necessitate reformandae Ecclesiae, CO* 6, col. 479; *CTS* 1:153.

115. In my view, Butin is correct to question Carlos Eire's assertion that Calvin employs the neoplatonic antithesis between spiritual-material in his doctrine of worship. As Butin shows, false worship is false for Calvin not because it is material per se, but because it is both "carnal" and external, and thus at odds with God's Spirit. See Butin, "John Calvin's Humanist Image of Popular Late-Medieval Piety," 422–23.

116. Comm. John 4:23 in *CNTC* 4:101.

117. See Eire, *War Against the Idols,* 73–88; and Wandel, "The Reform of the Images," 105–24.

118. Quoted in Grosse, *Les rituels de la cène,* 260.

119. Beza, *Sermons sur les trois premiers chapitres de Cantique des Cantiques de Salomon,* 341–42.

120. La Faye, "Sainct exercice sur la mort et passion de Nostre Seigneur Iesus Christ," 6.

121. Luther, "Lectures on the Epistle to the Hebrews" (1517–18), *LW* 29:224.

122. R. Consist. 21 (1564), fol. 56; and ibid., 17 (1560), fol. 121.

123. R. Consist. 13 (1558), fol. 41; and ibid., 14 (1558), fol. 121.

Chapter 2

1. For Beza's conversion to Protestantism, see Geisendorf, *Théodore de Bèze,* 16–31; Meylan, "La conversion de Bèze ou les longues hesitations d'un humaniste chréstien"; Manetsch, "The Journey Toward Geneva."

2. Calvin to Anonymous, June 30, 1551, *CO* 14, col. 145.

3. See Naphy's excellent description of the difficulties Calvin faced in recruiting pastoral colleagues in the 1540s. *Calvin and the Consolidation of the Genevan Reformation,* 55–73.

4. Calvin to Myconius, March 14, 1542, *CO* 11, col. 377; *CTS* 4:314.

5. Calvin to Farel, July 28, 1542, *CO* 11, col. 417 (*CTS* 4:338); and Calvin to Viret, August 19, 1542, *CO* 11, col. 428 (*CTS* 4:341–42).

6. See Naphy, *Calvin and the Consolidation of the Genevan Reformation,* 58.

7. See Olson, "Nicolas des Gallars, Sieur de Saules."

8. The participation of the professors in the Company of Pastors was occasional and sporadic. For the data presented in this chapter, I have not included these professors unless they served a city or rural parish during their tenure in Geneva. Thus, my figures include Pierre Chevalier, Jean Diodati, and Théodore Tronchin, but not François Portus or Isaac Casaubon.

9. My data is drawn from the registers of city and countryside ministers which appear in Heyer's *L'Église de Gènève,* 195–229 and 417–530, supplemented and corrected by details drawn from the *RCP,* vols. 1–13; *LR,* vols. 2–4; Borgeaud, *Histoire de l'Université de Genève*; and Haag and Haag, *La France protestante,* vols. 1–9 (Geneva: Slatkine Reprints, 1966). Haag is hereafter abbreviated as *FP.*

10. According to Catherine Santschi, Jacques Baud came from "une famille du 'patriciat local'" in nearby Satigny. See her article "Être religieux à Genève," 21.

11. Graph 2.1 permits us to resolve the contested issue of when the vacuum of native pastoral leadership in Geneva was rectified. For example, E. William Monter has claimed that "by the end of the [sixteenth] century a very high percentage of Geneva's Venerable Company of Pastors and Professors were composed of Genevan-born citizens," (*Calvin's Geneva*, 174). William Naphy, by contrast, has argued that "the ministers remained overwhelmingly French well into the seventeenth century," ("The Renovation of the ministry in Calvin's Geneva," 126–27). Diarmaid MacCulloch states the matter even more dramatically, noting with astonishment that "between the 1540s and 1594, the Genevan ministry did not include a single native Genevan," in *The Reformation: A History*, 239. Graph 2.1 makes clear that none of these generalizations is altogether accurate.

12. See Burnett, "A Tale of Three Churches," 99, 106–107; Meylan, "Le recrutement et la formation des pasteurs dans les églises réformées du XVIe siècle," 143–44.

13. Burnett, *Teaching the Reformation*, 40–41.

14. Gordon, *Clerical Discipline and the Rural Reformation*, 117–18.

15. Geneva was not entirely unique in the preponderance of foreign-born clergy leading the church. Bernard Vogler has shown that reformed churches in the Rhineland were also slow in recruiting local ministerial candidates, with 80 percent of the clergy being foreign as late as 1577. See his *Le clergé protestant rhénan*, chapter 1.2. Henri Meylan has observed a similar pattern in the Pays de Vaud. See his "Le recrutement et la formation des pasteurs dans les églises réformées du XVIe siècle," 127–50.

16. Beza to Gwalther, June 3/13, 1584, Zurich, Zentralbibl., ms. F 37, fols. 71–72. This was not the first time that Beza expressed such concerns. See his letter to M. de Mouy, March 10, 1567, *CB* 8:81.

17. Beza lodged this indictment in a published sermon in the early 1590s, see his *Sermons sur l'histoire de la passion et sepulture de nostre Seigneur Iesus Christ*, 784. See my discussion of this passage in *Theodore Beza and the Quest for Peace in France*, 217–18.

18. The churches of Basel and Württemberg, for example, developed extensive stipendiary systems for students. On this, see Burnett, *Teaching the Reformation*, 99–103; Tolley, *Pastors & Parishioners in Württemberg*, 24–43.

19. For student scholarships, see *RCP* 3:126, 139; ibid., 5:7, 11; 7:45–46, 77, 79. The two native sons who became pastors in Geneva through the assistance of student scholarships were Pierre Bioley and Gabriel Cusin. A third scholarship holder named Jean-Baptiste Rotan, from the Grisons, also served as a pastor in Geneva.

20. *RCP* 5:82–83.

21. *RCP* 10:4, note 5.

22. *RCP* 10:5–6.

23. Scarron was younger and had less parish experience than Samuel Perrot.

24. See Geisendorf's discussion of the evidence in support of the nobility of the Trembley family in *Les Trembley de Genève*, 11–15.

25. These noble ministers were Lambert Daneau, Antoine de Chandieu, and Jean Diodati. Daneau and Chandieu found refuge in Geneva following the St. Bartholomew's Day massacres of 1572. Diodati, whose father was a patrician of Lucca and the Count of Sarsano, arrived with his family in Geneva in the early 1570s.

26. Greengrass, *The French Reformation*, 55–60, 81. See also Benedict, *Christ's Churches Purely Reformed*, 137–39.

27. Pierre Viret's father was a tailor, Osée André's father was a merchant from Troyes, and Jean de Brunes's father was a merchant-goldsmith.

28. The number of candidates admitted to the Company of Pastors who came from clerical homes is plotted out per decade as follows: 2 (1570s), 3 (1580s), 1 (1590s), 3 (1600s).

29. Among Calvin's earliest colleagues, Antoine Marcourt and Jean Morand both had earned doctorates from the theological faculty of the University of Paris, Christophe Fabri had studied medicine at Montpellier, and Farel and Viret had been trained in the humane letters.

30. See *RCP* 10:102, note 229, citing the minutes of the Small Council.

31. Maag, *Seminary or University?* 28–29. That is not to say that the Academy was merely a seminary to prepare students for careers in the church. During the sixteenth century, the Academy also prepared students for careers in law (from 1566), medicine (briefly, from 1565–67), and civil service. Nonetheless, as Maag shows, during the sixteenth century, the majority of students at the Academy studied theology in preparation for church vocations. See ibid. 15, 29, 33, 55, 56, 84.

32. Borgeaud, *L'Académie de Calvin*, 52, quoting Daneau's *D. Aurelii Augustini Hipponensis Episcopi liber De haeresibus* (Geneva, 1576).

33. Beginning in October 1584, foreign students were charged a small matriculation fee at the Academy. See *RCP* 5:38.

34. Quoted in Maag, *Seminary or University?* 186.

35. For theological instruction at the universities of Heidelberg and Leiden during this period, see Maag, *Seminary or University?* 154–85. An excellent overview of the theological faculty at the University of Basel is found in Burnett, *Teaching the Reformation*, 127–54.

36. Dixon and Schorn-Schütte, *The Protestant Clergy*, 23, 128; Vogler, *Le clergé protestant rhénan*, 77–78. Burnett has shown significantly higher educational levels among ministerial candidates in reformed Basel. See *Teaching the Reformation*, 38, and Table 1.2 on page 280.

37. The most detailed description of Cop's life and ministry in Geneva is found in Doumergue, *Jean Calvin: Les hommes et le choses de son temps*, 3:576–88.

38. Calvin announced Cop's arrival in Geneva in a letter to Farel, April 1545, *CO* 12, col. 64.

39. Calvin to Oswald Myconius, April 25, 1547, *CO* 12, col. 514.

40. "Congrégation sur l'Election Eternelle," *CO* 8, cols. 130–31.

41. Cited in *RCP* 3:11, note 5.

42. Geisendorf, *Les Trembley de Genève*, 27, note 3. John Calvin served as the godfather of Trembley's first son, Jehan, who also died in infancy.

43. See Geisendorf, *Les Trembley de Genève*, 15–38.

44. These two controversies are discussed in Choisy, *L'État Chrétien Calviniste*, 16, 123. See also Geisendorf, *Les Trembley de Genève*, 25–27.

45. Beza to Jean-Baptiste Rotan, December 28, 1595, *RCP* 7:238.

46. See Posthumus Meyjes, "Charles Perrot (1541–1608): His Opinion on a Writing of Georg Cassander," 235. The fullest treatment of Perrot's life is still J. E. Cellerier's *Charles Perrot, pasteur genevois au seizième siècle.*

47. The register of the Company of Pastors reports in December 1566 that Denis Perrot was discharged "à cause de son indisposition et debilité de sens." *RCP* 3:12.

48. Cellerier, *Charles Perrot, pasteur genevois,* 23–30.

49. Ibid., 36–37. See also *RCP* 5:139, note 194.

50. Quoted in Posthumus Meyjes, "Charles Perrot," 235.

51. On November 23, 1610, the Company of Pastors judged "par la pluralité des voix que les escripts de nostre feu frere Monsieur Perrot seront rendu à nos Seigneurs, ne trouvant le Compagnie expedient que lesdits escripts voyent lumiere, tant à cause qu'en iceux ledit defunct accuse nos Eglises d'avoir fait chisme tenant ceste opinion qu'il falloit gemir et demeurer en l'Eglise Romaine, qu'à cause de plusieurs autres erreurs contenus auxdits escripts." *RCP* 11:36.

52. Evidence of this respect for Perrot is found in a dossier presented to Geneva's magistrates in 1588, in which the Company of Pastors noted that "Monsieur Perrot a de grandz dons de Dieu pour servir à l'Eglise...." *RCP* 5:352.

53. For this strange affair, see Cellerier, *Charles Perrot, pasteur genevois,* 44–68. Finally, on December 7, 1610, the register of the Company of Pastor notes that "qui ont fidelement rapporté ce qu'ils ont trouvé d'incommode, d'erronné et de dangereux èsdits escripts, est d'advis que tous tels passages, incommodes, erronnés et dangereux, seront raturés et bien expressement effacés; ains repurgés seront, soub ceste condition, remis aux heritiers, scavoir qu'ils s'obligeront soub leur foy et serment de ne jamais faire imprimer lesdits escrips, n'estants en forme ni disposition convenable pour voir la lumiere." *RCP* 11:36, 38.

54. For the life and literary contribution of Simon Goulart, see L. Chester Jones, *Simon Goulart, 1543–1628.* Robert Kingdon provides a short précis of the life of Goulart in *OER* 2:184.

55. Goulart to Josias Simler, May 10, 1576, found in Jones, *Simon Goulart,* 360, letter XIII.

56. Beza to Jacqueline d'Entremont, 1572, *CB* 13:19.

57. An annotated bibliography of Goulart's writings is found in Jones, *Simon Goulart,* 553–650. See also the bibliography found in *FP* 5:329–336.

58. Such was the judgment of the Provincial Synod of Dauphiné, when it attempted to procure Goulart for the church of Grenoble. See its letter to the Company of Pastors, March 5/15, 1605, *RCP* 9:271.

59. This phrase appears in an address delivered by Beza and David Le Boiteux to the Small Council in 1594. Cited in *RCP* 6:134, note 36.

60. Beza named "mes bon amys" Jean Favre and Pompée Diodati as executors of his estate. See *RCP* 9:137. For Beza's relationship to the powerful Jacques Lect, see Geisendorf, *Théodore de Bèze* (passim); and Lect's letter to Isaac Casaubon, October 16, 1605, in *RCP* 10, appx. 2, p. 346. For Beza's friendship with Caracciolo, see Dufour, *Théodore de Bèze,* 128. Caracciolo's history in Geneva is described in Kingdon, *Adultery and Divorce in Calvin's Geneva,* 143–65.

61. François Morel, who served as pastor in Geneva for two years in the early 1560s, had been one of the original reformed ministers in France and was elected president of the first National Synod of Paris (1559). See *FP* 7:500.

62. Jean-Raymond Merlin, once a professor at Lausanne, occupied the parishes of Peney and Geneva from 1559 to 1561, before being sent to France as a chaplain to the Huguenot captain Gaspard de Coligny and missionary to La Rochelle and Béarn. Merlin returned to Geneva in August of 1564, only to be deposed from the ministry in November for his unbridled criticisms of the magistrates, accusing them of being tyrants over the church. See *FP* 7:385–87; and especially Choisy, *L'État Chrétien Calviniste*, 20–24.

63. Raised in a noble home near Anduze, Pierre d'Airebaudouze was an archdeacon of the cathedral in Nîmes before fleeing to Geneva in 1553. He served the Genevan church six years before returning to France, where he had prominent pastoral positions in Lyon, Montpellier, and Nîmes. See *FP* 1:19, 26; and Greengrass, *French Reformation*, 50.

64. For the life and theological contribution of Lambert Daneau, see Félice, *Lambert Daneau*; Fatio, *Méthode et théologie*; Fatio, "Lambert Daneau."

65. Félice, *Lambert Daneau*, 62.

66. See Fatio, "Lambert Daneau," 107–108, 111–13.

67. A bibliography of Daneau's writings during this period is found in Fatio, *Méthode et théologie*, 7*–60*.

68. Beza's assessment of Daneau is found in his *Réponse de M. Th. de Bèze aux Actes de la conférence de Mombelliard*, 257. This passage is cited in Félice, *Lambert Daneau*, 84–85, note 1.

69. The best biography of Chandieu remains Bernus, *Le Ministre Antoine de Chandieu*. For Chandieu's significant literary contribution to French Protestantism see Barker, *Protestantism, Poetry and Protest*. See also *FP* 3:327–32; and *OER* 1:300–301. For Chandieu's theological contribution, see Sinnema's "Antoine de Chandieu's Call for a Scholastic Reformed Theology (1580)."

70. From Chandieu's *Ode sur les misères des églises françaises*, found in Bernus, *Le Ministre Antoine de Chandieu*, 54.

71. See Sinnema, "Antoine de Chandieu's Call for a Scholastic Reformed Theology." In one of his treatises against Torres, Chandieu defined his theological approach as follows: "I believe and affirm that the main points of religion and faith are to be taught, expressed, and defined from the Scriptures alone. But philosophy, if it is subservient to Scripture, is not to be neglected…. Therefore, when I assert and confirm our view, I use only the plain and express testimonies of Scripture which are the most certain and secure foundations of the truth; but when I demolish and refute Torres's view, which rests especially upon sophistic arguments, then I am compelled to disprove his errors and fallacies also from the laws of true philosophy" (cited in ibid., 167, note 37).

72. Beza to the Viscount of Turenne, March 9/19, 1591, *BSHFP* (1853): 279. See also Manetsch, *Theodore Beza and the Quest for Peace in France*, 215–16.

73. Goulart to Josias Simler, May 10, 1576, published in Jones, *Simon Goulart*, 359, letter XIII.

74. Burnett notes that by the 1540s, Basel's ministers and citizens were largely insulated from direct contact with the Catholic world: "Catholicism was

a specter to be denounced in sermons rather than something personally experienced." See *Teaching the Reformation*, 86. The case of Geneva was thus entirely different.

75. For a discussion of Diodati's life and theological contribution, see Budé, *Vie de Jean Diodati, theologien genevois*; McComish, *The Epigones*, esp. 1–27; and Campi, "Giovanni Diodati et sa traduction de la Bible en italien," Association des ami-e-s du Musée international de la Réforme (2007), at www.musee-reforme.ch/uploads/conference-e-campi.pdf. Accessed January 15, 2010.

76. *RCP* 10:85, 87.

77. McComish asserts that Diodati earned a doctorate in theology at age nineteen before assuming his teaching responsibilities. See *The Epigones*, 1.

78. For the Genevan theologians' role at the Synod of Dort, see McComish, *The Epigones*, 56–59.

79. Ibid., 3.

80. Ibid., 4, 40–41.

81. Ibid., 6–20, 167–208.

82. On the life of Théodore Tronchin, see ibid., 32–34.

83. Ibid., 33.

84. *RCP* 9:194–96.

85. Several older works (including *FP* and Heyer's *L'Église de Genève*) incorrectly state that Tronchin married the niece of Beza. Rather, Tronchin's wife Théodora Rocca was the daughter of Anna Taruffo (wife of Jean-Baptiste Rocca), whose widowed mother Catherine Del Piano had married Theodore Beza in 1588 when Anna was seventeen years old. See Geisendorf, *Théodore de Bèze*, 326; and Dufour, *Théodore de Bèze*, 251.

86. Tronchin's speech was during the 94th session of the Synod. He was chosen for the task when his colleague Jean Diodati fell ill. In his *Historie der Reformatie, en andre Kerkelyke Geschiedenissen, in on ontrent de Nederlanden* (1671–1704), the Remonstrant historian G. Brandt judged Tronchin's speech to be "very confused" and off-subject. See McComish, *The Epigones*, 48, 58–59.

87. McComish, *The Epigones*, 32, 34.

88. See Lambert, "Preaching, Praying and Policing the Reform," 491–96. A Jesuit priest named Luca Pinelli called Beza the "pope among the Calvinists." See Scaduto, "La Ginevra di Teodoro Beza nei ricordi di un gesuita lucano, Luca Pinelli (1542–1607)," 137. Likewise, Pierre Charpentier accused Beza of vaunting himself over Geneva as if it were his "royaume et pontificat," in his *Lettre de Pierre Charpentier Iurisconsulte, addressee à François Portes*, 15r.

89. A good example of Calvin's willingness to submit to the decision of his pastoral colleagues is seen in the Venerable Company's debate over whether the Genevan authorities should allow religious plays to be performed in the city. See Doumergue, *Jean Calvin*, 3:581–87.

90. See *RCP* 1:58–61 and Lambert's helpful discussion of this case in "Preaching, Praying and Policing the Reform," 234–36.

91. *RCP* 1:60.

92. *RCP* 2:102–103. Beza had defended the concept of a "president" or "superintendent" among a group of ministers in his *Confession de la foi chrestienne*, 152–53.

93. The controversies sparked by Colladon and Le Gaigneux occupy much space in the registers of the Company of Pastors during 1571–1572 (see *RCP* 3, passim). Disciplinary action taken by the Consistory is reported briefly in the R. Consist. 28 (1571), fol. 84v; ibid. (1572), fols. 140v, 156v, 160v. In a letter to the classis of Neuchâtel in October 1571, the Company of Pastors offered a detailed defense for its censure of Le Gaigneux, Colladon, and Urbain Chauveton (see *RCP* 3:269–70). For more on these and related controversies, see Manetsch, "Ministers Misbehaving"; and Kingdon, *Geneva and the Consolidation of the French Protestant Movement*, 20–28.

94. See Choisy, *L'État Chrétien Calviniste*, 58.

95. Details from RC 66 (May 22, 1571), fol. 73v; cited in Kingdon, *Geneva and the Consolidation of the French Protestant Movement*, 25–26.

96. See Choisy, *L'État Chrétien Calviniste*, 169–78, and especially Labarthe, "En marge de l'édition des Registres de la Compagnie des pasteurs de Genève."

97. RC 74 (1579), fols. 7v–8r.

98. RC 75 (1580), fols. 50r–v.

99. For more on Jacques Lect's strategic role in reconfiguring the balance of power between Geneva's state and church, see Campagnolo, "Jacques Lect"; and Borgeaud, *L'Académie de Calvin*, 296–312.

100. *RCP* 9:35–36. That the Company had discussed the effectiveness of the weekly presidency on several previous occasions, see *RCP* 8:188 and 9:8–9.

101. Ibid., 9:159.

102. See ibid., 9:164–65.

103. For an excellent discussion of the diminution of the Company's power after Beza's death, see Choisy, *L'État Chrétien Calviniste*, 365–75.

104. See *RCP* 10:58–66.

105. Jones, *Simon Goulart*, 232–49. The weekly presidency of the Company was retained in Geneva's churches until 1831.

Chapter 3

1. *RCP* 3:140; ibid., 4:14–15.

2. *RCP* 4:67–68, 77.

3. This succinct description of Luther's understanding of *Beruf* is drawn from Kenneth Hagen, "A Critique of Wingren on Luther on Vocation," 249. The classic study of Luther's doctrine of vocation, which Hagen both summarizes and critiques, is Wingren, *Luthers lära om kallelsen*; English edition, *The Christian's Calling: Luther on Vocation*, trans. Carl C. Rasmussen. Also helpful on this subject are Althaus, *The Ethics of Martin Luther*, 36–42; and Witte Jr., *Law and Protestantism*, 107–108.

4. *Institutes* III.xxiv.8, p. 974.

5. *Institutes* III.x.6, p. 724.

6. Luther defended the doctrine of the "priesthood of all believers" throughout his theological writings, but especially in his "Appeal to the German Nobility" (1520). See in Luther, *Martin Luther: Selections from His Writings*, 407–12. See Brian Gerrish's helpful discussion in "Priesthood and Ministry in the Theology of Luther." For Calvin on the "priesthood of all believers," see the *Institutes* II.xv.6, p. 502, and ibid., IV.i.12, p. 1026.

7. See Calvin, *Sermons on the Epistle to the Ephesians*, 457. For Calvin's doctrine of vocation, see McGrath, "Calvin and the Christian Calling"; Bouwsma, *John Calvin*, 181–82.

8. *Institutes* III.x.6, p. 725.

9. Calvin comments: "But since men would fight rashly and to no purpose if they did not have God to direct their course, to stimulate them into activity, he mentions also their *calling*. Nothing can fill us with courage more than the knowledge that we have been called by God. For from that we may infer that our labor, which is under God's direction and in which He stretches out His hand to us, will not be in vain." Comm. on 1 Timothy 6:12, *CNTC* 10:277.

10. Alister McGrath rightly notes: "Calvin's 'secularization of holiness' (Henri Hauser) involved bringing the entire sphere of human existence within the scope of divine sanctification and human dedication. It is this sanctification of life, of which the sanctification of work is the chief pillar, which stamped its impression upon Calvin's followers," *A Life of John Calvin*, 220.

11. Daneau, *Brième Remonstrance sur les jeux de sort*, 6–7.

12. Beza, *Sermons sur l'histoire de la résurrection*, 615–18. Beza also discusses the subject of vocation in his lectures on Romans 10. See Beza, *Cours sur les épîtres aux Romains et aux Hébreux, 1564–66*, 185–89.

13. *Institutes* IV.iii.2, p. 1055. See also Bouwsma, *John Calvin*, 219.

14. Beza, *Response aux cinq premiers et principales demandes de F. Iean Hay*, 37.

15. Beza, *Sermons sur l'histoire de la passion*, 784.

16. *RCP* 3:84–85.

17. Calvin, *Institutes of the Christian Religion, 1536 Edition*, ed. and trans. Ford Lewis Battles, 172. Hereafter abbreviated *Institutes* (1536).

18. Ibid., 167.

19. Ibid., 164.

20. Ibid., 165. Similarly, in his treatise *On the Necessity of Reforming the Church*, Calvin insists that "no man is a true pastor of the Church who does not perform the office of teaching....no man can claim for himself the office of bishop or pastor who does not feed his flock with the Word of the Lord." See *CO* 6, cols. 469–70; *CTS* 1:140, 41.

21. For Calvin's discomfort with the titles "cleric" and "clergy," see *Institutes* IV.iv.9, pp. 1076–77.

22. Beza, *Sermons sur le Cantique des Cantiques*, 201, 204, 447–48. See also *RCP* 2:55; ibid., 9:157; ibid., 8:133.

23. *RCP* 3:175, letter no. 12. See also ibid. 8:468, letter no. 99.

24. *RCP* 4:72. See also ibid., 8:468, letter no. 50.

25. Comm. John 3:29, in *CNTC*, 4:81. I am grateful to my former student Monique Cuany for calling my attention to this passage.

26. Beza, *Sermons sur le Cantique des Cantiques*, 203. Beza develops this point in his *Confession de la foi chrestienne*, 144–47 and *Traicté des vrayes essencielles et visibles marques de la vraye Eglise Catholique*, 26. See also Maruyama, *Ecclesiology of Theodore Beza*, 165–66.

27. Beza, *Sermons sur l'histoire de la résurrection*, 391–93.

28. First published in French, this volume was thereafter translated into Latin, Italian, Dutch, and English. Gardy indicates that more than thirty editions of this

work had appeared before 1600. See Gardy, *Bibliographie des oeuvres théologiques, littéraires, historiques et juridiques de Théodore de Bèze*, 60–80.

29. Beza, *Confession de la foi chrestienne*, 147–49.

30. This list is substantially the same as the conception of ministry articulated by ministers in other reformed cities. For Heinrich Bullinger's understanding of the duties of the pastoral office, see Biel, *Doorkeepers at the House of Righteousness*, 216.

31. See Grosse's helpful description of the codification of Geneva's public faith, in *Les rituels de la cène*, 428–40.

32. "Confession des Escholiers," in *CO* 9, cols. 721–30. Required subscription to this Confession of Faith was abandoned in 1576 to make it possible for students from non-Reformed backgrounds to study at the Academy. *RCP* 4:54, 58.

33. *EO* (1541), 262.

34. *RCP* 1:143–44. In this decree, the Council "a pronounce et declairé ledict livre de l'Institution du dict Calvin estre bien et sainctement faict, et sa doctrine estre saincte doctrine de Dieu, et que l'on le tient pour bon et vray ministre de ceste cité, et que dés yci à l'advenir personne ne soit osé de parler contre ledict livre ny la dicte doctrine," (ibid., 144).

35. *Catechism*, in *CO* 6, cols. 109, 110. "Catechism of the Church of Geneva," in Calvin, *Calvin: Theological Treatises*, 130.

36. *Confession de la foy*, in *CO* 9, col. 693.

37. *Catechism*, in *CO* 6, cols. 9, 10. "Catechism of the Church of Geneva," in Calvin, *Calvin: Theological Treatises*, 91–92.

38. *Confession de la foy*, in *CO* 9, col. 694.

39. *Catechism*, in *CO* 6, cols. 45–48. "Catechism of the Church of Geneva," in Calvin, *Calvin: Theological Treatises*, 105–106.

40. *Catechism*, in *CO* 6, cols. 19–24. "Catechism of the Church of Geneva," in Calvin, *Calvin: Theological Treatises*, 95–96. See also the *Consensus Tigurinus*, article 4, in *CTS* 2: 213.

41. *Confession de la foy*, in *CO* 9, col. 696.

42. *Catechism*, in *CO* 6, cols. 47, 48. "Catechism of the Church of Geneva," in Calvin, *Calvin: Theological Treatises*, 106.

43. *Catechism*, in *CO* 6, cols. 51–82. "Catechism of the Church of Geneva," in Calvin, *Calvin: Theological Treatises*, 107–19.

44. *Catechism*, in *CO* 6, cols. 39, 40. "Catechism of the Church of Geneva," in Calvin, *Calvin: Theological Treatises*, 102.

45. *Confession de la foy*, in *CO* 9, col. 698.

46. See the *Consensus Tigurinus*, article 7, in Calvin, *CTS* 2:214. See also *CO* 6, cols. 111, 112, "Catechism of the Church of Geneva," in Calvin, *Calvin: Theological Treatises*, 131.

47. *Catechism*, in *CO* 6, cols. 117, 118. "Catechism of the Church of Geneva," in Calvin, *Calvin: Theological Treatises*, 132.

48. See *Confession de la foy*, in *CO* 9, col. 697. *Catechism*, in *CO* 6, cols. 119–122. "Catechism of the Church of Geneva," in Calvin, *Calvin Theological Treatises*, 134–35.

49. *Consensus Tigurinus*, articles 9 and 14, in Calvin, *CTS* 2: 215, 216. The Genevan *Catechism* explains the nature of Christ's presence in these terms: "Minister: 'Have we in the Supper a mere symbol of those benefits you mention,

or is their reality exhibited to us there?' Child: 'Since our Lord Jesus Christ is the truth itself, there can be no doubt but that the promises which he there gives us, he at the same time also implements, adding the reality to the symbol. Therefore, I do not doubt but that, as testified by the words and signs, he thus also makes us partakers of his substance, by which we are joined in one life with him.'" See *CO* 6, cols. 127, 128. Calvin, *Calvin: Theological Treatises*, 137.

50. *Confession de la foy*, in *CO* 9, cols. 698–699; *Catechism*, in *CO* 6, cols. 133–134.

51. Thus, for example, in 1540 the Small Council reprimanded the minister Aimé Champereau for preaching that the remission of sins is achieved through baptism, and that the sacramental bread in the Lord's Supper is the actual body of Christ. See Lambert, "Preaching, Praying and Policing the Reform," 378–79.

52. For more on this, see chapter 8.

53. *RCP* 7:254–57, letter no. 33 bis. Ironically, it was a former Genevan minister named Pierre Merlin who raised the question at the fourteenth National Synod of Saumur (1597) whether Geneva's *Catechism* should continue to be "exposé publiquement" in the French churches. The Synod resolved to change nothing for the moment, and referred the question to the next synod. At the fifteenth National Synod of Montpellier (1598), after reading aloud Geneva's letter of concern, the assembly "declare que l'on ne fera aucun changement dans la Liturgie de nos Eglises, dans le Chant des Psaumes, ni dans le Formulaire de nos Catechismes." See Aymon, *Tous les synodes*, 1: 200, 219.

54. For Calvin's interchange with Louis Du Tillet, see Gordon, *Calvin*, 92–94; and Selderhuis, *John Calvin*, 66–67.

55. Louis Du Tillet to Calvin, September 7, 1538, *CO* 10.2, cols. 241–42; and Du Tillet to Calvin, December 1, 1538, *CO* 10.2, col. 293.

56. Calvin to Louis Du Tillet, October 20, 1538, *CO* 10.2, cols. 269–72; *CTS* 4:94–99.

57. Quoted in Nugent, *Ecumenism in the Age of the Reformation*, 135–36. For further discussion of this confrontation at Poissy, see Maruyama, *Ecclesiology of Theodore Beza*, 51–55.

58. Aymon, *Tous les synodes*, 1:78. See also Quick, *Synodicon in Gallia Reformata*, 74; and Maag, "Called to Be a Pastor," 74–75.

59. Méjan, *Discipline de l'Église Réformée de France*, 214. That Lutheran churches also struggled with the problem of self-made preachers, see Luther's "On the Sneaks and Furtive Preachers" (1532), in *WA* 30.III, 518–27; and, Gerrish, "Priesthood and Ministry in the Theology of Luther," 406–407.

60. Beza, *Sermons sur l'histoire de la résurrection*, 377. The Company of Pastors addressed the problem of *coureurs* in the reformed church of Castres in May 1593. See *RCP* 6:117–18 and letter no. 69 (303). For more discussion of these *coureurs*, see Maag, "Called to be a Pastor," 73–78.

61. *Institutes* (1536), 170.

62. The 1543 edition of the *Institutes* includes this paragraph: "We therefore hold that this call of a minister is lawful according to the Word of God, when those who seemed fit are created by the consent and approval of the people; moreover, that other pastors ought to preside over the election in order that the multitude may not go wrong either through fickleness, through evil intentions,

or through disorder." This statement was retained in the 1559 edition of the *Institutes* (IV.iii.15, p. 1066).

63. *Institutes* IV.iii.11, pp. 1062–63.

64. *Institutes*, IV.iii.4, p. 1057. This concept of extraordinary vocation also figures in Beza's theology. See, for example, his *Confession de la foi chrestienne*, 147–48; *Sermons sur l'histoire de la résurrection*, 391–99; and especially his *Ad tractationem de ministrorum evangelii gradibus ab H. Saravia....Responsio*, 11–19. On this latter work, see Maruyama, *Ecclesiology of Theodore Beza*, 188–89.

65. *EO* (1541), 263.

66. Calvin notes: "Today true pastors do not rashly thrust themselves forward at their own will, but are raised up by the Lord." Comm. Eph. 4:11, in *CNTC* 11:178.

67. See the Company of Pastor's letter to [André?] Pelade, June 17, 1565, *RCP* 3:175, no. 12.

68. *RCP* 10:117. The Company of Pastors made this statement to counter the attempt of Geneva's magistrates to woo Michel Le Faucheur from his church in France. See the final section of this chapter.

69. Of fifty pastors between 1559 and 1609 whose age is known or can be calculated with some precision, commencement of ministry in Geneva is distributed as follows: 20–24 years (15 ministers), 25–29 years (16 ministers), 30–34 years (5 ministers), 35–39 years (7 ministers), 40–44 years (5 ministers), 55–59 years (1 minister), 65–69 years (1 minister). From this sample, the average age at which men began pastoral ministry in Geneva was 30.6 years (median age 27). My data appear to follow quite closely the age distribution that historians have observed for commencement of ministry in other regions of Protestant Europe during the period. See Dixon and Schorn-Schütte, *Protestant Clergy of Early Modern Europe*, 26–28.

70. Note that Tronchin and Diodati were in their early twenties when they were appointed to academic posts at the Academy and admitted to the Company of Pastors. Both were somewhat older when they were assigned pastoral roles in the Genevan church.

71. *RCP* 8:294, letter no. 6. See also ibid., 307, letter no. 13; and ibid., 379, letter no. 50.

72. Nicolas Le More to the Church of Geneva, November 1, 1561, *BSHPF* 46 (1897): 466–48, quoted in Maag, *Seminary or University?* 22.

73. *EO* (1541), 262.

74. Although Calvin's Academy had no formal curriculum, the general subject areas treated by the professors each week are described in Gillian Lewis, "The Geneva Academy," 42–44; Maag, *Seminary or University?* 116–18; and Fraenkel, *De L'Écriture à la dispute*.

75. Hay, *Certain Demandes Concerning the Christian Religion and Discipline*.

76. Beza, *Response aux cinq premières et principales demandes de F. Iean Hay*, 42–44. Beza argued in a similar fashion in several of his sermons. See in particular his *Sermons sur le Cantique des Cantiques*, 213–14 and *Sermons sur l'histoire de la résurrection*, 527–28, 556. For a fuller treatment of Beza's commitment to the humanistic educational program, see my article "Psalms before Sonnets: Theodore Beza and the *Studia Humanitatis*."

77. Goulart, *Seconde partie des Discours Chrestiens*, 17–18.

78. Maag, "Called to Be a Pastor," 75–78.

79. Quoted in Bernus, *Le ministre Antoine de Chandieu*, 122.

80. *RCP* 5:247, letter no. 19.

81. Nicolas Le More to the Church of Geneva, November 1, 1561, *BSHPF* 46 (1897): 466–68, quoted in Maag, *Seminary or University?* 22. Emphasis added.

82. See *RCP* 2:111.

83. For an example of this pastoral charge, see the election of Simon Garnier, *RCP* 9:176.

84. *RCP* 4:70–72. Unfortunately, Pierre Servier died the following spring (see *RCP* 4:83).

85. These examples are drawn from *RCP* 8:250; 2:67; 6:81; and 7:12–13, 104, 106, 113.

86. *RCP* 4:72, 74–75, quoting from the minutes of the Small Council (RC 71, fol. 162v).

87. *RCP* 8:133. For more details on Gautier's troubled history, see ibid. 6:136–37, 8:28–29, 36.

88. The *Ecclesiastical Ordinances* (1576) for the first time affirmed the right of the magistrates to evaluate the trial sermons of ministerial candidates. For an example of senators intervening in a theological examination, see *RCP* 7:11.

89. *RCP* 5:50–51. Ten years later, Petit was once again considered for a pastoral post, and once again denied. In 1598, he abjured the Protestant faith through the preaching ministry of François de Sales. See *RCP* 7:10.

90. *RCP* 5:53.

91. See *EO* (1576), 278–80. This provision that granted the congregation the right of reporting objections to the magistrates first appeared in the revision of the *Ordinances* in 1561, but without the detail stipulated in the revision fifteen years later. See *CO* 10.1, col. 94.

92. See Aymon, *Tous les synodes*, 1:264, article 8. By the end of the sixteenth century, the Discipline of the Reformed Church of France required that candidates for ministry be ordained by the laying on of hands. See Méjan, *Discipline de l'Église Réformée de France*, 194–95. Accordingly, the seventeenth National Synod of Gap (1603) requested that the Genevan Church henceforth refrain from sending French students at the Academy to countryside parishes to preach and administer the sacraments without first ordaining them with "l'imposition des mains…" (Aymon, *Tous les synodes*, 1:264). The magistrates of Geneva appear to have used this incident in 1605 to force the issue with the city ministers, demanding that all candidates for ministry in Geneva receive the laying on of hands at their installation. See *RCP* 9:91, 129–30, 157, and ibid., 10:85, 87.

93. The "Formule du serment prescrit aux ministres" was approved by the Small Council on July 17, 1542. The text is found in *CO* 10.1, cols. 31–32 and Heyer, *L'Église de Genève*, 275–76.

94. Register of the Small Council, cited in Choisy, *L'État Chrétien Calviniste*, 17. See also *RCP* 3:149, ibid., 9:161–62.

95. *RCP* 2:98–99.

96. This was not the first time that the Small Council attempted to wrest control of pastoral assignments from the Company of Pastors, however. Already

in 1553, the magistrates transferred the minister François Bourgoing from his post in Jussy to a city church without the knowledge or consent of Calvin and his colleagues. The Company of Pastors sent two ministers to the Council to protest this action, but in the end decided to accept it. See *RCP* 1:160–61, and ibid., 2:1–2.

97. For more on this controversy, see Jones, *Simon Goulart*, 143–46.

98. *RCP* 8:216–17.

99. *RCP* 8:217, and note 173.

100. *RCP* 8:223–24.

101. See *RCP* 8:252.

102. RC, August 1, 1603. Cited in Jones, *Simon Goulart*, 149.

103. *RCP* 8:242, 244.

104. *RCP* 8:241.

105. This episode is described in Choisy, *L'État Chrétien Calviniste à Genève*, 369–70.

106. *RCP* 9:72.

107. *RCP* 9:74.

108. For more on Le Faucheur, see "Pasteurs et Prédicateurs" [anonymous]; and Olson, "Nicolas des Gallars, Sieur de Saules." The first article lists Le Faucheur's year of birth as 1585.

109. *RCP* 9:186. I found no reference to the elder Michel Le Faucheur in the register of the Consistory for 1606.

110. Pierre de L'Estoile records the remarkable effect that Le Faucheur had on the congregation of Charenton in October 1609: "Il prit son thème sur le passage du Psaume: *J'aime mon Dieu*, lequel il traita fort gentiment et pathétiquement; chose propre pour un peuple qui se prend il vint à sa péroration, il tira les larmes des yeux de la pl:uspart de ceux de l'assistance….encore que les compunctions en ceux de sa qualité soient fort rares. Ceux qui m'en ont parlé sans passion….m'ont dit qu'à la vérité son esprit et sa doctrine passoient bien son âge, et que son hardiesse, éloquence et passion par-dessus tous ses compagnons, voire les plus anciens et renommés, promettaient quelque chose de grand et non vulgaire." Cited in "Pasteurs et Prédicateurs," 423–24.

111. *RCP* 10:103.

112. *RCP* 10:100. This is the statement of the Council's position, as reported by the secretary of the Company of Pastors.

113. *RCP* 10:102 and note 229.

114. *RCP* 10:115–16.

115. *RCP* 10:117–19.

116. *RCP* 10:118.

117. From RC 105, fol. 182, quoted in *RCP* 10:122, note 301.

118. *RCP* 10:261–62, letter no. 72.

119. *RCP* 10:138–39.

120. Aymon, *Tous les synodes*, 1:383.

121. *RCP* 10:156, and letter no. 88.

122. See Choisy, *L'État Chrétien Calviniste*; and Campagnolo, "Jacques Lect."

123. Choisy, *L'État Chrétien Calviniste*, 374–75, 412.

124. *RCP* 8:223–24.

125. See Schilling, "Confessional Europe"; and Reinhard, "Pressures towards Confessionalization?" For an excellent summary and evaluation of the confessionalization thesis, see Ute Lotz-Heumann's chapter, "Confessionalization," in *Reformation and Early Modern Europe: A Guide to Research*.

126. Schorn-Schütte correctly observes: "The image of the clergyman as an agent of the state, which has long been employed to characterize both Protestant and Catholic structures, urgently requires revision, especially for the era under discussion here [i.e., early modern Europe]. Even if it is true that Protestant and reformed Catholic states prescribed a role for the clergy that was useful to the temporal authorities, this did not preclude the clergy of either confession from viewing the authorities critically." Quoted in "Clergy in the Early Modern Holy Roman Empire," 727. See also Schorn-Schütte, "Priest, Preacher, Pastor," 1, 29–36.

127. "Formule du serment prescrit aux ministres, 17 juillet 1542." Cited in Heyer, *L'Église de Genève*, 275.

Chapter 4

1. Chandieu, *Octonaires sur la Vanité et Inconstance du Monde*, 78. Barker describes this collection of poems as "Chandieu's masterpiece...the apogee of his poetry," Barker, *Protestantism, Poetry and Protest*, 225.

2. The belief that virginity was superior to marriage emerges from the earliest period of the Christian era. As St. Cyprian commented in the third century: "You, virginity, are the most beautiful part of holy church, and merit the hundredfold fruit, while widowhood merits only sixty, and marriage thirty." This viewpoint became commonplace thereafter, defended by such leading churchmen as Augustine, Thomas Aquinas, and Jean Gerson during the next millennium in the Christian West. For a succinct summary of Catholic attitudes toward marriage and celibacy in the Middle Ages, see Brown, *Pastor and Laity in the Theology of Jean Gerson*, 226–238; and Ozment, *When Father's Ruled*, 9–12. For the Protestant reformers' critique of the Catholic teaching on marriage and celibacy, see Witte Jr., *Law and Protestantism*, ch. 6; and Witte Jr. and Kingdon, *Sex, Marriage, and Family in John Calvin's Geneva*, 38–48.

3. *Institutes* (1536), 172–73. For Luther's view, see McLaughlin, "The Making of the Protestant Pastor," 64–67.

4. Farel, *Sommaire*, quoted in Louis Aubert's chapter "Mariage de Farel et nouveaux voyages," in *Guillaume Farel, 1489–1565*, 673.

5. Karant-Nunn, "The Emergence of the Pastoral Family," 98.

6. Santschi, "Être religieux à Genève," 1–27.

7. R. Consist. 31 (1577), fols. 96v–97, 98v, 103v, 122v–123. The Small Council investigated and deposed Druson from his pastoral office on September 16, 1577. See RC, 72, fols. 124–25v.

8. According to Anne-Marie Piuz, social demographers have established that at the beginning of the seventeenth century, Genevan women were married at 21.4 years, on average. See Piuz, "Les gens," in Mottu-Weber, Piuz, and Lescaze, *Vivre à Genève*, 70. E. William Monter proposes an older age for women at first marriage: "in both the city of Geneva and its hinterland, the median age at first marriage for women rose suddenly and permanently from twenty/twenty-one years

to about twenty-four years at the very end of the sixteenth century." "Historical Demography and Religious History in Sixteenth-Century Geneva," 419.

9. Jones, *Simon Goulart*, 7.

10. Doumergue, *Jean Calvin*, 3:578.

11. See Oberman, "Calvin and Farel: The Dynamics of Legitimation in Early Calvinism," in *John Calvin and the Reformation of the Refugees*; Gordon, *Calvin*, 281–82.

12. Piuz, "Les gens," in Mottu-Weber, Piuz, Lescaze, *Vivre à Genève*, 69–70.

13. Jones, *Simon Goulart*, 47.

14. Barnaud, *Pierre Viret*, 313–15.

15. See Beza to Johann Piscator, August 27 /6 September 6, 1588, in Cyprian, *Catalogus codicum manuscriptorum bibliothecae Gothanae*, 51–52. For more information about Beza's second marriage, see Geisendorf, *Théodore de Bèze*, 325–27.

16. Cottret, *Calvin*, 139–40.

17. Geisendorf, *Théodore de Bèze*, 28.

18. Greengrass, *French Reformation*, 50.

19. Geisendorf, *Les Trembley de Genève*, 30.

20. Dardier, *Jean de Serres*, 10–11.

21. The account of the marriage troubles of Honoré and Marie Blanchard appears in *RCP* 5: 4–5, 7, 12, 14–15, 22, 28–29, 109, 163, and 217. Note that the *Ecclesiastical Ordinances* (1576) allowed for annulment of marriage in cases of impotence. See Heyer, *L'Église de Genève*, 277–313, art., 143.

22. Quoted in Bernus, *Le Ministre Antoine de Chandieu*, 85.

23. See Barnaud, *Pierre Viret*, 319. These accidents involving little Marie occurred while Pierre Viret and his family lived in Lausanne, around a decade before they immigrated to Geneva.

24. Hilarius Grubbe to Beza, May 20, 1585, Rigsarkiv, Copenhagen XIII. Grubbe was the chancellor of the Danish king, who sent his son to Geneva for studies in 1585.

25. Theodore Beza's letters contain frequent discussion of such matters. See, for example, his interaction with Zurich's pastoral company regarding reports of the misbehavior of Josiah Simler, grandson of the Zurich pastor Rudolph Gwalther. Beza to Rudolph Gwalter, August 26/September 5, 1584, Statdtbibl. Zurich, ms. F 37, fol. 64; Heinrich Wolf to Beza, August 31/September 10, 1584, mss. B. Gotha (Cod. Chart. A 405, fol. 154); Heinrich Wolf to Beza, October 11/21, 1585, Mss. B. Gotha (Cod. Chart. A. 405, fol. 153).

26. This passage is found in a letter that Baduel wrote to the Magistrates of Bern in the 1540s, quoted in *FP* 2nd ed., 1:698.

27. Thomas Cartwright to Beza, July 25 [1577?], in *CB* 18:143. See also Dufour, *Théodore de Bèze*, 171. For the student boarders in Daneau's home, see Fatio, *Méthode et théologie*, 32, note 160.

28. This list of daily household responsibilities is corroborated by a fascinating document entitled "studiorum ratio," written by Beza's one-time colleague, Jean Ribit, professor of theology at the Academy of Lausanne from 1547–1558/9. In his daily schedule, Ribit envisioned that at 11 a.m. he would devote himself to "household matters" (including looking over the family's financial records and attending to family correspondence); at 1 p.m. he would listen to his wife read

the Bible (while he followed along in the Greek and Hebrew texts); at 7 p.m. he would "listen to the children's lessons"; at 8 p.m. he would conduct household devotions. This latter responsibility must never be neglected, Ribit noted, "if you want God to show favor on your household management." See Meylan, "Professeurs et étudiants,", 70–71.

29. *Institutes* III.xx.50, pp. 917–18.

30. See Manetsch, "A Mystery Solved?" 280–81.

31. *Maister Beza's Houshold Prayers*, B8v, B11v-B12r. For more on this prayer book, see Dufour, "Une oeuvre inconnue de Bèze?" 402–405.

32. Pierre Viret to Calvin, August 1, 1550, *CO* 13, col. 614.

33. "Vie de Calvin par Nicolas Colladon," *CO* 21, col. 113. Colladon writes: "Quant au ieu, il est bien vray que quelque fois, quand cela venoit à propos et ne compagnie familiere, il se recreoit au palet, à la clef ou autre tel ieu licite par les loix et non defendu en ceste Republique: mais encore c'estoit bien peu souvent, et plustost à l'incitation de ses familiers amis, que de son propre movement."

34. Jones, *Simon Goulart*, 289–90. Goulart edited for publication a half dozen collections of French music, including the *Thrésor de musique d'Orlande de Lassus* (1576) and *Mélange des Pseaumes* (1577). On these works, see Droz, "Simon Goulart, éditeur de musique."

35. Dufour, *Théodore de Bèze*, 169.

36. Beza, dedicatory epistle to *Les Psaumes* (1553). Reprinted in Beza, "Les Psaumes et l'épître dédicatoire de Théodore de Bèze," 99.

37. Chandieu, *Octonaires sur la vanité et inconstance du monde*, 46.

38. Theodore Beza to Jean-Jacques Grynaeus, June 24 /July 4, 1595, in *BSHPF* 3 (1855): 146–57.

39. On this point see Shawn D. Wright's book *Our Sovereign Refuge*, which demonstrates in convincing fashion that, for Beza, the doctrine of God's sovereignty was a pastoral doctrine intended to comfort and fortify God's people. Wright, *Our Sovereign Refuge*.

40. The phrase *Dominus providebit* appears regularly in Beza's letters. See Manetsch, *Theodore Beza and the Quest for Peace in France*, 54, note 11. Goulart also employed this phrase from time to time. See Goulart to Isaac Casaubon, October 10/20, 1604, in Jones, *Simon Goulart*, 408, letter no. 32.

41. Beza, *Sermons sur l'histoire de la passion*, 494.

42. Beza, *Chrestiennes Méditations*, 92.

43. Goulart to Sébastien Schobinger, December 27, 1624, in Jones, *Simon Goulart*, 429, letter no. 42.

44. *Catechism*, in *CO* 6, cols. 8, 9. "Catechism of the Church of Geneva," In Calvin, *Calvin: Theological Treatises*, 91.

45. Beza, *Sermons sur l'histoire de la passion*, 480.

46. Jones, *Simon Goulart*, 45.

47. For Geneva's ministers as "personnes de qualité," see *RCP* 9:129.

48. PC #1288 (June 15–22, 1565); R. Consist. 18 (1561), fol. 173v; 33 (1582), fol. 60r-v; 20 (1563), fols. 6v, 9v; 34 (1592), fols. 41v–42.

49. R. Consist. 25 (1568), fol. 70v; 32 (1581), fol. 226; 34 (1594), fol. 320v. None of these rumors was substantiated.

50. R. Consist. 20 (1563), fol. 26; 24 (1567), fol. 45v; 25(1568), fol. 142v; 28 (1572), fols. 163v–164.

51. R. Consist., 33 (1589), fol. 146v.

52. R. Consist. 25 (1568), fols. 176, 180v.

53. R. Consist. 24 (1567), fol. 3.

54. See Ariès, *Centuries of Childhood*. Scholarship that embraced or built on Ariès's thesis includes Mause, *History of Childhood*; Stone, *Family, Sex and Marriage in England, 1500–1800*; and LeGoff, *Medieval Civilization*, 285–88.

55. The classic statement of this viewpoint was Edward Shorter, *Making of the Modern Family*, esp. 54–78. Shorter asserts that "popular marriage in former centuries was usually affectionless, held together by considerations of property and lineage; that the family's arrangements for carrying on the business of living enshrined this coldness by reducing to an absolute minimum the risk of spontaneous face-to-face exchanges between husband and wife; and that this emotional isolation was accomplished through the strict demarcation of work assignments and sex roles." Shorter concluded that this "lovelessness was a common feature of the petty bourgeois and peasant marriage everywhere" in early modern Europe. Ibid., 55, 61.

56. For helpful surveys of more recent interpretations of marriage and family life in early modern Europe, see Spierling, *Infant Baptism in Reformation Geneva*, 14–16; Schultz, *Knowledge of Childhood in the German Middle Ages, 1100–1350*, 1–13; Nichols, *Domestic Life of a Medieval City*; Ozment, *When Fathers Ruled*; and Wiesner, "Family, Household, and Community," 2:51–70.

57. On this sad affair, see Kingdon, *Adultery and Divorce in Calvin's Geneva*, 71–97.

58. *R. Consist.* III, 28–29.

59. R. Consist. 6 (1551), fol. 32. See also Santschi, "Être religieux à Genève," 24.

60. These ministers were Simon Moreau (deposed 1545), Aymé Méigret (deposed 1546), Jean Fabri (deposed 1556), Louis de La Maisonneuve (deposed 1583), and Jean Guérin II (deposed 1587). We have already noted the deposition of Honoré Blanchard in 1583 for, among other things, lying about his impotence. See chapter 7 for more details.

61. R. Consist. 27 (1570), fol. 162r–v and 28 (1571), fol. 12v. See also Geisendorf, *Théodore de Bèze*, 256–58; and Choisy, *L'État Chrétien Calviniste*, 40–44. Beza was away on a journey during the consistorial hearing and was not a key participant in this affair. However, on his return to Geneva, Beza expressed his anger and disappointment at the harsh treatment that his wife's niece received from the Consistory.

62. Calvin to Bucer, July 4, 1549, CO 20, col. 394. For a discussion of this passage, see Selderhuis, *John Calvin*, 172.

63. Pierre Viret to Pierre de Watteville, 1546, CO 12, col. 306. See Barnaud, *Pierre Viret*, 313–14.

64. Beza, "Les vertus de sa femme fidele et bonne mesnagere, comme il est escrit aux proverb de Salomon, chap. XXXI," in *Poemes, Chrestiens et Moraux*, D4–D4v.

65. Beza to Constantine Fabricius, April 30/May 10, 1588, Paris, Bibl. Ste. Geneviève, ms. 1455, fols. 19v–20v.

66. See Beza, *Theodori Bezae Vezelii Poemata Varia*, 58, 60. Beza's last will and testament is found in Geisendorf, *Théodore de Bèze*, 325.

67. Comm. Ephesians 5:28, *CTSNT*, 21:322. For Calvin's view of the roles of husbands and wives in marriage, see Bouwsma, *John Calvin*, 76–77, 137–38.

68. Beza, *Sermons sur l'histoire de la passion*, 708.

69. According to Piuz, between 1590 and 1609, 1,055 deaths were recorded in Geneva due to smallpox, of which 1,047 were infants below the age of fourteen years. See "Les gens," in Mottu-Weber, Piuz, Lescaze, *Vivre à Genève*, 72.

70. Quoted in Bernus, *Le Ministre Antoine de Chandieu*, 91.

71. Quoted in ibid., 85.

72. Comm. 1 Timothy 5:17, *CTSNT*, 21:139.

73. Comm. 1 Timothy 5:18, *CTSNT*, 21:140.

74. Comm. Galatians 6:6, *CTSNT*, 21:112.

75. Goulart, *Seconde partie des Discours Chrestiens*, 231.

76. This general description appears all the more plausible given our knowledge of the alternative residence which the Small Council considered assigning to Calvin in 1541. This home, known as *maison de la Chanterie*, included four kitchens, a study, a sitting room, five bedrooms, two cellars, and two stables. See Doumergue, *Jean Calvin*, 3:496–500. Similarly, the residence assigned to Pierre Viret in 1541 included a study, three bedrooms, a dining room, and a kitchen. Ibid., 3:499.

77. Doumergue cites the inventory of furnishings loaned to Calvin, dated December 27, 1548. See his *Jean Calvin*, 3:497. At the time of Calvin's death, all these items were returned to the city.

78. Calvin to Piperin, October 18, 1555, *CO* 15, cols. 825. See Selderhuis's discussion of this passage in *John Calvin*, 220.

79. Beza's "Protestant art gallery" became the cause of a minor polemical skirmish. In 1597, after visiting Beza's home and observing the reformer's paintings, the Catholic polemicist Antoine de Saint-Michel, Sire of Avully, rushed to publish his *Lettre d'un gentil-homme Savoysien, à un gentil-homme Lyonnois* (n.p., 1598), in which, among other things, he accused Beza of idolatry and vanity for owning and displaying these portraits (see pp. 19–20). Beza responded to these charges in his anonymous *Response à la letter d'un gentilhomme Savoisien*, 59–60. For more details on this controversy, see Manetsch, *Theodore Beza and the Quest for Peace in France*, 318–20.

80. For a map of the rue des Chanoines in the sixteenth century, see Monter, *Calvin's Geneva*, 175.

81. See *RCP* 4:64–65, 161; ibid., 9:198.

82. See, for example, *RCP* 4:71.

83. *RCP* 9:198; ibid., 5:142; ibid., 4:43.

84. *RCP* 10:113, ibid., 11:3–4. See also Jones, *Simon Goulart*, 238.

85. See, for example, the kinds of clerical support reported in the rural bailliage of Chablais in 1567, "Registres des Pensions et Prébendes," in Gaberel, *Histoire de l'Église de Genève*, vol. 2; Pièces Justificatives, 243–48.

86. See Naphy, *Calvin and the Consolidation of the Genevan Reformation*, 64–65.

87. *RCP* 5:208.

88. *RCP* 8:166.

89. AEG, Finances O, no. 6, fols. 6, 38v, 102.

90. AEG, Finances O, no. 6, fols. 40, 83, 145v.

91. See *RCP* 7:38, 49–50, 173, 179; ibid., 8:13, 104–105. The parish of Cartigny-Chancy was formally subdivided into separate parishes in 1598.

92. *RCP* 8:104–105.

93. *RCP* 9:9.

94. Piuz, "Salaires, Prix, Monnaie," in *Vivre à Genève*, Mottu-Weber, Piuz, Lescaze, 225–26.

95. These figures are drawn from Table II in Jean-François Bergier's article "Salaires des pasteurs de Genève,"170.

96. Bergier, "Salaires des pasteurs de Genève,"177–78.

97. See *RCP* 4:5. There was precedent for paying Geneva's ministers "in nature." In 1558, the magistrates decided to provide each of the city ministers with twelve coupes of wheat, but this practice appears to have been discontinued before 1575. See *RCP* 2:80–81. A coupe of wheat was 79.3452 liters.

98. *RCP* 9:68. See Lescaze, *Genève, sa vie et ses monnaies aux siècles passes*, 112.

99. The ministers with some regularity complained about the inferior quality of the wheat they received from the city. See, for example, *RCP* 6:139; 7:171, 172; 8:13–14; 9:68, 169; 10:13. Bergier estimates that by the beginning of the seventeenth century, the value of these grain supplements represented from 35 to 55 percent of the ministers' monetary salaries. See Bergier, "Salaires des pasteurs de Genève," 170–71.

100. *RCP* 9:81. White wine was believed to be superior to red wine and thus was the choice of social elites. See Piuz, "Se nourir," in Mottu-Weber, Piuz, Lescaze, *Vivre à Genève*, 191.

101. See *RCP* 4:81; ibid., 6:111, 114.

102. Anne-Marie Piuz estimates that, in 1604, assistants to cobblers earned 2 florins per day, or 600 florins per year, based on 300 days of labor. By contrast, countryside ministers received a salary of 540 florins per year. Although Geneva's magistrates supplemented the ministers' salaries by providing them with 324 florins worth of wheat each year, those who assisted craftsmen could expect lodging and board during their period of employment. See Piuz, "Salaires, prix, monnaie," in *Vivre à Genève*, Mottu-Weber, Piuz, Lescaze, 213–19. Piuz is summarizing data presented in Mottu-Weber, *Économie et refuge à Genève*.

103. By way of comparison, salaries of Geneva's professors in 1597 were as follows: Hermann Lignaridus (theology; 1,500 florins); David Colladon (law; 700 florins); Jean Diodati (Hebrew; 800 florins); Isaiah Colladon (philosophy; 800 florins); Gaspard Laurent (Greek; 800 florins). See AEG, Finances O, vol. 8 (1592–97), fols. 83–84, and Piuz, "Salaires, prix, monnaie," in *Vivre à Genève*, 219.

104. See Robert Kingdon, "The Economic Activity of Ministers in Geneva in the Middle Sixteenth Century."

105. Olson, *Calvin and Social Welfare*, 120–26.

106. *RCP* 6:114, 110, 38.

107. *RCP* 3:136.

108. *RCP* 6:111.

109. RC 50, fol. 91, quoted in Doumergue, *Jean Calvin*, 3:463–64.

110. These gifts are recorded in the city's account books, found at AEG, Finances O, no. 6 (1563–1569), fols. 71v, 117, 134v, 166v; ibid., no. 7 (1572–1580), fols. 42v, 77.

111. Commenting on the great poverty of the minister Jean Du Perril (minister of Neydens from 1561), the registers of the Company of Pastors noted that this could not help but "l'affliger et empescher grandement à son ministere." RCP 4:135–36.

112. RCP 3:137–38.

113. RC 86, fol. 235r–v.

114. RC 87, fol. 108.

115. For more on Beza's financial hardship in old age, see Manetsch, *Theodore Beza and the Quest for Peace in France*, 213–15, 343.

116. Beza, *Sermons sur l'histoire de la passion*, 990–91. For a similar discussion, see his *Sermons sur l'histoire de la résurrection*, 526–28.

Chapter 5

1. *La forme des prières et chantz ecclésiastiques*, j8r–v.

2. See Muir, *Ritual in Early Modern Europe*, 62–79; Scribner, *Popular Culture and Popular Movements in Reformation Germany*, chs. 1 and 2.

3. The seven major feasts devoted to the Virgin Mary commemorate her purification (Feb. 2; also known as Candlemas), Annunciation (March 25), Visitation (July 2), Assumption (Aug. 15), Birth (Sept. 8), Presentation (Nov. 21), and Conception (Dec. 8).

4. Benedict, *Christ's Churches Purely Reformed*, 495–96.

5. Ibid., 31, 42. Zwingli's recommendation, however, was seen as too radical, and the Zurich City Council set the number of holidays at thirteen in 1526. In 1550, a new city council reduced the number of religious festivals to six. See ibid., 31.

6. R. Consist. 8 (1554), fol. 82v.

7. R. Consist. 20 (1563), fol. 168v.

8. R. Consist. 25 (1568), fol. 65. See also ibid., 24 (1567), fol. 158v.

9. For disciplinary cases related to Christmas observance, see R. Consist. 18 (1562), fols. 190v–191v; 21 (1565), fol. 197; 23 (1566), fol. 24; 33 (1582), fol. 95. For disciplinary cases related to the observance of the feasts of Epiphany and Ascension, see R. Consist. 28 (1572), fol. 121; 31 (1579), fol. 280v; 34 (1594), fols. 228, 230v; 25 (1568), fol. 102. For disciplinary cases related to Lenten observance, see R. Consist. 26 (1569), fol. 52; and 27 (1570), fol. 64.

10. See the vivid description of this celebration in January 1579, described in R. Consist. 31 (1579), fol. 278. In this case, the Consistory suspended five men from the Lord's Supper for "making the king."

11. "Charles Perrot's Description of Parish Life, circa 1564," appendix 4 in Lambert, "Preaching, Praying and Policing the Reform," 540–41.

12. RCP 9:56.

13. RCP 9:81–82.

14. See EO (1541), 9.

15. The requirement of an annual household visitation at Easter was introduced in the revision of the *Ecclesiastical Ordinances* (1561). See CO 10.1, col. 116, and Grosse's discussion in *Les rituels de la cène*, 400–408

16. *RCP* 11:14. Also see Grosse's discussion, "'Le mystère de communiquer à Jésus-Chirst,'" 169–70.

17. *La forme des prières et chantz ecclésiastiques*, l4v–l5r.

18. The censure was mandated by the *Ecclesiastical Ordinances* (1541): "Pour maintenir cette discipline en son état, que, de trois mois en trois mois, les ministres aient spécialement regard s'il y a crime à redire entre eux, pour y remédier comme de raison," (265).

19. The practice of the censure went through some minor modifications between 1559 and 1609. Beginning in 1576, the Company of Pastors decided to hold the censure on Fridays, nine days before the celebration of the Lord's Supper, to make it more convenient for countryside pastors to attend. So too, during periods of plague or famine, the Company sometimes cancelled the communal meal after the censure. See *RCP* 4:67, 75–76, 128; and 5:67.

20. *RCP* 1:58–61. See my discussion of this case in chapter 2.

21. *RCP* 2:82.

22. See *RCP* 4:31; 5:73, 139–40; 7:7; 8:69. For Beza's controversy with Gilbert Genebrard, see Geisendorf, *Théodore de Bèze*, 336.

23. *Institutes* IV.xii.17, p. 1243.

24. *RCP* 4:115.

25. *RCP* 4:115–16.

26. For more on the "Genevan Fast," see Fatio, *Le jeûne genevois*. Fatio estimates that around fifteen public fasts were observed between 1567 and 1620.

27. Grosse, *Les rituels de la cène*, 472–73.

28. R. Consist. 23 (1566), fol. 34v.

29. The best statement of Calvin's view of the fourth commandment is found in the *Institutes* II.viii.28–34, pp. 394–401. A more succinct statement is found in Geneva's *Cathechism* (1542), see *CO* 6, cols. 61–68; Calvin, *Calvin: Theological Treatises*, 111–13. For a helpful examination of Calvin's broader treatment of this subject, see Gaffin Jr., *Calvin and the Sabbath*.

30. Sermon on Deuteronomy 5:12–14, *CO* 26, col. 292.

31. Beza, *Les Pseaumes de David et les cantiques de la Bible*, 460.

32. Sermon on 1 Timothy 3:16, in *CO* 53, cols. 320. On this passage, see Leith, "Reformed Preaching Today," 228, note 8.

33. See R. Consist. 32 (1581), fol. 244v; 24 (1567), fol. 165; 22 (1565), fol. 121v; 31 (1579), fol. 283v; 31 (1577), fols. 70, 98v.

34. See R. Consist. 27 (1570), fols. 65, 88; 30 (1576), fol. 44; 23 (1566), fols. 21v, 49v; 16 (1559), fol. 194v; 16 (1559), fol. 230v; 22 (1565), fols. 85, 87.

35. R. Consist. 18 (1561), fol. 59v.

36. See R. Consist. 18 (1561), fol. 24; 24 (1567), fols. 80v, 99v; 28 (1571), fol. 41v; and PC #1639 (March 30–April 3, 1571).

37. See R. Consist. 28 (1571), fol. 59. Elsewhere, the Consistory minutes describe Sunday as "le jour du repos." See R. Consist. 32 (1581), fol. 272v.

38. For the locations of the weekly Congregation and the Company of Pastors meetings, see *RCP* 7:80–81. The statement by Peter Paul Vergerius in note 52, however, indicates that at least sometimes the weekly Congregation was held in the temple of St. Pierre itself.

39. *EO* (1541), 264.

40. Calvin to Farel, April 20, 1539, in *CO* 10.2, col. 337, *CTS* 4:132, discussed in Selderhuis, *John Calvin*, 220.

41. RC, vol. 79, fol. 130v–131; quoted in *RCP* 5:37–38.

42. Calvin to Anonymous, 1540, *CO* 11, cols. 56–57, discussed in Kraus, "Calvin's Exegetical Principles," 11.

43. Beza, *Sermons sur l'histoire de la passion*, 454, 319–20.

44. Beza, *Sermons sur le Cantique des Cantiques*, 48–49.

45. See Peter, *Jean Calvin, Deux Congrégations*; and de Boer, "Congrégation." The model of Zurich's *Prophezei* was duplicated not only in Geneva, but in Strasbourg, Bern, the Low Countries, England, Scotland, and Eastern Europe. See Benedict, *Christ's Churches Purely Reformed*, 30, 71, 163, 250, 266.

46. *EO* (1561); *CO* 10.1, col. 96.

47. Calvin to Wolfgang Musculus, October 22, 1549, *CO* 13, cols. 433–34.

48. Calvin to Wolfgang Musculus, December 7, 1549, *CO* 13, col. 491; *CTS* 5:252.

49. Calvin to Wolfgang Musculus, October 22, 1549, *CO* 13, col. 434.

50. "Congrégation faite en l'église de Genève, en laquelle a esté traittée la matière de l'élection éternelle de Dieu," in *CO* 8, col. 93. See Peter's discussion of the format of the Congregation, in *Jean Calvin, Deux Congrégations*, x–xi.

51. AEG, Ms. Fr. 40a, f. 76b, quoted in De Boer, "Congrégation," 72–73. Ten years later the Company of Pastors mandated that long invitations for public comment should be abbreviated to this succinct statement: "This concludes what God has given me on this passage. I invite the brothers to add what they think necessary for the edification of the Church." See *RCP* 3:104.

52. Gaberel includes (in French translation) a letter written by the Italian marquis Peter Paul Vergerius, describing his attendance at a Congregation during a brief visit to Geneva around 1556: "On Friday morning they hold in the cathedral a service called the Congregation, which all of the ministers and a lot of citizens attend. A pastor reads the scripture and explains it briefly. Next one of his colleagues expresses his views on the subject and then all the members of the assembly who wish to make a contribution speak in turn. As you can see, this is an imitation of the custom in the Corinthian church of which Paul speaks, and I have received great edification from these public colloquies." Gaberel, *Histoire de l'Église de Genève*, 2:512–13.

53. *RCP* 7:180–81.

54. *RCP* 1: 47.

55. See *RCP* 1:81. For a detailed discussion of this affair, see Gordon, *Calvin*, 205–209; and Cottret, *Calvin*, 209 12

56. Some of the books studied included Psalms (1555–59), the harmony of Exodus through Deuteronomy (1559–62), Galatians (1562–63), Joshua (1564), Isaiah (begun 1564), Judges (begun 1569), Romans (begun 1577), Job (concluded 1600), Isaiah (1600–1604), and Jeremiah (begun 1604). See Peter, *Jean Calvin, Deux Congrégations*, xv–xvi; and *RCP* 3:23; 4:88; 7:81; 8:8; 9:5.

57. *RCP* 10:86. See also ibid., 9:218.

58. *RCP* 10:166. See also ibid., 10:88.

59. *RCP* 10:173–74.

60. Thus, in 1610, Gaspard Laurent, the professor of Greek at the Genevan Academy, received permission from the Venerable Company to no longer attend the weekly Congregation. The rationale given was that the Friday morning service now resembled more a regular weekday sermon. See *RCP* 11:12.

61. Such was the case with the vibrant parish of Bossey-Neydens in 1600. See *RCP* 8:26.

62. *RCP* 2:6. In the same year, Jean de Montliard was forced to leave his post at Draillans because his bad feet made it impossible for him to acquit his ministry in a parish where "the houses of his parishioners were few and spread far apart from one another."

63. *RCP* 4:48. See also ibid., 8:26, 240.

64. See AEG, Finances O, vol. 9, fols. 20, 77.

65. See *RCP* 4:48–49; and RC, vol. 71, fols. 56v–57. It is possible, though not certain, that the death of the minister of Russin, Pierre Servier, was due to complications from this accident.

66. Lambert Daneau, pastor at Vandoeuvres from 1572–1574 expressed these sentiments in a letter in 1572. See Daneau to Pierre Daniel, [end of 1572], in Félice, *Lambert Daneau*, 305–306, letter XXV.

67. Scholars who have studied pastoral ministry in other regions of Reformation Europe have noted similar social and intellectual challenges for ministers assigned to rural parishes. For example, see Tolley, *Pastors & Parishioners in Württemberg*, 64–82, 113–14.

68. *RCP* 2:98–99.

69. AEG, EC Genthod, vol. 1 (1564–1630, 1696–1700), fols. 1–15. A transcription of this document appears in Lambert, "Preaching, Praying and Policing the Reform," appx. 4, 539–48.

70. AEG, EC Genthod, vol. 1, fols. 9–11.

71. AEG, EC Genthod, vol. 1, fol. 11.

72. AEG, EC Genthod, vol. 1, fols. 13–15.

73. AEG, EC Genthod, vol. 1, fol. 15.

74. Monter, *Calvin's Geneva*, 193–208.

75. *RCP* 5:125. See also ibid., 4:122–23.

76. *RCP* 5:187, note 65.

77. *RCP* 6:13, 35. See also Du Perril, *Journal de la guerre de 1589.*

78. For details about Catholic missionary activities in Chablais during this period, see Martin, *Trois cas de pluralisme confessionel aux XVIe et XVIIe siècle*, 73–106; Gonthier and Letourneau, *Vie de Saint François de Sales*, 120–60; Manetsch, *Theodore Beza and the Quest for Peace in France*, 318–28; and Fehleison, *Boundaries of Faith.*

79. The forty-hour devotion proved a particularly effective evangelistic method in Chablais. Formally recognized by Clement VIII in 1592, this devotional practice was a forty-hour period of special prayers, processions, and litanies leading up to the high Mass. See *New Catholic Encyclopedia*, vol. 5 (New York: McGraw-Hill, 1967), 1036.

80. See Beza's letter to Abraham Schultheiss, October 22/November 1, 1598, Paris, Bibl. Ste. Geneviève, ms. 1455, fols. 266v–268v. Manetsch, *Theodore Beza and the Quest for Peace in France*, 323.

81. *RCP* 7:89, 90, 92. Osée André, the minister of Chancy, was able to escape after three months. The minister of Bossey, Jean Gervais, was ransomed for 400 écus. See Geisendorf, *Les annalistes genevois au début du XVIIe siècle*, 566–69.

82. *RCP* 7:101–102, and notes 84 and 87. Geneva's magistrates hastily wrote a letter to the Savoyard official, demanding that he leave the villagers "in the freedom of their consciences." Ibid.

83. *RCP* 7:86.

84. For a poignant description of the Catholic conversion of Gaillard, see *RCP* 8:82.

85. *RCP* 8:90–91.

86. *RCP* 8:133.

87. *RCP* 7:91–93.

88. *RCP* 7:118, 125, 131, 138, 141.

89. *RCP* 7:185. See a similar complaint several years later, at ibid., 8:240.

90. *RCP* 8:24; ibid., 9:142, 188; ibid., 11:26.

91. *RCP* 9:114.

92. *RCP* 9:192.

93. *RCP* 9:33, 181; ibid., 10:112.

94. RCP 9:142–43.

95. *FP* 5:256.

Chapter 6

1. The Juranville–Martinville affair is described in detail by Choisy, *L'État Chrétien Calviniste*, 303–314; and Jones, *Simon Goulart*, 76–105. (Note that both authors mistakenly identify Madame Martinville as the step-sister of Madame Juranville.) Jones includes a transcription of the minutes of the criminal case against Simon Goulart, see PC #1798, no. 6; ibid. 441–47. For the response of the Company of Pastors, see *RCP* 7:15–20, 25–28.

2. PC #1798, no. 6, in Jones, *Simon Goulart*, 446.

3. *RCP* 7:18.

4. PC #1798, no. 6, in Jones, *Simon Goulart*, 444.

5. RC 90, fols. 154r–v.

6. RC 90, fols. 158v–159.

7. See Naphy, *Calvin and the Consolidation of the Genevan Reformation*, 5.

8. Karant-Nunn, "Preaching the Word in Early Modern Germany," 194–95.

9. For a description of this homiletic revolution, see the helpful survey by Phyllis Roberts, "The *Ars Praedicandi* and the Medieval Sermon." Johann-Baptist Schneyer has catalogued 140,000 extant Latin sermons for the period 1150–1350 in his *Repertorium der lateinischen Sermones des Mittelalters für die Zeit von 1150–1350*, 11 vols. On this see Hanska, "Reconstructing the Mental Calendar of Medieval Preaching," 299–300.

10. This figure is suggested by Hervé Martin, as reported by Lambert, "Preaching, Praying and Policing the Reform," 284.

11. On this, see O'Malley, *Praise and Blame in Renaissance Rome*. The main arguments of this book are summarized elsewhere, notably in Worcester, "Catholic Sermons," 10–11; and O'Malley, "Content and Rhetorical Forms in Sixteenth-Century Treatises on Preaching."

12. In his influential study of the preaching office during the later Middle Ages, Hervé Martin identified 1,849 clergymen who are known to have preached in France between 1350 and 1520. Of this number, 1,601 (87 percent) were from the mendicant orders. Martin identified an additional 849 church leaders who might have preached during this period. See Martin, *Le métier de prédicateur à la fin du Moyen Age, 1350–1520,* 23–77.

13. This general conclusion of historians is borne out by Martin's findings. Of the 1,849 preachers that he identifies in France from 1350–1520, only 263 (14 percent) were known to come from the ranks of the secular clergy. And it is unlikely that many of these secular clergy who preached were parish priests. Martin, *Le métier de prédicateur,* 23–77. See also Taylor, *Soldiers of Christ.* These conclusions, however, may not hold true of Catholic parish life in the Holy Roman Empire during the age of the Reformation. See Frymire, *The Primacy of the Postils,* 15–22.

14. Binz, *Vie religieuse et réforme ecclésiastique,* 1:390–92.

15. Binz, "Le fin du Moyen Âge (1260–1536)," 78. For more on Vincent Ferrier and his dramatic homiletical style, see Kienzle, "Medieval Sermons and their Performance," 108–109.

16. Fellay, "Les évêques, princes, et pasteurs," 121.

17. Ibid.; Eire, *War Against the Idols,* 133–34.

18. *SC* 8:210.

19. See, for example, *RCP* 2:88, 89, 90, 91.

20. R. Consist. 13 (1558), fol. 121.

21. Lambert indicates that in 1538 there were a total of five sermons in the city's churches on Sundays, and two sermons the rest of the week. Lambert, "Preaching, Praying and Policing the Reform," 285.

22. *EO* (1541), 266. On Geneva's early preaching schedule, see Lambert, "Preaching, Praying and Policing the Reform," 285–91. For a slightly different enumeration of weekly sermons, see McKee, "Calvin and his Colleagues as Pastors," 17–19.

23. The *Ecclesiastical Ordinances* (1541) are rather cryptic on this point: "Et jours ouvriers, outre les deux predications qui se font, que trios fois la semaine, on prêche à Saint-Pierre, à savoir lundi, mercredi et vendredi, et que ces sermons soient sonnés l'un après l'autre à telle heure qu'ils puissant être finis devant qu'on commence ailleurs," (ibid., 266). See Lambert's helpful discussion of this passage, "Preaching, Praying and Policing the Reform," 285–86, note 12.

24. Lambert, "Preaching, Praying and Policing the Reform," 286–87.

25. See *Ecclesiastical Ordinances* (1561), in *CO* 10.1, cols. 99–100. The schedule of services was as follows: At the Madeleine, sermons were held Monday through Saturday at 6 a.m. or 7 a.m., and Sunday at 8 a.m., noon (catechism), and 3 p.m. At St. Gervais, preaching services were conducted Wednesday at 4 a.m. or 5 a.m., Monday through Saturday at 6 a.m. or 7a.m., and Sunday at 4 or 5 a.m., 8 a.m., noon (catechism), and 3 p.m. At St. Pierre, sermons were given Monday, Wednesday, and Friday at 4 a.m. or 5 a.m., Monday through Saturday 7 a.m. or 8 a.m., and Sunday 4 a.m. or 5 a.m., 8 a.m., noon (catechism), and 3 p.m. See also Grosse, *Les rituels de la cène,* 178.

26. Regulations for worship and discipline in the countryside parishes were first formalized in 1547 in the *Ordonnances sur la police des églises de la campagne.*

This document is found in *CO* 10.1, cols. 51–58. For an English translation of this text, see Calvin, *Calvin: Theological Treatises*, 76–82.

27. See *RCP* 4:179–80.

28. The *Ecclesiastical Ordinances* of 1561 and 1576 gave the Consistory authority to admonish and, if necessary, discipline adults and children who were consistently negligent in attending sermons. See these provisions in the *Ecclesiastical Ordinances* (1561), *CO* 10.1, col. 117, and *Ecclesiastical Ordinances* (1576), in Heyer, *L'Église de Genève*, 295–296.

29. On January 16, 1537, the city council ruled that "pendant les sermons la dimenche boutiques ouvertes quelque sorte qu'elle soyent, ny bochiers, ny tripiers, ny aultres, ny revendery; mais chascung soit tenu serré incontinent que sonnera la grosse clouche pour le dernier coup." The magistrates issued a similar decree for the Wednesday prayer meetings in 1545: "les mescredi soyent faict comme la dimenche jusques après le sermon." Quoted in Lambert, "Preaching, Praying and Policing the Reform," 307.

30. Thus, for example, in August 1559, Calvin and Viret had primary duties at St. Pierre; Beza, and Chauvet were assigned to St. Gervais; Nicolas Des Gallars, François Bourgoing, and Jean Macard served at the Madeleine; and Michel Cop and Nicolas Colladon shared responsibility for the early morning sermons at St. Pierre's and St. Gervais. This reconstruction is based on McKee's data in "Calvin and his Colleagues as Pastors," 288–91, with supplemental data drawn from R. Consist. 15 (1559), fols. 147–151v.

31. McKee, "Calvin and his Colleagues as Pastors," 25–32.

32. In 1560, both the ministers François Morel, Sieur de Collonges, and François Bourgoing were sent to preach at the church of Vandoeuvres in place of the sick minister Claude Baduel. See R. Consist., 17 (1560), fols. 134v, 145v. Similarly, in 1587, Antoine de La Faye was sent to Chancy as a temporary replacement for the minister Jean Guérin who had been accused of committing adultery. See *RCP* 5:167.

33. For example, when Antoine Chauve was injured in a fall in January of 1585, the preaching schedule at St. Pierre was organized as follows: Jean Trembley was assigned the 8 a.m. Sunday service and catechism at noon; Beza was to preach Sunday afternoons; Jean-Baptiste Rotan was responsible for the Monday morning sermon; Charles Perrot was given the sermons on Tuesday and Wednesday mornings; Simon Goulart was assigned the sermon on Thursday morning; various countryside pastors would fill in on Fridays; and Jean Jaquemot was responsible for the Saturday morning service. This preaching schedule appears to have remained in force until Chauve regained his health in October 1585. See *RCP* 5:53.

34. McKee, "Calvin and his Colleagues as Pastors," 40–41.

35. RC 40, fol. 222, quoted in Lambert, "Preaching, Praying and Policing the Reform," 359. In a similar fashion, Jaques Varin decided to leave the service when he discovered that Antoine de La Faye, against whom he had a grudge, was the preacher of the day. R. Consist. 34 (1596), fols. 422v, 423v.

36. See Parker, *Calvin's Preaching*, 62–63. In his *Ad Claudii de Sainctes responsionem altera apologia*, Beza estimated that Calvin preached 290 sermons per year. This treatise is found in Beza's *Tractationes theologicae*, 2:353.

37. As late as 1594, Beza indicates that he (like Calvin) customarily preached on Sundays and every day of the work week on alternate weeks. See Beza to Caspar Peucer, August 26/September 5, 1594. Bibliothèque Sainte-Geneviève, ms. 1455, fol. 595v–597. This schedule is corroborated by the summary of Beza's preaching ministry in François Portus, *Response de François Portus Candiot,* 59–60.

38. *RCP* 5:151, 153. This request was granted, and Trembley was transferred to the less demanding post at St. Gervais.

39. *RCP* 6:51.

40. The ministers' commitment to successive exposition of biblical books appears somewhat problematic given Geneva's practice of regularly rotating pastors between parish assignments. On this problem, see McKee, "Calvin and his Colleagues as Pastors," 32.

41. The register of the Company of Pastors reports that, when Beza completed his sermon series on Hebrews, he "a demandé à la Compagnie qu'il pourroit prendre doresenavant l'epistre de St. Jacques. A semblé propre." *RCP* 3:137.

42. Around 800 of Calvin's sermons were printed during his lifetime, with another 1,500 remaining in manuscript. On this see Stauffer, "Un Calvin méconnu," 189–90. For a summary of Calvin's preaching activities from 1549 to 1564, see Parker, *Calvin's Preaching,* 63–64.

43. Cop's sermon series were subsequently published as *Sur les Proverbes de Salomon, exposition familière* (Geneva, 1556) and *Le livre de l'Ecclésiaste...esposé fidèlement et familièrement* (Geneva, 1557). Barnaud identified five manuscript copies of Viret sermons on Isaiah (one from 1556, the others from 1559) in Geneva's archives. See Barnaud, *Pierre Viret,* 540–43. Four of these sermons by Viret have been published by Henri Meylan, *Quatre sermons français sur Esaie 65 (mars 1559).* In addition to these sermons, Jean-Raymond Merlin's published exposition of the Ten Commandments, entitled *Les dix commandemens de la Loy de Dieu...exposez* ([Geneva], 1561), may well have been sermons first delivered from a Geneva pulpit.

44. See *RCP* 3:137 and 4:114. It is likely that Beza's paraphrases on the Old Testament books of Psalms (1579) and Ecclesiastes (1588), and his partial commentary on Job (1589) also served as preparation for homiletic activity. In a similar fashion, it is probable that Nicolas Des Gallars's commentary on Exodus (1560); Lambert Daneau's commentary on 1 Timothy (1577); and Antoine de La Faye's commentaries on Romans (1608), Ecclesiastes (1609), and 1 Timothy (1609) anticipated, or were related to, preaching series delivered in one of Geneva's pulpits.

45. See *La forme des prières et chantz ecclésiastiques* (Geneva, 1542). The best study of liturgical practice and developments in Geneva during the sixteenth and seventeenth centuries is Christian Grosse's *Les rituels de la cène,* esp. 115–240.

46. Lambert shows that, at least in the 1550s, very few if any marriages took place during the main 8 a.m. worship service on Sunday morning. Rather, couples usually chose to be married at early morning services during the week or at the Sunday afternoon services. See Lambert, "Preaching, Praying and Policing the Reform," 292–93. For the liturgy for marriages, see *La forme des prières,* L8v–M3v.

47. References to these cantors appear frequently in archival records of the city and church of Geneva during this period. See Pidoux, *Le Psautier Huguenot,* 2:140–70.

48. "Articles concernant l'organisation de l'église et du culte à Genève," *CO* 10.2, col. 12; Grosse, *Les rituels de la cène*, 185–86.

49. In his summary of Psalm 91, Beza recalled that this Psalm "fut le premier lequel i'oui chanter en l'assemblée des Chrestiens la permiere fois que ie m'y trouvay: & puis dire que ie me senti tellement resioui de l'ouir chanter à ceste bonne rencontre, que depuis ie l'ay tousiours porté comme engrave en mon coeur." *Les Pseaumes de David et les cantiques de la Bible*, 455.

50. Beza offered this prayer of illumination as a model: "Let us pray to our good God and Father...that it might please him to illumine us by the grace of his Holy Spirit, to have true understanding of his Holy Word, so that it might not be corrupted by our fleshly sense and understanding, but rather be faithfully preached and received in our hearts. Hence, we might learn by this to renounce ourselves and to place our complete confidence in him, so that we might honor him and serve him as is right, paying him the fear and honor that true children owe to their fathers, and servants to their masters." This prayer is included in the liturgy found in Beza's *Sermons sur le Cantique des Cantiques*, 2. For examples of Calvin and Viret's prayers of illumination, see Grosse, *Les rituels de la cène*, 666–69 (annex III). McKee includes several English translations of these prayers in *John Calvin, Writings on Pastoral Piety*, 112, 160.

51. This prayer is found in Grosse, *Les rituels de la cène*, 671 (annex IV). McKee provides a collection of more than three dozen of Calvin's prayers in her anthology *John Calvin, Writings on Pastoral Piety*, 220–39. Similar prayers are found following many of Beza's (published) sermons. See, for example, Beza's *Sermons sur l'histoire de la passion*, 20, 40, 120, 407, 757, 1022, 1058. As a general rule, however, Beza's prayers following his sermons are shorter and less-developed than Calvin's.

52. Lambert demonstrates that the majority of baptisms in the early 1550s were celebrated during early morning services on Wednesdays and Sundays. For the baptismal liturgy, see *La forme des prières*, K8–L4v and chapter 9 of this book.

53. Other types of worship services in Geneva followed the basic outline of the Sunday morning *culte*, though with slight modifications. On Sunday mornings when the Lord's Supper was celebrated, Calvin and his colleagues supplemented the regular order of worship with a Eucharistic prayer, congregational singing of the Ten Commandments, an explanation of the meaning of the Supper, and a public statement identifying members of the congregation who had been excommunicated from the Table. On the other hand, the liturgy for weekday services was significantly shorter: the Psalter was not sung and the intercessory prayer shortened, though it appears that in some parishes special prayers were recited for members of the congregation suffering illness. The one exception to this pattern was the Wednesday Day of Prayer, which followed the normal Sunday liturgy almost exactly, with the minor addition of a formal prayer of repentance after the sermon. See the helpful table provided by Grosse, *Les rituels de la cène*, 658–665 (annex II).

54. *RCP* 3:118–19. See also ibid. 3:57, 89, 96. The pastors at St. Gervais during this period were Simon Goulart, Jean Trembley, and Antoine Chauve.

55. *RCP* 4:170, citing RC 75, fols. 129–30. Hourglasses were sometimes used in Geneva's churches before 1580, however. See the case of Pierre Ruffy, accused

in 1568 of stealing hourglasses from both the temples of St. Gervais and the Madeleine. R. Consist. 24 (1568), fol. 206.

56. See *RCP* 8:48–49, 187.

57. RC 79, fol. 116, cited in *RCP* 5:36. Calvin himself approved the practice of kneeling during prayer, but did not prescribe it. See *Institutes* IV.x.29–30, pp. 1207–208.

58. *RCP* 5:188.

59. *RCP* 3:99. The magistrates conceded to the ministers' point of view.

60. *RCP* 10:147–48, 275–79 (letter no. 85).

61. *RCP* 5:143, 161; ibid. 8:178.

62. *RCP* 3:99, note 5; R. Consist. 20 (1563), fol. 157.

63. R. Consist. 15 (1559), fol. 213.

64. For distractions caused by crying babies, see *RCP* 4:216 and R. Consist. 34 (1595), fol. 406v. For coughing and vomiting (often an indication of drunkenness), see R. Consist. 16 (1559), fol. 197v; 20 (1563), fols. 88, 101; 24 (1568), fol. 30; 28 (1571), fol. 69. There are dozens of cases where people are called before the Consistory for sleeping during worship services. For the distraction of barking dogs, see RC 92, fol. 47 and *RCP* 4:216. As the latter reference shows, in 1582 the Small Council dispatched several men from the city hospital to guard the doors of the city churches to prevent dogs from entering the sanctuaries.

65. R. Consist. 17 (1560), fol. 174v.

66. R. Consist. 23 (1566), fol. 121v.

67. R. Consist. 20 (1563), fols. 100, 114v, 128.

68. For example, Claude Chirondat confessed to the Consistory in 1564 that he rarely attended services at St. Pierre because "il est impossible qu'il puisse ouyr." R. Consist. 21 (1564), fol. 45.

69. Christian Grosse reports that Catholic authorities had experimented with benches in Geneva's churches before the Reformation, but it did not become an established practice until 1536. See Grosse, *Les rituels de la cène*, 268–69.

70. For the arrangement of seating in Geneva's temples, and the social status that it connoted, see Grosse's discussion in *Les rituels de la cène*, 269–84.

71. R. Consist. 35 (1605), fols. 72v–73.

72. R. Consist. 36 (1607), fols. 41v, 42–43.

73. R. Consist. 24 (1567), fols. 155v–156, 163; ibid. 25 (1568), fol. 11v.

74. *RCP* 3:56.

75. *RCP* 4:106–107.

76. R. Consist. 36 (1607), fol. 104.

77. *Theodori Bezae Vita Calvini*, CO 21, col. 132. Beza later rendered this succinct description of the preaching ministries of Calvin, Farel, and Viret into Latin rhyme in the second edition of his *Poemata* (1569). See Dufour, *Théodore de Bèze*, 129.

78. Millet, *Calvin et la dynamique de la parole*.

79. On Melanchthon's *genus didascalicum* see O'Malley, "Content and Rhetorical Forms," 238–52; Burnett, *Teaching the Reformation*, 158–160; and Millet, *Calvin et la dynamique de la parole*, 138–51, 873–80.

80. For Calvin's reliance on Melanchthon, see the sustained discussion in Millet, *Calvin et la dynamique de la parole*, 113–51.

81. For Calvin's attitude toward Chrysostom, see Lane, *John Calvin: Student of the Church Fathers*, 12, 57, 70–74. Lane notes that Calvin owned and marked in his own hand the collection of Chrysostom's sermons published in Claude Chevallon's edition of Chrysostom's *Opera omnia* (1536). Ibid., 12.

82. Calvin's preface to Chrysostom's homilies is found in *CO* 9, cols. 831–38. For an English translation of this work, see McIndoe, "John Calvin: Preface to the Homilies of Chrysostom."

83. *CO* 9, col. 835. McIndoe, "John Calvin: Preface to the Homilies of Chrysostom," 23.

84. *CO* 9, cols. 834–35. See McIndoe, "John Calvin: Preface to the Homilies of Chrysostom," 22–23.

85. This point is accented by James Thomas Ford in his article "Preaching in the Reformed Tradition," 69. For excellent summaries of Calvin's hermeneutics, see Thompson, "Calvin as Biblical Interpreter"; and Kraus, "Calvin's Exegetical Principles."

86. Scholars have sometimes drawn a sharp contrast between Calvin's dynamic doctrine of Scripture in which believers encounter Christ through Word and Spirit, and the overly philosophical and "scholastic" doctrine of verbal inspiration championed by later reformed churchmen such as Beza, Chandieu, and Daneau where (it is argued) Scripture becomes little more than a sourcebook of timeless propositional truths about God. This approach was popularized a generation ago by authors such as Hall, "Calvin against the Calvinists"; and Rogers and McKim, *The Authority and Interpretation of the Bible*. It is now clear that such a juxtaposition is unwarranted. There is strong evidence that Calvin himself believed the very words of Scripture were inspired by God and infallible, even as it is clear that Beza and his Genevan colleagues affirmed the personal and subjective power of the Word in the believer's life. On this see Kantzer, "Calvin and the Holy Scriptures"; Woodbridge, *Biblical Authority*; Puckett, *John Calvin's Exegesis of the Old Testament*, 45–47; and especially Muller, *Post-Reformation Reformed Dogmatics*, 2:63–148.

87. *Institutes* IV.viii.9 and Comm. on Matthew 3:7(*CTSNT* 16:188). For references to the biblical authors as "mouths" of God or the Holy Spirit, see Calvin's comments on Ezekiel 13.1–3, *CTSOT* 12:8; Micah 6:9, *CTSOT* 14.2:347, and in the *Institutes* I.vi.2–3, vii.5.

88. For a discussion of these passages, see Kantzer, "Calvin and the Holy Scriptures," 142–45. See also *Institutes* I.xiii.3 ("the unerring standard"), Comm. on Amos 2:4–5 (*CTSOT* 14.1:177; "the pure Word of God"), Dedicatory Epistle *to* Comm. on Hebrews (*CTSNT* 22:xxi; "infallible rule of his holy truth"), *La forme des priers et chantz ecclésiastiques*, l3v ("the certain Word of God coming from heaven"), and *Institutes* IV.xvi.16 ("infallible Word of God"). It is clear that Calvin ascribed infallibility to the *autographs* of Scripture, not to the copies of Greek or Hebrew manuscripts of Scripture transmitted thereafter. Hence, Calvin occasionally identifies "copyist errors" in the biblical text. See, for example, Calvin's Comm. on Joshua 15:17 (*CTSOT* 4:206–207) and Comm. on Matthew 27:9 (*CTSNT* 17:272).

89. For Calvin on divine accommodation, see Battles, "God was Accommodating Himself to Human Capacity"; and the recent work by Jon Balserac, *Divinity Compromised: A Study of Divine Accommodation in the Thought of John Calvin*.

90. Calvin, "Reply to Sadoleto," 61, 86. In a similar fashion, Beza noted that Scripture should be "the rule of all our thoughts, words, and actions." *Sermons sur l'histoire de la résurrection*, 132.

91. The themes of Scripture's authority, unity, sufficiency, and clarity are found throughout Calvin's writings. See, for example, *Institutes* I.vi–vii and II.x; and *Acta synodi Tridentinae cum antidote*, in *CO* 7, cols. 411–418. An English translation of the *Antidote* is found in *CTS* 3:17–188. A generation later, Antoine de Chandieu summarized these themes in his succinct definition of Holy Scripture: "The sacred Scripture is the divinely inspired Word of God, breathed out by the Spirit of God to the Prophets, Apostles, and Evangelists, and written in the canonical books of the Old and New Testaments, so that the truth of God might be protected from the forgetfulness and corruption of men, and so that the Church might be perfectly instructed and confirmed in all those things for which knowledge and faith are necessary for eternal salvation." In *Locus de Verbo Dei Scripto, Adversus Humanas Traditiones*, 39. For an English translation of this work, see Chandieu, *A Common Place Touching the Word of God Written, Against the Traditions of Men*.

92. "Sed hoc tantum postulo, ut fideli populo Deum sum loquentem audire liceat, et a docente discere." Calvin, "Preface to Pierre Olivétan's French Bible," in *CO* 9, col. 788.

93. See *Institutes* IV.i.10, pp. 1024–25.

94. Sermon on 1 Timothy 3:1–4, *CO* 53, col. 266. See Parker's discussion of this topic in *Calvin's Preaching*, 23–25.

95. *Institutes* I.vii.4, pp. 78–79. For the relationship between Word and Spirit in Calvin's theology, see Hesselink's helpful discussion in his article "Word and Spirit," 300–302. Theodore Beza also emphasized the crucial role of the Holy Spirit in the illumination of God's Word in the heart of the believer. See his *Confession de la foi chrestienne*, 29, 80–83, and his *Sermons sur l'histoire de la passion*, 784–85.

96. *Institutes* IV.viii.9, pp. 1156–57.

97. Comm. on Galatians 4.22, in *CNTC* 11:85.

98. Peter, "Rhétorique et Prédication," 258–59.

99. Comm. on John 5:39, in *CNTC* 4:139. On this point, see Gerrish, *Grace and Gratitude*, 78–79.

100. Sermon on Titus 2:15–3:2, *CO* 54, col. 550.

101. Sermon on 1 Timothy 4:12–13, *CO* 53, col. 416.

102. For Calvin's comparison of human and spiritual eloquence, see especially Millet, *Calvin et la dynamique de la parole*, 225–56; and Peter, "Rhétorique et prédication selon Calvin."

103. Comm. on 1 Corinthians 1:17, *CNTC* 9:33.

104. Ibid., 32–33.

105. Ibid., 35.

106. Parker, *Calvin's Preaching*, 81, 172–78.

107. Ibid., 81–84.

108. Calvin's sermon on Acts 2:39–40 is found in Calvin, *Sermons on the Acts of the Apostles*, in *SC* 8:28–37.

109. Classical rhetoricians had identified six parts to an oration: the exordium, the narration, the proposition and division into parts, the confirmation, the refutation, and the peroration or conclusion.

110. *Sermon on Acts* 2:39–40, SC 8:36.

111. Ibid., 35.

112. Ibid., 35.

113. Ibid., 28–29.

114. Ibid., 36.

115. Ibid., 36.

116. Ibid., 35.

117. Badius's preface to Calvin's *Plusieurs sermons* (1558) is found in *CO* 35, cols. 587–88. See Rodolphe Peter's discussion in "Rhétorique et prédication selon Calvin," 257.

118. The Discipline of the Reformed Churches in France mandated this "simple and ordinary style" of preaching in 1578. See Méjan, *Discipline de l'Église Réformée de France*, 197–98.

119. Beza to Louis Courant, July 2, 1601, in Archives Tronchin, fonds. Bèze, vol. 5, fol. 296–97.

120. For biographical information on Andreas Hyperius, see *OER* 2:299–300. In addition to the writings of Melanchthon and Hyperius, the most important Protestant texts devoted to the formation of theological students as well as exegetical and homiletic method were Bullinger's *Ratio Studiorum* (1528) and Hemmingsen's *De Methodis Libri Duo* (1559). See Burnett, *Teaching the Reformation*, 159–61.

121. For more on Hyperius's method, see Sinnema, "The Distinction Between Scholastic and Popular"; and Bayley, *French Pulpit Oratory*, 61–62.

122. Bayley, *French Pulpit Oratory*, 61–62.

123. Hyperius, *De Recte formando theologiae*, 400, quoted (in French translation) in Fatio, *Méthode et théologie*, 70.

124. *CDM*, 57, 59.

125. Beza, *Icones, id est Verae Imagines Virorum Doctrina Simul et Pietate Illustrium*. I consulted Beza's French translation of this work, *Les vrais portraits des hommes illustres*, 66–67.

126. Beza's unpublished "Brevis Concionandi Methodus," along with a second text entitled "Ratio studii theologici ad Th. Beza instituta," are located in manuscript form in the Bibliothèque de Grenoble (ms. 1949). A transcription of these documents is found in Fatio, *Méthode et théologie*, annex IV, 119–21. Fatio describes the similarities between Beza's "Brevis Concionandi Methodus" and the writings of Hyperius and Daneau in ibid., 71. It is at least possible that the original recipient of Beza's "Brevis Concionandi Methodus" was the reformed pastor of Nîmes, Christian Pistorius. In 1582, Pistorius sent Beza a letter in which he requested the reformer to write a "concionandi methodum" for use in the church of Nîmes. See Pistorius to Beza, April 19, 1582, *CB* 23:42.

127. See Fatio's sustained discussion of this matter in *Méthode et théologie*, 63–98.

128. For Beza's preaching ministry, see Dückert, *Théodore de Bèze, Prédicateur*; Delval "La doctrine du salut dans l'oeuvre homilétique de Théodore de Bèze; Delval "La prédication d'un réformateur au XVIe siècle"; and Wright, *Our Sovereign Refuge*, 87–115.

129. For development of this point, see my article "'The Most Despised Vocation Today.'"

130. *Sermons sur le Cantique des Cantiques*, 244. See also ibid., 341–42.

131. *Sermons sur l'histoire de la résurrection*, 507. See also *Sermons sur le Cantique des Cantiques*, 101. In his *Confession de la foi chrestienne*, Beza notes: "[T]he preaching of the Word of God...is totally necessary to the salvation of those who are of the age of discretion," (95).

132. Beza, *Sermons sur l'histoire de la résurrection*, 439. See also Beza's discussion in his *Confession de la foi chrestienne*, 83.

133. Beza, *Sermons sur le Cantique des Cantiques*, 345.

134. Beza, *Sermons sur l'histoire de la résurrection*, 95. See also Beza, *Confession de la foi chrestienne*, 92. For Calvin's view of the "real presence" of Christ in Christian preaching, see Gerrish, *Grace and Gratitude*, 82–86.

135. Beza, *Sermons sur l'histoire de la passion*, 74–75.

136. Beza, *Sermons sur l'histoire de la résurrection*, 247.

137. Ibid., 294–95.

138. Ibid., 244–45.

139. Ibid., 294–95.

140. Michel Delval has provided the most detailed study of the structure and theological content of Beza's sermons. See especially his article "La prédication d'un réformateur," 61–86. Delval shows that in many of his published sermons, Beza interpolated lengthy doctrinal discussions or shorter exposés of a dogmatic or ethical nature that were probably not in the sermon when delivered from the pulpit. So too, in Beza's published sermons on the Song of Songs the editor has provided a numerical summary of the chief exegetical and doctrinal points in the passage. Even so, the extent of the editorial changes Beza made in publishing these sermons should not be overstated. Throughout these sermons one finds chronological markers that must have appeared in the original version of the sermon ("as we learned last Thursday..."). Likewise, Beza makes occasional allusions to the war with Savoy that were contemporaneous to the sermon's delivery. So too, the terse introductions and conclusions to each sermon indicate minimal redaction.

141. It is not clear whether Beza preached extemporaneously or used notes in the pulpit. This statement in Beza's introduction to his sermons on the Song of Songs may indicate that at least on occasion he, like Calvin, preached without notes: Several people "m'ont faict tresgrand instance de revoir & rediger par escrit ce que j'auroys dit en chaire, aultant que ma memoire le pourroit porter..." (*Sermons sur le Cantique des Cantiques*, A.iii.r).

142. Beza, *Sermons sur l'histoire de la passion*, 251. For similar statements, see his *Sermons sur l'histoire de la résurrection*, 420, 437.

143. Beza, *Sermons sur le Cantique des Cantiques*, 279.

144. In the thirty-five sermons included in the collection *Sermons sur l'histoire de la passion*, for example, Beza explicitly mentions only Josephus, Ignatius of Antioch, and Bernard of Clairvaux. By contrast there are hundreds of allusions to and quotations from the Scripture.

145. Richard Stauffer reports that in more than one thousand extant sermons, Calvin only discusses the doctrine of the Trinity in five passages; in Calvin's homiletic, "le dogme trinitaire n'y jouait, pour ainsi dire, aucun rôle." Stauffer suggests that this is due to Calvin's desire to avoid technical vocabulary,

retain divine mystery, and stay within the bounds of the biblical text. See his "Un Calvin méconnu," 201–202. Beza employs Trinitarian language much more readily.

146. Beza, *Sermons sur l'histoire de la passion*, 286; *Sermons sur l'histoire de la résurrection*, 217.

147. Beza, *Sermons sur l'histoire de la passion*, 722, 968.

148. I have found only two explicit personal references in Beza's eighty-seven published sermons.

149. Beza, *Sermons sur l'histoire de la passion*, 363.

150. Ibid., 800.

151. Beza, *Sermons sur le Cantique des Cantiques*, 270.

152. Dückert's summary of Beza's preaching style is appropriate: "on sent très bien chez notre prédicateur qu'il ne recherché ni la forme, ni l'élégance; son but n'est pas de plaire à l'oreille et à l'imagination, mais d'intéresser ses auditeurs, de les frapper, de les exciter, de les fortifier." *Théodore de Bèze, prédicateur*, 65.

153. *RCP* 10:103.

154. *RCP* 8:241–42.

155. *RCP* 8:266–67.

156. *RCP* 9:131–32. The ministers who were particularly antagonistic toward Cusin were Jean Pinault and Antoine de La Faye.

157. *RCP* 9:65–66.

158. *RCP* 9:215.

159. *RCP* 10:180, letter no. 2.

160. *RCP* 10:189–90, letter no. 8.

161. *RCP* 10:32.

162. For Viret as preacher, see Barnaud, *Pierre Viret*, 539–42. The homiletic gifts of Calvin, Viret, and Farel were recognized not only by friends, but also by Catholic opponents. The Catholic polemicist Antoine Cathelan, while highly critical of the reformers' teaching, nonetheless, gave implicit praise to their preaching abilities, noting that "ny Calvin avecques son sçavoir, ny Viret avecques son éloquence, ni Farel avecques son zèle" can justify their actions. Cited in Lambert, "Preaching, Praying and Policing the Reform," 375, note 224.

163. In a letter to Calvin on December 12, 1561, Beza reports preaching to a crowd of six thousand people in the pouring rain in a suburb of Paris. See *CB* 3:235. This episode is described by Geisendorf, *Théodore de Bèze*, 178–79.

164. Isaac Casaubon may have been thinking in part of Beza's homiletical gifts when he commented that "it was daily possible to learn something, or rather, many things from your words and by them I became a better and more learned man," in *Isaaci Casauboni Epistolae*, 63–64. This letter to Beza is dated February 17, 1597. Similarly, Urbain Chauveton noted that, as a professor, Beza displayed the "dazzling clarity" of Philip Melanchthon, the "sound and solid common sense" of John Calvin, and the "rich teaching and methodology" of Peter Martyr Vermigli. See *CB* 19:163.

165. La Faye, *Les vies de Iean Calvin & de Theodore de Bèze*. The section on Beza is a translation of *De vita et obitu...Th. Bezae*.

166. Quoted in Jones, *Simon Goulart*, 128.

167. Quoted in Bernus, *Antoine de Chandieu*, 122–23.

168. Extract from P. Perin, "Histoire de Genève," found in Geisendorf, *Les annalistes genevois du début du dix-septième siècle*, 660. The homiletic skill of Abraham Grenet and Antoine de La Faye is suggested by *RCP* 5:15 and 7:36.

169. See *RCP* 1:150; 2:66–67; 3:138.

170. See Lambert, "Preaching, Praying and Policing the Reform," 359–60.

171. R. Consist. 17 (1560), fols. 17v, 64v.

172. R. Consist. 32 (1581), fol. 243v.

173. R. Consist. 6 (1551), fol. 69. See Lambert's discussion of this and other criticisms of the ministers' harsh sermons in "Preaching, Praying and Policing the Reform," 367–69.

174. R. Consist. 12 (1557), fol. 44v.

175. Hence, in 1582, the Small Council advised the ministers "that they should all be advised to control themselves in their sermons so that they might not scandalize, but edify people." RC 77, fol. 39.

176. RC 41, fol. 104–104v, quoted in Lambert, "Preaching, Praying and Policing the Reform," 368.

177. See, for example, *R. Consist.* III (1547), 9–10, 171, 195; R. Consist. 7 (1552), fol. 58; ibid., 14 (1559), fol. 157v.

178. This detail is found in Lambert, "Preaching, Praying and Policing the Reform," 368.

179. *R. Consist.* II (1546), 300–301.

180. *R. Consist.* IV (1551), 35.

181. *R. Consist.* III (1547), 29–30.

182. *R. Consist.* III (1547), 195.

183. R. Consist. 20 (1563), fol. 117.

184. *R. Consist.* I (1543), 204–205.

185. R. Consist. 24 (1567), fol. 35v.

186. R. Consist. 9 (1555), fols. 203, 211 and 10 (1555), fol. 2.

187. For attacks on the ethnic background of Geneva's ministers, see *R. Consist.* III (1547), 21, 182; ibid., IV (1548), 56; R. Consist. 5 (1550), fol. 21.

188. See for example *R. Consist.* II (1546), 229; ibid. III (1547), 22 154–55.

189. R. Consist. 8 (1553), fol. 19. For similar accusations, see *R. Consist.* I (1543), 200 and PC #1454.

190. R. Consist. 25 (1569), fol. 117v.

191. R. Consist. 21 (1564), fol. 122v.

192. R. Consist. 17 (1560), fols. 111v–112.

193. *R. Consist.* IV (1548), 45.

194. R. Consist. 11 (1556), fol. 43. This anecdote appears in Lambert, "Preaching, Praying and Policing the Reform," 381.

195. R. Consist. 11 (1556), fol. 42v.

196. R. Consist. 32 (1581), fols. 213–214v.

197. R. Consist. 28 (1572), fol. 166.

198. *R. Consist.* II (1546), 202.

199. R. Consist. 22 (1565), fol. 89v.

200. See chapter 7 where suspension rates for absence from sermons are documented.

201. See RC 91, fol. 68; RC 92, fol. 110; RC 95, fol. 212; *RCP* 3:91; *RCP* 5:16, 184.

202. R. Consist. 23 (1566), fol. 146. In this interview, it is not clear whether Sunday services or weekday services are in view.

203. RC 78, fols. 111v–112, quoted in *RCP* 5:16–17.

204. RC 83, fol. 236.

205. Beza, *Sermons sur le Cantique des Cantiques*, 260.

206. R. Consist. 34 (1592), fol. 48.

207. For more on this controversy, see the beginning of this chapter.

208. RC 91, fol. 68; *RCP* 7:35.

209. RC 95, fol. 212; *RCP* 8:48–49; R. Consist. 35 (1605), fol. 48.

210. This protracted struggle is described in detail in Choisy, *L'État Chrétien Calviniste*.

211. RC 76, fols. 78v–82, cited in *RCP* 4:184–85. The image of the "silent dog" who does not bark at wrong doing, drawn from Isaiah 56:10, is also found in Beza's *Sermons sur l'histoire de la passion*, 590.

212. *RCP* 8:272–74.

213. This protracted case appears in *RCP* 9:187–93 and annex no. 83.

214. *RCP* 9:327.

215. *RCP* 10:110.

216. *RCP* 10:111.

Chapter 7

1. These statements are reported in Dufour, "Le mythe de Genève au temps de Calvin," 503; and in Kingdon, *Geneva and the Coming of the Wars of Religion*, 21.

2. Pinelli published an account of his visit entitled "Alcune cose più notabili e pericoli accaduti a me Luca Pinelli della Compagnia di Giesù," (1596). Part of this account is found in Scaduto, "La Ginevra di Teodoro Beza nei nicordi di un gesuita lucano, Luca Pinelli (1542–1607)." A partial English translation is found in Martin, *The Jesuit Mind*, 84–88.

3. A German transcription of this passage from Valentin Andreae's *Respublica Christianopolitana* (1619) is found in Schaff, *The Creeds of Christendom*, 460, 1:460, note 2.

4. Notable in this growing literature are Kingdon, "The Control of Morals in Calvin's Geneva"; Estèbe and Vogler, "Le genèse d'une société protestante: Étude compare de quelques registres consistoriaux languedociens et palatins vers 1600"; Monter, "The Consistory of Geneva, 1559–1562"; Mentzer, "*Disciplina nervus ecclesiae*: The Calvinist Reform of Morals at Nîmes"; Schilling, "'History of Crime' or 'History of Sin'?"; Garrisson, *Protestants du Midi, 1559–1598*; Watt, "Women and the Consistory in Calvin's Geneva"; Mentzer, *Sin and the Calvinists*; Kingdon, *Adultery and Divorce in Calvin's Geneva*; Graham, *The Uses of Reform*; Kingdon, "The Geneva Consistory in the Time of Calvin," 21–34; Thomas Lambert, "Preaching, Praying and Policing the Reform"; Didier Poton, "Les institutions consistoriales: I. Les exemples des XVIᵉ et XVIIᵉ siècles"; Murdock, *Beyond Calvin*, 76–101; Grosse, *Les rituels de la cène*; Manetsch, "Pastoral Care East of Eden." Timothy Nyasulu's recent dissertation on Presbyterian church discipline in modern-day Malawi offers intriguing parallels and comparisons. See Nyasulu, "'Bringing the Sheep Back to the Corral': Moral Discipline in the Church of Central Africa Presbyterian (CCAP) Synod of Livingstonia, Malawi, 1995–2005."

5. Gorski, *The Disciplinary Revolution*.

6. My research thus bears out the conclusion of Kingdon: "Discipline to these early Genevans meant more than social control. It also meant social help." Kingdon, "The Geneva Consistory in the Time of Calvin," 21–34.

7. For the influence of Oecolampadius and Bucer on Calvin's theology and practice of moral discipline, see Graham, *The Uses of Reform*, 1–27; Kuhr, "Calvin and Basel"; and Wendel, *Calvin*, 60–69.

8. *Institutes* IV.xii.1, p. 1230. This passage appeared in all subsequent editions of the *Institutes*.

9. *EO* (1541), 273.

10. *EO* (1541), 274. Although the concept of suspension from the Lord's Supper appears in this document, the word "excommunication" does not. Most likely, Calvin avoided using this word out of fear that reformed discipline would be likened to the practice of excommunication in the medieval church.

11. *EO* (1541), 275.

12. Ibid.

13. This opaqueness is seen when one compares paragraphs nos. 78, 79, 82, 83, 84, and 85 (each of which recognizes the power of the church to suspend offenders from the Lord's Supper) to paragraph no. 87 (where the Consistory, after admonishing the sinner, is required to send the offender to the Small Council for judgment "according to the exigencies of the case"). In cases of misbehavior of ministers, however, the Ordinances stated clearly that "le dernier jugement de la correction soit toujours reserve à la Seigneurie" (paragraph no. 21). See *EO* (1541), 265, 273–75.

14. Charles Parker has perceptively noted that the struggle to define the boundaries of authority between church and state usually reflected a more fundamental disagreement over the nature and definition of the Christian community. See his *The Reformation of Community*, 3.

15. For a more detailed account of this struggle, see Naphy, *Calvin and the Consolidation of the Genevan Reformation*, 144–207; and Grosse, *Les rituels de la cène*, 353–69.

16. Grosse, *Les rituels de la cène*, 358–59.

17. For more on this naming controversy, see chapter 9 in this book.

18. R. Consist. 5 (1551), fol. 100v.

19. R. Consist. 6 (1551), fols. 22, 24. For similar cases, see ibid., 5 (1550), fol. 37; 7 (1552), fol. 117; 8 (1553), fol. 30v.

20. See R. Consist. 7 (1552), 103. For a helpful discussion of the Berthelier affair, see Naphy, *Calvin and the Consolidation of the Genevan Reformation*, 152–53, 173–75, 182–87, and Grosse, *Les rituels de la cène*, 365–69.

21. See *RCP* 2:48–54.

22. RC 47, fols. 175v–176, quoted in Grosse, *Les rituels de la cène*, 367.

23. Naphy describes this as "a calculated political move to pack the Genevan electorate." See *Calvin and the Consolidation of the Genevan Reformation*, 192.

24. Naphy, *Calvin and the Consolidation of the Genevan Reformation*, 208–32.

25. *RCP* 2:68.

26. Grosse, *Les rituels de la cène*, 372–76.

27. For Geneva's sumptuary ordinances of the 1560s, see Monter, *Calvin's Geneva*, 216–17.

28. Beza writes in his *Confession de la foi chrestienne*: "La marquee de la vraye Eglise, c'est la predication de la Parole du Fils de Dieu, voire selon qu'elle a este revelee aux Prophetes & Apostres, & par iceux annoncee au monde, y comprenant par consequens les Sacremens, & l'administration de la police Ecclesiastique telle que Dieu l'a ordonnee"(121). Bucer, John Knox, and Chandieu also affirmed discipline as a "third mark" of the true church. See Maruyama, *The Ecclesiology of Beza*, 23–25, 162.

29. *Institutes* IV.xi.1–2, pp. 1211–14.

30. *Institutes* IV.xii.8–9, pp. 1236–39. Calvin here criticizes as too harsh both the practice of canonical penance in the early church, as well as the Catholic punishment of anathema.

31. *Institutes* IV.xii.10, p. 1238.

32. Beza, *Sermons sur l'histoire de la résurrection*, 129–30.

33. *Institutes* IV.xii.10, p. 1238.

34. *Institutes* IV.xii.5, pp. 1232–34. See also Beza, *Confession de la foi chrestienne*, 175; and Maruyama, *The Ecclesiology of Theodore Beza*, 31.

35. *Institutes* IV.viii.12, p. 1161.

36. *Institutes* IV.xii.11, p. 1238–39.

37. *EO* (1541), 292.

38. *EO* (1561), in *CO* 10.1, col. 116.

39. *R. Consist.* 11 (1556), fol. 29v.

40. The responsibilities of the *garde* were detailed in one of the first sessions of Calvin's Consistory. See *R. Consist.* I (1542), 126.

41. *EO* (1561), in *CO* 10.1, col. 98. These rural visitations became less frequent as the century wore on. In 1576, the magistrates ruled that commissioners visit the rural parishes once every three years. Despite the ministers' objections, the magistrates discontinued these visitations entirely after 1584. For more on rural visitations, see Grosse, *Les rituels de la cène*, 408–12 and *RCP* 4:15; 5:48–49, 198; 7:156; 8:16.

42. Originally, the head elder—one of the syndics—was responsible by law to preside over the Genevan Consistory and conduct the interrogation. This practice was modified by the Edict of 1560, which stipulated that the two lay elders drawn from the Small Council need not include a ruling syndic. See Grosse, *Les rituels de la cène*, 373–76.

43. *R. Consist.* 32 (1580), fol. 154.

44. *R. Consist.* 32 (1580), fol. 154r–v.

45. *R. Consist.* 32 (1581), fol. 170v.

46. *R. Consist.* 18 (1561), fol. 43r-v.

47. *R. Consist.* 31 (1578), fol. 170v. See also the case of Jaquème Favre, *R. Consist.* II (1546), 135–36.

48. *R. Consist.* 34 (1592), fol. 53v.

49. See for example *R. Consist.* 22 (1557), fol. 93v; 25 (1568), fol. 67; 27 (1570), fol. 94v; 33 (1582), fol. 45.

50. This scale of penalties was similar to that evidenced in other reformed churches. See Benedict, *Christ's Churches Purely Reformed*, 465.

51. *R. Consist.* I (1548), 305.

52. *R. Consist.* 25 (1568), fol. 163.

53. R. Consist. 31 (1578), fol. 135r–v.

54. R. Consist. 32 (1580), fol. 154v.

55. R. Consist. 31 (1578), fols. 249v–250.

56. See, for example, *EO* (1541), 273–74. In a speech before the Small Council in 1576, Beza delineated not two but three degrees of excommunication. The "first" or lightest degree of excommunication, he argued, was when the Consistory advised a defendant to abstain from the Lord's Supper until they first returned to Consistory and repented of their error. In this chapter, we have not counted this type of excommunication as a "full suspension," since defendants often reconciled themselves to the church without missing a Communion service. On this see RC 71, fol. 15v, quoted in *RCP* 4:39 note 3.

57. R. Consist. 18 (1561), fol. 159v; 28 (1572), fol. 121; 31 (1579), fol. 384; 27 (1570), fol. 123. Monter assesses the work of the Consistory in the late 1560s this way: "it is hard to escape the impression that many people were excommunicated for trivial reasons." Monter, "The Consistory of Geneva," 383.

58. R. Consist. 22 (1565), fol. 97.

59. Beza to Bullinger, November 13, 1571, *CB* 12 (1571), 218.

60. R. Consist. 26 (1569), fol. 2v.

61. R. Consist. 34 (1593), fol. 196.

62. Christian Grosse has shown that, according to the Edict of 1560, the names of excommunicated persons were to be announced in the church "affin que chescun s' abstienne de leur compagnie." Furthermore, the Edict stipulated that "ceux qui auront esté excommuniez par le Consistoire, s'ils ne se rengent après avoir esté deuement admonestez, mais qu'ils persistent en leur rebellion, soyent declarez par les temples estre rejettez du troupeau jusques à ce qu'ils viennent recognoistre leur faute et se reconcilier à toute l'Eglise." On this, see Grosse, *Les rituels de la cène*, 375; and *EO* (1561), in *CO* 10.1, cols. 122–123. Scholars disagree as to whether social ostracism was actually practiced against excommunicated persons in Geneva and other reformed communities, see Grosse, *Les rituels de la cène*, 395–96.

63. R. Consist. 17 (1560), 7.

64. *RCP* 2:138–39.

65. R. Consist. 25 (1568), fol. 209v. For Chautemp's support of Calvin during the Perrinist crisis of 1555, see Naphy, *Calvin and the Consolidation of the Genevan Reformation*, 190–91. Several days before the Consistory's action, the civil case against Chautemps was dismissed due to the statute of limitations. See PC #1507.

66. These cases involved Esaië Baldin, Lucas Cop, the son of Adam Dorival, and the daughters of François Bourgoing and Hugues Roy. See R. Consist. 22 (1565), fol. 184v; ibid., 24 (1567), fol. 121; *RCP* 8:184; R. Consist. 18 (1561), fol. 143; ibid., 37 (1608), fol. 30v.

67. See chapter 4 in this book.

68. Thus, for example, a niece and two nephews of Jean Trembley were called to Consistory on multiple occasions between 1565 and 1582. The tragic case of Trembley's niece Pernette de Roche is described at the end of this chapter. The sister of Nicolas Colladon was called to Consistory in 1575. The son-in-law of Pierre Merlin was investigated for fornication in 1561. And, as we have already

noted, Calvin's brother and sister-in-law were called to Consistory on several occasions before their divorce of 1557.

69. The figure of twenty-two depositions includes those ministers that were removed from office by Geneva's magistrates without being subject to the Consistory's discipline. These ministers include Antoine Courauld (1538), Nicolas Vandert (1542), Jacques Baud (1543), Edme Champereau (1545), Pierre de Lescluse (1545) Henri de La Mare (1546), Philip de Ecclesia (1549), and Jean Ferron (1549). For a description of these depositions, see Naphy, *Calvin and the Consolidation of the Genevan Reformation*, 68–71.

70. In her study of reformed churches in the south of France from 1559 to 1598, Janine Garrisson identified forty-two pastors—or 10 percent of her sample—who were censured or deposed. See Garrisson, *Protestants du Midi*, 146–47. By contrast, Bernard Vogler found that between the years 1557 and 1619, 17 percent of the clergy in the duchy of Deux-Pons and 14 percent of the clergy in the county of Sponheim were removed from office. This rate of turnover is partly explained by action taken against reformed clergymen during the Palatinate's confessional shift in 1588–90. See Vogler, *Le Clergé Protestant Rhénan*, 100–105.

71. The one possible exception to this statement, of course, was Calvin himself, who was dismissed from Geneva's pastoral company in 1538, only to be restored to his office in 1541. Calvin and his colleagues insisted, however, that the reformer had not been *deposed* from office.

72. For a more detailed discussion of consistorial discipline against Geneva's ministers during the sixteenth century, see Manetsch, "Ministers Misbehaving."

73. On this point, see Karen E. Spierling, *Infant Baptism in Reformation Geneva*, 105–57.

74. Sometimes the Consistory granted special permission for offenders to contract marriages or serve as witnesses at baptism, while leaving them in a state of suspension from the sacrament. See for example R. Consist. 25 (1568), fol. 189.

75. R. Consist. 17 (1560), fol. 5.

76. R Consist. 32 (1581), fol. 194.

77. R. Consist. 25 (1568), fol. 145.

78. R. Consist. 27 (1570), fol. 22v.

79. R. Consist. 35 (1605), fol. 17.

80. R. Consist. 26 (1569), fol. 169v.

81. R. Consist. 9 (1554), fol. 72. For the evolution of the practice of public reparation before the church (*l'amende honorable*) see Grosse's discussion, *Les rituels de la cène*, 453–66.

82. The Consistory registers sometime refers to restoration in these terms: "reintegre en la communion des fideles" (R. Consist. 17 [1560], fol. 53v), "l'admettre au rang des fidelles" (12 [1557], fol. 34v), "mise au rang des fideles" (12 [1557], fol. 94), "recepvoir au rang des fideles et a la communion des fideles" (12 [1557], fol. 134v).

83. R. Consist. 25 (1568), fols. 152v, 161v–162.

84. The Consistory reminded Alexandre Campagnole of this fact when he tried to avoid the humiliation of a public confession of sin. See R. Consist. 32 (1580), fol. 10r–v.

85. Monter, "The Consistory of Geneva, 1559–1569," 476–77.

86. McGrath, *A Life of John Calvin*, 113–14.

87. There is one small lacuna in the data set since we were not able to consult twenty folio pages of the Consistory minutes for the period November 10–December 1, 1558.

88. Efforts to count and categorize disciplinary cases are admittedly fraught with difficulties, and scholars have rightly advised caution when attempting to quantify materials like these. However, even if our tabulations necessarily present "soft" numbers, reflecting a degree of interpretive judgment, they nonetheless allow us to draw some general conclusions about the overall landscape of church discipline in Geneva over nearly seven decades. In our study of Geneva's documents, two interpretive difficulties have been particularly evident. First, from time to time the registers are unclear as to whether an offender is actually suspended. This confusion may result from opaque language used by the secretary, uncertainty about the offender's age (youthful offenders who had not yet been admitted to the Table could not be suspended from it), or cases in which the Consistory reaffirms a prior suspension of a recidivist. Fortunately, the secretaries of the Consistory normally denote a suspension with a marginal note, such as "suspendu du Cene." Second, the specific reasons for a suspension are not always self-evident, particularly when a defendant is guilty of multiple infractions. The case of Gaspard Bally illustrates the problem: he was suspended in 1580 for appearing in Consistory drunk and spewing forth a string of blasphemies and curses against the pastors (R. Consist. 32 [1580], 6v). Was he disciplined for drunkenness, or rebellion, or blasphemy, or perhaps all three? In these cases, I have consulted (when available) the statement of reconciliation, which usually sheds light on the primary reason for the suspension. Thus, the record of Bally's restoration reports that he was originally censured for "ivrognerie et irreverences" (ibid., 32 [1580], 22v). Additional difficulties with quantifying disciplinary records are described by Pollmann, "Off the Record: Problems in the Quantification of Calvinist Church Discipline."

89. See Graham, *The Uses of Reform*; Mentzer, "Excommunications in the French Reformed Churches," in Mentzer, ed., *Sin and the Calvinists*; Murdock, *Beyond Calvin*, 97–98. By way of comparison, Raymond Mentzer reports that the reformed church of Montauban (with around 8,000–10,000 adherents) suspended only 80 people from 1595–1598, while the Consistory of Nîmes (with approximately the same number of adherents) censured a total of 104 people from 1561–1563 and 1578–1583. Comparisons like these are suggestive, but must be made cautiously given the substantial differences between the "autonomous" churches of southern France and a "state" church in Geneva (with a magistracy willing to enforce ecclesiastical discipline). See Mentzer, "Excommunications in the French Reformed Churches," 100, 124.

90. "Endangerment" is the term chosen to identify the act of exposing oneself or another person to physical danger (usually the plague) through negligence or ill-will. We have also included attempted suicide under this rubric.

91. This percentage of male-female offenders is consonant with disciplinary patterns seen elsewhere in reformed Europe during this period. See Mentzer, "Excommunications in the French Reformed Churches," 124. Michael Graham's study of the caseload of kirk sessions in Scotland during this period also finds

a significantly larger number of men disciplined than women. See his *The Uses of Reform*.

92. R. Consist. 38 (1609), fol. 105v.

93. R. Consist. 30 (1576), fol. 48v.

94. In the Consistory minutes, these sins are frequently labeled as *paillardise*, from the French word *paille* (straw), with the connotation of sexual debauchery. See Mentzer, "The Calvinist Reform of Morals," 103.

95. Raymond Mentzer observes a similar pattern in the Consistory registers of the reformed churches of Montauban: "Although sexual activities, such as adultery and fornication, frequently came to the Consistory's attention, behavior that church officials would have considered outrageous or even criminal—homosexuality, incest, infanticide, and abortion—is virtually absent from their discussions." In "Morals and Moral Regulation in Protestant France," 14.

96. R. Consist. 23 (1566), fol. 61r–v. For other cases of incest, see R. Consist. 27 (1570), fol. 134; 29 (1575), fol. 102; 31 (1579), fols. 295v–296. Several instances of incest also appear in Geneva's criminal record during this period. See PC #1516 and #1683.

97. See R. Consist. 23 (1566), fol. 81, and the civil trial and condemnation of Jean de La Tour in PC #1452. On another occasion, the magistrates consulted the Consistory as to whether Barthasard Romey should be permitted to return to Geneva following his banishment. Romey had been banished from Geneva for failing to report to city officials "l'abominable crime de sodomie" that a sodomite had attempted to commit with him. The sodomite himself was executed by hanging. See R. Consist. 19 (1562), fol. 10v.

98. See R. Consist. 23 (1566), fol. 33, and PC #1339, #1340. The account of Loise Maistre appears in Kingdon, *Adultery and Divorce*, 135–39.

99. For Geneva's legal statutes against fornication, including premarital sex, see Witte and Kingdon, *Sex, Marriage, and Family in John Calvin's Geneva*, 1:414–18.

100. R. Consist. 30 (1578), fol. 147v.

101. R. Consist. 27 (1570), fol. 184v. Although cases of simple fornication are frequent in the Consistory registers, demographic figures indicate that the rate of illegitimate births in reformed Geneva was still significantly below the rates found elsewhere in Europe. See Monter, "Historical Demography and Religious History," 414–18.

102. R. Consist. 15 (1559), fol. 2v; *RCP* 3:287.

103. See Kingdon, *Adultery and Divorce*, 116–17. The "Ordinances for the Supervision of the Churches in the Countryside" (1547) stipulated that convicted adulterers should be imprisoned for nine days on bread and water, and subject to a fine. See Calvin, *Calvin: Theological Treatises*, 82.

104. Emile Rivoire and Victor van Berchem, *Les sources du droit du canton de Genève*, 3:170. The law enforced a double-standard in adultery cases. If the man alone was married, both he and his partner were to be punished with twelve days in prison on bread and water. If the woman alone was married, she was to be executed by drowning and her partner whipped and banished. If both the man and woman were married, they were both executed, with the woman drowned and the man beheaded. See Kingdon, *Adultery and Divorce*, 117.

105. These treatises usually appeared under the single title *Tractatio de polygamia, et divortiis* (Geneva: Jean Crespin, 1568). Kingdon summarizes the argument of these treatises in his book *Adultery and Divorce*, 166–74.

106. R. Consist. 34 (1595), fol. 408v.

107. R. Consist. 31 (1579), fol. 298r–v; 12 (1557), fol. 94. For more on Catholic behavior and belief in Geneva, see Grosse, *Les rituels de la cène*, 446–51.

108. That the ministers themselves distinguished between voluntary and involuntary contact with Catholic rites, see the case of Jean Dimon, R. Consist. 31 (1577), fol. 89v.

109. See Hoffman, *Church and Community in the Diocese of Lyon, 1500–1789*, 30–35.

110. R. Consist. 25 (1968), fols. 98v, 141v; ibid., 26 (1569), fols. 58v, 80v.

111. When a tide of refugees arrived in Geneva in the aftermath of St. Bartholomew's Day (1572), the city's ministers invited all those who had been "polluted with idolatries" to appear before the Consistory and to make public reparation. Over one hundred people responded. They were not, however, banned individually from the Lord's Table in a formal act of suspension. See *RCP* 3:95–96. One wonders if Geneva's more lenient stance toward confessional infidelity was prompted, in part, by the more liberal policy hammered out at the seventh National Synod of La Rochelle (1571), a synod over which Theodore Beza presided. See Aymon, *Tous les synodes*, 1:110.

112. R. Consist. 27 (1570), fol. 92r–v.

113. R. Consist. 28 (1572), fol. 121r–v. This case also appears in the minutes of the Venerable Company; see *RCP* 3:57–58. Though not suspended from the Supper, the suspects were imprisoned by the magistrates.

114. R. Consist. 28 (1572), fol. 156v.

115. For a discussion of charivari, see Muir, *Ritual in Early Modern Europe*, 106–11.

116. R. Consist. 32 (1580), fol. 107v.

117. R. Consist. 27 (1570), fol. 170r–v.

118. R. Consist. 20 (1563), fol. 88; ibid., 23 (1566), fol. 66v; *RCP* 7:194; R. Consist. 10 (1555), fol. 33v; ibid., 27 (1570), fol. 66.

119. R. Consist. 30 (1576), 28.

120. In his demographic study of sixteenth-century Geneva, E. William Monter shows that rates of illegitimate births in the rural parishes of Satigny and Jussy before 1600 were nine times higher than rates in the city between 1560 and 1580 (36 illegitimate children among 2,605 baptisms, compared to 17 illegitimate children among 12,458 baptisms). Nevertheless, even the "elevated" rate of illegitimacy in Geneva's countryside was below the rate of illegitimacy found elsewhere in Europe during this period. See Monter, "Historical Demography and Religious History," 414–15.

121. The vulgar content of some of these songs is suggested by the case of Nicolas Borsat. The Consistory interrogated four witnesses who recalled in detail the lyrics of Borsat's "chanson profanes et vilaines." Borsat was suspended, along with a companion who taught him the songs. See R. Consist. 27 (1570), fol. 101.

122. R. Consist. 31 (1577), fol. 49.

123. [Lambert Daneau?], *Traité des danses, auquel est amplement resolue la question, ascavoir s'il est permis aux Chrestiens de danser*, 12–20. On this topic, see Garrisson, *Protestants du Midi*, 302–305. The relatively large number of suspensions for dancing after 1570 may mirror patterns of behavior and discipline elsewhere in reformed Europe. In 1560, the second National Synod of Poitiers noted that "tous Consistoires seront avertis par les Ministres, de defender soigneusement toutes Danses." See Aymon, *Tous les Synodes*, 1:16. This provision also found its way into the Discipline of the French Reformed Church during this period, see Méjan, *Discipline de l'Église Réformée de France*, 296.

124. R. Consist. 17 (1560), fol. 195.

125. R. Consist. 34 (1596), fol. 444.

126. R. Consist. 25 (1568), fols. 99, 172v. The power to heal scrofula (the swelling of the lymph glands) was a supernatural gift sometimes ascribed to French and English kings. See Bloch, *Les rois thaumaturges; étude sur le caractère surnaturel attribué à la puissance royale, particulièrement en France et en Angleterre.*

127. Monter, *Witchcraft in France and Switzerland*, 42–66, 210–11.

128. The kirk sessions in Scotland played a similar role in witchcraft cases during this period. See Graham, *The Uses of Reform*, 298–308.

129. R. Consist. 24 (1567), fols. 137v, 149v, 151.

130. R. Consist. 36 (1607), fols. 76v–77. The registers indicate that the demoniacs returned to Geneva in the following years and continued to disturb religious life in the city. See R. Consist. 37 (1608), fol. 34 and 38 (1609), fol. 111.

131. See for example R. Consist. 35 (1605), fols. 6, 12, 47, 48v; 35 (1606), fol. 107; 36 (1607), fols. 45, 69v, 76v–77, 80v, 83v–84, 86v–87, 88, 90, 92, 93v; 37 (1608), fols. 3, 30v, 34, 43v, 52v; 38 (1609), fols. 6v, 82, 83v, 92, 94r–v, 96, 111.

132. R. Consist. 25 (1568), fols. 119, 182. This case appears in PC #1483.

133. See, for example, Jean Delumeau's *Catholicism between Luther and Voltaire*. My findings thus support the conclusions of Robert Kingdon: "Christianity was clearly not as dominant a force in the lives of the illiterate peasants in those villages [surrounding Geneva] as in the urban population. Even in Geneva's villages, however, while we find some evidence of folk religion or witchcraft, we find even more evidence of forms of Christianity." Kingdon, "The Genevan Revolution in Public Worship," 265.

134. *R. Consist. I* (1543), 294.

135. Alfred Perrenoud estimates Geneva's urban population to have been 16,000 in 1570, with another 4,000 people living in Geneva's countryside. See *La population de Genève du seizième au début du dix-neuvième siècle*, 1:36–37. Our data indicate that in 1569, an average of 41.6 people appeared before Consistory each week and a total of 657 people were suspended.

136. Michael Graham has noted a similar phenomenon in the disciplinary records of kirk sessions and presbyteries during the second and third decades of disciplinary activity of reformed churches in Scotland. See Graham, *The Uses of Reform*, 204–205.

137. Perrenoud estimates that Geneva's urban population increased from 13,100 persons in 1550, to 21,400 persons in 1560, and then dipped to 16,000 persons in 1570 due to the onset of the plague in 1568. See Perrenoud, *La Population de Genève*, 37.

138. R. Consist. 35 (1605), fol. 62v.

139. During the second half of the sixteenth century, the French reformed churches also prohibited and disciplined such popular behaviors as dancing, gambling, performing tragedies and comedies, banqueting, and participating in charivaris. See Meylan, *Discipline de l'Église Réformée de France*, 296–98 (articles 27–31). On this see Chareyre, "'The Great Difficulties One Must Bear to Follow Jesus Christ.'"

140. *RCP* 4:39.

141. RC 71, fol. 17, quoted in *RCP* 4:39, note 4.

142. "*Funus Consistori: o miserere.*" *RCP* 8:223. The unsatisfactory compromise that the Consistory ultimately agreed to was that Franc's wife would come to Consistory, and Franc himself would be interviewed by several ministers in the home of the pastor Antoine de La Faye. For the Franc controversy, see *RCP* 8:179–81, 183, 196–97, 210–11, 217, 222–23 and also Choisy, *L'État Chrétien Calviniste*, 340–41.

143. This account is found in R. Consist. 35 (1606), fols. 83v, 86, 94r–v, 97, 102–106, 108v, 110v, 112–13, 114v, and in *RCP* 9:187–92.

144. R. Consist. 35 (1606), fols. 101v–102.

145. R. Consist. 35 (1606), fol. 105v.

146. *RCP* 9:190.

147. This decree appears in annex no. 82 of *RCP* 9:325. The provisions of the *Ecclesiastical Ordinances* (1576) that address private and public vices are nos. 83, 84, 86. See *Ecclesiastical Ordinances* (1576), in Heyer, *L'Église de Genève*, 294–95.

148. R. Consist. 35 (1606), fol. 114v.

149. R. Consist. 27 (1570), fol. 123.

150. R. Consist. 19 (1562), fol. 83v.

151. R. Consist. 10 (1555), fol. 3v; 17 (1560), fols. 21v, 47, 138v; 26 (1569), fol. 143v; 33 (1589), fol. 129.

152. See R. Consist. 32 (1581), fol. 166 and 35 (1605), fol. 17.

153. R. Consist. 33 (1589), fol. 147v.

154. *R. Consist.* IV (1548), 44.

155. For cases where the ministers intervened on behalf of abused and neglected children, see for example *R. Consist.* I (1542), 92; II (1546), 299; IV (1548), 5; R. Consist. 17 (1560), fol. 110v; 18 (1561), fol. 77v; 25 (1568), fol. 157v; 27 (1570), fols. 49, 131; 28 (1572), fol. 208v; 30 (1576), fol. 60v; 31 (1580), fol. 81; 33 (1582), fols. 28v–29.

156. For the Consistory's intervention on behalf of illegitimate or abandoned children, see *RCP* I (1542), 53, 263; R. Consist. 5 (1550), fol. 40; ibid., 24 (1567), fol. 57v.

157. R. Consist. 6 (1551), fols. 49v, 52–53, 62v.

158. For a sample of cases where the Consistory intervened on behalf of elderly parents, see *R. Consist.* I (1543), 179; II (1546), 177; IV (1548), 5.

159. See R. Consist. 18 (1561), fol. 164v.

160. See R. Consist. 23 (1566), fol. 29v.

161. For despised refugees: *R. Consist.* III (1547), 35; R. Consist. 5 (1550), fol. 38v; 23 (1566), fol. 144. For poor laborers: R. Consist. 24 (1567), fol. 101; 25 (1568), fol. 142; 33 (1589), fol. 133. For mistreated prisoners: R. Consist. 34 (1594), fol. 237. For social misfits: *R. Consist.* III (1547), 128; R. Consist. 5 (1550), fol. 89v.

162. R. Consist. 33 (1589), fol. 145v. For a similarly shocking case, see ibid., 5 (1550), fol. 18v.

163. See for example, R. Consist. 25 (1568), fol. 164v; 32 (1580), fol. 27.

164. See for example, R. Consist. 17 (1560), fol. 146v; 19 (1562), fol. 92; 26 (1569), fol. 73v.

165. See for example R. Consist. 26 (1569), fols. 1, 2v, 50v.

166. See for example R. Consist. 16 (1560), fol. 259v; 18 (1561), fol. 154v; 23 (1566), fol. 62v; 26 (1569), fols. 20, 212; 28 (1572), fol. 185v; 30 (1577), fol. 112; (1596), fol. 469v; 35 (1606), fol. 127; 38 (1609), fol. 113v.

167. R. Consist. 32 (1580), fol. 27.

168. R. Consist. 31 (1578), fol. 220.

169. R. Consist. 18 (1561), fol. 36. See also ibid., 18 (1561), fol. 66v.

170. R. Consist. 28 (1571), fol. 83v. For other cases where the Consistory intervened on behalf of plague victims, see R. Consist. 27 (1570), fols. 127v, 131; 28 (1571), fols. 86r–v, 101.

171. Kingdon, "The Geneva Consistory in the Time of Calvin," 26–33. Christian Grosse discusses this dimension of the Consistory's ministry in detail, *Les rituels de la cène*, 503–65. See also Mentzer, "Moral Regulation in Protestant France," 7–8.

172. For example, *R. Consist.* I (1544), 356; III (1547), 18; R. Consist. 28 (1571), fol. 87; 29 (1575), fol. 1; 30 (1577), fol. 61.

173. For example, R. Consist. 31 (1579), fols. 351, 363.

174. R. Consist. 32 (1580), fol. 70.

175. R. Consist. 25 (1568), fol. 137v.

176. R. Consist. 32 (1580), fols. 3v, 57.

177. R. Consist. 18 (1561), fols. 172–172v.

178. R. Consist. 31 (1578), fols. 191v, 211.

179. R. Consist. 32 (1580), fol. 151v. I found no further evidence of conflict between these two women in later registers of Consistory.

180. R. Consist. 22 (1565), fol. 75, 109.

181. R. Consist. 22 (1565), fol. 149.

182. See R. Consist. 23 (1566), fols. 5, 16v, 25v, 109v; 25 (1568), fols. 79, 83–84.

183. R. Consist. 25 (1568), fol. 153.

184. See R. Consist. 30 (1576), fol. 7v.

Chapter 8

1. "Ad Bibliothecam," in Beza, *Les juvenilia*, 120–21. For an English translation and commentary on this work, see Summers, *A View from the Palatine*.

2. See Pettegree, *Reformation and the Culture of Persuasion*.

3. See Gilmont, *John Calvin and the Printed Book*, 138–43; and Ganoczy, *La bibliothèque de l'Académie de Calvin*, 17–19.

4. No comprehensive inventory of Beza's library is known to exist. However, scholars have discovered a list of thirteen books, annotated in Beza's hand, that were sold in Leiden in 1656. This list includes commentaries by Calvin (on Daniel) and Jean Mercier (on the poetic books of the Old Testament), theological works by Claude d'Espence, Flacius Illyricus, Wilhelm Holder, Adrianus Saravia,

François Bauduin, and Tileman Heshusius, a philosophical text by Pedro Nuñez, and Beza's own *Poemata*. See *CB* 9:9–10.

5. See Goulart to Sebastian Schobinger, November 26, 1626, in Banderier, "Documents sur Simon Goulart," 602.

6. Simon Goulart to Sébastien Schobinger, April 1, 1627, transcribed in Jones, *Simon Goulart*, 432–33, annex XLIII. Jones also includes a document listing ten books (and their prices) that Goulart sent to Schobiner between 1605 and 1627 (see annex XLII).

7. See Daneau to Simler, March 25, 1576, quoted in Fatio, *Méthode et théologie*, 25, note 66.

8. To my knowledge, the inventory itself has never been published. This survey is based on the summary article of Puyroche, "La bibliothèque d'un pasteur à la fin du XVIe siècle."

9. In his study of the libraries of more than one hundred Lutheran and Reformed pastors in the Palatinate, Bernard Vogler found that the average number of books owned by clergymen in 1580 was 71. Thirty years later, this number had increased to 111. See Vogler, *Le clergé protestant rhénan*, 239–54.

10. On censorship in sixteenth-century Geneva, see Santschi, *La censure à Genève au XVIIe si è cle*; Gilmont, *John Calvin and the Printed Book*; and Jostock, *La censure négociée*.

11. See Rivoire and Berchem, *Les sources du droit*, 3:87; and Santschi, *La censure à Genève*, 11. By 1588, primary responsibility for overseeing theological works printed in Geneva's print shops was given to the rector of the Academy, who as a member of the Company of Pastors represented the church's interests.

12. R. Consist. 31 (1577), fol. 47v.

13. *RCP* 5:210.

14. *RCP* 8:17, 27.

15. *RCP* 8:130, 142, 151. On this affair, see Jostock, *La censure négociée*, 259–60.

16. *RCP* 7:78. Dulco's book was later published as *Apologia chrysopoeiae et argyropoeiae, adversus Thomam Erastum* (Ursellis: Cornelius Sutorius, 1602).

17. Santschi, *La censure à Genève*, 22.

18. R. Consist. 17 (1560), fol. 41.

19. R. Consist. 20 (1563), fol. 104v.

20. R. Consist. 18 (1561), fols. 157, 161.

21. R. Consist. 31 (1579), fol. 335.

22. R. Consist. 15 (1559), fols. 15, 31v–32. This incident is described in Jostock, *La censure négociée*, 194.

23. See R. Consist. 27 (1570), fols. 26, 32. The ecclesiastical and civil cases against Lucas Cop are described in detail in Jostock, *La censure négociée*, 181–90.

24. Among his companions implicated in this affair were Pierre Enoch, son of Genevan minister Louis Enoch, the future pastor Jean-Baptiste Rotan, and Paul Chevalier, brother of the future minister and professor of Hebrew, Pierre Chevalier.

25. The criminal case is found in PC #1579.

26. Gilmont, *John Calvin and the Printed Book*, 284–285, and appx. I.

27. Calvin to Bullinger, March 13, 1551, *CO* 14, col. 51.

28. Calvin to the Queen of Navarre, April 28, 1545, *CO* 12, col. 67; *CTS* 4:455–56.

29. Beza to Josias Simler, September 19, 1575, *CB* 16:209. Eight years later, Beza urged his friend Chandieu to publish a response to the theological attack of the Jesuit Francisco Torres Turrianus. See Beza to Grynaeus, October 25, 1583, *CB* 24:281.

30. Chandieu, "Palinodie I," 141.

31. My calculations do not include multiple editions of an original title. Thus, this figure includes only a single edition of Calvin's *Institutes* or Beza's *Confession de la foi chrestienne*.

32. Among these dangerous volumes should be included Beza's *Du droit des magistrats* and Daneau's *Ad Petri Carpenterii...consilium...responsio*. On these two works, see Manetsch, *Theodore Beza and the Quest for Peace in France*, 63–73.

33. From 1559 to 1600, Calvin's *Institutes* were published in thirteen Latin editions, fifteen French editions, seven English editions, two German editions, three Dutch editions, one Italian edition, and one Spanish edition. See Peter and Gilmont, *Bibliotheca Calviniana* (vol. 3) for a description of each of these editions.

34. Beza, *Quaestionum et responsionum christianarum libellus*; Beza, *Quaestionum et responsionum christianarum pars altera, quae est de sacramentis*; Chandieu, *La responce à la profession de foy publiée contre ceux de l'Eglise réformée*. Lambert Daneau wrote another significant overview of reformed theology, his five volume *Christianae Isagoge* (1583–1588), the first volume of which was published two years after he departed Geneva for Leiden.

35. Beza, *Confession de la foy chrestienne*, 5, 10.

36. Gardy, *Bibliographie*, 60–80.

37. Geisendorf, *Théodore de Bèze*, 337–39.

38. *Harmonia Confessionum Fidei. Orthodoxarum, & Reformatarum Ecclesiarum*. The reformed confessions included the First and Second Helvetic Confessions (1536, 1566), the Confession of Basel (1534), the French Confession of Faith (1559), the Thirty-Nine Articles (1562), the Belgic Confession (1561), the Bohemian Confession (1573), the Tetrapolitan Confession (1530), the Saxon Confession (1551), and the Confession of Württemberg (1552). See Higman, "*L'harmonia confessionum fidei* de 1581."

39. Daneau, *Elenchi Haereticorum* (Geneva: Eustace Vignon, 1572). See Fatio, *Méthode et théologie*, 35–36.

40. This argument is found in the preface to Daneau's *In Petri Lombardi...librum primum Sententiarum...Commentarius*, described by Fatio, *Méthode et théologie*, 118–30.

41. Muller, *After Calvin*, 51–52.

42. For a helpful and concise summary of the theological issues separating Lutheran and reformed Christians on the subject of the so-called *communicatio idiomatum*, see Muller, *Dictionary of Latin and Greek Theological Terms*, 72–74; and Steinmetz, *Luther in Context*, 76–79.

43. The charge that Lutheran Eucharistic theology succumbed to the error of Eutyches was first made by Calvin himself. See *Institutes* IV.xvii.29, and the helpful discussion in Billings, *Calvin, Participation, and the Gift*, 135–36. See also Gerrish, *Grace and Gratitude*, 54–55.

44. Beza, *Ad acta colloquii Montisbelgardensis*, 253. For the long-term impact of this standoff, see Raitt, *The Colloquy of Montbéliard*, 155–56.

45. Goulart's preface to Guillaume Du Bartas's *La semaine* (1582), quoted in Jostock, *La censure negociée*, 203.

46. The most complete bibliography of Goulart's writings is found in Jones, *Simon Goulart*, 553–650.

47. See Droz, "Simon Goulart, éditeur de musique." The revisions in Goulart's edition of *Thresor de musique d'Orlande de Lassus* (1576) are described in greater detail in Jostock, *La censure négociée*, 203–208.

48. See Jostock, *La censure négociée*, 212–17.

49. This anecdote appears in Montaigne, *Essais* (1580), bk. II, ch. 29. For an English translation, see Michel de Montaigne, *The Essays of Montaigne*, 634.

50. Jostock, *La censure négociée*, 201–202, drawing on the conclusions of Ugo Rozzo.

51. For more on these biographies, see Backus, *Life Writing in Reformation Europe*, esp. 125–53.

52. Beza, *Icones, id est verae imagines virorum doctrina simul et pietate illustrium* (Geneva: Ioannem Laonium, 1580). The work appeared in French translation the following year as *Les vrais portraits des hommes illustrés* (Geneva, 1581).

53. Beza, *Les vrais portraits des hommes illustrés*, ii.

54. Beza to Nicolas Dürnhoffer, March 8, 1580, *CB* 21:65.

55. Jean de Serre, *Commentariorum de statu religionis et reipublicae in regno Galliae*; Beza, *Histoire ecclésiastique des Eglises réformée au royaume de France*; Goulart, *Mémoires de l'estat de France sous Charles neufiesme*; Goulart, *Mémoires de la Ligue*.

56. "Libertatem historiae, quam Divinae Providentiae ministram et tubam appellare debemus." From *Commenatariorum de statu Religionis et reipublicae in Regno Galliae* (5th edition, 1580), quoted in Dardier, *Jean de Serres*, 19.

57. Quoted in Dardier, *Jean de Serres*, 19.

58. Goulart to Josias Simler, November 20, 1575, quoted in Jones, *Simon Goulart*, annex 10, 349. In his poem "Ode sur le misères des Eglises Françoises" (1569), Antoine de Chandieu expressed similar thoughts regarding the importance of committing to writing the memory of the cruel massacres perpetrated against the Protestant churches in France. See Chandieu's *Epitaphe de la Mort de Tresillustre Prince Wolfgang, Comte Palatin du Rhin*, quoted in Barker, *Protestantism, Poetry and Protest*, 216.

59. For Calvin as a commentary writer, see Holder, *John Calvin and the Grounding of Interpretation*; Parker, *Calvin's New Testament Commentaries*; Parker, *Calvin's Old Testament Commentaries*.

60. Beza, Letter Preface to *Annotations*, in *CB* 6:266–67.

61. After Daneau departed Geneva, he also wrote commentaries on the Lord's Prayer (1582), the Gospel of Matthew (1583), the Epistles of John and Jude (1585), the Minor Prophets (1586), and the Gospel of Mark (1594). Daneau's commentaries and exegetical method are discussed by Olivier Fatio, "Lambert Daneau," 114.

62. For more on Daneau's *La Methodus tractandae sacrae scripturae* (1579), see chapter 6, and Fatio, *Méthode et théologie*, 64–84.

63. Chambers, *Bibliography of French Bibles,* vol. 1, *Fifteenth- and Sixteenth-Century French-Language Editions of the Scriptures.*

64. Beza, *Novum D. N. Jesu Christi Testamentum.*

65. See Dufour, *Théodore de Bèze,* 34–37. These subsequent editions of the *Annotations* appeared in 1565, 1582, 1589, and 1598. Likewise, beginning in 1565, Beza produced a smaller (and cheaper) in-octavo volume of this Latin-Greek New Testament, with a more concise collection of annotations. The French Catholic savant Richard Simon evaluated Beza's *Annotations* in these terms: "Il semble meme que sa principale application dans sa version & dans ses Notes, ait été de faire parler les Evangelistes & les Apostres la Theologie de ceux de Genève." *Histoire critique des principaux commentateurs du Nouveau Testament,* 751. For contemporary assessments of Beza's work as an exegete, see Backus *The Reformed Roots of the English New Testament* and Jan Krans, *Beyond What Is Written: Erasmus and Beza as Conjectural Critics of the New Testament.*

66. Beza to [Jean-Jacques Grynaeus], August 23/September 2, 1586, Basle, Universitätsbibl., Kirchen Archiv, C. I. 2, Bd. II, fol. 101.

67. Candaux, *Le Psautier de Genève, 1562–1865. Images commentées et essai de bibliographie,* 19.

68. On the militant use of the French Psalter, see Pettegree, *Culture of Persuasion,* 65–72.

69. *La Bible, qui est toute la saincte escriture du Vieil et du Nouveau Testament… Le tout revue et conféré sur les texts hébrieux et grecs par les pasteurs et professeurs de l'Eglise de Genève.* For this Bible's journey toward publication, see *RCP* 5: passim, as well as the ministers' and professors' preface (ibid. 340–53). The thirteenth National Synod of Montauban (1594) accepted the Bible of 1588 as the official version of the French reformed churches. See Aymon, *Tous les synodes,* 1:179.

70. Chambers, *Bibliography of French Bibles,* 1:480–81; and Chambers, *Bibliography of French Bibles,* vol. 2, *Seventeenth Century French-Language Editions of the Scriptures,* passim.

71. See Armstrong, "Geneva and the Theology and Politics of French Calvinism."

72. Diodati to M. de La Nou, July 13, 1605, quoted in Eugène de Budé, *Vie de Jean Diodati,* 169.

73. See Campi, "Giovanni Diodati et sa traduction de la Bible in italien," 15–21.

74. Diodati's annotations from the Sacra Bibbia were translated into English and published in 1643 under the title *Pious and learned annotations upon the Holy Bible.* See Campi, "Giovanni Diodati et sa traduction de la Bible," 10.

75. See Mottu-Weber's article "Jean Diodati," 65–66 and McComish, *The Epigones,* 167–75.

76. Letter Preface, Beza to Walter Mildmay, March 15, 1582, in *CB* 23:30.

77. Beza makes this point forcefully in his preface to *Valentini Gentilis teterrimi haeretici impietatum ac triplicis perfidiae et perjurii, brevis explicatio* (1567). See *CB* 8:244. For a discussion of this passage, see McPhee, "Conserver or Transformer of Calvin's Theology?" 120.

78. Viret, *Traittez divers pour l'instruction des fidèles qui resident et conversent ès lieus et pais esquels il ne leur est permis de vivre en la pureté et liberté de l'Evangile.* On this work, see Barnaud, *Pierre Viret,* 551–56.

79. Daneau's production of practical ethical writings include *Brieue remonstrance sur les ieux de sort* (1573), *Response au cruel, et pernicieux conseil de Pierre Charpentier.... Traitte duquel on apprendra en quell cas il est permis à l'homme Chrestien de porter les armes* (1575), *Traticte contre les baccanales* (1582), *Traité des danses* (1579), *Traité de l'estat des Chrestiens en leur accoustrement* ([Geneva], 1580). Fatio has recently questioned Félice's conclusion that the last two treatises were, in fact, written by Daneau. Lambert Daneau also wrote a general study of ethics entitled *Ethice chrestiana* (Geneva, 1577). For Daneau's ethical writings, see chapter 6 of Fatio's *Méthode et théologie*.

80. Daneau, *Les sorciers*.

81. Ibid., 29–30.

82. Ibid., 129.

83. See Parker, *Calvin's Preaching*, 180–87. For Calvin's reticence in publishing his sermons, see Gilmont, *John Calvin and the Printed Book*, 77–81.

84. Quoted in Gilmont, *John Calvin and the Printed Book*, 80.

85. For a concise summary of the publication history of Calvin's sermons after his death, see Gilmont, *Bibliotheca Calviniana*, 3:648–50.

86. "Calvinus, inquam, ille cuius summa in interpretandis fides, acerrimum in asserenda veritate iudicium, eruditio eximia, diligentia nusquam dormitans." Preface to Calvin's Sermons on Job, *CO* 33, cols. 11–12.

87. Preface to Calvin's Sermons on Job, *CO* 33, cols. 13–14. See also Gilmont, *Bibliotheca Calviniana*, 3:533–36.

88. Cop, *A Godly and learned Exposition vppon the Proverbes of Solomon*, *ij.

89. As noted in chapter 6, Beza's published sermon collections were *Sermons on the Song of Songs* (1586), *Sermons on the History of the Death of Jesus Christ* (1592), and *Sermons on the History of the Resurrection of Jesus Christ* (1593).

90. Beza, *Sermons sur le Cantique des Cantiques*, A.iii.r.

91. Beza, *Sermons sur l'histoire de la passion*, ¶.ii.v–¶.iij.

92. Ibid., ¶.viij.

93. On Beza's *Chrestiennes méditations* (1581) see Richter, "La meditation en prose à la Renaissance." Chandieu's *Méditations sur le psalme XXXII* (1583) is described in Baker, *Protestantism, Poetry and Protest*, 247–56. Goulart's work is entitled *XXV Méditations chrestiennes* (1608).

94. "Jean Jaquemot," in *FP* 6:39.

95. Chandieu, *Octonaires sur la vanité et inconstance du monde*, 22–28.

96. Ibid., 95.

97. Goulart, *XXVIII Discours Chrestiens, touchant l'estat du monde & de l'Eglise de Dieu; Seconde partie des discours Chrestiens*.

98. Goulart, *Seconde partie des discours Chrestiens*, 240–42.

99. This woodcut is found in the English translation of Goulart's work, entitled *The Wise Vieillard, or Old Man* (London, 1621), P2v. I have not been able to consult the original French version.

100. This observation has recently been highlighted by Alain Dufour in his biography *Théodore de Bèze*, and by S. K. Barker in her study of Antoine de Chandieu entitled *Protestantism, Poetry and Protest*.

101. Olivier Fatio makes this point forcefully in the introduction to his study on Daneau: "Existe-t-il position plus inconfortable que celle des epigones? D'une

part les historiens déplorent leur absence d'originalité, d'autre part ils crient à la trahison à la moindre différence d'avec le modèle!" Fatio, *Méthode et théologie*, ix.

102. Muller has identified three phases of Protestant Orthodoxy: Early Orthodoxy (1565–1640), High Orthodoxy (1640–1725), and Late Orthodoxy (1725–1770). See *After Calvin*, 4.

103. A helpful summary of the scholarly debate over the relationship between Calvin and later reformed orthodoxy is provided by Carl Trueman, "Calvin and Reformed Orthodoxy"; and Van Asselt and Dekker, *Reformation and Scholasticism*.

104. Kickel, *Vernunft und Offenbarung bei Theodor Beza*, esp. 167–68. Kickel's views are summarized and assessed positively in Armstrong, *Calvinism and the Amyraut Heresy*, 38–42. Shawn Wright, in his book *Our Sovereign Refuge*, is more critical in his assessment of Kickel's argument (see especially 50–51, 59–61).

105. This chart has been reproduced in several places, including in Olivier Fatio "Théodore de Bèze ou les débuts de l'orthodoxie réformée," 22–23.

106. Hall, "Calvin Against the Calvinists."

107. Armstrong, *Calvinism and the Amyraut Heresy*, 32.

108. Armstrong writes: "This new outlook [Beza's theological method] represents a profound divergence from the humanistically oriented religion of John Calvin and most of the early reformers. The strongly biblically and experientially based theology of Calvin and Luther had, it is fair to say, been overcome by the metaphysics and deductive logic of a restored Aristotelianism." *Calvinism and the Amyraut Heresy*, 32.

109. McGrath, *Historical Theology*, 169.

110. Spykman, *Reformational Theology*, 23. Spykman continues: "As we have seen, the dualist-dialectical synthesis of Thomas became dominant first in the medieval era. It became dominant again in the pseudo-Protestant thought of the early modern period in its reaction to the Counter-Reformation. As a result, much of the heritage regained in the sixteenth century was lost during subsequent centuries. Protestant theology came under heavy pressure from a resurgent Thomism. This was also true of theology as carried on in the Reformed wing. It, too, abandoned the newly discovered evangelical style of theologizing so characteristic of the work of Luther and Calvin. It opted instead to counteract the reactionary theology of Roman Catholicism with a reactionary theology of its own. As a result, instead of growth, stagnation set in" (24).

111. Holtrop, *The Bolsec Controversy on Predestination*, 2:835.

112. Ibid., 2:835, 858–59.

113. Scholarship challenging the "Calvin against the Calvinist" paradigm is burgeoning. Especially important is Raitt, *The Eucharistic Theology of Theodore Beza*; Fatio, *Méthode et théologie*; McPhee, "Conserver or Transformer of Calvin's Theology?"; Anderson, "Theodore Beza: Savant or Scholastic?"; Letham, "Theodore Beza: A Reassessment"; Sinnema, "Antoine de Chandieu's Call for a Scholastic Reformed Theology (1580)"; Mallinson, *Faith, Reason, and Revelation in Theodore Beza*; Trueman and Clark, *Protestant Scholasticism*; Wright, *Our Sovereign Refuge*. The work of Richard Muller remains indispensible in this regard. See particularly his *Post-Reformation Reformed Dogmatics*; *The Unaccommodated Calvin*; and *After Calvin*.

114. For this line of analysis, see especially Donnelly, *Calvinism and Scholasticism in Vermigli's Doctrine of Man and Grace*; McCoy and Baker, *Fountainhead of Federalism*; Trueman and Clark, *Protestant Scholasticism*; and Muller, *After Calvin*.

115. Muller, *After Calvin*, 8.

116. Muller counts twenty-six instances where the plural noun *scholastici* appears in the 1559 edition of the *Institutes*, usually referring to the theologians of the Sorbonne. See *The Unaccommodated Calvin*, 49–51.

117. See in particular the perceptive essays by Muller, "Scholasticism in Calvin: A Question of Relation and Disjunction," in *The Unaccommodated Calvin*, 39–61; and Steinmetz, "The Scholastic Calvin."

118. See *Institutes* II.ii.6, p. 263 and III.xiv.11, pp. 814–15.

119. See Muller, *The Unaccommodated Calvin*, 52–55. On this latter distinction, see Calvin's Commentary on 1 John 2:1–2, where the reformer distinguishes between the "sufficiency" and "efficiency" of Christ's atonement, and then adds: "This solution has commonly prevailed in the schools." *CO* 55, col. 310.

120. Steinmetz, "The Scholastic Calvin," 25.

121. Muller, *After Calvin*, 48. This conclusion is corroborated by a growing number of contemporary scholars. See for example Van Asselt and Dekker, *Reformation and Scholasticism*, especially 11–43.

122. See Muller, *After Calvin*, 75–76. The author provides this more detailed definition: The scholastic method "(1) identifies the order and pattern of argument suitable to technical academic discourse; (2) presents an issue in the form of a thesis or question; (3) orders the thesis or question suitably for discussion or debate, often identifying the 'state of the question'; (4) notes a series of objections to the assumed correct answer; and then (5) offers a formulation of an answer or an elaboration of the thesis with due respect to all known sources of information and to the rules of rational discourse, followed by a full response to all objections" (ibid. 27–28).

123. See Muller, *After Calvin*, 55.

124. Kristeller, *Renaissance Thought*.

125. Muller, *After Calvin*, 58–62. In fact, as Muller has shown, Calvin's *Institutes* after 1539 was structured according to established theological common places (*loci communes*). See Muller, *The Unaccommodated Calvin*, 62–78, 101–17. Beza also organized his two volume *Quaestiones et responsiones* (1570, 1576) around theological common places.

126. See Marvin Anderson, "Theodore Beza: Savant or Scholastic?" 320–32; Backus, "L'enseignement de la logique à l'Académie de Genève entre 1559 et 1565"; Fraenkel, *De l'Écriture à la dispute. Le cas de l'Académie de Genève sous Théodore de Bèze*.

127. See Dufour, *Théodore de Bèze*; Summers, "Theodore Beza's Classical Library and Christian Humanism"; Manetsch, "Psalms before Sonnets"; Fatio, *Méthode et théologie*; Barker, *Protestantism, Poetry and Protest*.

128. Table 8.1 illustrates this sustained humanistic concern of many of Geneva's pastors.

129. This statement is quoted in Gillian Lewis, "The Geneva Academy," 51. In a similar fashion, Michel Cop called Calvin a "pearl among us," and the Company of Pastors described the reformer as "nostre bon Pere." See Lambert, "Preaching, Praying and Policing the Reform," 483; and *RCP* 3:222.

130. Beza, *De aeterna Dei praedestinatione*, included in *Tractationes Theologicarum*, 1:422. See Mallinson's discussion of this passage in *Faith, Reason, and Revelation*, 24.

131. The first accusation was made by Claude de Sanctes, the second by Florimond de Raimond. See Mallinson, *Faith, Reason, and Revelation*, 24.

132. See Fraenkel, *De l'Écriture à la dispute*; and Beza, *Cours sur les Épîstres aux Romains et aux Hébreux*.

133. Calvin's legacy could be a contested one, of course, and it was not uncommon for Geneva's ministers and magistrates to debate Calvin's viewpoint on controversial questions related to religious practice: How had the reformer defined usury or blasphemy? What had Calvin believed to be the appropriate punishment for adultery? Did Calvin allow for leavened bread in the communion service? If Calvin's opinion on a particular question was not always entirely clear, the reformer's authority was never publicly questioned—at least by Geneva's leaders. Choisy, *L'État Chrétien Calviniste à Genève*, 42, 120, 129, 185, 359.

134. *RCP* 7:167–68, 182.

135. *RCP* 7:254–57, letter no. 33 bis. On this point, see also chapter 3.

136. Quoted in Jones, *Simon Goulart*, 239.

137. Cited in McPhee, "Conserver or Transformer of Calvin's Theology?" 353.

138. On this, see Muller, *Post-Reformation Reformed Dogmatics*, 2:435–36. By the 1582 edition of the *Annotationes*, Beza had revised his translation to be in line with the conventional Protestant interpretation taken by Calvin. See *Iesu Christi D. N. Nouum testamentum sive Nouum foedus*, 416. For Calvin's translation of this verse, see his comments on Acts 2:27, *CO* 48, col. 41.

139. Muller, *Post-Reformation Reformed Dogmatics*, 2:439–40. For Calvin's treatment of Hosea 6:7, see *CTSOT*, 13:233–35.

140. See Mallinson's table 2.1 "Proper names cited in Beza's *Tractationum Theologicarum*," in *Faith, Reason, and Revelation*, 39.

141. See Mallinson's table 2.2 "Proper names cited in Beza's *Tractationum Theologicarum* [sic, *Annotationes*]," in *Faith, Reason, and Revelation*, 40–41.

142. For example, in Daneau's *Ethice chrestiana* (1577), the author cites such extra-biblical sources as Aristotle, Cicero, the *Corpus of Civil Law*, Gratian's *Decretum*, Thomas Aquinas, Nicolas of Lyra, Calvin's *Institutes*, Beza, Viret, Vermigli, Melanchthon, Wolfgang Musculus, and Neils Hemmingson. Similarly, Chandieu's treatise *Locus de Verbo Dei Scripto, Adversus Humanas Traditiones* included quoted passages from the New Testament authors (identified as *perfecti Ecclesiae Doctores*), as well as more than two dozen early church fathers, most prominently Augustine (named no less than thirty-five times), Tertullian, Basil the Great, Irenaeus, Jerome, Chrysostom, and Gregory of Nazianzus. For the reference to the biblical authors as "perfectos Ecclesiae Doctores," see ibid., 68. For La Faye's use of early church authorities, see his *Replique Chrestienne, à la response de M. F. De Sales*.

143. Goulart, *Apophthegmatum Sacrorum Loci Communes*, index.

144. Bullinger to Beza, December 1, 1568, *CB* 9:198. This letter is discussed in Fatio, *Méthode et théologie*, 39.

145. See Mallinson, *Faith, Reason, and Revelation*, 75.

146. See Fraenkel, *De l'Écriture à la dispute*, 9–14 and Backus, "L'enseignement de la logique," 153–63.

147. "Letter Preface," *Epistolarum theologicarum, CB* 8:245. This passage is discussed by McPhee, "Conserver or Transformer of Calvin's Theology?" 161–67.

148. My translation, based on the Latin transcription found in Mallinson, *Faith, Reason, and Revelation,* 76, note 205.

149. See Beza, *Christian Questions and Responses,* 56 and Beza, *Sermons sur l'histoire de la passion,* 324–25. For Beza's selective appropriation of Aristotle, see Mallinson, *Faith, Reason, and Revelation,* 52–63.

150. Beza, *Iobus, Theodore Bezae partim commentariis partim paraphrase illustrates* "…qualis ex Prophanis illis Philosophis ac Aristoteles quidem illorum, meo quidem iudicio, facile principe, excepto discitur, ad horum sacrorum scriptorium normam esse exigendum, nisi a veritate aberrare volumus," (23–24).

151. *Tractationes Theologicarum,* 1:275, quoted in McPhee, "Conserver or Transformer of Calvin's Theology?" 172.

152. Daneau, *Paratitla in Augustini tomos duos praecipuos,* 84, quoted in Fatio, *Méthode et théologie,* 56 note 43.

153. La Faye, *Theses Theologicae.* We have only been able to consult this work in its English translation: *Propositions and Principles of Divinitie, propounded and disputed in the universitie of Geneva, by certain students of Divinitie.* A helpful summary of the preface of this work is found in R. Scott Clark's article "The Authority of Reason in the Later Reformation," 123–26.

154. La Faye, *Propositions and Principles,* A2.

155. Ibid., 4.

156. Chandieu, *Locus de Verbo Dei Scripto, adversus Humanas Traditiones.* I have also consulted an English translation of this work entitled *A Common Place Touching the Word of God Written, Against the Traditions of Men.* For more on this important treatise, see Sinnema, "Antoine de Chandieu's Call for a Scholastic Reformed Theology (1580)," 159–90.

157. Chandieu, *Locus de Verbo Dei Scripto,* 4.

158. Ibid., 5.

159. Ibid., 8–12.

160. Ibid., 9.

161. Ibid., 14.

162. Ibid., 18.

163. See Mallinson's detailed argument in *Faith, Reason, and Revelation.* At the same time, Beza affirmed with Calvin the crucial role of the internal witness of the Holy Spirit in conveying religious knowledge. On this basis, Mallinson has concluded that "despite many assessments, Beza—rather than Calvin—may have the better claim to a "'balanced' epistemology," (22–23).

164. See Fatio, "Lambert Daneau," 115–16; and Muller, *Post-Reformation Reformed Dogmatics,* 3:104. Muller argues, however, that Calvin had no fundamental objection to discussing the divine attributes and essence nor establishing an evidentiary basis for God's existence. See Muller, *Post-Reformation Reformed Dogmatics,* 3:88–89, 173. Note that Daneau's *Christianae Isagoges* was completed after Daneau had departed Geneva.

165. For Beza's treatment of church discipline as a formal "mark" of a true church, see Maruyama, *The Ecclesiology of Theodore Beza,* 23–24. Daneau addresses this subject in his *Compendium sacrae theologiae,* 79v–80v. For Beza

and Daneau's contribution to resistance literature, see Beza's *Du droit des magistrats*; and Daneau's *Ad Petri Carpenterii*. These works are described in detail in Manetsch, *Theodore Beza and the Quest for Peace in France*, 63–84.

166. Beza's supralapsarian doctrine is defended throughout his literary corpus, beginning with the *Tabula praedestinationis* (1555). The best treatment of Beza's supralapsarian doctrine is found in Donald Sinnema, "Beza's View of Predestination in Historical Perspective." For an excellent discussion of Beza's *Tabula praedestinationis*, see Richard Muller's "The Use and Abuse of a Document."

167. Beza to Calvin, July 29, 1555, in *CB* 1:170–71.

168. Muller, *After Calvin*, 12.

169. See Sinnema, "Beza's View of Predestination," 229.

170. The literature on the doctrine of assurance in the reformed tradition is substantial. See, for example, Beeke, *The Quest for Full Assurance*, 72–81; and Muller, *Christ and the Decree*. Donald Sinnema's article "Beza's View on Predestination in Historical Perspective" provides a convincing revision of Beza's doctrine of assurance, which is affirmed here. See esp. 235–38.

171. *Institutes* III.xxiv.5, p. 970.

172. See Sinnema's helpful discussion, in "Beza's View of Predestination," 237.

173. Beza, *Quaestionum & responsionum Christianorum libellus*, 1:703. An English translation of this passage is found in *A Little Book of Christian Questions and Responses*, 96–97.

174. Beza, *A briefe and pithie summe*, 19, quoted in Beeke, *The Quest for Full Assurance*, 79.

175. Beeke, *The Quest for Assurance*, 104–106, 131–42, 269–85. See also Hambrick-Stowe, "Practical Divinity and Spirituality."

176. An excellent introduction to the various positions in this debate is found in four opposing essays written by Torrance, Bell, Helm, and Lane, "Calvin and Calvinism."

177. See the evidence offered by Rainbow, *The Will of God and the Cross*; and especially Godfrey, "Reformed Thought on the Extent of the Atonement to 1618." Calvin's response to Tileman Heshusius is usually presented as the reformer's clearest statement on this subject: "But the first thing to be explained is, how Christ is present with unbelievers, as being the spiritual food of souls, and, in short, the life and salvation of the world. And as [Heshusius] adheres so doggedly to the words, I should like to know how the wicked can eat the flesh of Christ which was not crucified for them, or how they can drink the blood which was not shed to expiate their sins." Quoted in Rainbow, *The Will of God and the Cross*, 118.

178. An early reference to limited atonement appears in Beza's *Tabula praedestinationis* (1555): "Forasmuch therefore as he is merciful, & yet could not forget justice, before all other things it was necessary, that a Mediator should be appointed: by whom man might be perfectly restored, & that this should bee done by that free mercy and grace which doth appeare in the salvation of his elect.... And finally with one onely offering and sacrifice of himself, should sanctifie all the elect," (23, 25). See also Beza's comments in *A Little Book of Christian Questions and Responses* Q-A no. 31, 33, pp. 11–12.

179. "...propitiationis beneficium necessario ad solos electos, et, quia electi sunt, credentes pertinere.... Num vero Christus totius mundi peccata sustulit, ut vos de singulis hominibus interpretamini? Et certe nobis intolerabilis vox vestra visa est, Christum esse mortum pro damnatis, et homines non damnari propter peccata." In Beza, *Ad Acta Colloquii Montisbelgardensis Tubingae Edita... Pars Altera*, 215.

180. See Godfrey, "Reformed Thought on the Extent of the Atonement," 144–48; and Heppe, *Reformed Dogmatics*, 475–79.

Chapter 9

1. R. Consist. 33 (1589), fols. 150v-153. See also *RCP* 6:30–31. For a description of Beza's physical maladies during this period, see Manetsch, *Theodore Beza and the Quest for Peace in France*, 213.

2. The register of the Company of Pastors reports that Beza began preaching on the passion of Jesus Christ at the end of March 1589 (see *RCP* 6:8). This sermon series, which lasted more than a year, was published in 1592 under the title *Sermons sur l'histoire de la passion*.

3. Beza to Jacob Monau, December 14/24, 1589, in *Epistolarum historico-ecclesiasticarum seculo XVI a celeberrimis viris scriptarum semicenturia*, ed. Hummel, 92.

4. Calvin, "De La Visitation des Malades," in *La forme des prières et chantz ecclésiastiques*, M3v–M4.

5. Luther, *The Babylonian Captivity of the Church*, in *LW* 36. For helpful surveys of Catholic sacramental theology in the later Middle Ages, see Lindberg, *The European Reformation*, 181–91; and Evans, *A History of Pastoral Care*.

6. Calvin, *Institutes* (1536), 87–88, 91.

7. Ibid., 91–92.

8. *Institutes*, IV.xiv.1, pp. 1276–77. For Calvin's sacramental theology, see in particular Gerrish, *Grace and Gratitude*, 130–34; and Elwood, *The Body Broken*, 61–63.

9. Pelikan, *The Growth of Medieval Theology (600–1300)*, vol. 3 of *The Christian Tradition, A History of the Development of Doctrine*, 29–31, 205.

10. Spierling, *Infant Baptism in Reformation Geneva*, 8–9. See also Karant-Nunn, *The Reformation of Ritual*, 42–49.

11. This reconstruction of the Catholic rite of baptism depends upon Spierling, *Infant Baptism in Reformation Geneva*, 39–41; and Karant-Nunn, *The Reformation of Ritual*, 44–50.

12. For a careful comparison of Geneva's baptismal rite to the ceremony in other reformed churches, see the excellent study of Hughes Oliphant Old, *The Shaping of the Reformed Baptismal Rite in the Sixteenth Century*. My analysis has also drawn from the helpful essay of Egil Grislis, "Calvin's Doctrine of Baptism," as well as the studies of Pitkin, "'The Heritage of the Lord'"; Gerrish, *Grace and Gratitude*, 87–123; and Riggs, *Baptism in the Reformed Tradition*.

13. Calvin, *CNTC* 6:319. Calvin makes similar critical comments regarding the "theatrical pomp" of Catholic baptism in the *Institutes* IV.xv.19, p. 1319.

14. See *La forme des prières et chantz ecclésiastiques*, K8–L4v. This was not Calvin's first attempt at formulating a baptismal liturgy. In the first edition of his *Institutes* (1536), Calvin proposed a brief outline of a baptismal order. Later,

in Strasbourg, Calvin produced a baptismal liturgy for his French-speaking congregation that drew in part from Bucer's Strasbourg liturgy as well as Guillaume Farel's liturgy of 1533. See Old, *The Shaping of the Reformed Baptismal Rite*, 171–75 and *Institutes* (1536), 130.

15. Spierling, *Infant Baptism in Reformation Geneva*, 76. Interestingly, Elsie Anne McKee shows that the same minister did not always preach the sermon and officiate the baptismal service that followed. McKee, "Calvin and his Colleagues as Pastors," 37–38.

16. Geneva's liturgy did not specifically address the role of godparents in baptism, and the traditional presence of godparents was retained in reformed Geneva's baptismal practice. Karen Spierling shows that Calvin himself served as godfather at no fewer than forty-seven baptisms between 1550 and 1563. Spierling, *Infant Baptism*, 106, 115–117.

17. For a summary of Calvin's baptism liturgy, see Old, *The Shaping of the Reformed Baptismal Rite*, 172–75. I have relied on Calvin's original liturgy, *La forme des prières et chantz ecclésiastiques*, K8–L4v. For a contemporary Catholic description of Geneva's baptismal practice, see Cathelan, *Passevent Parisien*, 11–13.

18. Calvin's liturgy does not identify who was to present the child for baptism, the godparents or the parents. However, other Genevan sources (including Consistory minutes) make clear that both godparents and parents were expected to attend baptisms.

19. *La forme des prières et chantz ecclésiastiques*, L1v. For the significance of twofold grace in Calvin's baptismal theology, see Billings, *Calvin, Participation and the Gift*, 121–29.

20. *La forme des prières et chantz ecclésiastiques*, L1v–L2.

21. Ibid., L2.

22. On the reformed mode of baptism (sprinkling or pouring), see Old, *The Shaping of the Reformed Baptismal Rite*, 249–82. The contemporary Catholic polemicist Antoine Cathelan described the actual baptism in this fashion: "The ministers say 'I baptize you' once, and then throw water with their bare hands onto the face of the children, whom they have taken from the hands of the midwife." Cathelan, *Passevent Parisien*, 11–12.

23. *La forme des prières et chantz ecclésiastiques*, L4.

24. Baptisms in the countryside parishes were somewhat less common, though by no means infrequent. During Matthieu Scarron's ten-year ministry in the parish of Genthod-Moëns, for example, he officiated at seventy-one baptisms between the two congregations. See AEG, E.C. Genthod, Moëns, Magny, Malagny, vol. 1, fols. 63–78.

25. *Catechism*, in CO 6, cols. 117–18. "Catechism of the Church of Geneva," in Calvin, *Calvin: Theological Treatises*, 133. Italics added. For Zwingli's teaching on the significance of baptism, see Stephens, *The Theology of Huldrych Zwingli*, 199–206.

26. *Catechism*, in CO 6, cols. 119–20. "Catechism of the Church of Geneva," in Calvin, *Calvin: Theological Treatises*, 134. Similarly, in the *Institutes* (1559), Calvin notes, "it is not my intention to weaken the force of baptism by not joining reality and truth to the sign, in so far as God works through outward means. But from this sacrament, as from all others, we obtain only as much as we receive in faith," (IV.xv.15, p. 1315).

27. In the 1536 edition of his *Institutes*, Calvin endorsed Luther's view of infant faith, a position that he soon after abandoned. In later editions of the *Institutes*, Calvin argued that "infants are baptized into future repentance and faith, and even though these have not yet been formed in them, the seed of both lies hidden within them by the secret work of the Spirit," *Institutes* (1559), IV.xvi.20, p. 1343. On the matter of infant faith, see Grislis, "Calvin's Doctrine of Baptism," 52–53.

28. *Catechism*, in *CO* 6, cols. 119–20. "Catechism of the Church of Geneva," in Calvin, *Calvin: Theological Treatises*, 134.

29. *Catechism*, in *CO* 6, cols. 121–22. "Catechism of the Church of Geneva," in Calvin, *Calvin: Theological Treatises*, 135.

30. *Catechism*, in *CO* 6, cols. 122–23. "Catechism of the Church of Geneva," in Calvin, *Calvin: Theological Treatises*, 135.

31. To the question, "How are these benefits conferred on us through baptism?" the *Catechism* offers this response: "Because unless we render the promises unfruitful by rejecting them, we are fed with Christ and granted his Spirit." *Catechism*, in *CO* 6, cols. 119–20. "Catechism of the Church of Geneva," in Calvin, *Calvin: Theological Treatises*, 134. Elsewhere, Calvin states, "I grant, indeed, that many which are children of the faithful, according to the flesh, are counted bastards, and not legitimate, because they thrust themselves out of the holy progeny through their unbelief, " Comm. on Acts 3:25, in *CO* 48, col. 76 and quoted in Grislis, "Calvin's Doctrine of Baptism," 56. For Beza's view, see Raitt, "Probably They Are God's Children."

32. On the topic of emergency baptisms, see Spierling, *Infant Baptism in Reformation Geneva*, 67–78; and Benedict, *Christ's Churches Purely Reformed*, 503–504.

33. The Small Council prohibited emergency baptisms by midwives in January 1537 (Rivoire and Berchem, *Sources du Droit du Canton de Genève*, 2:333). A decade later, an ordinance for the supervision of countryside churches repeated this prohibition in the following terms: "If midwives usurp the office of baptism, they are to be reproved or chastised according to the measure of fault found, since no commission is given them in this matter, under penalty of being put on bread and water for three days and fined ten sous," Calvin, *Calvin: Theological Treatises*, 79. Calvin condemned the practice of emergency baptisms in the *Institutes* (IV.xv.20; p. 1320–21) as did Theodore Beza in his writings. The question of emergency baptisms became a point of controversy in Beza's debate with Jacob Andreae at the Colloquy of Montbeliard in 1586.

34. *R. Consist.* III (1548), 57. Spierling also discusses this passage in her book *Infant Baptism in Reformation Geneva*, 75.

35. *RCP* 7:158.

36. *R. Consist.* IV (1548), 126–127; R. Consist. 34 (1595), fol. 353v.

37. *R. Consist.* I (1542), 75. See Spierling's discussion of Baud's case and the popular practice of resuscitating dead infants before baptism in *Infant Baptism in Reformation Geneva*, 79–81.

38. R. Consist. 28 (1572), folio not noted (Oct. 16, 1572).

39. R. Consist. 32 (1581), fol. 250v. Flaignec's sin was all the more egregious given that he had abandoned his wife and infant child and returned to Geneva when the plague afflicted Lyon.

40. *Institutes*, IV.xv.17, p. 1316.

41. Spierling, *Infant Baptism in Reformation Geneva*, 144.

42. In November 1546, the Small Council enacted the ministers' list as law. See the city ordinance entitled "On the Imposition of Baptismal Names" (1546), found in *RCP* 1:29. The naming controversy in Geneva has been carefully studied by a number of scholars, including Spierling, *Infant Baptism in Reformation Geneva*, 140–152; Naphy, *Geneva and the Consolidation of the Genevan Reformation*, 144–53; Monter, "Historical Demography," 412–13; and the editors of the *R. Consist.* II (1546), 280–81, note 999.

43. See *R. Consist.* II (1546), 271, 277, 279–80, 284–85. The Consistory investigated (unproven) allegations that Ami Chapuis afterward took his son to a midwife for baptism and to receive the name "Claude." This case is described in greater detail by Spierling, *Infant Baptism in Reformation Geneva*, 144–46.

44. R. Consist. 5 (1550), fol. 74.

45. Monter, "Historical Demography," 412–14. Not all biblical names were acceptable, however. In 1565, the Consistory scolded a godfather who had named his brother's son Ishmael. The ministers and elders commanded him to choose a "good name" for the boy such as "Isaiah, Isaac, or Samuel." R. Consist. 21 (1565), fol. 199v.

46. *EO* (1561), in *CO* 10.1, cols. 103–104. Spierling, *Infant Baptism in Reformation Geneva*, 152.

47. On this see Benedict, *Christ's Churches Purely Reformed*, 504–506.

48. Thus, for example, in 1575 the ministers and elders confronted François Chapuis when his son still had not been baptized three weeks after birth—the delay was necessary, he insisted, because a godparent who lived in Chambéry had been detained. This excuse was unacceptable from the ministers' perspective, and they ordered him to present the child for baptism the following Sunday. See R. Consist. 29 (1575), fol. 31. A similar case occurred in 1561 when two fathers from the parish of Jussy delayed the baptisms of their children for three weeks. In addition to reprimanding the fathers and demanding the baptisms be performed immediately, the Consistory petitioned the Small Council to promulgate a law requiring that infants be baptized "two, three, or four days after birth." R. Consist. 18 (1561), fol. 136.

49. For Calvin's contact with Anabaptists and his theological interaction with Anabaptist theology, see Balke, *Calvin and the Anabaptist Radicals*.

50. *R. Consist.* III (1547), 177, 180–81.

51. *RCP* 1:75.

52. *RCP* 3:122.

53. R. Consist. 32 (1581), fols. 212v, 225v.

54. R. Consist. 33 (1582), fols. 13, 23.

55. The case of Abraham de La Mare is found in *RCP* 4:103 and R. Consist. 31 (1577), fols. 81, 130.

56. *RCP* 4:103.

57. See Old, *The Shaping of the Reformed Baptismal Rite*, 179–193. Old notes: "Almost all the Reformers tried their hand at a catechism at some time or another," (193). For early catechetical instruction in Basel, see Burnett, *Teaching the Reformation*, 52–55.

58. Old, *The Shaping of the Reformed Baptismal Rite*, 186–87. In his commentary on Matthew 28:19–20, Calvin notes: "Let us be sure, that it is by the power of teaching that signs put on their new nature, just as the outward washing of the flesh begins to be a spiritual pledge of regeneration when the teaching of the gospel goes before…. [Christ] couples baptism with a holy bond of teaching, that the one may be no more than an addition to the other." *CNTC* 3:252.

59. Calvin, *Articles Concerning the Organization of the Church and of Worship at Geneva Proposed by the Ministers at the Council* (January 16, 1537), in Calvin, *Calvin: Theological Treatises*, 54. Although usually ascribed to the pen of Calvin, Bruce Gordon argues that the tone of this document suggests the authorship of Guillaume Farel. See Gordon, *Calvin*, 71–72.

60. See *Instruction et confession de foy dont on use en l'église de Genève*, in *CO* 22, cols. 25–74. In 1538, Calvin published a Latin translation of this catechism under the title *Catechismus, sive christianae religionis institution* (see *CO* 5, col. 313–62). I. John Hesselink has recently published a fine English translation and commentary on the Latin edition of Calvin's catechism. See his *Calvin's First Catechism: A Commentary*.

61. Calvin to the Edward Seymour, Duke of Somerset and Regent of England, October 22, 1548, in *CO* 13, cols. 71–72; *CTS* 5:191.

62. *EO* (1541), 265, 272–73.

63. No copies of Calvin's 1541 *Catéchisme* have survived. Scholars therefore rely on the French edition of the catechism published in 1545, as well as a Latin translation published in the same year. For modern editions of the 1545 French and Latin editions, see "Le Catéchisme de l'Église de Genève" (1545) in *Confessions et catechisms de la foi reformée*, ed. Fatio; and *Catechismus ecclesiae Genevensis*, in *CO* 5, cols. 1–146.

64. Scholars continue to debate the degree to which Bucer's *Kurtze schriftliche erklärung für die Kinder* (1534) served as a model for Calvin's *Catéchisme* of 1541. Whereas J. Courvoisier pointed to Calvin's dependence on Bucer in his influential article "Le catéchismes de Genève et Strasbourg, étude sur le développement de la pensée de Calvin," Olivier Millet has recently argued that Calvin modeled his second catechism more on the French edition of his *Institutes* (1541). See Millet, "Rendre raison de la foi: Le Catéchisme de Calvin (1542)." It is noteworthy that Calvin's 1541 *Catechism* followed the same organizational scheme (Apostles' Creed—Ten Commandments—Lord's Prayer) that had appeared in Bucer's *Kurtze schriftliche*.

65. For Calvin's treatment of the so-called third use of the law, see Hesselink, *Calvin's First Catechism*, 81–84; Partee, *The Theology of John Calvin*, 136–42.

66. Old notes: "The inclusion of these prayers in the catechism makes it clear that instruction in the disciplines of prayer was an important part of fundamental training in Christian faith. The devotional aspect of the Christian life needed to be trained as much as the intellectual and the moral." *The Shaping of the Reformed Baptismal Rite*, 198.

67. *EO* (1541), 272; *EO* (1561), in *CO* 10.1, cols. 115–16. Emphasis mine.

68. With that end in view, beginning in 1549, published editions of the *Catechism* were organized into fifty-five weekly lessons to facilitate consecutive instruction in the household, school, and church. See Grosse, *Les rituels de la cène*, 490–91.

69. Beginning in 1576, Geneva's ministers were required to "tenir la doctrine des saints prophètes et apôtres, comme elle est comprise dans les livres du Vieux et du Nouveau Testament: de laquelle doctrine nous avons un sommaire en notre catechism" (*EO* [1576], in Heyer, *L'Église de Genève*, 278–79). Likewise, from 1559 to 1576, students at the Academy were required to promise to "suyvre et tenir la doctrine de foy telle qu'elle est contenue au Catechisme de ceste Eglise." See *CO* 9, col. 721. For an excellent discussion of the manner in which Calvin's *Catechism* functioned as doctrinal standard, see Grosse, *Les rituels de la cène*, 436–40.

70. In a letter to the fourteenth National Synod of Saumur in 1596, the Company of Pastors justified the use of summaries of Calvin's *Catechism* when instructing children. See *RCP* 7 (1596), 254, letter no. 33 bis.

71. See Gardy, *Bibliographie*, 167–70. Beza's small catechism was subsequently published in Latin, English, and Dutch editions.

72. Rodolphe Peter includes a reproduction of the text of *L'ABC François* in his article "L'abécédaire genevois ou catechism élémentaire de Calvin."

73. In the preface to the 1562 edition, the anonymous author explained the purpose of the pamphlet by identifying it with those "summaries and instructions which serve as memory-aids for people who are not capable of understanding and remembering what is taught in greater detail elsewhere." Quoted in Peter, "L'abécédaire genevois," 11.

74. For the parents' role in Christian instruction of their children, see especially Lambert, "Preaching, Praying and Policing the Reform," 429–37; Grosse, *Les rituels de la cène*, 481–82; and Pitkin, "Heritage of the Lord," 170–73.

75. Quoted in Grosse, *Les rituels de la cène*, 481.

76. Sermon 121 on Deuteronomy, in *CO* 27, col. 658, discussed in Peter, "L'abécédaire genevois," 18.

77. Beza, *Sermons sur l'histoire de la résurrection*, 206–207. Scriptural references have been removed from quotation.

78. *R. Consist.* I (1542), 54–55.

79. R. Consist. 31 (1579), fol. 309v.

80. This account appears in Gautier, "Un jeune Bâlois à Genève au XVIme siècle (1560–1563)."

81. See Grosse, *Les rituels de la cène*, 487; and Naphy, "The Reformation and the Evolution of Geneva's Schools."

82. See *L'Ordre du Collège de Genève* (Geneva: Estienne, 1559), bi–biv. The *Ordre* states that young students will be taught "their letters and syllables according to the *ABC Latinfrancois*." This document is no longer extant. See Grosse, *Les rituels de la cène*, 488.

83. R. Consist. 12 (1557), fol. 16v. Note the Consistory's line of questioning of François Mermiez in 1542: "Le Consistoire est de l'avis qu'on luy face les amonicions opportunes et remonstrances et qu'il face qu'il sache rendre rayson de sa foy en langue intelligible. Et s'il scet prier Dieu et s'il frequente les sermons." *R. Consist.* I (1542), 36.

84. *R. Consist.* I (1544), 378.

85. R. Consist. 17 (1561), fol. 217v.

86. R. Consist. 19 (1562), fol. 35v.

87. R. Consist. 32 (1580), fols. 47v–48.

88. R. Consist. 18 (1561), fol. 52.

89. R. Consist. 18 (1561), fol. 32.

90. R. Consist. 30 (1576), fol. 102v.

91. R. Consist. 18 (1561), fol. 37v.

92. R. Consist. 17 (1560), fol. 163.

93. R. Consist. 12 (1557), fol. 81. For other instances where defendants protested against adult attendance at the catechism sermon, see ibid., 16 (1559), fol. 220 and 22 (1565), fol. 26. Archival records indicate both that Geneva's ministers and magistrates expected adult attendance at the catechism, and that many adults refrained from doing so. Thus, in 1583, the magistrates commanded the elders and city guards to compel women, older children, and laborers to go to catechism (see RC 78, fol. 136, quoted in RCP 5:19). Similarly, in 1607, the Consistory complained to the Small Council that the city streets were crowded on Sundays at noon, and that "only children and chamber girls go to catechism," (R. Consist. 36 [1607], fol. 20v). That at least a few adults continued to attend the catechism sermon is demonstrated by the case of a widow named Jehanne Forest who, in 1605, was called to Consistory for fighting in the temple of St. Gervais "during the catechism" (ibid., 35 [1605], fol. 13).

94. This was made clear to a French immigrant named Antoine de La Grange in 1569, who was ordered to "give a hand so that his wife might be instructed" in the evangelical religion that she professed. R. Consist. 26 (1569), fol. 139. See also ibid., 26 (1569), fol. 65v.

95. See for example R. Consist. 12 (1557), fol. 133v; ibid., 13 (1558), fols. 45v, 56v. Invariably, the ignorant persons—not the ministers—were responsible for the cost of such private instruction.

96. R. Consist. 18 (1561), fol. 32.

97. R. Consist. 32 (1580), fol. 139v.

98. R. Consist. 17 (1561), fol. 214v.

99. R. Consist. 35 (1605), fol. 39v; ibid., 36 (1607), fol. 11.

100. See the data provided in chapter 7.

101. RCP 4:47.

102. R. Consist. 15 (1559), fol. 124r–v.

103. R. Consist. 15 (1559), fol. 167v.

104. R. Consist. 16 (1559), fol. 244.

105. In his Catechism, Calvin notes: "By Baptism the Lord adopts us and brings us into his Church, so that we are thereafter held to be of his household. After he has inscribed us in the number of his own, he testifies by the Supper that he takes a perpetual interest in nourishing us." CO 6, cols. 116, 118; Calvin, Calvin: Theological Treatises, 138. Note also Calvin's Institutes IV.xvii.1, pp. 1359–61.

106. Susan Karant-Nunn offers a helpful description of the different Eucharistic rituals practiced by Catholic, Lutheran, and reformed churches in the sixteenth century. See her The Reformation of Ritual, 108–35.

107. Cathelan, Passevent Parisien, 74.

108. In an initial draft of the Ecclesiastical Ordinances (1541), Calvin proposed that the Lord's Supper should be administered in the city once a month at

various churches in such a manner that each parish would host the communion service four times a year. See "Draft Ecclesiastical Ordinances," in Calvin, *Calvin: Theological Treatises*, 66–67.

109. For Calvin's liturgy for the Lord's Supper, see *La forme des prières et chantz ecclésiastiques* (1542), L4v–L8r.

110. Grosse, *Les rituels de la cène*, 227–29. The Genevan church continued to use unleavened bread in the sacrament until the beginning of the seventeenth century. Upon his return to Geneva, Calvin accepted the practice as a matter of religious indifference, though he warned against those "fanatics" who insisted that unleavened bread was required in the sacrament because of the parallel practice in the Jewish Passover.

111. Gerrish, "Sign and Reality," 122; see also Gerrish, "Gospel and Eucharist."

112. *Institutes* IV.xiv.8, p. 1284.

113. Calvin's liturgy describes the sacrament as "une medicine pour les poures maladies spirituelz" and "le pain celestial, pour nous repaistre & nourrir à vie eternelle." *La forme des prières et chantz ecclésiastiques* (1542), L6v, L7r.

114. Ibid., L7r–v.

115. Beza, *Confession de la foy chrestienne*, 102–103. For a developed statement and defense of Beza's understanding of the meaning and benefits of the Lord's Supper, see his *Adversus Sacramentariorum Errorem*. This work was subsequently translated into English under the title *Two Very Lerned Sermons of M. Beza, Together with a Short Sum of the Sacrament of the Lordes Supper*. Beza's theology of the Lord's Supper is described in detail by Raitt, *The Eucharistic Theology of Theodore Beza*.

116. See *RCP* 10:xxvi, 18, 32–33, 189. The Bernese church adopted the use of common (leavened) table bread in 1582 and imposed this change on the churches of the Pays de Vaud in 1605. In 1607, the Genevan church denied the request of the eighteenth National Synod of La Rochelle to conform to the practice of the French churches by adopting the use of common table bread. According to the editors of the *RCP*, the Genevan church finally began using leavened bread in the sacrament in 1623, followed by Basel (1642), and Schafhausen (1655). The common element in Geneva's attitude toward unleavened-leavened bread was the ministers' conviction that the church, not the magistrates, should decide the question.

117. R. Consist. 17 (1560), fol. 151.

118. R. Consist. 17 (1560), fol. 99v. For similar cases, see *R. Consist.* III (1547), 81; R. Consist. 10 (1555), fol. 8v; 14 (1558), fol. 54; 15 (1559), fol. 101v; 17 (1561), fol. 208; 21 (1565), fol. 193v.

119. R. Consist. 34 (1593), fols. 163, 166.

120. *RCP* 5:74–76.

121. See R. Consist. 17 (1560), fol. 148v; 22 (1565), fol. 25.

122. *RCP* 3:105. The sixth National Synod of Vertueil (1567) made a similar judgment. See Aymon, *Tous les synodes*, 1:76.

123. See *RCP* 4:31–32; ibid., 7:150; R. Consist. 22 (1565), fol. 41.

124. This was the advice that Theodore Beza gave to a Hungarian aristocrat named André Dudith in 1573, see *CB* 9:60. Beza justified his opinion by referring to the advice that Calvin had given to Jean de Léry and the Brazilian missionaries

in 1557 as to the protocol for the celebration of the Lord's Supper when wine was not available. On this interchange, see Dufour, *Théodore de Bèze*, 130.

125. Article 43 of the *Ecclesiastical Ordinances* (1576) stated that "les ministres distribuent le pain en ordre et avec reverence, et que les anciens ou les diacres distribuent la coupe," In Heyer, *L'Église de Genève*, 286.

126. *RCP* 8:6, 51.

127. *RCP* 9:19–20.

128. Calvin's *Catechism* addresses this topic as follows: "Minister: Does the administration of both Baptism and the Supper belong indiscriminately to all? Child: They are the proper function of those to whom the public office of teaching is entrusted. For the two things, feeding the Church with the doctrine of salvation and administering the sacraments, are joined to each other by a lasting tie." See *CO* 6, cols. 131, 132; "Catechism of the Church of Geneva," in Calvin, *Calvin: Theological Treatises*, 139. Royer stated his position in a series of "Theses" presented to the Company of Pastors in June 1604. See *RCP* 9:244–49, annex no. 17.

129. See *RCP* 10:xxiii; ibid., 9:86, 115.

130. For Royer's excommunication, see R. Consist. 35 (1605), fols. 34v–35v.

131. See Aymon, *Tous les synodes*, 1:328.

132. Comm. 1 Thessalonians 2:11, *CNTC* 8:345. Calvin's commitment to personal, pastoral engagement with his parishioners is described by Ronald Wallace in *Calvin, Geneva & the Reformation*, 168–75.

133. Beza, *Sermons sur l'histoire de la résurrection*, 567.

134. See Calvin to Farel, May 1540, in *CO* 11, cols. 41–42; *CTS* 4:184–85.

135. Gross, *Les rituels de la cène*, 400–402.

136. *EO* (1561), in *CO* 10.1, cols. 116–17.

137. The broader purposes of the annual visitation are described in the minutes of Company of Pastors for the year 1557. The visits were intended "pour cognoistre les personnes affin que la Cène du Seigneur ne fut prophanée, et d'exhorter ung chascung à faire son devoir envers Dieu et à ouir sa saincte parole." And, "pour s'informer de la foy, vie et conversacion d'ung chascung, et escripre les noms, pour donner courage et faveur aux gens de bien et cognoistre et regecter les iniques." See *RCP* 2:66, 72.

138. Selderhuis, *John Calvin*, 88.

139. Gautier, "Un jeune Bâlois à Genève," 415.

140. R. Consist. 9 (1554), fol. 36v; ibid. 34 (1596), fol. 424.

141. R. Consist. 5 (1550), fol. 96; ibid. 20 (1563), fol. 21v.; ibid. 26 (1569), fol. 39v.

142. *RCP* 6:21.

143. R. Consist. 36 (1607), fols. 76v–77, 104.

144. *RCP* 8:58.

145. *RCP* 6:42–43; ibid., 8: 58.

146. *EO* (1561), in *CO* 10.1, col. 115. Note that the 1576 edition of the *Ecclesiastical Ordinances* does not specify the day of this weekly visit.

147. R. Consist. 22 (1565), fol. 22; ibid., 34 (1594), fol. 237. Other examples where the ministers intervened on behalf of prisoners are found in *RCP* 5:107; ibid., 9:17; R. Consist. 34 (1596), fol. 461; ibid., 37 (1608), fol. 67; ibid., 38 (1609), fol. 10v.

148. *RCP* 9:14–15, 242 and annex no. 13.

149. See *CB* 23:268–72.

150. *EO* (1541), 10. This requirement was repeated in all subsequent editions of the Ordinances in the sixteenth century.

151. The Consistory minutes include a handful of cases each year where family members or friends of sick persons are reprimanded for failing to summon the minister to console their loved ones.

152. *La forme des prières et chantz ecclésiastiques*, M4.

153. Ibid., M4v.

154. RC 36, fol. 151v, quoted in Doumergue, *Jean Calvin*, 3:147.

155. Calvin to Viret, October 1542, in *CO* 11, cols. 457–458; *CTS* 4:358.

156. Doumergue, *Jean Calvin*, 3:147–48.

157. RC 37, fol. 110, quoted in Doumergue, *Jean Calvin*, 3:148.

158. See Naphy, *Calvin and the Consolidation of the Genevan Reformation*, 68–69.

159. *RCP* 2:106.

160. *RCP* 2:107.

161. *RCP* 2:107–109; and Choisy, *L'État Chrétien Calviniste*, 12–16.

162. For the year 1571 alone, I identified more than eighty people who were called before justice for suspicion of sorcery. Between May 10 and June 18, sixteen people were tortured, convicted, and executed for the crimes of sorcery or engraissement. See especially PC #1625.

163. RC 65, fols. 35–36, quoted in Geisendorf, *Théodore de Bèze*, 254.

164. Choisy, *L'État Chrétien Calviniste*, 18.

165. *RCP* 4:129–30.

166. Beza, *De peste quaestiones duae explicatae, una sitne contagiosa, altera an et quatenus sit Christianis per secessionem vitanda*. An English translation appeared the following year under the title *A Shorte Learned and Pithie Treatize of the Plague, Wherin Are Handled These Two Questions: The One, Whether the Plague Bee Infectious, or No: The Other, Whether and Howe Farre It May of Christians Bee Shunned By Going Aside.*

167. For historical background to this controversy, see Beza's letter to Rudolph Gwalther, November 19, 1579, in *CB* 20 (1579), 252, note 17.

168. Beza, *De peste quaestiones duae explicatae*, 6–7; *A Shorte Treatize of the Plague*, A4–A5.

169. Beza, *De peste quaestiones duae explicatae*, 6, 18; *A Shorte Treatize of the Plague*, A5, B7v.

170. Beza, *De peste quaestiones duae explicatae*, 15–16; *A Shorte Treatize of the Plague*, B5.

171. Beza, *De peste quaestiones duae explicatae*, 21; *A Shorte Treatize of the Plague*, C2r–v.

172. Beza, *De peste quaestiones duae explicatae*, 27–28; *A Shorte Treatize of the Plague*, C7v–C8v.

173. Beza, *De peste quaestiones duae explicatae*, 30; *A Shorte Treatize of the Plague*, D2v.

174. Beza, *De peste quaestiones duae explicatae*, 31; *A Shorte Treatize of the Plague*, D3v–D4.

175. Beza, *De peste quaestiones duae explicatae*, 31; *A Shorte Treatize of the Plague*, D4.

176. *Institutes* I.xvii.10, p. 223. For more on the difficulties and dangers of life in sixteenth-century Geneva, see Mottu-Weber et al., *Vivre à Genève*; and Bouwsma, *John Calvin: A Sixteenth Century Portrait*, 32–48.

177. Examples of this ministry of consolation are seen throughout Geneva's archival documents. See for example R. Consist. 19 (1562), fol. 47; 36 (1607), fol. 6v; 37 (1608), fol. 4v; *RCP* 6:21.

178. See Lambert, "Preaching, Praying and Policing the Reform," 393–479; Wallace, *Calvin, Geneva & the Reformation*, 210–14.

179. *Institutes* III.xx.50, pp. 917–18.

180. *Institutes* III.xx.2, p. 851.

181. *La forme des prières et chantz ecclésiastiques*, J8v–K1.

182. Ibid., K2r–v.

183. Elsie Anne McKee includes a rich sample of Calvin's extemporaneous prayers (in translation) in her *John Calvin: Writings on Pastoral Piety*, 220–39.

184. Goulart, *The Wise Vieillard, or Old Man*, 76, 201–205.

185. See Manetsch, "A Mystery Solved?" 275–88.

186. Beza, *Houshold Prayers*, M1or–v. The archaic English of all passages quoted from this work has been modernized.

187. Ibid., M12v.

188. Ibid., N1.

189. Scholars have recently estimated that Calvin wrote around 8,500 letters between 1530 and 1564. Beza probably wrote slightly fewer during his career in Geneva. See Miriam van Veen and Frans Pieter van Stam, "Letters," in *The Calvin Handbook*, ed. Selderhuis, 215.

190. A brief biographical sketch of Johannes Crato von Krafftheim is found in *OER* 1:451.

191. Beza to Crato, August 1, 1574, *CB* 15:130–37.

192. Crato to Beza, November 11, 1582, *CB* 23:200–201.

193. Beza to Crato, January 15, 1583, *CB* 24:6–7.

194. Ibid., 9. Beza here is quoting 2 Timothy 2:12 and alluding to 2 Corinthians 4:17–18.

195. Beza to Crato, January 15, 1583, *CB* 24:7.

196. Ibid., 13–14.

197. Ibid., 15.

198. Crato to Beza, February 25, 1583, *CB* 24:43.

199. Beza to Crato, October 30, 1583, *CB* 24:284.

200. Beza to Crato, December 31, 1583, *CB* 24:337. Beza is quoting Paul's words in Romans 8:28.

201. Beza to Crato, November 16, 1585, Bib. Ste. Geneviève (Paris), ms. 1455, fols. 16–17v.

202. For bibliographical information on the first of these volumes, entitled *XXVIII Discours Chrestiens*, see Jones, *Simon Goulart*, 607–608. Jones is ignorant of the existence of the second of these volumes, entitled *Seconde partie des Discours Chrestiens. Contenant XX Traitez divers, pour l'instruction et consolation des fideles*. These two volumes are found in the rare book room of the Bibliothèque Publique et Universitaire, Geneva.

203. Goulart, *XXVIII Discours Chrestiens*, ¶v, vii.

204. Goulart, *Seconde partie des Discours Chrestiens,* 299–301.

205. Goulart, *XXVIII Discours Chrestiens,* 275–76.

206. Goulart, *Seconde partie des Discours Chrestiens,* 160–61. Goulart returns to the matter of believers' assurance of their election at 291–93, 303–308.

207. Goulart, *Seconde partie des Discours Chrestiens,* 299; Goulart, *XXVIII Discours Chrestiens,* ¶iiii.

208. Goulart, *XXVIII Discours Chrestiens,* 322–27.

Epilogue

1. Febvre, *Au coeur religieux du XVIe siècle,* 267.

2. *RCP* 9:81.

3. *RCP* 8:223–24.

4. On this point, see Trueman, *Histories and Fallacies,* 109–40.

5. O'Donnell, *Augustine: A New Biography* 5. Emphasis in original.

6. Calvin's "Preface to Pierre Olivétan's French Bible," in *CO* 9, col. 788.

7. Whittingham's description of Geneva as the "mirror and model of true religion and true piety" is quoted in Dufour, "Le mythe de Genève au temps de Calvin," 503.

8. *Sermons sur l'histoire de la résurrection,* 568.

BIBLIOGRAPHY

Manuscripts and Archival Records

A<small>RCHIV</small> D'É<small>TAT DE</small> G<small>ENÈVE</small> (AEG)

E. C. Céligny, vol. 1.

E. C. Chancy, vol. 1. Baptisms (1598–1654).

E. C. Genthod, Moëns, Magny, Malagny, vol. 1 (1564–1630, 1696–1700).

E. C. Jussy, vol. 1. Register of Baptisms and Marriages.

E.C. Satigny, vol. 1. Register of Baptisms and Marriages.

Finances O, no. 6 (1563–69), no. 7 (1572–80), no. 8 (1592–97), no. 9 (1602–16).

Proces Criminel, first and second series. #1288 (1565), #1339 (1566), #1340 (1566), #1516, #1579 (1570), #1625 (1571), #1639 (1571), #1683, #1798 (1595).

Registres du Conseil, vols. 67–105 (1572–1609).

Registres du Consistoire, vol. 21 (1564), vol. 22 (1565), vol. 23 (1566), vol. 24 (1567), vol. 25 (1568), vol. 26 (1569), vol. 27 (1570), vol. 28 (Jan. 1571–Mar. 1573), vol. 29 (1575), vol. 30 (1576), vol. 31 (Jan. 1577–Feb. 1580), vol. 32 (Feb. 1580–Dec. 1581), vol. 33 (1582, Jan. 1589), vol. 34 (1592–1596), vol. 35 (1605–1606), vol. 36 (1607), vol. 37 (1608), vol. 38 (1609).

H.H<small>ENRY</small> M<small>EETER</small> C<small>ENTER FOR</small> C<small>ALVIN</small> S<small>TUDIES</small>

Registres du Consistoire, transcriptions (electronic version) by Robert M. Kingdon and his students Thomas Lambert, Jeffrey Watt, Isabella Watt, Glenn Sunshine, and David Wegener, vol. 6 (1551), vol. 7 (1552), vol. 8 (1553), vol. 9 (1554), vol. 10 (1555), vol. 11 (1556), vol. 12 (1557), vol. 13 and 14 (1558), vol. 15 and 16 (1559), vol 17 (1560), vol. 18 (1561), vol. 19 (1562), vol. 20 (1563), vol. 21 (Jan.–May 1564).

O<small>THER</small> A<small>RCHIVES</small>

Archives Tronchin, Bibliothèque Publique et Universitaire, Geneva, fonds. Bèze, vol. 5.

Bib. Gotha, Cod. Chart. A 405.

Bib. Ste. Geneviève, Paris, ms. 1455.

Rigsarkiv, Copenhagen XIII.

Stadtbibl. Zurich, ms. F 37.

Universitätsbibl. Kirchen Archiv, Basel, C. I. 2, Bd. II.

Primary Sources

Beza, Theodore. *Ad Acta Colloquii Montisbelgardensis Tubingae Edita, Theodori Bezae Responsionis, Pars Altera.* Geneva, 1588.

———. *Ad Acta Colloquii Montisbelgardensis Tubingae Edita....Pars Prior.* Geneva, 1588.

———. *Ad tractationem de ministrorum evangelii gradibus ab H. Saravia...Responsio.* Geneva: Jean le Preux, 1592.

———. *Adversus sacramentariorum errorem.* [Geneva: J. Stoer], 1574.

———. *Chrestiennes meditations.* Edited by Mario Richter. Geneva: Librairie Droz, 1964.

———. *Confession de la foi chrestienne.* Geneva: Conrad Badius, 1559.

———. *Correspondance de Théodore de Bèze.* Edited by Hippolyte Aubert, Fernand Aubert, Alain Dufour, and Henri Meylan. Vols. 1–35. Geneva: Librairie Droz, 1960–2011.

———. *Cours sur les épîtres aux Romains et aux Hébreux, 1564–66.* Edited by Pierre Fraenkel and Luc Perrotet. Geneva: Librairie Droz, 1988.

———. *Du droits des magistrats.* Edited by Robert Kingdon. Geneva: Librairie Droz, 1971.

———. *Ecclesiastes. Solomonis concio ad populum habita, de vita sic instituenda, ut ad veram aeternamque felicitatem perveniatur: Theodori Bezae paraphrasi illustrata.* Geneva: Jean le Preux, 1588.

———. *Epistola magistri Benedicti Passavantii.* N.p., 1553.

———. *Histoire ecclésiastique des Églises réformée au royaume de France.* 3 vols. [Geneva: Jean de Laon], 1580.

———. *Iesu Christi D. N. Nouum testamentum sive Nouum foedus...eiusdem Th. Bezae Annotationes.* [Geneva], 1582.

———. *Iobus, Theodore Bezae partim commentariis partim paraphrasi illustratus.* Geneva, 1589.

———. *Les Juvenilia.* Edited by Alexandre Machard. Geneva: Slatkine Reprints, 1970.

———. *A Little Book of Christian Questions and Responses.* Translated by Kirk M. Summers. Allison Park, Penn.: Pickwick, 1986.

———. *Maister Beza's Houshold Prayers.* London, 1607.

———. *Novum D. N. Iesu Christi Testamentum.* [Geneva]: Robert Estienne, 1556.

———. *De peste quaestiones duae explicatae, una sitne contagiosa, altera an et quatenus sit Christianis per secessionem vitanda.* Geneva: Eustache Vignon, 1579.

_____. *Poemata varia.* N.p. n.p., 1597.

———. *Les Pseaumes de David et les cantiques de la Bible, avec les argumens & la paraphrase de Théodore de Bèze.* Geneva: Iaques Berjon, 1581.

———. "Les Psaumes et l'épître dédicatoire de Théodore de Bèze." *BSHPF* 1 (1853): 95–99.

———. *Quaestionum & responsionum Christianorum libellus.* In *Tractationes theologicarum.* Geneva, 1570.

———. *Response aux cinq premiers et principales demandes de F. Iean Hay.* Geneva: Jean le Preux, 1586.

———. *Response à la lettre d'un gentilhomme Savoisien, ne se nommant point.* Geneva, 1598.

————. *Sermons sur les trois premiers chapitres de Cantique des Cantiques de Salomon*. Geneva: Jean le Preux, 1586.

————. *Sermons sur l'histoire de la passion et sepulture de nostre Seigneur Iesus Christ*. Geneva: Jean le Preux, 1592.

————. *Sermons sur l'histoire de la résurrection de nostre Seigneur Iesus Christ*. Geneva: Jean le Preux, 1593.

————. *A Shorte Learned and Pithie Treatize of the Plague, Wherin Are Handled These Two Questions: The One, Whether the Plague Bee Infectious, or No: The Other, Whether and Howe Farre It May of Christians Bee Shunned by Going Aside*. Translated by John Stockwood. London: Thomas Dawson, 1580.

————. *Tractationes theologicarum*. 3 vols. Geneva, 1573–1582.

————. *Traicté des vrayes essencielles et visible marques de la vraye Eglise Catholique*. Geneva: Jean le Preux, 1592.

————. *Two Very Lerned Sermons of M. Beza, Together with a Short Sum of the Sacrament of the Lordes Supper*. London: Robert Waldegrave, 1588.

————. *Le vrais portraits des hommes illustrés*. Edited by Alain Dufour. Geneva: Slatkine Reprints, 1986.

Beza, Theodore, and Antoine de Chandieu. *Poemes, chrestiens et moraux*. N.p., n.p. N.d.

Calvin, John. *Calvin: Theological Treatises*. Edited by J. K. S. Reid. Philadelphia: Westminster Press, 1954.

————. *Calvin's Commentaries*. *Calvin Tract Society*. 46 vols. Reprint. Grand Rapids, Mich.: Baker Books, 1989.

————. *Calvin's New Testament Commentaries*. 12 vols. Edited by D. W. Torrance and T. F. Torrance. Grand Rapids, Mich.: Eerdmans, 1959–72.

————. *Calvin's Old Testament Commentaries*. 3 vols. Edited by D. W. Torrance and T. F. Torrance. Grand Rapids, Mich.: Eerdmans, 1959–72.

————. *La forme des prières et chantz ecclésiastiques*. [Geneva], 1542.

————. *Institutes of the Christian Religion*. 2 vols. Translated by Ford Lewis Battles. Edited by John T. McNeill. Philadelphia: Westminster Press, 1960.

————. *Institutes of the Christian Religion, 1536 Edition*. Translated and Edited by Ford Lewis Battles. Grand Rapids, Mich.: Eerdmans, 1975.

————. *Ioannis Calvini opera omnia quae supersunt*. Edited by G. Baum, E. Cunitz, E. Reuss. 59 vols. Brunsvigae: C. A. Schwetschke, 1863–1900.

————. *John Calvin's Tracts and Treatises*. 7 vols. Edited by Henry Beveridge. 1844. Reprint, Grand Rapids, Mich.: Baker Books, 1987.

————. "Reply to Sadoleto." In *John Calvin-Jacopo Sadoleto: A Reformation Debate*. Edited by John C. Olin. Reprint, Grand Rapids, Mich.: Baker Books, 1987.

————. *Sermons on the Acts of the Apostles*. In *Supplementa Calviniana*, vol. 8. Edited by Willem Balke and Wilhelmus H. Th. Moehn. Neukerchen: Neukirchener Verlag des Erziehungsvereins, 1994.

————. *Sermons on the Epistle to the Ephesians*. London: Banner of Truth Press, 1973.

————. *Three French Treatises*. Edited by Francis Higman. London: Athlone Press, 1970.

Cathelan, Antoine. *Passevent parisien respondant à Pasquin Romain. De la vie de ceux qui sont allez demourer à Genève, et se dissent vivre selon la reformation de l'Évangile: faict en forme de dialogue*. 1556. Revised edition, Paris: Pierre Gaultier, 1875.

Casaubon, Isaac. *Isaaci Casauboni epistolae*. 3rd ed. Rotterdam, 1709.

Chandieu, Antoine de. *A Common Place Touching the Word of God Written, Against the Traditions of Men*. Translated by Coxe. [London]: J. Harison, 1583.

——. *Locus de Verbo Dei Scripto, Adversus humanas traditiones, theologicè & scholasticè tractatus*. Morge: Jean le Preux, 1584.

——. *Octonaires sur la vanité et inconstance du monde*. 1583. Revised edition, Geneva: Librairie Droz, 1979.

——. *La response à la profession de foy publiée contre ceux de l'Église réformée*. [Geneva?], 1585.

Charpentier, Pierre. *Lettre de Pierre Charpentier iurisconsult, addressée à François Portes*. N.p., 1572.

Cop, Michel. *A Godly and learned Exposition vppon the Proverbes of Solomon: Written In French by Maister Michael Cop, Minister of the Woorde of God, at Geneva. And translated into English, by M. O.* London, 1580.

——. *Le livre de l'Ecclésiaste…esposé fidèlement et familièrement*. Geneva, 1557.

——. *Sur les Proverbes de Salomon, exposition familière*. Geneva, 1556.

Daneau, Lambert. *A fruitfull Commentarie upon the Twelve Small Prophets, Briefe, Plaine, and Easie*. Trans. by Iohn Stockwood. Cambridge: Printed by John Legate, 1594.

——. *Ad Petri Carpenterii…consilium…responsio*. Neustadt, 1575.

——. *Brième remonstrance sur les jeux de sort*. Geneva: [Jacques Bourgeois], 1574.

——. *Compendium sacrae theologiae*. Montpellier, 1595.

——. *Les Sorciers. Dialogue tres-utile et necessaire pour ce temps. Auquel ce qui se dispute auiourdhui des sorciers & eriges, est traité bien amplement, & resolu*. Geneva: Jaques Bourgeois, 1574.

——. *Traicté contre les baccanales*. La Rochelle, 1582.

——. *Traité de l'estat honneste des Chrestiens en leur accoustrement*. Geneva: Jean de Laon, 1580.

——. *Traitté duquel on peut apprendre en quell cas il est permis à l'homme Chrestien de porter les armes, et par lequel est respond à Pierre Charpentier*. Geneva, 1576.

[Daneau, Lambert?]. *Traité des danses, auquel est amplement resolue la question, ascavoir s'il est permis aux Chrestiens de danser*. [Geneva: François Estienne], 1579.

De Saint-Michel, Antoine, Sire of Avully. *Lettre d'un gentil-homme Savoysien, à un gentil-homme Lyonnais*. N.p., 1598.

Du Perril, Jean. "Journal de la guerre de 1589." In *Mémoires et documents publiés par la Société d'Histoire et d'Archéologie de Genève*. Vol. 38. Edited by Alain Dufour, 127–87. Geneva: A. Jullien, 1952.

Goulart, Simon. *Apophthegmatum sacrorum loci communes. Ex sacris ecclesiasticis, & secularibus scriptoribus collecti*. Geneva, 1592.

——. *Seconde partie des Discours Chrestiens. Contenant XX. traitez divers, pour l'instruction & consolation des fideles*. [Geneva]: Jacob Stoer, 1595.

——. *The Wise Vieillard, or Old Man*. London: John Dawson, 1621.

——. *XXVIII Discours Chrestiens, touchant l'estat du monde & de l'église de Dieu. Nouvellement mis en lumiere, pour l'instruction & consolation des fideles affligez, & qui aspirant à la vie eternelle*. [Geneva]: Jacob Stoer, 1591.

Hay, John. *Certain Demandes Concerning the Christian Religion and Discipline.* In *Catholic Tractates of the Sixteenth Century*, edited by Thomas Graves Law. Edinburgh: William Blackwood & Sons, 1901.

Hummel, B. F., ed. *Epistolarum historico-ecclesiasticarum seculo XVI a celeberrimis viris scriptarum semicenturia.* Halle, 1778.

Jussie, Jeanne de. *Le levain du Calvinisme, ou commencement de l'heresie de Genève.* Geneva: Jules-Guillaume Fick, 1865.

La Faye, Antoine. *Brief traitté de la vertu de la croix et de la manier de l'honorer.* N.p., 1597.

———. *Propositions and Principles of Divinitie, Propounded and Disputed in the Universitie of Geneva, by Certain Students of Divinitie.* Edinburgh: Robert Waldegrave, 1591.

———. *Replique Chrestienne, à la response de M. F. De Sales, se disant evesque de Genève, sur Le traicté de la vertu & adoration de la croix.* Geneva, 1606.

———. "Sainct exercice sur la mort et passion de Nostre Seigneur Iesus Christ." In *Replique chrestienne, à la response de M. F. De Sales, se disant Evesque de Genève, sur Le traicté de la vertu & adoration de la croix.* Geneva: Jacob Stoer, 1605.

———. *Theses theologicae.* Geneva, 1586.

———. *Les vies de Iean Calvin & de Théodore de Bèze.* 1607. Reprint edition, Geneva: Jean Herman Widerhold, 1681.

Luther, Martin. *Martin Luther. Selections from His Writings.* Edited by John Dillenberger. New York: Doubleday, 1962.

Montaigne, Michel de. *Essais.* Paris, 1580.

Portus, François. *Response de François Portus Candiot, aux lettres diffamatoires de Pierre Charpentier advocat.* [Geneva], 1574.

Roset, Michel. *Les Chroniques de Genève.* Edited by Henri Fazy. Geneva: George & Co., 1894.

Salvard, Jean-François, Theodore Beza, Lambert Daneau, Antoine de Chandieu, and Simon Goulart. *Harmonia confessionum fidei. Orthodoxarum, & reformatarum ecclesiarum, quae in praecipuis quibusque Europae regnis, nationibus, & provinciis, sacram Evangelii doctrinam pure profitentur: quarum catologum & ordinem sequentes paginate indicabunt.* Geneva: Pierre St. André, 1581.

Simon, Richard. *Histoire critique des principaux commentateurs du Nouveau Testament.* Rotterdam, 1693.

Secondary Sources

Abray, Lorna Jane. *The People's Reformation: Magistrates, Clergy, and Commons in Strasbourg, 1500–1598.* Ithaca, N.Y.: Cornell University Press, 1985.

Althaus, Paul. *The Ethics of Martin Luther.* Philadelphia, Pa.: Fortress Press, 1972.

Anderson, Marvin. "Theodore Beza: Savant or Scholastic?" *Theologische Zeitschrift* 43 (1987): 320–32.

Ariès, Philip. *Centuries of Childhood: A Social History of Family Life.* Translated by Robert Baldick. New York: Vintage Books, 1962.

Armstrong, Brian. *Calvinism and the Amyraut Heresy: Protestant Scholasticism and Humanism in Seventeenth-Century France.* Madison, Wisc.: University of Wisconsin Press, 1969.

————. "Geneva and the Theology and Politics of French Calvinism: The Embarrassment of the 1588 Edition of the Bible of the Pastors and Professors of Geneva." In *Calvinus Ecclesiae*, edited by Wilhelm H. Neuser, 113–33. Frankfurt am Main: Peter Lang, 1984.

Aubert, Louis. "Mariage de Farel et nouveaux voyages." In *Guillaume Farel, 1489–1565*, 673–80. Neuchatel: Éditions Delachaux & Niestlé, 1930.

Aymon, Jean. *Tous les synodes nationaux des Églises réformées de France*. 2 vols. The Hague: Charles Deleo, 1710.

Backus, Irena. "L'Enseignement de la logique à l'Académie de Genève entre 1559 et 1565." *Revue de Théologie et de Philosophie* 111 (1979): 153–63.

————. *Life Writing in Reformation Europe: Lives of Reformers by Friends, Disciples and Foes*. Burlington, Vt.: Ashgate, 2008.

————. *The Reformed Roots of the English New Testament. The Influence of Theodore Beza on the English New Testament*. Pittsburgh, Pa.: The Pickwick Press, 1980.

————, ed. *Théodore de Bèze*. Geneva: Librairie Droz, 2007.

Baird, Henry Martyn. *Theodore Beza, the Counsellor of the French Reformation, 1519–1605*. New York: Burt Franklin, 1899.

Baker, J. Wayne. "Erastianism." In the *Oxford Encyclopedia of the Reformation*, edited by Hans Hillerbrand, vol. 2, 59. New York: Oxford University Press, 1996.

Balke, Willem. *Calvin and the Anabaptist Radicals*. Translated by William J. Heynen. Grand Rapids, Mich.: Eerdmans, 1981.

Balserac, Jon. *Divinity Compromised: A Study of Divine Accommodation in the Thought of John Calvin*. Dordrecht: Springer, 2006.

Banderier, Gilles. "Documents sur Simon Goulart." *BSHFP* 146 (2000): 571–606.

Barker, S. K. *Protestantism, Poetry and Protest: The Vernacular Writings of Antoine de Chandieu (c. 1534–1591)*. Burlington, Vt.: Ashgate, 2009.

Barnaud, Jean. *Pierre Viret, sa vie et son oeuvre*. Saint-Amans: G. Carayol, 1911.

Barthel, P., R. Scheurer, R. Stauffer, eds. *Actes du Colloque Guillaume Farel*. 2 vols. Geneva: Cahiers de la Revue de Théologie et de Philosophie, 1983.

Battles, Ford Lewis. "God Was Accommodating Himself to Human Capacity." *Inspiration* 31 (1977): 19–38.

————, ed. *The Piety of John Calvin*. Reprint. Grand Rapids, Mich.: Baker Books, 1978.

Bayley, Peter. *French Pulpit Oratory, 1598–1650*. Cambridge: Cambridge University Press, 1980.

Beeke, Joel. *The Quest for Full Assurance: The Legacy of Calvin and his Successors*. Edinburgh: Banner of Truth Trust, 1999.

Beeke, Joel, and Sinclair Ferguson, eds. *Reformed Confessions Harmonized*. Grand Rapids, Mich.: Baker Books, 1999.

Benedict, Philip. *Christ's Churches Purely Reformed*. New Haven: Yale University Press, 2002.

————. "Confessionalization in France? Critical Reflections and New Evidence." In *The Faith and Fortunes of France's Huguenots, 1600–1685*, 309–25. Aldershot: Ashgate, 2001.

Bergier, Jean-François. "Salaires des pasteurs de Genève au XVIe siècle." In *Mélanges d'histoire du XVIe siècle offerts à Henri Meylan*, edited by Henri Meylan, 159–78. Geneva: Librairie Droz, 1970.

Bernus, August. *Le Ministre Antoine de Chandieu d'après son journal autographe inédit, 1534–1591*. Paris: Imprimeries Réunies, 1889.

Biel, Pamela. *Doorkeepers at the House of Righteousness. Heinrich Bullinger and the Zurich Clergy 1535–1575*. Bern: Peter Lang, 1991.

Billings, J. Todd. *Calvin, Participation and the Gift: The Activity of Believers in Union with Christ*. New York: Oxford University Press, 2007.

Binz, Louis. *A Brief History of Geneva*. Translated by Jean Gunn. Geneva: Chancellerie d'Etat, 1985.

———. "Le Fin du Moyen Âge." In *Histoire du diocèse Genève-Annecy*, edited by Henri Baud, 50–97. Paris: Beauchesne, 1985.

———. *Vie religieuse et reform ecclésiastique dans le diocese de Genève pendant le Grand Schisme et la crise conciliare (1378–1450)*. Geneva: Alexandre Jullien, 1973.

Borel-Girard, G., L. Aubert, A. Piaget, et al. *Guillaume Farel, 1489–1565*. Neuchatel: Éditions Delachaux & Niestlé, 1930.

Borgeaud, Charles. *Histoire de l'Université de Genève: L'Académie de Calvin 1559–1798*. Geneva: Georg & Co., 1900.

Bouwsma, William. *John Calvin: A Sixteenth Century Portrait*. New York: Oxford University Press, 1988.

Brady Jr., Thomas A., Heiko A. Oberman, James D. Tracy, eds. *Handbook of European History 1400–1600*. 2 vols. Leiden: Brill, 1994.

Branderier, Gilles. "Documents sur Simon Goulart." *BSHFP* 146 (2000): 571–606.

Brown, D. Catherine. *Pastor and Laity in the Theology of Jean Gerson*. Cambridge: Cambridge University Press, 1987.

Brown, Peter. *Religion and Society in the Age of Saint Augustine*. New York: Harper & Row, 1972.

Budé, E. de. *Vie de Jean Diodati, théologien genevois*. Lausanne: Georges Bridel, Éditeur, 1869.

Burke, Peter. *Popular Culture in Early Modern Europe*. Reprint. Aldershot: Ashgate, 1994.

Burnett, Amy Nelson. "A Tale of Three Churches: Parishes and Pastors in Basel, Strasbourg, and Geneva." In *Calvin and the Company of Pastors*, edited by David Foxgrove, 95–128. Grand Rapids: CRC Product Services, 2004.

———. *Teaching the Reformation. Ministers and Their Message in Basel, 1529–1629*. New York: Oxford University Press, 2006.

———. *The Yoke of Christ. Martin Bucer and Christian Discipline*. Kirksville, Mo.: Sixteenth Century Essays & Studies, 1994.

Butin, Philip W. "John Calvin's Humanist Image of Popular Late-Medieval Piety and Its Contribution to Reformed Worship." *CTJ* 29 (1994): 419–31.

Cahier-Buccelli, Gabriella. "Dans l'ombre de la Réforme, Les membres de l'ancien clergé demeurés à Genève," (1536–1558). *Société d'Archéologie de Genève* 18 (1984–1987): 367–87.

Campagnolo, Matteo. "Jacques Lect, Juriste et Magistrat, 'Théologien et Évêque.'" In *Jacques Godefroy (1587–1652) et l'humanisme juridique à Genève*, edited by Bruno Schmidlin and Alfred Dufour, 149–73. Basel: Helbing & Lichtenhahn, 1991.

Campi, Emidio. "Giovanni Diodati et sa traduction de la Bible en italien." Association des ami-e-s du Musée international de la Réforme (2007). At https: www.zora.uzh.ch/24123.

Candaux, Jean-Daniel, ed. *Le Psautier de Genève, 1562–1865. Images commentées et essai de bibliographie.* Geneva: Bibliothèque publique et universitaire, 1986.

Cellerier, J. E. *Charles Perrot, pasteur genevois au seizième siècle.* Geneva: Jullien Frères, 1859.

Chaix, Paul, Alain Dufour, and Gustave Moeckli. *Les livres imprimés à Genève de 1550 à 1600.* Geneva: Librairie Droz, 1966.

Chambers, Bettye Thomas. *Bibliography of French Bibles.* Vol. 1. *Fifteenth- and Sixteenth-Century French-Language Editions of the Scriptures.* Geneva: Librairie Droz, 1983.

———. *Bibliography of French Bibles.* Vol. 2. *Seventeenth-Century French-Language Editions of the Scriptures.* Geneva: Librairie Droz, 1994.

Chareyre, Philippe. "'The Great Difficulties One Must Bear to Follow Jesus Christ': Morality at Sixteenth-Century Nîmes." In *Sin and the Calvinists: Morals Control and the Consistory in the Reformed Tradition,* edited by Raymond Mentzer, 63–96. Kirksville, Mo.: Sixteenth Century Journal, 1994.

Choisy, Eugène. *L'État Chrétien Calviniste à Genève au temps de Théodore de Bèze.* Geneva: Ch. Eggimann & Co., 1902.

Clark, R. Scott. "The Authority of Reason in the Later Reformation: Scholasticism in Caspar Olivetan and Antoine de la Faye." In *Protestant Scholasticism: Essays in Reassessment,* edited by Trueman and Clark, 111–26. Eugene, Or.: Wipf and Stock, 2005.

Corram-Mekkey, Sandra, Christophe Chazalon, and Gilles-Olivier Bron. *Crises et révolutions à Genève, 1526–1544.* Geneva: Foundation de l'Encyclopédie de Genève, 2005.

Cottret, Bernard. *Calvin: A Biography.* Translated by M. Wallace McDonald. Grand Rapids, Mich.: Eerdmans, 2000.

Courvoisier, J. "Le catéchismes de Genève et Strasbourg, étude sur le développement de la pensée de Calvin." *BSHPF* 84 (1935): 105–21.

Cyprian, E. S. *Catalogus codicum manuscriptorum bibliothecae Gothanae.* Leipzig: I. F. Gleditsch, 1714.

Dardier, Charles. *Jean de Serres, historiographe de roi.* Paris: Extrait de la Revue historique, 1883.

De Boer, Erik. "The *Congrégation*: An In-Service Theological Training Center for Preachers to the People of Geneva." In *Calvin and the Company of Pastors,* edited by David Foxgrover, 57–87. Grand Rapids, Mich.: CRC Product Services, 2004.

Deulumeau, Jean. *Catholicism between Luther and Voltaire: A New View of the Counter-Reformation.* Translated by Jeremy Moiser. Philadelphia, Pa.: Westminster, 1977.

Delval, Michel. "La doctrine du salut dans l'oeuvre homilétique de Théodore de Bèze." 2 vols. Ph. D. diss., University of Paris, 1982.

———. "La prédication d'un réformateur au XVIe siècle: L'activité homilétique de Théodore de Bèze." In *Mélanges de Science Religieuse* 41 (1984): 61–86.

De Mause, Lloyd, ed. *The History of Childhood.* London: Souvenir Press, 1974.

Deonna, W. "Cathédrale Saint-Pierre de Genève, cloches, horologes, orgues." *Genava* 28 (1950): 129–88.

———. "Cathédrale Saint-Pierre de Genève: La peinture." *Genava* 29 (1951): 56–87.

———. "Cathédrale Saint-Pierre de Genève: Les vitraux." *Genava* 29 (1951): 88–148.

Dixon, Scott C., and Luise Schorn-Schütte, eds. *The Protestant Clergy of Early Modern Europe*. London: Palgrave, 2003.

Donnelly, John Patrick. *Calvinism and Scholasticism in Vermigli's Doctrine of Man and Grace*. Leiden: Brill, 1975.

Doumergue, Émile. *Jean Calvin: Les hommes et les choses de son temps*. 7 vols. Lausanne Georges Bridel & Co., 1899–1917.

Droz, E. "L'Ecclésiaste de Théodore de Bèze." *Revue d'Histoire et de Philosophie Religieuses* 4 (1967): 338–46.

———. "Simon Goulart, éditeur de musique." *BHR* 14 (1952): 266–76.

Dückert, Armand. *Théodore de Bèze, Prédicateur*. Geneva: Imprimerie Romet, 1891.

Duffield, G. E., ed. *John Calvin*. Grand Rapids, Mich.: Eerdmans, 1966.

Duffy, Eamon. *The Stripping of the Altars: Traditional Religion in England 1400–1580*. New Haven, Conn.: Yale University Press, 1992.

Dufour, Alain. *La Guerre de 1589–1593*. Geneva: A. Jullien, 1958.

———. "Le mythe de Genève au temps de Calvin." *Revue Suisse d'Histoire* 9(1959): 489–518.

———. "Une oeuvre inconnue de Bèze?" *BHR* 22 (1960): 402–405.

———. *Théodore de Bèze, poète et théologien*. Geneva: Librairie Droz, 2006.

Eire, Carlos. *War Against the Idols: The Reformation of Worship from Erasmus to Calvin*. Reprint. Cambridge: Cambridge University Press, 1996.

Elwood, Christopher. *The Body Broken: The Calvinist Doctrine of the Eucharist and the Symbolization of Power in Sixteenth-Century France*. New York: Oxford University Press, 1999.

Estèbe, J., and B. Vogler. "Le genèse d'une société protestante: Étude compare de quelques registres consistoriaux languedociens et palatins vers 1600." *Annales: E.S.C.* 31 (1976): 362–88.

Evans, G. R., ed. *A History of Pastoral Care*. London: Cassell, 2000.

Fatio, Olivier, ed. *Confessions et catechismes de la foi reformée*. 2nd ed. Geneva: Labor et Fides, 2005.

———. *Le jeûne genevois. Réalité et mythe*. Geneva: Société d'Histoire et d'Archéologie de Genève, 1994.

———. "Lambert Daneau." In *Shapers of Religious Traditions in Germany, Switzerland, and Poland*, edited by Jill Raitt, 105–20. New Haven, Conn.: Yale University Press, 1981.

———. *Méthode et théologie. Lambert Daneau et les débuts de la scholastique réformée*. Geneva: Librairie Droz, 1976.

———. "Théodore de Bèze ou les débuts de l'orthodoxie réformée." *Hokhma* 28 (1985): 1–24.

Febvre, Lucien. *Au coeur religieux du XVIe siècle*. 2nd edition. Paris: S.E.V.P.E.N., 1968.

Fehleison, Jill. *Boundaries of Faith. Catholics and Protestants in the Diocese of Geneva*. Kirksville, Mo.: Truman State University Press, 2010.

Félice, Paul de. *Lambert Daneau, pasteur et professeur en théologie*. Paris: Librairie Fischbaucher, 1882.

Fellay, Jean-Blaise. "Les évêques, princes, et pasteurs." In *Encyclopédie de Genève*, edited by Catherine Santschi and Jean de Senarclens, vol. 5:121. Geneva: Association de l' Encyclopédie de Genève, 1986.

Ford, James Thomas. "Preaching in the Reformed Tradition." In *Preachers and People in the Reformations and Early Modern Period*, edited by Larissa Taylor, 65–90. Leiden: Brill, 2001.

Fraenkel, Pierre. *De l'écriture à la dispute. Le cas de l'Académie de Genève sous Théodore de Bèze*. Lausanne: Revue de Théologie et de Philosophie, 1977.

Frymire, John M. *The Primacy of the Postils. Catholics, Protestants, and the Dissemination of Ideas in Early Modern Germany*. Leiden: Brill, 2010.

Gaberel, J. *Histoire de l'église de Genève depuis le commencement de la réformation jusqu'à nos jours*. 3 vols. Geneva: Librairie Joël Cherbuliez, 1858.

Gaffin Jr., Richard. *Calvin and the Sabbath: The Controversy of Applying the Fourth Commandment*. Bristol: Christian Focus, 1998.

Ganoczy, Alexandre. *La bibliothèque de l'Académie de Calvin*. Geneva: Librairie Droz, 1969.

———. *The Young Calvin*. Translated by David Foxgrover and Wade Provo. Philadelphia: Westminster Press, 1987.

Gardy, Frédéric. *Bibliographie des oeuvres théologiques, littéraires, historiques et juridiques de Théodore de Bèze*. Geneva: Librairie Droz, 1960.

Garrison, *Protestants du Midi, 1559–1598*. Toulouse: Privat, 1991.

Gautier, A., ed. "Un jeune Bâlois à Genève au XVIme siècle (1560–1563)." In *Mémoires et documents publiés par la Société d'Histoire et d'Archéologie de Genève* 17 (1872): 412–16.

Geisendorf, Paul-F. *Les Annalistes genevois du début du dix-septième siècle. Savion—Piaget—Perin. Études et textes*. La Société d'Histoire et d'Archéologie de Genève. Vol. 35. Geneva: A. Jullien, 1942.

———. *Temples de la Campagne Genevoise*. Geneva: A. Jullien, 1955.

———. *Théodore de Bèze*. Reprint. Geneva: A. Jullien, 1967.

———. *Les Trembley de Genève de 1552 à 1846*. Geneva: A. Jullien, 1970.

Gerrish, Brian. *Grace & Gratitude: The Eucharistic Theology of John Calvin*. Minneapolis, Minn.: Fortress Press, 1993.

———. *The Old Protestantism and the New. Essays on the Reformation Heritage*. Chicago, Ill.: University of Chicago, 1982.

———. "Priesthood and Ministry in the Theology of Luther." *Church History* 34 (1965): 404–22.

Gilmont, Jean-François. *John Calvin and the Printed Book*. Translated by Karin Maag. Kirksville, Mo.: Truman State University Press, 2005.

Godfrey, W. Robert. "Reformed Thought on the Extent of the Atonement to 1618." *WTJ* 37.2 (1975): 133–71.

Gonthier, M. and M. Letourneau. *Vie de Saint François de Sales, évêque et prince de Genève*. Paris: Librairie Victor Lecoffre, 1920.

Gordon, Bruce. *Calvin*. New Haven, Conn.: Yale University Press, 2009.

————. *Clerical Discipline and the Rural Reformation. The Synod in Zürich, 1532–1580.* Bern: Peter Lang, 1992.

Gorski, Philip S. *The Disciplinary Revolution: Calvinism and the Rise of the State in Early Modern Europe.* Chicago, Ill.: University of Chicago Press, 2003.

Graham, Michael. *The Uses of Reform: "Godly Discipline" and Popular Belief in Scotland and Beyond, 1560–1610.* Leiden: Brill, 1996.

Greef, W. de. *The Writings of John Calvin.* Translated by Lyle D. Bierma. Grand Rapids, Mich.: Baker Academic, 1993.

Green, Ian. "'Reformed Pastors' and *Bons Curés*: The Changing Role of the Parish Clergy in Early Modern Europe." In *The Ministry: Clerical and Lay*, edited by W. J. Sheils and Diana Wood, 249–86. Oxford: Basil Blackwell, 1989.

Greengrass, Mark. *The French Reformation.* Oxford: Basil Blackwell, 1987.

Grislis, Egil. "Calvin's Doctrine of Baptism." *Church History* 31.1 (1962): 46–65.

Grosse, Christian. "'En esprit et en vérité?' La part du ritual dans la culture religieuse réformée." In *Calvinus Praeceptor Ecclesiae*, edited by Herman J. Selderhuis, 303–21. Geneva: Librairie Droz, 2004.

————. "'Le mystère de communiquer à Jésus-Christ,' Sermons de communion à Genève au XVIe Siècle." In *Annoncer l'Évangile (XVe–XVIIe siècle)*, edited by Matthieu Arnold, 161–82. Paris: Les Éditions du Cerf, 2006.

————. *Les rituels de la cène. Le culte eucharistique réformé à Genève (XVIe-XVIIe siècles).* Geneva: Librairie Droz, 2008.

Haag, Eugène, and Emile Haag. *La France protestante ou vies des protestants français.* 9 vols. Geneva: Slatkine Reprints, 1966.

Haag, Eugène, and Emile Haag. *La France protestante vies des protestants français.* 2nd edition. 6 vols. Paris: Sandoz & Fischbacher, 1877–1888.

Hagen, Kenneth. "A Critique of Wingren on Luther on Vocation." *Lutheran Quarterly* 16 (2002): 249–73.

Hall, Basil. "Calvin against the Calvinists." In *John Calvin*, edited by G. E. Duffield, 19–37. Grand Rapids, Mich.: Eerdmans, 1966.

Hambrick-Stowe, Charles. "Practical divinity and spirituality." In *The Cambridge Companion to Puritanism*, edited by John Coffey and Paul Lim, 191–205. New York: Cambridge University Press, 2008.

Hanska, Jussi. "Reconstructing the Mental Calendar of Medieval Preaching: A Method and its Limits: An Analysis of Sunday Sermons." In *Preacher, Sermon and Audience in the Middle Ages*, edited by Carolyn Muessig, 293–315. Leiden: Brill, 2002.

Heppe, Heinrich. *Reformed Dogmatics.* Translated by G. T. Thomson. London: George Allen & Unwin Ltd., 1950.

Hesselink, I. John. *Calvin's First Catechism: A Commentary.* Louisville, Ky.: Westminster John Knox Press, 1997.

————. "Word and Spirit." In *The Calvin Handbook*, edited by Herman Selderhuis, 299–312. Grand Rapids, Mich.: Eerdmans, 2009.

Heyer, Henri. *L'Église de Genève. Esquisse historique de son organization, 1535–1909.* Reprint. Nieuwkoop: B. de Graaf, 1974.

Higman, Francis. "L'*Harmonia Confessionum Fidei* de 1581." In *Catechismes et confessions de foi*, edited by Marie-Madelaine Fragonard and Michel Peronnet,

243–62. Montpellier: Le Centre d'histoire des réformes et du protestantisme de l'Université de Montpellier, 1995.

Hillerbrand, Hans. "Evangelical (Evangelisch)." In *The Encyclopedia of Protestantism*, edited by Hillerbrand, vol. 2:701–702. New York: Routledge, 2004.

Hoffman, Philip. *Church and Community in the Diocese of Lyon, 1500–1789*. New Haven, Conn.: Yale University Press, 1984.

Holder, R. Ward. *John Calvin and the Grounding of Interpretation: Calvin's First Commentaries*. Leiden: Brill, 2006.

Holtrop, Philip. *The Bolsec Controversy on Predestination, from 1551 to 1555*. 2 vols. Lewiston, Pa.: Edwin Mellen Press, 1993.

Janz, Denis. "Catechisms." In *Oxford Encyclopedia of the Reformation*, edited by Hans Hillerbrand, vol. 1:278. New York: Oxford University Press, 1996.

Jones, Leonard Chester. *Simon Goulart, 1543–1628. Étude biographie et bibliographique*. Geneva: Georg & Cie., 1917.

Jostock, Ingeborg. *La censure négociée. Le contrôle du livre à Genève 1560–1625*. Geneva: Librairie Droz, 2007.

Kantzer, Kenneth. "Calvin and the Holy Scriptures." In *Inspiration and Interpretation*, edited by John Walvoord, 115–55. Grand Rapids, Mich.: Eerdmans, 1957.

Karant-Nunn, Susan. "The Emergence of the Pastoral Family." In *The Protestant Clergy of Early Modern Europe*, edited by Scott Dixon and Luise Schorn-Schütte, 79–99. London: Palgrave, 2003.

———. *Luther's Pastors: The Reformation in the Ernestine Countryside*. Philadelphia, Pa.: American Philosophical Society, 1980.

———. "Preaching the Word in Early Modern Germany." In *Preachers and People in the Reformations and Early Modern Period*, edited by Larissa Taylor, 193–220. Leiden: Brill, 2001.

———. *The Reformation of Ritual: An Interpretation of Early Modern Germany*. New York: Routledge, 1997.

Kickel, Walter. *Vernunft und Offenbarung bei Theodor Beza. Zum Problem des Verhältnisses von Theologie, Philosophie und Staat*. Neukirchener: Verlag des Erziehungsvereins, 1967.

Kienzle, Beverly Mayne. "Medieval Sermons and their Performance." In *Preacher, Sermon and Audience in the Middle Ages*, edited by Carolyn Muessig, 89–124. Leiden: Brill, 2002.

Kingdon, Robert. *Adultery and Divorce in Calvin's Geneva*. Cambridge, Mass.: Harvard University Press, 1995.

———. "Calvin and the Government of Geneva." In *Calvinus Ecclesiae Genevensis Custos*, edited by Wilhelm H. Neuser, 49–67. Frankfurt Am Main: Peter Lang, 1984.

———. "Calvin's Ideas about the Diaconate: Social or Theological Origins?" In *Piety, Politics, and Ethics: Reformation Studies in Honor of George Wolfgang Forrell*, edited by Carter Lindberg, 167–80. Kirksville: Mo. Sixteenth Century Journal, 1984.

———. "The Control of Morals in Calvin's Geneva." In *The Social History of the Reformation*, edited by Lawrence P. Buck and Jonathan Zophy, 3–16. Columbus: Ohio State University, 1972.

―――. "The Deacons of the Reformed Church in Calvin's Geneva." In *Mélanges d'histoire du XVIe siècle offerts à Henri Meylan*, edited by Henri Meylan, 81–90. Geneva: Librairie Droz, 1970.

―――. "The Economic Activity of Ministers in Geneva in the Middle of the Sixteenth Century." *ARG* 50 (1959): 33–39.

―――. *Geneva and the Coming of the Wars of Religion in France, 1555–1563.* Geneva: Librairie Droz, 1956.

―――. *Geneva and the Consolidation of the French Protestant Movement, 1564–1572.* Geneva: Librairie Droz, 1967.

―――. "The Geneva Consistory in the Time of Calvin." In *Calvinism in Europe, 1540–1620*, edited by Andrew Pettegree, Alastair Duke, and Gillian Lewis, 21–34. Cambridge: Cambridge University Press, 1996.

―――. "The Genevan Revolution in Public Worship." *Princeton Seminary Bulletin* 20.3 (1999): 264–80.

―――. "Social Welfare in Calvin's Geneva." *AHR* 76 (1971): 50–69.

―――. "Was the Protestant Reformation a Revolution?" In *Transition and Revolution. Problems and Issues of European Renaissance and Reformation History*, edited by Kingdon, 53–77. Minneapolis, Minn.: Burgess, 1974.

Kingdon, Robert, Thomas Lambert, and Isabella Watt, eds. *Registers of the Consistory (1542–1544)*. Translated by M. Wallace McDonald. Grand Rapids, Mich.: Eerdmans, 2000.

Kraus, Hans-Joachim. "Calvin's Exegetical Principles." *Interpretation* 31 (1977): 8–18.

Kristeller, Paul Oskar. *Renaissance Thought: The Classic, Scholastic and Humanist Strains*. New York: Harper & Row, 1961.

Kuhr, Olaf. "Calvin and Basel: The Significance of Oecolampadius and the Basel Discipline Ordinance for the Institution of Ecclesiastical Discipline in Geneva." *Scottish Bulletin of Evangelical Theology* 16 (Spring 1998): 19–33.

Labarthe, Olivier. "En marge de l'édition des Registres de la Compagnie des pasteurs de Genève: le changement du mode de présidence de la Compagnie, 1578–1580." *Revue d'Histoire Ecclésiastique Suisse* 67 (1972): 160–86.

Lambert, Thomas. "Preaching, Praying and Policing the Reform in Sixteenth-Century Geneva." Ph.D. diss.: University of Wisconsin, 1998.

Lane, Anthony N. S. *John Calvin: Student of the Church Fathers*. Grand Rapids, Mich.: Baker Books, 1999.

Lee, Sou-Young. "Calvin's Understanding of *Pietas*." In *Calvinus Sincerioris Religionis Vindex*, edited by W. H. Neuser and B. G. Armstrong, 225–39. Kirksville, Mo.: Sixteenth Century Studies, 1997.

LeGoff, Jaques. *Medieval Civilization*. Translated by Julia Barrow. Oxford: Basil Blackwell, 1991.

Leith, John. "Reformed Preaching Today." *The Princeton Seminary Bulletin* 10.3 (1989): 224–57.

Lescaze, Bernard. *Genève, sa vie et ses monnaies aux siècles passés*. Geneva: Crédit Suisse, 1981.

Letham, Robert. "Theodore Beza: A Reassessment." *Scottish Journal of Theology* 40 (1987): 25–40.

Lewis, Gillian. "The Geneva Academy." In *Calvinism in Europe, 1540–1620*, edited by Andrew Pettegree, Alastair Duke, and Gillian Lewis, 35–63. Cambridge: Cambridge University Press, 1994.

Lindberg, Carter. *The European Reformation*. Oxford: Basil Blackwell, 1996.

———. *The Reformation Theologians. An Introduction to Theology in the Early Modern Period*. Oxford: Basil Blackwell, 2002.

Lotz-Heumann, Ute. "Confessionalization." In *Reformation and Early Modern Europe: A Guide to Research*, edited by David M. Whitford, 136–57. Kirksville, Mo.: Truman State University Press, 2008.

Maag, Karin. "Called to Be a Pastor: Issues of Vocation in the Early Modern Period." *SCJ* 35.1 (2004): 65–78.

———. *Seminary or University? The Genevan Academy and Reformed Higher Education, 1560–1620*. Aldershot: Ashgate, 1995.

MacCulloch, Diarmaid. *The Reformation: A History*. New York: Penguin Books, 2003.

Mallinson, Jeffrey. *Faith, Reason, and Revelation in Theodore Beza (1519–1605)*. Oxford: Oxford University Press, 2003.

Manetsch, Scott M. "The Journey Toward Geneva: Theodore Beza's Conversion, 1535–1548." In *Calvin, Beza and Later Calvinism*, edited by David Foxgrover, 38–60. Grand Rapids, Mich.: CRC Product Services, 2006.

———. "Ministers Misbehaving: The Discipline of Pastors in Calvinist Geneva, 1559–1596." In *Agir pour l'église. Ministères et charges ecclésiastiques dans les églises réformées*, edited by Didier Poton. Forthcoming.

———. "'The Most Despised Vocation Today': Theodore Beza's Theology of Pastoral Ministry." In *Théodore de Bèze*, edited by Irena Backus, 241–56. Geneva: Librairie Droz, 2007.

———. "A Mystery Solved? *Maister Beza's Houshold Prayers*." *BHR* 65.2 (2003): 275–88.

———. "Pastoral Care East of Eden: The Consistory of Geneva, 1568–1582." *Church History* 75.2 (2006): 274–313.

———. "Psalms before Sonnets: Theodore Beza and the *Studia Humanitatis*." In *Continuity and Change: The Harvest of Late-Medieval and Reformation History*, edited by Robert Bast and Andrew Gow, 400–16. Leiden: Brill, 2000.

———. *Theodore Beza and the Quest for Peace in France, 1572–1598*. Leiden: Brill, 2000.

Martin, Hervé. *Le métier de prédicateur à la fin du Moyen Age, 1350–1520*. Paris: Cerf, 1988.

Martin, Lynn A. *The Jesuit Mind: The Mentality of an Elite in Early Modern France*. Ithaca, N.Y.: Cornell University Press, 1988.

Martin, Paul E. *Trois cas de pluralisme confessionel aux XVIe et XVII siècles*. Geneva: A. Jullien, 1961.

Maruyama, Tadataka. *The Ecclesiology of Theodore Beza: The Reform of the True Church*. Geneva: Librairie Droz, 1978.

McComish, William A. *The Epigones: A Study of the Theology of the Genevan Academy at the Time of the Synod of Dort, with Special Reference to Giovanni Diodati*. Allison Park, Pa.: Pickwick Publications, 1989.

McCoy, Charles, and J. Wayne Baker. *Fountainhead of Federalism: Heinrich Bullinger and the Covenantal Tradition*. Louisville, Ky.: Westminster John Knox, 1991.

McGrath, Alister. "Calvin and the Christian Calling." *First Things* 94 (1999): 31–35.

———. *Historical Theology: An Introduction to the History of Christian Thought.* Oxford: Basil Blackwell, 1998.

———. *A Life of John Calvin.* Oxford: Basil Blackwell, 1991.

McIndoe, John H. "John Calvin: Preface to the Homilies of Chrysostom." *The Hartford Quarterly* 5 (1965): 19–26.

McKee, Elsie Anne. "Calvin and his Colleagues as Pastors: Some New Insights into the Collegial Ministry of the Word and Sacrament." In *Calvinus Praeceptor Ecclesiae,* edited by Herman J. Selderhuis, 9–42. Geneva: Librairie Droz, 2004.

———. *Elders and the Plural Ministry: The Role of Exegetical History in Illuminating John Calvin's Theology.* Geneva: Librairie Droz, 1988.

———. *John Calvin on the Diaconate and Liturgical Almsgiving.* Geneva: Librairie Droz, 1988.

———, ed. *John Calvin: Writings on Pastoral Piety.* The Classics of Western Spirituality. New York: Paulist Press, 2001.

McKim, Donald, ed. *Cambridge Companion to John Calvin.* New York: Cambridge University Press, 2004.

McLaughlin, R. Emmet. "The Making of the Protestant Pastor: The Theological Foundations of a Clerical Estate." In *The Protestant Clergy of Early Modern Europe,* edited by C. Scott Dixon and Luise Schorn-Schütte, 60–78. London: Palgrave, 2003.

McPhee, Ian. "Conserver or Transformer of Calvin's Theology? A Study of the Origins and Development of Theodore Beza's Thought, 1550–1570." Ph.D. diss.: Cambridge University, 1979.

Méjan, François. *Discipline de l'Église Réformée de France.* Paris: Éditions "Je Sers," 1947.

Mentzer, Raymond A. "*Disciplina nervus ecclesiae*: The Calvinist Reform of Morals at Nîmes." *SCJ* 18 (1987): 89–115.

———. "Morals and Moral Regulation in Protestant France." *Journal of Interdisciplinary History* 31.1 (2000): 1–20.

———, ed. *Sin and the Calvinists: Morals Control and the Consistory in the Reformed Tradition.* Kirksville, Mo.: Sixteenth Century Journal, 1994.

Meylan, Henri. "La conversion de Bèze ou les longues hesitations d'un humaniste chréstien." In *D'Érasme à Théodore de Bèze,* edited by Henri Meylan, 103–25. Geneva: Librairie Droz, 1976.

———. "Professeurs et étudiants, questions d'horaires et de leçons." In *La réforme et l'éducation,* edited by Jean Boisset, 67–75. Paris: Edouard Privat, 1974.

———. *Quatre sermons français sur Esaie 65 (mars 1559).* Lausanne: Librairie Payot, 1961.

———. "Le recrutement et la formation des pasteurs." In *Miscellanea Historiae Ecclesiasticae 3,* edited by Derek Baker, 127–50. Louvain: Publications Universitaires de Louvain, 1970.

———, ed. *Mélanges d'histoire du XVIe siècle offerts à Henri Meylan.* Geneva: Librairie Droz, 1970.

Michalski, Sergiusz. *The Reformation and the Visual Arts: The Protestant Image Question in Western and Eastern Europe.* London: Routledge, 1993.

Millet, Olivier. *Calvin et la dynamique de la parole*. Geneva: Éditions Slatkine, 1992.

———. "Rendre raison de la foi: Le Catéchisme de Calvin (1542)." In *Aux origins du catéchisme en France*, edited by Pierre Colin, Elisabeth Germain, Jean Joncheray, and Marc Venard, 188–203. Paris: Relais-Desclée, 1989.

Montaigne, Michel de. *The Essayes of Montaigne*. Translated by John Florio. New York: Random House, 1946.

Monter, E. William. *Calvin's Geneva*. New York: John Wiley & Sons, 1967.

———. "The Consistory of Geneva, 1559–1569." *BHR* 38 (1976): 467–84.

———. "Historical Demography and Religious History in Sixteenth-Century Geneva." *Journal of Interdisciplinary History* 9.3 (1979): 418–27.

———. *Studies in Genevan Government, 1536–1605*. Geneva: Librairie Droz, 1964.

———. *Witchcraft in France and Switzerland*. Ithaca, N.Y.: Cornell University Press, 1976.

Mottu-Weber, Liliane. *Économie et refuge à Genève au siècle de la réforme: la draperie et la soierie (1540–1630)*. Geneva: Librairie Droz, 1987.

———. "Jean Diodati." In *Dictionaire Historique de la Suisse*, edited by Marco Jorio, vol. 4:65–66. Hauterive: Éditions Gilles Attinger, 2005.

Mottu-Weber, Liliane, Anne-Marie Piuz, and Bernard Lescaze. *Vivre à Genève. La vie de tous les jours*. Geneva: Éditions Slatkine, 2002.

Muesig, Carolyn, ed. *Preacher, Sermon and Audience in the Middle Ages*. Leiden: Brill, 2002.

Muir, Edward. *Ritual in Early Modern Europe*. 2nd edition. Cambridge: Cambridge University Press, 2005.

Muller, Richard A. *After Calvin: Studies in the Development of a Theological Tradition*. New York: Oxford University Press, 2003.

———. *Christ and the Decree: Christology and Predestination in Reformed Theology from Calvin to Perkins*. Grand Rapids, Mich.: Baker Books, 1986.

———. *Dictionary of Latin and Greek Theological Terms*. Grand Rapids, Mich.: Baker Books, 1985.

———. *Post-Reformation Reformed Dogmatics*. 4 vols. 2nd ed. Grand Rapids, Mich.: Baker Books, 2003.

———. *The Unaccommodated Calvin: Studies in the Foundation of a Theological Tradition*. New York: Oxford University Press, 2000.

———. "The Use and Abuse of a Document: Beza's *Tabula Praedestinationis*, the Bolsec Controversy, and the Origins of Reformed Orthodoxy." In *Protestant Scholasticism, Essays in Reassessment*, edited by Carl Trueman and R. Scott Clark, 33–61. Eugene, Or.: Wipf and Stock, 2005.

Murdock, Graeme. *Beyond Calvin. The Intellectual, Political and Cultural World of Europe's Reformed Churches*. New York: Palgrave Macmillan, 2004.

Naef, Henri. *Les origines de la réforme à Genève*. 2 vols. Geneva: A. Jullien, 1968.

Naphy, William. *Calvin and the Consolidation of the Genevan Reformation*. Reprint. Louisville, Ky.: Westminster John Knox, 1994.

———. "The Reformation and the Evolution of Geneva's Schools." In *Reformations Old and New*, edited by Beat A. Kümin, 185–202. London: Scolar Press, 1996.

———. "The Renovation of the Ministry in Calvin's Geneva." In *The Reformation of the Parishes: The Ministry and the Reformation in Town and Country*, edited by Andrew Pettegree, 113–32. New York: St. Martin's Press, 1993.

Nichols, David. *The Domestic Life of a Medieval City: Women, Children, and the Family in Fourteenth-Century Ghent.* Lincoln, Neb.: University of Nebraska Press, 1985.

Nugent, Donald. *Ecumenism in the Age of the Reformation: The Colloquy of Poissy.* Cambridge, Mass.: Harvard University Press, 1974.

Nyasula, Timothy. "'Bringing the Sheep Back to the Corral': Moral Discipline in the Church of Central Africa Presbyterian (CCAP) Synod of Livingstonia, Malawi, 1995–2005." Ph.D. dissertation: Trinity Evangelical Divinity School, 2010.

Oberman, Heiko A. *John Calvin and the Reformation of the Refugees.* Geneva: Librairie Droz, 2009.

O'Donnell, James J. *Augustine: A New Biography.* New York: Harper, 2006.

Old, Hughes Oliphant. *The Shaping of the Reformed Baptismal Rite in the Sixteenth Century.* Grand Rapids, Mich.: Eerdmans, 1992.

Olin, John C. *John Calvin-Jacopo Sadoleto: A Reformation Debate.* Grand Rapids, Mich.: Baker Books, 1987.

Olson, Jeannine E. *Calvin and Social Welfare. Deacons and the Bourse Française.* London: Associated University Presses, 1989.

———. "Nicolas des Gallars, Sieur de Saules: Kith, Kin, and Aspects of His Work in Geneva with Calvin." *Reformation and Renaissance Review* 9.3 (2007): 277–303.

O'Malley, John. "Content and Rhetorical Forms in Sixteenth-Century Treatises on Preaching." In *Renaissance Eloquence, Studies in the Theory and Practice of Renaissance Rhetoric,* edited by James J. Murphy, 238–52. Berkeley, Calif.: University of California Press, 1983.

———. *Praise and Blame in Renaissance Rome: Rhetoric, Doctrine and Reform in the Sacred Orators of the Papal Court, c. 1450–1521.* Durham, N.C.: Duke University Press, 1979.

Ozment, Steven. *Protestants: The Birth of a Revolution.* New York: Doubleday, 1991.

———. *The Reformation in the Cities: The Appeal of Protestantism to Sixteenth-Century Germany and Switzerland.* New Haven, Conn.: Yale University Press, 1975.

———. *When Fathers Ruled: Family Life in Reformation Europe.* Cambridge, Mass.: Harvard University Press, 1983.

Parker, Charles. *The Reformation of Community: Social Welfare and Calvinist Charity in Holland, 1572–1620.* Cambridge: Cambridge University Press, 1998.

Parker, T. H. L. *Calvin's New Testament Commentaries.* Grand Rapids, Mich.: Eerdmans, 1971.

———. *Calvin's Old Testament Commentaries.* Edinburgh: T & T Clark, 1986.

———. *Calvin's Preaching.* Louisville, Ky.: Westminster John Knox Press, 1992.

Partee, Charles. *The Theology of John Calvin.* Louisville, Ky.: Westminster John Knox, 2008.

"Pasteurs et Prédicateurs." *BHSFP* 16 (1867): 422–29. [Anonymous.]

Pelikan, Jaroslav. *The Growth of Medieval Theology (600–1300).* Vol. 3. *The Christian Tradition. A History of the Development of Doctrine.* Chicago, Ill.: University of Chicago Press, 1978.

Perrenoud, Alfred. *La population de Genève du seizième au début du dix-neuvième siècle.* Vol. 1. Geneva: Éditions Société d'Histoire et d'Archéologie de Genève, 1979.

Peter, Rodolphe. "L'abécédaire genevois ou catechisme élémentaire de Calvin." *Revue d'Histoire et de Philosophie Religieuses* 45.1 (1965): 11–45.

———. *Jean Calvin, deux congrégations et exposition du Catéchisme*. Paris: Presses Universitaires de France, 1964.

———. "Rhétorique et prédication selon Calvin." *Revue d'Histoire et de Philosophie Religieuses* 55 (1975): 249–72.

Peter, Rodolphe and Jean-François Gilmont. *Bibliotheca Calviniana. Les oeuvres de Jean Calvin publiées au XVIe siècle*. 3 Vols. Geneva: Librairie Droz, 2000.

Pettegree, Andrew. *Reformation and the Culture of Persuasion*. New York: Cambridge University Press, 2005.

———, ed. *The Reformation of the Parishes: The Ministry and the Reformation in Town and Country*. Manchester: Manchester University Press, 1993.

Pettegree, Andrew, Alastair Duke, and Gillian Lewis. *Calvinism in Europe, 1540–1620*. Cambridge: Cambridge University Press, 1994.

Pidoux, Pierre. *Le Psautier Huguenot*. 2 vols. Basle: Éditions Baerenreiter, 1962.

Pitkin, Barbara. "'The Heritage of the Lord': Children in the Theology of John Calvin." In *The Child in Christian Thought*, edited by Marcia J. Bunge, 160–93. Grand Rapids, Mich.: Eerdmans, 2001.

Pollmann, Judith. "Off the Record: Problems in the Quantification of Calvinist Church Discipline." *SCJ* 33 (2002): 423–38.

Posthumus Meyjes, G. H. M. "Charles Perrot (1541–1608): His Opinion on a Writing of Georg Cassander." In *Humanism and Reform: The Church in Europe, England, and Scotland, 1400–1643*, edited by James Kirk, 221–36. Oxford: Basil Blackwell, 1991.

Poton, Didier. "Les institutions consistoriales: I. Les exemples des XVIe et XVIIe." *BSHPF* 148 (2002): 953–64.

Puckett, David. *John Calvin's Exegesis of the Old Testament*. Louisville, Ky.: Westminster John Knox, 2008.

Puyroche. "La bibliothèque d'un pasteur à la fin du XVIe siècle." *BSHPF* 21 (1872): 327–37.

Quick, John. *Synodicon in Gallia Reformata: Or, the Acts, Decisions, Decrees, and Canons of those Famous National Councils of the Reformed Churches in France*. London: Printed For T. Parkhurst and J. Robinson, 1692.

Rainbow, Jonathan. *The Will of God and the Cross: An Historical and Theological Study of John Calvin's Doctrine of Limited Atonement*. Allison Park, Pa.: Pickwick, 1990.

Raitt, Jill. "Beza, Guide for the Faithful Life." *Scottish Journal of Theology* 39 (1986): 33–107.

———. *The Colloquy of Montbéliard: Religion and Politics in the Sixteenth Century*. New York: Oxford University Press, 1993.

———. *The Eucharistic Theology of Theodore Beza: Development of Reformed Doctrine*. Chambersburg, Pa.: American Academy of Religion, 1972.

———. "Probably They Are God's Children: Theodore Beza's Doctrine of Baptism." In *Humanism and Reform: The Church in Europe, England and Scotland*, edited by James Kirk, 151–70. Oxford: Blackwell, 1991.

———, ed. *Shapers of Religious Traditions in Germany, Switzerland, and Poland*. New Haven, Conn.: Yale University Press, 1981.

Reinhard, Wolfgang. "Pressures towards Confessionalization? Prolegomena to a Theory of the Confessional Age." In *The German Reformation*, edited by C. Scott Dixon, 172–92. New York: Oxford University Press, 1999.

Richter, Mario. "La méditation en prose à la Renaissance." In *Cahiers V. L. Saulnier*. Vol. 7. Paris: Presses de l'École Normale Supérieure, 1990.

Riggs, John. *Baptism in the Reformed Tradition: An Historical and Practical Theology.* Louisville, Ky.: Westminster John Knox, 2002.

Rivoire, Emile, and Victor van Berchem. *Les sources du droit du Canton de Genève.* 3 vols. Aarau: Sauerländer, 1927–1935.

Roberts, Phyllis. "The *Ars Praedicandi* and the Medieval Sermon." In *Preacher, Sermon and Audience in the Middle Ages*, edited by Carolyn Muessig, 41–62. Leiden: Brill, 2002.

Rogers, Jack and Donald McKim. *The Authority and Interpretation of the Bible.* New York: Harper & Row, 1979.

Santschi, Catherine. *La Censure à Genève au XVIIe siècle, de l'Escalade à la Révocation de l'Édit de Nantes.* Geneva: S. A. Tribune de Genève, 1978.

———. "Être religieux à Genève à l'époque de la Réforme." In *Mythes et réalités du XVIe siècle, foi, idées, images*, edited by Bernard Lescaze and Mario Turchetti, 1–27. Alessandria: Edizioni dell'Orso, 2008.

Santschi, Catherine, et al. *Encyclopédie de Genève: Les Religions.* Vol. 5. Geneva: Association de l'Encyclopédie de Genève, 1986.

Scaduto, Mario, ed. "La Ginevra di Teodoro Beza nei ricordi di un gesuita lucano, Luca Pineli (1542–1607)." *Archivum Historicum Societas Iesu* 20 (1951?): 117–42.

Schaff, Philip. *The Creeds of Christendom.* Vol. 1. Reprint. Grand Rapids, Mich.: Baker Books, 1985.

Schilling, Heinz. "Confessional Europe." In *Handbook of European History 1400–1600*, edited by Thomas Brady, Heiko A. Oberman, and James Tracy, vol. 1, 641–81. Leiden: Brill, 1994.

———. "'History of Crime' or 'History of Sin'? Some Reflections on the Social History of Early Modern Church Discipline." In *Politics and Society in Reformation Europe*, edited by E. I. Kouri and Tom Scott, 289–310. London: Macmillan, 1987.

Scribner, Robert. "Pastoral Care and the Reformation in Germany." In *Humanism and Reform: The Church in Europe, England and Scotland, 1400–1643*, edited by James Kirk, 77–98. Oxford: Basil Blackwell, 1991.

———. *Popular Culture and Popular Movements in Reformation Germany.* London: Hambledon Press, 1987.

Schorn-Schütte, Luise. "The Christian Clergy in the Early Modern Holy Roman Empire: A Comparative Social Study." *SCJ* 29.3 (1998): 717–32.

———. "Priest, Preacher, Pastor; Research on Clerical Office in Early Modern Europe." *Central European History* 33 (2000): 1–39.

Schultz, James. *The Knowledge of Childhood in the German Middle Ages, 1100–1350.* Philadelphia, Pa.: University of Pennsylvania Press, 1995.

Selderhuis, Herman J. *John Calvin: A Pilgrim's Life.* Translated by Albert Gootjes. Downers Grove, Ill.: IVP Academic, 2009.

———, ed. *The Calvin Handbook.* Grand Rapids, Mich.: Eerdmans, 2009.

Shorter, Edward. *The Making of the Modern Family*. New York: Basic Books, 1977.

Sinnema, Donald. "Antoine de Chandieu's Call for a Scholastic Reformed Theology (1580)." In *Later Calvinism. International Perspectives*, edited by W. Fred Graham, 159–90. Kirksville, Mo.: Sixteenth-Century Essays and Studies, 1994.

———. "Beza's View of Predestination in Historical Perspective." In *Théodore de Bèze*, edited by Irena Backus, 219–40. Geneva: Librairie Droz, 2007.

———. "The Distinction Between Scholastic and Popular: Andreas Hyperius and Reformed Scholasticism." In *Protestant Scholasticism: Essays in Reassessment*, edited by Carl Trueman and R. Scott Clark, 127–43. Eugene, Or.: Wipf and Stock, 2005.

Spierling, Karen. *Infant Baptism in Reformation Geneva: The Shaping of a Community, 1536–1564*. Aldershot: Ashgate, 2005.

Spykman, G. J. *Reformational Theology: A New Paradigm for Doing Dogmatics*. Grand Rapids, Mich.: Eerdmans, 1992.

Stauffer, Richard. "Un Calvin méconnu: le prédicateur de Genève." *BSHPF* 123 (1977): 184–203.

Steinmetz, Daivd. *Calvin in Context*. New York: Oxford University Press, 1995.

———. *Luther in Context*. 2nd ed. Grand Rapids, Mich.: Baker Academic, 2002.

———. "The Scholastic Calvin." In *Protestant Scholasticism: Essays in Reassessment*, edited by Carl Trueman and R. Scott Clark, 116–30. Eugene, Or.: Wipf and Stock, 2005.

Stelling-Michaud, Sven, and Suzanne Stelling-Michaud, eds. *Le Livre du Recteur de l'Académie de Genève*. 6 vols. Geneva: Librairie Droz, 1959–1980.

Stephens, W. P. *The Theology of Huldrych Zwingli*. Oxford: Clarendon Press, 1986.

Stone, Lawrence. *The Family, Sex and Marriage in England, 1500–1800*. London: Weidenfeld and Nicholson, 1977.

Strauss, Gerald. *Luther's House of Learning: Indoctrination of the Young in the German Reformation*. Baltimore, Md.: Johns Hopkins University Press, 1978.

———. "Success and Failure in the German Reformation." *Past and Present* 67 (1975): 30–63.

Summers, Kirk. "Theodore Beza's Classical Library and Christian Humanism." *ARG* 82 (1991): 193–207.

———. *A View from the Palatine: The Iuvenile of Théodore de Bèze*. Tempe, Az.: Arizona Center for Medieval and Renaissance Studies, 2001.

Swanson, R. N. "Before the Protestant Clergy: The Construction and Deconstruction of the Medieval Priesthood." In *The Protestant Clergy of Early Modern Europe*, edited by C. Scott Dixon and Luise Schorn-Schütte, 60–78. London: Palgrave, 2003.

Taylor, Larissa. *Soldiers of Christ: Preaching in Late Medieval and Reformation France*. New York: Oxford University Press, 1992.

———, ed. *Preachers and People in the Reformations and Early Modern Period*. Leiden: Brill, 2001.

Thompson, John. "Calvin as Biblical Interpreter." In *Cambridge Companion to John Calvin*, edited by Donald McKim, 58–73. New York: Cambridge University Press, 2004.

Tolley, Bruce. *Pastors and Parishioners in Württemberg During the Late Reformation, 1581–1621*. Stanford, Calif.: Stanford University Press, 1995.

Torrance, J. B., M. Charles Bell, Paul Helm, and Anthony Lane. "Calvin and Calvinism," *Evangelical Quarterly* 55 (1983): 65–124.

Trueman, Carl. "Calvin and Reformed Orthodoxy." In *The Calvin Handbook*, edited by Herman Selderhuis, 472–79. Grand Rapids, Mich.: Eerdmans, 2009.

Trueman, Carl. *Histories and Fallacies: Problems Faced in the Writing of History.* Wheaton, Ill.: Crossway, 2010.

Trueman, Carl, and R. Scott Clark, eds. *Protestant Scholasticism: Essays in Reassessment.* Waynesboro, Ga.: Paternoster, 2005.

Van Asselt, Willem J., and Eef Dekker. *Reformation and Scholasticism: An Ecumenical Enterprise.* Grand Rapids, Mich.: Baker, 2001.

Vogler, Bernard. *Le clergé protestant rhénan au siècle de la réforme, 1555–1619.* Paris: Édition Ophrys, 1976.

———. "Formation et recrutement du clergé protestant dans les pays rhénans de Strasbourg à Coblence au XVIe siècle." In *Miscellanea Historiae Ecclesiasticae* 3, edited by Derek Baker, 216–21. Louvain: Publications Universitaires, 1970.

———. "Recrutement et carrière des pasteurs strasbourgeois au XVIe siècle." In *Revue d'Histoire et Philosophie Religieuses* 48 (1968): 151–74.

Wacker, Grant. *Heaven Below: Early Pentecostals and American Culture.* Cambridge, Mass.: Harvard University Press, 2001.

Wallace, Ronald. *Calvin, Geneva & the Reformation.* Eugene, Or.: Wipf and Stock, 1998.

Wandel, Lee Palmer. "The Reform of the Images: New Visualizations of the Christian Community at Zürich." *ARG* 80 (1988): 105–24.

Watt, Jeffrey. "Women and the Consistory in Calvin's Geneva." *SCJ* 24 (1993): 429–39.

Wendel, François. *Calvin, Origins and Developments of His Religious Thought.* Translated by Philip Mairet. Reprint. Grand Rapids, Mich.: Baker, 1997.

Whitford, David M., ed. *Reformation and Early Modern Europe: A Guide to Research.* Kirksville, Mo.: Truman State University Press, 2008.

Wiesner, Merry. "Family, Household, and Community." In *Handbook of European History 1400–1600*, edited by Thomas Brady, Heiko A. Oberman, and James Tracy, vol. 2, 51–70. Leiden: Brill, 1994.

Wingren, Gustaf. *The Christian's Calling: Luther on Vocation.* Translated by Carl C. Rasmussen. Reprint. Edinburgh: Oliver and Boyd, 1958.

Witte Jr., John. *Law and Protestantism: The Legal Teachings of the Lutheran Reformation.* Cambridge: Cambridge University Press, 2002.

———. *The Reformation of Rights: Law, Religion and Human Rights in Early Modern Calvinism.* Cambridge: Cambridge University Press, 2007.

Witte Jr. John, and Robert Kingdon. *Sex, Marriage, and Family in John Calvin's Geneva.* Grand Rapids, Mich.: Eerdmans, 2005.

Woodbridge, John. *Biblical Authority: A Critique of the Rogers/McKim Proposal.* Grand Rapids, Mich.: Zondervan, 1982.

Worcester, Thomas. "Catholic Sermons." In *Preachers and People in the Reformations and Early Modern Period*, edited by Larissa Taylor, 3–34. Leiden: Brill, 2001.

Wright, Shawn D. *Our Sovereign Refuge. The Pastoral Theology of Theodore Beza.* Carlisle, Pa.: Paternoster Press, 2004.

Zachman, Randall C. *John Calvin as Teacher, Pastor, and Theologian: The Shape of His Writings and Thought.* Grand Rapids, Mich.: Baker Academic, 2006.

CPSIA information can be obtained
at www.ICGtesting.com
Printed in the USA
BVOW03s1616081217
501987BV00003B/3/P